The Game of School

Robert L. Fried

The Game of School

Why We All Play It, How It Hurts Kids, and What It Will Take to Change It

JOSSEY-BASS
A Wiley Imprint
www.josseybass.com

Published by Jossey-Bass
A Wiley Imprint
989 Market Street, San Francisco, CA 94103-1741 www.josseybass.com

Jossey-Bass books and products are available through most bookstores. To contact Jossey-Bass directly, call our Customer Care Department within the U.S. at 800-956-7739, outside the U.S. at 317-572-3986, or fax 317-572-4002.

Jossey-Bass also publishes its books in a variety of electronic formats. Some content that appears in print may not be available in electronic books.

Library of Congress Cataloging-in-Publication Data

Fried, Robert L.
The game of school : why we all play it, how it hurts kids, and what it will take to change it / Robert L. Fried.—1st ed.
p. cm.—(The Jossey-Bass education series)
Includes bibliographical references and index.
ISBN 0-7879-7347-5 (alk. paper)
1. Active learning—United States. 2. Educational evaluation—United States. 3. Education—Aims and objectives—United States. 4. School improvement programs—United States.
I. Title. II. Series.
LB1027.23.F75 2005
370.15'4-dc22

2005001849

Printed in the United States of America
FIRST EDITION
HB Printing 10 9 8 7 6 5 4 3 2 1

The Jossey-Bass Education Series

For my brothers,
Marc and Richard, who keep me honest.
And for the teachers and students
who have enriched my work with theirs.

Contents

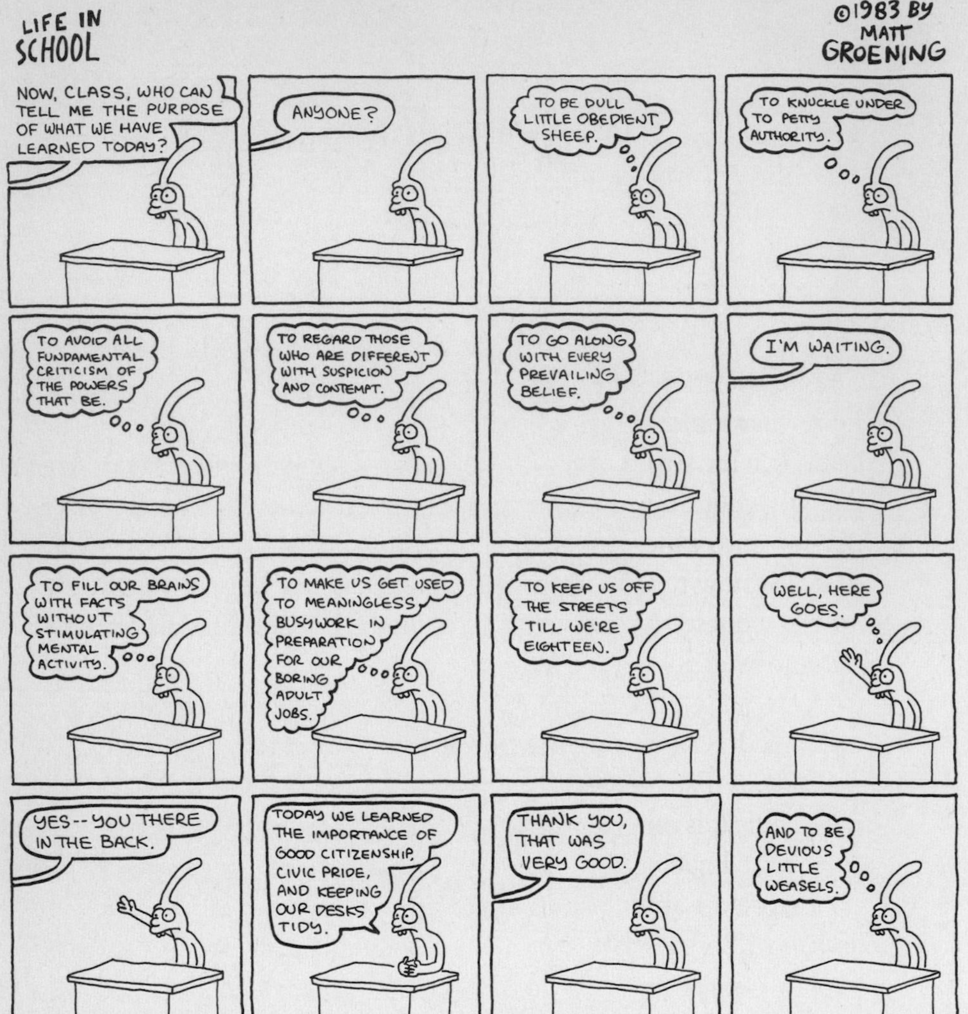
LIFE IN SCHOOL
©1983 BY MATT GROENING
NOW, CLASS, WHO CAN TELL ME THE PURPOSE OF WHAT WE HAVE LEARNED TODAY?
ANYONE?
TO BE DULL LITTLE OBEDIENT SHEEP.
TO KNUCKLE UNDER TO PETTY AUTHORITY.
TO AVOID ALL FUNDAMENTAL CRITICISM OF THE POWERS THAT BE.
TO REGARD THOSE WHO ARE DIFFERENT WITH SUSPICION AND CONTEMPT.
TO GO ALONG WITH EVERY PREVAILING BELIEF.
I'M WAITING.
TO FILL OUR BRAINS WITH FACTS WITHOUT STIMULATING MENTAL ACTIVITY.
TO MAKE US GET USED TO MEANINGLESS BUSYWORK IN PREPARATION FOR OUR BORING ADULT JOBS.
TO KEEP US OFF THE STREETS TILL WE'RE EIGHTEEN.
WELL, HERE GOES.
YES--YOU THERE IN THE BACK.
TODAY WE LEARNED THE IMPORTANCE OF GOOD CITIZENSHIP, CIVIC PRIDE, AND KEEPING OUR DESKS TIDY.
THANK YOU, THAT WAS VERY GOOD.
AND TO BE DEVIOUS LITTLE WEASELS.

Prelude

What's in a Game?

One of the things all kids learn in school is that it's often wise to keep your real feelings to yourself. It's not just about hiding that crush you have on a classmate from the gossipers in the cafeteria, or keeping your envy or contempt for "the Populars" from those with the power to exile you to social Siberia. You had also better be ready to know how to fake it properly when the teacher calls on you to answer a question to which you're sure he or she already knows the right answer.

Our guide in handling this tricky situation is a cartoon character named Bongo, from the pen of Matt Groening, years before he brought us *The Simpsons*. Opposite, from his 1990 book *The Big Book of Hell*, is one view of how we might cope with a teacher's predetermined query.

I have a name for this acquired wiliness: *playing the Game of School*. In Bongo's case, it is part of that larger game we feel we need to play to survive in this world. We get ahead by deciding mostly to go along with the power structure—at home, on the job, in social situations, even with friends—rather than reveal our true feelings, stick up for an unpopular point of view, or propose another way of responding to challenges. But there are other aspects of the Game even more frequently practiced, such that we all find ourselves playing along in one way or another.

A second manifestation of the Game occurs when teacher and students form a sort of unspoken pact: so long as the kids don't make trouble for the teacher, the teacher will make sure the students don't have to work all that hard.[1] Everybody pretends to keep busy, as assignments are handed out, notes are put up on the board, tests are given and graded, and students get their A's, B's, C's, or sometimes D's and F's. Cordiality in the classroom is achieved at the price of genuine and lasting learning by students. They "play at school" instead.

But even when teachers and students believe they are taking school seriously, as the teacher earnestly prepares her lesson plans and as students dutifully complete homework assignments and study for their tests, the Game may just be taking another form. While the teacher worries about making sure she covers her curriculum, and students scan the blackboard to determine what material is likely to be on the test, *authentic learning*—defined as *student engagement in ideas, concepts, skills, and activities that mean something to them and that lead both to a deeper understanding and to the ability to put ideas to work*—gets pushed so far into the background that it all but disappears.

People *think* they're teaching and learning. Students and teachers earnestly comply with what they feel to be their duty. But nobody is really learning much beyond what it takes to pass the next exam or to cover the textbook chapter. The Game begins whenever we focus on getting through the school day rather than actually *learning*.

In all of its manifestations, the Game of School is pretty much a fact of life, and virtually everyone who has made it up through the grades has had to play. It has become second nature: we don't even realize we're playing. We keep our eyes on what our teacher wants from us, rather than on what we want to learn; we first read the "focus questions" at the end of the chapter in our history textbook and then skim through the chapter to look for the answers, ignoring most of what's written there. And there are times, in grade school through graduate school, when, like our friend Binky, we sit on our true feelings while giving the teacher a dutiful if insincere response—especially when we're afraid we might be the only one there with a different way of seeing things.

When people succumb to the Game of School, the cheaper currency of unengaged compliance crowds out the gold standard of self-initiated learning. Played well enough and long enough, from first grade through our doctoral dissertations, we convince ourselves that the Game is all there really is, that *school learning* equals *game playing*. For one thing, it seems so obviously the thing to do; it helps us get through, get by, get over the obstacles that stand between us and our real goals of the moment (such as finishing our homework as quickly as possible so we can go out with our friends, or getting the term paper off our backs so we can study for the final). But its impact extends well beyond graduation, as we divert energy, intellect, and creativity away from *learning* and into *getting our education over with*.

The Game of School afflicts not only those classes where burned-out teachers baby-sit apathetic students. It is alive and well in honors classes and advanced placement courses, and the attitudes it fosters extend through college and graduate school. Its common denominator is that teacher and students have substituted some other goal for authentic learning. As I wrote back in the 1990s,

> The particular offense of playing the Game of School lies in the disengagement of our intellect and our feelings from tasks that deserve to be taken seriously: tasks like writing, reading, thinking, planning, listening, researching, analyzing, performing, applying, evaluating. We do harm when we reduce these acts of intellect, creativity, and judgment to rote exercises, perfunctory deeds, or meaningless gestures. Faced with the stresses of daily life in school, it can seem easier, at times, to *pretend* to believe rather than to *truly believe* in the value of what we are about.[2]

So We Learn to Do What Is Expected of Us—What's the Big Deal?

Will life demand of us, oftentimes, that we do things we'd rather not have to do? Of course it will. Is everything about learning supposed to be a joyful undertaking, requiring only enthusiasm but never any sweat? Of course not. Isn't it important for children to learn how to take direction, develop good work habits, meet deadlines, and measure up to standards set for them by people with the wisdom and experience to understand the challenges that lie ahead? Agreed. So what's the big deal? Why can't we simply accept that school is a place where young people go to accomplish the tasks that will lead them on to a brighter future?

We are dealing here with something both precious and vulnerable: a child's own sense of joy and competence as a learner, an inner force, a spirit of inquiry that a child is unlikely to repress until overcome by forces within school. Although parents and teachers do need to guide children as they mature, to help them learn to be successful in areas of academics and deportment that our society values, we must try to do this with minimal damage to the child's independent learning spirit and sense of personal worth.

Am I being overprotective of young learners, making far too much of the supposed "eclipse of the learning spirit" in the child and young adult due to the pressures of the Game of School? Consider this: amid all the accounts, throughout our lives in school, of kids complaining to each other about how bored they are with many of their classes, why do we accept this so passively, without arguing for the right to be learning something of value? Why don't students complain to the principal that so-and-so teacher in such-and-such course is wasting their time, abusing their intellect, and boring them to death? Why is no procedure set up in schools to adjudicate such charges (allowing a teacher to defend his or her practice, with options for mediation and compromise)?

It's not that kids are naturally passive: teenagers are hardly reticent when it comes to standing up for their rights (as any parent will testify). Yet, in school, they act like the academic equivalent of Soviet-era consumers standing in line for shoddy goods, rather than asserting their right to an education that will help them compete in the global marketplace of ideas. Is this not proof of the cumulative and numbing effect of this game?

The Stakes Are High

This paralysis of intellect and meaningful inquiry—the phenomenon that I call the Game of School—may be a figment of my imagination, or it may help us explain the wholesale failure of our education systems, worldwide, to engage and animate vast numbers of our students. Let us briefly examine both possibilities.

If I am fundamentally wrong, if the malaise that is palpable in classrooms all over our nation and the world can be explained by a group of factors, including poorly prepared or poorly paid teachers (or both), haphazard and uncoordinated instructional practices, or inadequate measures of accountability, or by students who are unmotivated (lazy), addicted to electronic toys, or afflicted with learning disabilities of one kind or another, then the solution to our problems is simply to ratchet up one or all of these factors. We need only to provide incentives and sanctions that will correct these deficiencies.

This appears to be the rationale behind our national movement called "No Child Left Behind." The argument is that if we provide a uniform curriculum, universal standardized testing, a pedagogy heavily based on teaching to those tests, and a requirement that progress on such tests be demonstrated on a yearly basis (with severe consequences for students, teachers, schools, and school districts that fail to maintain such progress), we will significantly improve the efficiency and effectiveness of our education system. We are betting billions of dollars and more billions of classroom hours in pursuit of this theory. I believe we are making a bad bet, but the results of our national gamble (whether constructive or destructive) are yet to be proven, at least to the satisfaction of most serious educational scholars.

But if I am correct; if the generally mediocre performance of our students—in all grades, and across the spectrum of abilities—is primarily due to their being locked into a classroom environment in which game playing has replaced authentic learning, then the potential for an explosion of creativity, motivation, excitement, and achievement among all students is within our reach. It will require mainly that we break the invisible walls that confine us within a ritualized and stultifying playing field, so that we can unleash the learning potential that is amply present within children and youth. If we break free of the tranquilizing atmosphere that dulls the learning spirit of even our high achievers, we open up vast possibilities for even the lowest-performing schools. Most of the resources needed to stimulate such growth are already present within our school communities. They consist of our teachers, parents, and most especially our students themselves. If such is the case, then No Child Left Behind is absolutely the wrong medicine, and politicians who prescribe it are guilty of doing great harm.

I do not make the mistake—even if my theory *is* correct—of assuming that it will be easy to change the Game and turn our schools into places that nurture and support the instincts for authentic learning that lie within each of us. The Game is strongly entrenched in our psychology of education as well as in our habitual practices. But if it should prove true that our students are now working at only a fraction of their true learning potential, think of how much power lies in reserve, untapped, beneath the crust of conventional practice! The mere possibility of such an outcome should be sufficient to induce even the skeptical reader to lend serious thought to my argument.

I contend that the Game of School victimizes each of us, to a greater or lesser degree. While we believe we must master that game in order to maximize our success or just to survive, we pay a penalty for losing sight of authentic learning. In this book I hope to confront the waste of human potential that is the true cost of playing the Game of School. Once we have assessed this waste and seen how insidiously it traps us, we will consider how to overcome it and regain our roles as learners and teachers who are true to our learning spirit.

The False Self of the Pseudo-Learner

Despite devoting three chapters to the Game of School in *The Passionate Teacher*, I seriously underestimated the Game's impact. I named the beast but didn't realize what a behemoth it truly is. It's not that people are always conscious of faking it or simply going through the motions (though there's plenty of that). After enough time has gone by in which little or no authentic learning has taken place, teachers and students both adopt what I call *the false self of the pseudo-learner* (or *pseudo-teacher*).

The student's false self evolves in the acceptance of routine within a culture of schooling that obscures learning in the pursuit of superficial rewards. There's a world of difference between the student whose "straight A's" are a reflection of engaged, thoughtful, and creative learning, and the student who has "psyched out" his teachers and agreed to do whatever it takes to get all A's (or who has replaced a personal sense of value with a fixation on external and symbolic reward). As is true of any child who becomes obsessed with pleasing adults in an uncritical manner, too much is lost of the child's sense of who he is.

The teacher's false self is experienced in failing to maintain a view of one's students as "natural-born learners" and adapting a defensive posture against the inevitable rebellion of children's spirits against the docile and reactive role they have been placed in. The false self emerges whenever teachers feel obliged to cut discussions short, to short-circuit a student's divergent or contradictory question, to gloss over a conflict between the textbook version and their own sense of the truth about history or science. It is seen in the teacher's upholding school directives—mandatory suspension for using the "F-word," the avoidance of books deemed "controversial," or assigning a mandatory thirty minutes of homework for every class—when he or she knows that these directives will undermine authentic learning for some or all students. It rears its head whenever teachers feel subservient to a state-mandated, test-based curriculum that they realize is unconnected to the lives and interests of their students.

In schools and colleges across the nation and throughout the world, students and teachers continuously adopt roles and postures that remind us of uncomfortable visits to unpleasant relatives. We play out our roles as if we have lost the sense that learning is an intensely exciting and enjoyable activity, a necessary and joyful part of our humanity.

Kathleen Cushman, in the introduction to *Fires in the Bathroom: Advice for Teachers from High School Students*, speaks of this spirit-crushing sense of anomie:

> Anyone who has made it out of their teens most likely remembers the feelings of anonymity and captivity that even the best high schools can convey. Whether in huge urban warehouses, sprawling suburban campuses, or newly consolidated rural schools, teachers with more than 125 students a day can't help but focus the majority of their attention on only the most urgent cases.
>
> In such settings, order trumps most other institutional aims. To keep the place running smoothly, students' behavior becomes more important than their understanding, acquiescence more valued than inquiry. In pursuit of order, school and classroom rules routinely supplant the disarray of kids' questions, objections, suggestions, and problems. High school becomes something done *to* kids, not *by* kids. This is the way it works; this is the way it has always worked.[3]

In contrast to attitudes and behaviors that are roundly criticized in school (for example, rude or insulting language, insubordination, cheating, fighting, etc.), pseudo-teaching and pseudo-learning usually fall below the radar screen of administrative supervisors. "Just keep the noise down in your room," the vice principal chastens a novice teacher. "And make sure you assign a detention for each tardy student." "Follow the district schedule in preparing students for the state tests," commands the principal. "After test week is over, you can go back to teaching whatever you teachers think is important."

My "Game Plan" for This Book

Still and all, why should I continue to belabor the point of schoolwide game playing, as I have already had my say about it? The answer, as I have discovered in the past ten years, is that the Game won't let me alone. With the advent of high-stakes standardized testing across the nation, the climate of game playing has, if anything, intensified. Principals exhort teachers to abandon exciting and successful instructional units if they are not strictly aligned with the test. Students come to learn that beating last year's test scores is the thing adults in school care most about. As if such pressures were not enough, competitive parents weigh in on school decisions, such as to abandon tracking or downplay class rankings, that may affect (however slightly) their child's competitive edge in college admission, heedless of the educational ramifications for other students. And in my university classes, students who seek careers in teaching continue to look at their courses as obstacles, requirements to be gotten out of the way.

I write this book because, perhaps as never before, the great majority of students at all levels of schooling and from all backgrounds find their days preoccupied with something besides learning, and we and they don't often realize it, or if we do, we feel hopeless to change it. The Game of School is so identified with the culture of our educational system as to seem both invisible and immutable. And yet our acquiescence virtually guarantees wholesale educational mediocrity, even where test scores are on the rise and dropouts on the decline.

This book is divided into eight chapters; interspersed are "interludes" that contain interviews and observations of teachers and students who are struggling to surmount the obstacles discussed in the chapters. The book ends with a "coda" to wrap up my observations.

In Chapter One, I describe aspects of contemporary schooling that result in an unseen, disastrous, and unnecessary waste of students' time, using Seymour Sarason's distinction between "productive and nonproductive contexts for learning" and Alfie Kohn's plea that we ought to send our kids to school to "learn," rather than to "work." The interlude is courtesy of Elcira Delgado, a former student now doing her student teaching, who writes about how she's grown up with the Game (and may not yet have outgrown it).

Chapter Two follows the nascent learner up through the grades, from kindergarten through college, to show how the Game evolves as students respond to the demands placed upon them. In our highly competitive society we have little choice but to play this game, although we can do much to lessen its negative impact once we have recognized the Game for what it is. The interlude examines how Heidi Thomas, an experienced teacher in a first-grade class, begins her school year in a way that promotes authentic learning.

Chapter Three builds on Evans Clinchy's unpublished research into the lessons to be learned from human evolution when considering formal education. In it, I create a tale in which several fifth graders initiate their own authentic learning quite apart from what goes on in school, and I call upon the words of naturalist Rachel Carson to help us consider what we may be sacrificing in our eagerness to provide instruction to children whose capacity to wonder and imagine and create can be so easily stunted or shortchanged. The interlude highlights the work of Melanie Livingston, a talented middle school English teacher in an urban bilingual school, whom I observed teach test prep to a class of seventh graders and Shakespeare's *Othello* to her eighth graders.

Chapter Four begins with a critique of our "state religion of achievement" that has pushed aside a deep and complex definition of learning in favor of a narrow but measurable emphasis on test scores. I also describe seven categories of learners who operate within the Game of School environment (including several groups who opt not to play). I speculate how each type relates to authentic learning versus playing the Game, and I invite student readers to place themselves somewhere within those categories. The interlude explores the work of Abd Al-Maalik, a beginning history teacher in a tough high school situation, as he copes with students who seem to have lost the knack of taking learning seriously.

Chapter Five has two purposes: the first is to reclaim the language of education from those who have imprisoned it within the dungeon of professional jargon—inviting teachers, students, and parents to consider what we truly mean by the terms *classroom management*, *curriculum*, *instruction*, *assessment*, *self-motivation*, and *family involvement*. My second purpose is to frame each of these terms so as to contrast practices that lead to authentic learning with those likely to perpetuate the Game. The interlude consists of an essay by Randy Wisehart, a friend and colleague who has twenty-eight years of experience in helping reluctant learners find their voice, and has in recent years worked with faculty at Earlham College to create a new master's-level teaching program based on passionate teaching.

I address Chapter Six to teachers who have become "stuck" in their professional lives, as the cumulative impact of the Game of School brings on a paralysis of spirit and a loss of passion. Those of you who are teachers are invited to assess yourselves on criteria that compare the attitudes of those who are stuck with those who have held on to their passion as teachers. The chapter concludes with ways to help teachers become unstuck. The interlude offers my own Joy and Misery Index, so that practicing educators can score themselves on how negatively or positively they are affected by external and internal factors that affect their classroom environments.

Chapter Seven asks what we each can do, as students, teachers, and parents, to change the Game in ways that promote authentic learning. I highlight the recent work and evolving philosophy of David Ervin, whom I first interviewed for *The Passionate Teacher* a decade ago; I report on an inspiring instance of students from Calgary taking on their local government on behalf of the homeless; and, drawing from my current teaching, I offer a few examples of how prospective teachers are learning to reach out to their students as partners in inquiry. The interlude is my interview with Jenny O'Neil from the City Year program in Boston, who has created the highly successful Building a Beloved Community initiative in Boston's most difficult middle schools.

The coda is titled "A Lesson Before Teaching," and in it I attempt to draw together my feelings about how readily the Game of School can be banished by students and teachers agreeing to challenge themselves with a true learning endeavor—yet how quickly the Game reappears when such authenticity is lost.

Throughout the book, I rely on the observations of learners from a variety of settings. Along with comments gleaned from essays and short papers of my current and former students at Northeastern University, I have greatly benefited from the work of three classroom teachers who have field-tested some of my ideas with their own students. I have also borrowed the voices of adolescent students who helped put together the book *Fires in the Bathroom*.

I invite you to immerse yourself in my critique of the Game of School, the better to reflect on your own willing and unwilling participation in it, in the hope that we can either change it or extricate ourselves and the young learners around us from its stultifying grip.

Chapter One

Wasting Time

Let's consider a frightening possibility: far too much of the time our children spend in school is wasted. It's not that nothing happens there or that kids spend their time just fooling around or that teachers don't try their best to present lessons they think are in our children's best interests. It's just that unless our children—of all ages—are truly engaged in their learning, most of what they experience during school hours passes over them like the shadow of a cloud, or through them like an undigested seed. They may be present in the classroom, but they are not really *there*. Their pencils may be chugging away on the worksheets or the writing prompts or math problems laid out for them, but their intelligence is running on two cylinders at best. They pay some attention to what their teacher happens to be telling them, but their imagination has moved elsewhere. Megan Flatley, a graduate student of mine, wrote in a recent short paper for class, "As a student, I remember being bored in 80 percent of my classes in high school. When something happened out of the ordinary, we all took pleasure in it. Whether this was a student acting up, a fire drill—any kind of distraction, really—it was more fun than what the teacher might be saying or the lessons I was supposed to be learning. Just the feeling of SOMETHING HAPPENING was exciting."

And, worst of all, by the time our kids have reached fourth or fifth grade, they think that what they are experiencing in school is *normal*.

Why *shouldn't* our kids be eager to head off to school each day, anticipating their next investigation, project, or performance? It can be agonizing for parents to see their imaginative, articulate, eagerly seeking young learner become, over the years, someone bored, passive, complaining, or compliant—focused on not making mistakes rather than on taking on new challenges.[1] Most kids in school listen and do what they're told, most of the time. They pick up stray facts and acquire some skills they wouldn't necessarily learn elsewhere. They learn about following rules in the lunchroom and about leaving one-inch margins on their papers. They even learn the Pythagorean theorem and how to write a five-paragraph essay with three supporting arguments and a conclusion.

But unless they view such activities as important, as having meaning to them in their lives *right now,* they aren't truly *learning*, in the sense of developing their minds and hearts as young people eager to embrace the world. Although it is true that many of us who have been successful in schools-as-they-are have fond memories of inspired teachers about whom the relevance of what they taught us only became apparent in retrospect (often years later), the odds are that too many of our fellow students never achieved such delayed enlightenment. I'm not insisting that everything we teach must be instantly relevant, only that we take very seriously our students' need to find purpose in what we ask of them. I am still shocked to hear so many young people express just how meaningless they find academic life in school and that they spend their time mostly just going through the motions. Andres, a young man who attends high school in San Francisco, put it this way: "In seventh grade my grades started slipping. I noticed I had a lot more freedom, and I stopped doing my work. But they kept on passing me, even though I wasn't doing anything. It's not like it was about my learning, it was about moving us through to high school. I hated that.[2]

What Is Authentic Learning?

Throughout these first pages, I have been using the word *authentic* to describe learning that is the alternative to playing the Game of School, and you have a right to know what I mean. Here are several examples, taken from a variety of sources:

- A history teacher leads a ninth-grade class on a field trip to an abandoned cemetery in the woods not far from their school. First, she and the kids spend some time cleaning up the site, removing dead limbs fallen from overhanging trees, righting headstones that have toppled over, cleaning the headstones with soap and water and brushes. Each student picks the name of someone from a headstone, and the class goes into the village to find what official records exist for that person. The students do their research, write it up, and present it as a booklet in a meeting with members of the town's historical society, who are enthusiastic about their work and talk with them about it. Their booklet becomes part of the town record.

- A fifth-grade teacher, mindful of how abstract such notions as "inequality" and "resources" and "poverty" can appear to kids, comes to class with exactly enough chocolate chip cookies for each of his students. He places students into groups, representing the relative populations of North America, South America, Europe, Asia, and Africa, with a large name tag for each group member listing their continent. He then distributes the cookies in a way that represents the "wealth" available to each group. The three students representing North America end up with six cookies each; the eight students representing Africa have one cookie between them. The students are asked to explore their feelings on the competing values of wanting to share the "good things" fairly, versus wanting to have all the cookies for themselves. They also get to speculate on how, if they ran the world, they might resolve this. Each student writes a response to the question, "How can we make the world a better place?"

- Children in a second-grade class take a trip to a nearby retirement home. They meet some of the residents and talk in small groups with them. When they return to school, they paint pictures that they think will be appreciated by their new older friends. When they return with their pictures, the residents have a tea party for them, and the student artwork is given to the residents to hang in their rooms.

- A seventh-grade math teacher, concerned about widely differing attitudes toward math among his incoming students, asks them to mark, anonymously on a 3-by-5 card, the number that best reflects how they feel: 1 = I love math; 2 = Math is pretty good; 3 = Math is so-so; 4 = I do it but don't like it; 5 = I hate math. A student is asked to tote up the scores while the teacher speculates as to how many kids might be in each category. The results are announced (everyone learns how good a predictor their teacher is). The class is then divided into five small groups, each with poster paper. One group has to reflect the results as fractions; the second, as percentages; the third, as decimals; the fourth, on a bar graph; the fifth, on a pie chart. Their *feelings* about math are given expression via math symbols. The teacher then talks about how their attitudes might change by Thanksgiving time, and the groups have to represent this, too, on poster paper. (The five groups switch methods of representing the new data.) Afterwards (or on following days), the students write, again anonymously, what they think it would take for each of them to be able to move up a number: what they need from their teacher, how their parents can help, what they themselves can do. The suspense generated by their attempt to achieve these new goals fuels the conversation of the classroom.

- An eleventh-grade civics teacher invites students to learn about the Bill of Rights by exploring what rights they *wish* were guaranteed by the Bill of Rights, from a twenty-first-century viewpoint. Each group can come up with two new "rights" that our Founding Fathers either didn't care enough about or couldn't possibly have predicted a need for. In exchange, the kids have to come to consensus about which two of the existing ten amendments they would be willing to let go of. A legal expert (lawyer, judge, legislator, or constitutional scholar) is invited into class to hear and comment on their proposals.

- I recently came across yet another example, offered by a high school student: "For our final exam in English and world history we had a mock trial with a real judge and a court typist. They separated us into defense and prosecution, with four lawyers on each side, and they set up a mock scene from *Animal Farm* in which the character Boxer supposedly dies. The defense was defending the guy who supposedly killed him. We had to dress up and go down to City Center for three or four hours. It was pretty fun. We learned more about the book, but we also learned how to follow court procedures, write direct testimony, and do cross-examination."[3]

If we look for them, we find dozens of similar examples in all subjects and at every grade level. What they share is that students recognize that knowledge and meaning have not been predetermined by teacher or textbook, but instead will emerge from their *own* efforts, guided and structured by their teacher. Students act as "junior partners" as they encounter academic content in a more or less realistic setting or through questions that seem cogent and not easily answerable. Nobody knows in advance what will emerge. Their role as students is to *speculate* about the unknown, to *seek* and to *synthesize* knowledge, and then to *share* it. Important people (their parents, local citizens, other students) care about what they will discover or create. Such engagement forms *genuine learning partnerships*.

Despite our children's strong innate capacity and zest for such authentic learning, the failure of our educational system to recognize and stimulate these great natural gifts causes educators to focus, instead, on presenting knowledge, or "delivering instruction," to students. As a result, children's desire to acquire information and skills takes a nosedive as they rise up through the grades. On a daily basis, kids are more likely to be influenced by how other kids behave toward them in the lunchroom or the playground, or by whether their teacher smiled at them or scolded them, than by the lesson plans their teacher followed and the knowledge he or she has "covered." The human interactions are what stand out, and it is these that are more likely to induce students to change or modify their behavior—to avoid that one or to get closer to this one or to try not to upset their teacher. Precious little of what they have supposedly learned has had as much of an impact.

The Attack on Our Learning Spirit

For nearly all of us, advantaged and disadvantaged, as we emerge from those preschool years of unabashedly enthusiastic learning and begin our careers as students, our inner drive to learn—what I would call our *learning spirit*—suffers a series of blows. Our freedom of physical movement is severely restricted, our curiosity is confined, our opportunity to talk to other kids about what we are learning is curtailed. We do not see these as attacks on our learning spirit; they are just the normal stuff that happens in school. In the classroom, we do not choose either to embrace or to reject "learning." We experience a pressure to do well, to be good, to be smart in school. Little by little, grade by grade, we find ourselves relating to school more and more in a way that sharply contrasts with the energy, purposefulness, and joy that young children bring to the challenge of learning how to talk, run, play games, ask questions, and investigate the world around them. Learning becomes a chore rather than an adventure.

In school we are more likely to learn *not* to talk, *not* to run, *not* to play, and *not* to ask questions. We are cautioned to "keep our hands to ourselves" and *not* to investigate anything that hasn't been placed before us on our desks. Our curiosity may be seen as impudence, our creativity misjudged as failure to follow directions. In *The Passionate Learner*, I documented just such a transfer of focus among a group of urban kids:

> I asked a group of third-grade students to tell me what were the most important things they were learning in school. They said, "not to run in the halls," "no pushing or fighting," "don't throw stuff on the floor." I agreed with them that these were, indeed, important things,

> and I wrote them on the board under the heading, "Good *Behavior*." But next to that I wrote "Good *Learning*" and asked them what important things they felt they needed to *learn*. After a few moments, two children raised their hands. One said, "to listen to the teacher." The other said, "to be good."
>
> Already, as third graders, learning had become a world of "good children" and "bad children." Good children listen to their teacher. The bad children don't. Thus far in their lives, these urban third graders still consider it *good* to "be good." For many of their older brothers and sisters, it has already become *cool* to "be bad."[4]

Not all children respond the same way, of course. There are plenty of kids in urban, suburban, and rural schools who will perk up and tell us that they are learning to read books, to write stories, to master long division, to care for classroom pets. School is clearly about more than just following the teacher's direction, as important as that is. But we should worry if our young people are beginning to confuse, or to blend in their minds, the idea of *obeying the teacher* with *learning*. For that tendency, if left unchecked by teachers and parents, will soon transform many children into youngsters whose resistance to obeying the teacher (which may be a normal aspect of their emerging adolescence) signals a parallel resistance to learning. Before we know it, the "resisters" become synonymous with "bad kids," even in their own minds. We don't find many kids who report, "I love what I'm learning in school—it's just that I don't like doing the stuff my teachers try to make me do."

There is a simple test we can perform to find out whether or not our children are truly learning. We can ask them, not the usual question, "How was school today, Honey?" or "What did she teach you in your math class?" but rather, "Did you learn anything in school today that you really want to know more about?" If the answer is often yes, your child has been primed to continue learning on her own. If it's usually no, you have cause for worry—even if your child brings home a good report card.

Megan Flatley recalls:

> I was a pretty good student, growing up, who didn't have to try very hard to get good grades. Looking back, I realize that I could have used my education for so much more than I did. Instead of really being involved in what was going on around me, I did the minimum necessary to get by. And, sadly enough, this "minimum" was more than enough . . . ! The subject matter was boring and irrelevant to me. My classes were something to get through, and I cannot recall ONCE going home and thinking, "I would like to look into that, to learn more about that."

I don't remember being asked such a question by my parents, or asking it of my kids as they moved through public school. It didn't occur to my parents or me to think that a child's time is as precious as that of a busy adult and that much of the time my kids and I were in school and doing homework was poorly spent. Looking back, I'd say that although most of the public schools my kids and I attended were deemed "pretty good" by local standards, at least 60 to 70 percent of the time spent in schools was wasted.

I have observed schools where, on average, the waste of time for students seemed closer to 90 to 95 percent. The teachers (or student teachers) knew *something* was wrong, but they rarely framed their concerns as a critique of their school culture or as a reflection on the enormity of time wasted. They were more likely to focus on deficiencies of aptitude or attitude on the part of significant numbers of students, or on the lack of interesting texts and materials, or on the inappropriateness of the curriculum they were being asked to deliver, or on the obstruction of a few troublemakers. Rarely, if ever, did they say to their classes, "This just isn't working. I can see that most of you aren't learning much—are you? Please tell me if I'm exaggerating the problem. But as I see it, whatever we're trying to accomplish, we're obviously not doing it very well. We need to rethink what we're doing. If *you* aren't learning much; if you're not engaged, not desirous of learning more about this topic, then obviously we're on the wrong track, and we should be doing something quite, quite different."

Such a statement is by no means a confession of ineptitude on the teacher's part, much less an expression of failure (though some might view it thus). It is an invitation for teacher and students to replace their false selves, their pseudo-educational roles, with new pathways to engagement in learning. Here is an instance where a student saw a teacher do just that: "I was sitting in history really bored, and I was wondering how could history help me? And he could tell that we were getting bored, so he asked us the same question! He didn't tell us the answer—the question was good enough. It kind of made me think."[5]

Going with the Flow

It's time to lift the veils from our eyes and contemplate the waste of time that has become endemic throughout our educational system. Those veils are everywhere; a search of available research on the topic offers little in the way of an examination of how children waste time by not being actively, intellectually, and emotionally engaged in their studies. In April 1994, a blue ribbon commission investigating our nation's education system in the aftermath of *A Nation at Risk* came up with a report titled *Prisoners of Time*, in which they documented what they saw as an obsolete structure of organization. Their report began,

> Learning in America is a prisoner of time. For the past 150 years, American public schools have held time constant and let learning vary. The rule, only rarely voiced, is simple: learn what you can in the time we make available. It should surprise no one that some bright, hard-working students do reasonably well. Everyone else—from the typical student to the dropout—runs into trouble.
>
> Time is learning's warden. Our time-bound mentality has fooled us all into believing that schools can educate all of the people all of the time in a school year of 180 six-hour days. The consequence of our self-deception has been to ask the impossible of our students. We expect them to learn as much as their counterparts abroad in only half the time.[6]

What is noteworthy in the commission's findings is that their focus is solely on how time is used and misused in schools (for example, "the fixed clock and calendar," the charge that "Academic time has been stolen to make room for a host of nonacademic activities," plus a plea for more planning time for educators, more interdisciplinary team teaching, individualized instruction, and more time for students to devote to ratcheting themselves up for the purpose of "mastering world-class standards" and meeting the global competition). The commission properly castigates our reliance on credits or "Carnegie units" as a basis for graduation, and demands that we "reinvent schools around learning, not time." However, they do not address the waste associated with *the failure to engage students in authentic learning*. They propose, sadly, only more of the same—more academic instruction aided by more technology—rather than a rethinking of how teachers and students might work to foster higher levels of learning.

Teachers, and the administrative staff who stand behind them, are powerful figures to young children.[7] When powerful people in our lives direct us to do something, some task, some function (be it lining up to go to lunch, opening our books to page 15, getting rid of our chewing gum, or solving the math problems on the handout), we usually have little choice but to obey. It would probably not be wise to say, "Mr. Knox, I'm not especially hungry, today, so I'd rather keep reading *Harry Potter* for a while and then come down to lunch a bit later." When asked to open our social studies textbook, a preteen is not likely to say, "I'm sorry, Miss Rodriguez, but to me it represents a biased view of history. Is it all right if I go to the library to look for another book on that topic that might be more interesting?" If told to spit out our chewing gum, it would probably not go over very well to respond, "But, Mr. Wilson, I never, *ever*, stick my gum under the desk. I chew it quietly because it helps me relax. It's also sugarless, so it won't hurt my teeth." If directed to start on the math handout, few students respond, "These problems are too easy [or too hard] for me, Ms. Chen. Do you think I could sit with my friend Kyle and work on some math that's at our level?"

Such responses might, in fact, be perfectly reasonable ones to use at home and, depending on our parents' style of child rearing, we might expect to receive positive or negative responses from them.[8] But in school, we soon learn, it's important for everyone to be doing things pretty much in the same way. There just isn't time for individual negotiation on assignments or other directives. We are schooled to "go along to get along." When we see one of our classmates openly defy a teacher, we learn how dangerous that can be. We don't want to get yelled at, kept inside for recess, sent to the time-out corner or principal's office, or threatened with a call home. So we line up for lunch, open our textbooks to page 15, throw the gum in the waste bin, begin tackling the math problems whether or not they are appropriately challenging. We soon fail to distinguish (if ever we did) between commands that have to do with rules of behavior and those that pertain to learning. You'd better "listen to the teacher" if you want to "be good."

The response of most of us is to play along. We may feel rebellious or bored, but, like Oliver Twist, we quickly learn not to ask for special favors. If our teacher is someone whom we admire and respect, we are more willing to acquiesce to his or her direction, especially if this teacher is sensitive to our own particular needs and makes a reasonable effort to tailor the assigned work to a level that challenges us without overwhelming us. Similarly, if we resent our teacher, we may continue to acquiesce, but we are likely to harden ourselves against that person and the learning she or he asks us to pursue.

In either case, we develop the habit of disengaging what we do in school and for homework from both the inner logic and the self-motivation that has heretofore driven us as learners to figure things out and learn new skills. We remove ourselves as the driver of our learning carriage, we succumb to the bit and bridle, we accept the blinders, and we learn to pull along with the other horses. We do our work to get it done. If something new and interesting emerges from an assignment, it is a pleasant surprise; but we learn not to expect such surprises as a concomitant of schoolwork.

Productive and Unproductive Contexts for Learning

Seymour Sarason reminds us of the distinction between "productive and unproductive contexts of learning." It is a central concept of his lifelong critique both of conventional schooling and of misguided school reform efforts. He explains, "by *productive* I mean that the learning process is one which engenders and reinforces [the child's] wanting to learn more."[9] Unproductive learning is almost everything else that goes on in school.

This is not a call to ban all instructional activities that students don't immediately and enthusiastically embrace. We don't want to turn our educators into slick salespeople who cater to the whims and fancies of their students (who are already too much influenced by the fads pushed by the media). We adults don't have to pander to our children's notions of what would be "easy" to do or "fun" to learn about. Children respond to good teaching even—especially—when it challenges them to think deeply, to aim high.

But unless we take very seriously the notion of productive and unproductive contexts of learning, we will find that the desired connection between a teacher's notion of what's worth teaching and a child's sense of what's worth learning more about will take place only rarely, or haphazardly, or with only a few "super teachers" or only a minority of youngsters who come to school ready and eager to soak up what we offer them.

Most of us who consider ourselves successful in life eventually regain at least some of our zest for learning, either in college or grad school; in preparation for a career that has captured our imagination; in the challenge of making a go of it in the business world; as artists and artisans or hobbyists of one kind or another; as advocates for political and environmental causes; as readers and writers. We humans love to learn, and we are never quite as invigorated as when we have carved out of our busy schedules some time to devote to our learning passions.

But this reemergence of a zest for learning cannot fully compensate for the loss that takes place during the years of our schooling. If we are fortunate enough to be raised in a home where love of learning is celebrated and modeled before our eyes, we may come to school well fortified to deal with lessons we find boring or meaningless, assignments we find confusing or tedious, or teachers who seem uninterested in how our own creativity exhibits itself. Our parents may comfort us with the idea that this, too, shall pass; they might assist us with our homework and help find creative solutions to tasks that seem absurd or pointless.

Defining What Children Do in School as "Work"

For most children in most schools on most days, such support cannot overcome the feeling that they are there simply to do what they are told. And then the Game, the act of feigning interest and putting forth only as much energy or thought as is necessary to meet the expectations set for us by those in command, envelopes our approach to school. We begin to see school, in a word, as our "work." After all, that's what everybody else calls it.

In his op-ed piece "Students Don't 'Work'—They Learn," writer and critic Alfie Kohn invites teachers to resolve, *From now on, we will stop referring to what students do in school as "work."*

> Importing the nomenclature of the workplace is something most of us do without thinking—which is in itself a good reason to reflect on the practice. Every time we talk about "homework" or "seat work" or "work habits," every time we describe the improvement in, or assessment of, a student's "work" in class, every time we urge children to "get to work" or even refer to "classroom *management*," we are using a metaphor with profound implications for the nature of schooling. In effect, we are equating what children do to figure things out with what adults do in offices and factories to earn money.[10]

I don't want to downplay the importance of work in our lives. I seek rather to elevate—to celebrate—the importance of *learning*, of productive learning, the kind of learning that makes the learner want to do more of it on her own.

Nobody's Fault: Crimeless Victims of a System That Hurts Learning

I see no despicable plot, no conspiracy by educators to deny children their right to learn. The problem is not that those who work within schools and colleges regularly force us to abandon our own learning goals and submit to their indoctrination. It's just that too many of us—students and teachers alike—agree to substitute lesser, symbolic goals for greater and truer ones. When we allow ourselves (or get convinced) to gear ourselves up so as to complete school tasks that have little meaning for us *aside from the value of getting them done and over with*, we lose touch with our own learning spirit. We become alienated from the natural learning desires and inquisitiveness within us. We tend to become compliant rather than creative, docile instead of courageous, inwardly passive instead of assertively engaged, cynical at a time in life when we should be idealistic. We become *game players* by reflex, and *learners* only on occasion.

Not everyone. And certainly not all the time.

There are inspiring teachers in our schools and colleges who want nothing more than for us to blossom as self-motivated and creative learners. For them, we are happy to perform the tasks they set for us (even if we might not have chosen those tasks ourselves). "Sometimes I can't wait to get up and go to school," reports Montoya, a high school student in Oakland. "Because at some points school is very interesting—like when we have exhibition night, where everybody shows their projects off."[11] We thrive on the praise that comes with compliance and hard work. Getting the assignment done well and on time can lead not only to a good grade but also to a genuine sense of achievement. Montoya reports, "I wouldn't even think I could do something and my teacher would push me farther and I would succeed and do really well. In those first two months we did tons of work, and at the end we had a big project to do. I couldn't believe all the work I did."[12]

And, to be fair, there is something about the nature of school that can offer a degree of structure, authority, and comfort to certain learners of all ages. For the youngest, it's a chance to gain recognition and praise from an adult not their parent who affords them a chance to perform well, within known boundaries, on tasks that challenge them to show just how "grown-up" and conscientious they are. For some teenagers faced with the confusions of growing up, school can be that place where they take a break from their hormones, their family struggles, and their peer group pressures and apply themselves to concrete, specific tasks within guidelines set forth by an adult figure to whom they do not need to prove how independent or cool they are. And for some adults who return to school for a course or a degree, a syllabus provides them with structure, boundaries, and intellectual challenge, along with a comforting sense of hierarchy, of someone deservedly "in charge"—qualities that may be missing in other parts of life.[13] But I worry that when too many students get in the habit of focusing, reflexively, on the "work" their teachers are asking them to do, their independence as learners begins to atrophy.

My argument with the Game of School is not an argument against *school*, much less against the teaching profession. Teachers, schools, and school systems are themselves often the victims of this self-same game, played out according to the rules set down by those who have power over us. My hope is to bring this phenomenon to the attention of educators and learners at all levels; it is most destructive where least acknowledged. Those caught in the Game soon lose awareness of it; it begins to seem like the only way of doing business.

Although we all play to one degree or another, the Game affects each of us quite differently. And though it can result in a significant or even a tragic loss of our own power as learners, it is a loss that is recoverable at every stage of life. It is never too late to learn, never too late to recover one's own learning power and initiative from the habits and practices that subdue and subvert that power. Learning on our own (or with chosen colleagues) or developing our own goals for the learning we do in school becomes an empowering act of discovering the truth; and it is the truth that makes us free.

Let's examine a view of the Game from a former student of mine, Elcira Delgado. Although quite contemptuous of the circumstances that have nurtured her role as a player in the Game of School, she's evidently not quite ready to give up playing.

~ Interlude ~

Elcira Delgado's Show

"Welcome to The Game of School! *I'm your host, Johnny Doe, and today our guest is college student Elcira Delgado. Elcira hails from the middle-class, suburban town of West Hartford, CT, a town known for its excellent school system. She enjoys long walks on the beach, listening to music, and no, school does not fit into her extracurricular activities. She's been a participant in our game now for about eight years. She's won every game so far and never gets sick of playing! How does she do it?"* . . .

Ladies and gentlemen, I would like to welcome you to *my* Game of School. It all began back in good old elementary school. Ah, the joys of being a fifth grader, you get to rule the school, you'll be in middle school soon and you don't have to use that stupid jar of paste. What? No paste? Wait, wait, wait. Why no paste? Oh yeah, now I remember. It's all becoming clear to me, or unclear to me. Fifth grade was the beginning of the downfall of my motivation to learn. Slowly but surely all those fun hands-on projects began to disappear (hence no more paste), and lectures became commonplace. But that's OK, because we still had a couple of science projects here and there, we got to move to another classroom to do history, and we still had recess. Besides, our report cards did not show us A's or F's, but simply showcased our work with an "excellent," "satisfactory," or "unsatisfactory." I had always been an "excellent" student and never needed a reminder from my parents to do my homework.

Yeah, I was *that* kid. You know the kind, the kid that always did their homework, 100 on every spelling bee, the student teachers show off to the administration. I did well because I enjoyed learning. But elementary school couldn't last forever, so I graduated from Braeburn Elementary school to begin my glory days as a middle schooler on the road to success.

Sixth grade? Ah yes, I remember it well: The institution of Homeroom; different teachers for different subjects; our first school dance; that kid with the cute hair (I must keep my focus on school); my first C—and in *English,* of all subjects.

You'd think after speaking English for a good 11 years I'd be getting A's. But back to that C. Ouch! Yeah, that one hurt. Yeah, those C's, you can't even change them into any other letter with your own red pen. Maybe you could make it a curvy B, but that's a stretch. Now I'm not saying that the C was the *beginning* of my game. Simply that it hurt. Up to now, I was "Little Miss Excellent" in school, and this C was a huge blow to my perfect record. Not only was it difficult for me to cope with my "satisfactory" grade, but my almost nonexistent social life was hurting too. Not being able to go outside and play kickball with the rest of the neighborhood sucks, especially when instead you are stuck inside, *grounded.*

My parents were not so pleased with this grade and began monitoring my schoolwork. I tried to tell them it wasn't my fault, but the fault of my evil, "She-never-even-smiles-at-me" English teacher. This did not fly so well. There was only one way out of this, to do all my work to the best of my ability. This lasted till about halfway through the year, when I had my parents convinced that I was once again a great student. School was still kind of interesting to me, but as my interests began to shift from learning to sleeping, shopping, and boys, my attention was no longer focused on the different cultures of the world, but instead on whom I was going to sit with at lunch that day. The fact that my classes had begun to drag on and on, with a teacher standing at the front of the class droning on for forty-five minutes, was no help either.

Seventh grade was the year of the lying, cheating, and stealing. You are not new to the school anymore, but you're no closer to the end than you were last year. This was the year that we began to learn algebra, the history of the world, and to read books longer than 150 pages. This is when I began to play the Game of School full tilt. I couldn't help it. Drilling of math problems, pages upon pages of wars, grammar, I couldn't take it. Do you think I really read every chapter of my textbooks to answer questions? Of course I didn't. Besides, the Cliff's Notes were not as time-consuming and had all the answers right there. Do you think I paid attention in class? Well that was 50/50, but still, I should have been attentive 100 percent of the time. Like that would ever happen . . .

Oh wait, it did, once! During my history class. I can't remember exactly what I was studying, but I wrote a wonderful paper on the topic. My parents even helped me proofread my masterpiece. I brought the disk to school and printed it out in the computer lab. The next week went along wonderfully, till, as luck would have it, I sanded a few layers of skin off during Tech Ed. As I walked to the nurse's office with a bleeding thumb and blackened skin, I was stopped by my history teacher (who didn't seem to notice my festering wound). He asked to speak with me after school, something about plagiarism and copying someone else's paper.

Are you kidding me?! Someone had handed in the same paper as I had?! Who'd done it? Oh, of course, the Goody Two Shoes of our class. *He* didn't have *time* to write a paper of his own, so he found mine in the computer lab and handed it in as his! Lucky for me, he confessed, but of course, since he was such a Kiss Ass he never got in trouble for it (but you know if it had been anyone else in our class, it would have been cause for instant out-of-school suspension). Forget working hard. If people are going to try to steal my work and take my A, there is no point in creating such masterpieces. So, I continued on my path of doing almost nothing, but fortunately for me succeeding with straight A's.

Eighth grade, not so important. Just a whole lotta doing nothing and passing classes. I slept a lot in class, too. Either that, or I pretended to look really interested. My parents didn't bother me about a thing. As long as the A came at the end of the semester, I could do what I wanted. This same mentality lasted into my high school years. Classes were b-o-r-i-n-g. Lectures became commonplace and essay tests were taking over. Luckily, by now I had perfected my "do-hardly-anything/still-get-an-A" skills. I was a Master. My friends never did understand how I did so well in school without lifting a finger to do my work. That empty A filled my soul with pride. I wasn't learning much, but colleges don't ask what we have truly learned. They simply read some b—s— essay we write and check out our grades . . .

And here I am today, a proud student in college, where I continue to play my Game of School. Why can't I study? Why do I settle for the mediocre grades? What is wrong with me?

Ah, the answer is simple, my friend. I have no motivation. "What?!" you say. "No motivation?" Isn't pleasing my parents and becoming a successful career woman enough? Apparently not. Some might say that I am still immature and have not learned the true value of higher education, and to them I would say, "You're partially right." But what is the point of doing my best, when I can get my degree, go out into the work field, perfect the necessary skills and become a master at what I do, without being a 4.0 student? Can't answer that one? Nah, me neither. Maybe that's why I never lose at my game . . .

OK, now I'm just dragging this out, like the rest of my educational experiences. Let's review what we've learned:

1. Elcira doesn't like doing schoolwork.
2. Elcira does the minimum necessary to succeed.
3. Elcira is still playing the Game of School as a sophomore in college.

Chilling facts, aren't they? I shudder myself when I read this list. As a future educator I should love school and learning, but that enthusiasm was lost somewhere in the halls of Sedgwick Middle School. All I know is that I've learned from my past education the type of teacher I DON'T want to be. And besides, it's difficult to be boring in an elementary classroom. I just hope that all those teachers teaching the secondary grades out there can realize how important it is to keep their students motivated, even in a boring subject like algebra, or you might end up with a classroom full of little Elciras.

Will I ever get back my motivation to learn? I don't know how likely that is to happen. You'd think that someone who does so little schoolwork would be hanging off the back of a garbage truck right now. But no, up to this moment in my life, the game has worked to my advantage, and I'm happy where I'm at. So, as I continue to pursue my education, the game will continue to be played. There's only one thing that could stop me dead in my tracks, which would be to receive a grade lower than a C. Until then? "Play on, Playa—the Game of School is goin' strong. Holla!"

Chapter Two

The Game of School up Through the Grades

We begin to play the Game of School from the moment we enter kindergarten or first grade, although if we observe most young children, it's difficult to see, in their enthusiasm and eagerness to learn, that the Game has already begun to take hold of their imaginations and their attitudes toward learning. The Game, at this stage, can be defined as "How do I get to be on the good side of my teacher? How do I make sure she likes me?" There is no shortage of motivated young learners in kindergarten or first grade, when, it seems, all the kids want to do and know everything. We hear proud teachers speak of them as "eager little sponges." But the ranks of motivated learners drop off sharply in the years from early childhood through elementary school, and they often seem to disappear in middle school, when social concerns predominate and academics seem "such a drag."

Elementary School: Let the Game Begin!

Unless restricted by severe emotional or cognitive disabilities, every child entering school does so as a naturally enthusiastic learner, one who can't wait to do new things and learn new skills. But that enthusiasm may be short-lived. School too often insists that this young child turn her attention away from the joy and spontaneity and purposefulness of learning and focus instead on pleasing the teacher and doing her work obediently. Ira Glass, host of the radio program *This American Life*, formerly reported on public education for National Public Radio. Speaking recently about

Chicago's Washington Irving Elementary School during the mid-1990s, before an ambitious school reform program was instituted there, Glass observed, "As in most Chicago schools, the *longer* a child stayed in school, the *worse* he was likely to do." He quotes Madelyn Miraldi, the school's former principal: "Everyone always used to say, 'Oh God, by third grade? *Man!* Their eyes glaze over.' They shut down their speaking and listening—they don't *care* anymore."[1]

I remember asking a group of elementary teachers to identify at what stage they began to see their pupils "turn off" to school, and most of them agreed that it closely followed the introduction of "real grades" in third or fourth grade. "That's when they start comparing themselves to other kids, often kids who entered school with a lot more preparation from home," said one teacher. "They begin to feel that they are just not good at school, and some of them stop trying." One of my students, Kate O'Regan, put it this way:

> I was an avid reader through fourth grade. I read every "Babysitter's Club" book ever made. When I went to fifth grade, I was faced with *grades!* My teacher had the reputation of being extremely strict. I was no longer allowed to read any Babysitter's Club–type books. Every semester if we wanted an A in reading, we had to read 1,000 pages. Now, I loved reading, yes; but I wasn't a fast reader. Yet I wanted that A. I started complaining of my "eyes hurting" when I read, and I stopped reading. I lied about the books I read, and I faked all the book reports. I didn't read a book from fifth grade until my junior year in high school.

As the child proceeds through school, he may, in fact, learn many useful and interesting things. But he also learns to undervalue his own learning in favor of "doing the work," pleasing his teachers, getting good marks on his report cards so his parents will be happy. Chris, a former student of mine, wrote:

> Basically, the game of school is a con game that you play against the education system—everything a student does to do well in school

> while doing as little work as possible. It is all those fake excuses students use to get out of exams or homework. The game has a lot to do with the notion that if parents see good grades, they automatically assume that their child is doing all of their schoolwork. My parents had no idea how little work I was actually accomplishing. . . . Just as long as I was getting A's and B's, they chose not to interfere.

The Games of Middle School, and a Visit to the Land of "the Losers"

In the middle school grades, there are two games that most of us play. One is the game of getting ahead, maneuvering ourselves (often with a push from our parents) into the top group academically, being placed up there with "the smart kids." Getting placed in the right classes, chasing straight A's—that's what counts. Creativity and outspokenness may jeopardize our chances. "Gifted and talented" too often comes to mean "compliant and diligent" if not "parentally pushed."

The second kind of game requires quite a different set of skills. This is the game of getting in with the popular kids, of being cool. By definition, not all of us will be popular, because for some kids to be "in with the Populars" requires keeping the rest of us out. What we are likely to see is, again, a sublimation of one's unique personality and the rejection of any kind of learning that isn't considered cool (the "geek-avoidance" syndrome). Both middle school games do damage to young intellects. Both demand conformity and obedience, as kids try to push ahead of others to land in that top group, academically or socially, as they minimize their individuality in order to fit in. Such conformity is the enemy of learning and causes us to betray our true selves in seeking the acceptance of others.

Before moving on to high school, I want to take us on a side-trip to visit the *Land of the Losers*. This will not be pleasant, for there is pain in remembering what it was like to be thought of as a "loser," even as there is pain in remembering how eager we might have been to apply that label to someone else.

The environment of most schools regularly produces a crop of "losers," either temporary or permanent. Temporary losers (and I fit into that category) are children whose talents go mostly unrecognized by their teachers and fellow students but who manage to perform well enough to hang on until they find themselves in an environment—such as college, the fine or performing arts, or the marketplace—where those gifts can flourish. Your typical "nerd" is in this category. Scorned because they would rather stick their noses in a book or hack into a computer than "hang out" and try to be popular, many temporary losers grow up to find a world outside of school that values thoughtfulness, depth of inquiry, creativity, and hard work. Temporary losers usually recover a measure of their learning spirit, though they may still bear the scars of having been rejected and stereotyped by peers and others because they couldn't, or wouldn't, fit in.

Permanent losers rarely recover. For them, school is a disaster, a source of shame and humiliation, and they no longer even think of themselves as learners. The names we attach to them: "Dummies," "Scrubs," "Trailer Trash," "Buzzards," vary by geography and culture, but they remain as marks of their caste. Permanent losers drop out in all ways—not just from school, but from learning. As classmates go off to college, they remain behind to pick up whatever job, relationship, or group of friends is left over, whatever might come along. The spark that was there in their eyes as children has been dulled through the repeated experience of failure and shame, of rejection and ridicule, and they seek to dull the pain through self-medication—drugs, alcohol, or collective or solitary isolation from the larger community.

Lest we assume that such victims come exclusively from lower socioeconomic classes, Elliott Currie has written a compelling book called *The Road to Whatever*, about white, middle-class kids who go astray, starting (in most of his cases) with unsympathetic or neglectful parents, but exacerbated by inattentive or unsympathetic social services, or schools that label them as "troublemakers" and then collude as these youngsters fulfill that prophesy. Currie writes,

> For most of the teenagers in this book, the "ground truth" about school—at least from middle school onward, and sometimes earlier—was astonishingly bleak. Many describe high school in particular as a "horrible" experience; some spent little time in high school at all and were bored, angry, and disengaged when they were there. The schools, at best, failed to engage their interest or mobilize their abilities and, at worst, bred a painful sense of injustice that compounded the anger and alienation they felt as a result of their treatment at home. . . .
>
> [M]ost encountered in the schools the same neglectful individualism they had found in their families, and this experience affected their lives in several destructive and mutually reinforcing ways. It made them feel worse about themselves at a time when they desperately needed to feel better. It helped confirm their sense of themselves as failures, screw-ups, or outsiders. . . .
>
> Accordingly, it put them even more beyond the range of potential engagement and support from competent and responsible adults and thus solidified their sense that they were mostly on their own, with few people to lean on or ask for guidance. . . . It chipped away at their expectation of a clear and attainable future of increasing competence, of steady integration into a stable and approving society. . . . More subtly, by failing to engage their spirits or tap their abilities, the school deprived them of the emotional sustenance and the self-esteem that the life of the mind and creative achievement can bring. . . . The bottom line was that the schools functioned less as actively nurturing institutions, committed to building the competence and intellectual capacity of all their students, than as instruments for sorting and categorizing them—sifting the good from the bad, the promising from the "losers," the troublesome from the "OK."[2]

Currie interviews a number of students who, like the "temporary losers" defined earlier, eventually had successful academic careers in college but who found themselves seriously at odds with their previous schooling: "It would be difficult to overstate the level of estrangement these extraordinarily bright and capable young people felt. They often entered high school with high expectations, a good deal of enthusiasm, and unusually strong abilities, but they soon discovered that those strengths were ignored or even undercut by teachers, while any acts of deviance or rebelliousness, however trivial, were magnified."[3]

There is another category of losers who fall somewhere in between those just described. They too are victims of the Game of School. These are the kids we label "average," the "good, quiet, obedient" kids who don't really "shine," who aren't considered "bright," whose parents never get to display a bumper sticker that says, "My Child Is an Honor Student at . . ." (carrying with it the implication, "and yours *isn't*").[4] These children too are victims of an education system that is focused on something it considers more important than self-motivated learning, whether that be behavioral conformity, worksheet completion, or pre-test memorization. Many young people struggle against the debilitating designation of being "just average." Lauraliz, born in Puerto Rico, moved to the Bronx; she describes herself thus: "I am one of the students that's in the crowd that teachers don't notice. I'm not liked and not disliked. It feels safer. I don't want to have people think I'm needy and I don't want to talk unless I'm sure I have the answer right."[5]

It can be very hard to maintain one's love for learning in the absence of the warmth and encouragement of teachers who reach out to you and recognize *your* creativity, *your* talents, *your* sensitivities, *your* special gifts, when so many others are content for you to sit there and not shine—quietly.

High School—Playing for Keeps

By the time we have reached high school, too many of us have become alienated from our learning spirit, that independent, inquisitive, creative side of our natures. In place of our independence and inquisitiveness, we have learned how to "psych out" our teachers to give them the least we can get away with and still get that A or C or whatever it will take to stay on the basketball team or keep the keys to the family car. We have learned how to compete with our fellow students for scarce opportunities, be they admission to a competitive college or a place on the varsity sports team—but we have not learned how to collaborate as learners, to teach and learn from one another (except when it comes to copying homework or studying together for tests). Our orientation toward authentic learning has atrophied. In its place, we have become expert game players.

By the time we are in high school, we are playing the Game of School with our future at stake. Now we are playing for keeps. Even in the most highly ranked schools, the Game proceeds mercilessly. Amanda, a former student of mine, attended Boston Latin High School (BLS), a public school open only to those who pass a competitive exam. Here's what she says about what it takes to play:

> How do honors students get where they are, particularly if they are not interested in actual learning? Many of them cheat shamelessly, such as by programming equations into their calculators. Some take papers offline. Copying homework happens daily during study periods and other classes. The amount of cheating that took place at BLS was disgusting, especially with the image that our school projects. Of course, non-honors "regular" students cheat as well, but not with the voracity and intensity of the honors students. . . . There was a boundary between students, teachers, and administrators. There was no adult to confide in about school issues. . . . I never felt as though there was any adult to talk to about my dreams, ambitions, or fears. And even among "the smartest students in Boston" we did not think it was kosher to be discussing ambitions. It wasn't ever about learning. It was about getting by, for some, and for others about stepping on others to get to the top.

For many high school students, the questions are "What courses shall I take, and what extracurricular activities should I engage in that will look good on my college application?" and "How can I make sure to suck up to my teachers so that I will end up with a grade-point average just a teensy bit higher than my classmates'?"

The competition can be especially fierce, with students vying to be among the top decile of grade-point average (which often requires *more* than straight A's, as in some schools teachers now give A-plus as their highest grade). A recent column by *New York Times* education writer Michael Winerip chronicles the woes and travails of top-ranked students at a Long Island high school, who are beset by horrific anxieties as they prepare for college. "The pressure's pretty miserable," says one. Another echoes this: "It's ridiculous. A 4.0 is an A, my average is 4.4, and I'm in the second decile. Everyone's stressed." According to a guidance counselor, "Parents hire tutors in ninth grade for the biology SAT II. They hire tutors for the state Regents tests the kids need for graduation." Winerip continues, "They hire tutors for $100 an hour to make sure their children get A's in A.P. courses, and they hire college admissions consultants to buff their applications."[6]

Students scan courses and teachers to see which ones are most likely to serve up high grades without too much effort. Teachers know that students (and their parents) will be watching their grading practices closely, so they grade defensively, focusing on criteria that are easily quantifiable, declining to pay as much attention to more in-depth or individualized student work whose assessment these teachers fear may be viewed as "subjective."

Extracurricular activities are likewise weighed as to their likely impact on college admissions officials. Students seeking to promote themselves as "leaders" often organize clubs or events that are lacking in substance (a one-day park cleanup or charity fundraiser, for example). The honors or AP classes become an elite school-within-a-school, and students who are not invited into these classes often feel decidedly second-class. Mathew Miller, another of my students, recalled, "When they cut the honors program in my high school, that left just AP classes and the regular college-bound track, which I was now assigned to. I noticed how much less challenging my classes were, but they didn't think I qualified for AP, so I just sat there, bored most of the time." It is often the case that some of the non-AP classes, such as those in biology and literature, involve more experiential learning than more "advanced" courses; because their teacher is not hurrying to make sure he or she covers all the topics likely to be on the AP exam, students have time to analyze the local water supply or to delve deeply into an author of their choice.

Learning *for Its Own Sake*? Get Real!

In the race for college, two things are likely to suffer: independence of mind and zest for learning. Vance, a high school student interviewed by Kathleen Cushman, points out, "If you're raised by teachers just telling you things and forcing them on you, it's hard or frustrating when teachers expect you to be proactive and take responsibility for your own education."[7]

The pressure to impress a college admissions officer overwhelms the pursuit of meaning. Rather than learn what interests us, we study, memorize, and give back what those who control our grades tell us to. We write papers that "give them what they want"; we use Cliff's Notes shamelessly. There's little time to read literature not on the approved list, no incentive to challenge the bias and distortions in our history textbooks. It won't be on the test, so fahgedaboudit.

Such cynicism about learning is rampant on most high school campuses, expressed in the age-old question, "Whadja get?" Never "Whadja learn?" Always "Whadja get." Some of this cynicism finds its expression in cheating. But the ultimate cost is that learning has become a dispirited, desensitized means to an end. And in the process of pushing kids on to meet those college requirements, we educators—parents and teachers—may be seen as coaches and cheerleaders for that Game, controlled by unseen Ivy League referees, rather than as adult models who show kids what it's like to think deeply and to search for meaning.

The biggest victim of such pressures is likely to be the most precious of our aspirations for young people, the hope that they will hold on to, even enhance, that love for learning so evident in preschool kids. Here is how Patricia Cadet, a current graduate student of mine, described her awakening to this issue:

During one of our class discussions something amazing occurred. We were discussing the love of learning. It was assumed that we all love to learn (after all, we plan to teach). I was startled by the realization that I have never thought of loving to learn, never asked if I loved to learn, never processed my pursuits as a love of learning, and never verbalized that I love to learn. I asked myself, "Do I love to learn?" and was not being able to answer that question. I felt uncomfortable, puzzled, then I allowed it to recede to some deep corner of my mind—confronting uncomfortable thoughts or feelings is not easy.

I was not taught to love learning, books, school. I despised school when I was a teenager—though I am sure those reasons were not because I hated to learn. School and learning have always been paired together. I had to attend school and I had to learn—no choice, no interest, no fun. How can one love something one does not enjoy, or under circumstances that do not allow one the luxury of fun? My parents always said school is something you take seriously; you do not play with school. The focus was never on learning but on school. But what is school without learning?—a daycare your parents send you to? a society within a larger society where the students are subjects to be governed and ruled by teachers and administrators in preparation for a predestined role in the larger society? or a process of demoralization that reshapes your enthusiasm and thirst for knowledge into indifference and impassivity? I remember it as a cold environment where, day in and day out, learn and love do not merge. You may love, and you may learn, but never love to learn. Since these were my experiences, how can I honestly say I love to learn?

Many years have passed since that period of my life; however, I seem to retain the effects of those years. I want to be free of them so that my contract with myself is not affected by the past. My students will hear about "love of learning." They will be asked about it. If they are not already on a path that at least offers a chance to fit love and learn together, then it is up to me to help them discover that loving to learn is not foreign and impossible. I will tell my students, "loving to learn is a relationship between the new information you gain through reading, debating, writing and thinking and who you are in your heart and mind and soul."

The place we call school or college, which should be our society's most vital promoter of learning, too often instead creates the field on which we learn to play a game that demoralizes us even when we are winners (and can permanently scar us when we lose). In the daily course of attending school, as they do what their teachers ask and strive to earn good grades, our children unknowingly substitute lesser goals for an invaluable goal they were born with: the pursuit of *learning for its own sake*.

That phrase! Talk about a custom "more honor'd in the breach than in the observance," as Hamlet put it. In our institutions of learning, we speak of "learning for its own sake" with the same inflection we use for phrases like, "back in my idealistic days when I used to *believe* in stuff like that." We assume that anyone in school who learns for the sake of learning is fondly foolish, someone so smart they can pretend not to be worried about grades, or too naïve to see the reality of grade-based competition, of learning in pursuit of the gold star, the honor roll, or the "almighty A."

Bringing the Game to College

A view in support of learning for its own sake comes from a young man who went off to college anticipating a profound intellectual experience and found quite the opposite. This is from an essay my nephew, Justin Fried, recently wrote about the difficulty of obtaining a true liberal arts education in today's world:

> Flipping through a college guidebook, one cannot help but be astounded by the number of institutions offering students the opportunity to study a variety of courses, sharpen their intellects with thought-provoking study, and cultivate a love of learning in an atmosphere that encourages debate and scholarship. But while this might be superficially true, what one actually finds at most liberal

arts colleges—including the most prestigious—is something very different. Lackluster students, money-driven pursuits, and a dearth of earnest intellectual striving are the more prevalent facets of contemporary liberal arts colleges. At the same time, an increasingly pragmatic approach to education threatens the vitality of the traditional liberal education, leaving the programs of many such colleges in a gray area between the "liberal arts" and "career training."

I experienced this firsthand as a freshman at Colby College in 2002. Brimming with enthusiasm for what I thought I would find at the "thirteenth best" small liberal arts college in the nation—a community of enthusiastic students and teachers exchanging knowledge and exploring truth—I was immediately shocked by the lack of academic interest and seriousness among my peers. Most students were more interested in getting drunk or going shopping than in discussing their intellectual pursuits or important issues of the world. There was also a severe segregation between what they talked about during class and with their friends during less formal times, so much so that mentioning academics outside the classroom was almost taboo. The students' social and intellectual lives seemed to exist in separate and even contradictory spheres.

While it would be untrue to say that nobody at Colby cared about what they were learning, it seemed that the primary motive for academic pursuits came from the desire to benefit financially from a Colby degree [along with] a boredom with and scorn for any type of education that seemed impractical or irrelevant, and so most students tried their best to bypass the liberal arts. Surprisingly, professors in many cases supported these efforts . . . . Countless times . . . I heard professors note the applicability of what they were teaching to various vocations, but not once did I hear one say, "this will make you a clearer, more independent thinker," or something like that. . . .

In the Summer '03 edition of *Colby* . . . a recently retired English professor describes teaching in the '60s: "Forty years ago classroom discussion was contentious and ideas were debated—and shot down—vigorously. If you had asked me, when I first started teaching in '63, if I had one word to tell what I wanted my classroom to be like, I would say, 'exciting.' If you ask me now I would say 'safe.' We want students to feel okay. . . ."

One of the results is that many students evince neither much interest in, nor much understanding of, subjects outside their major. Last year, during a visit to Colby, I was sitting in the dining hall with a good friend and a girl I hardly knew. My friend posed the question: "What are the obligations of a citizen living in a democracy?"

"To question and scrutinize its government," I responded. My friend turned to the other person.

"I'm a Bio major, honey," she replied.

Exactly.[8]

Many might recognize this as a familiar reaction of new college students to the realities of campus life and climate. I had a reaction similar to Justin's, back in 1959, when I arrived on campus prepared to "sit at the feet of the masters" only to face an orientation week of goofy games and cheerleading songs. As if to confirm his critique, many college students tell me that it's not until their junior year that they begin to go to college "for myself, for what *I* want to learn, for who *I* want to be in my life." Their freshman and sophomore years, they say, were spent in partying (celebrating being out from under their parents' watchful eye) or in wading through required courses and treating most of them as though they were still in high school. One girl named Alyson put it this way:

> The part of the game of school that makes me the most upset is the fact that now, as a sophomore in college, I continue to play it. Last year, as a freshman, I continually wrote my papers as quickly as possible to get them done just so I could go out that night. I would cram the night before a test and then, just like in high school, would forget most of the things I learned. The only difference is that now my parents are paying close to $40,000 a year, while back then, I could play for free.

Students Who Refuse to Play

What about those students who reject the Game almost from the first? I speak of the children who decide, from an early age (with or without the antischool influences of peers), not to go along. A friend who worked with families of preschoolers in a New Hampshire mill town (one that lacked a public kindergarten) reported that her school used to send a survey to parents who had registered their children for first grade, asking about their child's preparedness for school. One question on the survey, "Does your child understand and show proper respect for authority?" received the following reply: "Dana show respect for authority, okay, but he don't take s__ from nobody!"

Alice Warner, who is a new high school teacher in rural Oregon, tells me, "I only *wish* some of these kids would play the game well enough to have some choices in their lives. By the time they come to me, too many of them are just waiting out their sentence of compulsory education, waiting to drop out and get on with their lives." In America today, social scholars believe that the refusal to comply, to sit still and do the work, is largely a social class phenomenon. Children whose parents were themselves victims of school systems that gave up on them, or who acquiesced as they gave up on themselves, are often drawn to reiterate the emotions of failure, shame, and defiance regarding school that they have witnessed at home.

Unless students somehow make a connection between *the lessons we present to them* and *an interest they have in gaining new knowledge and skills*, the contexts of classroom learning will remain largely unproductive. Nor will this situation be corrected by the application of threats and bribes (frowns, warnings, notes sent home, grades, stickers, free pizzas)—the normal range of rewards and sanctions that teachers rely on to promote at least temporary compliance with "the task at hand."[9] A student's temporary compliance may be a lot more satisfying than his or her rejection or disobedience, but it is no substitute for self-directed and conscientious learning.

For the majority of students from economically impoverished neighborhoods or without a heritage of academic success in their family, year after year of unproductive learning creates huge obstacles to academic achievement. These in turn seriously limit their potential, under today's challenging economic conditions, to achieve a level of fiscal well-being that might allow their natural love of learning to reemerge. When one is limited to low-wage, demeaning employment options, to poverty or near-poverty living conditions, and to the shame and humiliation of having failed in school, one's potential to become a knowledgeable and active citizen may likewise be tragically reduced. Unproductive learning in school too often leads to an unproductive and unsatisfying life, and an increased likelihood of passing such attributes to one's children.

A Game We All Have to Learn to Play

Sadly, it is probably true that the Game of School is something that we have no reasonable choice but to master. We need to submit to the mandate of powerful people who want us to learn to read, write, use numbers, and behave appropriately with other children and with adults. It is in our own interest to learn these things—we need not feel that we are doing them just to "be good." We also should learn how to size up the demands on our time and to budget our efforts so that whenever timeliness is important, both in school and in adult life, we will be able to do things efficiently and to produce what people in authority are asking of us. We need to learn how to get along with our peers so that the pursuit of our own interests and desires, in class or on the playground, does not cause us to ignore the rights of those around us. And in an economy where our working parents are not as available to us as in previous generations, we increasingly rely on teachers and school to help shape us into good citizens.

We need to learn to play the Game of School because the consequences of opting out or dropping out are too severe for most of us to contemplate. This being an imperfect world, playing the Game turns out to be crucial to success in society, and it's unlikely that we can ever change it unless we first learn how to play it well enough. As Mahogany, a San Francisco high school student, puts it: "School is my way out, into taking care of myself. I can't see myself living in my grandmother's house any longer, depending on them. Also, I really want the college experience. My mom says the college years are the best of your life, and school is the way to get there. But out of six of my classes, three are interesting and three are a waste of time."[10]

As necessary as it may be to play this Game well, we can, as students, parents, and teachers—at any stage of life—free ourselves from its crippling aspects. If we understand this Game for what it is, and resist its demeaning, intellectually paralyzing side effects, we reemerge as authentic learners—better *students* because our creativity and inquisitiveness have not been hobbled by the necessity of playing the Game; better *parents* because we help our children remain enthusiastic and creative as learners as we help them distinguish busywork from real learning and adopt strategies appropriate for each; better *teachers*, who nurture a more active, enjoyable, and productive learning environment among our students, from first grade through graduate school. By delineating the necessary and the perfunctory aspects of the Game we encourage students to take pride in being real with us and with themselves.

We change the Game by putting it in its proper place—to enable us to cope with the often anti-intellectual, undemocratic, and unimaginative demands of institutionalized instruction while keeping our learning spirit intact. It helps us "give unto Caesar that which is Caesar's," while reserving for our own deeper benefit all other aspects of learning. Would that the world were different. But let us at least struggle not to become victims of the institutions set up to help us learn.

In the next chapter, we will concern ourselves with all of our children, who represent the human species in its evolution toward modern humankind, a path that educational writer Evans Clinchy and naturalist Rachel Carson believe is built on a natural love of learning that ought to be profoundly respected but often is not. But first, let us look in on the first day of first grade, in the classroom of Heidi Thomas, who teaches a diverse group of kids at Josiah Quincy Elementary School in the Chinatown section of Boston. I have supervised many student teachers working with Heidi Thomas over the years, and I never fail to be impressed at how well she manages to help children conform to the correct ways of being and behaving in school while she insists that they exercise choice and freedom in their pursuit of learning.

~ Interlude ~

Heidi Thomas's First Day of First Grade

The Josiah Quincy Elementary School was the first of Boston's public schools to have a separate classroom for each grade. Originally established in 1846, it was named after the man who was known as the "Great Mayor" of Boston, the second mayor in its history. Today, in its new incarnation, the school sits attached to a housing and multiservice complex in Boston's Chinatown. The complex serves both recent immigrants and long-established families from the surrounding community. The school also hosts some kids from the posh neighborhood of Beacon Hill, a larger number of African American children from Roxbury/Dorchester, and several children of Hispanic background. It maintains a Chinese language program; all students learn Mandarin as part of the shared cultural heritage. Quincy Elementary has a reputation as one of the finest and best-run schools in Boston.

Heidi Thomas is thirty years old and in her eighth year of teaching. I first met her when I supervised one of a stream of student teachers from Northeastern University who had been privileged to be assigned to her class. Most of the previous years, Heidi taught second grade or a blended two-three. This year, for the first time in her career, she is teaching first grade, assisted by Bev, a student teacher.

I have often had long discussions in my classes for preservice elementary teachers on how to balance a desire for kids to act on their own and take "ownership" of their learning with a need to help them learn how to behave appropriately and to respond to guidance from their teacher. This has often been viewed as an either-or proposition: either we focus on children's "freedom to learn" or we commit to principles of "responsible classroom management" as a way of ensuring a safe, friendly, productive classroom climate. Too many would-be teachers struggle with fears of "losing control" or, alternatively, of squelching the spontaneity of young learners who should be "free to choose," within reason, how and when to pursue their learning. I tend to keep images of Heidi's classroom in mind whenever I try to mediate between these conflicting values. Here is a partial record of the first day of school, September 9, 2004.

It's 9:30, and Heidi and Bev have just gone downstairs to meet the children and bring them up to their second-floor classroom. A photo of each child from last year remains displayed on a large green poster, with a clothespin under each (to clip on a sample of each child's work). Soon enough, these will be replaced with photos of this year's class. The photos show a rainbow of colors and features, all with big, bright smiles. On another poster are the names of the new class—unusual names (at least to me) like Wen Qi, Elijah, Yoav, Noni, Koray, Cai Ying, and Julissa, along with more common names like Cory, Betty, Tammy, Jordan, Jeffrey, and Andrew. Heidi has placed some easy-reading books on desks that are arranged in tables of four or five, with each child's name carefully spelled out on a bright yellow cardboard cutout of a pencil. She says she wants to continue the practice, begun in kindergarten, of "Shush-Reading" as the first thing children do when they arrive—"Even though, for some, 'reading' just means turning the pages and looking at the pictures. I've put enough books for children to share them with their neighbors, when they're done," she adds.

There is a large blue rug in one corner of the classroom, designed for group lessons, readings, and class meeting times, where children will be gently exhorted to "Make like a pretzel" with their eager, squirming bodies. A poster titled Help Wanted lists the classroom jobs of Calendar Counters, Line Leaders, Careful Cabooses, Tag Takers, Morning Messengers, Weather Watchers, Happy Helpers, and Room Readers. Cabinets and bookcases form room dividers.

At 9:50 the children enter. Heidi reconsiders her plan to have children sit down by their name plates and asks Bev to quickly collect them so that the children may sit where they like.

The children enter shyly, filling up one table before starting a new one. They look around, cautiously. Some talk quietly in English or Chinese. Others open their books. Bev distributes name labels to stick onto their shirts.

It's 10:10; everyone is reading quietly, and some are already exchanging books with neighbors. Another child arrives. "Nice to meet you, Tammy," Heidi says, "Oh, we're going to have such a *great* time in *first grade!*" She selects two children to be her "helpers." They approach the first table, and she recites with them: "Yellow Group, Yellow Group. Put your books away. Let's get up and answer the Question of the Day," which turns out to be a question about how they got to school today: by bus, by car, by subway train, or by walking. The children from the Yellow Group line up and slowly place their name in the appropriate column. This takes much longer than planned, and Heidi decides not to repeat the exercise. Meanwhile, Bev circulates around the room talking quietly to the children, some of whom have become a bit restless.

At 10:20 Heidi brings each table, by turns, to the meeting rug. They are asked to form a large circle. "We'll make room for everyone. It's great that almost everyone is crisscrossing their legs." Here she delivers her formal welcome to the class, and it comes *after* the children have experienced "reading" on their own, selecting their table, and conversing with others.

At 10:30 Heidi announces, "I'm going to play a very special game with you. Does everyone see I have a ball in my hand? Everyone put their hands on their knees. I'm going to throw this ball to Andrew." She throws the ball to him. "Who would you like to throw the ball to?" "Anthony," he says. After a child has received the ball, he crosses hands over his chest. Heidi challenges the class to repeat, in order, the names of everyone who has so far received the ball from a classmate. Each child chooses a person to throw to, one by one, as the children try to remember whom they threw the ball to. And, one by one, the children who've not yet had the ball receive it from a classmate. "Boys and girls," Heidi says, "Guess what! We just worked as a *team.* Are you ready for the *hard* part? Let's see how long it takes us to do this again, in the same order." She practices with them, first without the ball, a complex process with about twenty steps. "Do you guys think you can repeat this with the ball this time? Can you do this fast? We'll try our best."

It takes the children about a minute to go through the cycle by throwing the ball and announcing the name of the person they threw it to. Heidi asks if they think they can do it even faster, and most (but not all) of the children agree. They beat their record by ten seconds. "Pat yourself on the back and say 'Good Job' 'cause we're really a team," she says.

About twenty minutes later, Heidi announces, "Boys and girls, I'm going to give you a special seat on the rug right now and ask you to put on your best listening ears." She rearranges the kids in rows, on the rug, with a small aisle in-between. She has already memorized their names.

"Can I get your eyes on me? I have Noni's eyes, I have Jeffrey's eyes, I have Isaac's eyes. Oh, I'm waiting on . . ." and she mentions a child, who quickly focuses on her. "Take a look at this poster. What does this say?" They read aloud, "Eyes on me." "Zipper your lips." She comments, "This is another thing to remember when we're on the rug. If you'd like to talk, what do you do?" (They raise their hands.) "That's right. What do you think you need to do with your hands when you're not raising them to speak? I always tell my students that *this* hand can help the *other* hand be quiet by holding on to it. This is called your School Listening Look: Eyes on Me, Lips Are Zippered, Quiet Hands and Feet."

"Okay," she says, "Now that you all have your School Listening Look, I'm going to read to you one of my favorite stories. It's a story that I've read on the first day of school every day for years and years. It's called *Big Al.* Just look at the cover for a moment. Has anyone heard this story before? It's so much fun to hear stories again and again. What do you think when you see the picture on the cover?" (Several children raise their hands and make "predictions.") She invites them to speculate on the story and then reads it to them, a story about a big, scary-looking fish who doesn't know how to make friends with the smaller fish around him and is lonely. Everything Big Al tries to do to draw other fish to him just scares them off. In between reading the pages, Heidi asks them questions about what they think will come next in the story, about how fish breathe, about whether or not they are feeling sad for Big Al. Just before the denouement, she invites the children to find a "turn-and-talk buddy" so that they can talk about what they think will happen.

The children mostly talk to their buddy, but they keep their eyes on Heidi. "Boys and girls, something fascinating just happened in our classroom. Over here, two of you thought *different* things. Is it okay to think something different than your buddy? Give a thumbs-up if you think it's okay that Anthony and Edwin think different things might happen to Big Al." About half the class think it's okay; half think not. Heidi asks Anthony and Edwin to each say what they think will happen. "Is it okay that they think different things? It *is* okay," she says, reassuringly. She continues to read, finding another occasion to have them talk with their buddies. "Did Big Al finally make some friends?" "Yes," they all say.

At 11:20 Heidi says, "Boys and girls. You've been sitting quietly for a long, long time. I'm going to let you go back to your seats." Group by group, the children return to their tables. They are noticeably more enlivened and interactive than before. She asks them who needs to go to the bathroom, and all but four of them raise their hands and line up. Again, the children get to experience that they have some choice in what goes on, even as they are learning how to be "part of the team." As Heidi leads the larger group to the bathroom, Bev remains behind with the four children who have chosen not to go. They move around the room, looking at what's on the walls, measuring their height on the vertical scale. They seem to enjoy having the room to themselves, feeling free to explore and move about at will.

Heidi returns at 11:35 and asks them to sit down and pick up one of the books on their tables. "Raise your hand if you've seen this book before." She invites individual children to take initiative in describing a book they know. Soon it is time to line up for lunch, and the groups vie to see who is most ready to line up. All but one of the groups sits quietly, and this table lines up last (but without any spoken criticism).

About a month later, I have a chance to interview Heidi Thomas on how her practice and her principles coincide. Here is part of that interview:

> *RLF:* You were about to comment on how you see your class evolving from a more controlled to a more independent environment.
>
> *HT:* My goal as a teacher is to build a strong level of independence, to allow kids to really make their own choices within a given set of standards. I find I need to begin the year with a more structured climate, to teach them routines, to teach them responsibility—about being kind and helpful to each other. Once the kids are comfortable with that and they're feeling smart and feeling successful, I can start to release the structural aspects. For example, right now in my room each group of desks—each team—has a rotating "captain," and the captain is the one who gets materials for the whole team. I worry that at first, if all these first-graders were to all get out of their seats at once, it would be a little chaotic. But my goal is that by Thanksgiving we will have a more free-moving room, allowing them to take more initiative and more responsibility, not only for their own needs but also in being helpful to others and to me. I look forward to withdrawing some of the rules, lightening up on the—what shall I say?—the structure.
>
> *RLF:* "Structure" is the overarching term you use for the procedures that guide the kids?
>
> *HT:* Exactly. It would be great if I didn't have to teach that, if the kids just instinctively knew how to solve problems, say, of crowding at one of

the centers by telling one another, "Oh, why don't you get me some glue, as long as you're going to get some for yourself?" But they're not there yet. If we started off the year by kids having complete choice, I know that I would have a hard time handling it. But, again, one of my biggest goals for my students is that they become independent, that they start making choices in their learning.

RLF: Do you see a distinction between developing routines and fostering conformity?

HT: That's a good question. I'm thinking, now, about whether or not I see a difference. I think conformity is more authoritarian; it's saying to them, "*This* is how it needs to be done," whereas I try to be flexible with my routines. I might tell them: "This is how to hold and carry a chair—you put one arm *here,* and one arm *there,* and you keep it *in front* of you." But, after a while, if I see a kid who can safely carry a chair using only one arm, I would say, "Oh, *that* works, too!" It's like I want to model safe and useful procedures, but not impose a regime on them. But I worry that, in September and October in my room, it might look to an observer like I'm after "conformity."

RLF: You don't give that impression, even this early in the year. As I think about it now, I wonder: Is "routine" learning how to do things effectively and efficiently, whereas "conformity" means insisting on doing something a certain way for the *sake* of everyone doing it alike?

HT: Exactly. Yup. I agree.

RLF: And when some people talk about "structure," they may not understand the difference between establishing *routines* and promoting or instilling *conformity.* When I see you creating a structure, you are always looking to discover interesting alternatives the kids might bring up.

HT: It's interesting that you bring up the difference between these terms, because in the literacy class I teach for Northeastern University, just last week we were viewing some video clips of beginning teachers at work in different classrooms. A student who has been observing in my room said, "*Wow,* that teacher is being pretty strict; she's more traditional, much more *structured* than you are." I had to laugh, and I said, "Oh my gosh, you know, I see *myself* as very structured." And she said, "Oh, *you're* not structured. When I visit your classroom, I see kids *all over* the room—they're writing; they're playing games."

And this led to our discussing the difference between traditional and more open learning—where kids have choice and learn how to become independent. And we decided that, really, both the room in the video clip and my room have "structure"; it's just that my room is much more open. Maybe that's it—I have *structure,* but I'm not looking for *conformity.* My room can look very chaotic at times; the kids are loud and moving everywhere, but I'm thinking, "This is *organized* chaos. It's *structured* chaos. It makes sense for the purpose behind the lesson."

RLF: Structure on behalf of independence and interdependence?

HT: Yes, because my goal, by the end of the year, is to have the kind of room where kids decide what they want to study, within the broad guidelines of an activity. Kids need to be able to choose, but they need to learn to *have* that purpose. So I try to constantly model that for them, to say, "Can you make those choices?" and "If you can't yet, then, okay, I'll provide more guidance, more structure. But if you *can* do it—*by all means go ahead!*"

RLF: And that's the beauty of it; that's what I keep coming back to look at, that *balance.* You never are confused about where you want them to arrive. The structure—the routines—are pathways, toward making them not have to worry about—

HT: The *little* things, such as not worrying about what other kids are doing. To me, if you have that organization, then kids can build that independence. Often I've visited rooms that are very disorganized. If kids don't know what's going on, I feel it's hard for them to build independence, because they can't look at the *important* things; they get too stuck on the small stuff.

RLF: One other thing I'd like your comments on. I emphasize, here in this book, a contrast between the *Game of School* and *authentic learning.* It seems to me that when kids are busy playing the Game—you know, trying to please the teacher, doing what they need to get by, to get through—

HT: Then they're not engaged.

RLF: Yes, and that pattern can persist all the way to graduate school. Yet we know they don't come in to us learning in that way.

HT: No, no, they don't. It's funny. Even with first grade, we had a grade-level meeting, and some teachers were talking about giving a spelling test, and I said, "*Spelling* test!? *I'm* not giving a *spelling* test." What does *that* teach them? No! I don't want that. I'll assess their understanding of words we're working on through their *writing*. It's a more authentic way, to look at it in the context of things they're interested in and writing about. I don't *care* if they can memorize a particular word for a test on Friday. I care about why they need to know and use that word where it's needed. And maybe some of my kids can't spell that word on a spelling test. But if they're *using* it, they can learn where to go to find out how it's spelled.

RLF: You're saying that what's most important is that they should be able to say, "I am a writer, and I don't always get the words right" rather than "I stink at spelling. I'm no good at writing"?

HT: Absolutely. I've seen classrooms, throughout my career, where it's *all* about the Game of School. And it's so . . . sad. To see kids who began school so excited but are now losing that engagement, that excitement for learning. Their school life is just not authentic, not meaningful. I think, sadly, too many teachers come into the profession looking to continue playing the Game of School.

I taught sixth through eighth grades, my first years of teaching, and kids would come in asking, "What do we have to read? What pages are we going to be tested on?" And, being the literacy person that I am, *joy* in reading is the only thing I *care* about. My primary goal is for my kids to say, "I love to read." I mean, I believe in providing *some* explicit instruction around literacy skills—pointing out to them, "This is what good readers do. When they read things, they make pictures in their minds." But they don't have to do that by all of them mouthing "The *cat* that stepped on the *rat* that lay on the *mat*." Maybe it happens by telling them, "You know, when I was reading my novel last night in bed, I did this, too—I pictured what was happening." So explicit instruction doesn't necessarily equate to the Game of School. It's how you use it, and to what ends.

Chapter Three

Being Curious, Feeling Powerful, and Telling the World What You Know

> Exploring nature with your child is largely a matter of becoming receptive to what lies all around you. It is learning again to use your eyes, ears, nostrils and finger tips, opening up the disused channels of sensory impression.
>
> —*Rachel Carson*[1]

I had lunch with my good friend Evans Clinchy yesterday. Clinchy has served in almost every possible role in the field of education—journalist, program developer, school administrator, evaluator, reform advocate, and consultant, although he has never been a classroom teacher.

Aside from education, his great love as a scholar is evolution. Clinchy is certain that there's a dynamic connection between the sorry plight of education and our failure to learn the lessons of our human evolutionary history. His principal contention is that we have become human beings only because throughout our evolution we have been so passionate about learning. And if our education system has gone awry so as to stifle that passion in so many of us, it is because we have not begun to recognize the implications of our history. Day by day, Clinchy believes, our classrooms undermine the lessons of our evolutionary development.

The Mystery in the Hollow Tree: A Fiction

As I walk back to my university office after our lunch, a daydream collects about me, based on Clinchy's ideas. I imagine a scene from a children's movie, the kind one might see on public television during the after-school hours:

Three kids, ages ten and eleven, sneak away from recess at school one day because one of them, Caitlin, has discovered something in the local forest. She whispers to her two friends, Nate and Kyisha, and they slip away from the schoolyard, unseen, during noontime recess.

What Caitlin has found is a hollow log down near the brook several hundred yards from the school, a brook that is part of the twenty-five-acre forest that also borders the neighborhood where she and her mother reside. Yesterday before supper, when Caitlin peered into the log, she saw a pair of eyes staring back at her. At the time, she had to hurry back home to help prepare supper for her mom and herself, but she's so excited about her discovery that she can't wait for school to finish. She's got to find out more about who was looking back at her.

Caitlin, Nate, and Kyisha make their way quietly to the stream, and Caitlin leads them to the hollow log, perched on some rocks and leaning out over shallow water. When the three adventurers stand on some rocks in the stream, the open end of the log is about eye level. After warning her friends to be very, very quiet (so as not to disturb its occupant), they climb down the bank and, taking turns, bring their eyes up to the log. Sure enough, two small, bright eyes shine in the darkness of the log's interior.

The kids are ecstatic, and, backing away quietly, they repair to the bank of the stream and sit down. Their sense of wonder is enhanced by the smells and sounds of the forest and the brook. Nate wonders if it is a fox or a weasel; Caitlin thinks it might be a muskrat or an otter because she knows they live near water; Kyisha (who visits her granny down in Tennessee each summer) is pretty sure it's a raccoon. They hear the bell, signaling the end of recess, and hurry back to school. On the way, Nate, trying to show the girls how far he can jump, lands in a leaf-covered puddle and gets his sneaker full of mud.

The children briefly discuss whether or not to tell their teacher about their discovery. Nate argues that they should, because "she's pretty interested in science." Kyisha reminds them that math class begins right after recess, and their teacher doesn't allow anything to interfere with math lessons. Caitlin is worried that if word gets out, other kids will come down there and frighten the creature away. In the end they swear not to tell anybody about it, not until they've learned more on their own. As they arrive back at school, they agree to meet at Caitlin's house that afternoon to figure out what to do next.

The rest of the school day drags on impossibly slowly, it seems, despite the cheerful attempts of Caitlin's teacher to interest her in math and social studies. Shortly before the buses arrive, Kyisha and Nate beg the school secretary to use the office phone to ask permission to go to Caitlin's house "to study science" after school. Their only actual falsehood is telling their parents that Caitlin's mom will be there. (She doesn't come back from her job until 5:30.)

That afternoon on Caitlin's lawn, they discuss strategy. Nate wants to look up possible animals in a book, to learn more about them and their habits. Kyisha agrees, but wants to see if they can tempt it to come out by leaving some food for it nearby, to see what it chooses to eat. Caitlin likes both ideas. They ransack her mom's library and find only encyclopedia entries for *fox*, *muskrat*, and *raccoon*, which say little about their habitats or eating habits, so they agree they will ask the school librarian for help the next day.

Impatient to proceed, Caitlin suggests they bring a banana, some peanuts, and a hotdog, to see if they can tempt their elusive friend. Nate says they should only take food that would be natural to animals in this area. Kyisha says they must use rubber gloves, so the food won't be tainted with human scent.

Caitlin finds rubber gloves by the painting supplies in the garage. She also finds an old small plant stand that will allow them to put the food near the open end of the log, out above the stream-bed where other animals might find it first. They finally decide on an apple, a carrot, some earthworms dug from the compost pile, and a small can of cat food (chicken and chicken by-products). But Kyisha is adamant that they also need some fresh fish, because "raccoons will only eat fish if it's fresh." Caitlin finds an old fishing rod and, with their other menu items, they head for the stream.

After reaffirming that their mystery creature is still there, the trio heads downstream to where the water gets deeper. But their efforts to catch a fish prove unsuccessful. They return to the hollow log and, with some difficulty, set up the plant stand, weighted down with some rocks to keep its base from tipping over. Nate adds some mossy rocks, twigs, and old leaves, and they set out their buffet to look as natural as possible. By this time their shoes and pants are sopping wet.

Very pleased with themselves, the three amateur wildlife biologists sit together on the bank and watch to see if their dinner guest will emerge. They talk in near whispers, so as not to frighten it away. In their silence, they become aware of the forest's subtler noises, and their very quietness induces a sense of awe—something they feel but do not talk about.

Alas, after half an hour, nothing has happened. Kyisha says most animals only come out at night. Nate says he thinks they should all sleep out there and take turns watching. Caitlin says she'll ask her mom if she can invite them for a sleepover, but she guesses that it would be possible only on a weekend night. As they return to Caitlin's house, she promises not to peek at the log by herself before school next morning, but to wait until the three of them can come there together during recess.

Each of the three manages to get a library pass during reading period, early the next day. They explain their quest to the librarian, who directs them to a collection of nature books. They find two books that seem promising: *When Night Comes*, a book of wildlife photographs by Ron Hirschi and Thomas Mangelsen, and *The Kids' Wildlife Book*, by Warner Shedd. The first book seems a bit young for these fifth graders, but they open them both and pore over them with deep interest. In *When Night Comes*, they find a great photo of a raccoon, and learn that it eats frogs and salamanders. They also learn that the red fox and the badger live in dens. "But they might use a hollow log, to save having to dig a den," says Nate. Their list of possible animals expands to include martens and otters, because the book doesn't say where they live.

In *The Kids' Wildlife Book*, they learn a lot more about raccoons, foxes, porcupines, and the weasel family, including ermines, fishers, martens, and mink. Caitlin is fascinated by all the choices. They learn that porcupines love salt, eat only plants (including apples!), and spend a lot of time in trees, "but it sounds like they like to be *up* in live trees, not down in hollow dead ones," says Kyisha. "So it's probably not a porcupine. I still say it's a raccoon."

At lunch recess, the adventurous trio finds it impossible to slip away. They have been reminded that the forest is off-limits to schoolchildren (Nate's muddy sneaker alerted his teacher), so they gather at the edge of the playground to talk things over. Their group has grown by two: Kyisha's brother, Tonio, and Caitlin's best friend, Maria. Both have been sworn to secrecy. Plans for the Friday night sleepover are well under way.

Caitlin has been talking with her mom about the whole adventure. She has even brought her down to look in the log. Her mom is excited, too, and suggests that Caitlin phone up someone at the local Audubon Society. Caitlin wants her mom to make the call, but her mom says it's Caitlin's responsibility, as the originator of this whole adventure. They compromise; Caitlin's mom makes the initial call and asks to be referred to a staff wildlife specialist. Then she hands the phone to Caitlin.

What Caitlin learns is that although the idea of leaving food for the animal may work, she can never be sure what animal or animals have found the food and that the best idea may be to look for tracks. Caitlin remembers that in *The Kids' Wildlife Book* there are printed tracks of all the animals. But she says that the area near the hollow log is mostly stones, where footprints will be hard to discover. The Audubon specialist suggests that Caitlin and her friends build a sand tray to collect tracks from the mysterious animal. She also affirms that red foxes and members of the weasel family live in burrows dug into the ground. "It might be a bobcat," she tells Caitlin, adding, "They're very rarely seen around here."

By Friday, the school is abuzz with rumors of "a wild animal nearby in a hollow tree." Caitlin, Nate, and Kyisha are pestered with questions. Some kids talk about bears and mountain lions; others warn about snakes or spiders. But all are curious, and the three friends promise to let their schoolmates know what they discover—if anything. They repeat that the Audubon expert said it would be very easy to scare the animal away. Nate has signed out *The Kids' Wildlife Book* from the school library for the weekend, and on Friday afternoon, the five of them pick it up by turns to read about what the animals eat, where they live, and how they and their footprints look.

Kyisha and Tonio's father has agreed to bring two tents over to Caitlin's house and to spend the night with the five of them in the woods by the stream. Caitlin, Kyisha, and Maria will sleep in one tent; Nate, Tonio, and his and Kyisha's father will sleep in another tent. Caitlin's mom will stay at home in case anyone calls. That afternoon, they make a footprint-catching device by taking a pizza tray and covering it with a mixture of wet sand and mud. They keep adjusting the mixture so that it will catch the footprints as clearly as possible. Caitlin's cat, Gumball, is drafted to walk on the tray to test out the various mixtures.

When they arrive at the log, they discover that most of the food they left has been disturbed. The worm dish is in the water, upside down. The can of cat food has been dragged off downstream, and most of the food in it is gone. The apple and carrot are nowhere to be seen. Caitlin has brought another apple, carrot, and can of cat food to place on the tray. The eyes still shine out from the log. Tonio wants to use his flashlight to see if he can discover who the log's inhabitant is, but the others say that that might scare the animal off and that they should be patient. They set up their camp on the bank, back a hundred feet from the stream but with a good view of the log. Kyisha has looked in her almanac and found out that the moon will be three-quarters full that night.

They return to Caitlin's house for supper and then are anxious to get back to their campsite. As daylight fades, there is a combination of laughter and shushing coming from the tents, and the children alternately tell ghost stories and watch the streambed. For Maria and Nate, it's the first time they have slept in the woods. The children are captivated by the sense of doing scientific research while also camping in the wild, taking in the sounds, the smells, and the light that still penetrates the darkness. The moon does come up, but by that time all are fast asleep.

In the morning, the children rush down to the stream. The apple has been mostly eaten, but the cat food can remains untouched. On the tray are the footprints of . . . ? The children return to the campsite area, where they once again look over *The Kids' Wildlife Book*. They bring the book down to the stream and compare the tracks with those listed for raccoons, otters, foxes, porcupines, and bobcats. They quickly rule out the fox, the bobcat, and the raccoon. It's down to either a marten or a porcupine. The chewed apple argues for the porcupine, since it's a vegetarian. Finally, Tonio takes his flashlight and shines it into the log. All of the others crowd around. What they see looks like a dark, furry something with white or gray points. Again they look at the book. Then they feel pretty sure: it's a porcupine! Wow! Are they going to have a lot to tell their classmates come Monday!

Lessons from the Story

My imagination has carried me on its own journey, but what's the point? How does it connect to Clinchy's ideas about education and evolution? I see these kids hooked by an intense curiosity, drawn by an enhanced sensory awareness of the natural world around them, driven by the importance of acting as explorers and scientists, motivated by an irrepressible urge to share what they've discovered. Curiosity, sensory awareness, self-enhancement, talk. It's not hard to imagine myriads of children, stretching back beyond the dawn of civilization, powered by these same drives. It has led us to develop as a species of passionate learners.

I don't think children today are all that different in these respects than our ancestors. Kids still are curious. They think with all five of their senses. They feel powerful when in possession of important information and want to tell everyone about it. It occurs to me, as I construct this story, that children have always explored the world around them out of an intense desire to know what is "out there." They have used smell, taste, and touch as well as sight and hearing to bring that natural world into contact with their evolving intellect.

I see the ancestral "Caitlin" filled with a great sense of pride as she brings into her village some information—the location of a beehive, perhaps, or news of the arrival of a herd of caribou—that she knows will be treated by others as wonderful and valuable. After all, the most revered people in her village are those who are considered to be "wise in the ways of the world," the sachems, the wise women, the priests, those who chart the change of seasons and the movements of the stars. And were it not for the faculty of speech, whereby such vital information may be widely shared, human beings would not have become *Homo sapiens*. We are inveterate talkers. We can no more keep information to ourselves than hold our breath for five minutes. So with these children. They are the inheritors of our evolutionary gift of knowledge-seeking and information-sharing.

The problem our twenty-first-century Caitlins, Nates, and Kyishas contend with is that our schools and our media-driven society are not well suited to nurture the complex drives of children's curiosity, sensory awareness, self-importance, and talkativeness. As soon as organized public education became commonplace, in the nineteenth century, schools began to construct obstacles to inhibit or confine these hereditary instincts. Such a tendency persists. We have opted not to create schools as places where children's curiosity, sensory awareness, power, and communication can flourish, but rather to erect temples of knowledge where we sit them down, tell them a lot of stuff we think is important, try to control their restless curiosity, and test them to see how well they've listened to us. Let's examine in greater detail some of these evolutionary dynamics as they play out in contemporary society.

Curiosity and Sensory Awareness

Children's curiosity is natural. All kids have it. As parents, we find such curiosity to be engaging, entertaining, exhausting, and exasperating, by turns. But curiosity is a delicate, often individual phenomenon. It is spontaneous. It resists being preplanned or manipulated. It may be stimulated by a well-designed exercise, by a walk around the block or down the meadow to the woods, by a book or video, or by queries that hold forth the promise of surprise, intrigue, delight. But curiosity remains a personal option, not easily channeled into routine classroom activities.

Children's capacity for sensory awareness is vivid and intense. They squeal with delight as they enter the kitchen to smell their favorite supper cooking on the stove; they are dazzled by a flash of lightning on a stormy night and await with dread eagerness the terrible clap of thunder. And what parent or teacher has not contended with a child's irresistible urge to touch and taste things to discover what they are really like?

And yet might not our classrooms appear starkly vacant to a child of the African savanna, the South American jungle, the Australian bush—or, for that matter, to a child raised on a farm, or to one who hunts and fishes, or to a city child for whom the street provides music, light, and other sensory gifts? Where are the variations of light and color, the smells, the music, the stalking, hunting, and touching? These things are mostly deemed inappropriate—often for valid reasons of safety and orderliness—in the classroom environment. But it is just those constraints that our three contemporary explorers are determined to escape, so as to seek and to synthesize new knowledge in the world beyond.

In 1956, Rachel Carson wrote a book for her nephew, Roger, who was then four years old and whom she had taken on walks, in daylight and darkness, on sunny afternoons and rainy nights, to the seashore and through the forest, from the days of his infancy, carried in her arms. She describes her informal pedagogy this way:

> When Roger has visited me in Maine and we have walked in these woods I have made no conscious effort to name plants or animals nor to explain to him, but have just expressed my own pleasure in what we see, calling his attention to this or that but only as I would share discoveries with an older person. Later I have been amazed at the way names stick in his mind, for when I show color slides of my woods plants it is Roger who can identify them. "Oh, that's what Rachel likes—that's bunchberry!" Or "That's Jumer [juniper] but you can't eat those green berries—they are for the squirrels." I am sure no amount of drill would have implanted the names so firmly as just going through the woods in the spirit of two friends on an expedition of exciting discovery.[2]

Carson explicates her gently rebellious approach a few pages later, where she explains,

> We have let Roger share our enjoyment of things people ordinarily deny children because they are inconvenient, interfering with bedtime, or involving wet clothing that has to be changed or mud that has to be cleaned off the rug. We have let him join us in the dark living room before the big picture window to watch the full moon riding lower and lower toward the far shore of the bay, setting all the water ablaze with silver flames and finding a thousand diamonds in the rocks on the shore as the light strikes the flakes of mica embedded in them. I think we have felt that the memory of such a scene,

> photographed year after year by his child's mind, would mean more to him in manhood than the sleep he was losing.[3]

Later in this photo-filled book, Carson puts her beliefs about children and what I have been calling their "learning spirit" into the form, almost, of a prayer:

> A child's world is fresh and new and beautiful, full of wonder and excitement. It is our misfortune that for most of us that clear-eyed vision, that true instinct for what is beautiful and awe-inspiring, is dimmed and even lost before we reach adulthood. If I had influence with the good fairy who is supposed to preside over the christening of all children I should ask that her gift to each child in the world be a sense of wonder so indestructible that it would last throughout life, as an unfailing antidote against the boredom and disenchantments of later years, the sterile preoccupation with things that are artificial, the alienation from the sources of our strength.[4]

Although she has wisdom that deserves to be heeded by those of us who are formal educators, Rachel Carson does not mention school or education per se. Nor is she limited, in her outward reach, to parents privileged by having easy access to seashores and forests.

> If you are a parent who feels he has little nature lore at his disposal there is still much you can do for your child. With him, wherever you are and whatever your resources, you can still look up at the sky—its dawn and twilight beauties, its moving clouds, its stars by night. You can listen to the wind, whether it blows with majestic voice through a forest or sings a many-voiced chorus around the eaves of your house or the corners of your apartment building, and in the listening, you can gain magical release for your thoughts. You can still feel the rain on your face and think of its long journey, its many transmutations, from sea to air to earth. Even if you are a city dweller, you can find some place, perhaps a park or a golf course,

> where you can observe the mysterious migrations of the birds and the changing seasons. And with your child you can ponder the mystery of a growing seed, even if it be only one planted in a pot of earth in the kitchen window.[5]

Children's Sense of Power

Children's awareness of the power that accrues from having information of interest to others is apparent when some kid comes in with a story of a fire or accident just witnessed. Everybody crowds around to hear the details. The possessor of the information attains instant celebrity status. He instinctively feels the power of his knowledge. But all too often, the teacher will feel in competition with any student whose out-of-school adventures draw classmates away from the lesson at hand. "That's enough of that, now! We have work to do." I well remember, in fourth grade, standing at the window watching a crane move into place on the street below, only to have my teacher chide, "Come, come. We can't all be 'sidewalk superintendents.'" Caitlin and her friends know better, evidently, than to bring their discoveries to the attention of their classroom teacher, although I can easily imagine circumstances in which a sensitive and creative teacher could serve much the same role as did Caitlin's mother or the specialist from the Audubon Society in helping the children design an experiment to identify the mysterious pair of eyes.

As Caitlin brings her wonderful discovery to her two friends Nate and Kyisha, she undoubtedly experienced the surge of well-being that occurs when we feel we are in possession of some very important knowledge. Her "power" becomes their collective power, as they join her in her research. The shaping of their experiment is an expression of their exercise of the power of knowing. My colleagues and mentors Seymour Sarason and Deborah Meier have, each in their own way, much to say about this aspect of my imaginary scenario, the feelings of power that emanate from the discovery of knowledge and the shaping of ideas.

Deborah Meier's first book was, in fact, titled *The Power of Their Ideas*, and she has described to me her struggle with editors over her insistence on using *Their* in the title. "They wanted the title to read, 'The Power of *Our* Ideas,' giving credit to the grown-ups who had created our experimental school. But I told them that that was the whole point—that it's the power of *children's* ideas that our pedagogy should center on." The first page of her book includes an observation from her journals from the days when she taught kindergarten:

> I was certain that the distinction between living and nonliving was a "simple" idea. I chose the most obvious: a rock and our gerbil. I figured I'd leave the gray areas for later. But five-year-old Darnell insists on making it difficult. Is he putting us on? "Rocks change too, and rocks move." He reminds me that on our trip to Central Park, I described how the rocks had come down with the glaciers, and how they change shape over time. He won over some of the kids. They reproduce, said one: little rocks break off from big ones. I feel I'm losing the argument. So much for my neat chart.
>
> How can we show kids that it is precisely in such ideas that important discoveries are made, rather than closing the conversation off with an "explanation." We dismiss the mistakes as cute, the accidents of ignorance; but they are at the heart of the intellectually-curious child. . . . All kids are indeed capable of generating powerful ideas; they can rise to the occasion. It turns out that ideas are not luxuries gained at the expense of the 3 R's, but instead enhance them. . . .
>
> But there's a radical—and wonderful—new idea here—the idea that every citizen is capable of the kind of intellectual competence previously attained by only a small minority. It was only after I had begun to teach that public rhetoric gave even lip service to the notion that all children could and should be inventors of their own theories, critics of other people's ideas, analyzers of evidence, and makers of their own personal marks on this most complex world.[6]

Seymour Sarason's outlook on the issue of power in the contexts of learning becomes an investigation of the extent to which adults include children in helping organize and regulate the classroom itself. He is appalled at how, in a public educational system promoted by Thomas Jefferson to protect our fledgling democracy, teachers and administrators reserve for their exclusive say-so the establishment of rules of conduct for students. Here is what Sarason has to say about children's awareness of issues of power:

> Just as teachers are extraordinarily alert to issues of power—sensitive to the behavior that may or will require exercise of power, as well as to individual differences among students—so are the students. If substitute teachers have control problems, it says as much about the knowledgeability of students about power as it does about the substitute's unfamiliarity with the traditions of their classrooms and the casts of characters. Issues of power are always a function of the perceptions and actions of student *and* teacher. . . .
>
> How does power get defined in the classroom? What understanding of power do we want children to obtain? Should students have some kind of role in defining power, thus giving them some sense of ownership not only in regard to definition but also to implementation? Is the unilateral definition and exercise of power [by the teacher] desirable for the development of children? Does it tend to breed the opposite of what it intends to achieve?[7]

Sarason recounts a research experiment he attempted, years back, to measure the extent to which teachers in five suburban schools involved their students in developing the class rules they would live by. He had to terminate the experiment when his researchers reported *no evidence at all* that students were invited to offer their own suggestions as to rules. His work reminds me of a happier experience I had while researching *The Passionate Teacher*, when I was privileged to visit a high school class on sex education (it was called "Life Relationships," but it was mostly about sex) taught by the very talented Yvonne Griffin. Ms. Griffin had no doubt that her ability to reach and engage these urban teenagers on this most contentious of issues stemmed from her dedication to power sharing. She had them list *their* expectations for *her* as a teacher, posting it on the wall alongside her list of the attitudes and behavior she expected of them; she had them come up with the list of questions (some of them quite risqué) that would frame their inquiry about relationships, intimacy, and responsibility—even as she threw out her lesson plans from previous years.[8]

There is quite likely no substitute for the experience of feeling empowered, whether it is the power of kids' sallying forth in search of scientific discovery or of their being included as part of the structure of power within their school and classroom, if we hope for children to pursue learning enthusiastically within the structure of a classroom or a school.[9] Learning and power are inextricably linked. Powerless students often learn only that learning in school has little to offer them.

Children and Language

Happy children love to talk. They would rather talk to each other than do almost anything else (aside from run and jump around). What one of them knows (whether factual or not) soon becomes part of the common knowledge pool. The new information is digested, commented on, challenged, acclaimed, refuted—often simultaneously. A child's desire to communicate her own special knowledge, to share information that she senses others would be interested in, is universal. It is also the bane of many teachers' daily existence, often viewed as an unwelcome interruption. It gets in the way of what the teacher is trying to teach.

This linguistic aspect of the evolutionary nature of children's learning is treated by Frank Smith in *The Book of Learning and Forgetting*, where he posits that children's vocabulary expands at a terrific rate during their school years, quite aside from (or despite) the vocabulary and spelling lists their teachers impose on them. His research shows that children are likely to add up to twenty-five new words *per day* (few or none from their teachers' vocabulary lists) during their late elementary school years, as a result of their natural interaction with society and culture; higher levels of word growth occur for children who engage in independent reading, those whom Smith calls "members of the literacy club."[10]

Something very powerful must be occurring in the brains of children—a hunger for new words, for new ways of expressing who they are and what they know or seek to find out. Even as our three young explorers were swearing themselves to secrecy, there was no doubt in their minds that the knowledge they were accumulating would soon be shared with a wider audience. (It was, after all, only their desire to protect their unknown creature that kept them from running up to school shouting their discovery to one and all.) In their eagerness, they sought books to give them the words and directions they were missing. They became hunters of words as an inevitable consequence of their search to reveal the owner of the mysterious eyes.

We ignore this evolutionary evidence—reenacted, as it were, by Frank Smith in his research—at our peril. For in forcing our "official" vocabulary lists on children (while overlooking their natural appetite for language) and then testing them to see if they have memorized our words, we take their natural linguistic appetite and transform it through acts of subservience and drudgery. We curtail their own language acquisition by forcing them to do what they are already predisposed to do on their own. It might be far wiser, as Smith and others suggest, to stimulate children's acquaintance with diverse books and support them as they develop the habit of reading on their own for their own pleasure, rather than to teach them vocabulary or assign reading as homework. We ought to use evolutionary forces and predispositions (rather than substitute our own didactic schemes) if we seek to stimulate the growth of language and communication in children.

The Implications of Evolution for Education

Let's suppose that Evans Clinchy is correct that evolution teaches us vital lessons applicable to our nurturing of intellectual growth in children. If misguided politicians and school officials are indeed bent on an educational "delivery system" that repudiates hundreds of thousands of years of our journey to become human beings, it's no wonder so many of our children seem resistant to the knowledge and skills that we adults have devoted our professional lives to providing for them.

One way of considering the Game of School is to view it as an inevitable adaptation of the species to being placed in an intellectually alien and sensory-starved environment, one where children's curiosity, their capacity for sensory intelligence, their desire for heightened self-identities as discoverers and synthesizers of knowledge, and their proclivity to share "the power of their ideas" with their peers have been blunted by adult preoccupation with "the delivery of our instruction" and, these days, with the most narrow and constraining of assessment instruments, linked to state curriculum frameworks and tests. Faced with such obstacles, many young learners instinctively opt to seal themselves off from the sources of learning that are their evolutionary heritage. Instead, they join with their teachers in the exercise of pseudo-learning that mocks authentic learning through the rituals of passive ingestion, rote memorization, and indifferent recall, rituals also very familiar to college students.

Once locked into such behaviors, young people in their role as students—make the role of the teacher so much more difficult. After all, how can we teach the incurious? How can we awaken those whose senses have been dulled by the monotony of schoolwork? How can we reach those who feel decidedly unpowerful? How can we motivate the silenced children and youth among us to claim their share of the stage on which knowledge is brought to life in being shared?

One of my most impressive recent experiences, and one that gives me reason for hope in the midst of all the jargon, politics, and wrong-headed policies has been my observation of the work of several of our recent graduates, now serving as teachers in Boston schools. One of them is Melanie Livingston, who recently shared her experiences in an article titled "On Sucking, Being Easy, and Staying out of the Way."[11] What follows is a glimpse of Melanie Livingston at work.

~ Interlude ~

"Something So Good Wuz Neva So Deadly"

It is early on a spring morning, and I walk a half mile or so from the subway station to the Raphael Hernandez School in Jamaica Plain, a section of Boston with a large Hispanic population. For seventeen years, this building of four hundred or so students has been guided by Margarita Munez, a native of Puerto Rico and principal of this dual-language school, where students study in English and in Spanish on alternating days.

I am here to observe one of my former graduate students, Melanie Livingston, who is in her second year of teaching. The eighth graders whom I will see today were her students in seventh grade last year. All teachers in this public school (which has remained bilingual without changing status to a charter or magnet school) hold on to their students for two years, so the classroom ambience I will witness today has been two years in the making.

This is the class, Melanie has informed me, where all students received at least the minimal passing score in written English on the state test, the MCAS—all nineteen of them (even one boy who had been in a special education class but needed a transfer and was added to Melanie's roster this year). Across Boston, 17 percent of the students failed the MCAS in English. Her students are not, however, without deficiencies. "Over half our kids are in the 'Needs Improvement' category, so they have a long way to go." She says this is about the same percentage as eighth graders throughout Boston.

But the English part of the MCAS is over, and as a reward (to Melanie, at least) her eighth graders are free to study what she wants them to study: Shakespeare's *Othello*. "These kids have been reading the play for a little over two weeks now," she tells me. Today their eighty-minute class will focus on Acts IV and V. They are assigned a scene or two per night, using a text that features the original play on the right-hand page and explanatory notes on the facing page. Melanie amplifies their reading of the written text by playing a cassette recording of *Othello* that has dramatic acting, accompanied by music.

As the students wander in, around 8:30, they sit at desks grouped together in fours, with a small rug and pillows down at the end where I am perched, with my laptop on a table.

Melanie begins the class by reminding her students that they were supposed to have read act 4, scene 2, of *Othello* last night. Most (but not all) have their small paperback version of the play. Melanie announces that she thinks there is something quite special about lines 172–175 of act 4, scene 2, where Emilia challenges Iago about his motives. Melanie asks them to read those lines and see if they can come up with "an inference" from the imagery.

> *Emilia:* O, Fie upon them! Some such squire he was
> That turned your wit the seamy side without
> And made you to suspect me with the Moor.
> *Iago:* You are a fool. Go to!

She gives them ten minutes to study the text, while she confers with a student. There is a quiet buzz, as the kids try to decipher this somewhat familiar, often strange language. This is a tough passage in a difficult play, and the students struggle with it. After conferring with her student, Melanie circulates to see how they are progressing. She kneels at a group of desks, in deep conversation with a student. The rest of the class, by now a bit restless, chat with each other. About half of them have their books open to the play, and some are discussing what they have read.

At 9:00 Melanie calls them together, summarizing their struggle over this passage. "Why did I think this is important?"

One student offers, "Since Iago is such a liar, he wants to see everybody as false." This is followed by a lot of discussion about what may have been taking place offstage. When the level of chatter gets too loud, Melanie quiets the class by saying softly, "When Cristobal is ready, I'll be ready. When Gloria is ready, I'll be ready." Now attentive, they listen to a recording of act 5, scene 1, full of violence and Iago's treachery. The scene calls forth many responses from the students, who seem to relish the chance to guess what's going on.

The discussion continues, with Melanie challenging and questioning, then affirming and encouraging, always monitoring the discourse while also participating. She sits, cross-legged, on top of a desk, lending an air of campfire informality to the discussion. The students, emboldened by her confidence in them to be able to translate Shakespeare into modern English, put forward their ideas, impressions, interpretations.

As Othello's climactic monologue is about to be played on the cassette, the students "shush" each other so as be able to hear it clearly. There is absolute silence as they hear the actor say, "Put out the light, and, then, put out the light"; Melanie grins broadly as her students respond with gasps and titters, then friendly outrage as she turns off the tape just before the act of murder is committed.

At 9:30 Melanie assigns them the passage they've just listened to, act 5, scene 1, lines 1–24, in groups of three, to collaboratively translate Othello's monologue into modern-day English. One of the trio will focus on literal content, one on emotional tone, and the third on maintaining imagery so that it makes sense in a modern context without losing force. To show them how it's done, Melanie uses the phrase, "With wings of love, I o'erswept your walls," and illustrates how to find the literal meaning, ascertain the emotional tone, and translate it (in this case into something like, "I loved you so much I could fly over mountains to be by your side"). She gives them a half hour to do this. When she speaks with them, as she circulates, Melanie kneels so that her face is just about at the level of theirs as they sit.

I can sense that this is a tough assignment. There is the text, in Elizabethan English; there is the task, translating on both a literal and emotional level; there is the social context, working with two classmates to rewrite Shakespeare. These are, after all, eighth-grade kids from a mostly working-class Hispanic neighborhood. They're not college students or high schoolers in an advanced or honors section. I get up from my listening post and circulate around, looking at what they are writing. But first I listen as one boy, describing Desdemona to his group, exclaims "She's pure, a pure woman! Like water, she's 100 percent *pure!*"

The following are a few of the translations I see on their papers (spelling unedited):

> "You are the reason why I'm chocking you and I don't have to tell you why, you should already know. You are the reason why I'm doing what I have to do. Yet I won't make you bleed nor leave a scar on that beautiful white face."
>
> "This is what I must do for my peace."
>
> "O, Baby! My soul is the reason!"
>
> "Skin smoother than a baby's butt."
>
> "And I can't beleive a dude like me can cry a waterfall but its becuz I'm mad, not cause I'm sad."
>
> "You must die, you b****, cause otherwise you'll do the same to someone else."
>
> "Something so good wuz neva so deadly. I must cry, but they are man tears, this sadness is big just like my luv."

The students struggle with phrases like "skin like monumental alabaster," but also with "Put out the light, and, then, put out the light," which most come to understand as referring both to the torch Othello holds and the violent act he contemplates.

At 9:50 Melanie interrupts their investigation, their discourse, to urge them to pack up for their next class. It is she, not they, who has to remind them that the class period is almost over. She even has to nudge some of them that it's time to leave: "Let's go!" Melanie leads her class out the door at 10:00 and walks them to their science class next door.

For a full half hour, nineteen Hispanic eighth graders had immersed themselves in Shakespeare's prose, struggling to make it theirs. There was some frustration, some laughter, much earnest perusal of the text.

I have a few minutes to reflect with Melanie on her class. She is pleased with how they have responded. "It's not like this all the time, but it's been this good since I've started *Othello*. Something happened to them when I had them last year that I have been able to build upon during my second year with them. Something has clicked.

"They have their teachers for two years, so each teacher has a real influence. They are such caring kids; they listen to each other and applaud each other. They fight—oh, Lord, they fight—but they also work well together with each other."

When I return the following Monday to observe her seventh-grade English class in their "MCAS Monday" mode, Melanie explains, "This year's seventh-grade class is different. I had them last year, in sixth grade, but even so, I often need to take one class period a week for a class meeting. They're excited, but they can't contain themselves and focus on the work."

The children enter and sit at groups of desks, three or four students to a cluster. "This is MCAS Monday," she reminds them, before handing out a packet of a typical reading and interpretation exam, this one containing a three-page story, "Hearts and Hands," by O. Henry, plus short-answer questions and one essay question.

Melanie begins by reminding them what this is all about. "What's the only reason you're reading this passage? Is it to have fun? To read for pleasure?"

"It's to answer the questions they make us answer," a student calls out.

"Yes. This story, for example, is not something you are likely to choose to read at home. But it's the kind they will ask you to read on the test. What's the first thing you will read?"

"The questions," several say. The students have been through the routine before.

"Right! And then what?"

"We read the passage."

"Looking first at . . . ?"

"The words in italics at the beginning." This is the summary of the story, offered to help students navigate the anticipated difficulties and subtleties of the text.

"Yes, to give you a heads-up to what you will be reading. And only *then* will you read the passage, so you know what you're looking for. And there can't be any talking. Because if you talk during MCAS, I'm going to remove you so you can't interfere with anybody else's achievement. If you decide to give up, you put your head down. That's your business. But if you interfere with somebody else, that's my business, and I won't let you do it."

Melanie leaves the room to look for more books with which to begin her next thematic unit. She needs to round up five more copies for her class. There is near silence during her departure. Some of this may be due to my presence, but it is remarkable nonetheless. In her absence, I examine the text of O. Henry's story. It's quite subtle, with its nineteenth-century railroad car manners and police practices, not to mention O. Henry's plot twists, and there are lots of nuances that are foreign to twenty-first-century urban kids. Melanie returns with the extra books.

One boy, who was finding himself a bit distracted by the other two at his table (he himself, I observe, has largely been the cause of the distraction), gets up from his chair and announces that he wishes to read by himself. He lies on the floor, near the stacks of books.

It is now 9:00. The students have been working at this story, silently, for twenty-five minutes or so, and a few are getting restless. They whisper, but Melanie reminds them they'll get a chance to share answers later. Now is time for work.

At 9:10, Melanie asks if anybody needs more time. Three students raise their hands, and she says she'll give them five more minutes, warning the others to remain silent. She has a no-nonsense demeanor. "However we may question the ultimate value of this work," she seems to be saying, "we're going to take it seriously for now." For the first time, she circulates around the room, stopping off at tables to entertain students' individual questions. The noise level begins to rise.

It is now 9:20. "Sounds like everyone is done. Is everyone done?" In stark contrast to the half hour of silence, by this time the class is abuzz with chatter. There's a lot of jovial conversation, almost none of it related to the O. Henry story. I imagine that this exercise must be very frustrating. The story is so esoteric as to be almost gibberish to them. Melanie continues to circulate. From what I observe, her stance is to ally herself *with* the kids and *against* the test.

At 9:30, Melanie claps loudly to grab their attention, and the room settles down.

"All right: on a scale of 'no problem' to 'wicked hard,' this passage was . . ."

"*Wicked hard!*" is the response, and Melanie helps the group discover the clue that alerts readers to the story's twist at the end. Melanie reminds them that the passage in italics has indicated that the twist would be coming, and says, "Twenty-five percent of the answers are *right there* in the italics at the beginning!" The class gets noisy, and Melanie reminds them, "It's *one week* to the MCAS, and I need you to be with me, so that I can work with you and help you ace this."

Melanie tells them that in contrast to how they would behave in her English class, the conditions of the test require that they not explore all the possible meanings but instead pick the answer that most closely relates to the theme of the passage. One student asks about the term *foreshadowing,* and Melanie explains, with help from volunteers from the class, what the word means in the context of the story.

"Remember, sometimes you need to cover up all four of the possible answers and think things through for yourself. You're *much smarter* than the MCAS! You're smarter than the test. This was hard. It was a difficult passage, which means a number of things. First, that you have to really *read the italics;* also that you have to do more than 'play the game.' You need to use your best reading strategies to figure out what's really going on."

"Will all the questions on the test be this hard?" a student asks.

"There may be one or two of them this tough, but the rest should be easier," she says. "I've given you an especially tough one to work on today."

At 9:45, Melanie introduces the idea of a "book club" approach to the passage they've just read, prior to introducing their next thematic unit on fiction. She takes the role of facilitator and demonstrates the role of connector (who links the story to something they have experienced in real life); the image master (who searches out the key metaphors); the questioner (who asks the important questions about the text); and the quotation person (who picks out especially relevant quotations).

"If you show me that you can handle this book club format, you can be in control of your own learning. You will be in charge. But if you don't do the work, we can't do Book Club, and then *I* will do all the talking, and *you* will do all the listening, and *nobody* will do any learning."

Throughout, Melanie uses her own experiences, her affability, her willingness to talk about her own strengths and weaknesses, and her absolute reliance on their good will and cooperation in order to keep them in what Frank Smith calls the "literacy club."

"The way Book Club works is that you are totally in charge of your own learning. It's not me reading to you, or assigning you a section each day and checking up to see if you have read it. It's the group of you—all eight of you—acting the way grown-ups do when they decide to read a book for pleasure and talk about it with friends."

The class gets ready to leave. They have not by any means become fans of O. Henry stories, but quite likely each of them is feeling that he or she can absolutely rely on their teacher to help them cross this difficult "literacy" bridge to their future.

In both of the classes I've observed, and despite their stark differences in content (*Othello* versus O. Henry) and purpose (Shakespeare as an intriguing challenge versus MCAS test as crafty adversary), Melanie Livingston has maintained a stance that fosters authentic learning. She does this by being up-front honest and determinedly empowering. She is as energetic in her passion for Shakespeare as she is in her resolve not to let her students be victimized by The Test. She is so clearly *on their side* even as she exhorts them to stretch themselves beyond what they (and too many others) think they are capable of.

Perhaps most of all, she wants the material—the skills, the content, the challenge—to be *theirs,* so that they feel that learning is in their hands as emerging masters of the realm of knowledge, not as subjects or objects of systematic instructional delivery. This is apparent, for example, in her insisting that they translate Othello's soliloquy into their own idiom, while retaining its literal, poetic, and symbolic meaning. In this and in her MCAS coaching session, she helps her seventh and eighth graders triumph over the Game, even as they learn how to play it.

Chapter Four

Contemplating Our State Religion, and the Types of Learners Who Attend School Within Its Shadow

In recent years, our state and national push for "accountability" has lifted an important but decidedly secondary aspect of learning—assessment—onto center stage. Our political and educational leaders have let us know that it is not "learning" they are interested in promoting, but rather something called "achievement" or "annual progress," goals whose specific and measurable aspects can, in these leaders' minds, be determined only through standardized tests. I speak of this phenomenon as a state religion because, as is true of most state-imposed religions, the form has replaced the substance. Schools everywhere are being forced to bow down before idols of state-sanctioned curricula, to tremble in the shadow of all-powerful testing rituals, to replace their trust in the learning clerics of home and village (their teachers) with symbolic public worship of national gods (masquerading as standardized tests), in whose shadow our teachers are relegated to the role of altar boys. Because the state chooses not to appraise the souls of its flock (that is, to ask to what degree children are happily learning), it concerns itself with its own much less vital—and often superficial—accounting of what it considers to be "learning *achievement*." Test scores, rather than an enhanced emphasis on learning, become an end—become *the* end—in themselves (a rather common feature of government-organized religious activity).[1]

As writers from John Dewey to the present have warned us, such a substitution of goals (and gods) warps our view of learning and of ourselves as learners. It affects our youth without their even being aware that a severe transformation has taken place. We already suffer from the fact that by middle or high school, almost every kid has become wise to the ways of the academic world—expressed in terms of "What I have to do in order to get the grade I want." But now, on top of that, our students are victims of the trivialization of learning into test prep pedagogy, thrust upon them by the ecclesiastical functionaries of the school system, by people who have lost sight of the transubstantiation of society's goal of "learning" into the quest to "demonstrate measurable student progress." Like Jacob, the biblical youth who sold his patrimony to his brother Esau for the equivalent of a Big Mac, our youth are cajoled into giving up their independent spirit of learning, their spiritual heritage as self-motivated seekers, to get a test score burrito or a report card wrap.

The ultimate irony of this transference is that those few students who manage to retain their independent learning spirit, their innate curiosity, their pleasure in reading, exploring, or creating works of art are likely to be better positioned to blossom academically and vocationally than those who pursue academic achievement through the Game. It is from that minority unencumbered by pseudo-goals that we get most of our inventors, entrepreneurs, artists, and scientists. What leads to success at higher levels of abstraction and study is precisely this ability to turn from the expected to pursue the intriguing, to recognize the significance of the unanticipated result, to awaken to the new theory or pattern amid the cacophony of conventional thinking—precisely those qualities (so apparent in the learning of small children) that are most likely to be catechized out of young people as they learn what school "achievement" is all about.

And we who are parents bear a special burden (and may face an unbearable dilemma) in nurturing the continued curiosity and resourcefulness of our young learners, in the face of demands that we coach them in how to play the Game and wait upon their report cards to gauge how well they've done. We become so confused, so conflicted, so fearful that unless we keep our children's minds "on task," aiming for the honor roll, the advanced placement courses, the grade-point average of life, we will damage their chances to access the next set of elite learning venues, be they the elementary school's gifted-and-talented program, the high school's honors classes, an Ivy League college, or a top-ranked graduate program. Such pressures can easily thwart our desire to see the children in our lives as happy, curious, confident, and enthusiastic learners. We see the contrast between how our children respond to the things they love to learn and how they resist or rebel against the boredom and inanity of much of their schoolwork. But we bite our tongues and (still confused) become complicit in the atrophy of our children's learning spirit in furtherance of their academic careers.

In typical classrooms, where students have over time become much less focused on their own learning, on "making meaning," they and their teachers are inclined to view their efforts through the lens of the worker who produces things in order to get a reward (wages) or of the servant who labors with the objective of getting his or her tasks over with. When students are "put to work," Alfie Kohn points out, "the tasks come to be seen as—indeed, are often explicitly presented as—means to an end. What counts is the number of right answers, although even this may be seen as just a prerequisite to snagging a good grade. In fact, the grade may be a means to making the honor roll, which, in turn, may lead to special privileges or rewards provided at school or at home. With each additional inducement, the original act of learning is further devalued."[2]

This distinction between "learning for its own sake" and "working for the grade" is at the very core of this book. We generally pay lip service to the former—it's what every good teacher exhorts us to do. But the realities of school militate against it, and even the teachers who ascribe to its value often unwittingly undermine those ideals in the way they organize their instruction and, in particular, how learning becomes subservient to assessment strategies in the course or classroom.[3]

Seven Categories of Learners in an Education System That Belittles Learning

However bullying the high priests of our national education religion may be toward teachers and school officials, they may have only a limited affect on the young, who are not easily influenced by standardized tests that lead to yearly comparative ratings of schools on their test performance. Kids develop their own stance with regard to school, and by the time they hit high school, their postures, attitudes, and motivations are often well established. I remember one high school student telling me: "I know I coulda done better on that state test—I just didn't want to make this school look good."

Let me offer seven possible categories of learners to help gauge the extent to which students are affected by the Game of School. My categories are mostly geared toward kids in high school, but the descriptions could be adjusted to fit almost any age group from fourth or fifth grade through college. They are, inevitably, stereotypes or caricatures, and all the teenagers I know are complex, highly individual people who resist being categorized, and for good reason. Here is my list, to be fleshed out on the following pages:

1. True-Blue Learners (who love school for the learning they get out of it)
2. Go-Getters (who are in it for the grades, the honors, the advancement)
3. Cherry Pickers (who work hard only in subjects, and for teachers, they respect)
4. Pluggers (who put their noses to the grindstone and try to get through it)
5. Goof-Offs or Rebels (who think school is a cruel joke and become class clowns)
6. Socializers or Hang-Outers (who go to school mainly to be with their friends)

7. Give-Uppers (who are on their way out of school and of education)

My purpose in creating these categories is to stimulate conversation, not to make pigeonholes to stick kids in. So far, at least in the three high schools where students have looked over drafts of this chapter, the conversations have been most informative, and I am much indebted to three teachers, Tyra Pickering, from Muncie Central High School, in Muncie, Indiana; Alice Warner, from Newport High School, in Newport, Oregon; and Priya Sundaravalli, from the Future School, in Auroville, India, which she describes as "a polycultural school in our spiritual-intentional community, in southern India." They and their students looked at early drafts of the categories, discussed and wrote or drew their responses to them, many of which were mailed or emailed to me.

If you are a student in school, you may want to see which one or two of the following categories remind you most of yourself. If you are a parent, try to estimate where your child might be now, while reflecting on how your child's attitude has been evolving through the grades. If you are a teacher, you might ask your students to critique these categories and then talk together about the extent to which they see themselves as playing the Game of School.

Category 1: True-Blue Learners

You are a kid who really does love to learn, and your school provides you with opportunities that allow you to grow at your own pace and to be successful on your own terms. You may be considered "very smart," or you may be known as "a real hard worker," or both. You may be from an affluent family, destined for success, or you may be from a lower-income family, someone who sees school as an avenue of escape. Either way, you really love school and would probably do as well as you do even if there were no grades. Your teachers encourage you to learn what you are interested in learning, and you are eager to report what you've discovered to others in your class. The example you set spurs at least some other students to get excited about their learning. The learning activities you pursue on your own outside of school—reading, art or music, hobbies, nature studies, sports, church or civic groups—are also areas you bring lots of energy to; they provide a nice balance to your in-school learning. Life is a seamless web—learning just seems to come naturally to you.

For Tyra Pickering's ninth graders, this was a somewhat ambivalent category. Tyra wrote,

> One of my classes had a seminar-like discussion on this category, which focused on how students end up as true-blue learners and if true-blue learners were, in fact, the best category to be in to ensure success. Students began by labeling these students the "rich" kids whose parents (who had themselves gone to college and have instilled the work ethic into their kids' minds) supported, or forced them to do their homework. As a result, these kids know what they need to succeed. They have to get good grades in order to get into college, in order to get a good job, in order to get all of the things they need to be happy. But they also felt that this category could also include kids who come from bad homes and who see school as a way out of where they are now. They love school because it is an escape from the real world, a ticket out of where they are. As for the future of students in Category 1, my kids felt that they would succeed because they were truly happy and truly interested and focused on what they wanted.
>
> The pitfall to this category was that my students felt that it is a difficult place to be. Not every subject, according to them, is exciting. Not every teacher made them want to know more. Sometimes they had a hard time making the connections between what was being taught and the "real world" applications. "Learning for learning's sake" just isn't enough when you don't know what to do with the knowledge. They were also concerned about "time." How do

> these types of students find the time to be a part of so many things? Are they a part of them because they really want to be? Or are they are part of them because they are focused on the end prize which would place them more in Category 2 [Go-Getters]?[4]

Tyler R., a student from Oregon, included himself in this category because of his sense of mission:

"I love to learn. I really see school as a place to escape. I come from a family of high school dropouts . . . and I don't want that. I look at school as a place to pull ahead."

Category 2: Go-Getters

You "high achievers" do well in school, and everyone is proud of you. Some subjects are interesting and challenging, others not so much, but you work hard to be successful in all of them, and you have the grades to show it. Unlike students in the first category, grades are everything to you, and you know almost by instinct what each teacher expects of you and how to make sure you get those A's. You accept it as normal that some or most of your classes are dull and that many assignments make little sense, but that doesn't hold you back, and you are convinced that what you are learning is preparing you for the next grade, the next school, or college. You budget your time and energy well, giving each teacher what you know he or she expects from an A student. You make the honor roll every time.

As far as learning on your own, outside of school, is concerned, there's just not much time for that, aside from the clubs, sports, and activities you engage in, some because you genuinely enjoy them, others because you're sure they will look good on your academic record. You read a little on your own, especially if a book is recommended by a friend. But schoolwork always comes first, and there is plenty of that to occupy your available time.

From Tyra Pickering's journal:

This category seemed to appeal to my students more than the True-Blue Learners because it seemed to be more realistic. Many students could relate to it because it takes into consideration that not everything is interesting to everyone, but you tackle it all because you do want to succeed.

Students talked and wrote about how these Go-Getters are focused on pleasing others. Even the fact that they read things their friends recommend suggests that they are concerned with doing things to make others happy. The concern was that, while these students are technically successful, it is uncertain if they will ever be happy or if they will spend the rest of their lives trying always to do what is "right."

One student, Tyler, wrote about how he is both like and unlike the Go-Getter. He felt that he does try to make sure that his grades are good enough to get him into college, but that he felt it was important to "play" when he got home from school before he did his homework. He didn't want to focus all of his time on school work, but that didn't mean he wasn't a Go-Getter.

Another student, Garrett, sees this kind of student as a "geek" who is focused only on the grades and on the stereotypical geek activities such as chess. It never occurred to Garrett that he might be a Go-Getter. His interpretation says it all. These students are focused on school and could not possibly be "normal" kids.

However, in our discussion, students began talking about how Go-Getters will succeed because they have figured out what it takes to make it. In other words, they know the Game.

Another Tyler (Tyler C.), one of Alice Warner's students, commented, "I am a Go-Getter because I do pretty well in school, usually manage around a 3.5 GPA and also work very hard in school. I know what the teachers expect of me. I do play sports because I enjoy them, but I have to admit school work always comes first. . . . I am not going to lie and say I like school, but I think it is a great thing to have in life. That's why I am a Go-Getter."

Category 3: Cherry Pickers

Let's face it: there are good teachers and lousy teachers, interesting subjects and boring subjects. You have no problem staying on top of those subjects that interest you. It may be English and art, or physics and math, music or history; in those classes, you're one of the stars. It's clear to you why you do well—you find the stuff fascinating. The high grades you get in these subjects are welcome, but you'd probably do just as much work in those classes if there were no grades. In your other classes, those that hold little interest for you, you struggle to get by with a C, because you just don't like wasting time on stuff that seems meaningless.

Your counselor can't figure you out. You'd be an honors student for sure, she tells you, if you'd do as much work in *all* your subjects as you do in the ones you seem to love. "You're just not working up to your potential," she says. You think she's nuts. How can she not understand that to you some subjects and teachers are worth your best effort and others are not? So you end up with a B average, with most of your grades either A's or C's. Out of school, as in school, you keep on learning enthusiastically in the areas that mean something to you, and you ignore those that do not. Life's too short to waste time on junk.

Tyra Pickering reports:

> Most students, especially those who played basketball, immediately related to this category. They loved the name and felt that it perfectly described them. One student, Wesley, predicted that a Cherry Picker would most likely go to a public college because his grade-point average would not be high enough for anything else: "I believe that most students in this category will do just fine in life, I just don't know if they all will be able to handle the constant aggravation or not." I think he may be on to something. Yes, some subjects are more interesting than others, but life insists that you learn to deal

with both the good and the bad, and Wesley seems to have figured this out at fourteen.

Students also discussed and wrote about how a person becomes a Cherry Picker. While most students felt they related to this category, to some extent, they also felt that there was something missing but were unable to put their finger on what it was. No one wrote about being solely in this category, partially because that meant admitting that you couldn't deal with situations you did not enjoy.

Several of Priya Sundaravalli's fifteen- and sixteen-year-old students related to this category as well. Here are two excerpts from their statements, the first from Tez, a South Korean student, and the second from Sheila, who is German:

> I am a semi-Cherry Picker. I am specially interested in art and things connected to art. I grew up thinking that I'm always going to be an artist, so I put most of my attention to that kind of subject. . . . I do my best in most of the classes but I also think that there are very useless things sometimes and that one should not waste time on those things.

> I'm a bit of a Cherry Picker. In most of the subjects that I am interested in, like German, English, cooking . . . I try hard, maybe not always my best. I try and I have the will. Sometimes though I tend to give up. . . . I fear the classes I don't understand and I get scared and give up. Sometimes I try but I think it is impossible. I start to dislike the subject and pay less attention. . . . But when I like a subject, I try. I feel a certain specialness for that subject and look forward to going to class. My grades aren't exactly great in those subjects, but I enjoy them and I learn. I don't know what would make me more engaged in learning. Maybe if I would decide what I really want and put more effort into it, it would help.

A student of Alice Warner, in Oregon, suggested we name this group "Burger Kingers" because they like to "have it their way." Another, Yvonne, wrote this:

> I think that I am a Cherry Picker in a lot of ways. My grades are mostly A's and C's. Some classes just don't interest me. I think the teachers who make the classroom fun and involve the students in activities they can relate to have more students that succeed. I also think that the teachers who are the total opposite have students that fail, because . . . they think it's a "waste of time." If the teachers would try to change their teaching habits just a little to interest the students more, then maybe all of us could end up honor students. School is like a second home, and if we make our "home" a place where people don't want to be, where are we going to end up? To some people, school is all they have.

Category 4: Pluggers

School certainly has its ups and downs. In some classes you stay interested, do pretty good work, and get good grades. But in other subjects, it's a real struggle, sometimes, to do what they try to make you do, and you can't figure out why so much of school is so hard. You know you're not alone and that lots of kids feel this way. But the adults who run the school don't seem to care that most of the time you're just plugging along, doing what you're told, but not often engaged in what you'd call "real learning."

After all, what choice do you have? You and your parents know that you've just got to keep your grades up, although you wish everyone around you wasn't so focused on grades all the time. You push through your assignments, try to get around or get by those that don't interest you, and count the days until the next vacation. You hope (but you're really not sure) that things will get better as you move on up through the grades.

As far as learning on your own is concerned, by the time the school day is over and you've got most of your homework done, all you want to do is chill out, watch TV, listen to your music, surf the Internet, get together with your friends. You hardly ever read books not required for school, in part because it's such a struggle to read all the stuff that *is* required.

Tobey, who is German-Italian and one of Priya Sundaravalli's students, comments:

> I guess I would fall under the category of a Plugger. It sort of describes me in some way but it is quite superficial. There is no subject really that I am not interested in in some way, and my grades are most of the time pretty good. It is true that I often feel that I'm not making any real progress and just doing what the teacher says or sometimes not even that. Maybe it is just my fault and I'm too lazy and don't work up to my potential (as many of my teachers say). Basically I think that teachers could improve in some way by making the class more interesting, but generally it is up to the students to improve.

Zach S., from Oregon, includes himself in this category, with reservations: "After reading the different categories and the different types of learners, I've decided that I'm mostly a Plugger. . . . I really see myself in the situations you described, especially the 'You hope (but you're really not sure) that things will get better as you move on up through the grades' area. The only area in the Pluggers section that I'm not, is the part about other kids feeling the same. I kind of feel like I'm the only one."

A classmate, who elected not to disclose his or her name, offered this comment: "I am a person who does the work and tries to get it done on time. And some of the classes are dull, and I don't get the stuff we're doing and the teachers don't explain it that well, but I try to do as well as I can, and most of the assignments we do I don't get why we have to do it. . . . I really need to study, and I don't get good grades on tests, but sometimes I do."

Tyra Pickering writes:

> Most students feel that they fit into this category well. They are still young enough that many see their parents as pushing them to excel in school. However, while they feel they belong here, they also feel that they aren't really learning that much. What they learn is "how to make it." One student's visual representation depicted a horse tied

to a plow being led through the curriculum by the teachers. My interpretation of their reaction was that the image of "Work Horses" [now "Pluggers"] implies that they are being forced to complete tasks. This was the only complaint that many of them had. While they related to the idea of the ups and downs of school, the interesting and boring aspects of classes, I think they didn't like to think of themselves as being forced to plod through their days.

Category 5: Goof-Offs or Rebels

The same God who gave you a brain must have been half-asleep when He or She created schools, since nobody in their right minds would want to use such a wonderful instrument as your brain in such a mindless place as a school. You're too smart to fail, but you're also too ornery to just accept the stuff they dish out in most of your courses. You find most of what your teachers dish out to be amazingly dumb, hypocritical, repetitive, and totally useless. You see through it all: the kids and teachers just going through the motions; the adults who say one thing and do another; the teachers who play favorites and the kids who brownnose their way through it all; the kids who come from the wrong side of the tracks and are stuck into classrooms with the worst teachers. It's too painful to simply sit there and play along, so you become the class clown, the editor of the underground "truth teller" journal, the rebel, the cynic. In the classes of teachers you respect, you do good work, and you manage to keep your options for college open by not failing any important subjects. But, really, school is a joke.

Outside of school you tend to be a loner, one whose interest in books, sports, music, films, art, or nature finds you occasional friends in these activities but mostly leaves you by yourself to figure out why the world is as screwed up as it seems.

From Tyra Pickering:

Many students chose this category to write and/or draw about. Students seemed to equate this category with problems of "attitude."

Many, however, could relate to the Goof-Off in that they, too, have been so bored in class that they just wanted to do something—*any*thing—to make it more interesting. While some were annoyed by Goof-Offs, others were thankful because they did make the boring classes interesting. All agreed that this type of student would not be successful because being smart is just not enough unless you learn to apply it.

From Alice Warner:

Almost all the Goof-Offs felt this category was not accurately named—and mostly preferred the name Rebels [which I've since added]. One student said that category should be named Individual Realistic Thinkers, but another student, Alyssa, felt right at home:

"I, Alyssa, am a Goof-Off because I'm too smart to fail, but then again I never do my work and I know that I'm smart, but school is not my thing. I hate school. I hate it when teachers pick favorites, because I'm definitely not a favorite. All through seventh and eighth grade I was a class clown. It actually was pretty fun, even though I got into a lot of trouble for it.

"I am also a total [Socializer or Hang-Outer]. All through elementary school my nickname was 'Motor Mouth/Mega Lips.' I only go to school for the hot guys and my friends. I only do my work for the teachers I respect, and even then I barely do my work. Everything except my friends comes second. . . . I always know who's dating who and when and where the fights are gonna be. I sit at home every night and start on my homework and someone either calls me or gets online. After that I put my stuff away and talk to my friends. . . . I've had it with school! I give up. It's all a bunch of bull. . . . I'm so tempted to just quit school."

Category 6: Socializers or Hang-Outers

You go to school to be with your friends—everything else takes second place. A few of your teachers are "cool" enough to get you to do some work, and those who care and who "stay on your back" can usually get some work out of you. But you do it mostly just to please them, not because you feel you're learning anything important. You're considered "smart" in at least one subject (it might be writing stories; it might be math or science or art), but as for the rest, you give it the minimum necessary to keep your teachers and your parents from bugging you about it. Sometimes it works; sometimes they bug you anyway.

The social aspects of school—hanging out with your friends, getting to know some new kids, finding the people you like and who like you—seem so much more real than anything in the academic world. No tidbit of gossip passes you by; you always know who's dating who, who's cheating on who, who's bad-mouthing who. But most of the time, what your teachers talk about just goes in one ear and out the other. You're sorry, in a way, because some of your teachers are really "into" their subjects, and you kind of wish you could be there, too. But it seems like they're in a different world, a world of academic knowledge, and to you and your friends, that's just not "where it's at."

You'll try to stay in school and do what you need to do to graduate. But who knows what will happen—maybe college, maybe a job. As for doing any serious learning outside of school? Forget it. You're lucky if you can get through half of your homework on a given night, let alone anything else. Anyway, once your friends start to call on your cell phone, your mind is off learning for the night.

Tyra Pickering's response:

> Students seemed to have the most problems with this category [at least in its early drafts] simply because they couldn't separate the academic and social aspects of school. If they admitted they wanted to come to school to be with their friends (which seems only natural), then they had to admit that academics came second. I think that being with their friends and learning with their friends could not be separated for them. This category had us all confused.
>
> I *want* my students to be at least partially in this category; otherwise, they cannot make the connections to the real world. I am

> not saying that they should care only about the social aspects of school, but it seems they can learn some valuable knowledge by interacting with peers. Being social is a big part of becoming a valuable asset to a community, and I love it when students know enough of what is going on to be able to make connections between what we are learning and the real world out there (even out there in the hallways). Students who are so focused on the idea of the academics in the classroom often miss out on the essentials of growing up. I intentionally do not assign homework because I want my students to live life when they leave my room.

My response to Tyra's thoughtful dissenters is that of course school is a very important place for students to meet and make friends, and I agree that they can and do learn much from their schoolmates. So we are all, to a greater or lesser extent, Socializers. But there are some students for whom school is almost entirely *about* hanging out with friends, and there are many others who worry much more about their status in their peer group than the quality of the learning they do. As is true of sports—which also have many growth possibilities for young people and many worthwhile challenges, but which totally dominate the way some kids (and adults) look at education—whenever a student's social life comes to mean *everything*, it may indicate that teachers have not yet found a way to ignite a passion for learning in that student. Hanging out, being popular, teasing, flirting, getting "tight" with this one, "dumping" that one become the main reasons for coming to school.

Category 7: Give-Uppers

You've *had* it with school. It may be a place where other kids succeed, but it certainly isn't for you. You don't know if it's because you're just not very smart or because your teachers have it in for you or because it's all just a bunch of bull. Any way you look at it, the learning you do in school seems pointless or way beyond you or both. Sure, you could do better if you tried harder and if you had a teacher who really showed some interest in you and encouraged you. But that's not how you feel most of the time. Your parents are angry with you *and* with the school. They've tried just about everything—grounding you, taking away privileges, dragging you to see a counselor, arguing with the principal—but they're as upset and confused as you are.

The kids you hang with agree with the way you look at the whole school situation. They know that some other kids, and some teachers too, consider you a loser, but the way you and your friends see it, you guys are the only ones who see school as it *really* is—a club for the rich kids, the super jocks, and the real smart kids, and a big dump for everyone else. You know that no decent college would accept you with the grades you've got, and you're not even sure it's worth hanging around to graduate. If somebody came by with a better offer—like a decent job—you'd be tempted to quit school. The sight of books turns you off. Thankfully, there's some good music to be found, some sports or video games you like, and once in a while a movie that makes you feel as though you do understand how the world works. But, all in all, it's a pretty bleak picture.

Here is Tyra Pickering's reaction to this final category:

> This category produced the most interesting essays. To be honest, these are the students I'm most fascinated by. I assign a lot of reflective writing, and I always try to offer options that will appeal to all types of learners. When students in this category are given the freedom to express their opinions, they produce some of the best writing I have seen out of ninth graders. I would rather read an essay full of sincerity, though it may have a million misspelled words and terrible grammar, than an essay perfectly written that says little or nothing of what the writer truly believes. I have copied one of my students' papers here:
>
> "My name is Rob. I have been trying to get my grades right for the last two years. I figure that if other students can get good grades I can

too. I just don't work hard enough. Going through all four year of high school I have to understand that. I have to get my diploma so I can have a good job. Being a student at Muncie Central I have my ups and downs with stuff. All my classes are hard, well, most of them. All my friends make better grades then I do. I can't wait until summer vacation. I try to read the books that the school gives me but I just don't like reading them. I try to get around the teachers with my homework but it all catches up with me at the end. I've been slacking a little bit on my homework—I tried to get help but it seems like the teachers don't like me too well."

Tyra concludes, "My heart is with kids who identify with this final category of learners. It is not about playing the game for them. It is about surviving life. In the school where I am fortunate enough to teach, we are constantly striving to help them."

Student Comments on the Categorizing Process

A number of students could not find any one category that fit them. Alice Warner says that one of her students thinks we need a category for "Jocks who keep their grades up so they can play sports." She continues, "I thought this was very insightful. . . . As a teacher, I would say this is probably the most significant motivator for my students to play the Game of School—I have many combined Athlete/Go-Getting/Pluggers."

Several of her students were critical of the categories themselves or of the whole process, whereas others supported the effort. Here are some excerpts from their remarks:

> I like the fact you're trying to help people to teach better. The approach you are taking, however, is all wrong. . . . Teachers should not [prejudge] students and in my opinion, you and your book are doing this. But just to humor you, I will play your "game of school." I consider myself a Plugger; it basically describes me as a student. I like drawing, drafting and study hall, but the rest aren't "fun," for lack of a better phrase. . . . I hope that helps, I doubt it will, though [Walter S.].

When I was handed this little packet [describing the seven categories] I read the whole thing and had already made up my mind about what I was going to say. But, personally, I don't get why you are categorizing people. I know you are "studying" high school and us high-schoolers in it, but what are you trying to achieve here. . . ? I feel like by having us pick which category we fit under, you are trying to divide us all into groups that don't mix with each other [Kyla M.].

I believe there are not enough categories. . . . What about the class comedians who are really too smart for school? There are also kids like me who are really good students but hate school and have lazy habits about homework. I know a few more like me who are lucky enough to have this happen to them. I still think all your categories are very accurate. I just think you need more of them. I really find it humorous that some students in here say that categorizing is not right, and none of your stuff is accurate, and mostly that it just plain sucks. The people who say that stuff are the easiest to categorize—that's just plain funny. Your work is great. I just think you need more categories. Keep up the great work [Evan K.].

Prof. Fried, most of the categories don't fit me. Although I did find two that do. Categories 2 [Go-Getters] and 4 [Pluggers] fit me well . . . Category 4 was perfect in every way, I couldn't say it better myself. I have been trying to tell my Mom and Dad exactly the same thing for the last four years. I hope this essay will help you write your book and help you understand more about high school students [Tim G.].

There was another group of students whose critique was that their own experiences span more than one category. From India, Joey, who is German, writes,

I am half a Cherry Picker and half a Plugger. Sometimes at the end of the day I just feel like chilling out, sometimes I don't mind doing my homework. School definitely has its ups and downs, some subjects are kick-ass, some are hopeless, but I am pretty much an average student. Sometimes I get a C and sometimes an A. I used to be

> a Give-Upper before but I am happy to have changed. I am happy with my current state, and I think if I keep it up I will go far. In [middle school], I used to be a Goof-Off for some time, but it is all over now.

Blink, an Israeli boy at the same school, comments,

> I am a combination of most of the categories. I have a bad attitude about school but I study more, like the Plugger. I pay attention in class but I also try to remain social. I study like a Cherry Picker, only in the subjects I like, but I still work hard in other classes. Nothing would really get me "into" school except maybe a perfect society.

Spiff, who is Russian and their classmate, created his own definition:

> I will call my category Lonely Blue Dolphin. Someone who is looking for his own way, and until he finds it, he won't accept any other. Willing to work on interests, but like the Cherry Picker, "Life is too precious to waste time on junk." Not putting school down, not calling it a place for idiots, nor clever guys. School is school, the way it is—unchangeable like the bricks it is made with. It might be the way or might not. Doing homework always but a lot of time alone in the self. The biggest trap to avoid is the Road of Tomorrow and Castle of Nothing At All. This problem, once tackled, leads to a very peaceful, happy, joyful life. Unchangeable is the goal, a blind choice leads to a (maybe) fatal mistake.

My last contributor is Ivy S., from Oregon: "I found your theories on learning to be very interesting and accurate. However, the names confused me a bit. . . . I am a Cherry Picker; I love school, but not the classes part. I do my work well in the classes I love and struggle in those I don't. I like the social part of it quite a bit, and I love to learn; I just think that learning in a classroom at school is so boring and takes all the fun out of it."

Most schools want as many students as possible to be True-Blue Learners, Go-Getters, and Pluggers. If they don't love learning, let them at least work hard and aim for high grades. But what is it like when the majority of one's students identify as Rebels, Hang-Outers, or Give-Uppers? What does a teacher do when too many students won't play the Game at all, but come to school just to see their friends or to have fun at their teachers' expense or to do the minimum work necessary to stay out of trouble?

Last year I observed a teacher intern coping with one of the most difficult urban teaching situations I've ever encountered. It's not that this school was overrun with crime or gang violence; it's just that so many of the students were so discouraged by the spate of staff turnovers and policy changes that many of them no longer treated their classes as places where much learning happens. [I am given to understand that conditions in this school have improved considerably in the year following my observation of Al Maalik.] In observing this teacher at work, I was impressed both with the complexity of the challenge and with his quiet, dignified, persistent approach.

~ *Interlude* ~

Abd Al-Maalik, High School History Teacher

Abd Al-Maalik (not his real name; his school officials want him and their school to remain anonymous) is a young man with an intense, thoughtful look. He wears a sparse black beard on his dark, Semitic face, and his regular mode of dress includes a caftan or prayer cap and a white tunic that extends to his knees, worn over khaki slacks. Raised in Chicago by parents who emigrated from the Gulf States, he is a devout member of a particular Shiite sect and is deeply involved in religious affairs, both locally and throughout the world. His black-brown eyes radiate a soulful intensity, and he is one of the gentlest teachers I have ever observed.

Al-Maalik's entire persona—from mode of dress to mode of speech—is in sharp contrast to the culture that surrounds him in the urban high school at which he has interned, over the past year, and at which he has just been hired as a history teacher for the coming school year.

To say that Abd Al-Maalik's school has been buffeted by transitions would be a huge understatement. The turnover of faculty and staff during the past several years has been both rapid and often highly emotional. There have been four administrative heads in as many years. Turmoil at the top has been mirrored by a spirit of rebelliousness among the mostly African American student population, and problems of "attitude" and "behavior" are widespread.

It is one of Al-Maalik's theories, expressed in conversation with me, that these young people feel abandoned by the adults and that their sometimes arrogant and rude behavior stems, in part, from lack of trust that the adults care enough about them to stick around. With a curriculum designed to bring underachieving urban youth up to the point of college readiness, and a student body marked by significant deficiencies in literacy, work habits, and confidence, everyone has had to deal with a school culture marked by anger, frustration, tension, and failure.

The failure rate in some classes has been as high as 70 percent, and the faculty's refusal to "lower standards" in the face of a shifting population of students, a number of whom have already failed at other schools in the area, creates an often volatile atmosphere.

One aspect of Al-Maalik's stance that has attracted my interest is his focus on what he calls "the dignity of the work." As a teacher of history to students whose grasp of the subject is often spotty at best, he concentrates on emphasizing the value to inner-city youth of studying history, while focusing on the quality of their work. Now, in April, I am visiting Al-Maalik's eighty-minute class to see how his stance has evolved in response to what he sees as their need for him, as a teacher, to "take care of business" (that is, to take command of the class and to control wayward student behavior).

He is teaching history to tenth graders. In one recent observation of these students in another class, I saw practically no learning taking place, and at least a third of the students had been ejected from the classroom, at one time or another, during the eighty-minute class session. I am curious as to what Al-Maalik has in mind for these kids, in his unit on liberation movements of the twentieth century.

The class begins with Al-Maalik's greeting students at the door and handing them a "Do Now" (a brief topic-related assignment intended to engage students immediately in the work at hand). The tenth graders enter in a rambunctious mood; it takes them five minutes or so to settle down. A few are drumming on their desks, and one student challenges Al-Maalik on his announcement that their final paper on "anticolonial liberation movements" is due a month from now, on June 4. Al-Maalik explains they will be devoting lots of class time, between now and June, to this project because "it's the most important work you're going to be doing in history this year."

Today's focus will be on thesis statements. "What you owe me by the end of class today is your thesis statement and three supporting arguments. You have five minutes to get into Do Now mode. I will be coming around to check the notes you wrote for homework last weekend, so please have them ready." There is a friendly, no-nonsense tone here. He is neither threatening them nor berating them. He is just telling them how it is.

Miraculously, the class settles down. I say "miraculously" because I have seen this same group of students, in another classroom, keep the teacher and teaching intern at bay for an hour with a stream of interruptions, battles small and large, loudly voiced complaints, and heated exchanges over student behavior and teacher reactions. Even here, the potential for disruption of learning is ever present.

A student comes in late, crying "Who stole my chair!?" When there is no response, she loudly says, "*Excuse me!*" and Al-Maalik signals that she is to raise her hand, instead of calling out. He is walking around the classroom, checking the notes student have written, having quiet conversations with other students; he quietly tells several that they are to see him after school to talk about their notes. Although there is only a slight buzz in the room, he announces, "It's way too loud for Do Now." The late student again says, "*Excuse me!*" and Al-Maalik once more signals for her to raise her hand. He whispers to her about proper class decorum, but she brushes him off. Another student complains out loud about being put on the late list. Al-Maalik walks over to this one, and, after a few words from him (which cannot be overheard by me or anyone else), she reluctantly ceases complaining.

I notice that virtually all of his conversations with students are private, whispered ones. I have observed, in other classes, how a teacher's verbal response to a student's disrespectful words or behavior very often triggers a new round of even more raucous and angry interchanges, often leading to disciplinary action. Even here, I sense a powder keg of chaos that could explode at any moment, with three or four students willing to act as blasting caps. It is Al-Maalik's job to see that, whenever lit, these fuses get extinguished before the rest of the keg ignites.

At 9:05 Ms. G., Al-Maalik's mentor teacher, enters and, following the pattern he has established, quietly converses with individual students about their topics. Al-Maalik is not altogether pleased with their decorum and announces, "When we have guests in the room, I expect you to respect their presence." In an ever-so-slightly louder and sterner voice, he warns, "There is something I have to say: when Ms. G. comes in here, she is not to be demonized. You must respect adults in this building. I don't want to say any more about that. *Ever!* Whenever we have a Do Now, I expect you to do what's asked of you on the page."

Today's Do Now asks the students to use the notes they have written from their reading packets to answer one of three questions about the freedom movement in the country they've selected to study. The packets are groups of articles totaling twenty to sixty pages that serve as texts around the theme of national liberation movements. There are some dozen different movements represented in these background packets.

Al-Maalik is less than pleased about the quality of the notes he has been reviewing, and he announces, "Tonight is the first time I will be making phone calls to your home, unless you come in after school and finish your work. It is very important that you stay caught up with this project. And you must do your homework. Getting past this reading packet is the first obstacle. Judging by what I saw during the Do Now, it looks to me that lots of you are unprepared. But regardless, we will now spend the class time looking at how to construct a thesis and supporting arguments. Any questions?"

"Oh, could we *please* just move *on!*" says a restless student, tired of hearing the same directions repeated yet again, and Al-Maalik agrees. "The reason I can formulate a thesis statement and supporting statement is that I know the information that's in the case packet, which is why it's so important to read what's in your packet. I want to have you all working with me. I don't want anybody to be behind."

"You already *look* like someone's behind," a student mumbles in jest, scarcely audible. (Al-Maalik ignores the remark, if indeed he's heard it.) He turns on the overhead and says, "I set up a thesis and took apart the freedom movement in Kenya to create three statements that back up the thesis." He contrasts the experience of Kenya to that of Haiti and the Congo, saying that "the Kenyan people and leaders created a political system that remained stable after independence."

Al-Maalik announces, "During the next half hour, I want you to write three to five paragraphs on your research topic, practicing how to write a thesis statement and supporting arguments. I've made a model of how to answer the questions I want you to respond to, and today you will write a thesis and three supporting arguments." All this is delivered in a straightforward voice, without emotion.

During a previous conversation, Al-Maalik had questioned my advice to include students in the planning and decision-making process around important assignments. "For these kids, at this school, given the turmoil and frequent change of staff they've experienced, it won't work," he had argued. "They think it means that we don't know what we're doing, that we're asking them to do our work for us." Observing him, I understand the validity of his argument.

The first sentence on his overhead reads, "The freedom movement in Kenya was a success." Several students remark that it is too simple a statement. "Can't you jazz that up?" one asks. Al-Maalik assures them that these simple statements will lead to more complex ones. There is a spate of comments about who wants "simple" and who wants "harder" questions to be posed. Some try to make it a boy-girl issue. I can see how easily the fabric of academic work can unravel. But the students know they're just having a bit of fun and don't press the issue.

"Let's say you're doing India," Al-Maalik says, regarding the need for supporting arguments for the thesis statement. "You could say, 'Gandhi worked successfully with other nationalist leaders in challenging British rule' as a supporting argument." He jokes, "if *I* give you examples for your supporting statements, you better not use them, or that would be plagiarism." There is a gentle outcry that indicates their ambivalence toward his *helping* them but not doing their work *for* them. Some ask him to show them how to do it, but he insists that it has to be *their* work. He is taking a risk in raising the issue of plagiarism in a semi-joking way, but he gets away with it, and it seems to help them see him as less stern.

The underlying message seems to be, "I will treat you with respect, even joke with you, as long as everything we do enhances the dignity of the work before you. But make no mistake, my job is to see to it that you do your work and accomplish the task. You have no choice about this project, except as regards the country whose freedom movement you select and your manner of responding to the requirements I've announced. When you respect your work and the teachers who are here to guide you, we can treat each other in a friendly manner." It reminds me, somewhat uncomfortably, of the phrase often used by students who may be the first in their families to go to college: "If my teachers hadn't stayed on my back all the time, I wouldn't have made it through high school."

Al-Maalik now displays his third supporting argument on the overhead, this one a great deal more complex, and he uses it to answer the earlier charge that he was being too simple. "This one is much more difficult," he says, and asks two students to paraphrase it. He turns off the overhead and reiterates, "When you set up your supporting arguments, put them in chronological order. You should be writing these down in your notes, in your mind, in your heart. Here is today's assignment: develop a thesis and supporting argument. You will be turning this in at the end of today and I will read them all tonight and give them back to you. Background info and criteria for excellence are listed on the pages."

He asks one of the previously disruptive students if she understands and has any questions; she says she doesn't understand but has no questions. He checks in with one student who has kept his head down on his desk the whole time. He quizzes two students, who repeat his instructions. He reiterates: "I expect to see a complete set of notes on your reading packet before the end of the day, or else I will be calling home." Someone asks why he is threatening to call their parents, and he says,

"So not only me, but also someone at home will be on your case, urging you to work hard." A student comments, "At least you're being honest, not like Ms. ___ who says, 'I'm *only* doing this to *help* you.'" There is a tittering of laughter at his sarcasm.

Al-Maalik then goes over the details in rapid-fire Q-and-A fashion:

"What is the due date for the paper?"

"June 4."

"Will I accept late papers?"

"Yes," some students say. "No," say others.

"I *will* accept papers late, up to June 9, but I will not *like* it. I will be angry about it, but then I will forgive you." There is a twinkle in his eye. He is threading the needle, searching for the right balance between sternness and flexibility.

His two guiding principles, as I observe them, are as follows:

1. You students are capable of intellectual work, even though a number of you may not believe that you are. I must therefore hold you to a standard that is as high as you can reach, and urge you to put in reasonable effort to meet it.
2. It is my duty to make sure that the project I ask you to do is a worthy one. I will guide you every step along the way and support you with specific handouts and clear direction. I must continue to emphasize the dignity of the work that you do.

Again Al-Maalik declares, "It is time for you to begin work, alone or with any others who are working on the same liberation movement. By the end of class I expect to have a thesis statement and three supporting arguments from each of you. You may work alone or in groups." This is at least the fifth time he has repeated the same instructions, and there is a bit of ritual in it, but it also suggests a church service, with repartee back and forth with the minister.

This is a pivotal moment, as now that they are "on their own," so to speak, the potential for breakdown is greatest. Students are able to get up and move about the crowded room to form workgroups. But some choose to use the time for their own social purposes. There is some drumming on the table; a young man sashays down the center aisle, provoking a girl to call out, "What are you *doing,* you big tree!? You can't even *dance!*" She playfully pushes him toward his seat. Al-Maalik notices but does not comment. He realizes that he must cut them some slack if they are to accept the responsibility to motivate themselves.

One girl, who has obviously not done her homework, complains, "That packet don't tell us nothin'!" This to Al-Maalik, who patiently explains to her how Marcus Garvey, listed in her packet, has a direct relation to the liberation of Jamaica. Two minutes ago, a student had asked Al-Maalik if he has read all the background packets that he handed out to use for their individual research papers. He said, "Yes," and they believe him. If he is going to ask them to work hard, it counts for something that he works hard too.

He approaches a group and tells all three, sternly, that he needs to see better notes from them, "or else you will fall too far behind and not be able to get your work done in time." These are not students who usually do their assignments. They are kids who have learned how to fail, how to give up on themselves, how to turn a class period into party time.

Al-Maalik notices a student who has held his hand up for several minutes, "I'll get to you in three minutes, after I've talked to Takisha. Is that okay? *Three* minutes." Another student calls out that *she* asked for help, first. He ignores her and speaks quietly with Takisha, kneeling by her desk to do so. A student comes in late, and Al-Maalik hands her a packet, announcing, "Ten minutes! You have ten minutes to complete your assignment for today's class."

It appears that perhaps half the students are taking their assignment seriously. Another quarter drift in and out of attentiveness to the task. The remaining quarter are either goofing off (quietly) or just pretending to write. Al-Maalik squats on his heels in front of a student who flips through her packet carelessly, indicating by her body language that all this is just too much for her. She twists a clump of her hair in her hand and looks glum. I cannot hear what goes on between them, but their conversation goes on for more than five minutes. When he rises and leaves her table, she continues to hold on to and look at her packet before getting up and wandering to a nearby table. One student, also looking dismayed, claims that she has nothing else to do, since she has left her packet at home and cannot answer any of the questions. "Just leave me alone," she whines. "When I get home, I'll do it."

Al-Maalik announces "Five minutes. Five minutes left." The glum girl is now productively engaged. She is using words from her packet to develop supporting statements. Her lips move as she reads over the material.

Two students, working on the freedom movement of their native Cape Verde, seem puzzled, frustrated, as they read through the packet. "I think they're not doing as well now as they were before [independence]," one says. Her partner continues, "And we don't want to be seen as favoring, you know, the bad guys." Al-Maalik listens, attentively and patiently. He will not do their thinking for them.

"Mr. Al-Maalik? We are going to *die* in a cesspool of *shame,*" says one of the two Cape Verdians, who are not especially pleased with what they are learning. "This *sucks,* man! I'm mad. I'm gonna cry."

"You two feel ambivalent about the success of your country's independence movement?" Al-Maalik says. They ask if they can use that phrase in their papers and he says, "Those are my words; find your own." But it's clear that history has come alive for these two students, challenged by the ambiguities of their native country's gaining its independence.

As the class period draws to a close, Al-Maalik raises his hand to get their attention, informs them about their homework—two paragraphs on the background of your selected country's independence movement—and reiterates, "I *want* your thesis and supporting statements! No one in this class is going to fail for lack of effort. I will be here, after school, as long as you need me to be."

One student, on the way out, insists on reading his supporting statement about the Jamaican uprising. He asks Al-Maalik, "Is *that* a supporting statement?" and is told, "Prove it! If you can prove it from the text, you can use it." One student continues to write at his desk, diligently, as the others file out. In my eyes, this is a minor victory for the cause of the dignity of work.

Does Abd Al-Maalik's performance in this most difficult class rise to the level of what I have been calling *authentic learning?* Or is he busy training his students to at least play the Game of School with some attention to their academic careers? There is no easy answer, and you will come to your own conclusions. But this much is clear to me: given a situation that a number of others have viewed as nearly hopeless, Abd Al-Maalik has taken a stance that allows his students to believe that they can perform academic work on a serious topic. He has entered into a serious conversation with them. And he has signed on to come back to be with them another year as a full-time history teacher.

Chapter Five

Humanizing "School Talk" in Pursuit of Authentic Learning

A paper I have been asked to review for an educational journal, on the topic of cultivating creative minds in students (a topic that ought to be of interest and accessible to us all), illustrates the susceptibility of our profession to mind-numbing jargon (the names of authors cited have been changed, but the quantity of references remains as in the original):

> Available research in educational psychology (Maxfield, Duffy, & Forrest, 1994; Blunt, 1995; del Vecchio, 1988; Schwartzbaum & Zakari, 1998; Quartz, Engles, & Steem, 1993; Letterman, 1993; Flood, 1987; Flood & Rafts, 1990), in supplementation to life experiences, workplace experiences, and individual insights, uncovered deficiencies in educational teaching methods and strategies in which creative thinking and problem solving are taught at all educational levels. . . .
>
> Data collection, data analysis, member checking processes, and constructs emerging brought to the hermeneutic-dialectic process (HDP), a method used in naturalistic observation research to establish authenticity in which emerging constructions of all stakeholders (involved parties such as administration or teachers) have equal entry to the process to share conclusions, recommendations, and courses of action.

As one who is often called upon to read professional journals written in this style, I find such passages off-putting in the extreme, and I can only imagine how teachers, parents, and students might feel when faced with similar travesties of the mother tongue.

We have a right to access the language that regulates the lives of people in school and to thereby gain a clearer picture of how things can go right—or go wrong—for teachers and kids. I will examine six concepts—discipline and classroom management, curriculum, instruction, assessment, self-motivation, and family involvement—and show that there are two ways we can approach each of them: one path entrenches us more deeply in the Game of School; the other leads us toward authentic learning. But let us begin by examining a question related to these six concepts: What are the ingredients essential to allow a school to support authentic learning, even where such concepts operate effectively?

Thinking Beyond Questions of Resources

When we think of what it takes for young people to learn and thrive in a school setting, our thoughts are likely to go first to the matter of resources. Jonathan Kozol and other social critics have argued forcefully that shocking inequities exist in the resources we make available to students who live in poor and minority neighborhoods. Yet we make a serious mistake if we assume that all that is required to make learning happen is a professionally certified teacher presenting lessons from an approved curriculum to students in a well-lit, colorful room with textbooks, maps, computers, desks, and chairs—critical as those things are. Clearly, resource deficiencies play a role in the underachievement of children from economically disadvantaged circumstances. But we must also look for a child's readiness, confidence, and motivation to learn in both academic and nonacademic subjects. We must also acknowledge that each child has a spirit, a motivating energy, that may be either active or moribund.

Psychologist Jerome Bruner, in his landmark 1968 study, *Toward a Theory of Instruction*, ends his chapter "The Will to Learn" with this summary:

> The will to learn is an intrinsic motive, one that finds both its source and its reward in its own exercise. The will to learn becomes a "problem" only under specialized circumstances like those of a school, where a curriculum is set, students confined, and a path fixed. The problem exists not so much in learning itself, but in the fact that what the school imposes often fails to enlist the natural energies that sustain spontaneous learning—curiosity, a desire for competence, aspiration to emulate a model, and a deep-sense commitment to the web of social reciprocity.[1]

The child must *want* to learn what we adults desire to teach, must feel that school is a friendly, safe, socially affirming, intellectually challenging, and respectful environment in which to try out new ideas and practice skills that may be difficult to master. If one or more of those desired qualities is lacking for the child, all our resources, our good intentions, and our careful preparation may come to naught. Once a child comes to feel that school is a place of hostility, insecurity, shame, boredom, or disrespect, that child's response is likely to negatively affect not only his or her learning but that of other children as well, as nobody wants to suffer alone. If one child is uncomfortable, he or she is likely to feel less so if others around become distracted or "off task." By the same token, if most of one's classmates are happily engaged in learning, that spirit can be infectious, and a doubting, insecure, or unmotivated student is more likely to be carried along by the positive flow of classroom activity and seek to become "part of the crowd."

Classroom Management: Who's Managing Whom—and to What End?

Bruner's phrase, "the will to learn," resonates deeply in me. In my work with student teachers in urban elementary and secondary schools, I come face-to-face every day with their concerns about an apparent lack of motivation to learn, often coupled with irresponsible behavior, in children and young adults. Some students don't do their homework, or choose not to read the assigned books; they won't take risks in answering questions in class, preferring to wait until their teacher provides the answer. Some will put their names on a test paper and hand it back to the teacher blank, preferring to receive a zero than risk trying and failing—as if to say, "I'd rather be thought of as 'bad' than 'stupid.'" Through the antics of a few, goaded on by others, students challenge their teachers either to give way and abandon their lessons or to lose their cool and yell at or threaten the kids. "Learning is far from being a joy," these students seem to say. "It is a constant hassle that makes us feel humiliated, and if we can disrupt the class and undermine our teacher's agenda, that makes us feel strong."

For most inexperienced teachers, this struggle for power sooner or later comes down to a question of discipline, of deciding who's boss (even if being "the boss" was never something they had sought in deciding to enter this profession). Thus we come to the first of the "big issues" of school: *maintaining discipline*.

We all attempt to manage our environment. For a teacher, that may mean organizing learning activities to make them "manageable"—that is, to make it more likely that diverse children or young adults will be able to engage in the activity willingly and productively. Furthermore, each of us likes to feel in control of those situations where people above us expect us to exercise authority and judgment. This is especially so when we feel responsible for the productive efforts of people working under our direction. Conversely, none of us wants to feel "managed" by people who have undue power over us; it hurts our dignity and makes us feel we are being manipulated for someone else's purposes. Juxtapose these two sets of desires and you have the dilemma of *classroom management* for the novice teacher.

For new teachers working in our K–12 schools, there is perhaps no challenge more daunting, none more likely to keep them awake at night or bring tears of frustration to their eyes or indigestion to their gut, than what's usually called classroom management. The kids, it seems, all too easily fall out of control and are prone to take advantage of any perceived weakness on our part, ever ready to exploit a momentary lapse of discipline and steer our ship toward chaos. The responses—ranging from the old adage "Don't smile till Christmas" to more contemporary notions of positive or "proactive" discipline—tend to emphasize "behavior management," "positive reinforcement," and the judicious application of rewards and sanctions, all of them intended to limit the vulnerability of the classroom teacher to the antics of inattentive children and young adults in school.

Students' Thoughts on Classroom Management and Discipline

Here is a sampling of responses to the issue of classroom management, written by advanced undergraduate and graduate students preparing to be high school English and history teachers:

> Would-be teachers who approach the issue of discipline and classroom management as an issue of "control," or who think they can "master" it, are in for a big surprise. All the teacher preparatory classes and intellectual exercises cannot prepare a first year teacher for the visceral reactions of skyrocketing blood pressure and increased heart rate preceding the feeling that one's head is going to explode. This is usually followed by repetitions of whatever mantra works for the individual teacher, ranging from "Breathe, just breathe . . ." to "Remember, you *wanted* to be a teacher. You *wanted* to be a teacher . . ." [Ashot Gheridian].

> If students feel that you are belittling them or disrespecting them, they will not even entertain any ideas you may be presenting to them. However, if you respect them and hold them to high standards, education then becomes much more about assisting their performance, not managing students' behaviors. Because I facilitate so many conversations with high school and middle school students, I have learned that students just want to be heard and have their

opinions valued. I want my classroom always to be a place where students can speak their mind freely [Jarrod Chin].

For as long as I can remember, I have always worried about what other people thought of me and I have always wanted people to like me. However, as I spend more time in the classroom and I reflect on my experience, I am able to accept that I am not there to be my students' friend and, as much as I want them to, they don't have to like me for me to be an effective teacher [Ilsa Bruer].

Classroom management sets the teacher up for failure because the teacher goes into the classroom expecting to take charge of a situation that may not necessarily be out of control. If a teacher enters a situation defensively, then immediately the students pick up on that and, in turn, become defensive themselves [Anthony Erevia].

My students also look for any weakness they can find in a teacher, and they try to exploit it so students can dictate the way the class is run. It wasn't that long ago that I was in high school and, I'm not going to lie, I tried to do the same thing [Ian Connelly].

I do not agree that the only way to insure that the student will succeed is by staying "on their backs" and pushing them. I have found that if you are constantly pushing more and more information on the students, without any room for observation, exploration, questioning, activities, etc., it makes the students less interested and more likely to fail. It is very hard to motivate yourself with someone on your back all the time. Instead, the student may feel too pressured and intimidated to work at their best ability [Marcelle Irvine].

While a first instinct would be to either try to take complete control of the classroom or to create an environment where students feel equal to the teacher, both of these methods have serious consequences. In truth, teachers need to apply both of these theories to their classroom so that the students will know that they must respect their teacher, but an effort must be made to humanize the classroom by a teacher showing that they care about the students on a personal level, not just because they're paid to do it [Andrew Sullivan].

In the class discussion that followed my distribution of these selections, the most contentious issue had to do with the question of stance: Was it or was it not advantageous for beginning teachers to position themselves to be viewed by their students as a "friend"? Are "being a friend to students" and "being respected by students" mutually exclusive? We created a spectrum of views on the board, a range of stances on this issue, from Stern/Strict and Demanding/Expecting Respect on one end to what we called Laissez-Faire and Buddyhood on the other. There were perceived problems with each of these approaches to classroom management. In the end, many of my students seemed to agree that if what we seek is a *learning partnership* with students, we cannot remain aloof from them or be seen as demanding their respect as a matter of right. Nor can we be viewed as seeking to "buy them off" by offering them a light workload in exchange for minimal compliance and decent behavior on their part. The notion of Buddyhood was greeted with scorn. We have to earn their respect, the way a coach must earn it, by being willing to roll up our sleeves as learners ourselves and to engage them in the pursuit of knowledge worth knowing, of skills worth gaining.

This topic also elicited much commentary from the students interviewed by researcher Kathleen Cushman. Said one, "Don't be afraid to talk to us one on one, but don't try too hard to be our friend." Said another, "Any time an adult goes too far because they want to get to know you, it [our pulling back] happens. It's hard to go back and forth from being an authority to being a friend. To make a bond with your students you risk becoming too buddy-buddy."[2]

Opting for Mutual Respect Instead of "Management"

But the problem really begins with our use of that term *classroom management* to talk about our students and their deportment. Once we decide to think, plan, and act within the management mind-set, we put ourselves in serious danger of losing the war, no matter how adept we may become at winning the battles. Using this analogy, the war is our overall goal of creating what Sarason often speaks of as "contexts of productive learning," in which children want to learn more about themselves, others, and their world. The battle is our effort, on any given day, to create a safe, orderly, and respectful atmosphere in the classroom, one in which students "stay on task" and "do their work." But what if instead of focusing on *managing* our students, we chose to *enter into a partnership* with them?

To define each teacher's goal as "creating a mutually respectful learning partnership" rather than as "successfully managing the students" is to do more than engage in wordplay. It is rather to frame the relationship between teachers and students as one in which they are (or are aiming to be) on the same side in a struggle against ignorance, poor skills, low esteem, insecurity, prejudice, and the paralysis of low expectations—to view teachers and students as allies in the struggle for human dignity, self-respect, cooperation, and high achievement. Or, to put the goal in terms of productive contexts, it is to have students and teachers view each other as partners in pursuit of excitement, enjoyment, collaboration, satisfaction, and success in learning—something they are eager to do more of.

That being said, we must acknowledge that there are, of course, students who come to school with serious emotional or cognitive learning disabilities. There are children whose home life is in turmoil, children with serious physical and mental health problems, children who are bullied or tormented by others on the way to school or in the playground. These children bring those disabilities and traumas into class with them, and their behavior poses significant challenges for their teachers and fellow students, as well as for themselves.

All educators struggle with the question of how to successfully include students with disabilities into regular classrooms, how to balance the right of all children to be part of the learning community with the right of all children not to have their learning seriously impaired by those who consistently disrupt planned activities.

I have never found anyone who cannot imagine circumstances in which it is just not safe to keep a child with severe behavioral issues in the classroom, nor have I found many who wouldn't prefer to keep as many diverse children as possible learning productively together. And the efforts of teachers toward this goal are often genuinely heroic. Many, if not most, of the student teachers I supervise struggle with how to cope with classroom behaviors that result from children's disabilities and traumas. For some of them, this is their single greatest challenge.

I want to give beginning educators permission to focus their attention not primarily on "how to deal with those problem kids," the few persistent "troublemakers," but rather on how to create a positive, lively, enthusiastic, stimulating, and responsive climate for learning, such that virtually all children will want to become active participants, and those with particular disabilities or traumas will also seek, to the best of their abilities, to join in. I worry that in focusing so much on the minority of "problem kids," inexperienced teachers unwittingly foster an environment in which children discover that "making trouble" is what gets you the most attention.

Getting Out Beyond "Management"

Good teachers often fail to comprehend some of the basic opportunities and pitfalls of the teaching and learning process, even without factoring in the learning disabilities of particular students. By ignoring the lessons of our evolutionary heritage—our inherited disposition for passionate learning—we act in ways that diminish the desire of children to be the active agents of their own discovery and achievement. Amid our forgivable weaknesses (our insecurities, our cautions, our reluctance to divert from established school patterns and procedures), we are apt to reach for the control levers (or the panic button) as we try to avoid embarrassment or failure. We should be taking sensible risks in the other direction.

A parable: I am at best a novice alpine skier, and I often find myself on a mountainside where I am faced with a steeper slope than I am comfortable with. My whole body wants to tighten up and fight that mountain, but the tighter I become, the harder it is to ski down. Fortunately, I usually reach a point where my head tells me to just relax, go with the contours, lean forward rather than back on my heels, and let my skis do their job. There is no guarantee that I won't fall on my rear end anyway, no matter what I do, but I will enjoy skiing a great deal more if I am not fighting against myself by clinging to the illusion that I can be in total control of what's happening.

Beginning teachers, both at the stage of student teaching and in their first few years of classroom practice, inevitably face a situation not unlike what I experience on the ski slopes. An instinct for self-preservation leads them to tighten up, to reach for the mechanisms of reward or sanction. It is too easy to drift into an adversarial pattern of relationships, believing that "these kids have forced me into it by taking advantage of me when I relax with them or let up on the pressure." They look down the slope, with its icy patches and narrow turns, then lean back on their heels and stiffen their stance instead of accepting the inevitability of a slipup, here or there, on the path to success.

Sometimes we find children who have been raised to expect authoritative firmness (often called being "strict") from their teachers in order to help them feel secure in doing what's right. "You have to fill up the room with your presence," said Pattie Bailey, an experienced African American high school history teacher. "The kids have to know that you're in charge, that you see everything, and that they can rely on you to make sure they get their work done."

Caring about kids' learning and "taking charge" of the classroom are not mutually exclusive, especially in situations where culture and prior experience have left some children with the impression that those who truly care about them will not let them fall by the wayside, that strictness is a more reliable indication of a teacher's caring about her students than easygoingness. We have already seen, in the practice of Abd Al-Maalik and Melanie Livingston, a strictness that comes from total dedication to learning. But it is a strictness often coupled with humor and with an intense desire to relate to the learner as a person. For strict teachers like Melanie and Al-Maalik, caring always comes before anything else on their agenda, and if students have been socialized to equate caring with a more authoritarian stance, then their trust may well have to be built up with a more directive and authoritative approach before students can be helped to become more self-directive and self-motivated in their studies. It may well take more than one course, or one year, to make this happen. And, says Vance, a high school student from Harlem, there is also a certain respect due to a teacher who shows up each day and does her job, despite the harassment that may come her way: "You really affect kids when you just do your job day in and day out, do it well—and everything doesn't have to be about bonding with the kids and changing their lives. That's artificial. The bond will develop on its own if you just do your job well."[3]

Summarizing the points we've looked at in this section, Table 5.1 compares the approaches to classroom management that further the Game of School to those that foster authentic learning. But first, a note about my use of tables. Some readers are "visual learners" and understand best when they can visually compare contrasting philosophies and approaches. Other learners desire a more conversational treatment of such contrasts, finding devices like tables to be overly simplistic or confrontational (perhaps inviting a "good guys versus bad guys" dichotomy). I offer both treatments in this book, but urge you to view them as but two ways of addressing the same issue. Also, it is easy to view the tables as displaying opposites when, in fact, many good teachers find ways to combine some elements from both sides.

The Curriculum: Guiding Agenda or Ominous Threat?

Along with "classroom management," a great worry for inexperienced teachers (and some experienced ones) is that their very jobs depend on their "covering the material"—that they could get fired if they don't get through the textbook, don't "stay up there" with other classes (a threat made all too real by the advent of high-stakes

Table 5.1 Discipline and Classroom Management

Managing Kids Within the Game of School	*Creating a True Learning Partnership*
The teacher's first goal is to establish and maintain control of the class at all times.	The teacher's first goal is to establish a climate for productive learning among all class members.
Students need to be continuously managed so that they will behave appropriately in class.	Students deserve to be brought into a genuine learning partnership with each other and with adults.
Such control is deemed essential in order for students to stay "on task" and perform their work adequately.	Appropriate control is established through respect, caring, and sensitivity, leading to productive classes.
Although most students seem willing to learn, a few are disrespectful and don't seem to care about education.	All students want to learn; some who face particular challenges require thoughtful, caring strategies.
Good behavior in students results from the wise application of rewards and sanctions by teachers.	Good behavior in students results from a climate of self- and mutual respect, in which students act as citizens.

testing). When control of curriculum is seen as lying *outside* the classroom or school, and when the curriculum is loaded with so much material that it can only be "covered" through constant lecturing and note taking, students see the teacher as tied by marionette strings to an unseen, impersonal, yet constantly hovering master. Game-playing artificiality replaces authenticity, and enduring learning falls by the wayside.

A *Curriculum That Invites, Rather Than Commands*

There should be no big mystery about the word *curriculum*. It is basically a term of intent. Curriculum reflects the skills and knowledge that we *intend* students to learn from their experiences in our classrooms, as they perform activities we've designed so as to help them acquire skills and knowledge. I have argued elsewhere that curriculum is perhaps best seen as a *web of relationships:* of students to the material, teachers to the material, students and teachers to each other, and so on.[4] We would all do well to remember its limitations. To include something in the school's curriculum is no guarantee that it will be taught, much less that students will learn it. Curriculum is powerful when it speaks to students and their parents of our hopes and desires for student learning, in language they understand.

But in the world of the school, curriculum is commonly thought of as "what teachers are supposed to teach," or more particularly, "to cover," in their lesson plans and through "instructional delivery." Wherever that definition rules, the curriculum becomes a threat to children's learning. Whenever the teacher focuses on "what *I'm* supposed to *cover,*" rather than "what I *intend* for them to try to *learn,*" the locus of action is removed from the learner and placed on the instructor. Once displaced, it tends to remain there. We forget that curriculum is about kids "knowing" and become overly concerned with teachers "presenting."

But it's not enough just to focus on results, when the methods employed undermine authentic learning. Due to a perceived lack of public confidence in the ability of teachers to do their jobs well enough that our students will actually "know what they're supposed to," some business leaders and reform-minded officials did indeed attempt to shift the focus to what children have *learned*, rather than what teachers have "covered." Their efforts produced documents, sometimes called a "common core of learning," that indicated what students who graduate should know and be able to perform. But these serious reformers have recently had their work misused by politicians and bureaucrats who have, ironically, fixated on a most inappropriate tool—high-stakes standardized tests—to measure this otherwise worthy goal and supposedly to hold educators and schools "accountable." Instead of using such tests in a diagnostic way, to see what aspects of the curriculum a scientific sampling of our children actually understands (so that teachers can work together to adjust their methods and approaches), the tests are held over the heads of students, teachers, and entire schools, accompanied by dire threats (of retention in grade, loss of diploma, cuts in funding, state takeover).

The response of teachers and principals to such an externally imposed regimen has been the evolution of a new form of the Game of School, namely, "teaching to the test." As the cart of testing is placed before the horse of curriculum, our teaching becomes subservient to external assessment mechanisms, and the enterprise of learning declines.

Fending Off the "Curriculum Monster"

For inexperienced teachers, the curriculum—as an entity—can seem monstrous. It's all that stuff you're *supposed to know* so that you will teach it correctly to the kids. Such pressure induces even experienced teachers to cling to the teachers' edition of textbooks, so that they will *always* know where to find the right answer. Do you remember the episode of *The Simpsons* in which a rebellious Lisa removes all the teachers' editions from teachers' desks and hides them in her locker, precipitating panic in the teachers' lounge by those who had been relying on them for even the most obvious historical or mathematical information and who now had no idea how to respond to students' questions?

Intimidated, subservient teachers make poor role models for students. Thus "fear of curriculum" becomes another contributor to a diminished environment for learning. After all, who among us can possibly know everything we are supposed to teach? In the face of such an overwhelming challenge, why can't a teacher faced with what seems like a huge amount of material try to convey, in one manner or another, something like the following (I've pegged this to the elementary grades, but you could adapt it to an older audience):

> Here is an important topic we are going to be learning about in the next day [or week or longer period]. I remember how it was when I was your age, trying to learn about this, and I want us to try to find a way to make our learning interesting and useful. I will need your help in discovering those interesting ways to learn.

> Some of this material I already know well—because I apply it in my life [give an example]. Other stuff I still know about because I had a teacher who taught it in a very exciting way that made me want to learn and remember it [offer another example]. And other things I just plain forgot about, so I will learn them over again, along with you. Some parts may be easy; other parts may be hard. But I'm confident that we can do it.

The point of this little speech (one that I'm certain most teachers could improve on) is to ally teacher and students as partners in a common effort to make the curriculum a part of their world of excitement, adventure, confidence, and competence; to include the "unknowns" within our professional sphere of comfort; and to face challenges with team spirit. Table 5.2 summarizes the contrasts between curriculum as a function of the Game of School and curriculum as a vehicle for authentic learning.

Table 5.2 Curriculum

Game of School Curriculum	*Authentic Learning Curriculum*
Comes down from above and represents "what we have to cover" whether it makes sense or not.	Consists of learning objectives that the teacher has redefined so that they are worthwhile and challenging.
A rigid and tightly sequenced list of activities and topics from which no teacher is supposed to deviate.	A guideline of what students ought to be engaged with, offering flexibility in sequencing and emphasis.
Presented to students as requirements, not open to classroom discussion and possible adjustment.	Presented to students as "what's important for us to learn," inviting their comments and suggestions.
Focused on specific skills considered intrinsically important, whether or not they connect to students' lives.	Explained so as to help students see topics and skills as important because they are related to their lives.
The teacher avoids more intellectually complex aspects if he or she does not feel comfortable with them.	Teachers readily admit there are topics they find challenging; they model the "learner" role for students.

Instruction: Sharing and Showing, or Just Telling?

I share a common fault with many teachers—I get too much pleasure from talking to students about what I think I know something about. I hold on to the illusion that what I have to say is most important and that the best way for others to gain from my wisdom is to listen and take heed. This is a serious potential weakness, for my talking preempts the airwaves and demands attention from an entire class of learners who might have better ways to use this time. Even as I avoid the trick of warning students, "Listen up, because some of what I say may end up on a test," my ego is gratified when I observe students write notes as I speak.

In its purest form, instructing means "showing" or "sharing." Your ten-year-old wants to try to slice carrots with a big kitchen knife. He wants to learn how to wield something powerful and dangerous, and both you and he have an interest in his doing it safely and skillfully. So, with mixed feelings, you agree to teach him so he won't cut himself. You stand next to him, model the act while explaining its fine points, and pass the knife to him, perhaps keeping your hand on his arm (until he shakes it off). You are delighted as your son slices the carrots and then turns his face toward you with a smile of expectation. Instructing, here, is composed of a series of actions, including inviting and responding, explaining, modeling, observing, advising, correcting (if needed), and affirming.

How does this model apply as we extend instruction to a larger circle—say, a group of children? Here is how Bruner describes "instruction" taking place among the !Kung people of Africa:

> Among hunting-gathering humans . . . there is *constant* interaction between adult and child, adult and adolescent, adolescent and child. !Kung adults and children play and dance together, sit together, participate in minor hunting together, join in song and storytelling together. At very frequent intervals, moreover, children are party to rituals presided over by adults—minor, as in the first haircutting, or

> major, as when a boy kills his first kudu buck and goes through the proud but painful process of scarification. Children, besides, are constantly playing imitatively with the rituals, implements, tools, and weapons of the adult world. . . .
>
> Note, though, that in tens of thousands of feet of !Kung [documentary] film, one virtually never sees an instance of "teaching" taking place outside the situation where the behavior to be learned is relevant. Nobody teaches in our prepared sense of the word. There is nothing like school, nothing like lessons. Indeed, among the !Kung there is very little "telling." Most of what we would call instruction is through showing.[5]

Let us now contrast this with a typical fifth-grade classroom in an underresourced urban school visited by Jonathan Kozol:

> The children are doing a handwriting lesson when I enter. On a board at the back of the room the teacher has written a line of letters in the standard cursive script. The children sit at their desks and fill entire pages with these letters. It is the kind of lesson that is generally done in second grade in a suburban school. The teacher seems bored by the lesson, and the children seem to feel this and compound her boredom with their own. Next she does a social studies lesson on the Bering Strait and spends some time in getting the class to give a definition of a "strait." About half of the children pay attention. The others don't talk or interrupt or fidget. They are well enough behaved but seem sedated by the teacher's voice.[6]

In millions of classrooms the world over, it is telling that predominates, with only the explaining and correcting aspects added with any regularity. There is the efficiency argument, of course, that it is more economical to *tell* a group of children how to do something than to stand next to each of them and patiently model, explain, observe, and affirm. But experience shows us that such instructional efficiency comes at a price: we see inattention, uncaring, and forgetfulness among learners. Nor can such pitfalls be effectively countered by threats or bribes. We have, as Clinchy and Bruner remind us, too much human history of shared, modeled, playful, imaginative, and interactive teaching and learning for today's children to easily adapt to the conventional model of instruction through telling.

Where does this leave the teacher, faced with twenty-five to thirty students and forty minutes or so in which to instruct them? The best answer would be to replicate, to the maximum extent feasible, the "classroom" of the hunter-gatherers. And that is what I observe from the most talented teachers and student teachers. They are in constant motion, working with students singly, in pairs, and in small groups; briefly addressing the class as a whole; inviting, explaining, modeling, gently correcting, and sincerely affirming. They find ways for kids to help instruct others. There may not be much dancing and chanting, but more of the senses are at play than merely those involved in listening and writing. Moreover, the entire lesson has much that is in the spirit of happy ritual, wherein the growing competence of learners is celebrated, while the teacher is sparing and respectful in her correcting and redirecting functions. Table 5.3 lists some reminders of what it takes to make instruction lead to authentic learning in your classroom.

When teachers are able to instruct students well, the students experience it as immediate, relevant, and valuable. Veronica, a high school student from Oakland, California, comments on how one teacher offered her a dynamic link between the subject matter and issues facing her: "In biology class I have learned things I never heard about: biology and life, sexual viruses, things like that. It was important because you got to learn about what kind of diseases would happen if you didn't take care about yourself when having sexual relationships. That teacher changed my life."[7]

Tiffany, from Rhode Island, emphasizes the value of feeling included, culturally, in the teacher's approach to subjects: "You pay attention if the people you are identified with are represented. All my life I have been studying what Europeans and Americans do, but not Africans. So when we studied the Cold War, she gave us an article

Table 5.3 Instruction

Game of School "Teacher-Centered Instruction"	*Authentic Learning "Learner-Centered Instruction"*
The dominant instructional strategy is one of teachers' telling students what they think students need to know.	The dominant instructional strategy involves teachers' asking students to explore with them what they believe is important for students to learn.
Only the senses of sight and hearing are involved in instruction. Most learning is sedentary, and there is little attempt to make connections to students' lives.	Instruction involves more of the senses, allowing students to touch, smell, taste, and move around. Connecting topics to students' lives is essential.
Student boredom is seen as an inevitable part of teachers' front-loading "background information"; it results from inattentive students or poorly planned lessons.	Boredom is reduced to a minimum when children's sense of adventure is awakened and their natural curiosity about ideas and solving problems is nurtured.
Lesson plans are prepared well in advance, and teachers try to follow them as closely as possible. The focus is on the "scope and sequence" of instruction.	Lessons are planned but expected to evolve and change in response to student interests and initiative. Teachers leave room for spontaneity and engagement.
Teachers try to make sure they "cover" the required material by using effective "instructional delivery" strategies; texts and models used in class rarely reflect the backgrounds of the students being taught.	Teachers are concerned with students' receptivity and response to, and integration of, new ideas, knowledge, and skills; teachers strive to find culturally responsive course materials with which students can identify.
Teachers view themselves as the primary audience for the work that students do in response to instruction. Students "do their work" and show it to their teachers.	Teachers view themselves as facilitators or coaches. Students exhibit or demonstrate what they have learned to an audience of parents, fellow students, and others.

from an African textbook and we saw how differently they learn about it there. It gave us a sense of how different [studying history] could be."[8]

Assessment: To Support Learning or to Punish Non-Learners?

I've watched a group of rebellious urban high school students get quickly under control as soon as their teacher hands them a test. "Now she means business," they seem to say. "Now it's for real." And students normally take testing seriously because they know "it's going to count." Their doing so does not in any way ensure that what they do on the test reflects what they have actually learned, much less what they will remember and use a week, month, or year after the test is over. But the giving and grading of tests provides security for everyone: each knows what role to play.

What students do not realize is that the adversarial posture of the test—with the teacher giving it and grading it and the students submitting to it and hoping for the best—seriously limits the likelihood that teacher and students will join as partners in learning. Even when teachers try to be kind to their students, such as by going over all the specific areas of knowledge on which they will soon be tested, the whole exercise can seem superficial and fake: "We know why she's telling us what's gonna be on the test; it's because she wants us to do good, so she'll look good."

I've written extensively elsewhere about the perils and opportunities of alternative and authentic assessments, and I refer you to those texts in my notes, but two points are worth reiterating:

- We often give very mixed signals to our students with regard to assessment: we tell them, "This is the really important stuff I want you to learn well and retain," only to test them on a far more limited range of things that are much easier to assess objectively.

- We seriously underutilize student self-assessment as a means of looking at essential areas of skills and knowledge that are more subjective and, in so doing, we deprive students of a vital opportunity to develop ownership and responsibility for their learning.[9]

On this last point, Linda Darling-Hammond puts the goal quite succinctly, linking student self-assessment with the idea of portfolio development and workplace competence:

> A major goal is to help students develop the capacity to assess their own work against standards, to revise, modify, and redirect their energies, taking initiative to promote their own progress. Such self-directed work and self-motivated improvement is required of competent people in many settings, including a growing number of workplaces. Assessment strategies like portfolios take the concept of progress seriously—making the processes of product refinement and improvement a central aspect of the task and its evaluation. Thus they also allow students the opportunity to see, acknowledge, and receive credit for their growth, regardless of their level of initial competence.[10]

Table 5.4 lists characteristics that distinguish conventional testing aspects of assessment from the more convivial and cooperative relationship that can exist even amid the clearly differentiated power of student test taker and teacher test maker and grade giver.

Self-Motivation: Attribute of the Few or Necessary for All?

Let's repeat this until it becomes something of a mantra: *I can't truly teach unless my students want to learn whatever it is I'm teaching them*. But let us also remind ourselves of the evolutionary evidence: *the children and young people before me today are the products of untold generations of passionate and successful learners*. And if we need one more

Table 5.4 Assessment

Assessment Within the Game of School	*Assessment for Authentic Learning*
Exams signal that the period of instruction is over with; teaching ends and students get judged.	Assessment is ongoing and reflects a dynamic part of the teaching-learning process.
Tests and quizzes are summative; they reflect an assessment of what students know at test time.	Tests and quizzes are used diagnostically to see what students do and do not yet understand.
Tests and quizzes tend to focus on knowledge that can be memorized, even if it may soon be forgotten.	Assessment looks to see how well students have understood the material and can now apply it.
Teachers, as "proctors," watch over student behavior during exams and try to prevent cheating.	Teachers remain as "coaches" for students during tests, encouraging them to perform up to their potential.
Grades are a measurement of those aspects of a student's learning that can be objectively quantified.	Grades are based on student portfolios and exams that reflect the broad picture of student learning, both in and out of school.
Student self-assessment is rarely used, if at all, because students aren't trusted to assess themselves accurately.	Self-assessment is an integral part of helping students take responsibility for their own learning.

voice to reassure us, Frank Smith reminds us that there is no such thing as a young person who *isn't* learning:

> It is a frightening thought for many teachers that their students are learning all the time. Without any forgetting. And the students can't help it. They can even learn things they might be better off not learning. The problem in school is not that many students aren't learning, but *what* they are learning. They may not learn what their teachers teach them, but their teachers may not be teaching what they think they are teaching. To find out what students actually learn, look at the way they leave school. If they leave thinking that

> "school things"—such as reading, writing, mathematics, or history—are boring, difficult, and irrelevant to their lives and that they are "dummies," this is something they have learned both in school and outside. They *learn* to be nonreaders, or that they are nonspellers, or that they can't do mathematics. They learn who they are. If they learn they are leaders or geniuses (or clowns or fools) they behave accordingly.[11]

If we accept Smith's reasoning, the challenge before us is not "kids' learning versus kids' nonlearning." It's about how we enable these irrepressible learners to engage with the ideas, activities, and acquisition of skills that *we* want them to possess. (We acknowledge here that some scholars, such as Carl Rogers and A. S. Neill, argue that we should derive our agendas from those of the learners, not preempt them.)

When we approach a group of first graders with a welcoming smile, a happy song, and an exciting new book from the library; when we greet a group of middle schoolers with a few well-chosen references to popular TV shows and an intriguing question about why teenagers today tend to do what they do; when we address a class of rebellious high school sophomores in a firm tone, offering a well-structured agenda and a reminder that there is an exercise on the board that must be performed right now, in silence—we are essentially responding to the same challenge: How do I help these students attune their self-directed learning behaviors to an agenda that I believe is in their best interests? How do I help them motivate themselves to learn and practice—here today and beyond this class period—the knowledge and skills I believe will be valuable and also interesting to them?

It is a common misconception that self-motivation is only for smart, well-behaved, goal-directed, and confident kids and that all the rest have to be guided both by a commanding teacher presence and by the judicious application of rewards or threats. The truth of my experience—in rural, urban, and suburban schools and among students of diverse ages and backgrounds—is that *all* students are continuously motivating themselves with respect to their learning—even when they "motivate" themselves to goof off or drop out.

They also exhibit their responses in a great variety of ways. A seemingly "unmotivated" student dawdles, daydreams, or disrupts, depending on his or her age, personality, upbringing, and attitude toward this particular teacher or topic. A "motivated" student listens eagerly, asks pertinent questions, or writes down a personal response to the topic at hand, depending on the same variables. But aren't such responses really two sides of the same coin?

What we teachers must deal with is the degree of a student's self-motivation directed toward school-related learning that either has or has not been nurtured through parental modeling, inspirational teachers, and early recognition of a child's talents. The child's personality and learning style play their part. There are also factors that continue to shape motivation: interest in the topic, self-confidence in trying new things, expectations of approval by parents and peers, personal goals, and trust and respect between student and teacher. And all children are, in fact, self-motivated in some areas of knowledge and skills acquisition, be it athletics, art or music, social interplay, and so on. Simply put, we cannot avoid acknowledging that motivation is the key, even though (or especially because) we cannot control a student's willing response to instruction—as much as we might hope to encourage it.

Thus the problem for teachers comes when a few (or more than a few) of their students seem decidedly *un*motivated with respect to academics—the content and skill areas emphasized in the curriculum. The traditional approach that almost all of us have experienced from kindergarten through graduate school assumes that any lack of intrinsic motivation toward academics can be overcome by a good talking to, plus the judicious application of rewards and punishments. In too many classroom situations, teachers attempt to bypass the intrinsic motivation factor by threatening low grades, detentions, or phone calls to parents or by offering promises of extra credit, fun activities, gold stars, and the like. Both methods seem to work—that is, they achieve the *appearance* of student compliance with the teacher's academic learning agenda, allowing the teacher to reason, "If I can't make them *like* this material, at least I can make sure that most do the work, despite their apparent lack of interest."

This is a fallback stance that new teachers should consider how they might avoid, or how they can redirect their approach toward stimulating self-motivation, should the academic agenda provoke student resistance or rejection. Table 5.5 is my summary of the contrasting views regarding student motivation.

Table 5.5 Motivation for Learning

Approaches That Foster the Game of School	*Approaches That Foster Authentic Learning*
Teachers come to view academics as "content I've got to get across," rather than as intrinsically valuable.	Teachers view academics as "content I can help students engage in and relate to."
Teachers adopt a neutral stance: "You've got to learn this stuff, so we might as well get on with it."	Teachers are passionate about issues and ideas that underlie the material, and communicate that passion.
Once this neutral stance is taken, teachers announce various bribes and threats in hopes of spurring students to work.	Teachers understand that some students may need extra support as they encounter academic content.
These rewards and sanctions divert attention away from learning and toward the consequences of students' compliance or noncompliance.	Teachers continue to focus on ways that students can solve problems and overcome obstacles or resistance to academic learning.
Students come to view academics as "stuff we gotta do," rather than as an opportunity to discover and grow.	Students come to view academics as "stuff that will prepare us well for future educational opportunities."
Interest in school learning wanes as students grow older and become habituated to rewards and sanctions.	Interest and confidence in academic learning grows as students feel included in adult intellectual activity.

Here is some advice from the high school contributors to Kathleen Cushman's *Fires in the Bathroom* on what teachers can do to promote motivation in their students:

- Be passionate about your material and your work.
- Connect to issues we care about outside school.
- Give us choices on things that matter.
- Make learning a social thing.
- Make sure we understand.
- Respond with interest when we show interest.
- Care about us and our progress.
- Help us keep on top of our workload.
- Show your pride in our good work.
- Provide role models to inspire us.[12]

In their individual comments, the students interviewed reflected on the presence, or absence, of passion in their teachers' stance. Here are comments from, respectively, Vance, Mahogany, and Montoya:

> The mark of a good teacher is that no matter how weird or boring you might think their subject is, their love for it is what pushes you to learn something. It could be rat feces or some nasty topic, and the fact that their eyes are glowing when they talk about it makes you want to know something about it.
>
> If they have a passion for teaching kids, it's much easier for them to teach, period. I don't think most teachers have a passion, and you can tell if they do.
>
> Some teachers act like they don't want to be there. They don't have any spirit, they just make the class do work.[13]

We haven't yet solved or resolved anything with regard to student motivation. Insecure teachers will continue to be drawn toward a pedagogy of control, of bribes and threats (hiding behind the jargon of "consequences" and "positive reinforcement"), rather than toward an approach that nurtures academic self-motivation on the part of their students. I hope, throughout this book, to make it easier for new and renewing teachers to nurture self-motivation as a reasonable and practical goal for all students and to consider how they might build a classroom environment where students understand, *Nothing the teacher can do can substitute for my own will to learn*. When it comes to students' demonstrating their competence and meeting the standards, it is their self-motivation, supported by the teacher acting as mentor, guide, and coach, that will carry them through (perhaps with a little help from those on the home front).

Family Involvement: More Than a Slogan?

I hate the term *family involvement*. It's so weak, so vague, encompassing an entire spectrum of relationships, from casual or infrequent association to sincere engagement. When I hear calls for "parent and family involvement," I wonder if those making such an appeal know what kind of involvement they truly seek. Is it simple concurrence with what the teacher has already planned? Is it a call for "backup" from the home for homework policy and controversial school decrees like dress codes? Or does it indicate the teacher's desire—and need—for a genuine partnership, in which parents, students, and teacher agree to listen to one another and to work together to ensure success for the child?

Replacing "Involvement" with "Partnership"

The trouble that most school folk find with "family involvement" is that nobody really wants to have to deal with parents who have their own ideas about school or who differ among themselves about what holidays to celebrate, what controversial issues to expose students to, or how to group students in academic subjects. As Deborah Meier put it to me recently:

> Most schools truly don't look forward to more parent involvement—it can be disturbing, time consuming, inefficient, frustrating (parents say different things), and no one has time to do it well. Yet we are involved with families whether we want to be or not, and even if we never speak to them or meet with them, we are involved because we share this kid. And there is always the temptation to blame somebody else for what may be going wrong. At a point in our lives when we none of us have the time to meet the extraordinarily high expectations placed on us—as mother, as teacher—of course it's convenient to lay the blame elsewhere.

But at the school where Meier was founding principal (Mission Hill Pilot Elementary School, in Roxbury, Boston), teachers and staff pursue family involvement through weekly newsletters with news from each classroom sent to each home; monthly parent nights that feature exhibitions of student learning or educational topics (like standardized testing); and placing parents on committees to hire staff—all in addition to frequently scheduled meetings between teachers, students, and parents.

What we should all try to generate, in promoting parent and family partnership with teachers, is a friendly, forward-looking, and diverse array of activities aimed at establishing a trusting and productive relationship, a basis of understanding and cooperation, an open line of communication *before* any problems occur in a child's or teenager's school experience. We begin with recognition that students of all ages need the support of adults in the home and adults in the school and that these adults need to know and trust one another even—or especially—when parents and teachers come from different cultural backgrounds or when parents' lack of success in school has left a residue of shame or anger (or both) toward formal education.

I often pose the following actual dilemma to prospective elementary teachers in my Multicultural Children's Literature class:

You are a reading specialist working in rural Appalachia, and you're going around to the homes in your community, talking with parents about the value of reading to their children, offering to lend them books, and so on. And about half of the mothers you speak with—all of whom say they want their children to learn to read—confess to you that they themselves are illiterate. How do you respond? What are the next words out of your mouth?

The typical answers I get from my idealistic and well-intentioned students are to offer remedial programs, to suggest that parents get their children to read to them, to offer to come back and help teach the parent to read to their child. The reading specialist's actual response (I don't recall the source of this anecdote) was, "That's okay. Don't worry. You can fake it. I'll lend you books with pictures, stories you already know, like 'The Three Little Pigs' or 'Cinderella,' and you can have your child sit on your lap, with your arms around him, telling him the story as you turn the pages."

My students nod their heads. It makes sense, even if it's not what they expected to hear. Someone from a school has, at last, looked at this parent in terms of her strengths as opposed to her deficiencies. Not only did these Appalachian moms accept the invitation to fake read to their kids but, within months, half of them had volunteered for literacy classes. It makes us think how seldom we look at people, especially people who are poor or poorly educated, in terms of their strengths, rather than focusing on their weaknesses or deficiencies.

So how does a new teacher approach parents as partners who have much to offer, regardless of their formal education or the demands that jobs and family survival duties place on their time? That is the key question for teachers from kindergarten right up through high school. Even when teenagers seem embarrassed and uneasy about bringing parents into their school lives, deep down most of them want their parents and teachers to be there for them, working together. Such collaboration is easy to describe but rarely achieved.

There's no argument about the value of such a partnership; it's just that family involvement is often placed last on our list of priorities, another one of those things we have little time for and not much control over. Nor are we likely to get much support from those veteran teachers who have long ago lost patience with the many parents who seem unable to ensure that their kids come to school each day prepared to do their work or those who seem always ready to challenge—but rarely to support—actions by the teacher with which their child disagrees. Table 5.6 compares those school attitudes and practices that lead to family-school partnership with those that maintain a Game of School culture.

Beyond the items outlined in Table 5.6, there are some points that deserve a bit more explication, particularly for teachers unfamiliar with true parent-teacher partnership:

- Engaging parents as active partners with teachers and students is a *necessity*, not an option, even (or especially) when life circumstances make it difficult for all parties to meet and plan together. Teachers need to be creative, flexible, and proactive.
- The child, the teacher, and the parent should form a triangle of partnership (as with home, school, and community). A triangle is the most stable structure in nature. It is usually up to the teacher to initiate such a partnership, as students and parents may feel reticent about claiming their rightful roles in working for learning achievement.
- The core of building a partnership is to emphasize the strengths each party brings, rather than the problems or deficiencies of the situation. As in the case of the teacher in Appalachia, one looks at potential partners in terms of what they *can* do instead of what they appear unable to do.
- Sharing information between school and home is critical: newsletters, phone calls, notes, email, or a classroom-based answering machine. Reaching out to families in advance of

Table 5.6 Family Involvement

Approaches That Foster the Game of School	*Approaches That Foster Authentic Learning*
Many or most parents are viewed as ignorant, too busy, not caring enough, or unsupportive of teachers.	All parents are viewed as wanting the best for their children, despite constraints and hardships.
Efforts to "reach out" to parents are one sided, intended mainly to instruct or inform parents about how best to support the school's agenda.	Two-way communication between school and home invites parents to advise teachers in support of their child's unique approach to learning.
Administrators and teachers blame lack of family involvement on parents' past educational failures.	Teachers react with sensitivity and tact to parents' own past school experiences, and look to the future.
Parents' role in student learning is seen as backing up school directives and making sure their children get their homework done.	Parents are seen as essential partners in helping students learn in school and at home, and in supporting schoolwide initiatives.
Parent-teacher conferences too often focus on who is to blame for a student's lack of achievement or poor behavior.	Parent-teacher-student conferences focus on mutual efforts to support student achievement, with the child as an active participant in the conversation.
Parent-teacher organizations are dominated by teachers or a few outspoken parents (or both); relatively few parents attend.	Events for parents are keyed to student exhibitions and performances, as well as school and community issues. Food and child care encourage family attendance.
Parents rarely take part as volunteers, committee members, or advisers to the administration.	Parents feel comfortable and welcomed in the school, in whatever capacity they are willing to serve.

any problems helps teachers build a foundation for future cooperation.

- Allowing the student to help articulate his or her strengths and challenges (for example, by including the child in parent-teacher conferences) is a good way to overcome parents' or teachers' anxiety about "who's to blame" for lack of student achievement.

Reaching Out to the Community

Of course family involvement really means community involvement as well, and we will have a lot more to say about the latter during my interview with Jenny O'Neil of City Year, which is the interlude following Chapter Seven. But here is an email from Tyra Pickering, a first-year teacher at her hometown high school in Muncie, Indiana, whom we met in Chapter Four. Tyra's interest in one particular student led her to a part of her community into which she had never before ventured:

> Ashley [not her real name] is a girl in one of my classes. She came to me last week seeking advice. She wanted me to help her get emancipated. We talked and I spoke with her counselor about her options. I discovered that Ashley is currently living with an aunt who is trying to get temporary custody but that Ashley feels like a burden to the family. I was invited by the counselor to go to church and meet the aunt.
>
> I showed up Wednesday night and was amazed by the strong community I found there. I was shaking as I drove to the church. I have lived in Muncie my entire life and have never entered this particular neighborhood. This city is very segregated still and there are certain parts of town that I was raised to believe I didn't belong in. As I got out of my car I was greeted by a church member who took me in and introduced me to several other members.
>
> I have never felt so welcome or so much a part of anything in my entire life. There were my students singing in the choir, and their

> parents were sitting in the pews right next to me allowing me to be a part of their lives. I went to Sunday service today and the reverend spoke directly to me several times throughout the service. I met parents I would have never met had I not gone. I met students who can't wait to be in my class and I met students who wish they would have had me. It was a wonderful experience. It takes a village and to make the difference you have to be willing to put yourself out there, to take risks, to dare to be different for the sake of your students.

Keeping Our Eyes on the Prize

There ought to be no great mystery about the language of school. It must become our language, a language we are comfortable with in our own thoughts, in conversations with colleagues and young people, and in explaining to parents and other stakeholders what we are striving for on behalf of the children for whose nurturance we share responsibility. All of us who work closely with beginning teachers should do what we can to help them become comfortable with the language of school, so that they will not only survive those first, often bewildering years of practice but also grow in confidence and enthusiasm—thanks to their successes in working with children and youth, with families and neighborhoods.

We must try to prevent official jargon from obscuring the meaning of essential school themes. We must try to prevent teachers from becoming isolated within their classrooms and encourage them to share their joys and frustrations with supportive colleagues. We should help them acknowledge the dilemmas of power relationships in schools, so that they do not grow passive, resentful, or subservient in their dealings with administrators or veteran staff. We should acknowledge, as well, the complex range of young people's needs, so that such diversity does not overwhelm new teachers and prevent them from feeling confident, and comfortably challenged, in their work.

By understanding how vital self-motivation and natural learning appetites are in children, we take a huge step toward creating a classroom environment where students accept themselves as active, engaged learners and where the Game of School does not undermine the teaching and learning process.

Teaching is a complex and subtly nuanced undertaking. It is an art that is never mastered, no matter how adept one becomes at anticipating and responding to the panorama of attitudes and behaviors that students bring into class. There are indeed many books that attempt, as this one does, to help new teachers embrace the challenges of this profession. Perhaps too many of them focus on strategies and techniques to overcome a presumed adversarial or resistant posture by students toward academic learning. Whenever teachers and students feel disempowered and subservient, they both react by adopting a stance common to those who feel powerless and put upon: they try to get through their assigned tasks, get by them, get them over with. The meaning of what they are about is lost. Worse, the very capacity for learning is wounded. That stance is not only dysfunctional—it betrays an ignorance of the whole history of human learning. The Game of School must change. Teacher by teacher, student by student, class by class, we can restore learning to its exhilarating role in the evolution of the species.

Randy Wisehart, a veteran English teacher from Richmond, Indiana, is a colleague and friend who has often worked with student teachers. Wisehart possesses what I believe to be an exceptionally clear-sighted view of the balance needed to help aspiring educators hold on to their passions as they face the often bewildering messages of today's test-centered pedagogy. He wrote this piece for a special-focus issue of *Teacher Education Quarterly*, "Passionate Teaching and Learning in an Era of Test-Based Accountability." I present a large excerpt of it here, with his permission.

~ *Interlude* ~

Nurturing Passionate Teachers: Making Our Work Transparent

Randall Wisehart

At the beginning of the school year, the first year teachers and student teachers I will be working with will hear this typical statement from the principal of our high school: *We need to get those test scores up. We want our school to look good. Our goal is to increase the percentage of students passing the state test by 10 percent this year and another 10 percent next year. I expect all of us to be working toward this challenging goal.*

I don't even have to ask. I know what they're thinking. "Is this what teaching is about now, raising test scores? This isn't why I became a teacher. I'm not approaching my first year of teaching excited about the possibility of getting my students from a 465 (just below the cut score) to a 475 (just over the cut score). I can't imagine arriving at school each morning pumped at the idea of raising those test scores. I want to inspire students to become lifelong learners. I want to be a passionate teacher; I want to help students use their minds well. But I still want to be able to pay my rent. Help me. I'm confused. Do I build relationships with students or focus on raising those test scores?"

I have been a teacher in public schools for over 25 years. Over the last few years I have also taught students from Earlham College as well as mentoring beginning teachers. During 2002–2003, in my capacity as a mentor teacher, I worked with over a dozen beginning teachers and student teachers and got from them lots of feedback about what was helping them and what wasn't. They were very clear about what helped:

- Seeing me demonstrate lessons
- Asking me questions as I reflected on a lesson
- Sharing specific strategies and activities and discussing possibilities
- Reflecting with them after I watched them *teach*

Most important, they said, was having me share what was going on in my mind as I taught, asked questions, did professional reading, talked to my peers about what I was thinking and reflected on how it might impact my practice. When I was able to make my thinking transparent to them, they saw possibilities for themselves.[1] When I posed questions to them, they could see applications for their own practice. When they tried things in their own classrooms, they came back to me and I tried to help them make their own teaching, in turn, transparent.[2] They were learning how, in a world focused on standardized testing, to become passionate teachers.[3]

I believe strongly that the numbers and letters in our grading systems get in the way of what is important in classrooms.[4] When we reduce learning in our students' eyes to numbers and letters, we lose passion, we lose complexity, we lose fun, we lose depth, we lose the essence of learning.[5]

I do believe it is important that we learn specific classroom strategies that help students construct meaning, and that we analyze classroom data so students can understand what they do well and how they need to improve. I also want students to look at their scores on standardized tests as one way of understanding themselves as learners. However, I want them to be able to put that standardized test score in a context of learning that also includes rich classroom assessments, careful documentation of goals accomplished, and thoughtful self-assessments. What we seem to have lost is the scope of how students learn. This is what I want beginning teachers and student teachers to reflect on as they enter the profession of teaching.

Anyone who works with new teachers must let them know that they should not have to make a choice between bringing up test scores or promoting lifelong learning. Mentor teachers must show beginning teachers how to be "passionate teachers," which I define as living a life as a reflective educator, making it a priority to build positive relationships with students, creating a classroom community in which students share responsibility for their own learning and the learning of their peers, nurturing a climate that focuses on learning rather than rules, developing strategies that grow from students' emerging strengths as learners rather than by dwelling on learning deficiencies.[6]

Becoming a passionate teacher means more than merely being passionate about skills, content, and the habits of mind we may wish to engender in our students. First and foremost, it means making a commitment to recreating oneself as an educator—and continuing that regenerative process throughout a career. As I work with beginning teachers and student teachers, I try to demonstrate the habits of a reflective practitioner—living a life of inquiry, reading the research, analyzing my practice to make more of an impact on student learning. I must invite beginning teachers in by making my reasoning transparent so they can examine how I make decisions as a passionate teacher. We must discuss what excites us, what scares us, and what options they have as they begin to work in their own classrooms.[7]

Challenging the Game of School

During in-class workshop time, my ninth-grade students are either finishing drafts of writing or doing independent reading. I have brief conferences with students as three college students look on.

"Matt, what have you been doing well in the class over the last grading period?"

"I dunno."

"What about reading? What are you reading on your own time?"

"I'm still reading *IT* by Stephen King."

"Right. Well, how's that going?"

"I dunno."

I know from past conferences that Matt is often reluctant to be reflective, but I plunge ahead hoping that today will be the day I break through and get him to talk in specifics about what he is doing well and where he needs to improve in terms of Indiana English and language arts standards.

"Well, are you confused by anything or interested in any certain part?"

"The dialogue and description."

Finally, I have something to work with. "So you get lost in the descriptive passages and prefer the sections where there is more dialogue? How do you vary your reading strategies when you're reading the descriptive passages, then?"

"No, you've got it backwards. I like the descriptive part. I get confused by the dialogue."

When I debriefed this interaction, my college student observers asked if it was frustrating, and I said of course, it is. But conferencing is a cornerstone activity in nurturing dynamic relationships. Most of the kids in Matt's class are not confident readers. They all missed the cut score on the eighth-grade state exam and had come to my class for extra help with literacy. At this point in the year, they hadn't learned yet to articulate what they do well and what they need to do better. It takes months to get reluctant learners there. Even my stronger students are so used to playing the game of "guess what the teacher wants me to do and do that and nothing more" that an open honest discussion about their learning doesn't come easy.[8]

I want to tell beginning teachers how to create a community of learners in their classrooms, in stark contrast to the "game of school" that most students are used to.[9] I want to help them engage students in honest discussion about learning. I want them to see their students as co-learners who have much to offer, rather than as people with deficiencies. Passionate teaching isn't about correcting mistakes (although that is often part of it); it's about honoring what students bring to the classroom; it's about helping students demonstrate what they are learning and produce quality work; it's about showing students how to reflect on their work and continue to improve.

Lessons from the Classrooms of Passionate Teachers

Of course, one can be an impassioned lecturer, but passionate teachers remember that, ultimately, teaching is about building relationships. Dealing with content, skills, and habits of mind must come after teachers and students feel comfortable together. As with Matt, I try to model for newer teachers some specific strategies and practices that are more conducive to becoming a passionate teacher. I emphasize Socratic seminars, collaboration with students about most major classroom decisions, helping students relate what we're learning to state standards, and student self-assessment. This all sounds good, the beginning teachers and student teachers tell me, but how do we get students to do the work? Do we give lots of points to them if they "try"? Do we give separate grades for "effort"? How do kids even know what "quality work" is?

I invite them to watch me at work. I ask my ninth-grade students:

1. If you could talk to the author of this book, what would you say or ask?
2. What has the author done to help you enjoy the book so far?
3. What has surprised you most about a character?
4. What other author does this book remind you of?

One student's uncorrected response:

1. I would ask why would people give their lives up to save someone else.
2. He made the book adventeres.
3. They would go out to the ocean and save someone.

4. This book reminds me of tears of a tiger because they both try and save someone.

This does not show much depth of thought. I could have put a large red "F" on the paper since the student did not adequately respond to the prompts. Instead, as I read more and more responses, I reflected. Yes, I had made a gallant effort to model reading techniques while we read together, showing them my own responses and asking them to reflect on what could be added to make them better, etc.

I showed the first year teachers and student teachers samples of the reading responses. I shared with them my plan. I decided to revise a rubric based on the criteria I had already given out.[10] I had already established that students could "redo" their work at any time and receive "full credit" for their revised work if it was better than the original. After handing out the revised rubrics and my feedback to their responses, I met with some students and left others to work from my written comments. Following is the revised version of the student's response, albeit done only after a rather vehement protest:

1. This book reminds me of when I had to try out. I was nervous just like Mike was. Mike was scared that the coach was mean or something. I think it is scary to try out for a basketball team.
2. The author made this book joyful because it made me think. It almost feels like it is a true story. He tells a lot of good details and ideas.
3. Yes, because they felt scared when it came down to tryouts. A real person would feel that way too. I would be scared not to make the team.
4. I like the section where the coach was picking the players when he got to the last player he made it look like he was going to pick someone else. Instead, he picked Mike. He told some jokes as he picked the players. Everyone cheered for one or the other.

This is still not exemplary work, as I reminded the first year and student teachers. However, if my questioning during student conferences can help students like Matt, who are labeled "at risk" or "below standard" according to test scores, take small but significant steps to improve the quality of their work, I will help them get that much closer to being able to produce work that will help them continue to make progress as learners—and come closer to passing that high stakes test.

Passionate teachers continually reflect on the interplay of standards, student motivation, student learning, and grades. Given the current emphasis on standards and high stakes tests, more and more teachers wonder about giving "credit" for effort.[11] A passionate teacher wants students to achieve the standards and produce quality work, to complete their assignments but also to understand the importance of developing good habits of mind and habits of work.

If I give students "credit/points/grades" for effort, irrespective of performance, what I am really communicating is, "If you will be quiet and not bother me, I will give you a minimal passing grade or enough points for effort that it will make up for substandard work." If I do this, I am not helping students; I am perpetuating school as a game with minimal expectations. Instead, I show new teachers how to give students feedback on dispositions or habits of mind. A passionate teacher can explicitly discuss with students concepts such as "persistence" and describe what it looks like. Teachers and students could then collaboratively develop a rubric and use it to give students feedback on developing and sustaining qualities of persistence. In this case, giving students "credit" for persistence or effort takes on an entirely different tone. . . .[12]

As a year of working with beginning teachers and student teachers came to an end, I realized that wherever they went to teach, they would have to find a support network or else they would gradually slip into traditional practices and view passionate teaching as impractical if idealistic in today's schools.

If we believe that teachers, acting on their own, can create and maintain classrooms of passionate learning when isolated behind closed doors, we are kidding ourselves. A passionate teacher, for her own survival, must reach out to others, share her questions and inquiries, try to keep the professional conversation on teaching and learning. . . .[13]

The questions beginning teachers ask themselves are crucial. They must ask questions that help them navigate the dangerous terrain between being true to their students and focusing mainly on achieving higher test scores. Those of us who are veteran passionate teachers routinely recreate ourselves through our questions, our observations, our adjustments, our failures, our successes. Our gift and our responsibility to beginning teachers is to make our passionate teaching transparent. We must show them how building genuine relationships with students helps them score better on tests. Only with our support can beginning teachers hold onto the passion that brought them to this work.

Chapter Six

Getting Stuck

When the Game of School has become infused within and inseparable from the routines of one's daily practice, such that almost everyone (including you) views it as normal, you have, in my view, gotten stuck. When student resistance to classroom learning is seen as typical and inevitable, and teachers console each other to "just hang on till June," that, too, is being stuck. To be stuck is to feel that the world of school that surrounds you, your colleagues, your students, and their parents is a world that is acutely stressful to you and not very friendly to learning. The worst part of being stuck comes when you begin to think that what you are experiencing is the inevitable condition of being a teacher—in this school, in this neighborhood, in these times. "It comes with the territory," the voice of experience cautions you. "Get used to it."

To be stuck as a teacher is something other than feeling devastated or a failure. It's less dramatic, perhaps, but just as dangerous to your spirit. You feel that your school is a place where authentic teaching and learning happen only rarely. It is the rare student who seems to genuinely appreciate what you have to offer, the rare class that responds well to the instruction you have meticulously planned for them. You consider yourself lucky if "most of the kids are paying attention, most of the time," or if your latest lesson "seemed to go over okay." You face the daily grind of instructional delivery, content coverage, student apathy, and grade consciousness. Your own learning streams seem to have dried up even as each new school year presents its complement of pedagogical challenges.

To be stuck is more than just running into a problem—for example, when few of your students volunteer responses in class or when lots of them just don't do their homework or when too many do poorly on an important exam. In all those situations, everybody knows there's a problem, even if the solution may not yet be apparent. You may be facing an epidemic of spring fever or "senioritis," a rebellion against doing schoolwork outside of class, or perhaps a misunderstanding on your part of how much your students really understand about the content on which the exam was based. But to call it "a problem" is to assume that somewhere out there lies "a solution" that will lead the class back to productive learning.

When you are stuck, it is not at all clear that there is anything you can do to resolve the situation you're in. The horizons of your job look unchanging and unchangeable. It's the contrast between a teacher who says, "There's *something* not working here—I've *got* to figure out some way to turn this around," and one who implores, "Please, give me the strength to make it through this day [or this week, or this year]." In such cases teachers stop seeing students, colleagues, and administrators as individuals capable of enhancing their effectiveness, but instead view them as "forces I have to contend with." We are stuck when we no longer view ourselves as growing in our craft but, instead, feel criticized for our inadequacies without seeming to have adequate means of addressing them.

It is hard to overemphasize this point. As teachers, we pour incredible energy into our daily work. We care, and because we care so much, we worry. We worry about the kids who aren't doing well, about our standing in the eyes of our colleagues and administrators, about what happens to many of our students when they leave school each day and face a difficult home life. We also worry about our instruction: Are we helping students learn what we know they must? Are there better methods we ought to be using? And on and on.

Such an outpouring of energy and concern is tolerable as long as we are getting something back—so long as the flow of energy goes two ways, and we receive from our students and colleagues and, occasionally, parents as well, sufficient evidence that our efforts are having a real impact, that our caring is appreciated. But when the energy flow seems decidedly one directional—outward and away—we begin to burn out. Table 6.1 reflects a generalized picture of the differences between teachers who feel stuck in their professional lives and those who see themselves as evolving in authentic ways.

Seeing Ourselves as Victims Within a School Culture That Infantilizes Everyone

When conversation in the teachers' lounge becomes dominated by the kinds of attitudes and perspectives listed in the Feeling Stuck column of Table 6.1, an entire school culture can easily turn negative, cynical, hopeless, or all of these. I've seen it happen, and it's amazing how quickly such a culture turns new and idealistic teachers into pessimists.[1] There's almost no way of protecting oneself against such an attitude, once it becomes the dominant one. The kids pick it up, begin to call their school a dump, and pattern their negative behavior on the attitudes they sense emanating from the adults around them. The door to the teachers' lounge opens, and the first words one hears from the person who has just walked in are "Wait till you hear the *latest!*" often followed by "You think *that's* bad? Do you know what *I* overheard today?" The perpetrators of these supposed outrages may be students, parents, administrators, or a combination thereof. The teachers almost always see themselves as the victims.

Within the culture of failing schools one is likely to find that staff inertia and a penchant for victim-blaming prevail. In his broadcast report on a recently failed school reform effort in the Chicago public schools, Ira Glass pointed out, "One of the most common reasons that school reform fails is a reason that you *never* hear about in the press, or in the normal political debate about how to fix schools. School reform often fails because *teachers* kill it. The teachers don't want to do it; they don't agree it will work; they try it; it doesn't work at first, they fight among themselves. And it *dies*."[2]

Table 6.1 Attitudes That Make or Break a Teacher's Career

	Feeling Stuck and Staying Stuck in the Game of School	*Evolving Toward Authentic Teaching and Learning*
Teacher views of student attitudes toward learning: *How do you characterize the students you teach?*	A lot of students don't really care about education; many are lazy and unmotivated, and some are disrespectful of those who are there to help them learn.	Although problems with individual students (and some groups) exist, most are temporary and alterable, and may call for changes in our culture or strategy.
Teacher views of colleagues' attitudes toward teaching: *How do you generally see your fellow teachers?*	Other teachers are competitive, standoffish, or cliquish, leading to a desire to choose one's "buddies" and avoid others. Disputes are mostly hidden, except from one's intimates. Lots of negative gossip prevails.	Most teachers here are dedicated to the goals of the whole school. Although disagreements exist, they are treated respectfully, and people work to resolve them. Negative gossip is frowned on (though some of it gets repeated).
Teacher attitudes toward school administrators: *How much cooperation and trust do you think you get from the administration?*	There is an "Us vs. Them" atmosphere, characterized by a general lack of trust. Solidarity among teachers means we let the administration make the decisions (and then we gripe about them).	Administrators are educators who also have other duties (which they are more than willing to share with teachers). Faculty leadership is encouraged. "We teachers have to be part of the solution."
Teacher views of their subject areas and disciplines: *Who controls what you teach, and how are changes made to your curriculum?*	Our curriculum content is mostly fixed; we modify it rarely, and then only by faculty committee. There is little interdisciplinary teaching or student input into topics taught. "The stuff kids have to know hasn't changed all that much."	"Fluid" content is open for revision and renewal as dictated by student needs and the evolution of knowledge. Interdisciplinary teaching is encouraged, and students help plan the curriculum. "It's our job to help kids learn how to learn."
Teachers' sense of their future: *What's ahead for you as a teacher?*	We expect things to stay the same or get worse; there is much anxiety about "what they will do to us next" and a fear of losing control over our profession, as outside forces try to dominate us.	Although dangers lurk "out there," we are busy applying what we've learned to become ever more effective for more of our students. We need to be both positive and vigilant.

The uncomfortable truth is that the feelings associated with teachers' viewing themselves as victims are often sincere and well founded. It's almost impossible to refute such attitudes, and they have a way of becoming self-fulfilling prophesies. Distrust breeds distrust, cynicism anoints itself with ever new reasons for despair, victims find a renewable supply of justification for their sense of persecution. For a teacher to dissent from the prevailing negative attitudes is perceived as nothing short of betrayal by those who see themselves as victims. "Oh, so you've become one of *them!*" is the spoken or unspoken response.

Almost every veteran teacher I've met has either experienced such a negative culture personally or has friends among teachers who live out their lives under such a cloud. And well founded or not, such attitudes lead to a professional paralysis that has intellectual, operational, and emotional components. People stop thinking in new ways, they filter out evidence that might challenge old biases, and they stop reading in their field. Teachers no longer act collaboratively (except defensively), they feel either isolated or collectively paralyzed, and they lose any faith that they can make a difference outside their own classroom walls (and often, indeed, within the classroom). They feel depleted and afflicted, they look and act depressed (except when they take a cynical delight in the misfortune of those they consider their enemies), they fail to get energized by the successes of their students, and they feel jealous of any honors or achievements given to colleagues.

At schools where I have been asked to speak on Staff Development Day (often after having been invited by an administrator with little input from the faculty), I have seen rooms fill up with teachers who sit at both ends of the room or wedged into the rear seats, arms crossed on their chests, glancing at their watches, just waiting to see what irrelevancy or outrage I might utter. Even when I have met, as I always try to do, with a cross-section of faculty prior to my address and have tried to glean some of the prevailing issues and concerns of faculty, it avails me little in a school where the culture has become widely impregnated by the attitudes we have been talking about. And I do not blame such teachers.

My impression in such cases (and they are surprisingly widespread, especially at the middle and high school level) is of a group of adults who have over time been set back a full developmental stage by their school environment. They *look* like adults, but they *react* like adolescents: touchy, easily offended, cliquish, pouting at their inability to get their way, defensive about threats real or imagined to their prerogatives, obsessed by their routines and petty comforts, tough skinned yet strangely vulnerable, isolated within their rooms. This situation is not their fault. These people truly are victims of a system where power in schools has traditionally been allocated in a manifestly undemocratic manner and where teachers are often treated more like subjects of a monarchy than as intellectual workers in a free society. Unless there is a change in the culture, such infantilized adults will continue to play their versions of the Game of School, largely characterized by the universal teenage response to overpowering adults: "Whatever!"

Paralyzing the Passionate Teacher Within You

Even if you do not yet see yourself as a victim, the significance of being stuck is that it paralyzes the passionate teacher who lies within you. You no longer feel empowered by your love for your subject, your curiosity about how your students' minds work, your devotion to ideals and values that shape the world. You see teaching as "a job," and you grope for ways to make that job less onerous. You begin to see your profession through a view finder that searches for paths that avoid stress, paths that are convenient or comfortable even if they do not seem to work well for a number of your students, paths that protect you from disappointment but leave you more isolated the further down them you proceed. You note, in passing, that "teaching isn't all it's cracked up to be" or that "kids these days don't value the education we try to give them" or that "nobody respects us for the really tough job we have to do each day."

This paralysis can hit us after years of struggling in the classroom, as we find ourselves becoming fixated over proposed changes to our contracts or working conditions. I see many veteran teachers who've come a long, long way from the idealism of their early teaching careers and who now see that idealism as misplaced or naïve. They are very cautious about recommending a career as a teacher to their own children or to a friend's child.

I sympathize deeply with teachers who are rightfully frustrated by the conditions of their jobs, baffled by students who are openly disrespectful or who refuse to work, stupefied by parents who seem interested only in the achievement of their own child, or dismayed by administrators and officials who act in an arbitrary and capricious manner and who refuse to include teachers and teacher union representatives in decision making. We don't become stuck merely because we are upset or unhappy about the climate of teaching and learning at our school. (In fact, such a response may be a sign of your willingness to work for change.) We become stuck if the net effect of this harassment is to eclipse our vision of ourselves as vibrant and powerful players in the teaching and learning process at our school and if we cease to believe that we can act together with students, colleagues, and parents to create conditions for authentic learning.

Getting Unstuck

The trouble is that, once stuck, we are likely to experience an atrophy of just the confidence and zest we require in order to view our lot in life as capable of significant improvement. The energy that we ought to put into learning new ways to deal with our diverse students goes, instead, into complaining and feeling sorry for ourselves. It's so much easier to feel victimized by antagonistic forces and stresses than to become energized to confront and change the climate within which we teach.

For a percentage of those who are stuck in their careers as teachers there may be no way out except to leave their present school or quit teaching altogether and devote their lives to some other endeavor. If your appetite for the struggle for meaning and satisfaction within your classroom and school setting has withered, if the forces arrayed against you seem too formidable, if your collegial support seems weak and the sympathy of administrators is nonexistent, it may be time to look for some other way of pursuing your life goals.

I once facilitated a meeting of case workers who served as advocates for adults with disabilities (helping them find housing, employment, and other services). They were an astonishingly upbeat and energized group, and a number of them told me they were former schoolteachers. They had left teaching, they said, because they wanted to work with colleagues who shared their zest and passion to do good things; and here, unlike in their former schools, they had found just such a sense of advocacy and dynamism.

I suspect that the majority of teachers who feel stuck would like to remain as teachers, but they don't know how to reconcile their inner vision of good teaching and learning with the realities that surround them. For these people, there are two requirements for getting themselves unstuck. Both are essential, but they differ in emphasis. One is to see this quest as a personal and professional challenge. The second is to view the process as also a social and political one, to recognize that as is true of so many other aspects of good teaching, you can't do this alone. Both approaches require that we consider the following sets of assumptions and hypotheses. The first list may simply state the obvious:

- My situation, if not yet completely intolerable, is far from what I hoped to find when I became a teacher; if it is left unresolved, I am likely to experience disillusionment or burnout.
- I know that however hard I'm working now, I am not serving my students well so long as I feel disheartened and frustrated in my teaching. If I find myself blaming my students for not learning, or blaming their parents or MTV, I am on a downward slope.
- The situation is made worse by the participation of those around me in the Game of School, of people going through

the motions rather than teaching and learning in authentic ways.

- Teaching and learning will never be easy, but they were never meant to be as stressful, painful, and unrewarding as they now seem.
- If my situation—particularly in relation to my students—doesn't change for the better, my self-respect demands that I find something better to do with my life.

Having set forth these first five assumptions, we next need to consider the following five hypotheses:

- As long as I can breathe and think, I am capable of changing my life for the better.
- I am being weighed down—depressed—by the negative climate (internal and external) that surrounds my work as a teacher. I am not the teacher I might be if those clouds could lift.
- If I were able, somehow, to reverse this negative pattern, my students and I would recognize and appreciate the benefits of such a change. The cycle might move upward, in a positive direction.
- Although substantive change often takes time, I won't have to wait for months and years to feel the difference—there are indicators I can look for that will tell me, early on in the process, if I am on the right track.
- If I act wisely on my behalf, the effort I put into transforming my life as a teacher will pay off in significantly higher levels of job satisfaction, justifying the expense of my energy and the renewal of my faith in myself as a teacher.

Now comes the hard part: finding the motivation to enter the path leading out of paralysis and toward authentic teaching and learning. I don't want to minimize the difficulty of that fundamental first step, "getting out from under." Here is yet another list of five propositions to consider:

- I am neither the first nor the only teacher to feel stuck in this way. Others have managed to transform their professional lives, and it is likely that I will be able to do so, too.
- I am a valuable person who deserves a chance to begin this process and whose professional enhancement—if I am successful—will be recognized by others, particularly by my students.
- The path is neither easy nor always clear, and it's likely that I will stumble and make mistakes along the way. I don't expect to get it all right the first time, and I need to be patient with myself.
- People who care about the quality of teachers' lives have written books and articles that can help me begin the process of transformation. I need to find those sources of experience and inspiration and then give myself permission to set other tasks aside while I read them.
- There are people in my life (spouse, friends, mentors, colleagues, and even my students) who will welcome my struggle to transform my teaching. I need to discover who they are and figure out how they can support my endeavors.

It is on the next to last of these that I'd like to focus for a moment—the reading. There is a common perception that, by and large, teachers (as is true of many other professionals) don't read widely or in depth in their field. About this, Seymour Sarason has written, "Reading is more than desirable, it is crucial. If I were czar of education, I would seek to stimulate and support the professionals in each school to devote at least one hour each week to a meeting in which is discussed a published study, report, or book that everyone had read beforehand. Professionals should always be 'going to school.'"[3]

Unlike a few decades ago, when good writers about teaching and learning were few, there is now a wonderful selection of books and articles on virtually every aspect of our profession, available to the casual browser at a university bookstore or from the Web sites of the large book companies. These books (some of which are listed in the bibliography of this volume) offer varied perspectives on what it means to be a teacher in these troubled times.

It can be tremendously comforting and inspiring to find an author who speaks to your anxieties and laments or to your hopes and ideals (and sometimes to both), in a way that rings true and makes you feel much less alone. It can be wonderful to share a book with a colleague and then treat yourselves to lunch or dinner in a favorite restaurant while you discuss the book's impact on you. Part of being stuck is believing that nobody "out there" has walked for miles in your shoes or that most writers on education are starry-eyed idealists, teacher-bashing hacks, or ivory tower theorists, all of whom lack experience "in the trenches." But such cynicism only sinks you further into your current morass. Not reading keeps you paralyzed.

Liberating Yourself Within a School Culture That Isn't Changing

What do you do when you become aware of being stuck (and privately commit to escaping from the paralysis) while most of your colleagues still assume "That's the way it is around here"? You don't want to just turn your back on your fellow teachers or assume that you have "seen the light" while they still walk in darkness; but neither do you want to stay in the familiar rut of blaming, self-pitying, and making excuses for the lack of joy in your professional life. You want to step out of the Game in hopes of eventually attempting to change it, but you aren't happy about going it alone.

My suggestion is to search for the right words with which to pose a friendly challenge to those colleagues you are most comfortable with, those you hang out with over lunch. In your most low-key and humble way, let them know that you, for one, have set a goal of enjoying your teaching more this year, of lowering your level of stress and raising your level of satisfaction. Tell them you're not sure how you will attempt this but that one thing you are certain of is that whatever you try will have better results if others are working toward the same or similar goals. Here are some thoughts:

- Become your own researcher in the field of "student resistance to academic learning" and—most important—bring your students in on your investigation.
- Create a list of some of the things you hope to learn from your students, and invite students to post their own list of "what I have to do to get more out of learning."
- Invite colleagues to join you in a reading club, one that meets for 6:30 A.M. breakfast every other Thursday or for potluck supper on the first Wednesday of each month.
- Locate the nearest branch of a professional organization whose purposes you most identify with, be it a reading association, a math teachers' group, folks who address issues of social justice, or maybe a group affiliated with one of the national organizations to reform public education, such as the Coalition of Essential Schools or Phi Delta Kappa.

Of the items just listed, perhaps the most essential is also the most available. Your students are your most readily accessible source of expertise on what it takes to create a friendly, productive learning environment. They also have as much a stake as you have in creating a more pleasant and productive classroom climate. Just a peek into the words of wisdom collected in Kathleen Cushman's *Fires in the Bathroom* should be enough to convince you that students have many insights to offer and that they are ready to rise to the challenge of authentic learning, provided they respect the sincerity of your quest. The first hurdle may be the hardest—reaching out to your students, in a nonblaming way, with your honest questions and hopes. As I tell my teacher trainees: when in doubt, ask the kids.

Ultimately, none of these suggestions will work if you haven't yet found the will to reach out for authentic teaching and learning. And once you have found it, you are likely to find ideas of your own that are as good as or better than any of these. While you are enmeshed in the Game of School and feeling yourself a victim of a school culture that no longer sees itself as a community of learners, the pathway out may seem beyond your reach. It isn't, but it may seem that way. Your options are to continue to muddle through, to leave the profession entirely, or to begin to see yourself, once more, as a passionate teacher. It's not an easy choice.

Students and Parents

I recognize that in the last few pages I have addressed myself primarily to teachers and that they are not the only participants in this struggle. Space does not permit me to rework these lists from a student's or parent's viewpoint, but it ought not to be too difficult to look at each and imagine how the ideas could be translated for other stakeholders. An essential conversation is the one between parents and children, about how to keep the spirit of learning alive amid the confusing demands of Game of School habits. Parents should position themselves as advocates not just for their children's "doing well" in school but for their healthy evolution as young adults who love to learn. (I have written elsewhere, particularly in *The Passionate Learner*, about this issue from the perspective of parents and learners.)

Whoever we are, whatever our roles, if we remain stuck in negative, demeaning, or hypocritical postures, we are headed for failure, in both the short and longer term. There are resources at hand to help us emerge from such paralysis, but the critical first step is up to each of us: to look up from the morass of business as usual and demand something better.

Following is a little scale that can help teachers, at whatever stage of their careers, measure where they see themselves with regard to some of the challenges and potentialities of schools today.

~ Interlude ~

Fried's Joy and Misery Index for Educators

Guaranteed Unscientific: Participate at Your Own Risk!

Part One: "How Did Things Ever Get This Way?"

For each of the items that follow, rate yourself on a scale of 0 to 3, where 0 = No sweat, I can handle it; 1 = This has a moderate impact on me; 2 = This makes life really tough sometimes; 3 = If I don't get some relief soon, I'm gonna clobber somebody!

1. Today's kids seem a lot harder to handle; there's less parental guidance, which makes the educator's role much more difficult; and we rarely get consistent backup from administrators. _____
2. There's so much media and video technology available to kids that it makes it hard to hold their attention during class work. _____
3. The difficulty of responding to the range of abilities is much greater now that more kids with special needs are in regular classrooms. _____
4. There are a lot of good ideas and techniques we could use in our school, but it seems there's so much resistance to change around here, often from colleagues who have "seen it all before." _____
5. The push for "accountability" makes me feel that the public just doesn't respect educators these days or trust that we know what's right for kids. _____

6. The emphasis on standardized testing really limits my freedom as an educator to teach and work according to my values; I feel a lot of pressure to "teach to the test." ____
7. I tend to feel very alone in my job, with so much responsibility on my shoulders to "do right" by each of these diverse kids. ____
8. Optional: Write in your own. ____

   Your total score ____

Part Two: "It's Still the Best Job I Know—and Getting Better!"

For each of the items that follow, rate yourself on a scale of 0 to 3, where 0 = This is just not true, or, I get no joy from this at all; 1 = This has moderate positive impact on me; 2 = This makes my work here kind of exciting; 3 = I know why I love this job, and this is a big part of it.

1. I find the kids can really be counted on to help make our classroom and school an exciting, productive place to teach and to learn; their energy and enthusiasm are often exhilarating. ____
2. Despite (or due to) the impact of mass media, kids long for something real, for authentic relationships with adults who care about them. ____
3. The diversity of students and the support we have for inclusion make the classroom a rewarding, if challenging, community to work in. ____
4. I find a growing willingness on the part of the educators I work with to experiment with new approaches that promise better results. ____
5. More of our leaders accept the fact that we can't have high expectations only for the few; *all* our kids need to learn how to think. It's the responsibility of *all* of us to help children achieve. ____

6. If we put standardized tests in their proper perspective—as a tool, not as an end—I can still teach what I feel is most important. ____
7. I have opportunities to team with colleagues in my school or to take part in innovative or charter school efforts (or to do both); I don't feel isolated. ____
8. Optional: Write in your own. ____

Your total score ____

Part Three: Adding It All Up—and Reflecting on Where It Might Lead

Please subtract your total score on Part One from your total score on Part Two. I can't pretend to be scientific as to what the resulting score means, but consider these possible inferences:

7 or above: "I'm just where I should be and getting the most from it."

4 to 6: "Things could always be better, but I feel that I'm meeting the challenges of my profession and getting personal satisfaction from it."

2 to 4: "On the whole, I feel that I'm making headway in my work, despite the very real challenges that face me in this profession."

−2 to +1: "Although I can certainly find satisfaction in some or much of what I do, there are real obstacles I face that make this work quite frustrating."

−6 to −3: "There are some serious signs that I should rethink how I approach the challenges I face as an educator. The answers may not come easily."

−7 and below: "The frustrations I face are serious and potentially harmful to my effectiveness as an educator. I may need to consider making a change in what I do, where I work, or both."

Chapter Seven

No Time to Waste

For teachers, parents, and students at every stage of their schooling, the challenge to make our schools work comes down to a few questions:

> How can each person hold on to a view of *learning* as a wonderful extension of our natural human curiosity, rather than as an unending series of required tasks that seem fairly meaningless?
>
> How can each student see *school* as a community rich in opportunity and resources, rather than as a highly competitive obstacle course, a drudgery to be endured until it is over?
>
> How can each teacher invigorate the *passion* within, to create a true partnership with students and their families, rather than feeling locked into a structure in which game playing has replaced authentic learning?

Our challenge is that simple—and, of course, incredibly difficult. When we view these questions straight on, without the cushion of educational jargon, it's not hard to think of better ways for children and adults to learn together than what happens on most days in most classes in most schools. We can imagine settings both in school and in the community where kids, parents, and townspeople, led by a skilled and caring teacher acting more as facilitator than as presenter, are able to help make a number of exciting things happen. Learners of all ages can

- Explore ideas and issues of genuine interest
- Probe the mysteries of nature
- Read and discuss both classical and contemporary works of literature, poetry, nonfiction, and biography
- Compile and analyze data relevant to their lives as citizens
- Work to enhance the local environment and to participate in ecological practices
- Share the perspectives of diverse cultures and help community residents of various backgrounds feel welcomed and appreciated
- Create poetry and art, music and drama
- Debate the vicissitudes of individual freedom, social responsibility, and the pursuit of the common good
- Engage in spiritual exploration and the pursuit of personal and collective meaning.

Likewise, we can enter into a dialogue on how our schools can more sensitively respond to the desire for authentic learning on the part of students and teachers. We can

- Reflect on the *culture* of our schools
- Scrutinize our traditional school practices, our habituated responses to authority, our reactions to troublesome students
- Challenge the policies and practices of institutions whenever they seem to deprive children of their evolutionary heritage and inherent excitement about learning.

It is easy, even pleasurable, to speculate, criticize, and dream of how learning might be pursued in school and community settings. Yet when we face the inevitable routine of our next day's schedule, most of us tend to fall in line with the prevailing culture. We push our ideals off to the side and suit up for the Game of School.

Kicking Off the Comfortable Old Shoe of an Adversarial Stance

We live with our old habits and our habitual ways of thinking about school that include embedded images of the teachers who faced us from the front of the room, commanding the blackboard and the rank book, casting baleful looks at us and making us afraid of looking stupid. As teachers, we easily become preoccupied with images of students who resist learning, who can't stay in their seats or leave their neighbors alone, who talk back when reprimanded, who sullenly refuse to do their homework or hand us back blank test papers and dare us to flunk them. School seems made for a set-piece battle: students versus teachers, kids against grown-ups. Remember that old song grammar school kids sang on the last day of school each June: "No more pencils, no more books; no more teacher's dirty looks"? Has it changed all that much?

Whenever our insecurities or our habitual reflexes (depending on whether we are new teachers or old hands) lead us to define our students as the indolent or the unwilling or the inept, we slide into a stance that pushes aside those questions that begin this chapter. We fall back to a self-defensive posture from which we proclaim our authority as a matter of right. We are the *boss*, after all. We have a *job* to do. We *deserve* respect. We've been hired to get this stuff across to them, and we neglect that duty at our peril. We remind ourselves, "I'm not here to be their friend. I'm doing what I'm doing because these kids are too immature to see the value of this. We're going to get through this, one way or another. Hopefully, they will thank me later."

Perhaps most damaging to our hopes as teachers is that an adversarial stance (seemingly inevitable given the frame of mind just described) destroys our chance to develop a genuine partnership in learning. Instead of seeing, in front of us, rows of highly motivated students eager to claim their place in our knowledge-based world, we *expect* students to come in with an attitude of "Hey, what are you going to make us do today?" and we are unsurprised to hear, upon entering the teachers' lounge, "Boy, you wouldn't *believe* what I had to put up with in my fourth-period class!" Such resistance to learning seems to be a normal if not inevitable hazard of our system of compulsory education. The students *have* to be there—so of *course* some of them are gonna grumble, make trouble, and try to get around doing their work.

Can we find a way out of this paralyzing—if strangely comfortable—posture? We owe it to ourselves, as parents and educators, to offer children another path. We need to move with alacrity. We don't have time to waste.

But let us not delude ourselves. It won't be easy to change the Game of School so long as we accept the inevitability of an adversarial relationship. In this, we teachers are as likely as not to replicate the behavior of our offending students whenever we're put in their shoes, as a recent incident in my graduate course on preparing high school English and history teachers illustrates:

> Each week, three students volunteer to prepare an exercise around our assigned reading. The class has become increasingly relaxed with one another, and discussions are often lively.
>
> The week's threesome came up front, posted a review of the chapter on the board, and began, haltingly, to lecture to the class about the contrast between "teacher coverage" and "student understanding." They posed questions that seemed rather abrupt and tried to pull answers from their reluctant classmates, who watched passively as the threesome bumbled around in front of the room.
>
> Sitting on the side, I began to worry about their performance, hoping I would not have to intervene and redirect a floundering exercise. The three students then put us in small groups, handed each group a slip of paper with what seemed to be an unconnected quotation from some unknown source, and asked us to identify and analyze our respective passage. The class reluctantly fell to work, with lots of side conversations and very little contact with, or questions for, the presenters. Someone asked, "What's the purpose of all this?"

to which the three students replied, "We were all supposed to read the chapters from which these quotes were taken. You should be able to recognize them."

After ten minutes, the now-resistant class faced their three fellow students to find out what was what. The class was asked, "Have you identified your passage?" One group had done so and gave themselves a mock cheer, while the other groups looked on apathetically. Finally, the three presenters smiled and said, "This is the problem with aiming to 'cover the content,' isn't it?" They confessed that they had been role-playing the conventional stance of teachers trying to deliver instruction. Their role play had been perfectly executed, for all its apparent awkwardness. Most of the class relaxed, though some seemed a bit annoyed at having been "set up."

Sensing a "teachable moment," I came forward to hold up to the class a mirror on its behavior. "These are your *friends!*" I berated them, playfully. "These are your current and future *colleagues*, for heaven's sake. And yet you were content to sit back and watch them fumble around up here. Nobody said, 'Hey, Andrew, what are you trying to do? I'm confused.' Nobody asked, 'Patricia, can you tell us how what you want us to do connects with anything we've been talking about?' Nobody invited Ilsa to come over to their group and help clarify their task. Instead, you sat there muttering to yourselves, '*Boy*, are these guys screwing up. Glad it's not *me* up there in the middle of this mess.' Just watching your body language [and I leaned back with my arms crossed over my chest to illustrate the attitude of disengagement] told me how little responsibility you felt for their success or failure."

My mock tirade was greeted with embarrassed smiles and outright laughter. They realized I wasn't really criticizing them, that my explication had another purpose. Prior to the student-led exercise, we had been discussing the question of classroom discipline (or lack thereof), and one grad student (in his first year of full-time teaching) had confessed to having "lost it" in his own class this past week, berating his kids for their inattentiveness. Here we had just witnessed the same tendency among ourselves. "I wonder how long it would have taken," I mused, "before Ilsa, Andrew, and Patricia would have begun handing out detentions?" More laughter. "How primed we are—aspiring teachers though we be—to fall back into the 'passive-and-put-upon student' role whenever somebody in front of us tries to 'play teacher.' After all, what else is there for disempowered learners to do but sit back and hope that the dictator up front will somehow mess up or 'lose it'?"

A discussion ensued, in which students raised questions of instructional style, stance, and power relationships in the classroom. I related the words of my friend Dennis Littky, when he was principal of a rural high school in New Hampshire, who once told me that whenever a teacher came to him with a classroom discipline problem involving more than one or two disruptive kids, he would look for an instructional cause. What's not happening, learning-wise, that ought to be? How connected do the students feel to what's being taught? This, he said, is often disappointing to the teacher, who would prefer to have him come in and yell at the kids.[1]

Homeless in Calgary: "The Way We Learn Affects How We Act"

An incident from a school in Calgary, Canada, illustrates what we might expect when we are able to respond creatively to the questions posed at the beginning of this chapter. Sharon Friesen, co-founder of the Galileo Educational Network, told me the story:

> Pat [Sharon's partner at Galileo] and I had been working with a group of teachers in the Calgary region, and we had decided to have them read . . . *The Passionate Learner* as part of their ongoing study into creating inquiry-based classrooms. This group was in their second year of work with us and willing to try new ideas. They wanted to find ways to engage their students in deep and meaningful work, authentic work, work that mattered to their students and to the community.

Although they were being supported and encouraged within their school, they were continually frustrated with the slow pace of change in their school district and with the never-ending tug of war between teachers and students over meaningful, high-quality work. Two teachers in our group had started the school year with questions about heroes: What is a hero? Who were the heroes of the past? Who are the heroes today? What makes a hero, a hero? Are those we call heroes today truly heroes? Can anyone become a hero? If so, what does it take?

Through the heroes inquiry work, one class of students at Rocky Ridge School began to understand that a person's *actions* defined whether or not he or she was a hero. Wrote one student: "Sports figures and actors are not really heroes, because if you took away their money then they wouldn't play anymore. A hero doesn't do things for money, but for other people. The person who does something for others transforms who they are through their actions." The conversations that followed led to students wanting to do "something real—here in our community—that we can do something about." The holiday season was approaching, and the students came up with the idea of helping homeless people in their city.

The kids began with research on the problem of homelessness, what various agencies were doing about homelessness, how they as students could go about making a difference. The students each made a commitment to help a homeless person during the holiday season. Some served Christmas dinner at various homeless shelters, others brought coffee and donuts to homeless people wandering the streets, others collected money for the Salvation Army, and still others collected toys and clothing and with their parents delivered Christmas hampers to various families. Students also visited churches and shelters, discovering a lot about the variety of people who were either temporarily or chronically homeless.

When the students returned back to school after Christmas, they would not stop talking about what they had learned about themselves and the homeless people of their city through their

> "Take Action" project. One student captured the experience this way: "Things are so different here at our school. The way we learn is much different than that of other schools, I think that the way we learn affects how we act. The way we learn affects how we handle situations and problems. It is not our abilities that show us what we truly are; it is our choices. I think that inquiry is a better way to learn because of the freedom that you have. I think that all of us have grown since we first started."
>
> This particular class had been scheduled to go on a field trip to City Hall early in the new year, and although they were supposed to be taking on an environmental issue in their city, the students had become passionate about the problem of homelessness. Nothing could move them from their desire to investigate even further the problem of homelessness in their city. They decided to confront the mayor and aldermen, while at City Hall, with the following question: "If it is the local government's role to meet the citizens' needs, then why are there homeless people in our city?"
>
> The student then attended a weekly city council meeting, where the issue of the homeless was raised. One of the city councilors commented that the homeless were just a few alcoholics and vagabonds. A number of the students raised their hands and requested permission to speak. They stated that the councilor had his facts wrong. The demographics of the homeless in their city were quite different than just described. The students presented their findings to the city council and asked them to act to improve conditions for homeless people in their community. Their teachers, the mayor, and the city councilors were amazed by the intensity and thoroughness of the students' research and by the strength of the students' actions.

They needn't have been surprised. Most students crave opportunities to use their knowledge, their energy, and their sense of justice or injustice in a real-world setting where a teacher is guiding—but not dominating—their inquiries. We know this from our experience of students who voluntarily participate in extracurricular activities, such as athletics, music, and drama. Too often we tacitly assume that when students *have* to be in our classes, that same spirit will be difficult if not impossible to mobilize and maintain or that there will always be "a few kids who will spoil it for the rest." I, too, struggled with this oft-repeated rationalization, and I decided to bring it to one of the teachers I had interviewed in writing my first book, middle school music teacher David Ervin.

David Ervin: The Music of Passionate Teaching

David Ervin is quite possibly the happiest teacher I have ever known. With ten more years of teaching music and drama at Oyster River Middle School in Durham, New Hampshire, under his belt since I last interviewed him for *The Passionate Teacher*, plus a marriage, two small children, and a new house designed and built mostly by his father and himself, he shows no signs of slowing down.

Back in 1995, I had highlighted his work with seventh and eighth graders in helping them create, each year, an original musical play; the students write the script and the music, design the scenery, and put on a production for their school and community. Today, Ervin still devotes Sunday afternoons and quite a few Saturdays working with students on the musical plays they create together, and he hasn't had a school lunch period to himself for as long as he can remember. (It's his favorite in-school time to meet with groups of kids.)

Bittersweet, the students' latest production, is about the lives of child workers in the cocoa plantations of West Africa. It has just been recorded on CD, and he hands me a copy to take with me, along with two other recent works produced by his students: a musical play called *Eye of the Storm*, on the life of Elian Gonzales, the Cuban boy rescued from a sinking float off the Florida coast (his mother beside him, dead) who was fought over by anti-Castro family members in Miami and his father, back in Cuba; and *Requiem for Peace*, which his students created after the tragedy of September 11, 2001. As we talk, his eyes twinkle in a way that seems to say, "I can't believe how lucky I am to be doing this work with young teenagers." Our discussion got around to the topic of authentic learning, and here's what David Ervin told me:

> My philosophy of authentic learning begins by recognizing that from the first, the students have to have an emotional connection to what you're eventually going to be working on. I can't imagine starting any other way. The idea of introducing a topic without helping to create or discover an emotional connection is foreign to me. All of these projects come out of the kids' world. I feel it's my job to be continuously on the lookout for a topic that kids can connect with on an emotional, not just intellectual, level. I try to let myself be open to seeing those topics from any perspective, not just how adults might view it. All this is very different from a "curriculum," where you sit down and say, "Here are these things that need to be taught." What I bring to them as "curriculum" is small in comparison to the very large area I leave open for what the kids will create, the places their own commitment and passion will lead them.

I read to David one of his statements from *The Passionate Teacher:* "My basic premise is that I want every moment to be important enough to engage kids spiritually, emotionally, intellectually, even physically. When I create such an environment and keep it going, that's when education is happening." I ask, "Do you still believe this?"

> Absolutely. It's evolved in the sense that I think I better understand the stages that I expect to see in a meaningful group process. I think of my work as taking place over four stages:
>
> Stage One is the "connection stage." Any great project begins with this emotional-intellectual connection. When I think back to classes that I had when I attended junior and senior high school, they all just seem so emotionless. One of the sad things about public schools is that we are continually looking to *remove* emotion from our classrooms. The information we transmit is just so *factual*. The kids listen quietly because it's easy for them to be quiet—they're bored, their minds are elsewhere. I want none of that in my classroom.

I call Stage Two "exploration and creativity." I cannot emphasize too strongly the need for time together. Forget forty-five-minute classes—it's useless. I haven't had a lunch by myself in twenty years of teaching, and Sunday afternoon is my other regular "work day." In my classes, I try to have the students together in groups of twelve or so, so that every student feels needed, with an individual purpose, such that if they don't come through, an integral part of the whole picture would be missing. Once we have our topic, the kids are going to design a project that makes sure that we use every single person in the class.

On the Elian Gonzalez project, the kids decided that a CD would allow for some kids to focus on the technical aspects of the project, with all of them singing in some of the selections, and most of them eventually wanted to do a solo—not because they are such good singers, but because they are so passionately invested in the project that they want to be heard.

In this stage, my job is to have them have a number of group experiences, such as eating lunch together, playing Ping-Pong and foosball, here in my house, cooking pizzas together. I never do less than a six-hour rehearsal. What I want is to come together as a group so that when the really hard work starts, halfway through the process, they have a foundation of caring about each other.

We have to deal with moral and spiritual issues, to turn them over and even get into arguments about them, as we question, "Why are we here? Why commit our whole selves to this process?" We need to ask this so that when the really hard part comes, we will know why we're putting ourselves through all this. I'm always asking myself, "How can I make this even more fun—to encourage a level of solidarity among them that will keep them together as the stress builds up?"

I divide the total project time in half. After one month of a two-month project, we need to have a completed full draft. Then we celebrate that by spending group time together, perhaps on a camping trip, reading our draft around a campfire. This ends Stage Two.

Stage Three means one thing: "refinement." Hopefully, three things have already been achieved: (1) we have a strong emotional connection to what we've been working on—the kids feel they have something to say that they want to say to as many people as they possibly can; (2) the individual students have made a connection to a group that makes each feel needed and cared for; (3) they already have a sense of completion. They know: this is not going to fail. We won't have to suffer through and hope it comes together in the last few days.

At this point, I assume the role of the *Great Questioner,* the one who's never happy with where we are. I become a very tough coach. I explain this change to the kids: "*Now* you need me to play a different role—the perfectionist who never stops asking for more." We joke about this change in my role at this stage, but at heart it's very serious. I really emphasize the importance of discipline in the third stage, where the kids have to commit their work to memory and make it a part of them, part of a continuous circle of belonging, creating, perfecting, and performing. I remind the kids that all creativity comes courtesy of the Muses, in mythology, who are the daughters of Memory. We use discipline to incorporate all aspects of memory, and from that is born all forms of art—that's the way the metaphor works for me.

Stage Four is our public presentation, our exhibition. It's the key to great education for students. It's good to have a fixed date; it provides some safety, and makes some amazing stuff happen during the preparation. It's our chance to say, "This is how we tell the world about what we believe to be true about this topic or theme!"

I attempt to challenge David at this point—to try my hand at being a Great Questioner—by asking him, "If you were pulled out of teaching music and asked to teach English or math, what would you bring with you from your experiences with the kids in music?" (In my mind are all the people who have read his story in *The Passionate Teacher* but who have dismissed him because he doesn't face the pressure of a standard curriculum or a state proficiency test.) But Ervin won't budge from his stance.

I would *love* to teach math. I even proposed that the school let me teach the eighth-grade algebra class. The first thing is that just having math class would not be enough for me; I'd need more time to get to know the kids and let them experience through me what's so incredible about math. It's as exciting to me as music. Math is as emotional for me as any other educational endeavor. I would have sessions in which we'd invite in community members who have something to do with math.

I certainly love the freedom that being a music teacher gives me. I really don't have groups of state officials or anxious parents lined up to enforce the mandated curriculum. Nobody really cares about what music teachers teach, aside from what they witness during a performance. And I work to integrate the music with other key subjects. Nearly every project I do is collaborative—the play about Elian Gonzales was codeveloped with a social studies teacher.

"Ten years ago," I remind David, "you talked about patterning your teaching after the battlefield tactics of Alexander the Great: running headlong into a project with the expectation that your students will forget their self-consciousness or inhibitions and follow you to victory. Is this still your approach?"

The evolution of our *Requiem for Peace* is an example of how we can inspire kids to reach so much further than they initially think they can go. Our requiem is entirely in Latin, but it didn't begin that way. On 9/11, I happened to be auditioning a dozen eighth graders for our choral quartet. After we learned about the attack and its consequence, I proposed that instead of my picking the best four, all twelve of them, working with me, should commit ourselves to writing a requiem together, for peace. I talked about what requiems were, and we listened to four or five of them and then set off to write our own. A dozen kids got together for lunch every day for six months and three out of four Sundays. Their words began with anger, a desire for revenge. But after working with this theme for several months, all they wanted was peace.

We decided, initially, that our requiem would be at least one-third in Latin, the rest in English. But as the students worked further on it, only the Latin words seemed to express the emotions they felt

> from the tragedy. The students had, by this time, become what I call "super learners," when their appetite for knowledge is driven by their spiritual, emotional, intellectual commitment to an idea, a quest, a cause. They didn't know the Latin at all, but as super learners, those words they'd never heard before became the best way of describing the feelings they had. They wrote poem after poem, lyric after lyric, in English, but when the time came time, only the traditional Latin text seemed to work. The English poems remained in their folders. The kids ended up using the Latin text but creating new music for it.

After talking in his home, I listened in my car to *Requiem for Peace*. It brought tears to my eyes. The kids were by no means virtuosi performers, but their voices rang with a clarity and depth of feeling that were undeniably lovely.

It would be unfair to hold out David Ervin's experience as the template for all teachers to pattern themselves by. He is an unusually talented and devoted educator, a thoroughly passionate teacher, and he has had more than a decade to build a reputation in the school and community as one who elicits the maximum creativity and commitment from his students. But he is less unusual than it might seem in his devotion to children's learning. I know many teachers who aspire to similar qualities of intensity and partnership with their students. *Authentic learning is within our reach. We have no time to waste in figuring out how to make such an environment our own.*

Changing the Game: Getting from Here to There

There are no surefire remedies, no quick fixes. I have probably used these same phrases in all three of my books on education, and still they ring true. I continue to ask how we might inspire people in schools to say, "Let us resolve to look at our students as the dynamic natural learners that they *are*, rather than as the learning-averse creatures that schools have made them into!"

With my own advanced undergraduate and graduate students, in the courses I teach on instructional methods and curriculum, I insist that in developing model instructional units, they must address themselves directly to their students. Their goals, objectives, introductory remarks, teasing "hook" questions are to be directed *to* their students rather than *about* their students (as though their real audience is whatever administrator might be looking over the teacher's shoulder). I bluntly cross out statements that begin, "In this unit, students will be responsible for . . ." and replace them with, "In our unit, you will produce . . . while I will do my own research on . . ." More than a few of my students don't "get it" in their first or second attempts. But here are a few snatches from the latest batch of drafts:

From a unit on Toni Morrison and the social construction of identity, by Meghan Owens:

> Hi everybody! Do any of you think that you act a certain way just because, for example, you are a *cheerleader,* or a part of the *drama club,* or live in a *specific part of town?* Do personality characteristics come to mind when I give the labels of *band geek* or *prom king?* What about if I just gave the categories of *Asian, Black, White, Mixed,* or *Hispanic?* Are there dominant stereotypes inscribed in your mind for each of these groups?

From "The U.S. Government and the Electoral Process," by Thomas Sallee:

> I am looking forward to doing this unit with you because I believe that one of our greatest responsibilities is to act on behalf of each other as citizens of our country. I have done this, in the past, by swearing an oath to support and defend the Constitution of the United States. As a young college graduate, I earned a commission in the United States Marine Corps and swore to defend our country. For four years I served in uniform to protect the rights of other citizens, and I was called to war in Iraq. However, not all citizenship responsibilities are this dramatic. . . . I get discouraged when I vote and it seems to make no difference—sometimes I wonder why I even bother. I want to take a close look at politics in this country and see if there really is anything worthy of my time as a citizen.

From a unit on Chaucer by Anthony Erevia:

How do you pass the time on a long trip? Do you allow yourself to be open to other ideas when you are thrown together with people outside of your own social or family circle? Besides talking about yourself, how would you let other people know the kind of person you are? These are some of the questions we will be tackling as we discover a new author, a new unit, and a new device for storytelling. In fourteenth-century England, Geoffrey Chaucer wrote *The Canterbury Tales*, a collection of short stories told by twenty-nine people who have gathered together to take a pilgrimage from Southwark, England, to Canterbury, to seek inspiration from someone they called "the holy blissful martyr."

From a unit on the poetry of Maya Angelou, by Marcelle Irvine:

When I was a teenager, I hated poetry. It was not until I was an adult that I went back and found that I could really appreciate it. I hated poetry as a teenager because I never had a teacher who effectively taught poetry to me. It was never fun or engaging. Poetry was obscure, boring, something I just had to get through. My goal is to make sure that you do not have the same experience that I did. I want you to understand the many beautiful complexities of poetry. I want you to see the music in the words, and learn how to find your own voice. I want you to discover the importance of being able to express yourself, your "inner voice," through the art of poetry and music.

Introductory letters to students are followed by what I call hook questions, which I describe in detail in *The Passionate Teacher*. Here is a sampling from some of the units just described:

- "What are some of the different labels we apply to people in this classroom, school, and neighborhood? Do we treat each other differently based on these labels?" (Meghan Owens)
- "If you could elect absolutely anyone as president of the United States, who would it be—and why?" (Thomas Sallee)

- "In your opinion, what *is* poetry? Why should anyone care about, or write, poetry? Would someone like *you* ever write poetry—or is it only for the 'literary' types?" (Ilsa Bruer)
- "What can your family teach you about the past—that no textbook could?" (Andrew Sullivan)
- "Have you ever felt pulled in different directions by parents, other family members, or friends? What did you do about this—and how did it make you feel?" (Megan Flatley)
- "What would you do if, at your age right now, you were asked to go and fight for your country?" (Brian Caromile)
- "When might you be willing to take the risk of befriending an unpopular kid in school? What's the difference between everyone being *equal* and everyone being *the same*?" (Ashot Gheridian)

There's nothing revolutionary about any of these units or questions—teachers address students in this manner daily in thousands of classrooms. But for new teachers, such a stance lets students know, right off the bat, that their teachers also are curious and not necessarily convinced that what we are teaching them is "the truth" or "a classic." We want to engage them in a mutually respectful conversation based more on the fact that we share the title of "learner" with them, despite our responsibility as teachers to hand out grades when the unit is over and done with.

Criticizing What We Love: Another Aspect of Stance

One pattern discernable in a number of my students' unit plans is that they, as teachers, maintain a critical posture with respect to the material they are presenting. Even, or especially, when the material in our unit is something we really love—that author or poet who really speaks to us; that era of history full of implications for the social justice issues of today; intricacies of math or physics that still have the power to furrow our brows with delightful perplexity—we owe it to our students to adopt a critical posture, to raise questions about the importance or validity of our chosen topic.

What if we invite our students to grapple with our skepticism, rather than our enthusiasm? What if we adopt a stance that says,

> Here is a topic [or text or issue] that gets taught year after year [or that our department thinks we ought to introduce in your grade]. But I'm not sure we ought to teach it. It *may* be valuable or important, or it may be a waste of time. But we'll never know unless we scope it out, take it apart, subject it to our own critical analysis.
>
> And then, when we've come up with reasons to argue our case for or against learning this material, we'll present our findings to the department. We'll tell them that as *experts* in how *students like us* react to *material like this*, we suggest an alternative topic or approach. We think that next year's students should have a choice between this and some other topic, or that the school should drop this material even if we've nothing better to replace it with, so we can spend more time on another unit we had to rush through in order to get to this one.

We don't have to fake it. We need only remind ourselves that wherever students feel overwhelmed by their teacher's commitment to a given topic, student interest and commitment to that topic may weaken, often fatally. A healthy skepticism toward even those topics to which we're most loyal or committed is likely to spark student interest. It smells like freedom to them. They get to use their minds in a critical way, with their teacher acting as their coach (even while secretly hoping they will end up appreciating the topic).

At the point when we believe our students truly own their own views on the material, we may opt to show our true colors, because they now have enough of a stake in the topic to push back. We can say,

> Okay, you've all pretty much agreed to recommend to the department that they dump [topic, text, issue X] for the students who come after you. That's fine. I've invited the department chair [or a couple

> of my colleagues, or both] to come in tomorrow to hear you defend that position. You probably think future kids in this class will owe you a huge debt of gratitude. But first, let's see how discerning you are about *my* opinions. On the slips of paper I've handed out, I want you to anonymously write down what you believe is my true idea of the value of this topic, and what my reasons might be. Then let's compare notes.

Some might find such an approach manipulative or less than candid, but I beg to differ. My purpose is not to have us play tricks on our students in order to tease more effort out of them but to reduce the power differential between us as we engage in intellectual work. We teachers begin with most of the power: it's our role to tell them what they have to learn, and at this point in their school careers they are at least pretending to like it, finding ways of giving us back our own views of the subject. This power differential and the practices that come with it foster the Game of School. Authentic learning earns its name largely because it occurs in contexts that are comparatively free of teacher coercion or student grade-grubbing.

We get from here to there when we reduce the power differential between our students and ourselves by not only engaging them in authentic learning activities but also by taking our opinions off the table while our students are forming and defending their own.

I suspect that as students, parents, and teachers—*learners*, the lot of us—we get from here to there not so much by means of a comprehensive five- or nine-point "strategy" as by a combination of observation, instinct, and stance:

- *Observation.* We train ourselves to notice those instances when the learners around us (including us) truly buy in to the value of what we are learning, when the powerful forces of curiosity, exploration, and conversation indicate that the mind and the spirit are alert to the challenge of ideas.
- *Instinct.* We get into the habit of intuiting when these same learners (again, including us) have closed down a vital part of

their creative imaginations and are more or less going through the motions in order to put the task behind us. That's where we stop. We call a halt and deliberately change direction while at the same time reminding us all that our goal is *learning*.

- *Stance*. We promote such engagement by acting as coaches of our students' thoughtfulness, intellectual freedom, and creative risk taking. We let our passions serve our students' initiative, rather than overwhelm them.

To further illustrate the usefulness of these attributes, I invite you to sit in on a conversation I had recently with a young woman who represents, in my mind, this very combination of observation, instinct, and stance. Jenny O'Neil, who hails from Indiana, contacted me because she had read *The Passionate Teacher* in a course at Earlham College and has been attempting to put its philosophy into practice during her three years in the City Year program in Boston. But it is I who have been learning from her.

~ Interlude ~

Jenny O'Neil and City Year: Building a Beloved Community

Four years ago, fresh from her undergraduate work at Earlham College in Indiana, Jenny O'Neil joined the City Year program as a corps member. It is normally a one-year commitment. Jenny has been in City Year since 2001. After a year as a corps member, working in a middle school in Roslindale, she became a program manager of ten new corps members and now directs training for all 160 members, 100 of whom are in fifteen of Boston's most troubled middle schools. This year's corps consists of 60 percent urban folks, 40 percent from the suburbs. Two-fifths are college graduates; one-fifth have some college; another fifth have their high school diplomas; and the last fifth are working on their GEDs. Each corps member spends more than forty-five hours a week on the job. If Jenny O'Neil cannot make a convincing case that authentic learning can flourish in even our most troubled urban settings, then our cause may be without hope. Here's what she has to say:

When we first began to work in middle schools, here in Boston, we were focused on a literacy program for grades 3 through 8. It was supposed to be really cool for kids. But what they asked us to deliver was a random list of ideas they had come up with that they wanted us to get kids writing about, with topics like the United Nations Rights of Children, or Tibetan prayer flags. The folks organizing the initiative thought they could connect their topics to issues here at home, such as the "Peace Poles" erected locally to mark sites where there had been a shooting—symbols of the hope for peace and tranquility among people, similar to the Tibetan flags. They saw two communities, on opposite sides of the world, each voicing the same plea. The people developing the literacy program were really excited, but they had forgotten to involve the kids. So instead of using these preset topics, I decided to go back to some ideas that begin with the kids themselves—their perspectives, their experiences. And it was from this stance that we created the Building the Beloved Community (BBC) program.

This past summer, I faced a somewhat similar situation, working now as a trainer. One hundred sixty new corps members, seventeen to twenty-four years old, were coming into City Year, but we had no idea what their experience in school had been prior to coming to us. We had just one month before school started in September to turn them into teachers. So I decided that we should aim at something the kids would want to talk about, which is their own lives and their own communities. Instead of us trying to pass some information on to them, our focus would be on getting these young students to begin seeing themselves as active people, capable of doing something about an idea or issue they knew something about. But even that seemed too abstract.

A Model Bedroom, Complete with Swimming Pool and Car-Shaped Bed

What we did was to start off by having our corps members talk to the third through eighth graders about the kids' personal lives. Our purpose was literacy, but first we had to hook the kids. We asked the fourth graders, for example, "If you could design your ideal room, at home, what would it look like?" We actually remained faithful to the state curriculum requirement that students make dioramas in fourth grade, but instead of them making one about a book that they had been required to read, they began making dioramas about a part of their lives they wanted to improve upon. And they came up with these ornate rooms: "My bedroom has a swimming pool, and my bed is shaped just like a car," was a typical response. The dioramas were great; the kids were using their fine motor skills but applying them to something they cared about that was *theirs*. They spent three days completing the dioramas—the kids were so into it.

And then we said, "Okay, now that we know something about who you are, let's find out about your families. What songs did your mother sing to you?" And we wrote song lyrics based on that. And so it went. We asked questions that made a gradual transition from the kids' personal lives to the broader community that surrounds them. We asked, "If you could have anyone's eyes, ears, mouth, and nose, whose would you have? If you could have the ears of someone who has heard *amazing* things, or could have the eyes of someone in history who has *seen* amazing things—whose eyes would they be, and why? If you could have the mouth of someone who has made really great speeches . . ." And the kids really took off on those questions. They said things like, "I would have my grandmother's eyes, because she has seen three generations grow up." "I would have Mariah Carey's mouth, because she's the first biracial woman ever to really make it big in the world." They could identify the eyes and ears and voice they wanted to have from what they had experienced or heard about out in the world.

Mapping a Community of Support

Then we asked them, "Okay, let's talk about your day. If you could trace how you spend a typical day, what would that look like?" And we made maps that traced the routes they typically take. We might have a kid who wakes up in Mattapan, goes to school in Hyde Park on a bus, passing through Dorchester and Roslindale and Mission Hill. That's a long day for a kid. But just because they don't stay in one neighborhood doesn't mean that they're not "in the community." And we go on to ask, "Who in your life, throughout your day, has helped support you, has made you feel that you belong? Who are people you see every single day, who are part of *your* community, whom you *know* would notice you if you were gone?" In response, the kids mentioned the lady who drives the bus, the guy at the bodega down the street where they get juice and a snack. These are the people that kids knew would have to be around in order for their day to be successful. And so that kind of allowed them to help fill out a picture of their community.

Starting from there, we are finding that the possibilities are endless, because we've demonstrated to the kids that *we* are not trying to tell them who *they* are, that we want to know what's important to *them,* who's engaging them, what their ideal life is like. And we've respected them by allowing them to identify who their community is. It's not what usually happens when teachers bring forth a list of who they think is important—the doctors and judges and city officials. We discover that Mr. Garcia at the bodega is just as significant as Principal Delgado, in terms of being there for you.

And that has allowed us to do so many different things—to have conversations with the kids that begin, "So, that's your community? Well, tell me what you see there." And we talk about what keeps kids safe; we have them write up brochures for other kids on how to find what they need when they need it: "Here are all the places you can go if you need food; here is where kids can go to get medical care"—*they* made up those lists.

Building a Beloved Community

Initially, as I said, the focus was solely on literacy. I just knew intuitively, my first year, that I couldn't deliver the program handed to me, so I said, "Let me try *this.*" And it had worked. So I thought, *If it worked for me, let me try to have other corps members do it.* So in my second year in City Year, I changed my focus from literacy to learning habits for kids.

We don't have enough time to train our incoming corps members on how to be literacy tutors for kids. Anyway, it's more important for them to be role models for kids than to make them recognize what a homonym is. In the one month we have, we can train these new corps members—a number of whom lack their high school diplomas—in how to respect a child and discover together what that child's world is. That, we can do.

So, in 2002–2003, our entire program changed to BBC—Building a Beloved Community, after Dr. King's famous speech. And it was really rough at first. I never anticipated how hard it would be to write a curriculum for somebody else. I was now a program manager, directly in charge of a team of ten new corps members—but they asked me to develop the BBC program for six such teams. It was *so hard* to adapt my own lesson plans so that other people could use them!

How I failed to serve my corps members, in the first year I took over, was that I didn't really think about how *they,* the corps members, needed to be engaged in order to do the job right. Previously, my task was to write up something that I would implement the next day; now I had to write down all the specifics so that others could deliver it, and at each of the grade levels. I was sure that because *I* had done it, and it had worked out well, it would be good. But when I started to observe classes, I found myself asking, "Why is the same thing happening to these new corps members that had first happened to me with the preset literacy initiative? Why are the kids trying to get out of doing these great lessons I designed?" And I realized that I hadn't invested my corps members in it.

Then I had to do a lot of serious thinking: *Why don't the corps members care about this the way I do?* I had to assess how I had trained them and what was taking place in their classrooms. I traveled around, looking at the way corps members were teaching, and I began to ask them, "What do you like in this neighborhood, so far?" In Jamaica Plain, very near one of the really roughest middle schools, there's this fantastic bakery that sells these *unbelievable* Mexican desserts. There's a pizza shop called Imagine Pizza that's really incredible. And I asked the corps members, "Have you done your laundry here? Have you read the local newspaper? Because if you're going to *teach* about this community, then you have to *care* about this community *before* you can teach about it."

My visits showed me why I had failed my corps members, at first. I hadn't shown them how to love what they were teaching about, so they couldn't show that excitement to the kids. By my second year of running the BBC program I had learned my lesson. The *first* thing I did with my new corps members was to send them out to the community. They had a kind of scavenger hunt to find a bunch of things out in the community: What's the best spot from which to see the ocean? Where do you get the cheapest and best haircut? It was then up to *them* to design the lessons. I took a cue from Deborah Meier, that the best lessons are a combination of kindergarten and graduate school, and I started teaching them how to present the curriculum to the kids by my doing the curriculum with *them*—the corps members did the arts and crafts projects, the explorations. So by the time they got to teaching the kids, they knew how to feel comfortable, and they liked what they were talking about. That made finding a way for them to really connect to the students much, much easier.

"You Get My Class Too Riled Up"

The corps members talk to each other about the lessons, with the kids looking on, and then they step back and invite the kids to do the lesson. There's a real buzz in the room. And that's the number one criticism we get from their teachers: "You get my class too loud, too riled up." In schools where that kind of energy level is just not feasible—such as a school without classroom walls, where the sound really travels—a few corps members came up with an exercise we call a Readiness Check. We let them stomp out the energy, first. We check all the parts of the body (since we say you have to have all the parts of your body involved)—so we begin with a "feet check"; we do exercises to get our fingers moving; we stretch our necks. We've got these kids *moving,* however quietly, so that if they're not allowed to make too much noise, there are ways to modify the game and still make it engaging. We realize we cannot change a school. What we can change is how we get the kids engaged, under almost any circumstances.

Coda

A Lesson Before Teaching

As a teacher of teachers-to-be, I often experience melancholy as my students head off for student teaching and the world beyond. In this I am like every other teacher; I worry that I haven't quite reached them, haven't yet persuaded them of what I have wanted most to convey: that passionate teaching and authentic learning are worth going all out for, taking big risks for, betting the house on, so to speak.

My biggest fear is that the tentacles of the Game of School are already so well wrapped around them that they will be pulled from pursuing authentic learning even as they apply themselves energetically—even idealistically—to their students. I worry that my best arguments won't inoculate them against the notion that being a teacher consists, in the main, of making a good-faith effort to get reluctant kids to do their work, or to cover the state curriculum frameworks, or to match their lesson plans to the unique learning styles of diverse children. "Love for learning" sounds okay, but it's not something to count on. (And who knows how to measure it?)

It's not that I reject those more conventional goals; I just want *more*, and like teachers everywhere, I face the likelihood that I may never get that "more" from the majority of my students. Even when I invite someone like Heidi Thomas or Melanie Livingston into my seminar, as living proof that authentic learning works with even at-risk kids, my preservice teachers are apt to conclude, "I probably won't ever be *that* good, so I'd better play it safe and not stick my neck out quite that far, at least until I'm sure I can do the job I've been hired to do." And how can I blame them for that?

So here's what I really want to say to teachers everywhere: the Game of School may seem pervasive, but it's also a wobbly tyrant, vulnerable to the onslaught of any group of kids with active minds who are fired up to do their own learning. We *can* break out of the habits and patterns that confine us to the Game and open up new possibilities for teaching and learning. But we can only do so *with our kids as partners in the struggle*. Our students have to want it, too.

And the kids have to trust that when we strive, together, for excellence; when we go into battle against the prevailing forces of mediocrity or the racism of low expectations, we won't dominate or manipulate them. We'll open some pathways and develop strategies to counter some of the obstacles facing our students, so that they will view those obstacles as struggles they believe they can win. As teachers, we'll show them how to access books, films, and living role models from the community, so that they need not be shackled to boring textbooks or worksheets. But we won't patronize them or complain that we too are powerless pawns of the system. We'll make the plans and outline the challenges, but it is they who will do the real intellectual work, for it is only they who can make the learning *authentic*.

The Game Can Be Made to Disappear—but It Can Also Come Roaring Back

The really good news, as I see it, is that whereas the Game of School has a stranglehold on learning in schools and colleges everywhere, and even though so many of our kids seem to have tacitly accepted the idea that thinking deeply, searching for the truth, and acting on principle are values reserved for their lives outside of school, this Game is a fragile bully. It quickly folds its tent when confronted by authenticity. When a genuine learning situation presents itself, one that ignites the imagination, sets loose the curiosity, and taps into the energy of young minds, the Game melts like the Wicked Witch of the West. It cannot withstand the power of a really good question or the vitality of a creative performance to raise kids' eyes above the narrow horizon of business as usual. As David Ervin says, when working with diverse kids on a musical play they've created on a controversial topic, "I try to help kids show themselves how society might be."

But, sadly, the obverse is also true. If the Game is vulnerable, so also is authentic learning. If curiosity can drive the Game into a corner, then kids' frustrations or boredom or the imposition by adults of arbitrary power can quickly restore its potency. Our students will shrink back from their most ambitious learning endeavors if they suspect that we, their teachers, don't really support them, won't allow them the time or resources they need, or won't stick up for them if other powerful persons in the school or community question the value of their learning endeavors.

It All Comes Down to *Stance*

So before you enter the unavoidable chaos of that first classroom; before you are thrown into the fray of a hostile or just very trying group of kids, with perhaps your survival as a teacher at stake; before you set foot in that strangely subdued honors class, where the students sit so passively, awaiting orders and expecting A's in return—think about who you are and what you are passionate about, and try to resolve to stay true to that core, regardless of what's ahead in those first few weeks and months or even years of teaching.

If your stance is to first gain a firm sense of control, to make it clear who's boss (in preparation for loosening up and showing your students your softer side once they've gotten themselves under control)—then *do what you must do:* establish your leadership, pounce on the first miscreants who challenge your authority or disrespect your person. But never lose the twinkle in your eye, the lightness of your step, the sense of humor that rides in tandem with your sense of purpose. And hold on to the resolve that you and these kids are destined to do great things together.

If your stance is to approach your students candidly as a new teacher with much to learn, to engage them in dialogue, to ask them to tell you about themselves, their strengths, needs, preferences, and dreams (while telling them enough about yourself to arouse their interest and curiosity, if not their immediate respect)—then *do what you must do:* announce your openness to dialogue, to compromise, to give-and-take. But never lose the fierceness of your commitment to quality, or your pride in excellence of performance, or the fires of your aversion to mediocrity and the passive compliance with the Game. And hold on to the resolve that you and these kids are destined to do great things together.

If your stance is to lead with your devotion to your academic subject, to lay out clearly and forthrightly what you see as the real challenges that the material will present, to go over the syllabus in detail and make sure no student is confused about what they will be dealing with, or what your expectations and deadlines are regarding their competent execution of assignments (hoping all the while that they will acquire, by osmosis or by hard work, some of your passion for this subject)—then *do what you must do:* immerse them in the material, clarify your ground rules, lay out the schedule of the work ahead and the grading system that goes with it. But never lose your sensitivity to your students as people who are striving to make sense of the world, who are buffeted by the powerful and contradictory influences on their lives, who may well be more drawn to subjects other than yours, to ways of being and becoming in which your academic discipline may connect obliquely, if at all. And hold on to the resolve that you and these kids are destined to do great things together.

Passionate teaching and authentic learning are not dependent on only one pedagogical approach. They are not beholden to a narrow theoretical view of education. But they do require that we adopt a stance that supports our students, emotionally and intellectually, as we invite them to become partners in learning endeavors. We may not be able to *identify* with our students (their music, lifestyles, or social mannerisms belong to their generation), but we can accomplish much when we respect the quality of their minds and hearts—despite the bad habits and distorted horizons with which prior experiences of schooling may have left them.

If we adopt and hold on to our stance, the odds are pretty good that we can survive those bewildering first years of teaching with our values intact and our spirits high. We stand an excellent chance of convincing our colleagues, administrators, and our students' parents that we have the talent to do this most difficult job in these trying times and to help our students realize the potential for authentic learning with which their evolutionary heritage has endowed them.

Notes

Prelude

1. Sizer, Theodore, *Horace's Compromise* (2nd ed.), 1992a, p. 156.
2. Fried, Robert, *The Passionate Teacher,* 1995, p. 95.
3. Cushman, Kathleen, *Fires in the Bathroom*, 2003, p. iv.

Chapter One

1. See Fried, Robert, *The Passionate Learner,* 2001a, chap. 5, for a discussion of what parents can do to help children remain enthusiastic learners.
2. Quoted in Cushman, Kathleen, *Fires in the Bathroom*, 2003, p. 108.
3. Andres, student quoted in Cushman, 2003, p. 177.
4. Fried, 2001a, p. 2.
5. Mahogany, student quoted in Cushman, 2003, p. 126.
6. National Education Commission on Time and Learning, *Prisoners of Time*, 1994, p. 1.
7. Deborah Meier has said, on numerous occasions, that "children do what they see powerful adults around them doing, and they are unlikely to do what adults in their lives don't seem to want to do."
8. It is a theory of mine (as yet uninvestigated) that one of the positive aspects of home schooling is that parents are likely to be much more attuned to their children's pleas and concerns about how to make their learning more interesting, more appropriately

challenging. Children thus waste less time and continue to share responsibility, with their parent-teacher, for directing their own learning.

9. Sarason, Seymour, *And What Do YOU Mean by Learning?* 2004, p. viii.
10. Kohn, Alfie, "Students Don't 'Work'—They Learn," 1997, p. 60.
11. Quoted in Cushman, 2003, p. 109.
12. Quoted in Cushman, 2003, p. 108.
13. I am indebted to my brother, Richard Fried, for this insight.

Chapter Two

1. Glass, Ira, "Two Steps Back," broadcast Oct. 15, 2004.
2. Currie, Elliott, *The Road to Whatever,* 2005, pp. 192–194.
3. Currie, 2005, p. 213.
4. See Kohn, Alfie, "Only for My Kid," 1998.
5. Quoted in Cushman, Kathleen, *Fires in the Bathroom*, 2003, p. 163.
6. Winerip, Michael, "On Education: Lessons in the Fine Art of College Admissions," 2003, p. B9.
7. Quoted in Cushman, 2003, p. 131.
8. Fried, Justin, "Colby and the Liberal Arts," pp. 5–8.
9. See Kohn, Alfie, *Punished by Rewards*, 1993.
10. Quoted in Cushman, 2003, p. 101.

Chapter Three

1. Carson, Rachel, *The Sense of Wonder,* 1956, p. 52.
2. Carson, 1956, p. 18.
3. Carson, 1956, p. 22.
4. Carson, 1956, pp. 42–43.
5. Carson, 1956, p. 49.
6. Meier, Deborah, *The Power of Their Ideas*, 1995, pp. 3–4.
7. Sarason, Seymour, *The Predictable Failure of Educational Reform*, 1990, pp. 81–82.

8. Fried, Robert, *The Passionate Teacher* (2nd ed.), 2001b, pp. 30–44.
9. Fried, 2001b, pp. 30–44; see also the experience of Melissa Parent, pp. 277–300.
10. Smith, Frank, *The Book of Learning and Forgetting*, 1998.
11. Melanie Livingston's paper was published in *Teacher Education Quarterly*, Fall 2004, pp. 15–22.

Chapter Four

1. As Deborah Meier and others point out, those government officials who so earnestly push for mandatory testing of students decline to measure how the "rising test scores" they take so much pride in correlate with the intended outcomes of testing: graduation rates, success in college, and employer satisfaction. Likewise, they are mostly silent on whether the phenomenal cost of such testing, and the pushing aside of other learning activities to focus on test preparation, reflect a wise, efficient, or effective use of scarce resources.
2. Kohn, Alfie, "Students Don't 'Work'—They Learn," 1997, p. 60.
3. In *The Passionate Learner* (2001a, p. 199), I offer an exercise that asks teachers to select a course they currently teach, list the five most important long-term learning goals they have for their students (the ideas, concepts, and skills they most want their students to retain and apply after the course is over), and then compare this list with the five most important criteria that will determine a student's grade for that course (for example, tests and quizzes, homework completion, class participation, term papers and projects). The contrast between the two lists is usually dramatic and often shocking.
4. I adjusted this category after reading this response, so that it now includes students from a wider range of backgrounds and abilities who yet really enjoy the learning they pursue in and out of class.

Chapter Five

1. Bruner, Jerome, *Toward a Theory of Instruction*, 1968, p. 127.
2. Quoted in Cushman, Kathleen, *Fires in the Bathroom*, 2003, pp. 4, 169.
3. Quoted in Cushman, 2003, p. 170.
4. Fried, Robert, *The Passionate Learner*, 2001a, chaps. 7 and 8. These chapters deal with ways that teachers and students can survey themselves on how well or how poorly a particular instructional unit engages them.
5. Bruner, 1968, pp. 150–151.
6. Kozol, Jonathan, *Savage Inequalities*, 1991, p. 46.
7. Quoted in Cushman, 2003, p. 106.
8. Quoted in Cushman, 2003, p. 125.
9. See Fried, Robert, *The Passionate Teacher* (2nd ed.), 2001b, chaps. 17 and 19, and Fried, 2001a, chaps. 13 and 14.
10. Darling-Hammond, Linda, *The Right to Learn*, 1997, p. 116.
11. Smith, Frank, *The Book of Learning and Forgetting*, 1998, p. 10.
12. Cushman, 2003, p. 122.
13. Quoted in Cushman, 2003, pp. 103–104.

Interlude: Nurturing Passionate Teachers

1. Fullan, Michael, *Change Forces*, 1993.
2. Schön, Donald, *Educating the Reflective Practitioner*, 1987.
3. Fried, Robert, *The Passionate Learner*, 2001a.
4. Guskey, Thomas, "High Percentages Are Not the Same as High Standards," 2001.
5. Meier, Deborah, *In Schools We Trust*, 2002.
6. Sizer, Theodore, *Horace's School*, 1992b.
7. Barth, Roland, *Learning by Heart*, 2001.
8. Bomer, Randy, *A Time for Meaning*, 1993; Burke, Jim, *Writing Reminders*, 2003.
9. Fried, Robert, *The Passionate Teacher* (2nd ed.), 2001b.

10. Goodrich-Andrade, Heidi, "Using Rubrics to Promote Thinking and Learning," 2000; Stiggins, Richard, *Student-Involved Classroom Assessment*, 2001; Wiggins, Grant, *Educative Assessment*, 1998.
11. Guskey, Thomas, "How Classroom Assessments Improve Learning," 2003.
12. Guskey, 2003.
13. Barth, 2001; Fullan, Michael, *Change Forces: The Sequel*, 1999.

Chapter Six

1. Ira Glass's study of Cathy La Luz, a Chicago schoolteacher whom he had profiled ten years previously, details such a transformation in painful but realistic detail ("Two Steps Back," broadcast Oct. 15, 2004).
2. Glass, Oct. 16, 2004.
3. Sarason, Seymour, *You Are Thinking of Teaching?* 1993, pp. 129–138.

Chapter Seven

1. Dennis Littky has recently coauthored a book, *The Big Picture* (2004), which recounts his experiences.

Bibliography

Barth, R. *Learning by Heart*. San Francisco: Jossey-Bass, 2001.

Bomer, R. *A Time for Meaning*. Portsmouth, N.H.: Heinemann, 1993.

Bruner, J. *Toward a Theory of Instruction*. Cambridge, Mass.: Belknap Press, 1968.

Burke, J. *Writing Reminders*. Portsmouth, N.H.: Heinemann, 2003.

Carson, R. *The Sense of Wonder*. New York: HarperCollins, 1956.

Clinchy, E. *Transforming Public Education*. New York: Teachers College Press, 1996.

Clinchy, E. *Creating New Schools: How Small Schools Are Changing American Education*. New York: Teachers College Press, 2000.

Currie, E. *The Road to Whatever: Middle-Class Culture and the Crisis of Adolescence*. New York: Henry Holt, 2005.

Cushman, K. *Fires in the Bathroom: Advice for Teachers from High School Students*. New York: New Press, 2003.

Darling-Hammond, L. *The Right to Learn*. San Francisco: Jossey-Bass, 1997.

Duckworth, E. *The Having of Wonderful Ideas*. New York: Teachers College Press, 1996.

Fried, R. *The Passionate Teacher*. Boston: Beacon Press, 1995.

Fried, R. *The Passionate Learner*. Boston: Beacon Press, 2001a.

Fried, R. *The Passionate Teacher*. (2nd ed.) Boston: Beacon Press, 2001b.

Fullan, M. *Change Forces*. Philadelphia: Falmer Press, 1993.

Fullan, M. *Change Forces: The Sequel*. Philadelphia: Falmer Press, 1999.

Glass, I. "Two Steps Back." *This American Life*, no. 275, broadcast Oct. 16, 2004. [http://www.thislife.org].

Goodrich-Andrade, H. "Using Rubrics to Promote Thinking and Learning." *Educational Leadership*, Feb. 2000, pp. 13–19.

Guskey, T. "High Percentages Are Not the Same as High Standards." *Phi Delta Kappan*, Mar. 2001, pp. 534–536.

Guskey, T. "How Classroom Assessments Improve Learning." *Educational Leadership*, Feb. 2003, pp. 6–11.

Kohn, A. *Punished by Rewards*. Boston: Houghton Mifflin, 1993.

Kohn, A. "Students Don't 'Work'—They Learn: Our Use of Workplace Metaphors May Compromise the Essence of Schooling." *Education Week*, September 3, 1997, pp. 43, 60.

Kohn, A. "Only for My Kid." *Phi Delta Kappan*, Apr. 1998, pp. 568–577.

Kohn, A. *The Schools Our Children Deserve*. Boston: Houghton Mifflin, 1999.

Kozol, J. *Savage Inequalities*. New York: Crown, 1991.

Littky, D. *The Big Picture: Education Is Everyone's Business*. Alexandria, Va.: Association for Supervision and Curriculum Development, 2004.

Meier, D. *The Power of Their Ideas*. Boston: Beacon Press, 1995.

Meier, D. *In Schools We Trust*. Boston: Beacon Press, 2002.

National Education Commission on Time and Learning. *Prisoners of Time*. Washington, D.C.: U.S. Government Printing Office, 1994.

Sarason, S. *The Predictable Failure of Educational Reform: Can We Change Course Before It's Too Late?* San Francisco: Jossey-Bass, 1990.

Sarason, S. *You Are Thinking of Teaching? Opportunities, Problems, Realities*. San Francisco: Jossey-Bass, 1993.

Sarason, S. *Parental Involvement and the Political Principle: Why the Existing Governance Structure of Schools Should Be Abolished*. San Francisco: Jossey-Bass, 1995.

Sarason, S. *Revisiting "The Culture of the School and the Problem of Change."* New York: Teachers College Press, 1996.

Sarason, S. *Teaching as a Performing Art*. New York: Teachers College Press, 1999.

Sarason, S. *And What Do YOU Mean by Learning?* Portsmouth, N.H.: Heinemann, 2004.

Schön, D. *Educating the Reflective Practitioner: Toward a New Design for Teaching and Learning in the Professions*. San Francisco: Jossey-Bass, 1987.

Sizer, T. *Horace's Compromise*. (2nd ed.) Boston: Houghton Mifflin, 1992a.

Sizer, T. *Horace's School*. Boston: Houghton Mifflin, 1992b.

Smith, F. *The Book of Learning and Forgetting*. New York: Teachers College Press, 1998.

Stiggins, R. *Student-Involved Classroom Assessment*. Upper Saddle River, N.J.: Prentice Hall, 2001.

Wiggins, G. *Educative Assessment*. San Francisco: Jossey-Bass, 1998.

Winerip, M. "On Education: Lessons in the Fine Art of College Admissions." *New York Times*, Oct. 22, 2003, p. B9.

Index

About the Author

Robert L. Fried is associate professor of education at Northeastern University, in Boston. He is the author of *The Passionate Teacher* and *The Passionate Learner* (Beacon Press), as well as *The Skeptical Visionary: A Seymour Sarason Educational Reader* (Temple University Press). A frequent speaker on campuses and at conferences both in the United States and abroad, Fried also works with schools and school districts interested in passionate teaching and authentic learning. He lives in Concord, New Hampshire, with his wife, Patricia Wilczynski.

Acknowledgments

There are a number of people who have offered their wisdom and guidance throughout the process of my writing this book. The first who comes to mind is Deborah Meier, who has read the manuscript several times and offered most valuable assistance. Evans Clinchy and Seymour Sarason have also read drafts and lent me their encouragement, as have John Gunderson and Randy Wisehart. I am deeply indebted to Randy for his fine essay, which appears in the interlude following Chapter Five. I have borrowed much from Kathleen Cushman's *Fires in the Bathroom* and the voices of her high school student coauthors; I want to thank Kathleen for being so generous in allowing me to avail myself of quotations from her book.

My editor at Jossey-Bass, Lesley Iura, has been a most kind and patient recipient of the seemingly endless drafts and revisions with which I keep loading up her email "inbox." Lesley has provided me with early and continual encouragement for this book, as have other staff at Jossey-Bass. Only now can Lesley be certain she won't be receiving any more rewrites! The copyeditor, Michele D. Jones, has added much through her keen eye for punctuation, detail, and nuance. I felt as though she had truly read the book, not just examined it under a microscope.

To several classroom teachers I owe much; this book would be very much the poorer without their wonderful collaboration. Heidi Thomas, Melanie Livingston, and Ibrahim Al Qamari have each lent their wisdom to portions of the manuscript, as has Jenny O'Neil, whom I shall also call a teacher, as she does a wonderful job training and inspiring 160 corps members from City Year. Former teachers

Sharon Friesen and Pat Clifford brought me word of the application of some of my ideas to their work with teachers in Calgary, Alberta. (Sharon's story appears in Chapter Seven.)

Tyra Pickering (Muncie, Indiana), Alice Warner (Newport, Oregon), and Priya Sundaravalli (Auroville, India) are high school teachers who shared Chapter Four of the book with their students, many of whom gave very thoughtful responses to my proposed categories of learners. These teachers also offered their own reflections on both my writing and on their students' response to it. I wish to thank those students whose words found their way into the book, including Tyra Pickering's students Tyler, Garrett, Wesley, and Rob; Alice Warner's students Tyler R., Tyler C., Zach, Alyssa, Walter S., Kyla M., Yvonne, Evan K., Tim G., and Ivy S.; and Priya Sundaravalli's students Tobia, Jonas, Guy, Arseny, Tae-Beck, and Mohini; thanks also to all their classmates who volunteered commentary and drawings. These students' views led me to significantly revise my descriptions of the seven categories.

My current and former students from Northeastern University have also played an essential role in the formation of this work, beginning with Elcira Delgado, whose reflection on the Game of School appears as the first interlude. Contributions of ideas, portions of student papers, and excerpts from curriculum units lend, I hope, some illustration of how I have attempted to integrate these notions into my own practice (as well as ample testimony that my students persist in having their own minds about these things). I will not mention them all here, as their contributions are acknowledged in the chapters in which they appear, but I am sincerely grateful for their diverse and considered opinions.

I am also indebted to my brother, Richard Fried, for his wise addition to Chapter One, and to his son, Justin Fried, for permission to excerpt his essay reflecting on his first year of college, which appears in Chapter Two.

Last, I wish to thank my wife, Pat Wilczynski, for lending me every possible support during the writing of this book and for putting up with me so uncomplainingly during my frequent mental absences during its inception and editing.

Family Matters

How Schools Can Cope with the Crisis in Childrearing

ROBERT EVANS

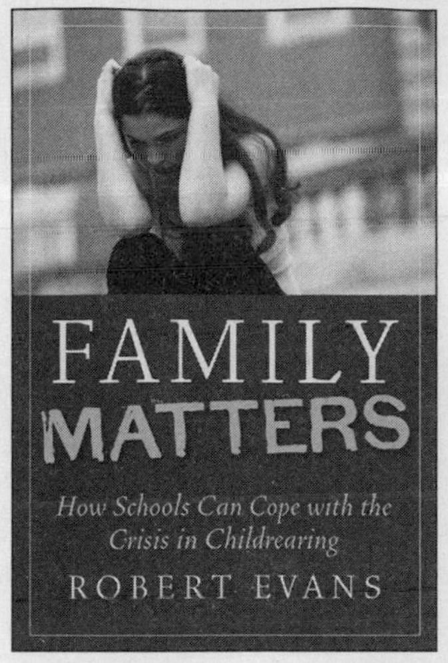

Cloth / ISBN: 0-7879-6656-8
www.josseybass.com

"In a brave and winning combination of information, analysis, anecdotes, and personal observations, Rob Evans makes a forthright, powerful case for renewed and respectful school-family collaboration on behalf of children."

—Theodore R. Sizer, *Coalition of Essential Schools*

In this provocative book, Robert Evans takes a sharp look at the enormous changes occurring among children and parents and the dilemma these changes pose for schools.

Students everywhere are harder to reach and teach, their attention and motivation less reliable, their language and behavior more provocative. This is largely because parents, suffering a widespread loss of confidence and competence, are increasingly anxious about their children's success, yet increasingly unable to support and guide them. And these parents are increasingly assertive and adversarial vis à vis the school. Examining these trends and their underlying causes, Evans calls for a combination of limits and leverage. At the policy level, we must rethink our notions of accountability, accepting the reality that schools cannot overcome all the forces that affect children's lives and learning. At the schoolhouse, educators can improve their impact by clarifying and asserting purpose (core values) and conduct (norms for behavior), and by becoming more appropriately parental vis à vis students and parents. Evans outlines concrete ways to implement these measures, and he closes with a reflection on ways to sustain hope and commitment in the face of unprecedented challenge.

Robert Evans is a clinical and organizational psychologist and the executive director of The Human Relations Service in Wellesley, Massachusetts. A former high school and preschool teacher, and a former child and family therapist, he has consulted in hundreds of public and private schools throughout the United States and internationally, working with teachers, administrators, and boards. His interests have focused on school change and resistance to it, on leadership, and on changes in families and their effect on schools. He is the author of many articles and the book *The Human Side of School Change* from Jossey-Bass. He lives near Boston with his wife, Paula.

Teaching with Fire

Poetry that Sustains the Courage to Teach

SAM M. INTRATOR AND MEGAN SCRIBNER

Cloth / ISBN: 0-7879-6970-2
www.josseybass.com

"Teaching with Fire *is a glorious collection of the poetry that has restored the faith of teachers in the highest, most transcendent values of their work with children . . . . Those who want us to believe that teaching is a technocratic and robotic skill devoid of art or joy or beauty need to read this powerful collection. So, for that matter, do we all.*"

—Jonathan Kozol, author of *Amazing Grace and Savage Inequalities*

Those of us who care about the young and their education must find ways to remember what teaching and learning are really about. We must find ways to keep our hearts alive as we serve our students. Poetry has the power to keep us vital and focused on what really matters in life and in schooling.

Teaching with Fire is a wonderful collection of eighty-eight poems from well-loved poets such as Walt Whitman, Langston Hughes, Billy Collins, Emily Dickinson, and Pablo Neruda. Each of these evocative poems is accompanied by a brief story from a teacher explaining the significance of the poem in his or her life's work. This beautiful book also includes an essay that describes how poetry can be used to grow both personally and professionally.

Teaching with Fire was written in partnership with the Center for Teacher Formation and the Bill & Melinda Gates Foundation. Royalties are used to fund scholarship opportunities for teachers to grow and learn.

Sam M. Intrator is assistant professor of education and child study at Smith College. He is a former high school teacher and administrator and the son of two public school teachers. He is the editor of *Stories of the Courage to Teach* and author of *Tuned In and Fired Up: How Teaching Can Inspire Real Learning in the Classroom*.

Megan Scribner is a freelance writer, editor, and program evaluator who has conducted research on what sustains and empowers the lives of teachers. She is the mother of two children and PTA president of their elementary school in Takoma Park, Maryland.

Guide to Operating Systems

Guide to Operating Systems

Fifth Edition

Greg Tomsho

Australia • Brazil • Mexico • Singapore • United Kingdom • United States

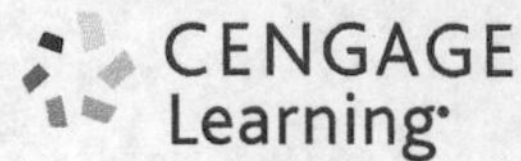

Guide to Operating Systems, 5th edition

Greg Tomsho

GM, Science, Technology, & Math: Balraj Kalsi

Senior Product Director, Computing: Kathleen McMahon

Product Team Manager: Kristin McNary

Associate Product Manager: Amy Savino

Director, Development: Julia Caballero

Content Development Manager, Computing: Leigh Hefferon

Managing Content Developer: Emma Newsom

Senior Content Developer: Natalie Pashoukos

Product Assistant: Abigail Pufpaff

Vice President, Marketing Services: Jennifer Ann Baker

Marketing Coordinator: Cassie Cloutier

Senior Content Project Manager: Brooke Greenhouse

Production Director: Patty Stephan

Art Director: Diana Graham

Cover Image(s): © iStock.com/xiaoke ma

Library of Congress Control Number: 2016942762

ISBN: 978-1-305-10764-9

Cengage Learning
20 Channel Center Street
Boston, MA 02210
USA

Cengage Learning is a leading provider of customized learning solutions with employees residing in nearly 40 different countries and sales in more than 125 countries around the world. Find your local representative at **www.cengage.com**.

Cengage Learning products are represented in Canada by Nelson Education, Ltd.

To learn more about Cengage Learning, visit **www.cengage.com**.

Purchase any of our products at your local college store or at our preferred online store **www.cengagebrain.com**.

Printed in the United States of America
Print Number: 02 Print Year: 2017

Brief Contents

Table of Contents

Introduction

If you use a computer, you also use a computer operating system to tap into the computer's power. The more you know about a computer's operating system, the more you are able to enjoy the full versatility of your computer. This book opens the door to understanding your computer's operating system. Also, the book enables you to understand many types of operating systems so you can compare the advantages of each for your personal and professional use.

In this book, you learn about the most popular operating systems in use today:

- Windows, with emphasis on Windows 10 and Windows Server 2012, and coverage of Windows Server 2016
- UNIX/Linux, with emphasis on Fedora 23
- Mac OS X, with emphasis on El Capitan

The book starts at a basic level and builds with each chapter to put you on track to become an accomplished user of each operating system.

You learn the operating systems in clear language through a hands-on, practical approach. An advantage of studying several operating systems is that you can compare the functions of each side-by-side as you learn. If you are taking an introductory operating systems course or an operating systems survey course, this book offers a strong foundation for mastering operating systems. Also, if you are preparing for one or more computer certifications, such as for hardware systems, networking, programming, or security, you'll find this book provides a vital background for your preparations. The book is particularly useful as background for the CompTIA A+ certification. If you are relatively new to computers, the book starts with the basics to build your confidence. If you are more experienced in computers, you'll find lots of useful information to further build your repertoire of knowledge and experience.

The Intended Audience

Guide to Operating Systems, Fifth Edition is written in straightforward language for anyone who uses a computer and wants to learn more. No prior computer experience is required, although some previous basic experience with a computer is helpful. The hands-on projects in this book use a variety of operating systems. You can learn the concepts if you have access to one or a combination of the operating systems presented. The more operating systems that are available to you, the better the opportunity to compare their features. For the most part, the projects can be performed in a classroom, computer lab, or at home.

What's New to this Edition

Guide to Operating Systems, Fifth Edition is extensively updated to include the most current operating systems and operating system features. This includes all-new coverage of Windows 10, Windows Server 2012, Windows Server 2016, Fedora Linux with the GNOME desktop, and Mac OS X El Capitan. Coverage of legacy operating systems is greatly reduced to provide mainly an historical perspective.

The book also includes extensive updates for new hardware and new operating system installation and management activities. New hardware coverage includes the latest CPUs and peripheral devices. The interaction of operating systems and new storage devices is also significantly updated, as well as new networking capabilities, including wireless networking advances and cloud computing. An entire chapter has been added for operating system virtualization, including VMware, Microsoft Hyper-V, and VirtualBox.

Screen captures, figures, and tables are virtually all new. The hands-on projects are fully updated or are all new for the new operating systems. A new end-of-chapter section called Challenge Labs gives readers one or more hands-on activities that require research and synthesis of information already learned.

Chapter Descriptions

The chapter coverage is balanced to give you a full range of information about each topic. The following is a summary of what you will learn in each chapter. Besides the instruction provided throughout the chapter text, you can build on your knowledge and review your progress using the extensive hands-on projects, challenge labs, case projects, key terms, and review questions at the end of each chapter.

- *Chapter 1: Operating Systems Fundamentals* gives you a basic introduction to operating systems, including the types of operating systems and how they work. You also learn about the history of operating systems.

- *Chapter 2: Popular Operating Systems* presents in-depth descriptions of modern Windows OSs, Linux and UNIX, and Mac OS X. You also briefly learn about earlier Microsoft operating systems. This chapter gives you a starting point from which to compare features of operating systems and to understand advancements in the latest versions.
- *Chapter 3: The Central Processing Unit (CPU)* enables you to understand how processors work and the essential characteristics of modern processors. The chapter concludes with an overview of popular modern processors.
- *Chapter 4: File Systems* explains the functions common to all file systems and then describes the specific file systems used by different operating systems, from a brief introduction to FAT to more in-depth coverage of NTFS, ufs/ext, HFS, and HFS+.
- *Chapter 5: Installing and Upgrading Operating Systems* shows you how to prepare for installing operating systems and then shows you how to install each operating system discussed in this book. You learn about installing operating systems from scratch and how to upgrade operating systems.
- *Chapter 6: Configuring Input and Output Devices* explains how devices such as monitors, keyboards, mice, disk drives, network cards, and other devices interface with operating systems. You learn about the latest input and output technologies for modern operating systems and computers.
- *Chapter 7: Using and Configuring Storage Devices* describes popular storage devices, including hard drives, removable drives, RAID, CD and DVD technologies, flash and solid-state drive storage, network storage, USB devices, and the latest emerging technologies. Storage device configuration is covered for the operating systems and you learn how to perform backups for Windows, UNIX/Linux, and Mac OS X operating systems.
- *Chapter 8: Virtualization and Cloud Computing Fundamentals* introduces you to virtualization, its terminology, and some of the popular virtualization products that can be used on the OSs this book discusses.
- *Chapter 9: Configuring a Network Connection* provides an introduction to how networks function, including network technologies and protocols. You learn how to configure protocols in each operating system and you learn about the basic structure of local and wide area networks. You also learn how operating systems interface with networks.
- *Chapter 10: Sharing Resources and Working with Accounts* shows you many ways to share resources through a network, including sharing disks, folders, and printers. Besides covering how to share resources, the chapter also discusses how to secure them through accounts, groups, and access privileges.
- *Chapter 11: Operating Systems Management and Maintenance* presents many techniques for maintaining systems, such as cleaning up unused files, defragmenting disks, making file system repairs, tuning virtual memory, and addressing problems. The chapter also addresses planning for backups and how to tune systems for top performance.
- *Appendix A: Operating System Command-Line Commands* shows you how to access the command line in each operating system and presents tables that summarize general and network commands. This appendix provides a place to quickly find or review the operating system commands.

Features

To aid you in fully understanding operating system concepts, there are many features in this book designed to improve its pedagogical value.

- **Chapter Objectives.** Each chapter in this book begins with a detailed list of the concepts to be mastered within that chapter. This list provides you with a quick reference to the contents of each chapter as well as a useful study aid.
- **Illustrations and Tables.** Numerous illustrations of operating system screens and concepts aid you in the visualization of common setup steps, theories, and concepts. In addition, many tables provide details and comparisons of both practical and theoretical information.
- ***From the Trenches* Stories and Examples.** Each chapter contains boxed text with examples from the author's extensive experience to add color through real-life situations.
- **Chapter Summaries.** Each chapter's text is followed by a summary of the concepts it has introduced. These summaries provide a helpful way to recap and revisit the ideas covered in each chapter.
- **Key Terms.** A listing of the terms that were introduced throughout the chapter, along with definitions, is presented at the end of each chapter.
- **Review Questions.** The end-of-chapter assessment begins with a set of review questions that reinforce the ideas introduced in each chapter.
- **Hands-On Projects.** The goal of this book is to provide you with the practical knowledge and skills to install and administer desktop and server operating systems as they are employed for personal and business use. To this end, along with theoretical explanations, each chapter provides numerous hands-on projects aimed at providing you with real-world implementation experience.
- **Critical Thinking Sections.** The end-of-chapter Critical Thinking section gives you more opportunities for hands-on practice with **Challenge Labs,** which enable you to use the knowledge you've gained from reading the chapter and performing hands-on projects to solve more complex problems without step-by-step instructions. This section also includes **Case Projects** that ask you to evaluate a scenario and decide on a course of action to propose a solution. These valuable tools help you sharpen decision-making, critical thinking, and troubleshooting skills.

Text and Graphic Conventions

Whenever appropriate, additional information and activities have been added to this book to help you better understand what is being discussed in the chapters. Icons throughout the text alert you to additional materials. The icons used in this textbook are as follows:

The Note icon is used to present additional helpful material related to the subject being described.

Tips are included from the author's experience to provide extra information about how to configure an operating system, apply a concept, or solve a problem.

Cautions are provided to help you anticipate potential problems or mistakes so you can prevent them from happening.

Each hands-on project in this book is preceded by the Hands-On Projects icon and a description of the practical exercise that follows.

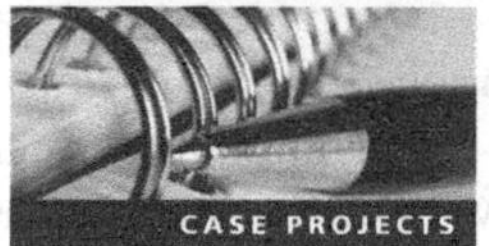

Case Project icons mark each case project. Case projects are more involved, scenario-based assignments. In each extensive case example, you are asked to implement what you have learned.

MindTap

MindTap for *Guide to Operating Systems* is an online learning solution designed to help students master the skills they need in today's workforce. Research shows that employers need critical thinkers, troubleshooters, and creative problem-solvers to stay relevant in our fast-paced, technology-driven world. MindTap helps users achieve this with assignments and activities that provide hands-on practice, real-life relevance, and mastery of difficult concepts. Students are guided through assignments that progress from basic knowledge and understanding to more challenging problems.

All MindTap activities and assignments are tied to learning objectives. The hands-on exercises provide real-life application and practice. Readings and "Whiteboard Shorts" support the lecture, while "In the News" assignments encourage students to stay current. Pre- and post-course assessments allow you to measure how much students have learned using analytics and reporting that makes it easy to see where the class stands in terms of progress, engagement, and completion rates. You can use the existing content and learning path or pick and choose how the material will wrap around your own content. You control what the students see and when they see it. Learn more at *www.cengage.com/mindtap/*.

Instructor Resources

Everything you need for your course in one place! This collection of book-specific lecture and class tools is available online via *www.cengage.com/login*. Access and download PowerPoint presentations, images, the Instructor's Manual, and more.

- *Electronic Instructor's Manual*—The Instructor's Manual that accompanies this book includes additional instructional material to assist in class preparation, including suggestions for classroom activities, discussion topics, and additional quiz questions.

- *Solutions*—The instructor's resources include solutions to all end-of-chapter material, including review questions and case projects.
- *Cengage Learning Testing Powered by Cognero*—This flexible, online system allows you to do the following:
  - Author, edit, and manage test bank content from multiple Cengage Learning solutions.
  - Create multiple test versions in an instant.
  - Deliver tests from your LMS, your classroom, or wherever you want.
- *PowerPoint presentations*—This book comes with Microsoft PowerPoint slides for each chapter. They're included as a teaching aid for classroom presentations, to make available to students on the network for chapter review, or to be printed for classroom distribution. Instructors, please feel free to add your own slides for additional topics you introduce to the class.
- *Figure files*—All the figures and tables in the book are reproduced in bitmap format. Similar to the PowerPoint presentations, they're included as a teaching aid for classroom presentations, to make available to students for review, or to be printed for classroom distribution.

About the Author

Greg Tomsho is director of the Computer Networking Technology Department and Cisco Academy at Yavapai College in Prescott, Arizona. He has earned the CCNA, MCTS, MCSA, A+, Network+, Security+, Server+, and Linux+ certifications. A former software engineer, technical support manager, and IT director, he has more than 30 years of computer and networking experience. His other books include *MCSA Guide to Installing and Configuring Microsoft Windows Server 2012/R2*; *MCSA Guide to Administering Microsoft Windows Server 2012/R2*; *MCSA Guide to Configuring Advanced Microsoft Windows Server 2012/R2 Services*; *MCTS Guide to Windows Server 2008 Active Directory Configuration*; *MCTS Guide to Microsoft Windows Server 2008 Applications Infrastructure Configuration*; *Guide to Networking Essentials*; *Guide to Network Support and Troubleshooting*; and *A+ CoursePrep ExamGuide*.

Acknowledgments

I would like to thank the team at Cengage Learning for this opportunity to improve and expand on the fifth edition of this book. This team includes Kristin McNary, Product Team Manager; Natalie Pashoukos, Senior Content Developer; Brooke Greenhouse, Senior Content Project Manager; and Serge Palladino, Nicole Spoto, and Danielle Shaw of Manuscript Quality Assurance, who tested projects for accuracy. Thanks also go to my development editor, Dan Seiter, for his guidance in creating a polished product. Additional praise and special thanks go to my beautiful wife, Julie; our daughters, Camille and Sophia; and our son, Michael. As always, they have been patient and supportive throughout the process and I truly appreciate their support.

Reviewers

Guy Garrett, M.S., M.B.A.
Associate Professor, Cybersecurity & Information Technology
Manager, Network Systems Technology/Cybersecurity Program
Gulf Coast State College
Panama City, FL

Emily Harrington
CIT Coordinator/Faculty
Pitt Community College
Winterville, NC

Todd Koonts, MSIT, CCE
Program Chair
CTI/Information Assurance and Digital Forensics
Central Piedmont Community College
Charlotte, NC

Before You Begin

The importance of a solid lab environment can't be overstated. This book contains hands-on projects that require a variety of operating systems, including Windows 10, Linux Fedora 23, and Mac OS X El Capitan. Using virtualization can simplify the lab environment. For example, you can use VMware Player, VMware Workstation, VirtualBox, and other products to install Windows and Linux in a virtual machine, regardless of the OS running on your physical computer. Installing Mac OS X in a virtual machine running on Windows requires some creativity, but it can be done. If you want to run El Capitan as a VMware virtual machine running on Windows, do a little Internet research on the topic. The following section lists the requirements for completing hands-on activities and challenge labs.

Lab Setup Guide

Most of the hands-on projects and challenge labs require a Windows 10, Linux Fedora 23, or Mac OS X El Capitan computer. The computers should have a connection to the Internet, but only a few of the activities actually require Internet access. The use of virtual machines is highly recommended.

Windows 10 Computers

- Windows 10 Enterprise or Education Edition is recommended, but other versions are acceptable
- An account that is a member of the local Administrators group
- Workgroup name: Using the default workgroup name ("Workgroup") is acceptable, but the name is not important
- Memory: 1 GB required, 2 GB or more recommended

- Hard disk 1: 60 GB or more (Windows installed on this drive)
- Hard disk 2: Unallocated 60 GB or more
- IP address via DHCP server or static if required on your network
- Internet access

Fedora 23 Computers

- Fedora 23 Linux locally installed (a live CD boot will work for some activities, but not all)
- An administrator account and access to the root password
- Memory: 1 GB
- Hard disk 1: 60 GB or more (Fedora 23 installed on this drive)
- Hard disk 2: 20 GB or more
- IP address via DHCP server or static if required on your network
- Internet access

Mac OS X Computers

- Mac OS X El Capitan
- An administrator account and access to the root password
- Memory: 1 GB
- Hard disk 1: 60 GB or more (Mac OS X El Capitan installed on this drive)
- IP address via DHCP server or static if required on your network
- Internet access

Additional Items

- Windows 10 installation media (DVD or .iso file)—Using an evaluation copy is acceptable. You can download evaluation copies of Windows from *www.microsoft.com/en-us/evalcenter/*
- Windows Server 2012 R2 installation media (DVD or .iso file)—Using an evaluation copy is acceptable
- Linux Fedora 23 installation media (DVD or .iso file)

chapter 1

Operating Systems Fundamentals

After reading this chapter and completing the exercises, you will be able to:

- Explain basic operating system concepts
- Understand the history of operating system development
- Discuss how operating systems work
- Describe the types of operating systems
- Discuss single tasking versus multitasking
- Differentiate between single-user and multiuser operating systems
- List and briefly describe current operating systems

Computers come in many and varied physical forms. There are supercomputers that perform complex computing tasks at incredible speeds, business servers that provide enterprise-level networked applications, desktop and laptop PCs, tablets, smartphones, and wearable computers. Plus, there are many devices you may not even think of as having a computer, such as those embedded in everyday devices like cars, televisions, and even dishwashers. Without an operating system, however, these devices are only a collection of electronic parts. It takes an operating system to turn a computer into a functioning device for work or play. The operating system is the software that starts the basic functions of a computer, displays documents on the computer's monitor, accesses the Internet, and runs applications—it transforms the computer into a powerful tool. There are many kinds of operating systems, but only a few have captured a wide audience. Server operating systems like Windows Server 2016 and UNIX run on network servers, and client operating systems like Windows 10, Mac OS X, and Ubuntu Linux run on desktop computers. Some operating systems are very specialized and rarely seen, such as those that run the electronics in a car. Others are ubiquitous, such as Android and iOS, which run mobile devices.

This book is your guide to the most popular operating systems. In the beginning chapters, you take an in-depth look at popular desktop or client operating systems: Windows 10, Windows 8.1, Windows 7, UNIX/Linux (particularly Linux), and Mac OS X El Capitan. Later in the book, you examine popular server operating systems: Windows Server 2016, Windows Server 2012, and UNIX/Linux. (Note that several distributions of Linux/UNIX can be either client or server operating systems.) This chapter sets the foundation for understanding desktop and server operating systems by introducing you to concepts that apply to most operating systems. With this knowledge under your belt, you will have a solid frame of reference to understand operating system specifics as they are discussed in later chapters.

About the Hands-On Projects

Be sure to read and complete the activities in the "Before You Begin" section of the Introduction. The Hands-On Projects in this book require that you first set up your lab environment so it is ready to go. The "Before You Begin" section gives you step-by-step instructions for the suggested lab configuration to use with all activities in this book.

Completing the Hands-On Projects is important because they contain information about operating systems that is best understood through hands-on experience. If for some reason you can't do some of the projects, you should at least read through each one to make sure you don't miss important information.

An Introduction to Operating Systems

Before we discuss how an operating system works, let's review the basic functions of any computer. A computer's functions and features can be broken down into the three basic tasks all computers perform: input, processing, and output. Information is input to a computer from a device such as a keyboard or from a storage device such as a hard drive; the central processing unit (CPU) processes the information, and then output is usually created. The following example illustrates the process:

- *Input*—A user running a word-processing program types the letter *A* on the keyboard, which results in sending a code to the computer representing the letter *A*.
- *Processing*—The computer's CPU determines what letter was typed by looking up the keyboard code in a table.
- *Output*—The CPU sends instructions to the graphics cards to display the letter *A*, which is then sent to the computer monitor.

The three functions described above involve some type of computer **hardware**, but the hardware is controlled and coordinated by the operating system. Without an operating system, every application you use would have to know the details of how to work with each of the hardware devices. Without the operating system to coordinate things, only one application could run at a time. So, you couldn't open a Web browser while working on a Word document, for example. The operating system can be seen as the go-between for the applications you run and the computer hardware.

In a nutshell, an **operating system (OS)** is a specialized computer program that provides the following features:

- *User interface*—The **user interface** provides a method for users to interact with the computer, usually with a keyboard and mouse or touch screen. A user clicks, touches, or types; the computer processes the input and provides some type of output.
- *File system*—The **file system** is the method by which an OS stores and organizes files and manages access to files on a storage device, such as a hard drive.
- *Processes and services*—A **process** is a program that's loaded into memory and run by the CPU. It can be an application a user interacts with, such as a word-processing program or a Web browser, or a program with no user interface that communicates with and provides services to other processes. This type of process is usually called a **service** in Windows and a *daemon* in Linux, and is said to run in the background because there's no user interface.
- *Kernel*—The **kernel** is the heart of the OS and runs with the highest priority. It schedules processes to run, making sure high-priority processes are taken care of first; manages memory to ensure that two applications don't attempt to use the same memory space; and makes sure I/O devices are accessed by only one process at a time, in addition to other tasks.

Each of the above OS components are discussed in more detail throughout this book. For now, let's look more closely at various types of OSs.

Desktop Versus Server Operating System

A **computer program** is a series of instructions executed by the computer's CPU. A computer program can be large and complex, like an operating system, or it can be small and fairly simple, such as a basic app running on a mobile device. What's special about an operating system program compared to an app is that the operating system is loaded when the computer is turned on and remains running until you turn the computer off. Its job is to make the computer useful so you can run apps, access the Internet, and communicate with other computers.

While there are many types of OSs, and they are designed for different purposes, this book focuses on desktop or client OSs, and server OSs. A **desktop operating system**, or *client operating system*, is typically installed on a personal computer (PC) that is used by one person at a time, and is almost always connected to a network, either wired or wirelessly. The hardware used with a client OS can be in several forms, such as:

- A full desktop computer consisting of separate components for the monitor, CPU box, keyboard, and mouse
- A portable or laptop unit that combines the monitor, CPU box, keyboard, and pointing device in an all-in-one device that is easy to carry
- A combination such as the iMac computer in which the monitor and CPU are in one unit with a separate keyboard and mouse
- A fourth category, often referred to as a 2-in-1, consists of a large tablet computer such as the iPad Pro or Microsoft Surface, along with a detachable keyboard

A **server operating system** is usually installed on a more powerful computer that typically has a wired connection to a network, and can act in many roles to enable multiple users to access information, such as e-mail, files, and software. The server hardware can also take different forms, including traditional server hardware, rack-mounted server hardware, and blade servers.

The traditional server, often used by small or medium-sized businesses, consists of a monitor, CPU box, keyboard, and mouse. **Rack-mounted servers** are CPU boxes mounted in racks that can hold multiple servers. Each rack-mounted server typically has its own power cord and network connection—but these servers often share one monitor and pointing device. Depending on the height of the rack and the height of the servers, one rack can hold a few servers or several dozen. **Blade servers** conserve even more space than rack-mounted servers; each blade server typically looks like a card that fits into a blade enclosure. The **blade enclosure** is a large box with a backplane that contains slots for blade servers; the box provides cooling fans, electrical power, connection to a shared monitor and pointing device, and even network connectivity, depending on the blade enclosure. A single blade enclosure can house over 100 blade servers. Medium-sized and large organizations use rack-mounted and blade servers to help conserve space and to consolidate server management.

Visit *www.hpe.com*, *www.dell.com*, or *www.supermicro.com* to view examples of traditional, rack-mounted, and blade servers. Also, note that the actual hardware design of rack-mounted and blade servers varies by manufacturer.

Modern desktop and server operating systems are designed to enable network communications so that the operating systems can communicate with one another over a network cable, through wireless communications, and through the Internet. Network communications enable sharing files, sharing printers, and sending e-mail.

Input and Output

One of the most basic tasks of an operating system is to take care of **input/output (I/O)** functions, which let other programs communicate with the computer hardware. The I/O functions take requests from the software the user runs (the application software) and translate them into low-level requests that the hardware can understand and carry out. In general, an operating system serves as an interface between application software and hardware, as shown in Figure 1-1. Operating systems perform the following I/O tasks:

- Handle input from the keyboard, mouse, and other input devices
- Handle output to the monitor and printer
- Manage network communications, such as for a local network and the Internet
- Control input/output for devices such as network interface cards
- Control information storage and retrieval using various types of storage media such as hard drives, flash drives, and DVDs
- Enable multimedia use for voice and video composition or reproduction, such as recording video from a camera or playing music through speakers

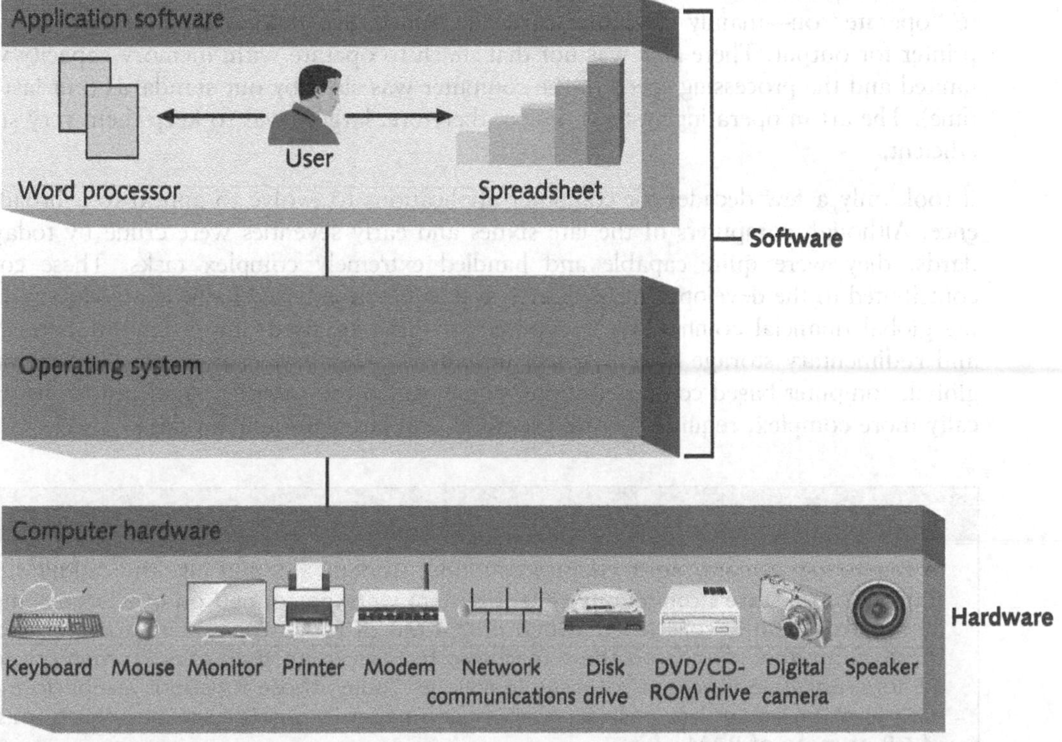

Figure 1-1 General tasks for all operating systems

A Short History of Operating Systems

The history of operating systems is a very elaborate subject. As a matter of fact, there are many books on this subject. This short history is not meant to be comprehensive; it merely presents enough background information to show how some of the features in modern PCs and PC operating systems developed.

Initially, computers were used as large automated calculators to solve all sorts of mathematical and statistical problems. Computers were extremely large, often taking up entire rooms. Although you can legitimately trace the history of today's digital computers back 100 years or more, no practical designs were used by significant numbers of people until the late 1950s. Scientists programmed these computers to perform precise tasks. The operating systems were rudimentary, often not able to do more than read punch cards or tape and write output to Teletype machines (machines resembling typewriters). A tape or deck of cards was loaded, a button was pushed on the machine to indicate the input was ready, and the machine started to read the tape and perform the operations requested. If all went well, the work was done and the output was generated. This output would be sent to the Teletype, and that was that.

Yes, there was computer history before this point, but it did not involve any sort of operating system. Any program that the computer ran had to include all logic to control the computer. Because this logic was rather complex, and not all scientists were computer scientists, the operating system was a tool that allowed non-computer scientists to use computers. The OS reduced programming work and increased efficiency. Obviously, there was not all that much to "operate" on—mainly the punch card and punch tape readers for input and the Teletype printer for output. There also was not that much to operate with; memory capacity was very limited and the processing speed of the computer was slow by our standards (but fast for that time). The art in operating systems design, therefore, largely was to keep them very small and efficient.

It took only a few decades for computer applications to evolve to appeal to a broader audience. Although computers of the late sixties and early seventies were crude by today's standards, they were quite capable and handled extremely complex tasks. These computers contributed to the development of space travel, submarine-based ballistic missiles, and a growing global financial community. Computers of this time used only a few kilobytes of RAM and rudimentary storage of only a few megabytes. This period also saw the beginning of a global, computer-based communications system called the *Internet*. Applications became logically more complex, requiring larger programs and large amounts of data.

From the Trenches ...

In the 1990s, student registration, accounting, student aid, and all other administrative functions in a state's community college system were performed on one large computer at each community college—that had only 4 MB of RAM. The system administrators of those computers considered these machines to have more than enough memory to run all administrative functions for a single college. Today, those functions are performed at each location on servers; each server is much smaller in physical size, and each uses tens of GB or more of RAM.

As always, necessity was the mother of invention. Input and output devices were created, and computer memory capacity and speed increased. With more devices to manage, operating systems became more complex and extensive, but the rule of thumb—small and fast—was still extremely important. This round of evolution, which really began to take off in the mid-seventies, included the display terminal, a Teletype machine with a keyboard that did not print on paper, but projected letters on a screen (commonly referred to as a *cathode ray tube* or *CRT*). The initial CRT was later followed by a terminal that could also show simple graphics; the terminal looked like an early computer, but it was only a monitor and a keyboard without a CPU or processing capability. The magnetic tape drive, used to store and retrieve data and programs on tape, could store more and was less operator intensive than paper tape. It was quickly followed by numerous manifestations of magnetic disks.

The next evolution was the ability to share computer resources among various programs. If a computer was very fast and could quickly switch among various programs, you could do several tasks seemingly at once and serve many people simultaneously. Some of the operating systems that evolved in this era are long lost to all but those who worked directly with them. However, there are some notable players that were responsible for setting the stage for the full-featured functionality we take for granted today. Digital Equipment Corporation's (DEC's) PDP series computers, for example, ran the DEC operating system, simply known as OS, in one version or another. A popular one was OS/8, which came in various versions, such as Release 3Q; OS/8 was released in 1968. PDP-8 computers were general-purpose machines that at one time were the top-selling computers across the world. The PDP series could also run Multics, which was the basis for the development of the first version of UNIX, a multiuser, multitasking operating system. (Multics is widely considered to be the first multiuser, multitasking operating system. You'll learn about multitasking later in the chapter.)

TIP

To find out more about the once popular PDP-8 computers, visit *www.cs.uiowa.edu/~jones/pdp8*.

The original UNIX was developed at AT&T Bell Labs in 1969 by Kenneth Thompson and Dennis Ritchie as an improvement on Multics. Later, DEC VAX computers used Virtual Memory System (VMS), a powerful, multitasking, multiuser operating system that was strong on networking. IBM mainframes made a series of operating systems popular, starting with GM-NAA I/O in the early sixties and later with System/360. Many others would follow, including CICS, which is still in use today.

Programming computers at this time was still a very complicated process best left to scientists. In the mid-1960s, right after the first interactive computer game was invented at the Massachusetts Institute of Technology (MIT), a simple programming language was developed at Dartmouth College, aimed at the nonprogrammer. It was dubbed **BASIC**, or **Beginner's All-purpose Symbolic Instruction Code**, and became a widely used programming language for many years to follow. A few years later, in 1975, Bill Gates discovered BASIC, and became interested enough to write a compiler for it. (A compiler is software that turns computer code written by people into code that is understood by computers.) Gates then sold the compiler to a company called Micro Instrumentation Telemetry Systems (MITS). MITS was the first company to produce a desktop computer that was widely accepted and could conduct useful work at the hands of any knowledgeable programmer. That same year, Gates dropped out of Harvard to dedicate his time to writing software. Other programming languages introduced around this time included Pascal, C, and other versions of BASIC supplied by various computer manufacturers. Only a couple of years later, Gates' new company (Microsoft) and others adapted popular mainframe and minicomputer programming languages, such as FORTRAN and COBOL, so they could be used on desktop computers. There were also proprietary languages that gained some popularity—languages primarily designed for database programming, for example—but they didn't last and aren't significant to this book.

The introduction of the microcomputer in the mid-1970s was probably the most exciting thing to happen to operating systems. These machines typically had many of the old restrictions, including slow speed and little memory. Many microcomputers came with a small operating system and Read-Only Memory (ROM) that did no more than provide an elementary screen, keyboard, printer, and disk input and output. Gates saw an opportunity and put together a team at Microsoft to adapt a fledging version of a new microcomputer operating system called *86-DOS*, which ran on a prototype of a new microcomputer being developed by IBM called the *personal computer*. 86-DOS was originally written by Tim Paterson (from Seattle Computer Products) as the Quick and Dirty Operating System (QDOS) for the new 8086 microprocessor. 86-DOS (or QDOS) evolved in 1980 through a cooperative effort between Paterson and Microsoft into the **Microsoft Disk Operating System**, or **MS-DOS**. MS-DOS was designed as a **command-line interface**, which means that users typed in commands instead of using the **graphical user interface (GUI)** point-and-click method that is common today.

The original MS-DOS did not offer a GUI desktop from which to click menus and icons. The command-line interface is available in modern Windows operating systems, as well as in Linux and Mac OS X. Some server administrators prefer to use a command-line interface because it offers more individualized and specialized control over the operating system. You'll have an opportunity to use command-line interfaces in Windows, Linux, and Mac OS X throughout the projects in this book.

MS-DOS became a runaway success for Microsoft, and it was the first widely distributed operating system for microcomputers that had to be loaded from disk or tape. There were earlier systems, including Control Program/Monitor (CP/M), that used some features and concepts of the existing UNIX operating system designs, but when IBM adopted MS-DOS for its PC (calling it PC DOS), the die was cast.

What did MS-DOS do? It provided the basic operating system functions described earlier in this chapter, and it was amazingly similar to what was used before on larger computers. It supported basic functions, such as keyboard, disk, and printer I/O—and communications. As time went on, more and more support functions were added, including support for such things as hard disks. Then along came the Apple Macintosh in 1984, with its GUI and mouse pointing device, which allowed users to interact with the operating system on a graphical screen. The mouse allowed users to point at or click icons or to select items from menus to accomplish tasks. Initially, Microsoft chose to wait on development of a GUI, but after Microsoft saw the successful reception of the interface on Apple computers, it developed one of its own.

When the Macintosh was introduced, it seemed light years ahead of the IBM PC. Its operating system came with a standard GUI at a time when MS-DOS was still based on entering text commands. Also, the Macintosh OS managed computer memory closely for the software, something MS-DOS did not do. And, because Mac OS managed all computer memory for the application programs, you could start several programs and switch among them. Mac OS was also years ahead in I/O functions such as printer management. In MS-DOS, a program had to provide its own drivers for I/O devices; MS-DOS provided only the most rudimentary interface. On Mac OS, many I/O functions were part of the operating system.

Microsoft, however, did not stay behind for long. In 1985, Microsoft shipped an extension to its DOS operating system, called Microsoft Windows, which provided a GUI and many of the same functions as Mac OS. The first Windows was really an operating "environment" running on top of MS-DOS, made to look like a single operating system. Today's Windows is no longer based on DOS and is a full-fledged operating system.

Although Apple was six years ahead of Microsoft in offering a friendly GUI-based OS, Apple ultimately fell well behind Microsoft in sales because it chose not to license the Mac OS to outside hardware vendors.

Numerous incarnations of operating systems have come and gone since those days. Today, both Windows and Mac OS X are very similar in what they can do and how they do it; they have a wealth of features and drivers that make the original DOS look elementary. Their principal functions are unchanged, however: to provide an interface between the application programs and hardware, and to provide a user interface for basic functions, such as file and disk management.

Let's review the important pieces of operating system development history. Although pre-1980s computing history is interesting, it doesn't hold much relevance to what we do with computers today. Tables 1-1 and 1-2 show the major milestones in operating system development. The tables summarize 8-, 16-, 32-, and 64-bit operating systems. In general, a 64-bit operating system is more powerful and faster than a 32-bit system, which is more powerful and faster than a 16-bit system, and so on. You will learn more about these differences in Chapter 2, "Popular Operating Systems," and Chapter 3, "Operating System Hardware Components."

Table 1-1 Operating system releases from 1968 to 1999

Operating system	Approximate date	Bits	Comments
UNIX (Bell/AT&T)	1968	8	First widely used multiuser, multitasking operating system for minicomputers.
CP/M	1975	8	First operating system that allowed serious business work on small personal computers. VisiCalc, a spreadsheet application released in 1978, was the first business calculation program for CP/M, and to a large extent made CP/M a success.
MS-DOS	1980	16	First operating system for the very successful IBM PC family of computers. Lotus 1-2-3 was to MS-DOS in 1981 what VisiCalc was to CP/M. Also in 1981, Microsoft introduced the first version of Word for the PC.

(continues)

Table 1-1 Operating system releases from 1968 to 1999 (*continued*)

Operating system	Approximate date	Bits	Comments
PC DOS	1981	16	IBM version of Microsoft MS-DOS.
Mac OS	1984	16	The first widely distributed operating system that was totally graphical in its user interface. Also, Mac OS introduced the use of a mouse to PC-based systems.
Mac System Software 5	1987	16	Mac OS implemented cooperative multitasking so that more than one application could be run at one time.
Mac System Software 6	1988	16	Mac OS was significantly stabilized and was also adapted to run on portable computers.
Windows 3.0	1990	16	First usable version of a graphical operating system for the PC.
Linux 0.01	1991	16	Linus Torvalds made the first version of Linux available through an FTP download site.
Mac System Software 7	1991	32	Mac OS was redesigned to have a new interface, more applications, and to use 32-bit addressing.
MCC Interim Linux	1992	16	The first actual distribution of Linux was offered through the University of Manchester in England.
Windows for Workgroups (Windows 3.11)	1993	16	First version of Microsoft Windows with peer-to-peer networking support for the PC.
Windows NT (New Technology)	1993	32	Microsoft's first attempt to bring a true 32-bit, preemptive, multitasking operating system with integrated network functionality to the world of personal computing. Windows NT was later offered in a Workstation version and a Server version.
Red Hat Linux, SUSE, and the Linux kernel 1.0	1994	16/32	Linux kernel version 1.0 was released, as were the first distributions of Red Hat Linux and SUSE Linux.
Windows 95	1995	16/32	An upgrade to Windows 3.x, mostly 32-bit code, with a much improved user interface and increased support for hardware. It offered native support to run 32-bit applications and many networking features. Windows 95 represented a different direction than Windows NT because it was intended to provide backward compatibility for 16-bit applications, and it continued to allow applications to directly access hardware functions.
Windows 98	1998	32	Implemented many bug fixes to Windows 95, more extended hardware support, and was fully 32-bit.
GNOME 1.0 desktop	1999	16/32	The GNOME 1.0 desktop (similar in function to Windows) became available as free software and grew to become one of the most popular UNIX/Linux desktops.

Table 1-2 Operating system releases from 2000 to the present

Operating system	Approximate date	Bits	Comments
Windows 2000	2000	32	A major revision of the Windows NT operating system; Windows 2000 was much faster and more reliable than Windows NT. The Windows 2000 kernel contained over twice the lines of code used in Windows NT. Windows 2000 came in several versions, including Professional, Server, Advanced Server, and Datacenter.
Windows Millennium Edition (Me)	2000	32	Microsoft's operating system upgrade of Windows 98, designed specifically for the home user, with improved multimedia capabilities.
Mac OS X	2001	32	Introduced as a significant departure from the earlier Mac OS versions because it was rewritten to have UNIX-based Darwin as the foundation for the operating system code. Updated versions of Mac OS X continue to be issued with the Snow Leopard version (Mac OS X 10.6) at this writing.
Linux kernel 2.4	2001	32/64	Enabled compatibility with Plug and Play devices, including USB devices.
Windows XP	2001	32/64	The successor to Windows Me and Windows 2000 Professional, available in four editions: Home, Professional, Tablet PC, and Media Center. The Home Edition was a 32-bit system that focused on home use for photos, music, and other multimedia files. The Professional Edition, available in 32-bit and 64-bit versions, was intended for office and professional users who needed more computing power and extensive networking capabilities. The Tablet PC Edition was tailored for tablet PCs that use speech and pen capabilities and offered great mobility, such as native wireless communications. Finally, the Media Center Edition was for enhanced digital media use involving television, audio, video, and graphics.
Windows Server 2003	2003	32/64	Available in Standard Edition, Web Edition, Enterprise Edition, and Datacenter Edition, this operating system was designed as a server platform for Microsoft's .NET initiative, which integrated all types of devices—PCs, handheld computers, cell phones, and home appliances—for communications over the Internet.
Linux kernel 2.6	2003	32/64	Provided support for larger file system storage, new CPUs, more stable 64-bit CPU support, and support for many more simultaneous users.
Windows Vista	2006	32/64	Introduced a newer security philosophy that employed a restricted user account control mode. Came in five editions: Home Basic, Home Premium, Business, Enterprise, and Ultimate.
Windows Server 2003	R2 2006	32/64	An interim release, called *Release 2* (R2), of Windows Server 2003 for compatibility with Windows Vista and to add new features, particularly for medium-sized and large organizations. Offered the same editions as Windows Server 2003.
Windows Server 2008	2008	32/64	Employed the new security philosophy begun with Windows Vista and extended security for servers in part by offering greater modularity to achieve a smaller attack profile. The main editions included Standard, Enterprise, Datacenter, Web, and HPC (High Performance Computing).

(*continues*)

Table 1-2 Operating system releases from 2000 to the present (*continued*)

Operating system	Approximate date	Bits	Comments
Mac OS X Snow Leopard	2009	32/64	Dropped support for PowerPC processors and switched to using only Intel processors.
Windows 7	2009	32/64	Employed enhanced security features, with fewer headaches and stumbling blocks for the user, compared to Windows Vista. Offered many new desktop features. The editions included Home Basic, Home Premium, Professional, Enterprise, and Ultimate.
Windows Server 2008 R2	2009	64 only	An interim release (Release 2 or R2) for Windows Server 2008 that included built-in compatibility with Windows 7. It had desktop changes similar to Windows 7. Offered the same versions as Windows Server 2008. Microsoft's current plans are only to develop new operating systems for 64-bit computers.
Chrome OS	2009	32/64	An OS based on the Linux kernel and developed by Google. Chrome OS is intended to be an online OS, meaning that you must be connected to the Internet to get the best use of it. Chrome OS runs primarily Web applications and is only available pre-installed on a device from a manufacturer, such as a Chromebook.
Linux Kernel 3.0	2011	32/64	New features include automatic defragmentation, a feature to wake up a computer from a wireless interface (Wake on WLAN), support for containers (a type of virtualization), and support for new devices.
Windows 8/8.1	2012/2013	32/64	Windows 8 was Microsoft's first attempt to unify the mobile and desktop computing space. The touch-centric interface was not well accepted; to mollify users, Microsoft quickly released Windows 8.1, which walked back some of the disliked user interface changes from previous Windows versions.
Windows Server 2012/ R2	2012/2013	64 only	Windows Server 2012 was released along with Windows 8 and had the same user-interface problems. Windows Server 2012 R2 was released along with Windows 8.1. Windows Server 2012/R2 made substantial enhancements to its virtualization engine, Hyper-V, and added cloud-centric features. Windows Server 2012/R2 had Standard and Datacenter editions along with Foundation and Essentials. Enterprise edition was later dropped.
Linux Kernel 4.0	2015	32/64	This release includes live updating of the kernel without requiring a system shutdown, a feature called *lazytime* that supports better file time stamping, and a number of driver and performance enhancements.
Windows 10	2015	32/64	Windows 10 finished walking back the user interface problems of Windows 8 while providing a single OS that worked well on the desktop as well as on touch-centric mobile devices like the Microsoft Surface. Speculation is that Windows 10 may be the last named version of Windows.
Mac OS X El Capitan	2015	32/64	This release includes the Split View feature, an updated Spotlight search app, and new swipe gestures.
Windows Server 2016	2016	64 only	Windows Server 2016 is slated for release about the time this book goes to press (fall 2016). This version emphasizes virtualization, flexible storage solutions, and cloud computing, and includes a version called *Nano Server* that has a very small footprint for embedded and virtual deployments.

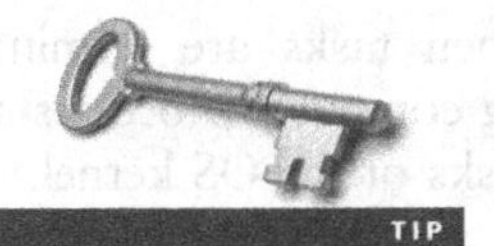

Check out Paul Thurrott's SuperSite for Windows at: *http://winsupersite.com/server/windows-server-0* to read about the latest in Windows 10 and Windows Server.

All of these PC operating systems changed the roles of the big machines' dynasty. Many big machines are now obsolete; others are used for calculation and data storage as back-end functions for the PC. Even in this arena, they are threatened today as PC operating systems and hardware extend further and further.

Many older operating systems are no longer around because of hardware changes. In Chapter 3, you look more closely at hardware architecture and what it means for the operating system. A good example of hardware that is no longer feasible to run an OS is the Z80 CPU produced by Zilog. Zilog manufactures semiconductors and created the first microprocessor.

When the cheaper and more flexible Intel 8088 and 8086 microprocessors were introduced in the IBM PC, the MS-DOS platform was a more attractive choice for most users. The Z80 and its CP/M operating system slowly died out. The same happened to some operating systems that used IBM PC hardware for other reasons. A prime example is IBM's own OS/2 operating system, first released in 1987 and developed jointly with Microsoft. The OS/2 system required extensive hardware, and it could not run older MS-DOS applications. Many people wanted to continue to run MS-DOS applications, so OS/2 was not a big hit. Because new software for OS/2 was slow to come and offered no substantial new features, people were hesitant to use it. Today, you will find OS/2 mainly in environments where it is used to interface to large IBM mainframes with custom-developed applications. For an operating system to be successful, many things must work together: availability of hardware and application programs, the right mix of features, and good timing. Try Hands-On Project 1-1 at the end of this chapter to learn more about the history of operating systems.

Understanding How Operating Systems Work

Many elements go into enabling an operating system to work with the computer on which it is loaded. These include:

- The kernel
- Resource managers
- Device drivers
- Application software
- BIOS

In the next sections you learn about each of these elements. The sections are followed by a summary to help you put the information together.

The Kernel

The kernel consists of the essential program code of the operating system. To help illustrate this concept, you might draw a parallel to a general contractor on a job site. The general contractor is there to schedule all the specific tasks that must be completed to finish the job and to ensure that all the subcontractors have the necessary resources and tools to do their jobs in a timely manner. Tasks are scheduled, resources are allocated, and then tasks are terminated and resources released so they can be used for other tasks. Scheduling computer processes and managing resources, such as memory and processing time, are key tasks of the OS kernel.

The term *kernel* has evolved from the UNIX operating system, but is also used to apply to the core code in the Windows and Mac OS X operating systems. In UNIX and Linux systems, the basic interface with the kernel is called the **shell**, which is a program that enables users to execute commands. You learn how to identify the UNIX/Linux shell in the Hands-On Projects in Chapter 2.

The jobs performed by the kernel can include:

- Managing interactions with the CPU
- Starting, managing, and scheduling programs that handle I/O activities, including device and networking activities
- Handling basic computer security
- Managing use of the computer's memory (RAM)
- Managing priority levels assigned to programs and computer processes

In Windows systems, the name of the kernel file is ntoskrnl.exe. In Mac OS X, the kernel is called *XNU*. The actual kernel name in Linux depends on the distribution and release of Linux. You can determine information about the kernel by using the *uname -sr* command in Linux (see Hands-On Project 1-5 to learn how to execute the *uname* command).

UNIX and Linux are available in distributions. A **distribution** is an issuance of UNIX or Linux that is based on a standard kernel, but that also has customizations added by a particular private or commercial development group. For example, Red Hat Enterprise Linux has customizations that are useful for organizations and businesses; this distribution is sold through the Red Hat company. GNU Linux is a distribution built on a Linux kernel, but with added tools from the GNU Project and the Free Software Foundation. GNU Linux is free. Fedora Linux is sponsored by Red Hat to serve as a development vehicle for testing customizations that may or may not be incorporated into Red Hat Enterprise Linux. Fedora Linux is offered free as a way to encourage the public to test new features prior to incorporating them into Red Hat Enterprise Linux.

Resource Managers

One of the functions of the operating system is to manage RAM and central processor use. For example, programs and devices require access to memory. If two devices or programs use the same memory space at the same time, they will not function properly, and they might cause the computer and operating system to hang. Even the computer's CPU contains memory that must be properly managed to avoid problems. The operating system uses specialized programs called **resource managers** to help ensure that memory is used properly and there are no memory conflicts.

The operating system also manages how programs access the processing capabilities of the CPU. Even if a computer has two or more CPUs, it is still important that one program not dominate the processing time on any one CPU. If one program were able to take over all of the time on a CPU, the computer might appear to hang and the work by other programs would come to a halt, possibly crashing the computer. When multiple programs and processes are running, the operating system manages the amount of time each is given by the CPU. For example, if there is one CPU and 10 programs that want to access it, the operating system will give each program a time slice on the CPU—as determined by the priority the CPU gives a particular program or process. Each program or process does a little work during its time slice, and then the kernel gives the next program or process CPU access for its time slice. Often programs associated with operating system tasks have a higher priority than user programs, because operating system programs are necessary for the smooth functioning of the computer.

Device Drivers and the Operating System

The operating system communicates and works directly with many devices, including the monitor, keyboard, disk drives, mouse, network adaptor, sound card, and so on. Some operating system programs exchange information with specific hardware (chips) inside the computer that control these devices. The code (instructions) for this information exchange is typically referred to as a device driver. A **device driver** translates computer code to display text on a screen, or translates movements of a mouse into action, for example. A separate device driver is usually present for each I/O device, as shown in Figure 1-2. In general, operating systems have a standardized way of communicating with a certain type of device driver. The device driver contains the actual code (instructions) to communicate with the chips on the device. This way, if another piece of hardware is introduced into the computer, the operating system code does not have to change. To enable the computer to communicate with the new device, you simply need to load a new device driver onto the operating system.

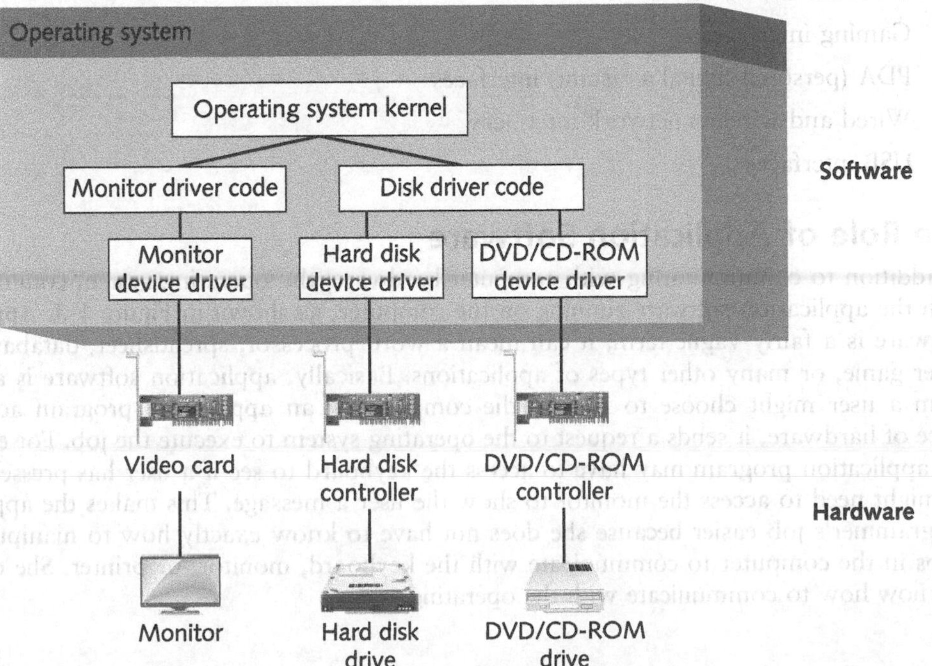

Figure 1-2 Device drivers provide communication between the OS and hardware devices

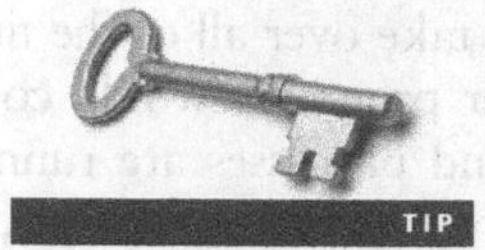

If a particular device is not working, one way to troubleshoot the problem is to obtain and install the latest driver for that device, which can usually be downloaded from the manufacturer's Web site.

For example, high-capacity removable hard drives that connect through a Universal Serial Bus (USB) were introduced after some earlier operating systems were written. Thus, earlier versions of operating systems did not natively support USB-based removable hard drives. However, because removable hard drives are similar to other types of disk drives, early versions of operating systems could be adapted to use removable hard drives by loading a few simple drivers for the operating system. You may encounter device drivers that interface with your operating system for other devices, including:

- Fixed internal hard disk drives (HDDs) and solid state drives (SSDs)
- Computer monitors
- Keyboards
- Mouse and trackball devices
- Remote communications modems
- Printers and scanners
- Tape drives, flash drives, hard drives, and other removable media
- Digital cameras and video hardware
- MP3 players or other audio hardware
- DVD/CD-ROM drives
- Gaming interfaces
- PDA (personal digital assistant) interfaces
- Wired and wireless network interfaces
- USB interfaces

The Role of Application Software

In addition to communicating with computer hardware, the operating system communicates with the application software running on the computer, as shown in Figure 1-3. Application software is a fairly vague term; it can mean a word processor, spreadsheet, database, computer game, or many other types of applications. Basically, application software is any program a user might choose to run on the computer. If an application program accesses a piece of hardware, it sends a request to the operating system to execute the job. For example, the application program may have to access the keyboard to see if a user has pressed a key, or might need to access the monitor to show the user a message. This makes the application programmer's job easier because she does not have to know exactly how to manipulate the chips in the computer to communicate with the keyboard, monitor, or printer. She only has to know how to communicate with the operating system.

1

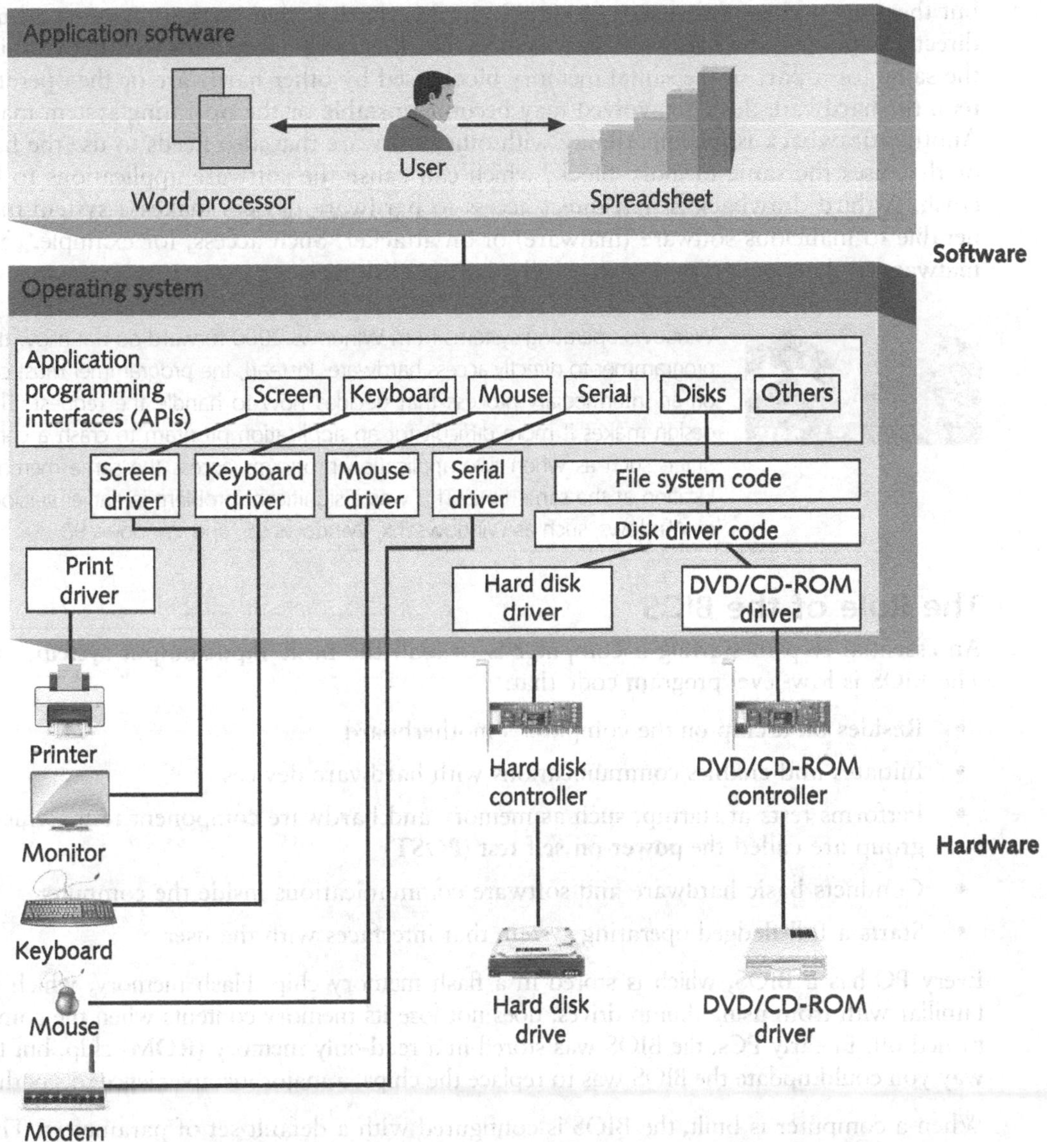

Figure 1-3 Application programs communicate with hardware through the operating system

In its most basic form, an operating system manages the communication among the application programs, the user, and the computer. This level of management allows application programmers to concentrate on applications that will run on any hardware, as long as the operating system can control them. In other words, an application program can submit a general request to the operating system, such as "write this information to disk," and the operating system handles the details. The application programmer doesn't have to worry about how to queue data, update the disk directory, or physically copy data from memory to the disk drive.

In early operating systems, programmers designed code to directly access hardware and improve overall application performance. This practice can make hardware response fast, but there are serious drawbacks. A significant drawback is that memory is often required for directly managing the hardware. If a memory block is programmed for use that conflicts with the same (or a part of the same) memory block used by other hardware or the operating system, the hardware devices involved may become unstable or the operating system may crash. Another drawback is incompatibility with other software that also needs to use the hardware or that uses the same memory block, which can cause the software applications to hang or crash. A third drawback is that direct access to hardware devices makes a system more vulnerable to malicious software (malware) or an attacker. Such access, for example, can allow malware to damage a disk or extensively damage disk files.

Windows operating systems from Windows 2000 forward do not allow the programmer to directly access hardware. Instead, the programmer must call on an intermediary process that decides how to handle the request. This design makes it more difficult for an application program to crash a computer, such as when two application programs access the same memory location at the same time. This was a significant problem in earlier versions of Windows, such as Windows 3.x, Windows 95, and Windows 98.

The Role of the BIOS

An essential step in starting a computer is to load the **basic input/output system**, or **BIOS**. The BIOS is low-level program code that:

- Resides on a chip on the computer's motherboard
- Initiates and enables communications with hardware devices
- Performs tests at startup, such as memory and hardware component tests, which as a group are called the **power-on self test (POST)**
- Conducts basic hardware and software communications inside the computer
- Starts a full-fledged operating system that interfaces with the user

Every PC has a BIOS, which is stored in a flash memory chip. Flash memory, which you are familiar with from using thumb drives, does not lose its memory contents when the computer is turned off. In early PCs, the BIOS was stored in a **read-only memory (ROM)** chip, but the only way you could update the BIOS was to replace the chips, a major inconvenience to say the least.

When a computer is built, the BIOS is configured with a default set of parameters. The BIOS configuration stores information about the amount of RAM, the storage devices, and other I/O devices on the computer. The BIOS configuration is stored in a memory chip called **complementary metal oxide semiconductor** (**CMOS**). A CMOS chip uses a low-power memory technology that is powered by a small battery. Users can make changes to the BIOS configuration by accessing the BIOS setup screen before the computer boots. Figure 1-4 shows a sample BIOS setup screen on a computer. Whenever you turn on your PC, the machine wakes up and begins executing the startup program inside the BIOS. This program initializes the screen and keyboard, tests computer hardware, such as the CPU and memory, initializes the hard disk and other devices, and then loads the main operating system—Windows 10 or Linux, for example—that provides more advanced functionality for application programs. Figure 1-5 illustrates the main operating system components, including the relationship of an operating system to the BIOS.

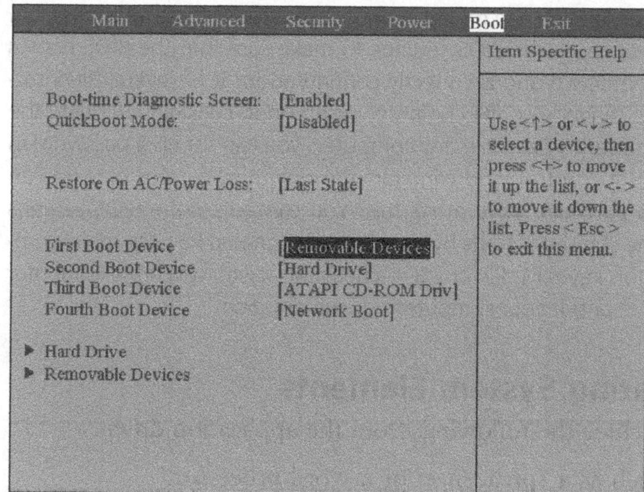
Main Advanced Security Power Boot Exit
Item Specific Help
Boot-time Diagnostic Screen: [Enabled]
QuickBoot Mode: [Disabled]
Restore On AC/Power Loss: [Last State]
First Boot Device [Removable Devices]
Second Boot Device [Hard Drive]
Third Boot Device [ATAPI CD-ROM Driv]
Fourth Boot Device [Network Boot]
▶ Hard Drive
▶ Removable Devices
Use <↑> or <↓> to select a device, then press <+> to move it up the list, or <-> to move it down the list. Press < Esc > to exit this menu.

Figure 1-4 Sample BIOS setup screen

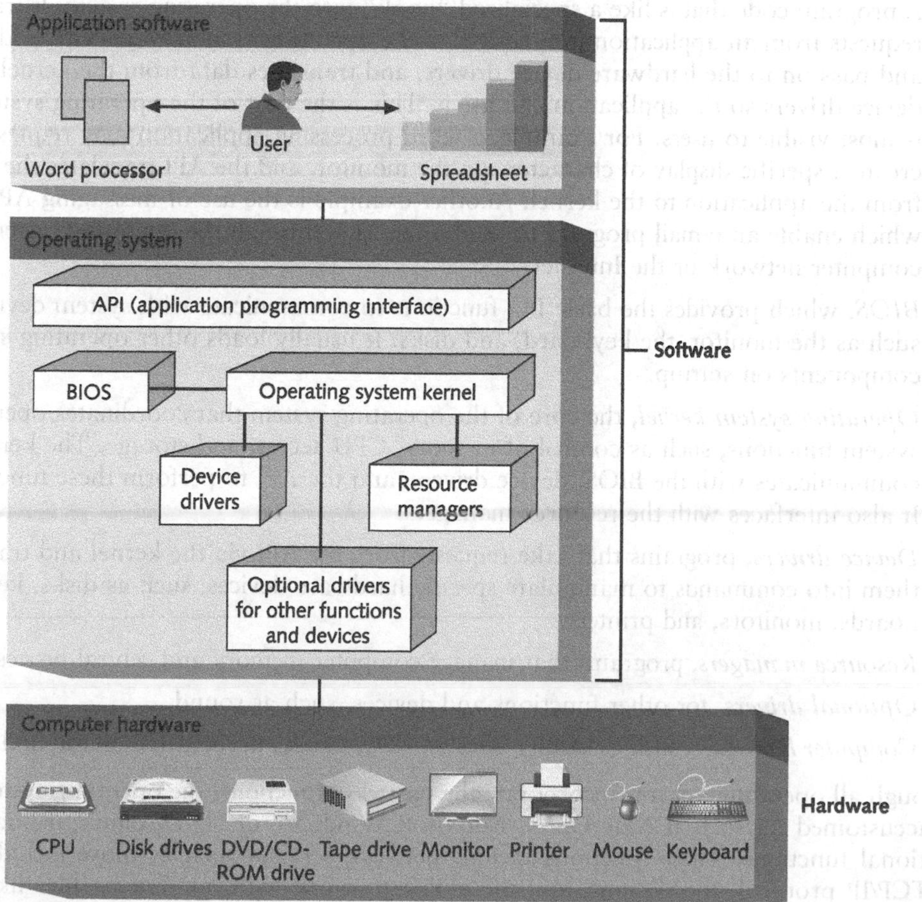
Application software
User
Word processor
Spreadsheet
Operating system
API (application programming interface)
BIOS
Operating system kernel
Device drivers
Resource managers
Optional drivers for other functions and devices
Software
Computer hardware
CPU
Disk drives
DVD/CD-ROM drive
Tape drive
Monitor
Printer
Mouse
Keyboard
Hardware

Figure 1-5 General operating system design

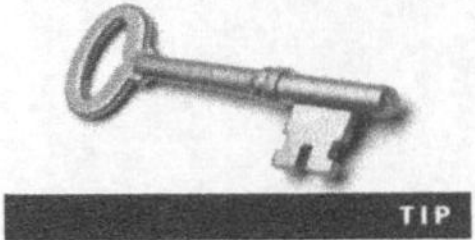

If a computer is turned on but cannot access a device, such as the main disk drive, check the BIOS settings to make sure that the BIOS knows about the device and is correctly configured for it. If several BIOS settings are changed or the computer won't boot, consider changing the CMOS battery. Also, on many computers you can set up a password in the BIOS to control who can start the operating system or who can access a particular drive at startup. You can access the BIOS settings when the computer starts by pressing a designated key. On many computers, this key is F1, F2, or ESC—check the screen when the computer boots, or consult your computer's documentation.

A Summary of Operating System Elements

The elements in Figure 1-5 include the following, from the application down:

- *Application software*, such as a spreadsheet or a word processor.
- *Application programming interface*. An **application programming interface (API)** is software designed to communicate with the application software and the user. The API is program code that is like a specialized "hook" into the operating system. It translates requests from an application into code that the operating system kernel can understand and pass on to the hardware device drivers, and translates data from the kernel and device drivers so the application can use it. This is the part of the operating system that is most visible to users. For example, a word-processing application may request to create a specific display of characters on the monitor, and the API translates the request from the application to the kernel. Another example is the use of messaging APIs, which enable an e-mail program to send a message through the operating system to a computer network or the Internet.
- *BIOS*, which provides the basic I/O functions to communicate with system devices, such as the monitor, the keyboard, and disks. It usually loads other operating system components on startup.
- *Operating system kernel*, the core of the operating system that coordinates operating system functions, such as control of memory, CPU access, and storage. The kernel communicates with the BIOS, device drivers, and the API to perform these functions. It also interfaces with the resource managers.
- *Device drivers*, programs that take requests from the API via the kernel and translate them into commands to manipulate specific hardware devices, such as disks, keyboards, monitors, and printers.
- *Resource managers*, programs that manage computer memory and central processor use.
- *Optional drivers*, for other functions and devices, such as sound.
- *Computer hardware*, such as storage devices, CPU, mouse, keyboard, monitor, and printer.

Although all operating systems incorporate the basic I/O functions, the operating systems you are accustomed to, such as Mac OS X, Microsoft Windows, or UNIX/Linux, include many additional functions. These functions include network services such as those included with the TCP/IP protocol, file systems, and the ability to work with multimedia files like audio and video files.

The Hands-On Projects at the end of this chapter enable you to view the interfaces (desktops) of Windows 10, Linux, and Mac OS X—all of which enable users to interact with the operating system.

Types of Operating Systems

There are many types of computer operating systems, which work in very different ways and are intended for very different purposes. To a large extent, the functions required by a computer dictate what the operating system will do and how. As an example, the computer in a microwave oven needs device drivers for the light-emitting diode (LED) display, numeric keypad, and door-closing switches, whereas the computer in a television needs drivers to monitor the remote control and tell the tuner to change the channel. The same goes for various types of small and large computers; a computer designed to handle a high volume of numerical operations for many users needs different functions than the PC used to run a word processor.

In general, operating systems are organized by the size, type, and purpose of the computer on which they run. For example, PC-class computers are designed for individual users to perform tasks, such as word processing, database and spreadsheet management, and networking with other computers. Over the years, PCs have become faster, more complex, and more powerful, offering the user more features. As a result, many PCs can now handle complex operations that go beyond simply running a user's application software. This ability has resulted in advanced operating systems that are designed to provide complex graphical user interfaces and advanced services and applications. The lines of division by size, type, and purpose are therefore getting more vague every day. Hardware is becoming more compact, but capable of doing more, and operating systems are getting larger and more complex.

One example of how PC operating systems have become more complex is the comparison of lines of code. Windows 3.1, released in 1992, had about 3 million lines of code, whereas modern OSs like Mac OS X and recent Windows versions have more than 50 million lines of code.

For instance, in the seventies, corporate computing was confined to mainframe- and minicomputer-class devices. These were refrigerator-sized or larger computers that required a full staff to manage them, and large, expensive air-conditioned rooms to hold them. The operating systems for these machines were quite complex and often included such intrinsic functions as text editing (not quite "word processing" by today's standards), database management, networking, and communications. There were few PC-class devices at the time. Those that were available were capable of minimal functionality, and used what could only be described as rudimentary operating systems. Many of those early devices didn't support any storage hardware (disk drives), or if they did, it was frequently serial, low-density tape. In this comparison, it should be easy to see that "in the old days," operating systems for large machines were very different from operating systems used for smaller machines.

From the Trenches ...

In the early 1990s, one of the authors managed the installation of a new IBM 9000-class mainframe. Installing the hardware and operating system, plus porting (relocating) programs and data from the previous mainframe, was such a complex process that it took several months to plan and many more months to test and execute. The computer equipment was so large that it was delivered by a moving van. Compare that task to setting up a new PC server and operating system, which requires very little space and can take as little as a few hours to a few days to complete.

At the same time, applications for these early large machines were written with efficient code so they could maximize all of the resources on the computer. As a result, appearance, programming, and management were very terse and basic.

To a lesser extent, this is still true today. There are still "big" machines and "small" machines, except that much of today's computer equipment is no longer physically large. The days of room-sized or even refrigerator-sized computers are nearly gone. A "big" machine today simply has more processing power, more memory, more storage (disk drive capacity), and better network connectivity. Very high-capacity computing is often accomplished by linking together several servers to appear as one.

Some of today's supercomputers are still physically large, such as those made by the Cray supercomputer company (visit *www.cray.com*). A **supercomputer** is one that has extreme processing power and speed to handle complex computations that are beyond the reach of other computers. A supercomputer might be used to simulate constantly changing and complex molecular structures, for example.

To operate today's more powerful computers, more powerful and more capable operating systems are employed. For example, a company that sells Internet access and Web hosting to thousands of other users—an Internet service provider (ISP), for instance—requires computers capable of performing multiple tasks for many users at the same time.

Although the computers used for such large installations typically don't look much different from the PC or Macintosh designed for a single user, they are quite different inside. They have powerful multitasking, multiuser capabilities with high-speed network connections. Also, they may include multiple CPUs and have more powerful I/O capabilities. The differences are significant, but also subtle. For example, Linux is a popular desktop operating system (used by a single person) based on UNIX, and it is also used to host Web servers, mail servers, and other Internet-related multiuser applications. Again, the hardware for a single-user Linux computer is likely much different from that of a Linux computer used to host Internet services, even though the operating system is the same. On the other hand, even with the enhanced hardware, an ISP wouldn't likely replace Linux or any other server operating system, such as Windows Server 2016, with a system intended for the desktop, such as Windows 10.

So-called high-end workstations are used by engineers for graphical design, or by editors for film design and animation. Again, these machines may look much like a school or home PC, but inside they include extremely fast hard disk controllers, 3D graphics interfaces, lots of memory, and often support for multiple CPUs. The needs of these workstations are very different from the multitasking, multiuser needs of an Internet server, but they too have special requirements that can't be met by some operating systems. Although some graphics applications use Linux or UNIX, the Windows and Mac OS X operating systems are more popular foundations for these applications, and can be used for powerful business applications as well.

So, there must be other factors that differentiate high-end and low-end computers. The main factor is the application software used with the computers. Again, the differentiation among computers is getting less defined. You have seen some of these factors, but the confusing concept is that even high-end applications can often run on what are considered low-end machines on the same operating system. When this is the case, the main differentiating factor is the hardware: the speed of the disk controller, size and speed of the storage media, amount and speed of memory, size of the data pathways in the computer (such as 32-bit, 64-bit, or larger), or speed and number of CPUs.

One way to look at computer and operating systems is to consider them in terms of one or more of the following characteristics:

- Time sharing
- Real-time
- Multiuser

Time Sharing

A **time-sharing system** is a central computer system that is used by multiple users and applications simultaneously. Mainframe computers typically fall into this category. These computers are used to conduct massive calculations or manipulate huge amounts of data. Mainframe computers, such as IBM System z mainframes, are used at scientific institutions, banks, and insurance companies. They are built to quickly perform tasks, such as keeping track of thousands of checking account balances. Most of their work is done in batches, using **batch processing**—such as clearing two million checks and updating their associated bank accounts—instead of single, sequential repetitive tasks. When the batch process is finished—all checks have been posted, for example—the statements can be printed. Contrast this approach to that of smaller computers, such as PCs, that are interactive and use **sequential processing**, where each process request is completed and the data returned before the next process is started.

Big batch processing jobs, or multiple batch jobs that must occur in a specific order on large computers, are often scheduled to run after work hours because they require so many machine resources. This makes batch processing less convenient than the instant response you get with a sequential process.

Besides batch processing, many clerks, customer representatives, and ATM machines often use a mainframe to do daily transactions. They all share the resources, or processor time, of the large machine, which is why such machines are called *time-sharing systems*.

From the Trenches ...

A downside of batch processing is that if the order of processing is inadvertently changed, the result may be a disaster to the data. A bank experienced this problem when performing its fiscal year-end closing. Some preliminary financial calculations and database updates were scheduled after all files were formally closed for the fiscal year. To restore the files to their year-end condition, it was necessary to restrict access to the mainframe the next day, and the batch processes were rescheduled. No new business could be done on the mainframe for a day until the data was restored and corrected.

Real-Time Systems

A **real-time operating system (RTOS)** receives and processes inputs and produces the required outputs in a specified amount of time. It is more important for the response time of an RTOS to be consistent than fast, although RTOSs are also built for speed. For example, an RTOS might be used in an industrial plant to control machinery. Inputs to the computer controlling the machinery dictate how the machines respond; the responses must be consistent and predictable, or the entire process may be thrown off.

Examples of RTOSs include VxWorks from Wind River Systems, QNX, and Windows CE. These OSs are typically used in **embedded systems**, which means the computer has a dedicated function within a larger system such as a piece of machinery. Examples of embedded systems include the computer that runs all the systems of a modern automobile or the computers that run the robots on an automated assembly line.

Multiuser Systems

A **multiuser system** supports multiple users who access the hardware and software of the computer and operating system. Both time-sharing and real-time systems can be multiuser systems. To review, time sharing is a method for enabling multiple users to share in using CPU resources, such as through terminals or computers with terminal software. A terminal consists of a keyboard and monitor without a CPU. For example, a time-sharing mainframe was originally accessed by running cables from terminals to a specialized communications box connected to the mainframe, creating a multiuser system, as shown in Figure 1-6. In time sharing, users may experience delays as the processor and operating system handle all of the processing requests and processing time becomes available. Today, multiple users typically access mainframes through a computer network.

Servers, such as a Linux server or Windows Server 2016, can provide computer access to multiple users over a network, as shown in Figure 1-7. In this environment, multiple users can do many different things on the multiuser computer at the same time. Access to resources is designed to be instantaneous by all users. Most modern OSs run both on personal computers and servers and are considered multiuser operating systems. Even though Windows 10, for example, doesn't typically have multiple monitors and keyboards attached to it with several users running applications, these OSs can support multiple user connections through a network.

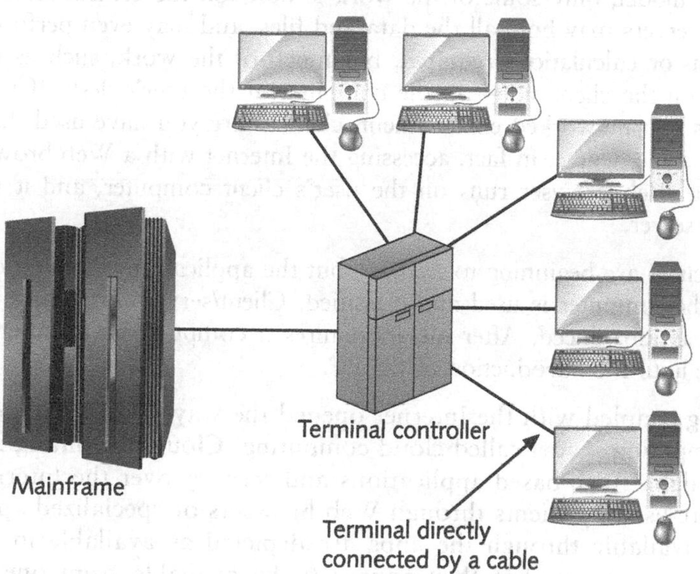

Figure 1-6 Time-sharing mainframe with terminals

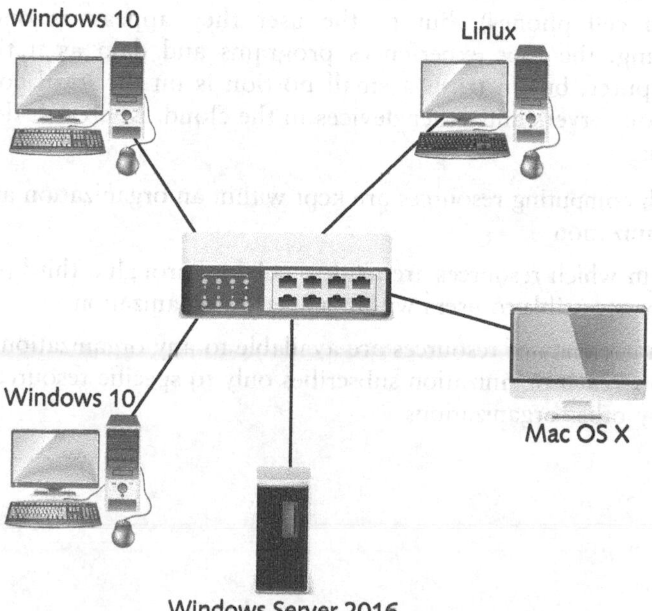

Figure 1-7 Using a network to access a Windows server

In a departure from mainframes and time sharing, one of the newer approaches to multiuser operations is the use of **client/server systems.** On a multiuser mainframe, all of the work is typically done on the big machine, including running programs, storing data, and accessing data. In the client/server model, only some of the work is done on the central servers. In a client/server system, the servers may hold all the data and files, and may even perform some of the database functions or calculations required, but much of the work, such as running programs, is performed on the client side—on the computer at the user's desk. If you have used PC-class computers in a networked environment, chances are you have used the client/server model, at least to some degree. In fact, accessing the Internet with a Web browser is a client/server activity. The Web browser runs on the user's client computer, and it requests Web pages from a Web server.

Operating system differences are beginning to narrow, but the applications that run on them help differentiate how the computer is used and classified. Client/server computing was not possible until the PC was introduced. After all, it requires a computer at the user's desk, which was not available until the introduction of the PC.

Client/server computing coupled with the Internet opened the way to an even more efficient and powerful computing model called cloud computing. **Cloud computing** involves providing a host of scalable Web-based applications and services over the Internet or a private network that are used by clients through Web browsers or specialized apps. The servers and resources available through the apps are depicted as available in a cloud because there are many resources, but they appear to be available from one unified resource (see Figure 1-8). You might compare this technology to using telephone services. There are many telephone companies and telephone technologies (such as land lines, satellite phones, and cell phones), but to the user they appear as one giant resource. In cloud computing, the user experiences programs and data as if they are installed on the user's computer, but in truth a small portion is on the local computer and all other resources are on servers and other devices in the cloud. Microsoft describes three types of cloud models:

- *Private cloud*—In which computing resources are kept within an organization and used exclusively by that organization
- *Hosted private cloud*—In which resources are made available through a third-party outsourcer, but are only accessible to users within a specific organization
- *Public cloud*—In which a variety of resources are available to any organization through a third party and each organization subscribes only to specific resources, which may be shared by other organizations

1

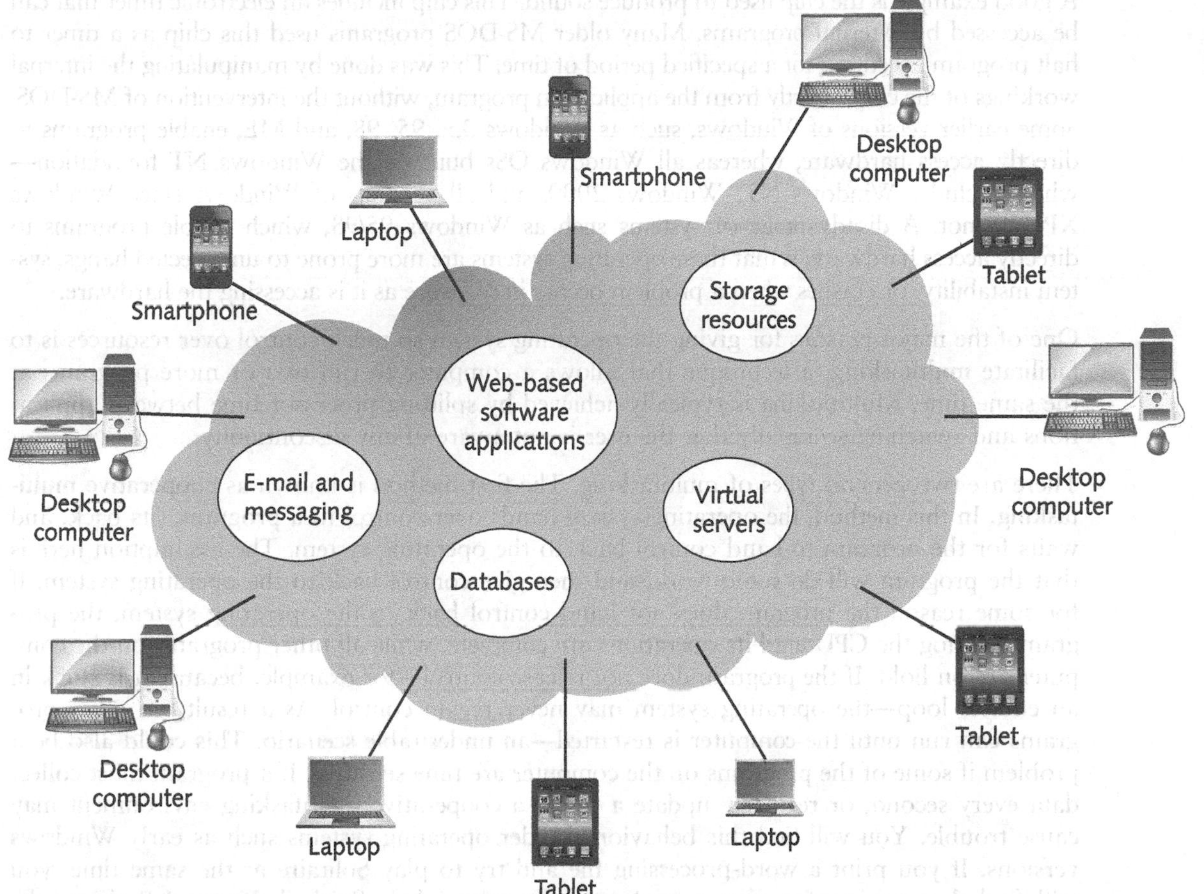

Figure 1-8 Cloud computing

Common cloud service providers include Amazon Web Services (AWS), Microsoft Azure, and Dropbox. AWS and Microsoft Azure are full-service cloud computing companies that can offer customers anything from cloud storage to an entire network of servers and services. Dropbox, as you may know, is a cloud storage company that provides seamless access to files through the Internet.

Single Tasking Versus Multitasking

A few aspects of operating systems deserve a closer look. As pointed out earlier, today's PC operating systems go way beyond basic I/O. In practice, almost every resource in the computer, such as the memory and the microprocessor (CPU), is managed by the operating system. This is both good and bad; it results in a lot more consistency and a lot of added functionality. However, application programs can no longer directly access hardware in creative ways as they could before, particularly under MS-DOS and in early Windows systems.

A good example is the chip used to produce sound. This chip includes an electronic timer that can be accessed by external programs. Many older MS-DOS programs used this chip as a timer to halt program execution for a specified period of time. This was done by manipulating the internal workings of the chip directly from the application program, without the intervention of MS-DOS. Some earlier versions of Windows, such as Windows 3.x, 95, 98, and ME, enable programs to directly access hardware, whereas all Windows OSs built on the Windows NT foundation—which includes Windows NT, Windows 2000, and all versions of Windows since Windows XP—do not. A disadvantage of systems such as Windows 95/98, which enable programs to directly access hardware, is that these operating systems are more prone to unexpected hangs, system instability, or crashes when a problem occurs in software as it is accessing the hardware.

One of the major reasons for giving the operating system so much control over resources is to facilitate **multitasking**, a technique that allows a computer to run two or more programs at the same time. Multitasking is typically achieved by splitting processor time between applications and switching so rapidly that the user is not aware of any discontinuity.

There are two general types of multitasking. The first method is known as **cooperative multitasking**. In this method, the operating system hands over control to a program, sits back, and waits for the program to hand control back to the operating system. The assumption here is that the program will do some work, and then give control back to the operating system. If for some reason the program does not hand control back to the operating system, the program will hog the CPU until its operations are complete, while all other programs on the computer are on hold. If the program does not release control—for example, because it is stuck in an endless loop—the operating system may never regain control. As a result, no other programs can run until the computer is restarted—an undesirable scenario. This could also be a problem if some of the programs on the computer are time sensitive. If a program must collect data every second, or regularly update a clock, a cooperative multitasking environment may cause trouble. You will find this behavior in older operating systems such as early Windows versions. If you print a word-processing file and try to play Solitaire at the same time, you will find that you cannot play a card until the print job is finished. Figure 1-9 shows the basic concept of cooperative multitasking.

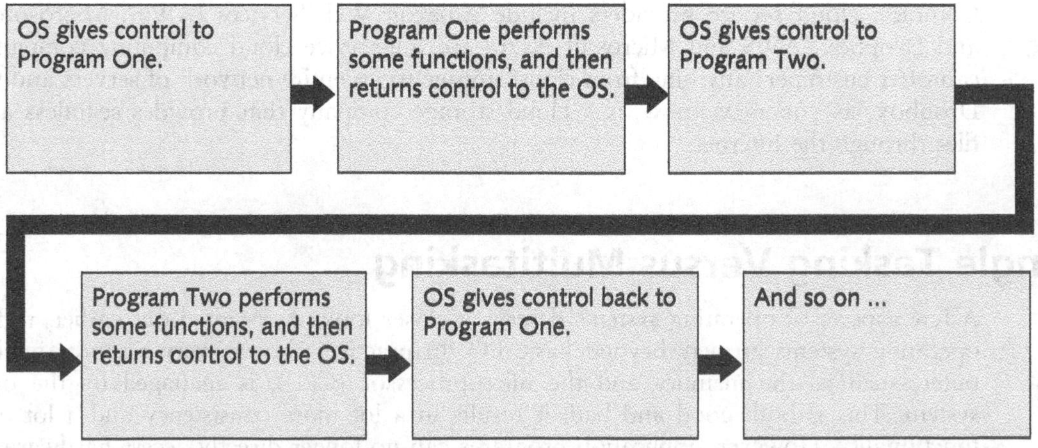

Figure 1-9 Cooperative multitasking basics

A better method is the second alternative, **preemptive multitasking**, illustrated in Figure 1-10. Modern operating systems developed since the early 2000s use preemptive multitasking. These systems include all Windows OSs since Windows XP, along with Mac OS X and all Linux/UNIX variations. In preemptive multitasking, the operating system is in control of the computer at all times. It lets programs execute a little bit of code at a time, but immediately after the code executes, it forces the program to relinquish control of the CPU back to the operating system. It then takes the next program and repeats the same process. Because the operating system is in charge, it has a lot of control over how much of the computer's resources are allocated to each program. As a result, the computer must use more of its processor power and memory to support the operating system, but the behavior of programs and the computer as a whole are a little more predictable. Playing Solitaire while printing a word-processing file within a preemptive multitasking system is not a problem—both processes get enough CPU time to do their jobs—and the user is often unaware that the system has been rapidly switching between tasks.

NOTE

Linux/UNIX OSs have always included preemptive multitasking since the original UNIX developed by Bell Labs in the 1970s.

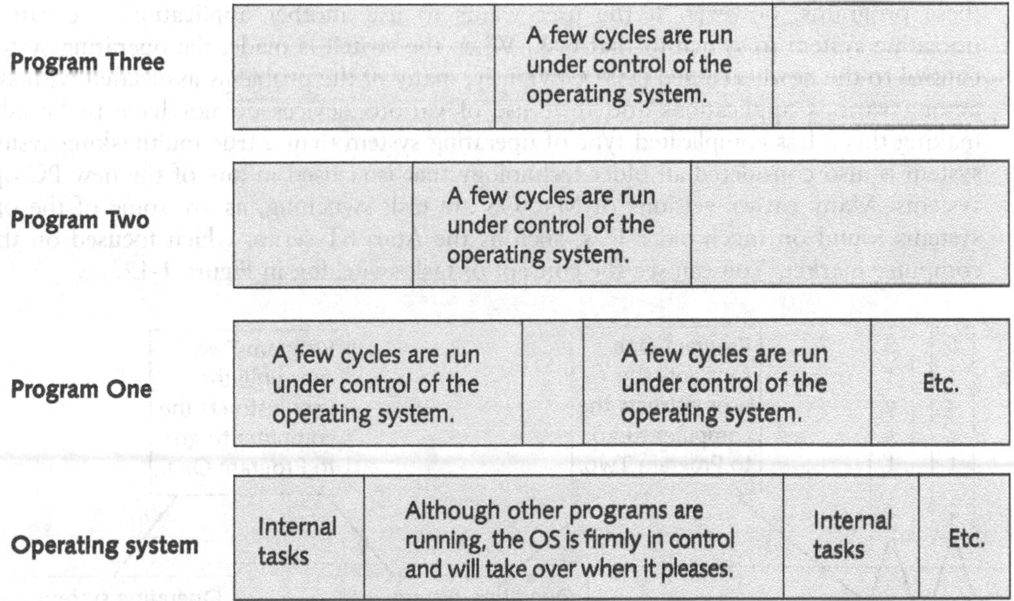
Program Three
A few cycles are run under control of the operating system.
Program Two
A few cycles are run under control of the operating system.
Program One
A few cycles are run under control of the operating system.
A few cycles are run under control of the operating system.
Etc.
Operating system
Internal tasks
Although other programs are running, the OS is firmly in control and will take over when it pleases.
Internal tasks
Etc.

Figure 1-10 Preemptive multitasking basics

Some older operating systems, such as MS-DOS, were single-tasking operating systems. A **single-tasking** operating system executes one program at a time (see Figure 1-11). To do something else, one program must be stopped and a new program must be loaded and executed. Because multiple programs are not trying to use the same resources, single-tasking operating systems are a lot simpler. These systems, however, are considered older technology, and as new operating systems are released, they are seldom single-tasking. New single-tasking operating systems are found only in computers with very limited processor capacity, such as older personal digital assistants (PDAs), which have long since been replaced by smartphones and tablets that sport their own multitasking OSs.

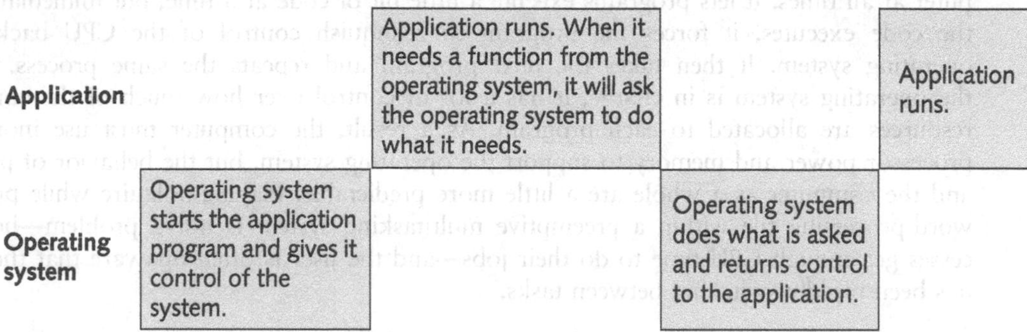

Figure 1-11 Single-tasking operating system

A special note must be made of a hybrid system called a **task-switching** operating system. This system offers many of the device management functions of the multitasking operating system, and it can load multiple application programs at once. It will actively execute only one of these programs, however. If the user wants to use another application, she can ask the operating system to switch to that task. When the switch is made, the operating system gives control to the newly selected task. Obviously, many of the problems associated with switching among various applications and their use of various devices do not have to be addressed, making this a less complicated type of operating system than a true multitasking system. This system is also considered an older technology that isn't used in any of the new PC operating systems. Many earlier versions of Mac OS are task switching, as are some of the operating systems found on much older PCs, such as the Atari ST series, which focused on the home computer market. You can see the concept of task switching in Figure 1-12.

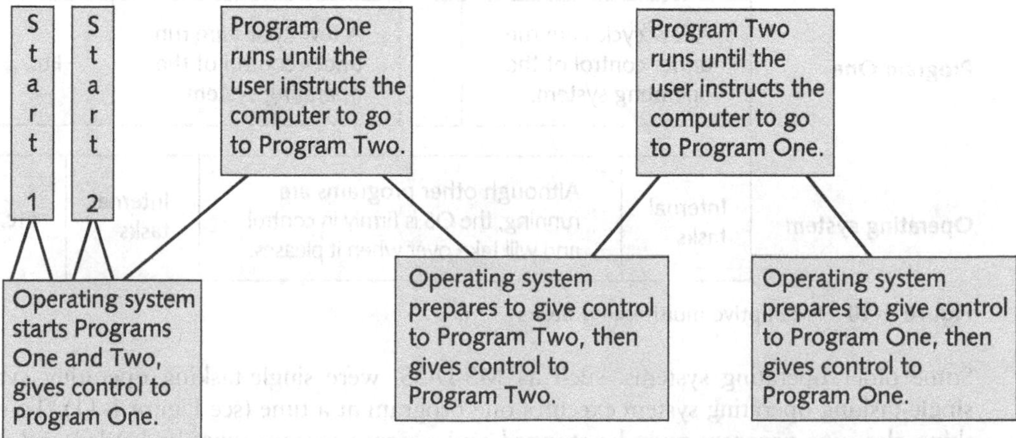

Figure 1-12 Task switching

Multitasking should not be confused with **multithreading**. Multithreading is the ability of programs to be written so that they run several program code blocks, called *threads*, independently. For example, a database program might run a thread to pull data from the database and another thread to simultaneously sum figures to create a subtotal. You learn more about multithreading in Chapter 3.

Single-User Versus Multiuser Operating Systems

Some operating systems, in addition to being able to run multiple programs at the same time with multitasking technology, allow multiple users to use an application simultaneously. These systems are known as *multiuser operating systems*. By definition, a multiuser system is almost a multitasking system. Most multiuser systems use preemptive, multitasking technology. The desktop operating systems covered in this book initially were designed as **single-user** systems (only one user at a time), with the exception of UNIX and Linux, which have always been multiuser operating systems by design. From the start, all Windows server systems, from Windows NT onward, were designed as full-featured multiuser systems. Mac OS X Server is also a full-featured multiuser system. The desktop versions of operating systems, such as Windows 10 and Mac OS X, are also multiuser systems, but they do not have the full multiuser capacity of the server systems. All of these desktop systems are intended to handle only 10 to 20 simultaneous users before they bog down under the load. A server system is designed to handle hundreds of users at once.

While modern OSs are multitasking as well as multiuser, Windows 98 was a good example of an operating system that was multitasking but not multiuser. Windows 98 could handily run a word-processing program while running a Web browser and an e-mail client for a single user, but it wasn't designed to run applications for multiple users simultaneously. Table 1-3 compares single-user and multiuser operating systems.

Table 1-3 Comparing single-user and multiuser operating systems

Single-user operating system	Multiuser operating system
Handles only one user at a time	Handles multiple users at a time
Some older desktop operating systems are only single-user	All server operating systems are multiuser, and some desktop operating systems have limited multiuser capability
Some single-user operating systems do not use multitasking and some do	Always employs multitasking
Single-user systems that can use multitasking may use either cooperative or preemptive multitasking	Uses preemptive multitasking

Current Operating Systems

The operating systems surveyed in this book are the most common in today's computing environments, and they fall into several families:

- Windows 7, 8.1, and 10
- Windows Server 2008, 2012, and 2016
- The different distributions of UNIX/Linux operating systems, focusing particularly on Fedora, which is used as a leading-edge development environment for the popular Red Hat Enterprise Linux (new features in Red Hat Enterprise Linux come from Fedora)
- Apple Macintosh Mac OS X (version 10.11 El Capitan)

Windows 8 was not well-received and almost all systems that were initially configured with Windows 8 were upgraded to Windows 8.1 when it became available, so this book does not cover features particular to Windows 8.

In Chapter 2, you learn about these families in more detail. This section provides a brief summary.

At the time of this writing, three popular desktop operating systems were used most frequently in corporate America—Windows 7, 8.1, and 10. These three operating systems offer a stable work environment that is appealing for office use. Further, Microsoft continually issues updates for Windows systems that increase their security and performance. It is also possible to find some corporate users hanging on to older versions of Windows and even MS-DOS, but they have become rare. The most popular Microsoft server operating systems are Windows Server 2008/R2 and Windows Server 2012/R2. Support for Windows Server 2003 has ended and most companies have upgraded or are upgrading to a newer version of Windows Server. Windows Server 2016 will be released about the time this book publishes, and features and screenshots will be based on preview release 4.

The multiuser UNIX operating system has been popular among industrial-strength users for many years. It is especially appealing to members of the scientific and research communities for its power to perform complex tasks and maintain large databases. There are many flavors of UNIX, but the two main design standards are the Berkeley Software Distribution (BSD) standard and the System V Release 4 (SVR4) standard. This book focuses on SVR4 UNIX. Linux is a UNIX look-alike system that is popular as a server operating system in business, education, and government and is rapidly replacing UNIX. Linux operating system distributions are particularly popular for servers and are gaining ground on the desktop, in part because they take advantage of a huge open source software community. Open source software is typically developed by hundreds or thousands of volunteers, relies on peer review, contains code in the public domain, and is typically distributed for free.

You can learn more about open source software at *www.opensource.org* and *sourceforge.net*.

The Mac OS X operating system for Apple Macintosh computers is popular in the educational and graphics sectors, particularly for video editing and desktop publishing. Its use in the corporate world is often for these applications, and it is also very popular among home users. Corporate users sometimes regard Mac OS X as difficult to set up for networking in a medium-sized to large organization with complex networks, although Apple has addressed many of these concerns. Mac OS X is popular with home users because the desktop is intuitive and home network setup is user friendly. Also, some home users are already familiar with Mac OS X from using it at school.

In Chapter 2, you will take a much closer look at the individual operating systems mentioned here. You will find out more about the hardware required to run each operating system, and which versions you will see in which environments. Try the Hands-On Projects at the end of Chapter 1 to learn more about the Windows-based, Linux, and Mac OS X operating systems, including how to use tools for obtaining system information, how to view device drivers, how to see multitasking in operation, and how to use desktop applications.

Chapter Summary

- All computers perform three basic tasks: input, processing, and output. An operating system is a specialized computer program that provides a user interface, file system, processes and services, and a kernel.
- An operating system provides the foundation upon which to run the components of a computer and execute applications.
- A basic task of an operating system is to enable a computer to perform I/O functions so that it can use software applications and communicate with computer hardware.
- Two common types of operating systems are desktop (or client) and server operating systems.
- The history of operating systems and computers represents a progression from physically huge computers to large computers to desktop-sized computers that have powerful processing capabilities and operating systems.
- Device drivers can extend the native functions of an operating system to provide access and control over different types of devices, such as printers and DVD drives.
- The BIOS is low-level program code that operates between the computer hardware and a higher-level operating system to initiate communications with hardware devices, perform hardware tests at startup, and enable the startup of the higher-level operating system.
- An operating system may be geared to run a large mainframe computer or a small PC. However, small PC systems can now be very powerful; when combined, they can be used in many places instead of mainframe systems.
- Operating systems can be understood in terms of characteristics such as time sharing, real-time operation, and multiuser capabilities.

- From a user standpoint, one of the most significant advances in operating systems was the refinement of the GUI, as seen in the development of Windows-based and Mac OS systems.
- Early operating systems tended to be single tasking, but modern systems are largely multitasking.
- A true multiuser system is one in which multiple users access and run a single application on a single computer at the same time.
- Current popular operating systems include Windows 7, 8.1, and 10, Server 2008/R2, Server 2012/R2, Server 2016, UNIX/Linux, and Mac OS X El Capitan. Of the systems listed, the server operating systems are primarily discussed in the last three chapters of the book, along with some networking basics.

Key Terms

application programming interface (API) Functions or programming features in an operating system that programmers can use for network links, links to messaging services, or interfaces to other systems.

application software A word processor, spreadsheet, database, computer game, or other type of application that a user runs on a computer. Application software consists of computer code that is formatted so the computer or its operating system can translate the code into a specific task, such as writing a document.

basic input/output system (BIOS) Low-level program code that conducts basic hardware and software communications inside the computer. A computer's BIOS basically resides between computer hardware and the higher-level operating system, such as UNIX or Windows.

batch processing A computing style frequently employed by large systems. A request for a series of processes is submitted to the computer; information is displayed or printed when the batch is complete. Batches might include the processing for all of the checks submitted to a bank for a day, or for all of the purchases in a wholesale inventory system, for example. Compare to *sequential processing*.

Beginner's All-purpose Symbolic Instruction Code (BASIC) An English-like computer programming language originally designed as a teaching tool, but which evolved into a useful and relatively powerful development language.

blade enclosure A large box with slots for blade servers; the box also provides cooling fans, electrical power, connection to a shared monitor and pointing device, and even network connectivity. The actual design depends on the manufacturer.

blade server A server unit that looks like a card that fits into a blade enclosure. Blade servers are intended to save space. See *blade enclosure*.

client/server systems A computer hardware and software design in which different portions of an application execute on different computers, or on different components of a single computer. Typically, client software supports user I/O and server software conducts database searches, manages printer output, and the like.

cloud computing A computing technology that provides a host of scalable Web-based applications and services over the Internet or a private network used by clients through Web browsers.

command-line interface An interface that enables the user to display a command line from which to enter commands. These interfaces include the Command Prompt window in Windows operating systems and the terminal window in Linux and Mac OS X.

complementary metal oxide semiconductor (CMOS) A type of memory that stores a computer's BIOS configuration. A CMOS chip uses a low-power memory technology that is powered by a small battery.

computer program A series of instructions executed by the computer's CPU.

cooperative multitasking A computer hardware and software design in which the operating system temporarily hands off control to an application and waits for the application to return control to the operating system. Compare to *preemptive multitasking.*

desktop operating system A computer operating system that is typically installed on a PC, usually used by one person at a time, and may or may not be connected to a network. Also called a *client operating system.*

device driver Computer software designed to provide the operating system and application software access to specific computer hardware.

distribution An issuance of UNIX or Linux that is based on a standard kernel, but that also has customizations added by a particular private or commercial development group.

embedded system A computer that has a dedicated function within a larger system, such as a piece of machinery.

file system The method by which an OS stores and organizes files and manages access to files on a storage device.

graphical user interface (GUI) An interface between the user and an operating system that presents information in an intuitive graphical format, including multiple colors, figures, icons, windows, toolbars, and other features. A GUI is usually deployed with a pointing device, such as a mouse, to make the user more productive.

hardware The physical devices in a computer, including the CPU, circuit boards (cards), disk drives, monitor, and modem.

input/output (I/O) Input is information taken in by a computer device to handle or process; an example is characters typed at a keyboard. Output is information sent out by a computer device after the information is handled or processed; an example is the display of typed characters on the monitor.

kernel An essential set of programs and computer code built into a computer operating system to control processor, disk, memory, and other functions central to a computer's basic operation. The kernel communicates with the BIOS, device drivers, and the API to perform these functions. It also interfaces with the resource managers.

Microsoft Disk Operating System (MS-DOS) The first widely distributed operating system for microcomputers, created by Tim Paterson and a team at Microsoft that included Bill Gates. This generic computer code was used to control many basic computer hardware and software functions. MS-DOS is sometimes referred to as DOS.

multitasking A technique that allows a computer to run two or more programs at the same time.

multithreading Running several program processes or parts (threads) at the same time.

multiuser system A computer hardware and software system designed to service multiple users who access the computer's hardware and software applications simultaneously.

operating system (OS) A specialized computer program that provides a user interface, file system, services, and a kernel to a computer. An OS runs on computer hardware and facilitates application execution.

power-on self test (POST) Tests, such as memory and hardware component tests, that are run by the BIOS when a computer starts and that must complete before the operating system is loaded. See *basic input/output system (BIOS)*.

preemptive multitasking A computer hardware and software design for multitasking of applications in which the operating system retains control of the computer at all times. See *cooperative multitasking* for comparison.

process A program that is loaded into memory and run by the CPU. It can be an application a user interacts with, such as a word-processing program or a Web browser, or a program with no user interface that communicates with other processes and provides services to them.

rack-mounted server CPU boxes mounted in racks that can hold multiple servers, each with its own power cord and network connection—and that often share one monitor and pointing device.

read-only memory (ROM) Memory that contains information that is not erased when the power is removed from the memory hardware.

real-time operating system (RTOS) An operating system that receives and processes inputs and produces the required outputs in a specified amount of time.

resource managers Programs that manage computer memory and CPU use.

sequential processing A computer processing style in which each operation is submitted, acted upon, and the results displayed before the next process is started. Compare to *batch processing*.

server operating system A computer operating system usually found on more powerful PC-based computers than those used for desktop operating systems. A server OS is connected to a network and can act in many roles to enable multiple users to access information via e-mail, files, software, and other means.

service A process that runs in the background because there is no user interface. See *process*.

shell An interface that enables users to interact with an operating system kernel. The shell enables the user to execute commands. See *kernel*.

single-tasking A computer hardware and software design that can manage only a single task at a time.

single-user system A computer hardware and software system that enables only one user to access its resources at a particular time.

supercomputer A computer that has extreme processing power and speed to handle complex computations that are beyond the reach of other computers.

task switching A hybrid between single-tasking and multitasking that permits the user or application software to switch among multiple single-tasking operations.

time-sharing system A central computer system, such as a mainframe, that is used by multiple users and applications simultaneously.

user interface A component of an operating system that provides a method for users to interact with the computer, usually with a keyboard and mouse or touch screen.

Review Questions

1. Which of the following is a basic function all computers perform? (Choose all that apply.)
   a. processing
   b. Internet access
   c. graphics
   d. input
   e. e-mail
   f. output
2. Which of the following executes instructions provided by computer programs?
   a. NIC
   b. USB
   c. CPU
   d. drive
3. The large bank where you work uses an older mainframe to make a customer service database available for complex reports and queries about customer profiles. Which of the following occurs when 12 users run large reports on the mainframe at the same time?
   a. batching
   b. interfacing
   c. overload
   d. time sharing
4. Which of the following is a feature typically provided by an operating system? (Choose all that apply.)
   a. file system
   b. spreadsheet
   c. database app
   d. kernel

5. What is another name for a client operating system?
   a. real-time operating system
   b. multiuser operating system
   c. server operating system
   d. desktop operating system
6. While on a coffee break, your colleague asserts that cooperative multitasking is the best operating system design. What is your response? (Choose all that apply.)
   a. A disadvantage of cooperative multitasking is that it relies on each program to decide when to give control back to the operating system.
   b. Cooperative multitasking can be faster than other forms of multitasking because it increases the clock speed of the processor.
   c. Cooperative multitasking OSs can get stuck in an endless loop.
   d. Modern operating systems use preemptive multitasking so that the operating system is fully in control.
7. You are called into a small business in which 25 people are using one Windows 10 computer to share files. The business wants you to diagnose why file sharing is often slow or seems to grind to a halt. What is your assessment?
   a. Windows 10 is only meant for 20 or fewer simultaneous users. The company should upgrade to a server system.
   b. Windows 10 is working in batch mode and should be reset for multitasking mode.
   c. The company should switch to Windows 7.
   d. Windows 10 is experiencing task locks and task locking should be turned off.
8. Which type of server plugs into slots in an enclosure that contains a backplane?
   a. rack-mounted
   b. blade
   c. tower
   d. mainframe
9. What is the core code of an operating system called?
   a. kernel
   b. blade
   c. driver
   d. bus

10. You are using e-mail to send a message over the Internet. Which of the following types of software acts like a hook in the operating system to enable e-mail transmissions over the Internet?
    a. software compiler
    b. hook driver
    c. Internet translator
    d. application programming interface
11. Which of the following operating systems only comes in a 64-bit version and not a 32-bit version?
    a. Mac OS X Leopard
    b. Linux
    c. Windows Server 2016
    d. Windows 10
    e. No current operating system operates only on a 64-bit computer.
12. Which processor was used in the original IBM PC?
    a. Zilog Z80
    b. Motorola 68000
    c. AMD Opteron
    d. Intel 8088
13. Which of the following operating systems are multitasking systems? (Choose all that apply.)
    a. MS-DOS
    b. Windows 10
    c. Mac OS X
    d. Linux
14. To help manage access to the CPU, programs and processes are assigned which of the following by the operating system?
    a. a time-stamp
    b. 100 KB of RAM
    c. a program unit interval
    d. a priority

15. Today's class discussion is a comparison of high-end computers and lower-end computers. Which of the following factors help to differentiate these types of computers? (Choose all that apply.)
    a. number of CPUs
    b. size of the monitor
    c. size of the data pathways in the computer
    d. number of USB ports
16. Where is a computer's BIOS typically stored in modern computers?
    a. RAM
    b. flash memory
    c. ROM
    d. hard disk
17. Which of the following is performed by the BIOS? (Choose all that apply.)
    a. runs the power-on self test
    b. starts the operating system
    c. manages the file system
    d. allocates memory to applications
18. Operating systems that give programs direct access to manipulating hardware are more susceptible to which of the following problems? (Choose all that apply.)
    a. malicious software vulnerabilities
    b. runaway BIOS
    c. memory block conflicts that make hardware devices unstable
    d. CPU clocking problems
19. Which type of operating system is most likely to be part of an embedded system?
    a. task-switching
    b. cooperative multitasking
    c. real-time
    d. time sharing
20. What are two types of cloud computing models? (Choose two.)
    a. private cloud
    b. public cloud
    c. preemptive cloud
    d. cooperative cloud

Hands-On Projects

Please read the "Before You Begin" section of this book's Introduction for details on the suggested lab configuration for all the projects.

At the end of each chapter in this book, Hands-On Projects give you direct experience in applying what you have learned about operating systems. As you are completing the Hands-On Projects, keep a lab book, notebook, or word processor handy so you can record your findings for later reference.

These projects use a variety of OSs, including a Windows client and a Windows server. For people who use a Windows client, note that the instructions apply to Windows 10. For projects that use a Windows server, instructions will apply to Windows Server 2012 R2. Projects that use Linux will use Fedora 23 with the default GNOME desktop, and those that use Mac OS X will use El Capitan. Other OS versions and releases can be used with small changes to the instructions. The Linux projects are tailored for the Fedora 23 distribution. If you choose to use a different Linux distribution, plan to use one with the GNOME desktop; the steps in the Hands-On Projects will still apply in most cases. All of the Linux commands you learn to use in the terminal window will work on any Linux distribution and desktop, and in many UNIX distributions as well. The Mac OS X projects primarily use the default Mac OS X desktop. Because Mac OS X is built on BSD UNIX (the Darwin distribution), some projects also use the terminal window in Mac OS X for practicing UNIX commands.

In some Windows projects, you may see the User Account Control (UAC) box, which is used for security to help thwart intruders. If you see this box, click Continue. Because computer setups may be different, the box is not mentioned in the actual project steps.

Table 1-4 Which operating system is used in each project?

Operating system	Projects
Any	1-1
Windows 10	1-2 through 1-4
Fedora Linux	1-5 and 1-6
Mac OS X El Capitan	1-7 and 1-8

Project 1-1: Explore the History of the Computer

The Internet can be a rich source of information about the history of computers. In this project, you use the Internet to review the history of computers, software, and the Internet. You will need a computer with any OS installed that has access to the Internet.

1. Start and log on to any computer with Internet access and a Web browser. Open a Web browser and go to *www.computerhistory.org/timeline*.
2. Determine the answers to the following:
   a. Which three PCs were released in 1977?
   b. What was the first non-kit PC developed in 1973?
   c. What important data storage medium was released in 1983?
   d. What does ASCII stand for, and in what year did it come out?
   e. What was the name of the first fully transistorized computer, which was developed in 1955?
   f. What input and output devices were used by the Manchester Mark I computer?
   g. In what year was the World Wide Web born via the development of Hypertext Markup Language (HTML), and who developed HTML?
3. Visit the Hobbes' Internet Timeline 10 (Hobbes' Internet Timeline Copyright © 1993–2016 by Robert H. Zakon) by accessing *www.zakon.org/robert/internet/timeline*. Determine the answers to the following:
   a. BITNET, one of the predecessors of the Internet, was launched in 1981. What does BITNET stand for?
   b. What worm struck the Internet in 2001?
   c. What food could you order through the Internet in 1994?
   d. What famous person sent an e-mail in 1976?
   e. What country offered Internet voting for local elections in 2005?
   f. In 2008, what kind of network did NASA test?
4. Close your browser.

Project 1-2: Explore the Windows 10 Interface

A good place to start learning about an operating system is to perform a preliminary exploration of its user interface and the tools available to work with and manage the system. In this project, you explore the Windows 10 interface and some of its tools.

1. Start your Windows 10 computer. If necessary, log on by pressing **Ctrl+Alt+Del**.
2. Enter your user name, password, and domain name (if required), and then press **Enter** or click the **Submit** button.
3. Notice the taskbar, which is at the bottom of the desktop on most systems.
4. Click **Start** to view the available applications you can run and tasks you can complete. Record some of the options.

5. On Windows 8.1 and Windows 10, you can right-click the **Start** button to see a list of administrative tasks that are particularly important to an IT administrator or computer technician (see Figure 1-13). Right-click **Start** and browse through the available tools. (Note: The same menu is also available in Windows Server 2012 R2 and later.)

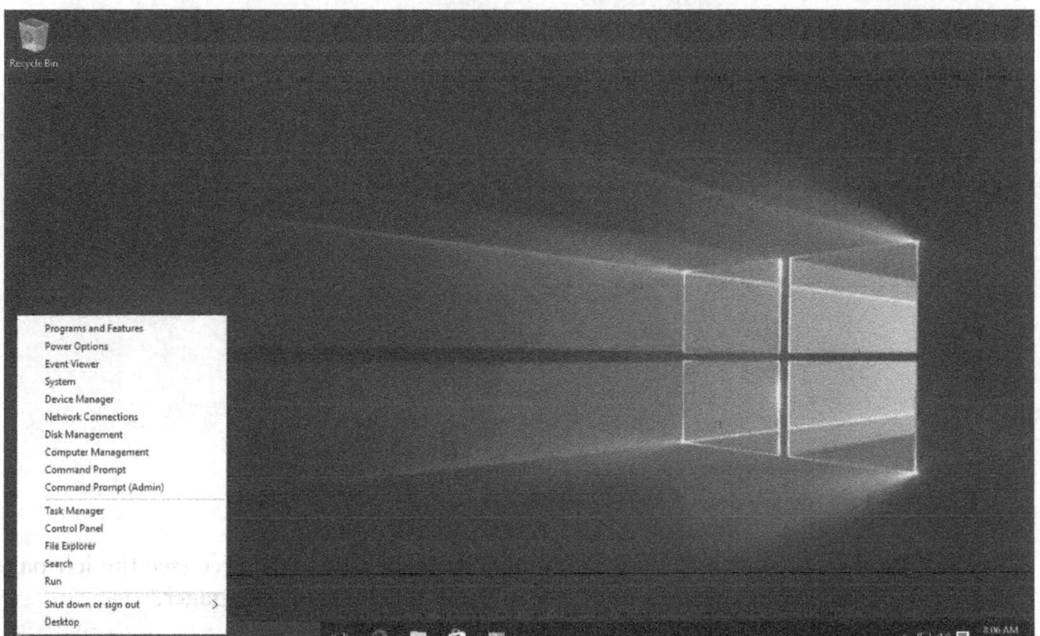

Figure 1-13 Right-clicking the Start menu in Windows 8.1 and Windows 10

6. Right-click the **Start** button, and then click **Command Prompt.** Notice the option for Command Prompt (Admin), which runs the command prompt with the administrative privileges required for some commands.

7. Type **help** and press **Enter** to see a list of commands you can run from the command prompt. Type **exit** and press **Enter** to close the command prompt.

8. Right-click **Start**, and click **System** (see Figure 1-14). This window displays information about the installed OS and the computer. From here you can change the computer name and join a workgroup or domain. This window also tells you whether Windows is activated. Close the System window by clicking the **X** in the upper-right corner.

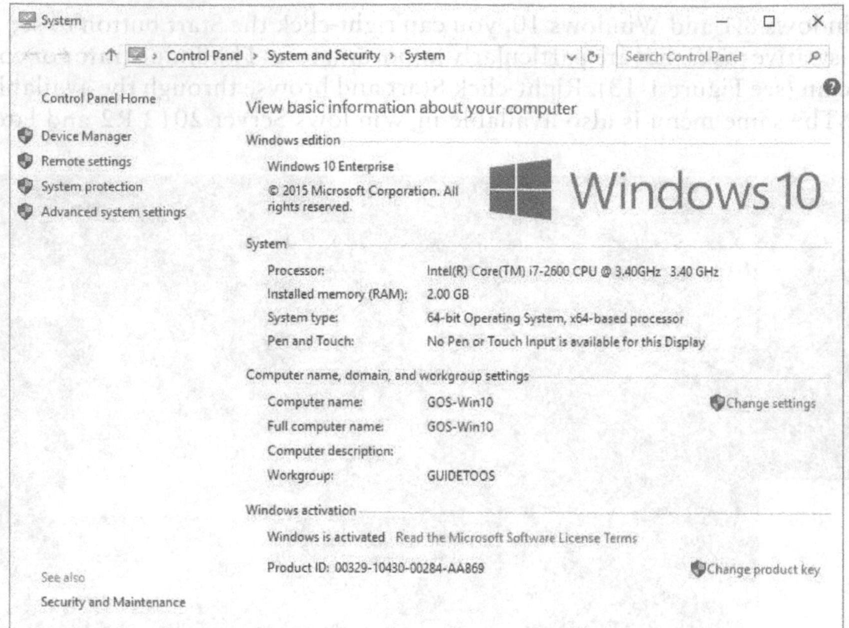

Figure 1-14 The Windows System window

9. Right-click **Start** and click **Computer Management.** In the tree (see the left pane) under Computer Management and System Tools, click **Device Manager.**
10. What types of devices that you can use with the computer are displayed in the right pane? Record some of your observations.
11. Double-click **Processors.** What type of processor or processors are installed in the computer? Double-click **Network adapters.** How many network adapters are installed? What kind are they?
12. Close the Computer Management window.
13. Stay logged on if you're going on to the next project.

Project 1-3: View Devices and Device Drivers in Windows 10

Devices connected to a computer, such as the keyboard, are linked into the operating system through device drivers. In this project, you view the keyboard device drivers installed in Windows 10.

1. Start your Windows 10 computer and log on, if necessary.
2. Right-click **Start,** and then click **Device Manager.**
3. Double-click **Keyboards.**
4. Double-click the keyboard description under Keyboards to open the keyboard Properties dialog box.

5. Click the **Driver** tab. Who is the provider of the keyboard device driver, and is the device driver digitally signed (for security)? Record your observations.

6. Click the **Driver Details** button to see the names of the driver files (see Figure 1-15).

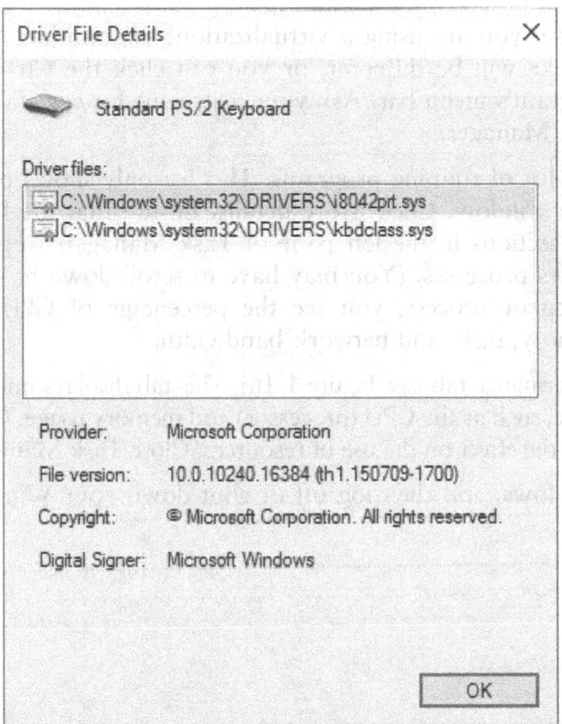

Figure 1-15 Driver details in Windows 10

7. Click **OK**, click **Cancel**, and then close the Device Manager window.

8. Stay logged on if you're going on to the next project.

Project 1-4: Examine Multitasking in Windows 10

Multitasking enables the user of a desktop operating system to perform many activities at once, such as running a word processor, using a spreadsheet, and running a Web browser. In this project, you take advantage of multitasking using Windows 10.

1. Start your Windows 10 computer and log on, if necessary.

2. Click in the **Search the web and Windows** text box next to the **Start** button, type **notepad**, and press **Enter** to start the Notepad program. (If Cortana is enabled, you will see "Ask me anything" in the text box instead of "Search the web and Windows.")

3. Click in the **Search the web and Windows** text box, type **calculator**, and press Enter to start the Calculator program.

4. Click in the **Search the web and Windows** text box, type **paint**, and press **Enter** to start the Paint program. You now have three programs running.
5. Notice that an icon appears for each application in the taskbar. Windows is now multitasking. Click the **Calculator** icon in the taskbar to bring its window to the front of the others.
6. Press **Ctrl+Alt+Del.** (Note that if you are using a virtualization program like VMware for these projects, this keystroke will be different, or you can click the Ctrl+Alt+Del icon on the virtualization program's menu bar. Ask your instructor for specific instructions, if necessary.) Click **Task Manager.**
7. In Task Manager, you see the list of running programs. This list only shows programs you started that have an open window. Click **More details.** Ensure that the **Processes** tab is selected. You see three sections in the left pane of Task Manager: Apps, Background processes, and Windows processes. (You may have to scroll down to see Windows processes.) For each app or process, you see the percentage of CPU each is using, and the amount of memory, disk, and network bandwidth.
8. In Task Manager, click the **Performance** tab (see Figure 1-16). This tab displays information about the system resources in use, such as the CPU (processor) and memory usage. Close one or two applications and observe the effect on the use of resources. Close Task Manager.
9. Close the remaining open windows, and then log off or shut down your Windows 10 computer.

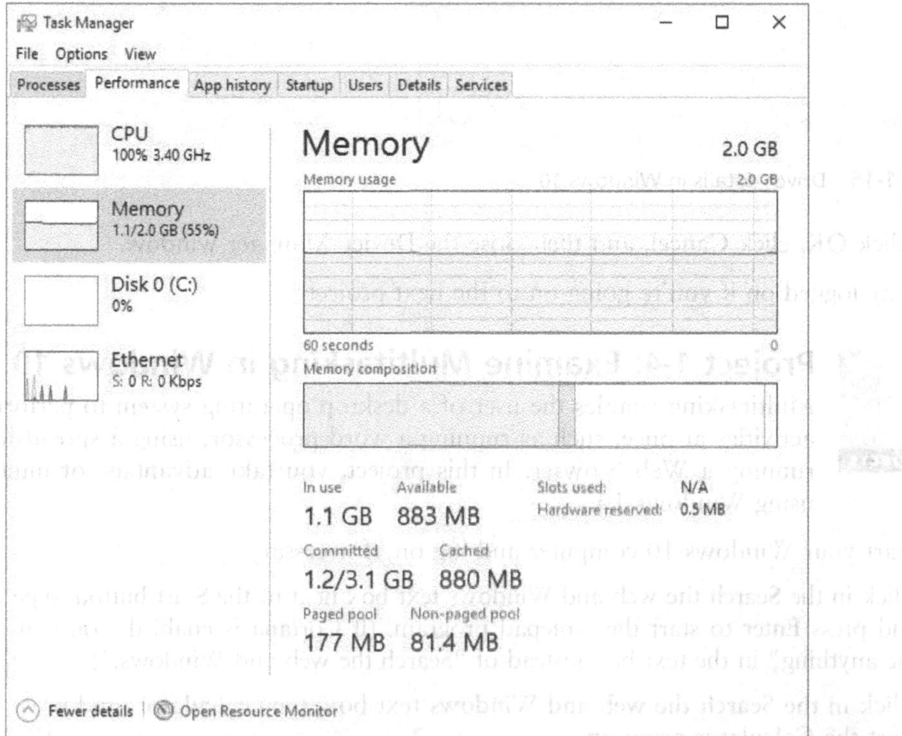

Figure 1-16 Windows Task Manager: Performance tab

Project 1-5: Explore the Fedora Linux Interface

In this project, you briefly explore the Fedora 23 desktop and view some of the common tools available in Fedora 23. While you can use other versions of Linux, Fedora 23 is suggested for these projects because they are written with that distribution in mind. Note that Fedora 23 comes with the GNOME desktop by default.

1. Start your Linux computer and log on.
2. Notice the bar at the top of the desktop. This is the top panel, which contains the Activities menu, a digital clock, and a place to access settings for the network, control the sound volume, and log on and off from the system. Click **Activities** to access common tasks.
3. In the Activities Overview window (see Figure 1-17), you have access to common applications such as a Web browser, e-mail client, image browser, and file browser. Click the **Show Applications** icon (it looks like a square grid of white dots) at the bottom of the screen to see more tasks and apps.

Figure 1-17 Fedora 23 with the GNOME desktop and Activities Overview window

Source: Fedora 23 (Linux)

4. Click **Settings** to see a list of settings tools. Click **Details** near the bottom of the All Settings window (see Figure 1-18). The Overview window displays basic information about the system hardware as well as the GNOME version. Close the Details window.

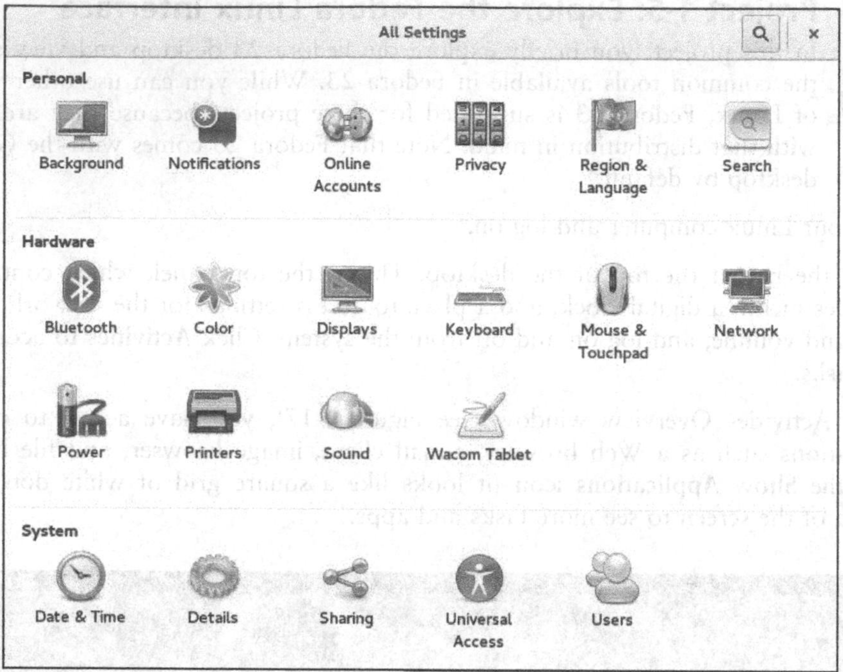

Figure 1-18 The All Settings window in Linux

Source: Fedora 23 (Linux)

5. Click **Activities** and click the **Show Applications** icon. Click **Utilities** to see a list of utilities that come with Fedora, including a calculator, disk management utilities, and system monitoring.

6. Click **Terminal** to open the terminal application, which provides a command-line interface to Linux, much like the command prompt in Windows. In the terminal window, type **uname –a** to see detailed version information for the Linux OS and the kernel.

7. Type **man ls** and press **Enter**. The resulting display provides documentation about the *ls* command that is used to list files. (The *man* command is used to access the Linux online help.)

8. Press the **Spacebar** to page through the manual information for the *ls* command. Keep pressing the Spacebar until you reach the end of the documentation. Press **q** to exit the manual documentation.

9. Type **ls -la** and press **Enter** to view information about files.

10. Click the **X** in the upper-right corner of the terminal window to close it and return to the desktop.

11. On the far right side of the top panel, click the **power icon**. A small panel opens. Here you can adjust the sound volume, manage network connections, view information about the current user, log off the system, and shut down or lock the system, among other things. On the lower-right side of the open panel, click the **power icon**. You are informed that the system will power off in 60 seconds. Click **Cancel** if you are continuing to the next project.

Project 1-6: View Device Drivers in Linux

In this project, you list the contents of a particular driver file in Fedora Linux, but the same procedures apply to many versions of UNIX/Linux. In this example, the *sda* file contains driver information pertaining to hard drives.

1. Start your Fedora Linux system and log on, if necessary. In the panel at the top of the desktop, click **Activities,** click **Show Applications,** click **Utilities,** and then click **Terminal.** (Remember these steps to open a Linux terminal window, as you will be doing so frequently throughout the book. Later instructions simply tell you to open a terminal window.)
2. Type **ls -l /dev** and press **Enter** to display the contents of the /dev directory, which contains the Linux device drivers.
3. To see information about the hard disk driver, type **ls –l /dev/sda** and press **Enter.** Notice in the output the word *disk*, which indicates the driver is for a disk device. Device drivers will be discussed in more detail in Chapter 6, "Configuring Input and Output Devices."
4. Type **exit** and press **Enter** to close the terminal window, or close the window by clicking the **X** in the upper-right corner.

Project 1-7: Explore the Mac OS Interface

This project enables you to briefly explore the Mac OS X El Capitan desktop. Depending on the setup of your Mac OS X system, you may or may not need an account and password to access the operating system.

1. Boot the Mac OS X system. If you need to provide logon information, enter your name and password and press **Enter** or **Return.** (If you are using a Mac keyboard, the key is labeled *Return*. On PCs, the key is labeled *Enter*. Throughout this book, the term *Enter* will be used, but just substitute *Return* if you are using a Mac keyboard.)
2. Notice the menu options in the menu bar at the top of the screen and record them (see Figure 1-19).
3. Next, observe the bar that appears at the bottom of the screen (by default on most systems). This is called the *Dock*.
4. Point to each icon in the Dock to see what it does and record some of the icon names. (Note that the contents of the Dock can be customized, so different systems may have different icons.)
5. Click the **Go** menu at the top of the desktop. From here, you can explore files, view the network, access the iCloud drive, and open applications and utilities.
6. Click an open area of the desktop to close the Go menu.
7. Click the **Apple** icon at the far left side of the menu bar. Click **About This Mac** to see information about the system. Explore each of the six tabs in the About This Mac

window (see Figure 1-19). Close the About This Mac window by clicking the red **X** at the top of the window.

Figure 1-19 Mac OS X El Capitan desktop and About This Mac window

Source: Mac OS X El Capitan

8. Click **Help** on the menu bar at the top of the desktop. Click **Mac Help.**
9. Type **Using USB devices** in the Spotlight search box, which includes a magnifying glass icon. Press **Enter** and notice the range of topics from which to choose.
10. Close the Mac Help window by clicking the **red button** on the upper-left side of the window. An X appears in the button when you point to it.
11. Click **Go** in the menu bar at the top of the screen. Click **Utilities.**
12. Double-click **Terminal.** Use the scroll bar, if necessary, to find the Terminal icon.
13. Type **man ls** and press **Enter** to view documentation about the *ls* command.
14. Press the **Spacebar** to page through the documentation.
15. Press **q** to exit the documentation and return to the command prompt in the terminal window.
16. Type **ls -la** and press **Enter** to see a listing of files similar to those you saw with Fedora.
17. Click the **Terminal** menu at the top of the desktop and click **Quit Terminal.**
18. Close the Utilities window. Stay logged on to your Mac OS X computer if you are continuing to the next project.

Project 1-8: Examine Multitasking in Mac OS X

Mac OS X is another example of a multitasking operating system in which you can run several applications at the same time. This project enables you to start three applications in Mac OS X to demonstrate multitasking.

1. Start your Mac OS X computer and log on, if necessary. Double-click **Macintosh HD** on the desktop.
2. Double-click the **Applications** folder.
3. Double-click **TextEdit**. Notice that TextEdit is added to the Dock when you start the program.
4. Click the **Applications** window to bring it to the front, and then double-click **Calculator**. Calculator is added to the Dock.
5. Click the **Applications** window and double-click **Safari**. Note that you can also start Safari from its icon in the Dock.
6. Click the **Applications** window to activate it. Note that Go is displayed as an option in the menu bar at the top of the screen. Next, click **Go** in the menu bar and click **Utilities**.
7. Double-click **Activity Monitor** in the Utilities window.
8. Make sure that **CPU** is selected at the top of the Activity Monitor window. Click the **% CPU** column heading to sort programs by activity. Notice the changes (or lack of them) in CPU activity as you close windows in the following steps. (If necessary, move or maximize the Activity Monitor window so it is not obscured by other windows as they are clicked.)
9. Click the **Utilities** window and close it.
10. Click the **Calculator** on the desktop or its icon in the Dock to bring it to the front. Click **Calculator** in the menu bar at the top of the desktop and click **Quit Calculator**. You can also click the red **X** on the upper-left side of the application's window.
11. Close TextEdit and Safari. Note any changes in Activity Monitor.
12. Close Activity Monitor.
13. Notice that the icons from the applications you just closed are removed from the Dock (except Safari, which is always on the Dock).
14. Shut down or log off your Mac OS X computer.

Critical Thinking

The following activities give you critical thinking challenges. Challenge Labs give you an opportunity to use the skills you have learned to perform a task without step-by-step instructions. Case Projects present a practical problem for which you supply a written solution. Not all chapters contain Challenge Labs. There is not always a specific right or wrong answer to these critical thinking exercises. They are intended to encourage you to review the chapter material and delve deeper into the topics you have learned.

Case Projects

Case Project 1-1: Basic Operating System Functions

The Lawson City and County Planning Department has recently received a new budget allocation to purchase new desktop and server systems. Because the budget has been strapped for many years, the department hasn't been able to upgrade its systems. Most of the desktop computers are running Windows XP or Windows 7. The server systems are Windows Server 2003 and Windows Server 2008. The department has network and Internet connectivity through a combination of older wired and wireless technologies.

Before they begin making decisions, the planning office managers ask you to make a presentation to cover the basics of operating systems. They ask you to begin the presentation by explaining basic functions that operating systems perform. Create a presentation and give it to the class or your instructor. Consider using diagrams or slides.

Case Project 1-2: Device Drivers

This is a follow-on case project to Case Project 1-1.

One of the managers has heard that current device drivers are important to consider when choosing an operating system. Improve your presentation by including an explanation of device drivers and why they are important.

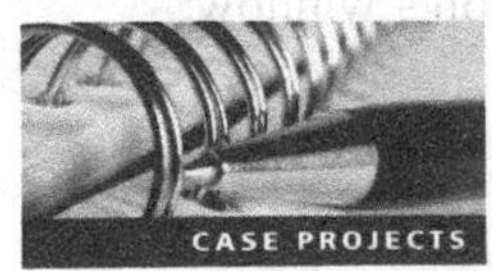

Case Project 1-3: Choose a New Server

This is a follow-on case project to Case Project 1-1.

High on the list of needs is implementing a new server. A small committee of planning department employees has been formed to look at options for a server operating system. What options should they consider, which do you recommend, and why do you recommend them? Write a short memo for your instructor.

Case Project 1-4: Choose New Desktop Systems

This is a follow-on case project to Case Project 1-1.

What desktop operating systems might be used to replace the Windows XP and Windows 7 computers? What operating system capabilities should the planning department look for when replacing these computers? Also, how might system costs affect the decision? Write a short memo for your instructor.

Case Project 1-5: A Problem with a Newly Released Operating System

While the planning department is researching computer options, a computer support person comes across an article in a computer magazine about a newly released operating system that is experiencing frequent memory and CPU problems, such as slow or no response when accessing disk drives or displaying characters on the monitor. What might be the cause of these problems? Write a short memo for your instructor.

chapter 2

Popular Operating Systems

After reading this chapter and completing the exercises, you will be able to:

- Describe early Microsoft operating systems and their characteristics
- Identify the features of modern Microsoft operating systems
- Identify the features and characteristics of UNIX and UNIX-like operating systems
- Identify the features and characteristics of Mac OS and Mac OS X

This chapter examines the features of the most popular operating systems as well as their general characteristics, strengths, and weaknesses. Chapter 1 provided a brief historical survey of operating systems. This chapter takes a closer look at early Microsoft operating systems that laid the groundwork for current desktop and server operating systems. You will then focus on these more recent operating systems, which include Windows 7 and later versions, Windows Server 2012 and later versions, as well as UNIX/Linux and Mac OS X El Capitan. This overview will provide the background you need to choose the operating system that is best suited for a particular work or home environment, and to determine which operating system to use when new computers are installed or existing computers are upgraded. Likewise, you will be able to identify situations in which the wrong operating system is used.

System hardware requirements for the current operating systems discussed in this book are listed in Chapter 5.

Early Microsoft Operating Systems

Earlier operating systems were very primitive compared to those available today. They laid the groundwork for the look and feel, features, and characteristics of current operating systems. This section describes some early Microsoft operating systems and shows the progression from these systems to more modern ones.

MS-DOS and PC DOS

Microsoft's original operating system for the IBM PC hardware platform was called MS-DOS, or more simply, DOS. The version of MS-DOS that ran on early IBM computers was called PC DOS because it was customized and marketed by IBM. Most programs operating under DOS used a simple text-based, command-line user interface similar to what you see when you open a command prompt on a modern Windows computer. Both versions could only access up to 640 KB of memory.

Windows 3.x

Microsoft released the first version of Windows in 1984, implementing a graphical user interface (GUI) to compete with the Apple Macintosh. This early version of Windows was quite slow and not well accepted. Windows 3.1 in the early 1990s was the first popular, usable Microsoft GUI, and it paved the way for Windows to become the dominant PC operating system (see Figure 2-1).

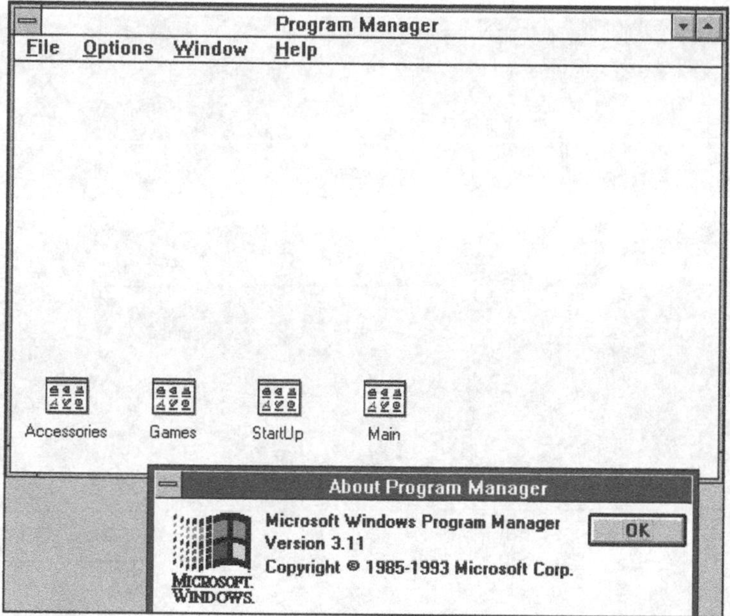

Figure 2-1 The Windows 3.x GUI

Windows 95

As the PC platform became more powerful and the Pentium architecture became more common, Microsoft created a true 32-bit operating system that could use the functionality of the new 32-bit computer architecture. Windows 95 eliminated the 640 KB memory limit and the 16-bit code. By being able to use more computer resources, Windows 95 could introduce several advanced functions that have now become standard Windows features:

- The Windows desktop
- Plug and Play
- ActiveX and the Component Object Model (COM)
- The registry
- Multitasking
- Enhanced network and Internet capabilities

The Windows Desktop Windows 95 introduced a new GUI, now called the *desktop* (see Figure 2-2), which became the foundation for the GUI used in all later versions of Windows. The Windows 95 GUI introduced the Start button that provides direct access to system utilities and application programs. Other desktop features included the taskbar at the bottom of the screen, which contains icons that represent currently running programs and other information about the system's operation, and shortcut and program icons to seamlessly run programs, manipulate files, and access network connections from one place.

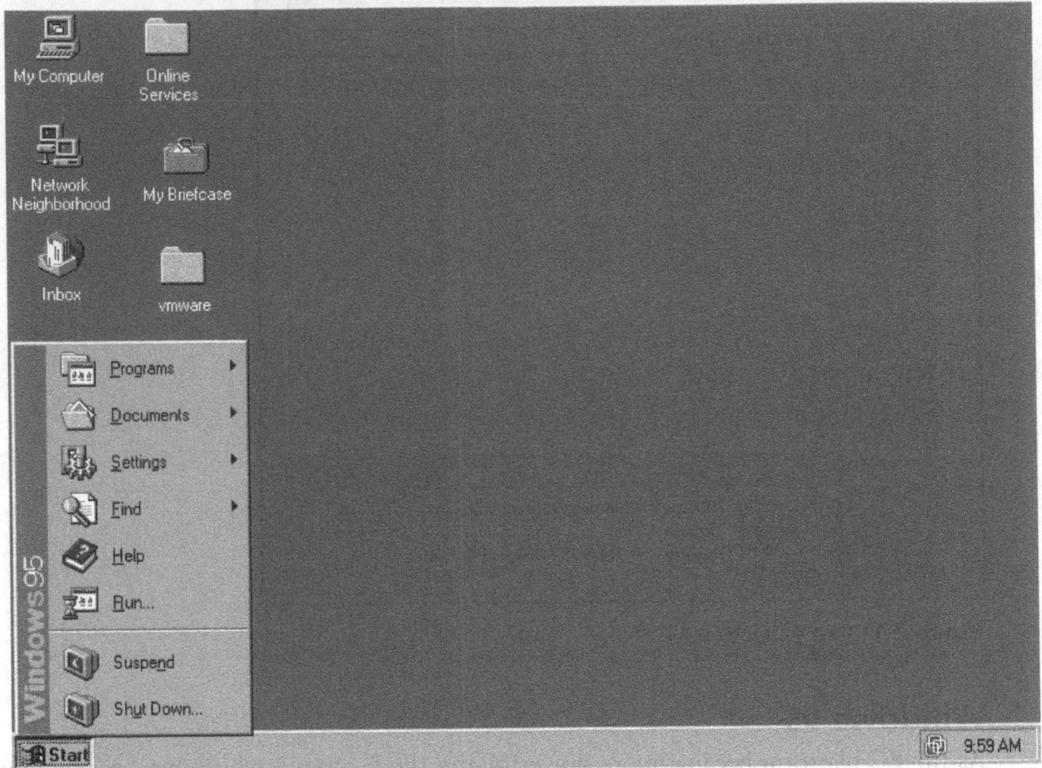

Figure 2-2 The Windows 95 desktop shortcuts, Start button, and taskbar

Plug and Play Plug and Play (PnP) was possibly the most exciting hardware feature introduced in Windows 95 and continued in later versions of Windows (except Windows NT). PnP enables the operating system to automatically detect newly installed hardware. Before PnP, devices had to be configured using hardware in the form of little switches or jumpers on the expansion card or motherboard. This manual configuration was fraught with difficulties due to resource conflicts and the risk of incorrect switch or jumper settings. PnP put the configuration of devices in the hands of software, which is not a perfect solution, but it is considerably better than manual configuration.

ActiveX and the Component Object Model (COM) Much of the easy manipulation of the user interface in Windows 95 was made possible by a Microsoft technology called ActiveX. **ActiveX**, along with its parent, the **Component Object Model** (COM), is a standardized way for objects to communicate with each other. These objects include programs, files, computers, printers, control panels, windows, and icons.

The Registry Windows 95 also introduced a new way of storing and managing operating system information. Up to this point, such information was kept in files in various locations on the hard disk. The new concept was called the **registry**, a database that stores operating system information, information about hardware and software configuration, and general information that is shared by parts of the operating system or application programs to make COM and ActiveX work. You explore the registry in Hands-On Project 2-2.

The registry is a hierarchical database that provides the following information:

- Operating system configuration
- Service and device driver information and configuration
- Software and application parameters
- Hardware configuration
- Performance information
- Desktop configuration

Multitasking Multitasking in Windows 95 was cooperative for 16-bit applications, but preemptive for 32-bit applications. Windows 95 introduced a **task supervisor,** which detects tasks that appear stuck, and presents the option to close hung tasks without having to restart the operating system. A hung task occurs when an application no longer responds to keyboard or mouse input. In earlier versions of Windows, and sometimes even with Windows 95 and later, a hung task could hang the entire OS, requiring a restart and reboot of the computer. Starting with Windows 95 and preemptive multitasking, a hung task did not hang the entire system and only the problematic task had to be restarted.

Enhanced Network and Internet Capabilities The networking functionality in Windows 95 was substantially extended from earlier versions of Windows. Unlike earlier versions of Windows, in Windows 95 the network drivers were part of the Windows operating system. In all but the early versions of Windows 95, all the networking code was written as a 32-bit application. This resulted in a significant boost in network performance. When Windows 95 was released, Microsoft did not support Internet connectivity, but by 1997, Microsoft integrated Internet access through its Web browser, Internet Explorer, and the ability to share computer resources over the Internet into its operating systems.

Windows 98/Me

Windows 98 and its slightly newer sibling, Windows Millennium Edition (Me), were similar to Windows 95 in many ways. They ran on similar computers and provided roughly the same capabilities. Windows Me included all Windows 98 features but expanded multimedia and networking capabilities.

Windows 98 The Windows 98 user interface differed slightly from Windows 95, with little changing of the desktop's appearance except for the ability of Windows 98 to view items on the desktop as a Web page, a feature called Active Desktop.

Some of the additional changes from Windows 95 to Windows 98 included:

- Expanded PnP support
- Automatic registry checks and repairs
- Advanced power management features

- Support for new hardware standards such as Universal Serial Bus (USB)
- Improved cooperative multitasking for 16-bit applications
- Greater integration of Internet and networking features
- Extended multimedia support
- Expanded support for high-speed networking
- Ability to perform upgrades over the Internet

Windows 98 also supported newer hardware standards, such as **Universal Serial Bus (USB)** 1.0, a relatively high-speed (at the time) input/output (I/O) port, and updated standards for multimedia, data storage, and networking.

USB is a bus standard that enables you to attach all types of devices—keyboards, cameras, pointing devices, telephones, tape drives, and flash memory, for example—to one bus port on a computer. Up to 127 devices can be attached to one port, and it is not necessary to power off the computer when you attach a device. USB was developed to replace the traditional serial and parallel bus technologies on computers.

Windows Millennium Edition (Me)

Windows Millennium Edition (Me) was developed for home computer users, not office or professional users, and it implemented applications that appealed to home users more than Windows 95 or 98. These applications included playing music, storing family photos, playing games, and accessing the Internet. Windows Me offered better support for infrared devices, such as **Infrared Data Association (IrDA)** support, and implemented the enhanced PnP standard, called **Universal Plug and Play (UPnP)**. UPnP is a set of protocols that allows network devices to be automatically discovered and configured by network client computers. While Windows Me brought a number of enhancements to the Windows OS, its hardware support and reliability problems hampered its success in the marketplace. Customers opted to stay with Windows 98 until Windows XP came out in late 2001.

Windows NT

While Microsoft was developing the Windows line of operating systems to run on the lower end of IBM PC hardware, it also developed a high-end operating system intended for powerful workstations and servers. This OS was called Windows New Technology, or Windows NT. Over the course of its development, Windows NT supported the IBM PC architecture, the Alpha architecture, and for a while, the PowerPC architecture, as each of these hardware platforms gained its time in the industry spotlight. The idea was to make an operating system that could be used on some very powerful computers. One very significant difference between Windows 95/98 (often referred to as Windows 9x) and Windows NT was that the operating system kernel in Windows NT ran in **privileged mode**, which protected it from problems created by a malfunctioning program or process. Privileged mode gives the operating system an extra level of security from intruders, and prevents system crashes due to out-of-control applications.

Windows NT 4.0 was the first widely successful version of Windows NT. It was released at about the same time as Windows 95 and sported the new Windows 95 look.

Windows NT was offered in two versions: Windows NT Workstation and Windows NT Server. Windows NT Workstation was the operating system for users who needed a high-end, stable, and secure graphical operating system. Windows NT Server was designed as a multiuser server operating system for access over a network. For all the changes inside the operating system, however, Windows NT looked remarkably like Windows 9x on the outside. Users could easily move from the Windows desktop OS (Windows 9x) to Windows NT because of the familiar user interface.

Networking Support Windows NT supported network connectivity protocols that were compatible with IBM mainframes, UNIX computers, Macintosh computers, Novell NetWare servers, all Windows-based computers, and others. It also supported high-speed networking connectivity and remote access over telephone lines or the Internet.

Security Security was a significant feature of Windows NT. The operating system required the user to log on and be authenticated by submitting a username and password to gain access to the computer. Windows NT 4.0 Server had a C2 top-secret security rating from the United States government. The C2 rating means that the Windows NT Server network operating system provided security at many levels, including the following:

- File and folder protection
- User accounts and passwords
- File, folder, and account auditing
- File server access protection on a network
- File server management controls

The domain was an integral part of the Windows NT security model. In every Windows NT domain, there was one Primary Domain Controller (PDC). The PDC computer was responsible for keeping all usernames and passwords for all users who wanted to contact the domain. Any other server that was part of the domain could request password and permission information from the PDC. This allowed a user to sign on to the domain once and gain access to any server that was a member of the domain, a feature called ***single sign-on***. In addition to user and password information, the PDC could also contain system policies, which provided general information on what users were allowed to do on certain computers on the network, down to what function and features of the user interface should be enabled.

Windows 2000

Built on the Windows NT technology, Microsoft Windows 2000 was a more robust operating system. The operating system represented a significant rewrite of the Windows NT kernel, and ran about 30 percent faster than Windows NT. Also, like its Windows NT predecessor, Windows 2000 used preemptive multitasking and multithreading, and the kernel ran in privileged mode.

Windows 2000 had more advanced networking support than Windows NT and supported new networking technologies, such as **virtual private networks (VPNs)**. A VPN is a private network that is like an encrypted tunnel through a larger network—such as the Internet, an enterprise network, or both—and is restricted only to designated member **clients**. With a VPN, you can securely access network resources on a private home or company network from anywhere you have Internet access.

People who have experience troubleshooting problems with mismatched drivers, or who have overwritten portions of the operating system in previous versions of Windows, appreciated the built-in protection of the core operating system files and driver-signing features of Windows 2000. Windows 2000 kept a copy of operating system files in a safe place, so if a critical file was overwritten or deleted, the operating system automatically replaced it. **Driver signing** means that you can set up all drivers so they cannot be inadvertently overwritten by earlier driver versions, and only certified versions of drivers can be installed.

New features in Windows 2000 included:

- *Active Directory*—**Active Directory** is a database used to store information about resources such as user accounts, computers, and printers; it groups resources at different levels (hierarchies) for local and universal management. These groupings are called *containers* because they are like storage bins that can hold network resources and other bins at lower levels. Active Directory also provides a centralized means to quickly find a specific resource through indexing. Active Directory was only available on the server version of Windows 2000.
- *Distributed network architecture*—Windows 2000 offered new ways to distribute network and management resources to match the needs of most types of networks. In Windows 2000 Server, multiple servers could be designated as domain controllers, each containing a copy of Active Directory and able to verify a user who wanted to log on to the network. This was an important change from Windows NT Server 4.0, in which one server, the PDC, maintained the master copy of account and security information; and one or more servers, called *backup domain controllers (BDC)*, kept copies of this information as a backup. On Windows 2000 Server, each computer that had Active Directory installed was referred to as a Domain Controller (DC).
- *Kerberos security*—**Kerberos** is a security system and authentication protocol that authenticates users and grants or denies access to network resources based on a user's log-on name and password. The primary goal of Kerberos is to prevent unauthorized users from accessing computer and network resources. Kerberos works through a special communications protocol that enables a client to initiate contact with a server and request secure communication. The server responds by providing an encryption key that is unique to that communication session, and it does so by using a protected communication called a *ticket*. Windows 2000 Server and Professional and all successive versions of Windows support Kerberos.
- *IntelliMirror*—IntelliMirror was a concept built into Windows 2000. It was intended to enable Windows 2000 clients to access the same desktop settings, applications, and data from wherever they accessed the network, even if they were not on the network. IntelliMirror also used information in Active Directory to ensure that consistent

security and group policies applied to the client, and that the client's software was upgraded or removed on the basis of a central management scheme.

- *International language compatibility*—Windows 2000 supported more languages and language capabilities than previous versions of Windows, and included Hindi, Chinese, and multiple versions of English. This feature was important because servers are used all over the world.

Windows 2000 Server and Windows 2000 Professional

Microsoft offered versions of Windows 2000 designed for server and workstation implementations. The basic server version was called Windows 2000 Server, and Windows 2000 Professional was designed for workstations. When it introduced Windows 2000, Microsoft's overall goal was to combine Windows 2000 Server and Windows 2000 Professional on a server-based network to achieve a lower **total cost of ownership (TCO)**. The TCO is the total cost of owning a network, including hardware, software, training, maintenance, and user support costs. Windows 2000 Professional was intended as a reliable, easy-to-configure, workstation operating system to be used in a business or professional environment. Recognizing that professionals are highly mobile, Windows 2000 Professional was designed to work equally well on a desktop computer or a notebook computer. Windows 2000 Server was intended to play a key management role on the network by administering Active Directory and a multitude of network services. By combining Windows 2000 Professional workstations and Windows 2000 Server on the same network, along with Active Directory, it was possible to centralize software updates and workstation configuration via a server.

Windows 2000 Server supported up to four processors, while Windows 2000 Professional supported up to two. Windows 2000 Server also offered more services and user connectivity options that are appropriate for a server instead of a workstation. These services included the following:

- The capability to handle virtually unlimited numbers of users simultaneously (depending on the hardware platform; Windows 2000 Professional is designed for up to 10 simultaneous users only)
- Active Directory management
- Network management
- Web-based management services
- Network-wide security management
- Network storage management
- Remote network access, network-wide communications services, and high-speed network connectivity
- Application services management
- Network printer management through Active Directory

Windows 2000 Server, Advanced Server, and Datacenter Server

Windows 2000 Server was divided into three different products to match the network application: Windows 2000 Server, Windows 2000 Advanced Server, and Windows 2000

Datacenter Server. Windows 2000 Server provided a comprehensive set of server and Web services for up to four processor systems, and supported up to 4 GB of RAM. Windows 2000 Advanced Server was intended for high-end enterprise networks that require up to eight processor servers, clustered servers, or both. Clustering is a technique in which two or more servers are linked to equally share the server processor load, server storage, and other server resources (see Figure 2-3). Windows 2000 Advanced Server also had the ability to handle up to 8 GB of RAM. Windows 2000 Datacenter Server was targeted for large database and data manipulation services. The Datacenter version supported 64 GB of RAM, clustering, and individual servers with up to 32 processors.

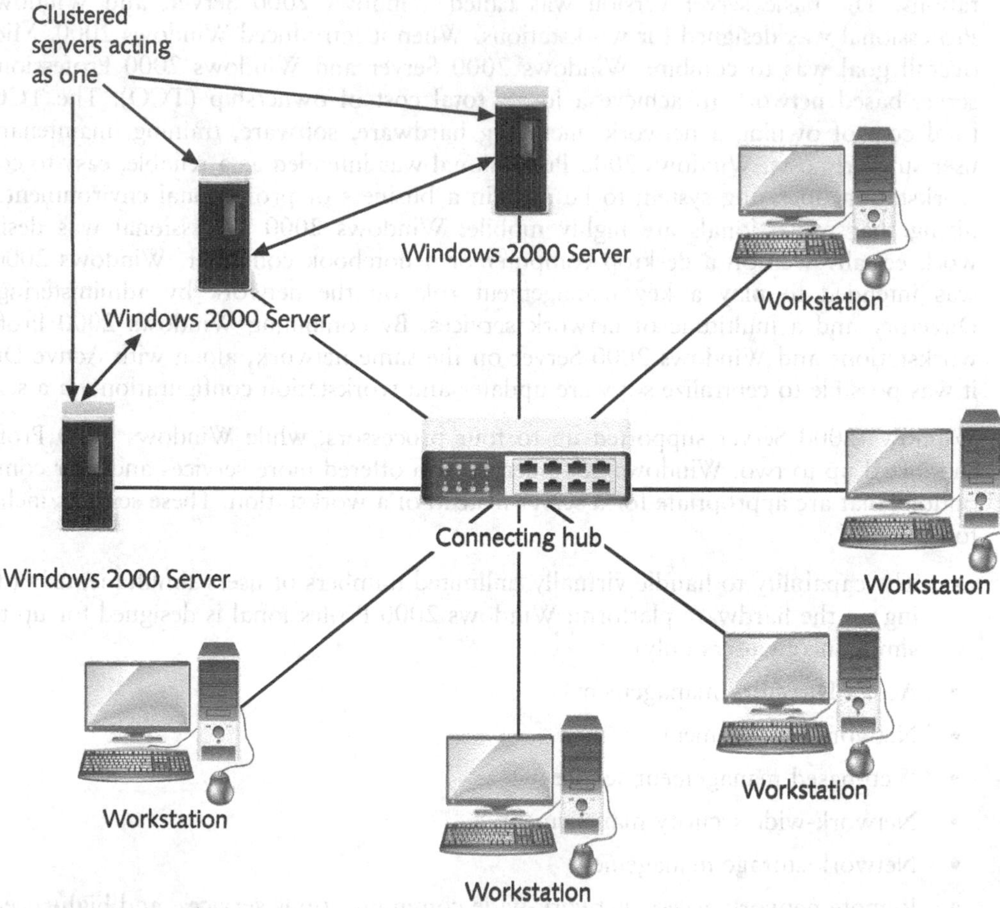

Figure 2-3 Server clustering

Microsoft discontinued support for all versions of Windows 2000 Server in 2010.

Windows XP and Windows Server 2003

Windows 2000 evolved into two products, both containing the core elements of the Windows 2000 kernel: Windows XP and Windows Server 2003. Windows XP was the desktop version of the operating system, while Windows Server 2003 was the server version. Both of these operating systems offered a refreshed desktop GUI, with changes apparent in the two-column Start menu, as shown in Figure 2-4.

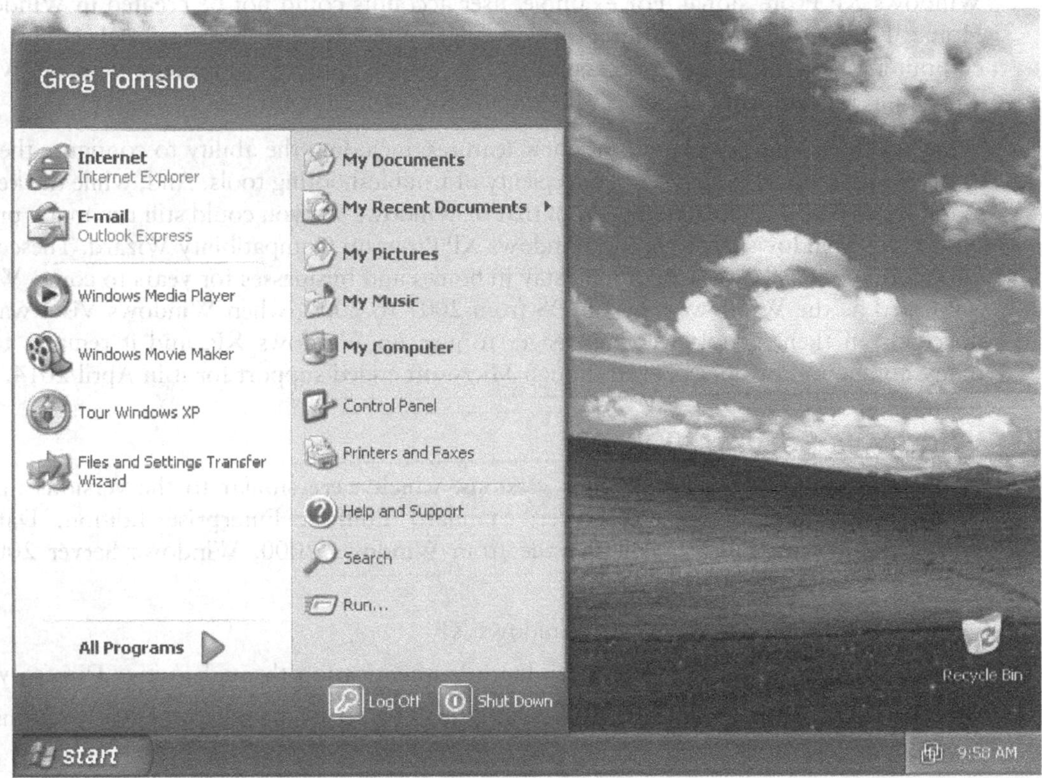

Figure 2-4 The Windows XP desktop and Start menu

In addition to the new GUI, Windows XP and Windows Server 2003 offered more capabilities for keeping photo albums, playing music, running video and audio files, playing games, and using other multimedia applications. Windows XP and Windows Server 2003 also offered better Internet security through a built-in firewall and the ability to remotely control the computer over an Internet connection via a tool called Remote Desktop. Remote Desktop is designed to be secure; the computer being controlled must first grant access. Another feature introduced with Windows XP was that you had to **activate** it after installation. The OS could be activated automatically online or by calling Microsoft with the activation key that came with the system. The activation code is linked to a particular computer on which the operating system resides. System activation is a mechanism to help ensure that software is not pirated.

Windows XP came in several versions, including Windows XP Home, Windows XP Professional, Windows XP Tablet PC, Windows XP Media Center, and Windows XP 64-Bit.

Windows XP Home and Professional Editions Windows XP, which stands for "Windows Experience," originally came in two versions: Windows XP Professional and Windows XP Home Edition. Windows XP Professional was intended for office and professional use. This version of Windows XP had the ability to create accounts for different users who might use the operating system. Windows XP Professional, like Windows 2000 Professional, could be used as a small server for up to 10 users. Windows XP Home Edition was meant to be the next upgrade from Windows 9x/Me, and was a scaled-down version of Windows XP Professional. For example, user accounts could not be created in Windows XP Home Edition. Another difference was that Windows XP Professional could run on computers using up to two processors and on 64-bit Itanium computers, whereas Windows XP Home Edition ran only on 32-bit single-processor computers.

Windows XP contained many other new features, including the ability to configure themes for the desktop, a better help system, and plenty of troubleshooting tools. And, while the kernel for Windows XP was vastly different from that of Windows 9x, you could still run many programs written for Windows 9x using the Windows XP Program Compatibility Wizard. These features and more made Windows XP a mainstay in homes and businesses for years to come. Windows XP lasted as the Windows flagship OS from 2001 to 2007, when Windows Vista was introduced. Even then, people were not eager to give up Windows XP, and it remains today in many homes and businesses even though Microsoft ended support for it in April 2014.

Windows Server 2003/R2

Windows Server 2003 came in four versions, which were similar to the versions that were available for Windows 2000 Server: Standard Edition, Enterprise Edition, Datacenter Edition, and Web Edition. An upgrade from Windows 2000, Windows Server 2003 contained new features, including:

- The GUI interface used with Windows XP
- Improvements for faster network logon authentication through Active Directory
- Several hundred new group policies that can be set to manage user workstations via Active Directory
- New tools for managing server resources
- Ability to run on 64-bit Itanium processors
- Remote server management through the Remote Desktop tool
- Enhanced ability for users to run programs on the server, through Microsoft Terminal Services
- Runtime code for the Windows .NET development environment to run applications through the Internet on all types of devices

Microsoft listened to the demands for tighter security in their operating systems. With Windows Server 2003, they took a step in that direction. After the initial installation, most Windows server features had to be set up manually, which was a change from previous versions of the operating system, where many functions were set up by default. In Windows Server 2003, you set up only the functions you wanted to use. (Operating system installation is covered in Chapter 5.)

Windows Server 2003 Release 2 (R2) was an interim version of Windows Server. It upgraded Windows Server 2003 with many new features that were then incorporated into Windows Server 2008 and beyond. Some of the Windows Server 2003 R2 enhancements included a new version of the **Microsoft Management Console (MMC)**, faster code execution (depending on the server hardware), a new **Print Management Console**, strong integration with **.NET Framework**, and improved security. Organizations that used Active Directory, **Distributed File System (DFS)**, clustered servers, and group policies found valuable new features for managing their enterprise networks. Microsoft continued to emphasize improvements in security for all of its operating systems, and Windows Server 2003 R2 was no exception. From the security standpoint, the R2 version came with a new Windows Firewall, first introduced in Windows XP Service Pack 2. The R2 version also integrated new security patches into the operating system code, and added a new feature, called Post-Setup Security Updates, to guide server managers through new configuration activities related to patches and updates.

Windows Server 2003 R2 offered many new features that organizations wanted for even more reliable, heavy-duty, and uninterrupted computing. Some of these features are summarized here:

- Better performance
- Improved group policy management
- MMC 3.0 and the Print Management Console
- New server clustering capabilities
- Virtual server options
- Dynamic Systems Initiative
- Better identity and access management
- Better options for branch office servers
- DFS enhancements
- Subsystem for UNIX-based applications
- Improved storage management

From the Trenches ...

A college had limited IT server staff who were familiar with the Windows Server 2003 operating system. With the release of Windows Server 2003 R2, they used the Print Management Console to give access to the help desk personnel. The help desk was able to set up, reset, check status, and customize printers on the network. All of this took place remotely at the help desk. Customers were happy that they got immediate assistance and did not have to wait for a technician to come to their office. The server staff were also pleased that they did not have to make as many trips out of the office to fix problems.

Microsoft ended support of Windows Server 2003 in July 2015, and has urged companies to move to Windows Server 2008 or Windows Server 2012.

Modern Windows Operating Systems

While many Windows XP and Windows Server 2003 computers are still operating, both OSs are now considered legacy systems. Microsoft no longer supports them or earlier Windows versions, and users should update their computers to more recent versions to ensure better reliability and security. Even Windows 7 and Windows Vista, which are described next, no longer receive mainstream support from Microsoft. Extended support ends for Vista in April 2017 and in January 2020 for Windows 7.

Windows Vista/Windows 7

Microsoft Windows Vista, released in January 2007, is a workstation operating system that followed Windows XP. Features in Windows Vista grew out of Windows XP and the development process for Microsoft Windows Server 2008. Not long afterward, in July 2009, Windows 7 was introduced. Like Windows Me, Windows Vista was not well received, which is why Windows 7 was introduced fairly quickly after it was apparent that Windows Vista was struggling in the marketplace (people still loved Windows XP). This section focuses on Windows 7, which is far more prevalent in homes and businesses even in 2016, even though most of what is discussed applies equally to Windows Vista as well. In addition, most features were carried forward from Windows 7 to Windows 8/8.1 and Windows 10.

Windows 7 was geared to make desktop computing more intuitive and more reliable for users than previous versions of Windows. For example, every computer user has had trouble finding a specific document or file they know is buried in a folder somewhere. Windows 7 is designed to enable users to quickly find documents, files, and resources—even if they don't remember the exact location. This is accomplished through enhanced search facilities and new ways to organize information.

In terms of security and reliability, Windows 7 has more built-in security features than previous versions and requires less rebooting. For instance, the Windows 7 firewall is enhanced to monitor both incoming and outgoing communications. When used with Windows 7, Internet Explorer has stronger security to avoid spyware and malicious software attacks. Further, when you install a software patch to enhance security or for other reasons, there are fewer instances that require you to reboot the computer right away, which makes your system more reliable.

Code enhancements "under the hood" in Windows 7 make this operating system about a third faster than Windows XP and Windows 2000. In terms of what you see on the desktop, Windows 7 provides what Microsoft calls a "unified presentation subsystem for Windows," which means that the windows you see are consistently designed and offer many new features for quickly accessing information. The new desktop presentation, called Aero (Authentic, Energetic, Reflective, and Open), also enables organizations to more effectively manage user desktops for uniformity and to reduce common problems in computer use. To the developer, the unified subsystem means there is a more consistent set of application programming interfaces (APIs) for linking programs with the operating system. Visually, Aero can use 3D graphics accelerators to render transparent and other visual effects called "Glass" display effects.

For most users, the reasons to upgrade to Windows 7 include greater speed, more productivity through the use of intuitive features, uniformity of the desktop, and greater security and reliability. These factors are particularly important to users who rely on a computer for school, work, entertainment, and important functions in a home.

While many home users upgrade their OS for new features, corporate IT departments often upgrade only when there is a business reason for doing so. Business reasons may include new features that increase employee productivity, but many businesses only upgrade because the OS is no longer supported with security and reliability enhancements.

Windows 7 implements many new features that represent changes from earlier Windows operating systems. A sampling of new features includes:

- Desktop and windows interface
- Libraries
- Folder resource sharing options
- Reliability features
- Security features
- User Account Protection
- Management options

Each of these is explained in the following sections.

Desktop and Windows Interface When you use Windows 7, you'll notice that, as in Windows XP, there is a Start button on the taskbar. The taskbar can contain icons for currently running programs or ones you can choose to run. A notification area on the right side contains the time and other elements, such as the speaker volume. Windows 7 also has a feature called desktop **gadgets** (first introduced with Vista), or small applications for readily accessing information and tools, such as a clock, calendar, or weather updates.

Desktop gadgets posed a security risk, and support for them ceased starting with Windows 8.

The Windows 7 Search box at the bottom of the Start menu is an important feature that enables fast searching for a specific document or file. The Search feature provides very fast searches for resources. Figure 2-5 shows the Windows 7 Start menu with the Search box at the bottom and the desktop with a clock gadget and a CPU meter gadget running on the right side.

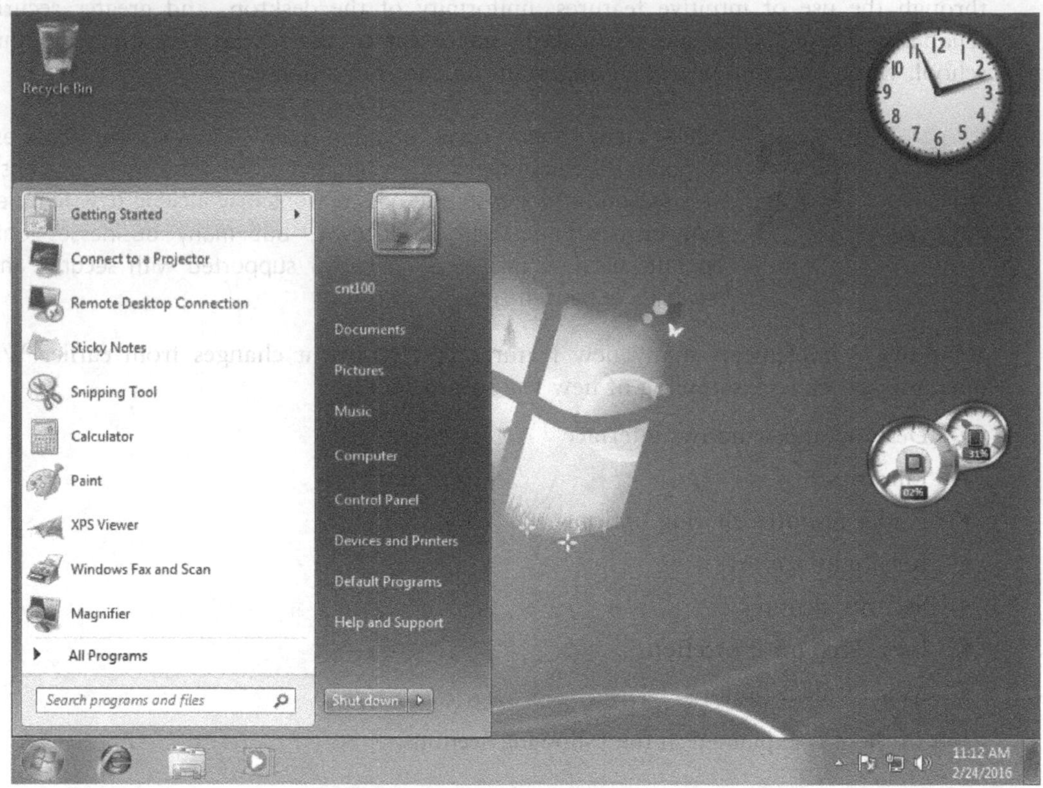

Figure 2-5 The Windows 7 desktop and Start menu

As in previous Windows versions, the Windows 7 Control Panel is the place to configure your computer. Control Panel still offers the Classic view, which is comparable to pre-Windows XP versions. You can also see Control Panel contents in the Category view introduced in Windows XP. When you use the Category view, the presentation of information is designed to more quickly address a specific task, such as configuring a network connection. Figure 2-6 shows a list of the Control Panel categories in Windows 7.

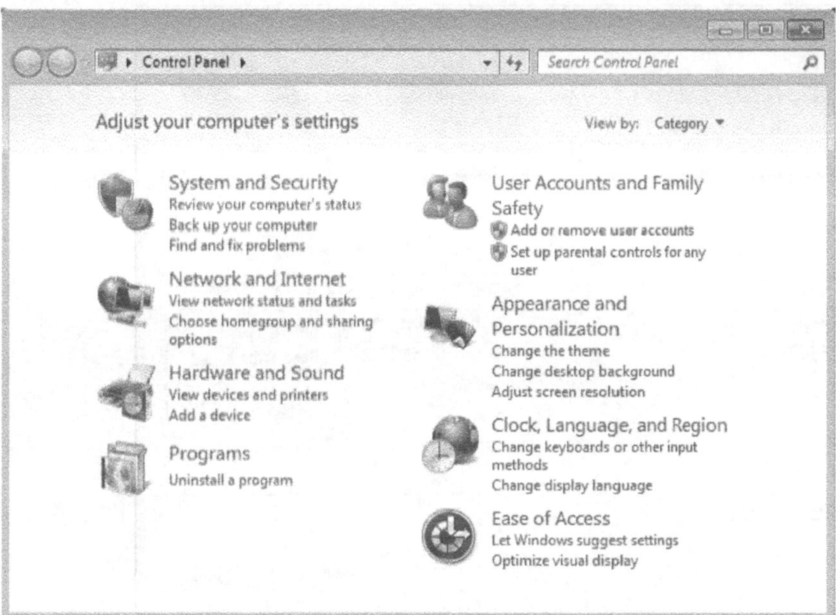

Figure 2-6 Windows 7 Control Panel categories

Libraries A library is an innovation for organizing files from multiple locations on your computer and the network. Libraries can be optimized based on the content of the files, such as documents, music, pictures, and videos. A library is not really a folder in the traditional sense, such as Documents. It is a dynamic folder that houses files from one or more different locations.

Folder Resource Sharing Options Sharing folders over a network is a powerful tool for making information resources available to multiple network users (see Chapter 10). In Windows 7, you have the option to configure folder sharing in one of two ways: (1) by selecting the folder and clicking the Share with button in the Explorer window or (2) by right-clicking the folder and clicking Share with. After you elect to share a folder, you see the Sharing Wizard that enables you to specify which users can access the folder (see Figure 2-7). You can choose from a list of users who have accounts on the computer or you can use the Find button to locate other users on a network, such as those in Active Directory. There are three permission levels:

- *Read*—Permissions to open and view the file
- *Read/write*—Permissions to view, use, and change the file contents, and to remove the file
- *Owner*—Permissions to view, use, and change the file contents as well as change permissions on the file

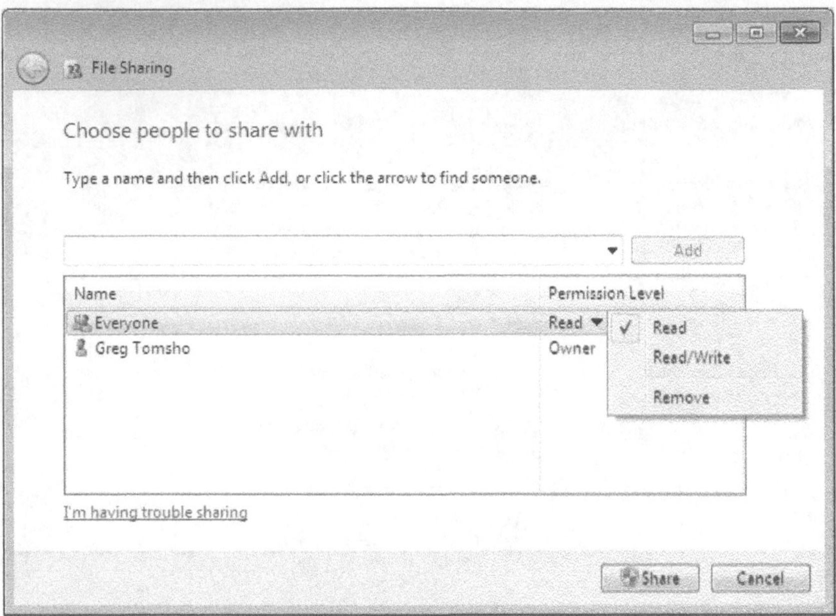

Figure 2-7 Sharing a folder in Windows 7

As in Windows XP, a Windows 7 folder or file also has file permissions that control who accesses the folder or file. If the file permissions deny access to a user or group, that person or group will not have share access. File permissions are configured by right-clicking the folder or file, clicking Properties, and clicking the Security tab.

In addition to the Sharing Wizard, users can specify the use of a file on the basis of a personal or public profile established on their computers. Files not to be shared can be saved into a personal profile and files to be shared can be saved into a public profile.

Reliability Features Windows 7 has features for increased reliability so users experience fewer interruptions and information is kept intact. These features include the following:

- *Startup Repair Tool*—Automatically launched when a boot problem is detected. It can detect and solve driver problems, incorrect startup settings, and corrupted startup information on the disk.
- *New code to prevent interruptions*—Additional safeguards to prevent system crashes and hangs.
- *Self-diagnosis for problems*—Built-in diagnostics for common hardware problems, such as disk or memory failures.
- *Restart Manager*—Reduces the number of times you have to reboot your computer due to installed updates or patches. Instead of rebooting the entire computer, certain processes that are updated can simply be restarted.
- *Service-failure recovery*—The operating system can automatically detect when a service has failed and attempt to restart it.

Security Features Building a secure operating system means building in security from the ground up. If you are a user of earlier Windows operating systems, you are probably aware of the continual need to install security updates and patches. Because computer attackers use a multitude of ways to invade operating systems, manufacturers have had to plug all kinds of unanticipated holes. Today we know more about how systems are attacked and there are more available defenses. In Windows 7 and beyond, Microsoft is working to change coding structures at the foundation of the operating system to reduce the opportunities for attackers. Besides locking down the code, Microsoft has implemented additional security features, including:

- A more comprehensive firewall
- User Account Protection
- Built-in security software to find and eliminate malicious software
- Status information

The Windows firewall monitors traffic going into and coming out of the computer. This capability was initially implemented in Windows XP with Service Pack 2. Another firewall element used in Windows 7 is the ability to link it to the use of group policy settings. This means that a server manager can set up a group policy to have consistent desktop and system settings on that server's clients. In an office or organization, the group policy configuration can be used to ensure that all users have enabled the firewall and are using exactly the same security settings within the firewall. Even if a user changes his or her firewall settings, the group policy ensures the settings are back the next time that user logs on (or the group policy can be set to prevent users from changing firewall settings). Having consistent firewall settings is vital for an organization, because its network is no more secure than the least secure client.

Another feature of the Windows firewall is that it is compatible with IP Security (IPsec). IPsec is a set of secure communications standards and standards for encryption to protect network communications between computers. IPsec is supported by Microsoft and other server systems, such as all Windows systems since Windows 2000 Server and Linux.

User Account Protection (UAP) was introduced in Windows Vista and is intended to make user accounts more secure. UAP enables the user account administrator to better protect accounts by controlling permissions and by limiting the software applications that can be run from an account. UAP protects the registry and specified folders so their contents are only available to a specific user. If you regularly use virus checking or other system protection software, you have probably noticed that the software often corrects changes to a computer's registry that have been introduced by malicious software. UAP is designed to address this important security problem.

Some users log on to their computers using an account that has Administrator permissions. Because this type of account can make significant changes to the operating system, there is a risk in running all applications with Administrator permissions in effect. UAP limits the permissions given to applications so that system-wide changes are not made inadvertently or through malicious software. One downside to UAP is that some applications you could formerly run in Windows XP may not run in new versions of Windows.

In Windows 7, Microsoft has integrated programs to search for and eliminate malicious software, including viruses, worms, and Trojan horses. If the integrated programs cannot successfully delete specific malicious software, they may instead be able to block the effect of the malicious software on the local computer.

Windows 7 also includes what Microsoft calls Windows Service Hardening. One common avenue for attackers is through an open service, such as through FTP. Windows Service Hardening limits the effect a service can have in Windows, so attacks are limited or thwarted.

It can be difficult for a user to determine if new security patches and other updates are implemented on a computer. Windows 7 provides status information to show whether recent patches and updates have been installed. This is part of Microsoft's Network Access Protection initiative for networks using Windows client OSs (Windows Vista and later) and Windows Server OSs (Windows Server 2008 and later). These servers have the ability to set up network access protection that is enforced on all clients, such as maintaining security patches and updates.

Windows 7 Management Options Windows 7 and later extend the TCO initiatives of Microsoft to save on support costs incurred by users and organizations. Windows 7 comes with more group policy settings than earlier Windows versions, which means that computers in an office, department, or organization can be standardized for easier use. For example, if all users in the customer service department in a business use the same order entry program, that program can be set up to start the same way on all department computers via group policy. A customer service representative can go to any computer in the department and access the program in a familiar way. By creating consistency in the way computer systems are used, group policy saves on support costs.

Sometimes one computer is used by many people, such as a public computer in a coffee shop or library. In this situation, one computer might have different group policies, depending on who logs on. Windows 7 includes the Group Policy Management Console (GPMC). The GPMC enables the computer's administrator to configure different group policies for different kinds of users.

In Windows 7 it is more difficult to change system settings and files, such as the registry, because the system can be configured so that only an authorized installer makes these changes—instead of users or software that do not have authorization. This system protection is accomplished through the Windows Resource Protection (WRP) feature.

For more versatile management, Windows 7 brings back the Administrative Tools menu first introduced in Windows NT. To access the Administrative Tools menu, click Start, click Control Panel, click System and Security, and click Administrative Tools. Some of the Administrative Tools that are available include:

- *Computer Management*—Opens the Computer Management tool that provides access to many general management functions, such as Event Viewer, Shared Folders, Task Scheduler, Reliability and Performance, Device Manager, Disk Management, and Services and Applications.
- *Performance Monitor*—Shows monitors for utilization of the CPU, disk, network, and memory.
- *Task Scheduler*—Permits you to set up tasks or applications to run at a certain time, such as starting a backup at 6:00 p.m.
- *Event Viewer*—Enables you to access the computer system's logs to track activities and errors.

Windows Server 2008/R2

Windows Server 2008 was released by Microsoft in February 2008 and Windows Server 2008 R2 was released in October 2009. It is available in versions similar to Windows Server 2003. Windows Server 2008 and Windows Vista share the same code base and thus the same new features, as do Windows Server 2008 R2 and Windows 7.

Windows Server 2008 R2 is the first Windows OS not to be available in a 32-bit version; it is only available in a 64-bit version.

Compared with its predecessors, Windows Server 2008 and Windows Server 2008 R2 include some new and enhanced features:

- Active Directory
- Failover clustering
- Hyper-V
- Self-healing NTFS
- Server Core
- Server Manager

Active Directory With Windows Server 2008, a read-only domain controller (RODC) was implemented. This is great for servers in locations that do not have the desired security for a domain controller. Hackers cannot make changes at remote locations that would then be replicated to the main domain controller at the corporate headquarters. In addition, RODCs limit the amount of sensitive information stored on the server, such as user passwords.

Failover Clustering Failover clustering is a server OS feature in which two or more servers are tightly linked; one server is the active server and the others are considered standby servers. The active server provides services to network clients while the standby servers monitor the availability of the active server. If the active server fails, one of the standby servers (as determined by an algorithm) begins providing its network services. Failover clustering is enhanced significantly in Windows Server 2008 Enterprise and Datacenter editions with the addition of a cluster validation wizard. This wizard runs validation tests on the servers you are going to cluster. It tests the software and hardware on each server and provides a report on how well failover clustering will run.

Hyper-V Microsoft rolled out Hyper-V in Windows Server 2008; a stand-alone release of Hyper-V Server is available. It allows the server to run multiple independent operating systems at the same time on the same hardware. Hyper-V allows server administrators to combine multiple virtual servers on one physical server.

Self-Healing NTFS In the past, if you experienced problems with NTFS volumes on a disk, you used Chkdsk.exe to fix the problem. This meant taking down the volume to run the utility. With self-healing NTFS, the utility runs in the background to correct hard disk problems. The availability of the file system is far greater than the previous way of using the Chkdsk.exe utility, data is preserved as much as possible, and better reports are provided to describe modifications made to the volume.

Server Core Microsoft describes Server Core as being "designed for use in organizations that either have many servers, some of which need only to perform dedicated tasks but with outstanding stability, or in environments where high security requirements require a minimal attack surface on the server." Server Core is a bare-bones installation with a limited GUI that is meant to reduce hacker attacks to the operating system. It is ideal for branch offices, remote locations, and office servers.

Server Manager Server Manager combines and replaces the Manage Your Server, Configure Your Server, and Security Configuration Wizards found in Windows Server 2003. It centralizes these features and provides one location to set up, deploy, and manage servers, add server roles, and check the status of servers. Figure 2-8 shows the Server Manager.

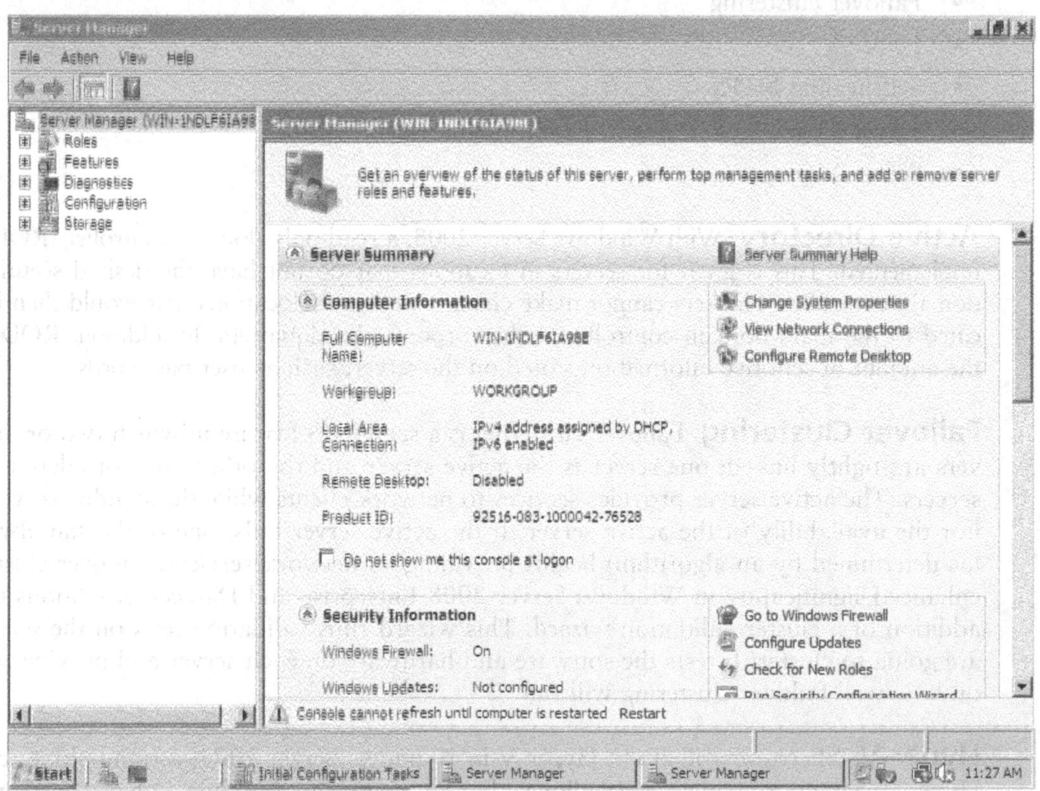

Figure 2-8 Windows Server 2008 Server Manager

Windows Server 2008/R2 supports up to 64 physical processors in a system and up to 64 TB of RAM. Windows Server 2008/R2 is available in Datacenter Edition, Enterprise Edition, Standard Edition, and Web Server Edition. The Web Server edition does not support Windows Hyper-V and cannot be configured as a domain controller.

Some of the new, updated, and enhanced features found in Windows Server 2008 R2 include:

- Integration with Windows 7
- File services management
- Scalability
- Reliability
- Virtualization
- Web platform updates

Integration with Windows 7 The features described here are only available to Windows 7 client computers attached to Windows Server 2008 R2 systems. Mobile connectivity is becoming more important as organizations are finding ways to do more with fewer resources. As discussed under Windows 2000, a popular way to remotely connect to the corporate servers is via a VPN. Users will most likely need to install a VPN client on their mobile device and then establish a connection. This can be time-consuming and difficult. Many times, it requires the assistance of the company help desk or even the server administrator.

Microsoft introduced DirectAccess to provide the functionality of a VPN without the hassles of setting one up and then initiating it each time you want access to the remote network. The remote computer is automatically authenticated before the user logs on. Thus, when the user logs on, the process is very fast and requires very little effort. This allows Windows Server 2008 R2 to manage the Windows 7 client without waiting for the client to log on. DirectAccess uses IPsec encryption over the Internet to protect the organization's data.

Organizations are turning more to centralized applications on the corporate server. This reduces the costs of remote and branch IT groups. It also puts a greater burden on the connections between the branch group and organization headquarters. On one hand, centralized applications save money, but on the other, there is the additional cost of increased bandwidth. The BranchCache feature allows the remote network to cache frequently accessed applications and information at the branch office, greatly reducing the traffic over the network link.

File Services Management With the price of server storage declining and the centralization of data in storage area networks (SANs), the management and security of this data is becoming increasingly important. A SAN is a fast network that contains components that can be shared for storage and access to the storage. Windows File Classification Infrastructure (FCI) provides the information you need to manage the data. It automates the classification of data based on predefined categories, including what is contained in the data. If the data contains sensitive information, FCI may move this information to a more secure server and even encrypt it.

Scalability Windows Server 2008 R2 includes components to help reduce the number of physical servers. This reduces the organization's costs for servers, administrators, physical space, and power consumption. Windows Server 2008 R2 supports up to 256 logical processors along with Hyper-V, which supports up to 64 logical processors.

Reliability Windows Hardware Error Architecture (WHEA) now supports memory and cache error recovery. This is done without the application or the operating system being aware of the process. Windows Server 2008 R2 also supports "hot add" capabilities for memory, processors, and I/O resources. A server administrator can add memory, processors, and I/O resources to a server when the need arises without taking the server down, reconfiguring it, and then rebooting it. In today's 24/7 world of operations, reliability and uptime are critical to the success of the organization. This is accomplished through Dynamic Hardware Partitioning.

Virtualization Modern data centers rely heavily on virtualization to keep operational costs as low as possible both for power consumption and the purchase of new physical servers. Windows Server 2008 R2 provides Hyper-V for server virtualization, which includes Live Migration. This allows the server administrator to move a virtual machine from one physical server to another. The users of the server will see no service interruption.

Virtual machines are growing in popularity because it is easy to set them up quickly on servers already in the data center. Management of virtual machines becomes a growing task as the number of these machines increases. Windows Server 2008 R2 provides enhancements that assist the server administrator, such as Hyper-V Management Console and System Center Virtual Machine Manager 2008.

Web Platform Updates Internet Information Services (IIS) 7.5 and enhanced support for .NET on Server Core are two of the Web platform updates in Windows Server 2008 R2. IIS 7.5 provides centralized Web management, more reliability, and improved security.

There is also a new administration console called IIS 7.5 Manager. This console allows for both local and remote administration. Configuration management allows Web site administrators to delegate control over content to the owners of the information. IIS 7.5 comes with enhanced troubleshooting tools such as the failed request tracing tool, which keeps a record of failed requests based on a set of rules the server administrator creates. Finally, IIS 7.5 provides a better server footprint. It has a modular architecture so that the server administrator can load just the modules needed for the specific type of Web services being offered. This, along with the Windows Server 2008 R2 Server Core option, reduces the amount of code and thus the vulnerability to attack.

Windows 8/8.1

Windows 8 was released in October 2012 and was intended to unify the operating system user interface and code base to work on mobile touch-centric devices as well as traditional desktops. Just a year later, in October 2013, Microsoft released Windows 8.1 to correct for some egregious miscalculations, not the least of which was the abandonment of the beloved Start button. The touch-centric interface of Windows 8 was not well received, particularly because so few Windows mobile devices were in use and very few people had a touch screen as their desktop or laptop monitor. The mouse and keyboard were still the input devices of choice on the vast majority of Windows systems.

In Windows 8, the Windows Start button is replaced by the Start screen (see Figure 2-9), which contains live tiles you can press or click to start applications or access the desktop.

When Windows 8 boots, users are placed directly into the Start screen rather than the desktop. To get to the desktop, users must click a live tile on the Start screen. With no Start button on the desktop, users must find a spot in a corner of the screen and touch or click it to bring up the Start screen.

Figure 2-9 Windows 8 Start screen

Despite the shortcomings of the user interface, Windows 8 and its immediate successor, Windows 8.1, have a number of improvements over Windows 7 under the hood, most of which would carry forward to the better-received Windows 10. Some of the new and improved features include the following:

- User interface changes
- Storage enhancements
- Security enhancements
- Client Hyper-V
- Integration with online services

User Interface While the user interface is the primary knock on Windows 8, there are some notable and well-received changes. Windows Explorer is renamed File Explorer and gets a ribbon-style interface to replace the traditional command bar. Task Manager got a facelift, making it easier to see what processes are running and what resources are being used. Also, a new touch-optimized Settings app provides access to common PC settings without making users wade through all of the options in Control Panel (although the full Control Panel remains). While the Start button was missing from Windows 8, Microsoft brought it back in a reduced form in Windows 8.1. In Windows 8.1, clicking the Start button opens the Start screen, but right-clicking it gives administrators and power users quick access to frequently used administrative tools such as Programs and Features, Power Options, Event Viewer, System, Device Manager, Network Connections, Disk Management, Computer Management, and several more (see Figure 2-10).

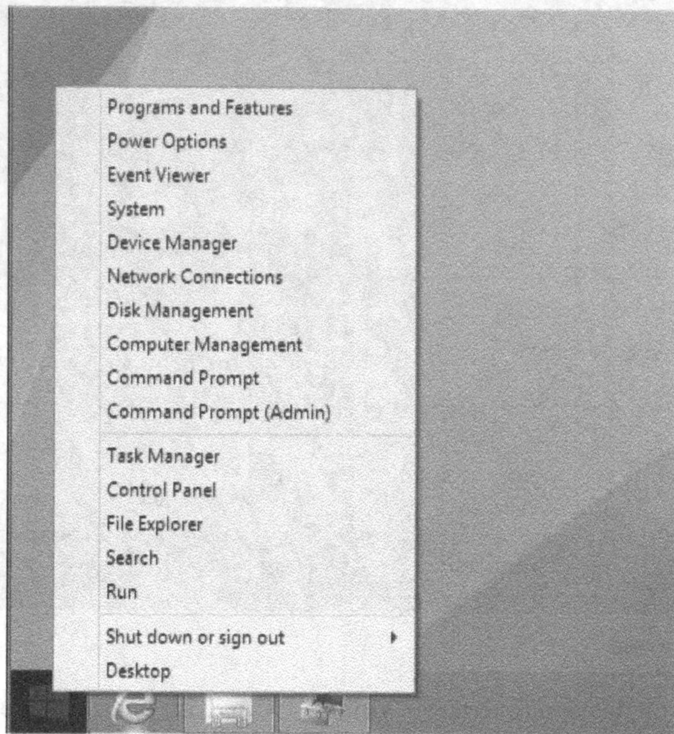

Figure 2-10 The Windows 8.1 Start button and right-click menu

Storage Enhancements Windows 8 introduces Storage Spaces, a storage management and configuration tool that allows users (and server administrators on Windows Server 2012) to manage disks of different sizes and interfaces (including external disks) as a single pool of storage, creating virtual disks and virtual volumes from the storage pool as necessary. Another nice feature in Windows 8 is the ability to mount CD and DVD images with a simple double-click on an ISO file. After double-clicking (or right-clicking and clicking Mount), a new drive letter is created and the ISO file is opened in a File Explorer window. This feature allows you to explore the contents of a DVD image without burning it to a disk. In a similar fashion, you can mount virtual disks if they are in the Microsoft VHD or VHDX format used by Hyper-V and Storage Spaces. Mounted virtual disks can then be used as if they were a physical disk attached to the system with a drive letter assigned. Storage and storage devices are discussed in more detail in Chapter 7.

Security Enhancements Windows 8 adds the option to sign in with a Microsoft online account rather than using a local user account and password. In addition, you can sign in using a PIN or a picture password instead of a traditional password. To use a picture password, you choose a picture and then use a touch screen to create a combination of lines, circles, and taps. To use the picture password when you sign in, you repeat the pattern you created on the displayed picture. Windows 8 also offers a variety of controls to allow parents to monitor their children's activities. And, if your system starts acting up, new recovery options allow you to refresh your PC without losing any files or reset the machine to factory settings and completely start over.

Client Hyper-V Microsoft brings the success of Hyper-V on Windows Server OSs to its client line of OSs starting in Windows 8. Client Hyper-V uses the same virtualization technology that is found on Windows Server, allowing you to run multiple OSs on a single physical computer. This feature allows you to upgrade to the latest Windows version and still be able to run older versions of Windows in a virtual machine. For example, if you have an application designed for Windows XP, Windows Vista, or even earlier versions that will not run in Windows 8 and later versions, you can run the application in a virtual machine with the required guest OS installed.

Online Services Users who choose to sign in using a Microsoft online account gain the benefits of synchronized applications and settings between devices. In addition, the client necessary to access Microsoft's OneDrive cloud storage service is built into Windows 8. As part of the Windows 8 user interface makeover, Microsoft introduced Windows Store apps that run on desktop and mobile computers alike. These touch-centric apps run full-screen in Windows 8, but Microsoft changed course in Windows 10, allowing Windows Store apps to be run in a window like most other programs.

Windows Server 2012/R2

Windows Server 2012/R2 is Microsoft's deep dive into the private cloud. This new version is chock-full of new tools and features designed to help server administrators increase the availability of network services and limit security risks. Microsoft has also emphasized features that help datacenter operators deploy and manage a private cloud. Windows Server 2012/R2 comes in two primary editions and two special editions. Standard and Datacenter editions return from Windows Server 2008, but there is no longer an Enterprise edition. Standard Edition is suitable for most mid-sized to large companies, while Datacenter Edition is designed for organizations that rely heavily on Hyper-V virtualization. The two special editions are Essentials and Foundation. Essentials is aimed at small businesses with 25 or fewer users. It supports most of the roles and features in Standard and Datacenter editions, but some roles have restrictions or limited functions. Essentials Edition is automatically configured as a root domain controller, which is the first domain controller installed in an Active Directory forest. Foundation Edition, the entry-level Windows Server 2012/R2 edition, is suitable for small businesses that need to purchase a complete server solution for file and printer sharing, centralized control over user accounts and network resources, and common services used in most networks, such as Web services, DNS, and DHCP. Foundation Edition is available as an OEM version only, installed on a server by the manufacturer, and supports only 15 users. The features already discussed in the Windows 8/8.1 section are present in Windows Server 2012/R2, with the exception of some of the user-specific features. Also, Windows Server 2012/R2 boots directly to the desktop instead of the Start screen.

Windows Server 2012/R2 maintains all the core technologies used in Windows Server 2008, including Server Manager, NTFS, Active Directory, and Windows file and printer sharing and networking features, although many of these technologies later received enhancements, as discussed in the following sections.

Server Manager Server Manager has been updated to allow administrators to manage all the servers in the network from a single management console. The left pane of Server Manager displays the major views: Dashboard, Local Server, and All Servers. You use the Local Server view to manage just the server where you're running Server Manager, and the All Servers view to manage aspects of all servers. To add servers you want to manage, right-click All Servers and click Add Servers or use the Manage menu. When you click All Servers in the left pane, you see a list of servers you can manage in the right pane (see Figure 2-11).

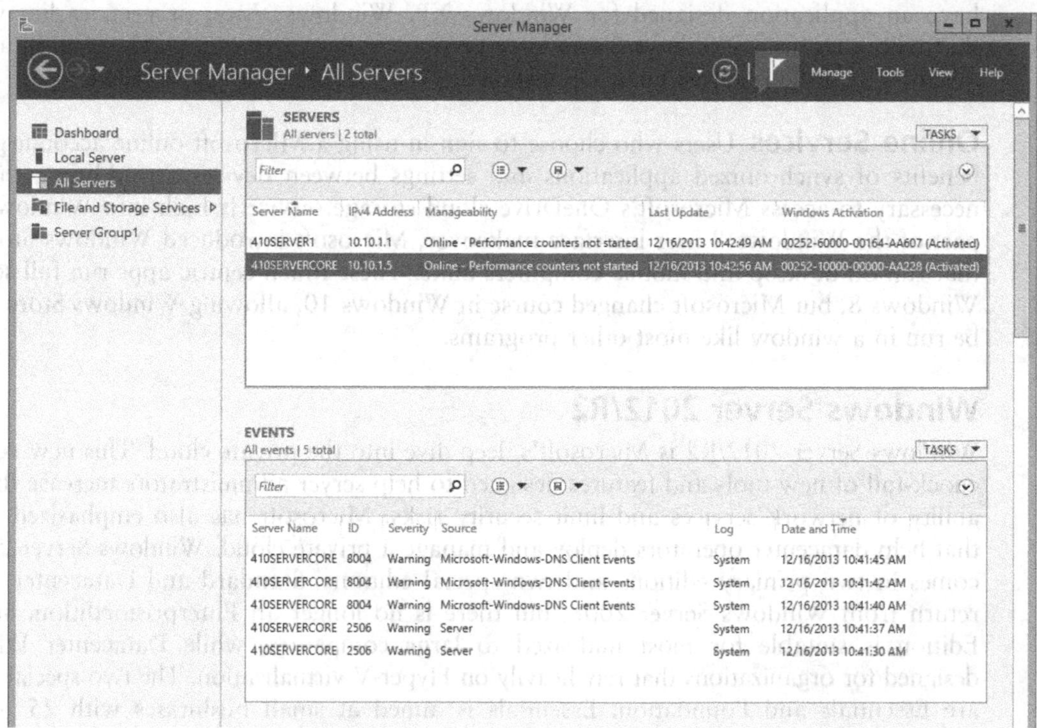

Figure 2-11 Windows Server Manager in Windows Server 2012/R2

NTFS File System NTFS was introduced in Windows NT in the early 1990s. Although it has been updated throughout the years, NTFS has remained a reliable, flexible, and scalable file system. One of the most noticeable improvements of NTFS versus its predecessor,

FAT32, is file and folder permissions. Since its debut in Windows NT, NTFS has added many new features, including disk quotas, built-in file compression and encryption, BitLocker drive encryption, and a host of performance and reliability improvements.

Active Directory Active Directory is the foundation of a Windows network environment. This directory service enables administrators to create and manage users and groups, set network-wide user and computer policies, manage security, and organize network resources. With Active Directory, you transform a limited, nonscalable workgroup network into a Windows domain with nearly unlimited scalability. Windows Server 2012/R2 continues to add features to Active Directory, including an easy-to-use Recycle Bin to restore deleted objects, and a user interface to create password policies that can be applied to individual users and groups.

New Features in Windows Server 2012/R2 Microsoft has added several new features and improved a host of existing features to make Windows Server 2012/R2 a secure, highly available, enterprise-class server OS. Microsoft's emphasis on the private cloud is clear, with several features focused on this burgeoning sector of IT. Some of the new and improved features are discussed briefly in the following list and covered in more detail in later chapters.

- *Server Core*—Server Core has no taskbar or Start screen, just a command prompt window on a black background. Its use might not be obvious, but Server Core has quite a bit going on under the hood. Server Core's lightweight interface hides powerful server capabilities that aren't encumbered by a resource-intensive GUI. A fresh installation of Server Core uses a little more than 5 GB of disk space compared with more than 9 GB for a fresh installation of Windows Server 2012/R2 with a GUI. A major enhancement made to Server Core in Windows Server 2012/R2 is the ability to switch between Server Core mode and GUI mode. In the Windows Server 2008 version, after you installed it in Server Core mode or GUI mode, you couldn't switch to the other mode.
- *Minimal Server Interface*—The benefits of Server Core mode are substantial, but some people just can't live without being able to point and click. Microsoft recognized this fact and found a happy medium between Server Core mode and the full GUI: Minimal Server Interface (also called MinShell). Minimal Server Interface allows users to perform most local management tasks with a GUI tool but lacks many aspects of the full user interface.
- *Hyper-V 3.0*—Hyper-V is the Windows Server virtualization environment introduced in Windows Server 2008. Although it's not new, the enhancements in Hyper-V version 3.0 make Windows Server a leader in virtualization software. Hyper-V 3.0 is a major component of Microsoft's private cloud initiative and includes these new features: multiple concurrent live migrations, Hyper-V Replica, support for up to 32 virtual processors, virtual machines with up to 32 GB of RAM, and several additional performance and reliability enhancements.
- *PowerShell 4.0*—PowerShell is a command-line interactive scripting environment that provides the commands for almost any management task in a Windows Server 2012/R2 environment. It can be used much like a command prompt, where you enter one command at a time and view the results, or as a powerful scripting engine that enables

you to create and save a series of commands for performing complex tasks. Although PowerShell 1.0 was introduced in 2006, it has been substantially enhanced in Windows Server 2012/R2 with more than 50 new cmdlets, job scheduling, enhanced auto-completion, and improved performance.

- *Storage Spaces*—As discussed in the sections on Windows 8, Storage Spaces provides administrators with the ability to manage storage of different sizes and interfaces, creating virtual disks that can be anything from a simple volume to a fault-tolerant RAID 5.
- *Resilient File System*—Resilient File System (ReFS) is a new file system in Windows Server 2012/R2 that's intended for large data storage applications that require a high degree of reliability. It's largely backward-compatible with NTFS but doesn't support some features, such as file-based compression, disk quotas, and Encrypting File System (EFS).
- *Dynamic Access Control*—Dynamic Access Control (DAC) gives you fine-tuned control over shared resources without some of the limitations of traditional file permissions. DAC works alongside traditional permissions, giving administrators more flexibility in assigning access to resources. Traditional permissions are based on user and group accounts, and in a large network with hundreds or thousands of users and resources, group-based permissions can be limiting and complex. DAC allows classifying data and assigning permissions by user attributes rather than group memberships. As a simple example, a folder can be classified as belonging to the Accounting Department, making access available only to users whose Department attribute equals Accounting, or the folder can be classified as highly sensitive so that its contents are encrypted automatically, relieving an administrator from having to encrypt it manually.

From the Trenches ...

The Computer Networking Technology department at a college runs its own network, including routers, switches, and Windows servers. The servers used hardware RAID controllers for fault-tolerant disk storage. However, every time the OS was updated or a disk needed to be replaced, the RAID controllers seemed to have problems. For example, when the servers were upgraded from Windows Server 2008 R2 to Windows Server 2012, the drivers for the RAID controllers weren't available. The department turned to Storage Spaces, the new feature in Windows Server 2012, so that standard disk controllers could be used while maintaining fault tolerance with virtual RAID disks. Now, disk space can be expanded simply by adding a new disk without the need to worry about compatibility with the existing disks. In addition, there is no further need to be concerned about updated drivers for finicky RAID controllers.

Windows 10

Windows 10 is the current release of the client version of Windows, and some say it may be the last numbered release of Windows, with enhancements coming as regular feature updates automatically when they are released. Windows 10 was released in July 2015. What, no Windows 9, you might ask? Microsoft decided to forego Windows 9 and leap directly from

Windows 8.1 to Windows 10. The official explanation is that the new Windows was too big a leap forward to advance just one version number, but some suspect it was a way for Microsoft to distance itself from what is considered a poor showing with Windows 8. In fact, Microsoft offered a free upgrade to Windows 10 during its first year of availability to anyone who possessed a valid license for Windows 7 or Windows 8/8.1.

Windows 10 builds on the successful features of Windows 8/8.1, discards some of the less successful, and brings back some popular Windows 7 features that had been left out of Windows 8. Some of the key features of Windows 10 include:

- *Virtual desktops*—A feature long available on Linux desktop managers, virtual desktops let users create multiple desktops and switch between them to access open application windows that were started in each desktop. To create a new desktop, click the new Task View icon on the taskbar, and click the plus sign that appears in the bottom right of the screen. Alternatively, press Windows+Ctrl+D to create a new desktop and switch to it. To move an open application window to a different desktop, press the Task View icon, right-click the window you want to move, click Move to, and select the desktop you want (see Figure 2-12). In the figure, you see the Task View icon to the right of the Search bar on the taskbar, and you can see two desktops. The window with Microsoft Edge, the new Windows Web browser, is about to be moved to Desktop 2. Virtual desktops help you organize your workspace and easily switch between sets of applications you are working on, making multitasking more efficient.

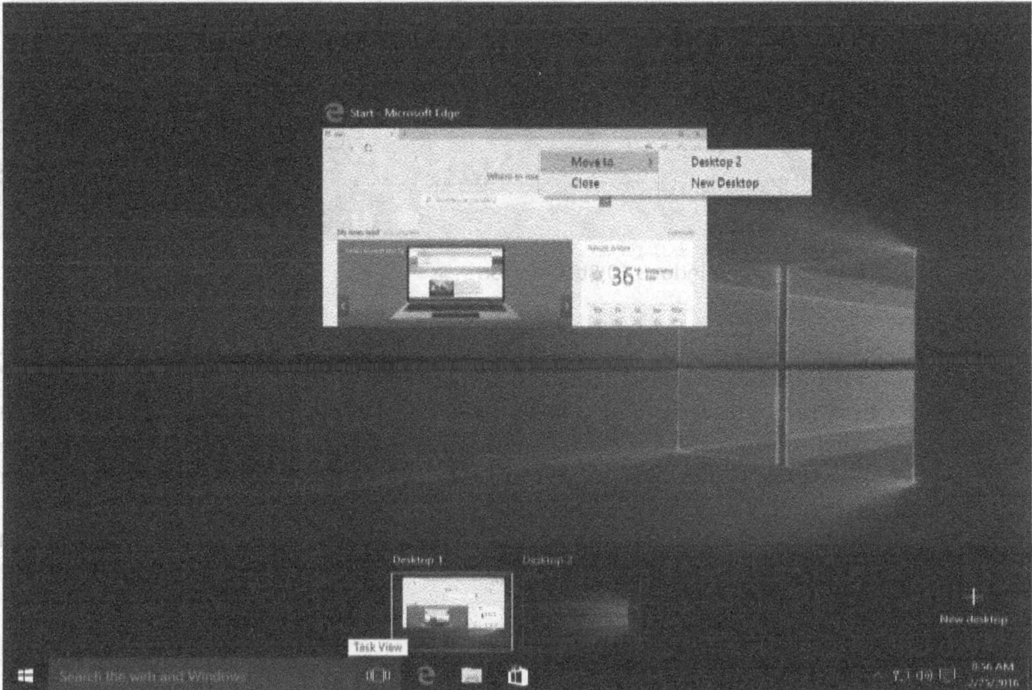

Figure 2-12 Windows 10 virtual desktops

- *Return of the Start button*—The Start button is back and is a hybrid between the Windows 7 Start button and the Windows 8 Start screen. There are essentially two columns; the left column looks somewhat like the old Windows 7 Start button, with frequently used applications and shortcuts to settings and a power button for log-off/shutdown options. The right pane looks like a scaled-down version of the Start screen from Windows 8, with live tiles pointing to apps you can run (see Figure 2-13). For IT pros and power users, the right-click functionality of the Start button added with Windows 8.1 remains.

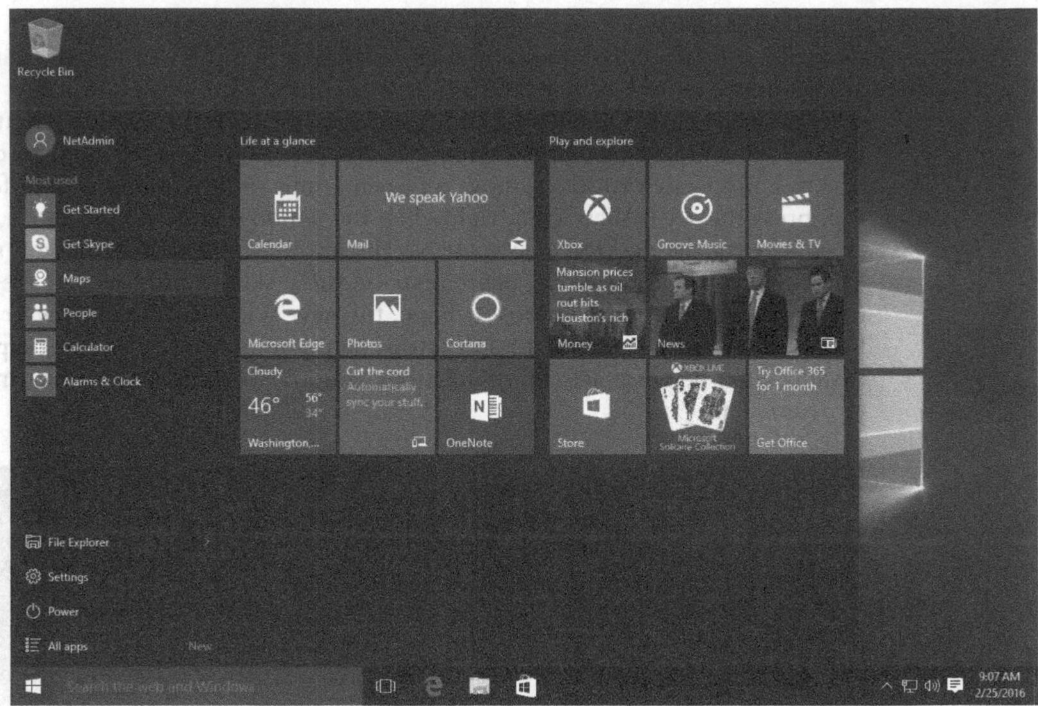

Figure 2-13 Windows 10 Start button

- *Microsoft Edge Web browser*—Microsoft started from scratch to come up with Microsoft Edge, an eventual replacement for Internet Explorer. Edge is a slimmed-down Web browser built around standards such as HTML5, but it doesn't support ActiveX controls, so you can't get rid of Internet Explorer right away if you need those capabilities. However, it does have a built-in PDF reader and Adobe Flash Player. It integrates nicely with Microsoft's new digital assistant, Cortana (discussed next), has a reading mode, and supports annotations directly on Web pages that can be stored and shared in the cloud (see Figure 2-14).

Figure 2-14 Microsoft Edge Web browser

- *Cortana digital assistant*—If you have ever used an iPhone or iPad to talk to Siri, or said "Okay Google" into your Android phone, you have some ideas what Cortana is all about. In order to use Cortana on your computer, you must be signed in with a Microsoft online account. With Cortana, you can use voice commands to ask questions (Cortana uses Bing as its search engine), open applications, set reminders and appointments, and so forth.
- *Quick access*—File Explorer adds a feature called Quick access that lets you pin any folder or search result to the Quick access section in the left pane of File Explorer.
- *Universal application architecture*—The Metro-style apps that Microsoft first released with Windows 8 are designed to run across Windows 10 desktops, tablets, smartphones, and other portable devices—even Xbox One. Windows 10 automatically recognizes whether you are on a device with a touch screen and selects between a mouse-oriented interface and a touch screen interface.
- *Sign-in options*—A new feature called Windows Hello allows you to expand your sign-in options. Aside from using a password or PIN, you can now sign into your device using your facial features or fingerprint if your hardware supports it. To use the face recognition option, you'll need an Intel RealSense 3D camera; a regular Web cam won't work. For fingerprint sign-in, you'll need a compatible fingerprint scanner, which you can buy as a USB device for as little as $15.

There are many more features in Windows 10, and Microsoft will be releasing new features as updates as they are completed.

Windows Server 2016

Still under development at this writing, Windows Server 2016 comes with the Windows 10 user interface and builds upon features found in Windows Server 2012/R2. Here are a few of the highlights you can expect to find in Windows Server 2016, which was due to be released in the fall of 2016:

- *Hyper-V*—A host of improvements to Hyper-V are included in the new Windows Server 2016, including nested virtualization (the ability to run a virtual machine in a virtual machine), Linux Secure Boot, production checkpoints, hot add and remove for memory and network adapters, and many more.
- *Nano Server*—Nano Server is a new install option for Windows Server 2016. It goes beyond Server Core, with an even smaller footprint, and doesn't support a local logon—all management tasks are done remotely. Nano Server is designed for single-task virtual machines, a DNS server, a storage host, or a Web server.
- *Failover clusters*—Failover clusters can now be upgraded from Windows Server 2012 R2 to Windows Server 2016 without Hyper-V or file server cluster downtime.
- *Windows Containers*—Windows Server 2016 expands its virtualization options with Windows Server Containers and Hyper-V Containers. Containers allow you to run applications that are isolated from one another, improving reliability. Windows Server Containers provide a moderate level of isolation while sharing various system libraries and Hyper-V Containers give you virtual-machine levels of isolation without the resource overhead of an actual virtual machine.

UNIX and UNIX-like Operating Systems

The UNIX operating system comes in many different formats. Of all the operating systems covered in this book, it is the oldest, most diverse, and most complicated. The reason for this is that one manufacturer does not have the exclusive license for UNIX. After UNIX was developed at AT&T, the company never formally licensed the kernel to prevent others from using it and implementing their own specialized utilities. AT&T used the operating system within the company and made the source code available outside the company. The end result is that there are many UNIX versions with many diverse utilities.

Versions of UNIX today adhere to one of the two main design standards: the **Berkeley Software Distribution (BSD)** standard or the **System V Release 4 (SVR4)** standard. Examples of BSD-style UNIX include the freely available NetBSD and FreeBSD operating systems, as well as the commercially available BSDi UNIX. SVR4 versions include freely available versions of Linux and commercial versions such as Oracle (formerly Sun Microsystems) Solaris and SCO UNIX. All UNIX systems include security features. Table 2-1 lists several versions of UNIX or UNIX-like OSs, along with the manufacturer and origin. It also includes Web addresses to check for additional information.

2

Table 2-1 UNIX or UNIX-like OSs

Version	Manufacturer/source	Origin	Web address
AIX	IBM	A combination of SVR4 and BSD	*www-03.ibm.com/systems/power/software/aix/*
Debian	Debian	BSD	*www.debian.org*
Fedora	Fedora (supported by Red Hat)	SVR4	*https://getfedora.org*
FreeBSD	The FreeBSD Project	BSD	*www.freebsd.org*
HURD	GNU	BSD	*www.gnu.org/software/hurd/hurd.html*
Mac OS X	Apple Computer	BSD (Darwin UNIX)	*www.apple.com*
NetBSD	The NetBSD Project	BSD	*www.netbsd.org*
OpenBSD	The OpenBSD Project	BSD	*www.openbsd.org*
Red Hat Linux	Red Hat	SVR4	*www.redhat.com*
Solaris	Oracle	BSD	*www.oracle.com*
openSUSE	MicroFocus	SVR4	*www.suse.com*
Turbolinux	Turbolinux, Inc.	SVR4	*www.turbolinux.com*
Ubuntu	Canonical	BSD	*www.ubuntu.com*

This book uses Linux for its UNIX examples; Linux is modeled after UNIX and shares many of the same features and commands. Most Linux versions are available free of charge, but some enhanced versions of Linux must be purchased. Linux is considered "UNIX-like" based on standards that were developed after UNIX originally came out. Linux runs on Intel-based and AMD-based processors.

There are a number of Linux versions available worldwide. Red Hat Linux, Ubuntu, and Debian are well known in the United States, but are also popular worldwide. OpenSUSE Linux is another popular product, especially in Europe. The product comes in both a professional and personal version. Turbolinux is the leading Linux distributor in the Asian-Pacific region. It provides workstation, desktop, and server versions of its product.

Because UNIX comes in such a wide variety of implementations, it runs on almost any hardware. There are UNIX versions available for all hardware mentioned up to this point. For this reason, it is hard to define exactly what specifications a platform should meet to run UNIX.

UNIX is a true multitasking, multiuser operating system. This means, as explained before, that it can fully serve all the computing needs of multiple users running multiple applications at the same time. Depending on the hardware, a single UNIX computer can support from one to several thousand users.

After startup, UNIX typically presents you with a request for a login, or username, followed by a request for a password. The username and password you provide determine what privileges you will be granted on the system. When your identity has been verified, you are presented with a shell—that is, the user interface. This is another point where UNIX is substantially different from most other operating systems: by default, most UNIX versions come with several different shells, and it is up to users to pick the shell they want to use. Different shells provide different levels of functionality, but all of the shells function much like the shell in a Windows command prompt, with a series of built-in commands and the ability to call **external commands** (operating system commands that are stored in a separate program file on disk) and application programs simply by typing commands at the command line.

The most popular UNIX shells are the Bourne shell (sh), its cousin the Bourne Again shell (bash), and a version of the Bourne shell called the C *shell* (csh), in which some of the commands are formatted to be similar to the C programming language. Overall, these shells function in the same way: you get a prompt, you type a command, and they do what you ask. When you are done with the shell, you can exit using the *exit* command. Typically, this returns you to the login prompt. Try Hands-On Project 2-5 to determine which UNIX shell you are using.

Many versions of UNIX can also provide you with a GUI. The most popular interface is the X11 Window System, known commonly as X Window. **X Window** is similar to other windowed interfaces. A unique feature of X Window is that it is network enabled. Using an X terminal, it is possible to run X Window and all the application programs on a remote UNIX computer, and to remotely interact with your applications. One UNIX system can support many X terminals and users. X Window, however, is an optional part of many UNIX versions. Just as there are many different UNIX versions, there are also many different versions of X Window. Linux generally uses a version called Xfree that can be obtained for free. X Window, by default, does not include programs analogous to Windows Explorer for managing files, or the Windows-based Start menu for starting programs, but many utilities are available to provide file and application management.

Fedora Linux, for example, offers an X Window-like GUI interface called GNOME (see Figure 2-15), which can be installed or omitted. Even when GNOME is installed, you can still execute regular Linux commands by starting the terminal emulation program window shown in Figure 2-16. To start the terminal emulation program in Fedora, for instance, click Activities, Show Applications, Utilities, and then click Terminal. Hands-On Project 2-6 enables you to learn more about the Fedora GNOME interface, while Hands-On Project 2-7 helps you to learn about the *find* command in a terminal window.

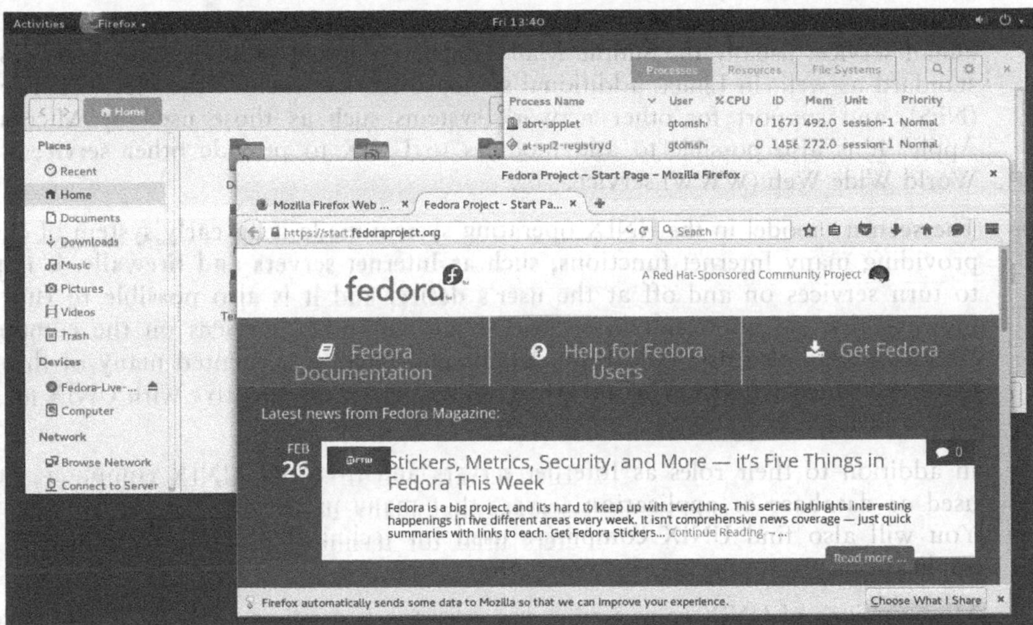

Figure 2-15 The GNOME desktop in Fedora

Source: Fedora Linux

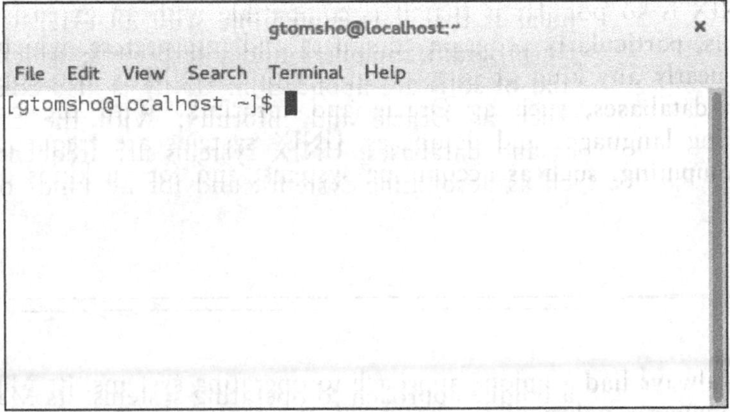

Figure 2-16 A terminal window in Linux

Source: Fedora Linux

All networking functions in UNIX are based on the BSD networking model, which provides support for the Transmission Control Protocol/Internet Protocol (TCP/IP). This is the standard protocol in use on the Internet, and as such, UNIX computers are qualified to provide numerous Internet services. (Network protocols are discussed later in this book.) The standard UNIX operating system does not provide many network functions. Most of these functions are provided by add-ons. The standard functions include login services, which allow a user to connect to the UNIX computer from another remote computer on the network; file transfers through the File Transfer Protocol (FTP); and some form of e-mail service, usually the Simple Mail Transfer Protocol (SMTP). Other services can be standard as well. In Linux, additional standard services include the Network File System (NFS), and support for other network systems such as those used by Microsoft and Apple. It is also possible to add modules to UNIX to provide other services, such as World Wide Web (WWW) service.

The security model in the UNIX operating system made it an early system of choice for providing many Internet functions, such as Internet servers and firewalls. It is possible to turn services on and off at the user's desire, and it is also possible to run services in ways that do not result in security issues for other services on the computer. All Windows OSs also use TCP/IP by default and have implemented many of the security features found in UNIX. This makes Windows Server competitive with UNIX as Internet and Web servers.

In addition to their roles as Internet servers and firewalls, UNIX computers are often used as database or application servers that many users can access at the same time. You will also find UNIX computers used for technical design and industrial control applications.

Most versions of UNIX come with a line editor, a text editor, or both. A line editor is an editor used to create text one line at a time. Line editors are often used to create scripts, programs in which each line executes a specific command. A text editor enables you to edit text in a full-screen mode.

One reason that UNIX is so popular is that it is compatible with an extensive range of programming tools, particularly program compilers and interpreters, which means that you can create nearly any kind of software application. UNIX is also compatible with many popular databases, such as Oracle and Informix. With the combined power of programming languages and databases, UNIX systems are frequently used for administrative computing, such as accounting systems, and for all kinds of scientific applications.

Mac OS

Apple Computer has always had a unique approach to operating systems. Its Macintosh line of personal computers revolutionized the world of operating systems with its all-graphical user interface and an all-graphical shell. Although there are subtle differences between Microsoft Windows and Mac OS in the way they function, you will see many similarities as well, which many would say is because Windows was designed to mimic the look and feel of Mac OS. Mac OS X is built on Darwin UNIX, which is a distribution of the BSD UNIX version. The Mac OS X El Capitan desktop is shown in Figure 2-17.

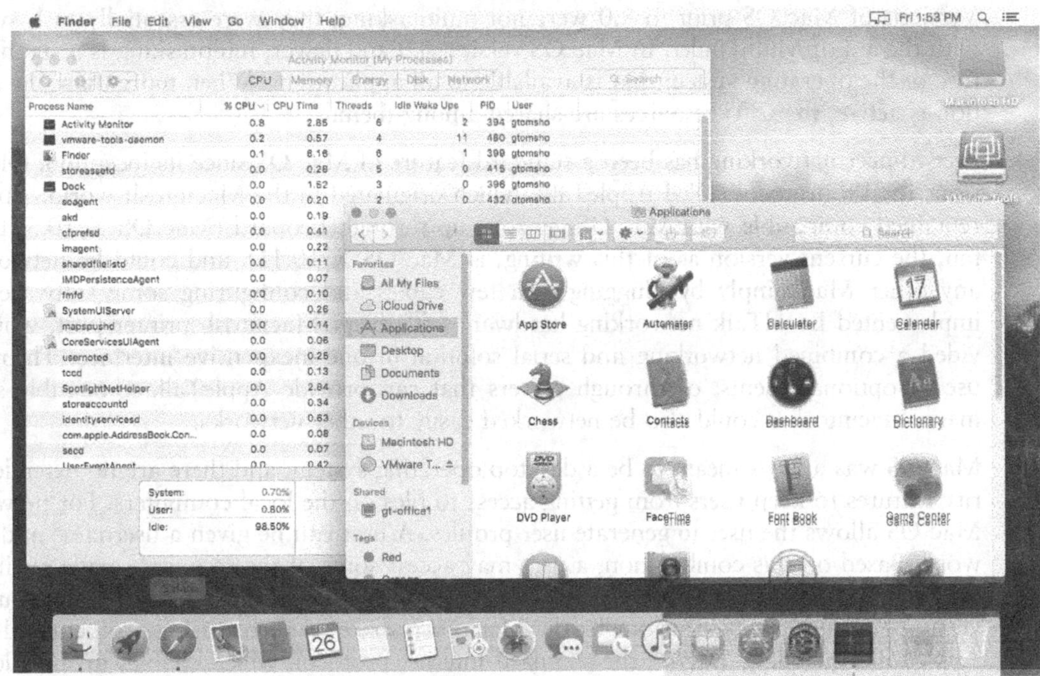

Figure 2-17 The Mac OS X El Capitan desktop

Source: Mac OS X El Capitan

The hardware architecture of Mac OS is substantially different from the architecture used on most other platforms, especially because many of the graphical functions are included in the basic input/output system (BIOS) functions, which are located in the read-only memory (ROM) of the hardware. (Apple calls this "firmware.") Beginning with System 7.1, Apple began using system enabler files that allowed the previous version of the operating system to support new hardware. When the next version of the operating system was released, support for the most recent Macs was included so the enabler file was no longer needed for that model. The hardware architecture needed to run Mac OS is very dependent on the version of the operating system. If you run version 7.0, you could be using any Macintosh hardware architecture, except for the PowerPC platform, which is supported as of version 7.5. If you are running the newest generation of hardware (Intel-based), you are required to run Mac OS X. Apple has always made the hardware and software closely interconnected, which results in strict requirements when it comes to operating system/hardware coordination.

One significant difference between Mac OS and other operating systems covered in this chapter is that only one company (Apple) makes hardware capable of running Mac OS. Mac OS runs on Intel processors, but the hardware is still Apple hardware. Several years back, Apple licensed Power Computing, Motorola, and other companies to make Mac OS-compatible hardware, but that is no longer the case. In short, using Apple software means using Apple hardware.

Versions of Mac OS prior to 8.0 were not multitasking; they were essentially task switching with the aid of MultiFinder. In Mac OS version 8.0 and newer, multitasking is a standard feature of the operating system that is available to all applications. When more than one application is active, the CPU resources are shared among them.

Peer-to-peer networking has been a standard feature of Mac OS since its inception. Older versions used a protocol called AppleTalk, which originated in the Macintosh world. AppleTalk remained compatible with Mac OS versions up through Leopard (Mac OS X 10.5; El Capitan, the current version as of this writing, is Mac OS X 10.11), and could be networked to any other Mac simply by plugging in a few cables and configuring some software. Apple implemented LocalTalk networking hardware with every Macintosh printer port, which provided a combined networking and serial solution in one inexpensive interface. Through the use of optional clients, or through servers that can provide AppleTalk-compatible services, many Macintoshes could also be networked easily to other networks.

Mac OS was always meant to be a desktop operating system, and there are no extended security features to keep users from getting access to files on the local computers. For networking, Mac OS allows the user to generate user profiles. A user can be given a username and a password. Based on this combination, a user may access some of the resources made available on the network. Mac OS can use its networking features to share printer and disk resources. In version 8.x and later, extensions let the Macintosh share resources using protocols other than AppleTalk, including TCP/IP, the standard Internet protocol, which enables greater flexibility in how Macs can be networked. Beginning with Mac OS X version 10.6 (Snow Leopard), AppleTalk is no longer supported. Snow Leopard supports TCP/IP networking.

Throughout its history, Mac OS has been known for its support of graphics, video, and sound capabilities. In this respect, Mac OS has been ahead of the industry. Because Apple has had tight control over both the Macintosh hardware architecture and operating system, and because it chose to actively enhance the audiovisual functions of both hardware and software, the Mac and the Mac OS are favored by people in the graphics, sound, and video fields. Macintosh computers are used in many different environments, especially those that deal with the creative process. The Mac font management and ColorSync color matching technologies have endeared it to graphic arts and prepress professionals, while QuickTime has made the Mac popular for multimedia sound and video production. You will also find many Macs in educational environments. The home computer market has a small but substantial share of computers running Mac OS. MacBook Air notebook computers continue to be popular, even in organizations that have settled primarily on the Windows-Intel platform.

Mac OS 9.x introduced features for better hardware and Internet access. For example, version 9.1 introduced a Printer Sharing panel to manage and share a USB printer on a network. There is a capability to connect to another computer over the Internet by using the Point-to-Point Protocol (PPP), a network communications protocol designed for remote communications. (You will learn more about protocols later in this book.) Mac OS 9.x added Personal Web Sharing for creating a Web page that others can access over the Internet or through a private network. Also, Mac OS 9.x included a runtime execution tool for running Java applets from the Finder tool. The Network Assist Client tool can be used by network administrators to control the computer.

2

Mac OS X

Mac OS X, where X means version 10, is a significant update because it sports the "Aqua" interface. One of the main changes for users of Mac OS 9.x and earlier is that some programs and utilities were replaced. The Apple menu can no longer be customized as in the past. New menu features include System Preferences, which is similar to the Control Panel on Windows systems. System Preferences enables you to set functions such as the time and date, display settings, startup functions, energy saving functions, and network functions. The Dock function can be customized through the System Preferences tool for the applications you want to include. Through Dock, you can start multiple applications and switch between them in a multitasking environment.

Out of the box, Mac OS X is configured so that different users can access the operating system in their own workspaces, without affecting other users. If one user wants to log out so that another user can access Mac OS X, the first user can now select the new Log Out option from the Apple menu, instead of turning off the computer and then rebooting.

Many windows in Mac OS X now can be customized so that their contents appear in columns, similar to Windows-based systems. Also, the title bar in a window displays buttons to close, minimize, or maximize (zone) that window. Throughout each window, the icons have a modern look. Also, some windows have "drawers" that slide out like file cabinet drawers to offer information.

Internet connectivity is enhanced in Mac OS X through the Internet Connect tool, which performs functions that users of previous Mac OS versions associated with the Remote Access tool. Internet Connect enables you to set up an Internet connection, configure a modem, and monitor the status of a connection. Internet applications include the Mail application from Apple, which is used for e-mail; and Internet Explorer, a Web browser from Microsoft. Some notable changes and enhancements of Mac OS X that have occurred through the years include:

- *Mac OS X 10.6 Snow Leopard*—This was the first version of Mac OS X that would support only Intel-based processors. A download called Rosetta could be installed to retain support for PowerPC applications.
- *Mac OS X 10.7 Lion*—With the success of the iPad and iOS, it was only natural for Apple to incorporate some of the popular features found in iOS into Mac OS X. Mac OS X Lion included Launchpad to easily browse installed applications, and the use of multi-touch gestures was expanded for hardware that supported it. Mission Control unified a number of utilities into a single interface.
- *Mac OS X 10.8 Mountain Lion*—The success of iOS on mobile devices continued to color Mac OS X with support for iMessage, iWork, and iCloud, along with Notification Center. In addition, all software updates were available only through the App Store.
- *Mac OS X 10.9 Mavericks*—Running on Intel 64-bit processors, Mavericks was a modest release with mostly minor feature and performance improvements. This was also the first departure from using big cat names for each Mac OS X release. From here on, at least for a while, well-known California locations would be used to name the OS.
- *Mac OS X 10.10 Yosemite*—Yosemite gave Mac OS X a face lift, with a user interface that was based on iOS 7, giving window edges a more flat appearance. Probably the biggest new feature is called Handoff, which allows users of iOS 8.1 and later mobile

devices to "hand off" work in progress (such as SMS messages, e-mails, and phone calls) from their mobile device to their Mac.

Mac OS X 10.11 El Capitan

Mac OS X 10.11 El Capitan is the current release of Mac OS X that started shipping in September 2015. Most would not call this a major release, but there are some improvements to features and performance. A feature called Split View lets you work in two applications at the same time, with each application snapped to opposite sides of the screen (see Figure 2-18). The Spotlight search app was updated, Pinned Sites lets you easily recall your favorite Web sites, and some new swipe gestures were added to apps. Finally, El Capitan introduces Metal for Mac, a set of 3D development tools for designing games and other 3D apps.

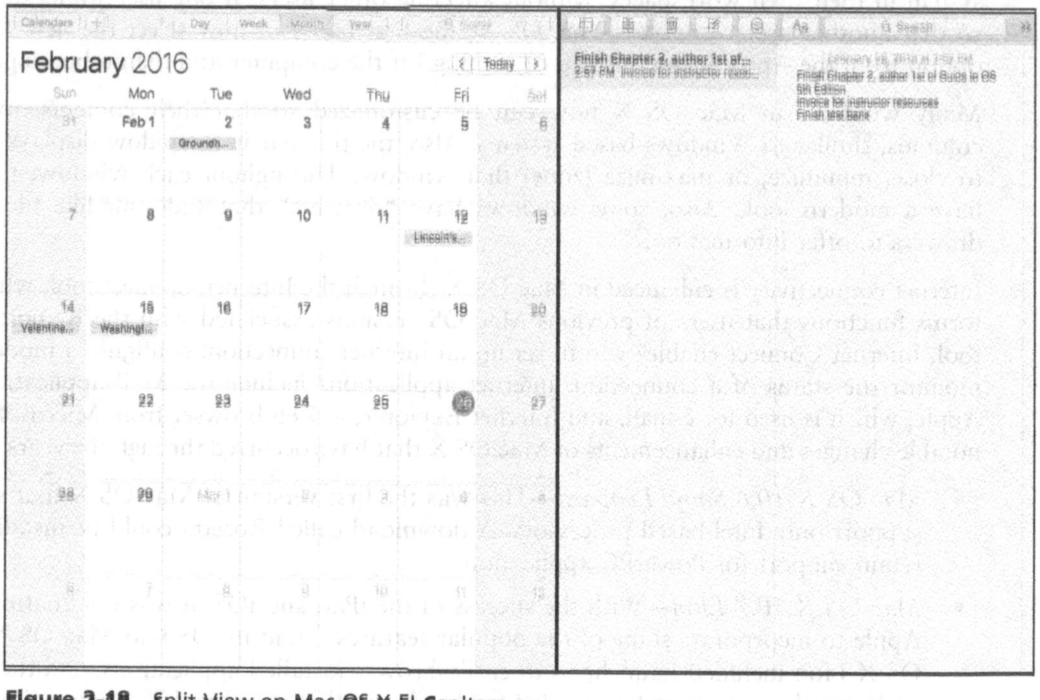

Figure 2-18 Split View on Mac OS X El Capitan

Source: Mac OS X El Capitan

Chapter Summary

- Early computer operating systems were primitive compared to current operating systems, but they were significant during their time and moved us toward a desktop computing environment. Server operating systems followed to allow for file sharing and printing.
- Windows, Macintosh, and Linux/UNIX are popular current operating systems, with new releases announced on a regular basis. Each release has new features and enhancements.

- Server operating systems have evolved to allow clustering, virtual servers, self-healing NTFS, a storage manager for SANS, single sign-on, network management, and security features.
- Mac OS X is built on Darwin UNIX, which is a distribution of the BSD UNIX version. Mac OS X 10.11 El Capitan is the latest Mac OS X release.

Key Terms

activate To register your copy of a Windows operating system, starting with the Windows XP version. Without this activation, you can only run your operating system for a very brief time.

Active Directory A Windows Server installable service that consists of a database of computers, users, shared printers, shared folders, and other network resources and resource groupings used to manage a network and enable users to quickly find a particular resource.

ActiveX An internal programming standard that allows various software running under the Windows operating system to communicate with Windows and other programs.

Berkeley Software Distribution (BSD) A variant of the UNIX operating system upon which a large proportion of today's UNIX software is based.

client In a networking environment, a computer that handles certain user-side software operations. For example, a network client may run software that captures user data input and presents output to the user from a network server.

clustering The ability to share computing load and resources by linking two or more discrete computer systems (servers) to function as though they are one.

Component Object Model (COM) Standards that enable a software object, such as a graphic, to be linked from one software component to another one.

Distributed File System (DFS) A set of client and server services to organize distributed shared files into a logical file system.

domain A logical grouping of Windows computers and computer resources that helps manage these resources and user access to them.

driver signing Setting up all drivers so that they cannot be inadvertently overwritten by earlier driver versions and only certified versions of drivers can be installed.

external commands Operating system commands that are stored in separate program files on disk. When these commands are required, they must be loaded from disk storage into memory before they are executed.

failover clustering A group of two or more servers configured so that if one server fails, another server can resume the services the first one was providing.

File Classification Infrastructure (FCI) A system that allows files to be located on servers in an organization based on predetermined naming conventions.

gadgets Small applications for readily accessing information and tools.

Hyper-V A Windows feature that allows a server to run multiple independent operating systems at the same time and to run multiple virtual servers on one physical server.

Infrared Data Association (IrDA) A group of peripheral manufacturers that developed a set of standards for transmitting data using infrared light. Printers were some of the first devices to support the IrDA specifications.

IP Security (IPsec) A way to secure Internet Protocol (IP) traffic by encrypting and authenticating each packet.

Kerberos A security system and authentication protocol that authenticates users and grants or denies access to network resources based on a user's log-on name and password. Kerberos creates a unique encryption key for each communication session.

library A combination of folders that can be in any location on the local computer or the network.

line editor An editor that is used to create text one line at a time.

Microsoft Management Console (MMC) A flexible system that allows server administrators to configure the servers and monitor their function in one place.

.NET Framework A large library, available to all programming languages supported by .NET, that allows multiple programming languages to use code from other languages.

peer-to-peer networking A network setup in which any computer can communicate with other networked computers on an equal or peer-like basis without going through an intermediary, such as a server or network host computer. Mac OS is a peer-to-peer operating system.

Plug and Play (PnP) Software utilities that operate with compatible hardware to facilitate automatic hardware configuration. Windows versions starting with 95 recognize PnP hardware when it is installed, and in many cases can configure the hardware and install required software without significant user intervention.

Print Management Console A console that allows a system administrator to manage printers and printing throughout the network.

privileged mode A feature of the operating system kernel introduced in Windows NT that protected it from problems created by a malfunctioning program or process.

registry A Windows database that stores information about a computer's hardware and software configuration.

Server Core A scaled-back version of Windows Server 2008 in which all configurations and maintenance are done via the command-line interface.

storage area network (SAN) A set of storage devices that appear to the server to be locally attached, but in fact are on their own network with access granted to the server.

System V Release 4 (SVR4) A variation of the UNIX operating system. It is very popular today along with the Berkeley Software Distribution (BSD).

task supervisor A process in the operating system that keeps track of applications running on the computer and the resources they use.

total cost of ownership (TCO) The cost of installing and maintaining computers and equipment on a network. TCO includes hardware, software, maintenance, and support costs.

Universal Plug and Play (UPnP) An initiative of more than 80 companies to develop products that can be quickly added to a computer or network. These products include intelligent appliances for the home. For more information, go to *http://openconnectivity.org/upnp*.

Universal Serial Bus (USB) A serial bus designed to support up to 127 discrete devices with data transfer speeds up to 5 Gbits/s (gigabits per second).

User Account Protection (UAP) A feature of some Microsoft operating systems that allows for better protection of user accounts by controlling permissions and limiting the software applications that can be run from an account.

2

virtual private network (VPN) A private network that is like an encrypted tunnel through a larger network—such as the Internet, an enterprise network, or both—and is restricted to designated member clients.

Windows Hardware Error Architecture (WHEA) An architecture that supports memory and cache error recovery without the operating system being aware of the process.

X Window A windowed user interface for UNIX and other operating systems.

Review Questions

1. What was the original Microsoft operating system for the IBM PC?
   a. Windows 3.1
   b. Windows 1.0
   c. MS-DOS
   d. Windows 95
2. Windows 2000 Server was the first Windows server to contain Active Directory. True or False?
3. What does it mean if a driver is signed?
   a. The driver file contains a digital certificate.
   b. Only certified versions of drivers can be installed.
   c. The driver can only work in Windows 10 and later versions.
   d. The driver must be installed on a server.
4. What is the default authentication protocol used by Windows 2000 Server and later versions?
   a. Kerberos
   b. MS-CHAP
   c. PAP
   d. IntelliMirror
5. In Windows Server 2003, most features and services are installed and enabled by default. True or False?
6. With which client OS does Windows Server 2008 share the same code base?
   a. Windows Server 2003
   b. Windows XP
   c. Windows Vista
   d. Windows Server 2003 R2

7. Self-Healing NTFS is a process to repair disk drives on an off-line server. True or False?
8. What feature introduced with Windows Server 2008 provides only a limited GUI?
   a. Active Directory
   b. Server Core
   c. Plug and Play
   d. RODC
9. Which of the following best describes a virtual private network (VPN)?
   a. a stand-alone virtual network
   b. a virtual network residing within one computer
   c. a private network that is like an encrypted tunnel through a larger network
   d. a network that can only be observed from the outside on rare occasions
10. Windows Server 2008 R2 supports up to 64 physical processors. True or False?
11. What features available starting with Windows Server 2008 R2 provide the functionality of a VPN without requiring users to initiate a connection each time they want one?
    a. remote desktop protocol
    b. IntelliMirror
    c. Hyper-V
    d. DirectAccess
12. FCI automates data classification based on predefined categories. True or False?
13. Windows 8 has a Start button that supports only right-click functionality. True or False?
14. The X Window-like GUI interface in Red Hat Linux is called which of the following?
    a. KDE
    b. RDP
    c. BSD
    d. GNOME
15. Which of the following best describes Hyper-V?
    a. the fifth version of the overdrive section on the Intel chip
    b. a method to increase the speed of memory access on a personal computer
    c. the server virtualization code used to create multiple logical servers on one physical server
    d. extremely fast communication over the USB port
16. Looking at Windows Server 2008 R2, which of the following statements is true?
    a. It was released in both a 32-bit and 64-bit version.
    b. It shares a core operating system with Windows Vista.
    c. It supports Live Migration.
    d. It has integration features with Windows XP and Windows Vista.

2

17. What was the first version of Windows Server to come in Essentials and Foundation editions?
    a. Windows Server 2016
    b. Windows Server 2012
    c. Windows Server 2008
    d. Windows Server 2003
18. What are the two main design standards to which most versions of UNIX adhere? (Choose two.)
    a. BSD
    b. USB
    c. SVR4
    d. SCO
19. What company supports Fedora Linux?
    a. Oracle (formerly Sun Microsystems)
    b. Red Hat
    c. IBM
    d. Hewlett-Packard (HP)
20. Virtualization allows you to do which of the following?
    a. Combine multiple physical servers into one logical server.
    b. Run a live and test environment on separate physical servers.
    c. Set up multiple operating systems on one physical server.
    d. Access multiple physical servers through one virtual console.

Hands-On Projects

In some Windows projects you may see the User Account Control (UAC) box, which is used for security to help thwart intruders. If you see this box, click Yes to continue. Because computer setups may be different, the box is not mentioned in the actual project steps.

Project 2-1: Use the Windows Search Function

Windows 10 offers a convenient search program to quickly find files and start applications. In this project you learn how to use the "Search the web and Windows" search box in Windows 10.

1. Start and log on to your Windows 10 computer. Click the Search the web and Windows text box next to the Start button. (Note that if Cortana is enabled, the search box will display the prompt "Ask me anything.")

2. Type **file**. Notice that the operating system interactively searches as you are typing (see Figure 2-19).

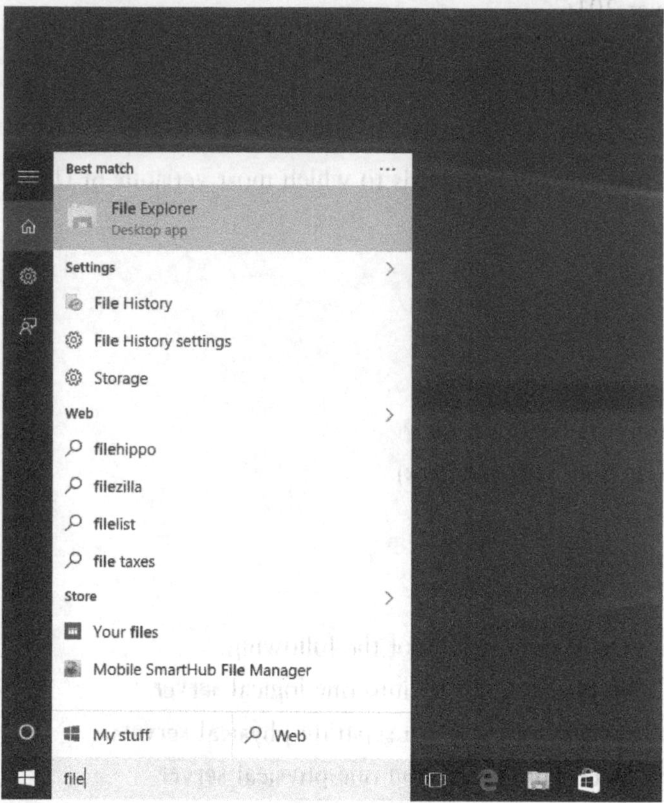

Figure 2-19 Windows 10 "Search the web and Windows" search box

3. Click **File Explorer** in the search results menu to start File Explorer.
4. Close the File Explorer window.
5. As an alternative, you can start a program by entering its file name in the search box. Click the **Search the web and Windows** text box. Type **explorer.exe.** Press **Enter** or click **explorer.exe** in the search results to start File Explorer.
6. Close File Explorer.
7. Click the **Search the web and Windows** text box.
8. Type **cmd** and press **Enter**. You'll see the Command Prompt window.
9. In the Command Prompt window, type **dir** at the command prompt and press **Enter** to list the directories and files in your current directory. Type **dir /a** and press **Enter.** You will see a long list of files and directories, including system and hidden files. The */a* option in the *dir* command specifies that all files should be listed.

10. Close the Command Prompt window.
11. Stay logged on if you are continuing to the next project.

Project 2-2: Browse the Windows 10 Registry

In this project, you browse the registry of Windows 10. Be careful not to make any changes to the registry. The Registry Editor does not have a Save or OK function, so any changes you make take effect immediately. Also, there is no Undo key.

1. Log on to Windows 10, if necessary.
2. Click the **Search the web and Windows** text box, type **regedit,** press **Enter,** and click **Yes.**
3. You see an interface like File Explorer that shows five folders, called *keys*. Each key contains information about different aspects of the system, such as hardware settings, user environment settings, application settings, and Windows system settings.
4. In the left pane, click to expand **HKEY_LOCAL_MACHINE\SOFTWARE\Microsoft\Windows\CurrentVersion\Authentication** and then click **LogonUI.** The right pane displays a number of values related to the current user (see Figure 2-20).

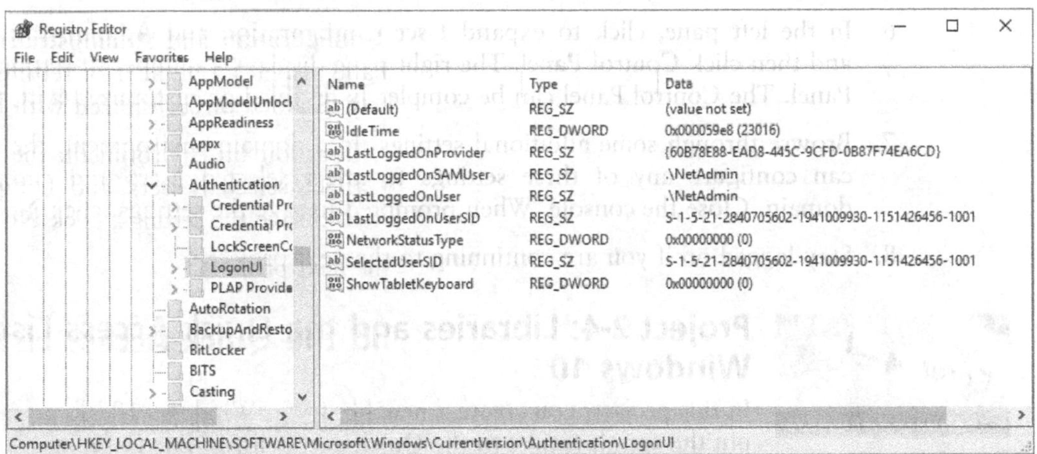

Figure 2-20 Windows 10 registry

5. In the left pane of the registry editor, navigate to **HKEY_CURRENT_USER\Control Panel.** Right-click **Control Panel** and click **Find.** In the Find dialog box, click to uncheck Keys and Data, leaving only Values checked. In the Find what box, type **Wallpaper** and click **Find Next.** The value shows the path to the wallpaper used by the current user.
6. Close the Registry Editor.
7. Stay logged on if you are continuing to the next project.

Project 2-3: Work with MMC and Group Policy Editor

In this project, you use the Microsoft Management Console (MMC) and load a snap-in called Local Group Policy Editor. Group Policy is used to configure aspects of your system, including the working environment. In a Windows domain, the IT administrator can configure Group Policy on Windows servers that are pushed down to domain members to maintain a consistent security and working environment for all client computers.

1. Log on to Windows 10, if necessary.
2. Click the **Search the web and Windows** text box, type **mmc**, press **Enter**, and click **Yes**.
3. In the console that opens, click **File** and click **Add/Remove Snap-in**. In the Add or Remove Snap-ins dialog box, browse through the available snap-ins. Scroll down and click **Group Policy Object Editor** (part of the name may be cut off), and then click **Add**.
4. In the Select Group Policy Object window, click **Finish**. Click **OK**.
5. In the left pane of the console, click to expand **Local Computer Policy**, **Computer Configuration**, and **Windows Settings**. Then click **Security Settings**. In the right pane, double-click **Account Policies** and then **Password Policy**. This is where policies are configured that control password and account lockout settings.
6. In the left pane, click to expand **User Configuration** and **Administrative Templates**, and then click **Control Panel**. The right pane displays a number of settings for Control Panel. The Control Panel can be completely disabled or customized with these settings.
7. Browse through some additional settings. In a domain environment, the administrator can configure any of these settings to affect selected users and computers in the domain. Close the console. When prompted to save the settings, click **No**.
8. Stay logged on if you are continuing to the next project.

Project 2-4: Libraries and the Quick Access List in Windows 10

In this project, you create a new library in Windows 10, do a search, and then pin the search results to the Quick access list in File Explorer.

1. Log on to Windows 10, if necessary.
2. Open File Explorer by right-clicking **Start** and clicking **File Explorer**.
3. To work with libraries, you must enable them in the Navigation pane. To do so, click **View** in the File Explorer menu bar, and then click **Navigation pane**. Click to select **Show libraries**. (If Show libraries is already checked, skip this step.)
4. In the left pane of File Explorer, right-click **Libraries**, point to **New**, and click **Library**. Type **Programs** and press **Enter** to give the new library a name.
5. Right-click **Programs**, and click **Properties**. Click **Add** to add a new folder. Navigate to the C: drive and click **Program Files (x86)**. Click **Include folder**.

6. Click **Add** to add a new folder. Navigate to the C: drive and click **Program Files**. Click **Include folder.**
7. Click **Change library icon.** Choose an icon from the list and click **OK.** Click **OK** to finish creating your library. Click to expand **Programs.** In the right pane, you see a list of files and folders contained in the two folders.
8. Click the **Search Programs** text box at the top right of the File Explorer window, and type **Internet**. This search will show all files and folders whose name or contents contain the word "Internet."
9. Click the **Home** menu in File Explorer and then click **Pin to Quick access.** A new item is added under the Quick access list in the left pane of File Explorer. You see a search icon named Internet. Click **Internet** to see the search results in the right pane. From now on, you can click the Internet search icon in the Quick access list to repeat the search results. Close File Explorer.
10. Log off or shut down your Windows 10 computer.

Project 2-5: Determine the Shell in Linux

In this project, you learn how to determine what shell you are using while in the Linux operating system. The shell serves as an interface between the user and the operating system—for example, when the user instructs the operating system to execute a program or command.

1. Start your Linux computer and log on.
2. Access the shell prompt by opening a terminal window in the Linux GNOME interface. To open a terminal window, click **Activities**, click the **Show Applications** icon, click **Utilities**, and click **Terminal**.
3. Look at the shell prompt. The $ prompt means that you are in either the Bourne, Bourne Again, or Korn shell.
4. At the shell prompt, type **echo $SHELL**, making sure that the word "SHELL" is in all capital letters. Press **Enter**. A response of /bin/bash means you are using the Bourne Again shell. If /bin/sh appears, you are in the Bourne shell. A response of /bin/ksh signifies the Korn shell.
5. If you got an error message in Step 4, enter **echo $shell**, making sure that the word "shell" is in all lowercase letters. You should see the response /bin/csh, which means that you are in the C shell.
6. At the shell prompt, type **man bash** and press **Enter** to read the online manual information about the Bourne Again shell, which is the default shell used in Fedora and Red Hat Linux distributions.
7. Press the **Spacebar** one or two times to continue reading the introductory information about the Bourne Again shell. When you are finished reading the first few pages, press **q** to exit the documentation.
8. Close the terminal window, but stay logged on to Linux for the next project.

Project 2-6: Create a Shortcut on the Linux Activities Dash

In this project, you start a program from the Activities dash and then create a shortcut on the Activities dash.

1. From your Linux desktop, click **Activities**. You see a list of icons in a panel called the dash on the left side of the screen.
2. Click **Files** (the icon that looks like a filing cabinet) to open Files, the Linux GNOME file manager.
3. Notice that a new item is placed next to the Activities menu. The active application is shown here. Click **Files** next to Activities to see a list of options. You can open a new window, perform tasks specific to the application, view the application's preferences, get help, and quit.
4. Click the Files window again. Click **Computer** in the left pane to open the root of the file system. Double-click **Home** to open the home folder for the current user. Close **Files**.
5. Click **Activities**, click **Show Applications**, and then click **Utilities**. Right-click **Terminal** and click **Add to Favorites**. From now on, you can open a terminal window directly from the Activities dash. Click the **Activities** menu to show the desktop again.
6. Click **Activities** and then click the **Terminal** icon to start a shell prompt in a terminal window. Type **gedit** and press **Enter** to start the GNOME text editor. This editor is like Windows Notepad but has more features. Type your name and the name of the class you are taking, and then click **Save**.
7. When prompted, type **myfile** as the name of the file, click **Documents** in the left pane, and click **Save**.
8. Open Files by clicking **Activities** and clicking **Files**. Double-click **Documents** in the right pane to see the file you just created. Also notice that Files appears in the Applications menu next to Activities. Close Files. Notice that gedit now appears in the Applications menu. Close **gedit**. Close the terminal window.
9. Stay logged on if you are continuing to the next activity.

Project 2-7: Find Files in Linux

In Linux, you can search for a file using the *find* command from the Terminal window. Alternatively, you can use the search tool in the GNOME Activities menu.

1. Open a terminal window. (Hint: You just created a shortcut to it in the previous project.)
2. At the shell prompt, type **find /home -name Desktop** and press **Enter** to search for the desktop directory within your account's home directory (see Figure 2-21). In this

context, *find* is the command to search for one or more files, */home* tells the *find* command to search for files in the /home directory, which is the parent directory for all user account directories, and *-name Desktop* is an instruction to look for all files that contain *Desktop* as part of the name.

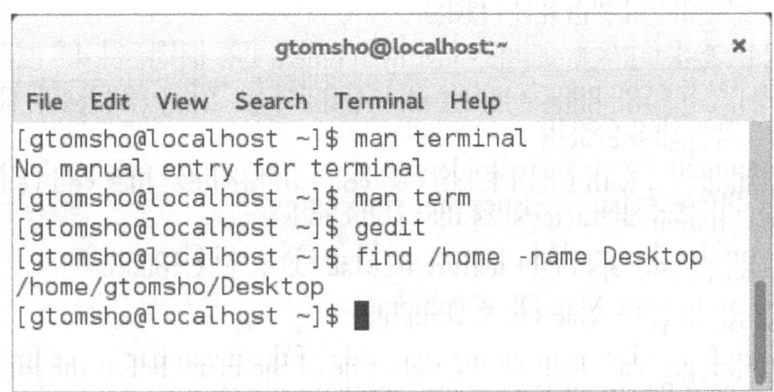
gtomsho@localhost:~
File Edit View Search Terminal Help
[gtomsho@localhost ~]$ man terminal
No manual entry for terminal
[gtomsho@localhost ~]$ man term
[gtomsho@localhost ~]$ gedit
[gtomsho@localhost ~]$ find /home -name Desktop
/home/gtomsho/Desktop
[gtomsho@localhost ~]$

Figure 2-21 Using the *find* command in the Linux shell

Source: Linux

3. Type **man find** and press **Enter** to see the manual pages for the *find* command. Scroll through the man pages to see the options available with the *find* command. Press q when you are finished.
4. Type **locate Desktop | more** and press **Enter**. This *locate* command uses an index to find all files and folders on the disk that include the word *Desktop*. The | *more* part of the command pipes output to the *more* command, which paginates the output. Press the **Spacebar** if necessary to scroll through the files.
5. Type **touch myDesktopfile** and press **Enter** to create a new file named myDesktopfile. Type **locate Desktop** and press **Enter**. The command does not find the file because the index has not been updated.
6. Type **sudo updatedb** and press **Enter** to update the index. Type your password when prompted, if necessary. The *updatedb* command must be run as the superuser and therefore requires you to enter your password in most cases.
7. Type **locate Desktop | more** and press **Enter**. You should see the myDesktopfile in the listing. Close the Terminal window.
8. Click **Activities**, click the **Type to search** text box, and type **Desktop.** Don't press Enter. Linux finds all items related to the desktop and all files that have the word *Desktop* as part of the name. If you press Enter, you will run any applications found that are related to Desktop.
9. In the search results, click the folder named **Desktop** to open the folder in Files.
10. Close **Files**.
11. Log off or shut down your Linux computer.

Project 2-8: Use Spotlight in Mac OS X

Mac OS X was among the first operating systems to offer faster searches by providing Spotlight. Spotlight offers the following:

- Indexes files so you can find them faster
- Enables you to search for something just by typing a few letters of the name
- Quickly searches the computer's nooks and crannies for what you want, even if you're not sure how to spell it exactly
- Works in conjunction with smart folders so you can organize files you've found according to different characteristics that you choose

In this project, you use the Spotlight feature in Mac OS X El Capitan.

1. Start and log on to your Mac OS X computer.
2. Click the magnifying glass icon on the right side of the menu bar at the top of the desktop. Read the message about the services Spotlight offers.
3. Type d. Notice that Spotlight starts an instant search (see Figure 2-22).

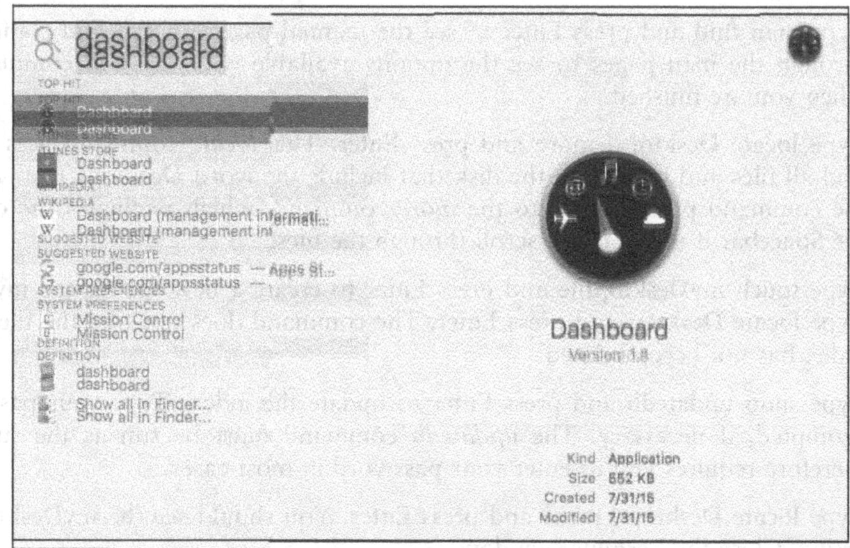

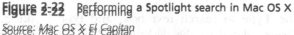

Figure 2-22 Performing a Spotlight search in Mac OS X

Source: Mac OS X El Capitan

4. Slowly type the remaining letters, **ashboard**, to see how Spotlight changes its display.
5. In the right pane, double-click **Dashboard** to open it. Dashboard is a collection of widgets. Close Dashboard by clicking the circle icon with the arrow in the lower-right corner.
6. Open Spotlight again by clicking the magnifying glass icon.
7. Delete **dashboard** in the search box.

8. Type **itunes**. The item under Top Hits is Spotlight's best guess about which item is most likely the one you want.

9. Delete **itunes** and type **jpg**.

10. Click one of the images listed (with a .jpg extension). Notice that the picture is previewed in the right pane.

11. Click somewhere on the desktop to close Spotlight.

12. Stay logged on if you are continuing to the next project.

Project 2-9: Examine the Menus in Mac OS X

In this project, you examine the Mac OS X menu bar options on the desktop.

To view the Mac OS X desktop and menu bar options:

1. Log on to your Mac OS X computer, if necessary.

2. Click **Finder** in the menu bar to display the Finder menu selections. Finder enables you to manage features on the desktop as well as empty the trash (deleted files and folders) or secure emptied trash. Click **Preferences** in the Finder menu. The Finder Preferences window enables you to set up preferences for desktop features, such as specifying items to display on the desktop, including disk drives (see Figure 2-23).

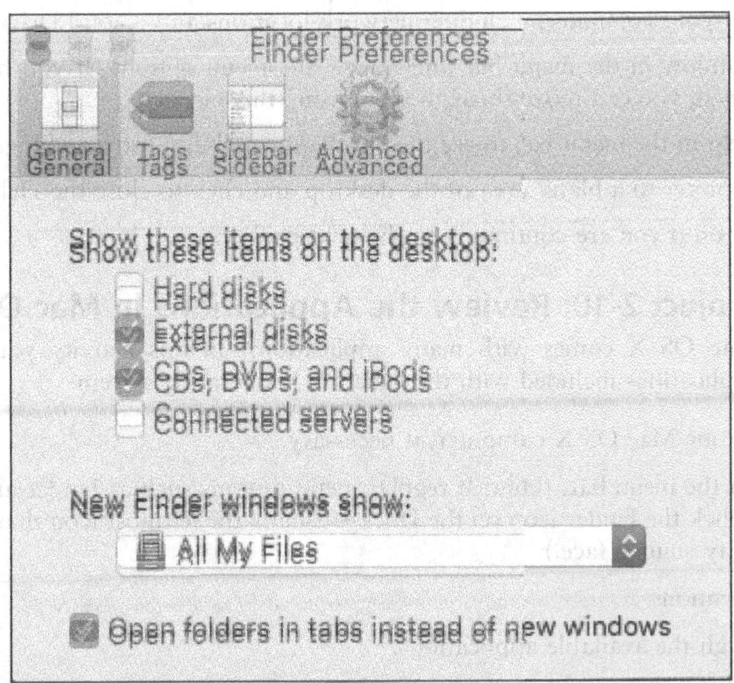

Figure 2-23 Finder preferences

Source: Mac OS X El Capitan

3. Click each of the buttons in the Finder Preferences window as listed below:
   - **General**—Specify items to display on the desktop, such as hard drives, and determine where to open windows and set folder properties.
   - **Tags**—Color-code labels used in windows so that windows can be sorted by color.
   - **Sidebar**—Designate what appears in the Sidebar shown in open windows. For example, you can display links for quick access to devices, documents, and shared resources.
   - **Advanced**—Configure options for file extensions, emptying the trash (deleted files), and where to perform searches.
4. Close the Finder Preferences window.
5. Click **File** in the menu bar and review the options in the File menu. From here you can open a new Finder window, open and create files, and save items to a portable drive.
6. Point to **Edit** in the menu bar and notice the options that can be used while editing, such as cut and copy. (These options are only available if you are editing a file.)
7. Point to **View** in the menu bar. Notice the options that can be used to manage the presentation of items in a window, such as displaying items as icons or a list.
8. Point to **Go** in the menu bar and notice its options. From here, you can open various locations on your computer, including network locations and iCloud Drive.
9. Point to **Window** in the menu bar and review the menu options. If you have multiple windows open, you can move through them using this menu.
10. Point to **Help** in the menu bar to see the Spotlight capability for searching.
11. Move the pointer to a blank area of the desktop and click to close the Help menu.
12. Stay logged on if you are continuing to the next project.

Project 2-10: Review the Applications in Mac OS X

Mac OS X comes with many applications. In this activity you review the applications included with the Mac OS X operating system.

1. Log on to your Mac OS X computer, if necessary.
2. Click **Go** in the menu bar. (Hint: If regular menu options such as Finder and Go aren't displayed, click the Finder icon on the Dock—usually the leftmost icon that looks like a blue and gray smiling face.)
3. Click **Applications.**
4. Scroll through the available applications.
5. Double-click **Dictionary.** Dictionary is an application that enables you to quickly look up the meaning of a word or determine its spelling.
6. Type **folder** in the Spotlight box.

7. Read the definition for *folder*. Close the Dictionary window.
8. Double-click **TextEdit** in the Applications window. Like most OSs, Mac OS X has a basic text editor. Close TextEdit.
9. Double-click **Safari** in the Applications window. Safari is the native Mac OS X Web browser. Close Safari.
10. Double-click **LaunchPad** in the Applications window. LaunchPad provides another method for starting applications in Mac OS X. Click **Notes**. Notice that you only need to single-click the application icon to start it. Leave Notes open.
11. Click the **Safari** icon in the Dock. Press and hold the green maximize button in Safari, and then slide the Safari window to the left side of the screen until it snaps into place. Double-click the Notes window; it snaps into place on the right side of the screen. This is called Split View.
12. Close the Safari window and the Notes window. Close the Applications window.
13. Log off or shut down your Mac OS X computer.

Critical Thinking

The following activities give you critical thinking challenges. Challenge Labs give you an opportunity to use the skills you have learned to perform a task without step-by-step instructions. Case Projects present a practical problem for which you supply a written solution. Not all chapters contain Challenge Labs. There is not always a specific right or wrong answer to these critical thinking exercises. They are intended to encourage you to review the chapter material and delve deeper into the topics you have learned.

Case Projects

The following scenario is used for Case Projects 2-1 through 2-6:

Darts is a sporting goods company with outlets in most of the western states. This company has a network of 10 servers and 273 client computers that have the following operating systems:

- Eight Windows Server 2008 servers
- Two Linux servers running Red Hat Linux Enterprise
- 20 computers running Mac OS X version 10.7 Lion
- 32 computers running Windows 10
- 80 computers running Windows 8.1
- 46 computers running Windows Vista
- 95 computers running Windows XP

Darts realizes that with the projected growth of the company, they need to upgrade the computers and servers on their network.

112 Chapter 2 Popular Operating Systems

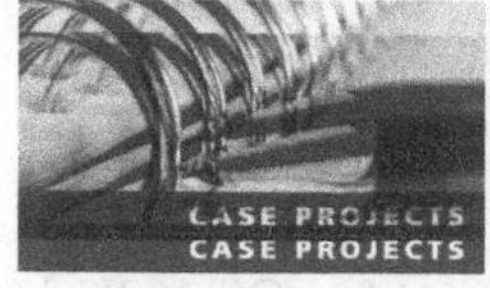

Case Project 2-1: Accounting Department Upgrade

The Accounting Department has all of the Windows XP computers. The accounting director wants to upgrade to Windows 10. What are the advantages of upgrading for this department in terms of the enhanced operating system functions that are available in Windows 10? What are some possible disadvantages?

Case Project 2-2: Legacy Billing System

If the Accounting Department does upgrade to Windows 10, will the department be able to run a legacy 16-bit billing program that was designed for Windows XP?

Case Project 2-3: New Computer for the Marketing Department

The Marketing Department uses the Mac OS X version 10.7 Lion computers. Because they plan to purchase new computers, what is the newest Mac operating system to which they can upgrade? What would be the advantage of this upgrade for their department?

Case Project 2-4: President's Problem

The president of Darts is convinced that the processor on his Windows Vista system is overloaded. How can you help him determine if there is a problem with the processor?

Case Project 2-5: Chief Financial Officer's Concerns

The new chief financial officer believes that all of the Windows XP computers should be upgraded to Windows 10 because Windows 8.1 was not well received in the marketplace. What are the advantages and disadvantages of upgrading to Windows 10 compared to Windows 8.1? Include a discussion of the total cost of the upgrade (TCO).

Case Project 2-6: Server Upgrades

What would be the advantage of upgrading the Windows Server 2008 servers, and if you recommend upgrading them, what operating system do you recommend? Why?

chapter 3

The Central Processing Unit (CPU)

After reading this chapter and completing the exercises, you will be able to:

- Describe the function and features of CPUs
- Identify features of popular CPUs from various manufacturers

Operating systems and hardware work together to make computers useful for business, educational, personal, network, and cloud computing applications. The features of an operating system used for a particular application depend on the capabilities of the hardware. In many cases, modern operating systems do not support older hardware. When you upgrade an operating system, you may need to upgrade the hardware to match the new operating system's capabilities.

This chapter focuses on the CPU and its surrounding electronics, including CPU architecture, clock speeds, and buses. In addition, you learn how CPUs are used by particular operating systems.

Understanding CPUs

As you learned in Chapter 1, "Operating Systems Fundamentals," one of the main functions of the operating system is to provide the interface between the various application programs running on a computer and the hardware inside. Central to understanding the hardware is the system architecture of the computer, which is built around the CPU, or processor. The **system architecture** includes the number and type of CPUs in the hardware, and the communication routes, called buses, between the CPUs and other hardware components, such as memory and disk storage. A **bus** is a path or channel between a computer's CPU and the devices it manages, such as memory and I/O devices.

The CPU is the chip that performs the actual computational and logic work. Most modern PCs have one such chip, and are referred to as **single-processor computers**. In reality, to ensure complete functionality, the CPU requires several support chips, such as chips that help manage communications with devices and device drivers.

Chip technology continues to develop with the addition of multicore processors. A processor **core** is the part of a CPU that reads and executes very basic instructions, such as reading and writing data from and to memory or executing an arithmetic operation. CPUs were originally created to have only one core and thus perform only one instruction at a time. A multicore processor has two or more cores—for example, a dual-core processor contains two cores and a quad-core processor has four. The most processor cores used in traditional PC desktops and servers is 16 as of this writing, but high-end CPUs, such as Intel's Knights Landing, have up to 72 cores. Development continues in this area, and scientists so far have put as many as 1000 cores on a single CPU chip.

Some computers have multiple physical CPUs; many have two, and some have as many as 128 or more. This type of computer is generally referred to as a **multiprocessor computer**. You will take a closer look at single-processor, multiprocessor, and multicore computers later in this chapter.

Basic CPU Architecture

We will discuss different design types of CPUs and various components of a CPU, but before we do, let's take a look at its basic architecture. Most CPUs are composed of the following elements (see Figure 3-1):

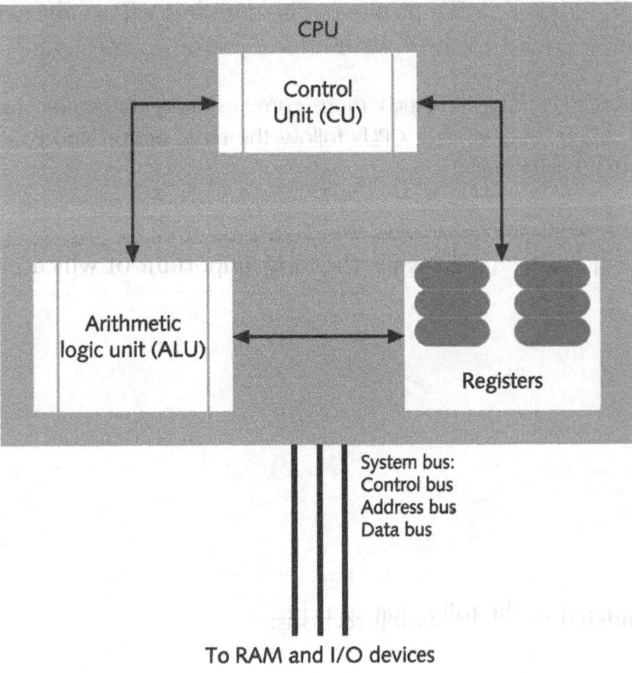

Figure 3-1 Basic architecture of a CPU

- *Control unit*—The **control unit** (CU) is the director of operations in the CPU. The control unit provides timing and coordination between the other parts of the CPU, such as the arithmetic logic unit, registers, and system bus. For example, when a new instruction should be executed, the control unit receives and decodes the instruction and tells the arithmetic logic unit to execute it.
- *Arithmetic logic unit*—The **arithmetic logic unit (ALU)** performs the primary task of any CPU, which is to execute instructions. These might be arithmetic instructions, such as addition or multiplication of integers, or logic instructions, such as binary AND or binary OR instructions. Most CPUs also contain a **floating point unit** (FPU) that performs floating point operations.
- *Registers*—A **register** is a temporary holding location on a CPU where data must be placed before the CPU can use it. There are instruction registers that hold the instruction the CPU executes, such as add, multiply, or store. Also, the CPU uses address registers to access data stored in RAM, and data registers that hold the data the CPU is currently working with, such as two numbers used in an add or multiply instruction.
- *System bus*—The system bus is a series of lanes that are used to communicate between the CPU and other major parts of the computer, such as RAM and input/output (I/O) devices. There are actually three types of buses: the control bus, address bus, and data bus. The **control bus** carries status signals between the CPU and other devices. Status signals inform the CPU that a device needs attention; for example, when an input device has data ready, the CPU must execute the device driver code to read the data from the device. The **address bus** carries address signals to indicate where data should

be read from or written to in the system's memory. The data bus carries the actual data that is being read from or written to system memory.

While modern CPUs are much more complex than the simple block diagram in Figure 3-1, most CPUs follow the basic design and contain the elements described.

CPUs can be classified by several hardware elements, the most important of which are:

- Design type
- Speed
- Cache
- Address bus
- Data bus
- Control bus
- CPU scheduling

Each of these elements is considered in the following sections.

Design Type

Two general CPU designs are used in today's computers: Complex Instruction Set Computing (CISC) and Reduced Instruction Set Computing (RISC). The main difference between the two is the number of different instructions the chip can process and the complexity of the instructions. When a program executes on a computer, the CPU reads instruction after instruction from the program to perform the tasks specified in the program. When the CPU has read such an instruction, it carries out the associated operations. The CPU can process as many as 20 million complex operations per second on the low end, and several billion on the high end. Clock speed and CPU design are the factors that determine how fast operations are executed. It is convenient for the programmer to have many instructions available to perform many different operations.

Let's say, for example, that the programmer wants to multiply two numbers. It would be convenient to give the CPU the two numbers, then tell it to multiply them and display the result. Because different kinds of numbers (such as integers and real numbers) must be treated differently, it would be nice if there were functions to perform this multiplication on all number types. You can see that as we require the CPU to perform more and more functions, the number of instructions can rapidly increase. The **instruction set**, or the list of commands the CPU can understand and carry out, can become quite complex as programs perform more functions. A processor that works like this is called a CISC CPU.

CISC and RISC CPUs differ in the following ways:

- *Complex versus simple instructions*—CISC CPUs are generally more complex, meaning each instruction does more work than a single RISC instruction. Some instructions carried out by CISC CPUs may require several RISC instructions to perform the same task. For example, say you want to add two numbers that are stored in memory locations X and Y and store the result back in memory location X. The CISC CPU code might look like the following:

```
add X, Y
```

Behind the scenes, the CPU must load the data from location X into one of its registers, load the data from location Y into another one of its registers, perform the calculation, the result of which is stored in another register, and then move the result back into memory location X. To perform the same task with a RISC processor, you might have several instructions:

```
load R1, X
load R2, Y
add R1, R2
stor R1, X
```

In the above example, the RISC CPU requires four instructions: two to load the numbers to be added from memory (X and Y) into registers (R1 and R2), one to perform the addition, and one to store the result from its register (R1) back to memory (X). As you can see, CISC instructions are much more complex because they do a lot of work that doesn't require specific instructions, whereas RISC CPUs require the programmer (or compiler) to explicitly write those instructions. Based on the above example, what advantage is there in using a RISC CPU? It has to do with clock cycles.

- *Clock cycles*—The single add instruction on a CISC CPU might take four CPU clock cycles, whereas each of the four instructions carried out by the RISC CPU will take one clock cycle each. In this example, it takes both CPU types the same number of clock cycles to perform the same task. Some instructions on CISC CPUs might require one clock cycle; others might need two, four, or more clock cycles. Conversely, most instructions on RISC CPUs take only one clock cycle. Because the instructions on RISC CPUs take a uniform number of clock cycles, designers can use this fact to their advantage with pipelining.
- *Pipelining*—Pipelining is the ability of the CPU to perform more than one task on a single clock cycle. For example, if you have a series of additions to perform, a RISC processor doesn't have to wait for all four instructions to complete before it moves on to the next addition. While the second load instruction of the first addition is being performed, the RISC processor can be loading the first value for the next addition. While pipelining does occur in CISC CPUs, the varying number of cycles it takes to complete each instruction makes pipelining more difficult and not as effective, compared to RISC CPUs. Figure 3-2 shows how pipelining and the number of cycles required per instruction can affect execution time. In the figure, a CISC CPU and RISC CPU are each performing a series of three additions. With the CISC CPU, only three instructions are required, but each instruction takes four clock cycles and the first instruction is completed before the second instruction is started. With the RISC CPU, each addition takes four instructions of one clock cycle each, but using pipelining, the second addition is started while the first addition is still under way, allowing the RISC CPU to complete all three additions in only six cycles, as opposed to 12 cycles for the CISC CPU.

3

CISC CPU

Three additions in 12 clock cycles

Clock cycles											
1	2	3	4	5	6	7	8	9	10	11	12
add (1st addition)				add (2nd addition)				add (3rd addition)			

RISC CPU

Three additions in 6 clock cycles

Clock cycles						
1	2	3	4	5	6	
load	load	add	stor			1st addition
	load	load	add	stor		2nd addition
		load	load	add	stor	3rd addition

Figure 3-2 CISC processing versus RISC processing using pipelining

- *Hardware versus microcode*—Because CISC instructions are so complex, there is actually a small program inside the chip that must interpret and execute each instruction. This small program is called **microcode.** RISC instructions are all executed directly by the CPU hardware, with no microcode middleman. This approach makes for faster execution of individual instructions.
- *Compiler*—A **compiler** is a computer program that takes a high-level language like C# or Java and turns it into assembly code that is executed by the CPU. Due to the complexity of CISC-based instructions, the compiler has less work to do because the high-level language code need not be broken down into as many assembly language steps. Taking the example of an addition instruction from before, the C# or Java code might look like the following:

  ```
  X = X + Y;
  ```

  The compiler then translates that statement into assembly code for a CISC CPU. The assembly code might also be a single line of code:

  ```
  add X, Y
  ```

  By comparison, several lines of code might be needed when the compiler translates the statement into assembly code for a RISC CPU:

  ```
  load R1, X
  load R2, Y
  add R1, R2
  stor R1, X
  ```

After a high-level language program is compiled to assembly language, another step called *assembly* is needed before it can be executed by the CPU. Assembly translates assembly code into machine code. With machine code, each assembly language statement is translated into a series of numbers—for example, the statement *load R1, X* might be translated to something like 09 101 2215. Remember, computers can only interpret numeric values; the software they run translates numbers into human-readable form, and vice versa.

- *Number and usage of registers*—As mentioned, a register is a temporary holding location on a CPU where data must be placed before the CPU can use it. Because so much room is used for microcode on CISC CPUs, there are far fewer registers than on a RISC chip, which doesn't use microcode. The more registers there are, the more simultaneous operations the CPU can perform, as you saw with pipelining. One of the reasons pipelining is easier with RISC CPUs is because there are more registers to store data for pipelined instructions. In addition, CISC CPUs erase their registers after each instruction and require them to be reloaded with each successive instruction, whereas RISC CPUs can leave data in registers until the register is needed for another operation.

CISC and RISC CPUs continue to be produced. The debate between which is better is muddied by the inclusion of CISC features in RISC CPUs and RISC features in CISC CPUs. Intel processors are still considered to be CISC.

Speed

The speed of a CPU defines how fast it can perform operations. There are many ways to indicate speed, but the most frequently used indicator is the **internal clock speed** of the CPU. As you may know, a CPU runs on a very rigid schedule along with the rest of the computer. The clock provides this schedule to make sure that all the chips know what to expect at a given time. The internal clock speed tells you how many clock pulses, or ticks, are available per second. Typically, the CPU performs some action on every tick. The more ticks per second there are, the faster the CPU executes commands, and the harder the electronics on the CPU must work. The clock speed for a CPU can be lower than 1 million ticks per second (1 megahertz or MHz) or higher than 4 billion ticks per second (4 gigahertz or GHz). The faster the clock is, the faster the CPU, and the more expensive the hardware. Also, as more components are needed to make a CPU, the chip uses more energy to do its work. Part of this energy is converted to heat, causing faster CPUs to run warmer, which requires more fans in the chassis. Overheating of computer components in general and CPUs in particular is a constant battle faced by IT departments; it requires considerable investment in the cooling systems of data centers.

From the Trenches . . .

A college upgraded from 1.8 GHz computers to a model running at 3.06 GHz. The computers were plugged in and ran for about five minutes before the video became scrambled and stopped working. Several calls were made to customer service; after four days of work, technicians determined that the computers had a heating problem. The computers were built at sea level, where they worked just fine, but the college was in a city at an elevation of over 5000 feet. Air contains fewer molecules as the altitude increases. Molecules hitting the surface of the CPU carry away the heat, and at higher elevations, there aren't as many molecules, so there is less air movement to cool the warmer CPUs. These warmer CPUs were overheating the video circuitry and causing the problems. The manufacturer's addition of dual-chassis fans to each computer corrected the problem.

In addition to performing fast operations inside the CPU, the chips must be able to communicate with the other chips in the computer. This is where the external clock speed of the CPU comes in. While a CPU may run internally at a speed of 3 GHz, it typically uses a lower clock speed to communicate with the rest of the computer. The reason for the lower speed is again cost, to a large extent. It would be extremely expensive to make every component in the computer run as fast as the CPU. Therefore, the other components in the computer typically run at a reduced clock rate. Usually, the external clock speed is one-half, one-third, one-fourth, or one-eighth the speed of the internal CPU clock.

Cache

If a CPU wants to get a few numbers out of memory, and its internal clock speed is four times faster than its external clock speed, it obviously must wait on the external clock, which could be very inefficient. To avoid this problem, modern CPUs have cache memory built into the chip. Cache memory works by providing extremely fast access to data so the CPU doesn't have to wait for main RAM. While the CPU is executing program code, instructions or data that are most likely to be used next are fetched from main memory and placed in cache memory. When the CPU needs the next bytes of data or the next instruction, it looks in cache first. If the information cannot be found, the CPU then fetches it from main memory. The more often the CPU can find the data in cache, the faster the program will execute. There are different levels of cache, with each successive level becoming larger, but slower:

- *Level 1 cache*—Level 1 (L1) cache is the fastest of the cache types; usually it runs at the same speed as the CPU, so the CPU won't have to wait for data if it can be found in L1 cache. However, L1 cache is the least plentiful—typically 8 to 32 KB per processor core—so it can't hold much data. L1 cache is usually divided into two parts: instruction cache and data cache. L1 cache is always an integral part of the CPU chip on modern CPUs.
- *Level 2 cache*—Level 2 (L2) cache is somewhat slower than L1 cache, but much larger. Many CPUs today have 256 KB of L2 cache per processor core. The combination of L1 cache and L2 cache greatly increases the chances that the data the CPU needs will

Basic CPU Architecture 121

be located in cache, so the CPU will not have to access much slower main memory. L2 cache is also an integral part of the CPU chip on modern CPUs.

- *Level 3 cache*—Level 3 (L3) cache, until the last several years, was not part of the CPU chip, but was instead a part of the motherboard. This meant that L3 cache could be fairly large, but considerably slower than L1 and L2 cache. On the more advanced CPUs, L3 cache is part of the CPU and is shared among the CPU cores. L3 cache can often be found in sizes of 8 MB, 16 MB, and greater.
- *Level 4 cache*—Level 4 (L4) cache, if it exists, will usually be found on the motherboard. If a CPU has L1, L2, and L3 cache and is installed on a motherboard that has built-in cache, the cache on the motherboard will become L4 cache. If a CPU only has L1 and L2 cache, the motherboard cache will become L3 cache. The exception is the high-end version of some CPUs that are starting to come with on-board L4 cache. Some of these high-end CPUs have as much as 128 MB of L4 cache that is shared among the CPU cores.

The amount of cache, especially for larger CPUs, determines the speed of the CPU. In many cases, up to 95 percent of the data a CPU needs to transfer to and from memory is present in one of the caches when the CPU needs it. A specialized piece of hardware called the cache controller predicts what data will be needed, and makes that data available in cache before it is needed. Most modern CPUs can also use the cache to write data to memory and ensure that the CPU will not have to wait when it wants to write results to memory. You can see that intelligent, fast cache controllers and large amounts of cache are important components for increasing the speed of a CPU.

Address Bus

The address bus is an internal communications pathway that specifies the source and target addresses for memory reads and writes. It is instrumental in the transfer of data to and from computer memory. The address bus typically runs at the external clock speed of the CPU. The address, like all data in the computer, is in digital form and is conveyed as a series of bits. The width of the address bus is the number of bits that can be used to address memory. A wider bus means the computer can address more memory, and therefore store more data or larger, more complex programs. For example, a 16-bit address bus can address 64 kilobytes, or KB (65,536 bytes) of memory, and a 32-bit address bus can address roughly 4 billion bytes, or 4 gigabytes (GB) of memory. Modern processors have a 64-bit address bus, allowing them to address 16 terabytes (TB) of memory.

Data Bus

The data bus allows computer components, such as the CPU, display adapter, and main memory, to share information. The number of bits in the data bus indicates how many bits of data can be transferred from memory to the CPU, or vice versa, in a single operation. A CPU with an external clock speed of 1 GHz will have 1 billion ticks per second to the external bus. If this CPU has a 16-bit data bus, it could theoretically transfer 2 GB (2,000,000,000 bytes) of data to and from memory every second. (One byte consists of 8 bits, so 1 billion × 16 bits/8 bits per second = 2 GB per second.) A CPU with an external clock speed of 1 GHz and a 64-bit data bus could transfer as much as 8 GB per second (1 billion × 64 bits/8 bits per byte). That is four times as much data in the same time period, so in theory, the CPU will work four times as fast.

There are a couple of catches here. First, the software must be able to instruct the CPU to use all of the data bus, and the rest of the computer must be fast enough to keep up with the CPU. Most CPUs work internally with the same number of bits as on the data bus. In other words, a CPU with a 64-bit data bus can typically perform operations on 64 bits of data at a time. Almost all CPUs can also be instructed to work with chunks of data narrower than the data bus width, but in this case the CPU is not as efficient because the same number of clock cycles is required to perform an operation, whether or not all bits are used. All Windows versions from Windows XP forward include a 64-bit version, and starting with Windows Server 2008 R2, all server versions are 64-bit only.

Control Bus

The CPU is kept informed of the status of the computer's resources and devices, such as the memory and disk drives, by information transported on the control bus. The most basic information transported across the control bus indicates whether a particular resource is active and can be accessed. If a disk drive becomes active, for example, the disk controller provides this information to the CPU over the control bus. Other information that may be transported over the control bus includes whether a particular function is for input or output. Memory read and write status is transported on this bus, as well as **interrupt requests (IRQs)**. An interrupt request is a request to the processor to "interrupt" whatever it is doing to take care of a process, such as a read from a disk drive, which in turn might be interrupted by another process, such as a write into memory.

CPU Scheduling

CPU scheduling determines which process to execute when multiple processes are waiting to run. For example, if you have three applications open on your computer, each application must be scheduled to get CPU time. The CPU switches between the applications very quickly based on factors like priority, so users don't typically notice that this switching, or *time-slicing*, is occurring. CPU scheduling is not a function built into the CPU; rather, it is a function of the operating system. However, the architecture of the CPU can greatly facilitate a system's ability to efficiently schedule multiple processes. Recall from Chapter 1 that a process is a program that's loaded into memory and run by the CPU. Most PC operating systems of the 1970s and 1980s were basically single threaded, meaning they could only schedule the process to run as a whole. Beginning with the Windows NT operating system, the use of CPU scheduling algorithms began to evolve to allow **multithreading**, which is the ability to run two or more parts of a process, known as threads, at the same time. A **thread** is the smallest piece of computer code that can be independently scheduled for execution. For example, if a user is running a word processor, one thread might accept input from the keyboard and format it on the screen while another thread does a spell check as the user types. Switching between threads takes a considerable number of CPU instructions to accomplish, so it was only practical to begin including this feature in OSs when CPUs became powerful enough to support it. Modern CPUs with multiple cores are designed specifically for multithreading, so switching between threads is extremely efficient when compared to the operation in older CPUs. Some Intel CPUs contain a feature called Hyper-Threading.

Hyper-Threading (HT) allows two threads to run on each CPU core simultaneously. In some ways, this feature doubles the amount of work a CPU can do. When monitoring a CPU with a program such as Task Manager, each CPU core is actually seen as two logical processors, so a 4-core CPU will be reported as having 8 logical processors.

3

Popular PC Processors

The following sections provide an overview of the CPUs found in PCs and of more powerful 64-bit processors that are available for PCs and servers.

Intel

The most popular CPUs used in PCs today are designed by Intel. The first player in this line of processors was the 8088, the CPU found in the original IBM PC. Early Intel CPUs were identified by model numbers: 8088, 8086, 80286, 80386, and 80486. The model numbers are sometimes shown without the 80 prefix, or are preceded by an "i," as in 80486, 486, or i486. The Pentium family of chips followed the 486 (*penta* means five in Greek). Pentium chips are sometimes identified with just a P and a number—for example, P4 for Pentium 4. Table 3-1 lists single-processor Intel CPUs, including the Celeron, Pentium III, and Pentium 4. The Intel Itanium and Itanium 2 are 64-bit processors designed for higher-end PCs and servers. Notice the trends in Table 3-1 toward ever-faster internal and external clock speeds, more and larger cache, and increasing capability to handle multimedia and large amounts of data.

Table 3-1 Single-core Intel CPUs

CPU	Year introduced	Data bus/ address bus bits	Internal clock speed	External clock speed	Cache	Comments
8088	1978	8/20	4–8 MHz	4–8 MHz	No	CPU of the first IBM PC.
8086	1978	16/20	4–16 MHz	4–16 MHz	No	First Intel CPU to have a 16-bit data path.
80286	1982	16/24	8–40 MHz	8–40 MHz	No	Beginning of the 80x86 line.
80386SX	1985	16/24	16–40 MHz	16–40 MHz	No	Less expensive version of 386 chip; supported only 16-bit data bus.
80386DX	1985	32/24	16–40 MHz	16–40 MHz	No	Introduced 32-bit data bus.
80486SX	1989	16/24	16–80 MHz	16–40 MHz	Yes	Less expensive version of 486 chip; supported only 16-bit data bus.
80486DX	1989	32/24	16–120 MHz	16–40 MHz	Yes	First Intel chip to use different internal and external clocks, include a math coprocessor, and include L1 cache on the chip as well as features for external L2 cache.
Pentium	1993	32/28	16–266 MHz	16–66 MHz	Yes	More instructions added and L1 cache was made more efficient.

(*continues*)

Table 3-1 Single-core Intel CPUs (*continued*)

CPU	Year introduced	Data bus/ address bus bits	Internal clock speed	External clock speed	Cache	Comments
Pentium Pro	1995	64/28	33–200 MHz	33–50 MHz	Yes	Optimized for running 32-bit instructions. Intel also released the Multimedia Extension (MMX), with new instructions to deal with multimedia and handling large amounts of data.
Pentium II	1997	64/36	66–550 MHz	66–100 MHz	Yes	Inclusion of L1 cache running at internal clock speed as well as L2 cache running at external or twice the external clock speed; both were built right onto the CPU module.
Xeon	1998	64/36	500 MHz–3.66 GHz	400–800 MHz	Yes	Offered as a version of the Pentium II and Pentium III processors. Used a new L2 caching technique that was twice as fast as non-Xeon processors. The newer Xeon MP chips also had a new instruction set that improved video, encryption, and authentication performance—features important for busy Web servers. It also used Hyper-Threading technology, and L3 cache of 512 KB, 1 MB, or 2 MB was available.
Celeron	1998	64/36	850 MHz–3.06 GHz	66–800 MHz	Yes	Low-end processor for PC multimedia and home markets.
Pentium III	1999	64/36	600 MHz–1.2 GHz	100–133 MHz	Yes	Introduced Streaming SIMD Extensions. SIMD, which stands for *single-instruction, multiple-data* stream processing, is an instruction set designed to provide better multimedia processing.
Pentium 4	2001	64/36	1.3–3.88 GHz	400–1066 MHz	Yes	Included two math coprocessors; also used execution-based cache. Extreme Edition supported Hyper-Threading, a technology that enables a single processor to appear to the operating system as two separate processors. The Pentium 4 had a similar architecture to the Xeon MP but added an execution-based cache, which was even faster than the original Xeon cache.

Table 3-1 Single-core Intel CPUs (*continued*)

CPU	Year introduced	Data bus/ address bus bits	Internal clock speed	External clock speed	Cache	Comments
Itanium	2001	64/128	733–800 MHz	266 MHz	Yes	First RISC-based Intel chip, 64-bit with EPIC architecture; designed for high-end PC workstations and servers.
Itanium 2	2002	64/128	1.3–1.5 GHz	400 MHz	Yes	Extended the Itanium family of CPU chips; optimized for dual-processor servers and workstations.
Pentium M	2003	64/36	900 MHz–2.26 GHz	400–533 MHz	Yes	Pentium M referred to a group of mobile single-core processors.
Multicore processors	Table 3-2 lists Intel multicore processors starting with the Pentium D.					

A very important feature of Intel CPUs is **backward compatibility,** which means that a significant number of features from an older chip can function on a newer chip. For example, code written to run on an 8088 processor runs on a newer CPU without change. Because the 8088 code is 16-bit code, it does not use many of the advanced features of the newer CPUs, and it runs more slowly than code written especially for the CPU. Backward compatibility is one of the major reasons for the success of the Intel line of CPUs. The Itanium line of Intel CPU chips is not backward-compatible.

The Intel Itanium and Itanium 2 processors are a significant departure from previous Intel processors in two respects: they are built on the RISC-based EPIC architecture and they are 64-bit chips. The Itanium features the complete EPIC design allotment of 256 64-bit registers that can operate as rotating registers. In order to use the capabilities of the Itanium 64-bit processor, the operating system and applications must be recompiled or rewritten to use 64-bit processing.

The Intel Itanium processor is intended for very large-scale operations that match powerful mainframes. For this reason, the chip architecture and bus design include the capability to run more than 1000 processors as a group.

Initially, processors were developed with one core, which executed the program instructions. Today, these cores are independent of each other and are packaged on a single chip. Some processors today contain 6, 8, 12, 16, and even more cores. Multicore processors are the norm today, and even smartphones and tablets frequently contain two or four cores.

Table 3-2 lists multicore Intel CPUs along with the number of cores and the cache size. Notice that the Intel Core i3, i5, and i7 processors have bus speeds referred to in terms of GT/s, or gigatransfers per second.

These tables are not intended to be comprehensive; rather, they are intended to show the progression of CPUs and CPU architecture through the years.

Table 3-2 Multicore Intel CPUs

CPU	Year introduced	Cores	Speed	Bus speed	Cache
Pentium D	2005	2	2.64–3.60 GHz	533–1055 MHz	1–2 MB
Xeon	2005	2–8	1.68–3.73 GHz	667–1600 MHz	2–24 MB
Itanium	2006	2–4	1.40–1.73 GHz	400–667 MHz	8–24 MB
Intel Core Solo	2006	1	1.06–1.86 GHz	533–667 MHz	2 MB
Intel Core Duo	2006	2	1.06–2.33 GHz	533–667 MHz	2 MB
Pentium Dual-Core	2007	2	1.60–3.33 GHz	800–1066 MHz	1–2 MB
Intel Core 2 Duo	2007	2	1.86–3.33 GHz	800–1333 MHz	3–6 MB
Intel Core 2 Quad	2007	4	2.33–3.00 GHz	1066–1333 MHz	4–12 MB
Intel Core 2 Extreme	2008	2	2.00–3.20 GHz	1066–1600 MHz	6–12 MB
Atom	2008	1	800 MHz–2.13 GHz	400–533 MHz	512 KB–1 MB
Intel Core i7	2009	4–6	1.06–3.33 GHz	2.5 GT/s–4.8 GT/s	4–12 MB
Intel Core i5	2009	2–4	1.06–3.76 GHz	2.5 GT/s	3–8 MB
Intel Core i3	2010	2	1.20–3.06 GHz	2.5 GT/s	4 MB

Table 3-2 stops with processors released in 2010, but that doesn't mean Intel stopped developing new CPUs. For the most part, Intel has maintained the same naming structure for its products, with new processors named Pentium, Core i3, Core i5, and Core i7. Intel differentiates its models by adding a number and microarchitecture code name after the name of the CPU. **Microarchitecture** is the description of a CPU's internal circuitry, defining characteristics such as the technology used to create the chip, the supported instruction set, the bit size, and so forth. For example, the Intel Core i7-5820 Haswell-E is a 6-core process running at 3.3 GHz based on the Haswell microarchitecture, which was released in 2013. The most current microarchitecture, released in 2015, is called Skylark. It has bus transfer speeds up to 8 GT/s, up to 128 MB L4 cache, and four cores; it runs at speeds up to 4 GHz.

Try Hands-On Projects 3-1 through 3-6 to practice monitoring processor usage and obtain information on the CPU in Windows-based, Linux-based, and Mac-based operating systems.

AMD

Advanced Micro Devices, Inc. (AMD) manufactures CPU chips that compete with Intel PC chips. Table 3-3 lists single-core AMD chips, some of which are still being manufactured. More recent versions of these chips use multicore technology, and are listed in Table 3-4.

Table 3-3 Single-core AMD processors

Processor	Latest clock speeds (MHz or GHz)	Compares to Intel chip	System bus speed (MHz)
AMD-K6-2	166–475 MHz	Pentium II, Celeron	66, 95, 100
AMD-K6-III	350–450 MHz	Pentium II	100
Duron	1–1.3 GHz	Celeron	200
Athlon	Up to 1.9 GHz	Pentium III	200
Athlon Model 4	Up to 1.4 GHz	Pentium III	266
Athlon MP	1.4–2.1 GHz	Pentium III	200 to 400+
Athlon XP	Up to 2.2 GHz	Pentium 4	266, 333, 400
Opteron (64-bit)	1.4–2.0 GHz	Itanium	244

Table 3-4 Multicore AMD processors

Processor	Clock speeds (MHz or GHz)	Cores	Compares to Intel chip
Athlon II	1.8–3.3 GHz	2–4	Intel Core 2 Duo
Phenom II	2.5–3.5 GHz	2–6	Intel Core 2 Quad
Phenom	1.8–2.6 GHz	3–4	Intel Core 2 Quad
Athlon X2	2.3–2.8 GHz	2	Intel Core 2 Duo
Opteron 4000 Series	1.7–2.8 GHz	8–12	Itanium/Xeon
Opteron 6000 Series	1.7–2.4 GHz	6	Itanium/Xeon

Like Intel, AMD continues to develop CPUs with names based on the series, such as Athlon and FX, and the core architecture, such as Zambezi and Vishera. As of 2016, one of AMD's most current processors for desktop computers is the FX-8320 Vishera, which sports 8 cores running at up to 4.7 GHz, with 8 MB L2 and 8 MB L3 cache.

Other Processors

In addition to Intel and its direct competitors, several other manufacturers produced processors for various types of computers, including Motorola, PowerPC, SPARC, and Alpha chips.

Motorola Motorola chips were typically found in Macintosh computers. Its line of CISC CPUs is used in many older Macintosh computers, as well as in many older UNIX computers. The popular models were the 68000, 68020, 68030, and 68040. The development of the chips' features was roughly similar to the development in the Intel line; the 68020 showed many similarities to the 80286, the 68030 was similar to the 80386, and the 68040 was similar to the 80486. Motorola has discontinued these chips.

PowerPC This line of chips used different instruction sets and a different general architecture than the Motorola 68xxx line, and was developed jointly by Apple Computer, IBM, and Motorola, an alliance referred to as AIM. These RISC chips were known as the PowerPC line. In 2005, Apple moved to using Intel chips and Motorola left the CPU manufacturing business.

SPARC SPARC, which stands for Scalable Processor Architecture, is a RISC processor designed by Sun Microsystems and continued with Oracle Corporation's acquisition of Sun Microsystems. SPARC CPUs have gone through many incarnations, and the RISC processor is the most popular on the market today. The SPARC M7 from Oracle is the current version of the SPARC processor. It is a 64-bit chip with 64-bit address and data buses. The SPARC M7 contains 32 cores, runs at speeds up to 4.1 GHz, and has an L3 cache of 64 MB.

Primarily, you will see various implementations of the UNIX operating system running on these CPUs, performing high-end engineering and networking duties. The most popular operating system that uses the chip is Oracle Corporation's Solaris. (Solaris is SunOS with a desktop window system.) Dell and HP have announced they will resell Oracle Solaris for their platforms.

Alpha Another CPU of interest is the Alpha CPU, originally designed by Digital Equipment Corporation (DEC). DEC was purchased by Compaq, which in turn was purchased by HP. The Alpha CPU was found in older high-end HP Compaq servers; it had a 64-bit data bus and a 64-bit address bus. The internal clock speed could be as high as 1.3 GHz. It was the first chip to reach a speed of 1 GHz. The Alpha used a traditional 64 KB L1 cache and an external L2 cache that could go up to 8 MB. Similar to the SPARC, Alpha chips were widely used in the UNIX environment. Also like the SPARC, Alpha chips were found in computers that had heavy networking, engineering, and graphics duties. Many proprietary devices, such as file servers, firewall products, and routers, ran custom operating systems based on an Alpha architecture.

HP has moved away from Alpha chips in its high-end server computers, replacing the Alpha with the Intel chipset. HP continued development of the Alpha into 2004, production through 2006, and support through 2011.

There are many other CPUs, but many of the details about these chips are beyond the focus of this book. The CPUs discussed here are the most popular in PCs today and the most often used by the operating systems covered in this book.

Chapter Summary

- One of the main functions of the operating system is to provide the interface between the various application programs running on a computer and the hardware inside. Processor hardware improvements have marched steadily from the early 8088 chip to the modern 64-bit multicore processors. Operating systems paralleled these changes to take advantage of the capabilities of new processors at each stage of development. Processors continue to become faster and more efficient.
- Most CPUs are composed of a control unit, arithmetic logic unit, registers, and a system bus, which is composed of a control bus, address bus, and data bus.
- CPUs can be classified by several elements, including design type, speed, cache, address bus, data bus, control bus, and CPU scheduling. Design types include CISC and RISC. CISC makes programming less complex but RISC can be faster in many instances.
- The amount of cache is critical to a CPU's overall speed because it is much faster than RAM. Modern CPUs have L1, L2, L3, and sometimes L4 cache built into the processor chip.
- CPU scheduling allows an operating system to schedule multiple processes or threads. Multicore processors facilitate efficient CPU scheduling.
- Intel processors are the most popular CPUs in PCs today, but AMD processors are also frequently used. Some processors come with 16 or more cores. The most current Intel microarchitecture is called Skylake, which has bus transfers up to 8 GT/s. Among the most current AMD processors is the FX Vishera line of processors, which have up to 8 cores.
- Other processors include the Motorola, PowerPC, the SPARC, and the Alpha.

Key Terms

address bus An internal communications pathway inside a computer that specifies the source and target address for memory reads and writes.

arithmetic logic unit (ALU) A component of a CPU that executes instructions.

backward compatibility The ability of features from an older chip to function on a newer chip.

bus A path or channel between a computer's CPU and the devices it manages, such as memory and I/O devices.

cache controller Internal computer hardware that manages the data going into and loaded from the computer's cache memory.

cache memory Special computer memory that temporarily stores data used by the CPU. Cache memory is physically close to the CPU and is faster than standard system memory, enabling faster retrieval and processing time.

compiler A computer program that takes a high-level language like C# or Java and turns it into assembly code that is executed by the CPU.

Complex Instruction Set Computing (CISC) A computer CPU architecture in which processor components are reconfigured to conduct different operations as required. Such computer designs require many instructions and more complex instructions than other designs. Compare to *Reduced Instruction Set Computing (RISC)*.

control bus An internal communications pathway that keeps the CPU informed of the status of particular computer resources and devices, such as memory and disk drives.

control unit (CU) A component of a CPU that provides timing and coordination between the other parts of the CPU, such as the arithmetic logic unit, registers, and system bus.

core The part of a processor used to read and execute instructions.

data bus An internal communications pathway that carries data between the CPU and memory locations.

external clock speed The speed at which the processor communicates with the memory and other devices in the computer; usually one-fourth to one-half the internal clock speed.

floating point unit (FPU) A component of a CPU that executes floating point mathematical operations.

Hyper-Threading (HT) A feature of some Intel CPUs that allows two threads to run on each CPU core simultaneously.

instruction set In a computer CPU, the group of commands (instructions) the processor recognizes. These instructions are used to conduct the operations required of the CPU by the operating system and application software.

internal clock speed The speed at which the CPU executes internal commands, measured in megahertz (millions of clock ticks per second) or gigahertz (billions of clock ticks per second). Internal clock speeds can be as low as 1 MHz or more than 4 GHz.

interrupt request (IRQ) A request to the processor so that a currently operating process, such as a read from a disk drive, can be interrupted by another process, such as a write into memory.

level 1 (L1) cache Cache memory that is part of the CPU hardware. See *cache memory*.

level 2 (L2) cache Cache memory that is somewhat slower than L1 cache but is much larger. See *cache memory*.

level 3 (L3) cache Cache memory that is slower than L1 or L2 cache but is much larger. L3 cache is located on the CPU chip on most modern CPUs, and is shared among multiple cores. See *cache memory*.

level 4 (L4) cache Cache memory that is found on some advanced modern CPUs. See *cache memory*.

microarchitecture The description of the internal circuitry of a CPU that defines characteristics such as the technology used to create the chip, the supported instruction set, and the bit size.

microcode A small program inside a CISC CPU that must interpret and execute each instruction.

multiprocessor computer A computer that uses more than one CPU.

multithreading Running several processes or parts (threads) of processes at the same time.

pipelining A CPU design that permits the processor to operate on one instruction at the same time it is fetching one or more subsequent instructions from the operating system or application.

Reduced Instruction Set Computing (RISC) A computer CPU design that dedicates processor hardware components to certain functions. This design reduces the number and complexity of required instructions and often results in faster performance than CISC CPUs. Compare to *Complex Instruction Set Computing (CISC)*.

register A temporary holding location in a CPU where data must be placed before the CPU can use it.

single-processor computer A computer capable of supporting only a single CPU.

system architecture The computer hardware design that includes the processor (CPU) and communication routes between the CPU and the hardware it manages, such as memory and disk storage.

thread The smallest piece of computer code that can be independently scheduled for execution.

Review Questions

1. Which component of the CPU is responsible for executing arithmetic and logic instructions?
   a. CU
   b. ALU
   c. data bus
   d. control bus
2. Instruction pipelining is a processing technique that allows the processor to operate on one instruction at a time with the pipeline keeping the instructions in order. True or False?
3. Which part of a CPU carries signals to indicate where data should be read from or written to in the system's memory?
   a. register
   b. data bus
   c. control unit
   d. address bus
4. Which of the following is true about CISC CPUs?
   a. They have a simple instruction set.
   b. They require a more complex compiler.
   c. They use microcode.
   d. Pipelining is easy.

5. Which of the following is used to keep the CPU informed of the status of resources and devices connected to the computer?
   a. control bus
   b. ALU
   c. microcode
   d. pipeline
6. What type of computer program takes a high-level language and turns it into assembly code?
   a. interpreter
   b. compiler
   c. assembler
   d. translator
7. What was the first widely used personal computer CPU manufactured by Intel?
   a. RISC
   b. 80286
   c. Alpha
   d. 8088
8. Where must data be placed on a CPU before it can use the data for arithmetic instructions?
   a. FPU
   b. register
   c. data bus
   d. CU
9. Manufacturers rate their CPU speeds based on which characteristic?
   a. external clock speed
   b. pipelining speed
   c. internal clock speed
   d. core speed times the number of cores
10. Which of the following is true about RISC CPUs versus CISC CPUs? (Choose all that apply.)
    a. They use microcode.
    b. They use a complex compiler.
    c. They use more registers.
    d. They have complex instructions.

11. Which cache level provides the fastest access to its data?
    a. L1
    b. L2
    c. L3
    d. L4
12. A CPU with an external clock speed of 2 GHz and a 64-bit data bus can transfer how much data per second?
    a. 8 GB/s
    b. 16 GB/s
    c. 32 GB/s
    d. 128 GB/s
13. The list of commands a CPU can execute is referred to as which of the following?
    a. instruction set
    b. instruction cache
    c. data set
    d. data cache
14. AMD manufactures which of the following chips? (Choose all that apply.)
    a. Atom
    b. Duron
    c. Xeon
    d. Phenom
15. Which manufacturer developed the Celeron line of CPUs?
    a. Intel
    b. Apple
    c. Motorola
    d. AMD
16. Which line of CPUs is a RISC processor?
    a. 68000
    b. Atom
    c. SPARC
    d. Pentium D

Hands-On Projects

Project 3-1: Monitor Processor Usage with Task Manager

Use Windows Task Manager to monitor processor usage.

1. Start your Windows 10 computer and log on.
2. Right-click the **taskbar** and click **Task Manager** on the shortcut menu. Click the **More details** button, if necessary.
3. Click the **Performance** tab and click **CPU** in the left pane, if necessary (see Figure 3-3).

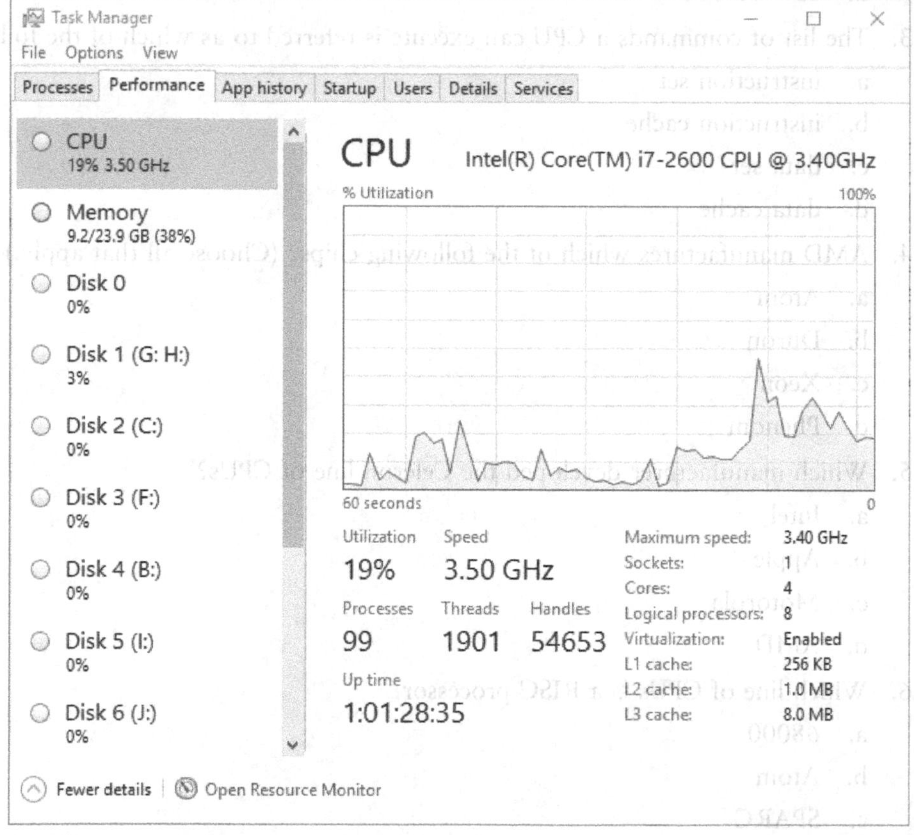

Figure 3-3 The Performance tab in Task Manager

4. Watch the CPU history graph and note how it changes over time. Open and close a Web browser three or four times. Look at the CPU history graph now. You should see a distinct increase in CPU utilization.
5. Review the other information you can learn about the CPU. In Figure 3-3, you see the CPU model at the top of the graph. Below the graph, you see the maximum speed of the CPU, the number of cores, the number of logical processors, and the amount of L1, L2, and L3 cache, as well as other information. Your display will likely look different depending on the type of CPU running on your system. Can you tell by looking at Figure 3-3 if the CPU that is being monitored supports Hyper-Threading? How can you tell?
6. Close Task Manager. Stay logged on if you are continuing to the next project.

Do not leave Task Manager running in the background when you are not using it. Task Manager uses CPU and memory resources and could slow down the computer.

Project 3-2: Check Processor Status in Device Manager

Most Windows-based systems can report on whether the processor (or any other hardware device) is working properly. This project shows you how to check the status of the processor.

1. Log on to your Windows computer, if necessary.
2. Right-click **Start**, and click **Device Manager**.
3. Double-click **Processors** (see Figure 3-4). How many processors are displayed? Double-click a processor in the list.

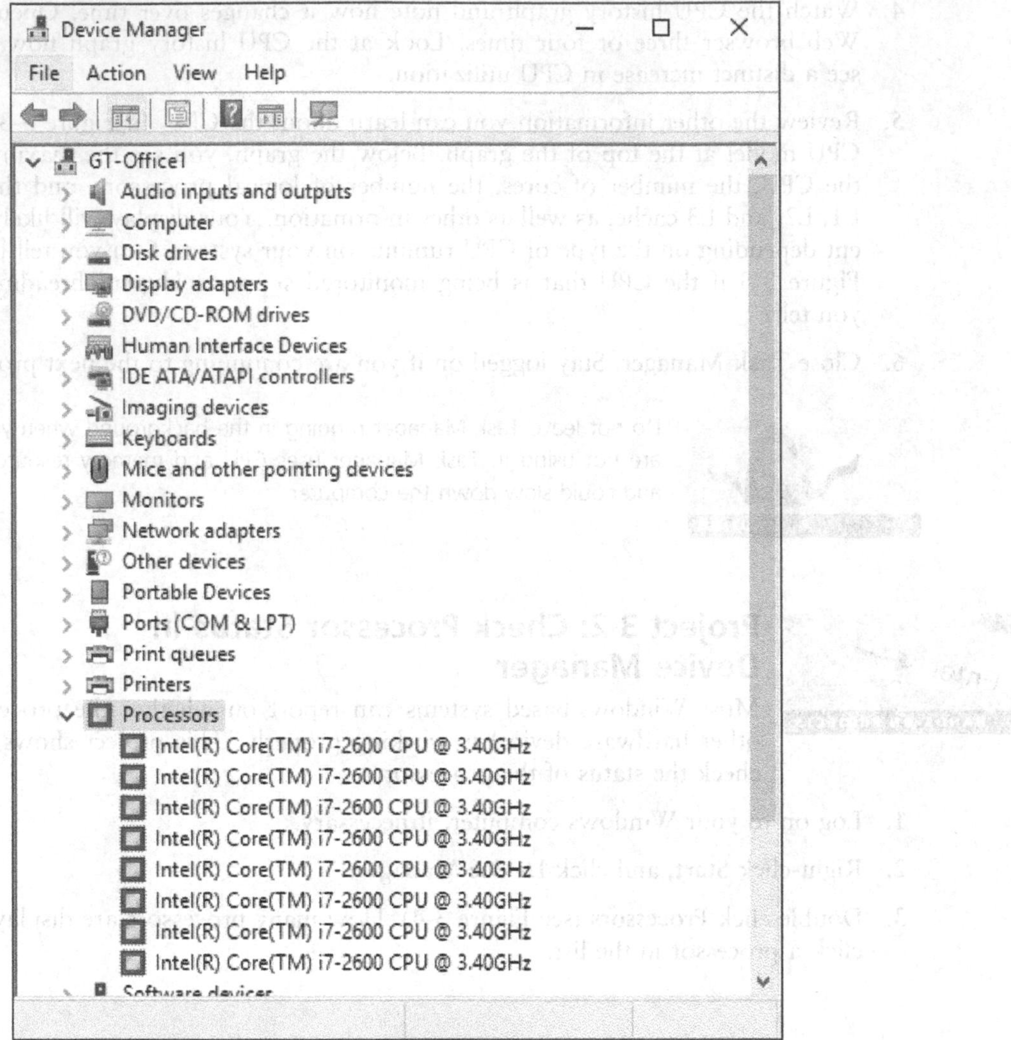

Figure 3-4 Viewing processors in Device Manager

4. Click the **General** tab, if necessary. The General tab shows the manufacturer and model of the CPU, and the Device status box shows the status.
5. Click the **Details** tab. Here, you can see a variety of information about the device and the device driver. Click the selection arrow under Property and browse through the properties. Click **Power data** to see the various power states supported by the CPU.
6. Click **Cancel** to close the Processor Properties dialog box, and then close Device Manager.
7. Log off or shut down your Windows computer.

Project 3-3: Use System Monitor in Linux

The GNOME desktop in Linux offers the System Monitor tool for tracking processor activity. In this project, you learn how to use the System Monitor tool.

1. Start your Linux computer and log on.
2. Click **Activities** and click **Show Applications.** Click **Utilities** and then click **System Monitor.**
3. Click the **Resources** tab, if necessary (see Figure 3-5).

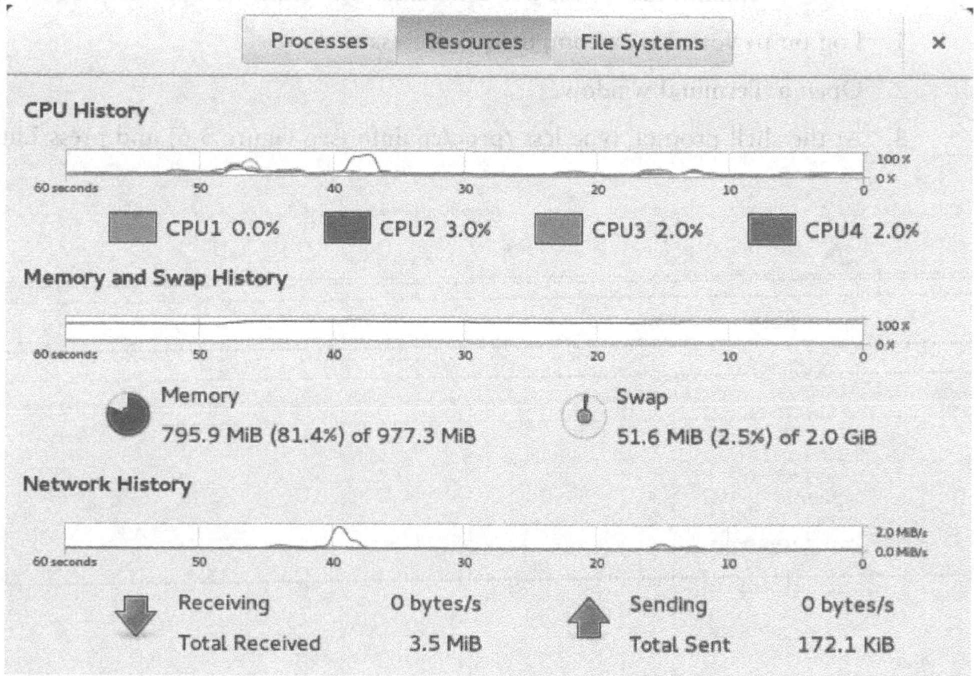

Figure 3-5 System Monitor in Linux

Source: Linux

4. If your computer has more than one processor, you'll see a color-coded line for each processor in the CPU History section of System Monitor. (Figure 3-5 shows there are four processors.)
5. Notice the Memory and Swap History section of System Monitor. The Memory information shows the amount of memory that is currently in use, as a percentage of the total amount of memory. In Figure 3-5, 795.9 MiB (or MB), or 81.4 % of the total memory is in use in a computer that has 977.3 MiB (or MB) of RAM. Review the memory statistics for your computer.
6. Open and close several applications, such as a Web browser, terminal window, and file editor. Return to System Monitor to see the changes in the graphs. Close System Monitor and any open windows.

7. Click **Activities**, click **Show Applications**, and then click **Settings**. Click **Details** in the System section. The Overview window shows basic system information, such as the amount of memory installed, the CPU, the bit size of the OS (32-bit or 64-bit), and the GNOME version. Close the Details window.

8. Stay logged on if you are continuing to the next project.

Project 3-4: View the cpuinfo File in Linux

In addition to using the GNOME System Monitor, you can determine information about the CPU in a Linux computer by displaying the contents of the /proc/cpuinfo file via the *less* command. You learn how to do so in this project.

1. Log on to your Linux computer, if necessary.
2. Open a **Terminal** window.
3. At the shell prompt, type **less /proc/cpuinfo** (see Figure 3-6) and press **Enter**.

```
gtomsho@localhost:~
File  Edit  View  Search  Terminal  Help
processor       : 0
vendor_id       : GenuineIntel
cpu family      : 6
model           : 42
model name      : Intel(R) Core(TM) i7-2600 CPU @ 3.40GHz
stepping        : 7
microcode       : 0x29
cpu MHz         : 3400.026
cache size      : 8192 KB
physical id     : 0
siblings        : 4
core id         : 0
cpu cores       : 4
apicid          : 0
initial apicid  : 0
fpu             : yes
fpu_exception   : yes
cpuid level     : 13
wp              : yes
flags           : fpu vme de pse tsc msr pae mce cx8 apic sep mtrr pge mca cmov
pat pse36 clflush dts mmx fxsr sse sse2 ss ht syscall nx rdtscp lm constant_tsc
arch_perfmon pebs bts nopl xtopology tsc_reliable nonstop_tsc aperfmperf pni pcl
mulqdq ssse3 cx16 pcid sse4_1 sse4_2 x2apic popcnt tsc_deadline_timer aes xsave
/proc/cpuinfo
```

Figure 3-6 Viewing /proc/cpuinfo in Linux

Source: Linux

4. Press the **Page Down** key or press the **Spacebar** to view more of the file's contents one page at a time. The **Page Up** key takes you back through the previous pages of the file. You can also use the up or down arrows to navigate through the file one line at a time.
5. This file shows you how many processors are in the computer, indexed by 0. If you see only one section of information under processor 0, then you have one processor. A second section, showing processor 1, would mean you have two processors, and so on. Look for the model name, speed, cache size, and number of cores.
6. Press **q** to exit the display of the /proc/cpuinfo file's contents.

7. Type **top** and press **Enter**. Top is an interactive task manager that runs in a terminal window. Look for the Tasks field. It should be displayed in the second row on the left side of the window.
8. To toggle from task mode to thread mode, press **H**. (A capital H is required, so you probably need to press **Shift-H**.) The Tasks field is changed to Threads and the number increases because many tasks contain two or more threads.
9. Press **q** to quit the top task manager.
10. Close the Terminal window and log off or shut down your Linux computer.

Project 3-5: View Hardware Information in Mac OS X

In Chapter 1, "Operating Systems Fundamentals," you briefly used the About This Mac feature in Mac OS X. This feature is worth reviewing because it provides a fast way to determine what processor is in a Macintosh computer and the amount of memory. This information can save you time, for example, if you are planning to upgrade multiple computers to the latest version of Mac OS X and you want to determine which ones have Intel processors and whether they have enough RAM for the upgrade. In this project, you review how to open the About This Mac window for information about the processor(s) and RAM.

1. Start your Mac OS X computer and log on.
2. Click the **Apple** icon in the top left corner of the menu bar.
3. Click **About This Mac** on the menu.
4. The About This Mac window not only shows the operating system version, as you learned in Chapter 1, it also shows the number of processors, the model name and speed of the processors, plus the amount and type of memory installed (see Figure 3-7).

Figure 3-7 The About This Mac window

Source: Mac OS X El Capitan

5. Click **System Report** in the About This Mac window.

6. Make sure that **Hardware** is highlighted in the left pane. Here you learn more about the processor, including the speed, the number of cores, and the amount of L2 and L3 cache, if present (see Figure 3-8).

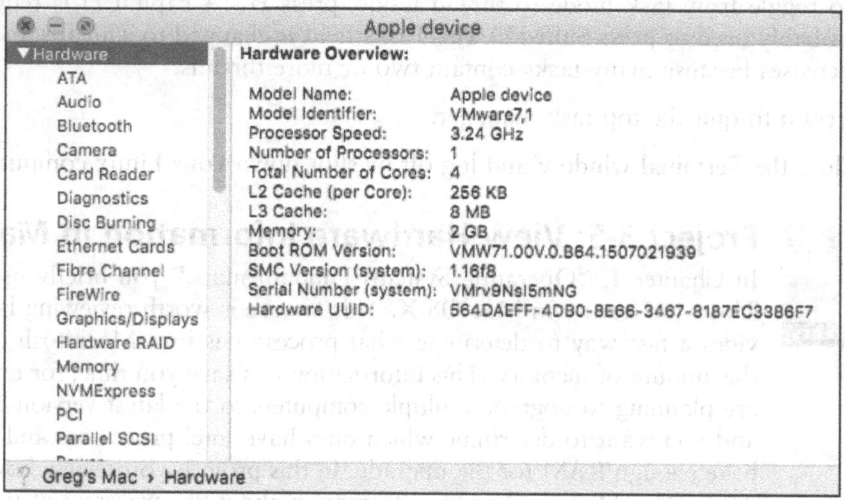

Figure 3-8 Mac OS X hardware overview

Source: Mac OS X El Capitan

7. In the left pane, click **Memory** under Hardware. The right pane shows information about the number of memory slots and the RAM (if any) plugged into each slot (see Figure 3-9).

Apple device

▼Hardware: ATA, Audio, Bluetooth, Camera, Card Reader, Diagnostics, Disc Burning, Ethernet Cards, Fibre Channel, FireWire, Graphics/Displays, Hardware RAID, Memory, NVMExpress, PCI, Parallel SCSI, Power, Printers, SAS, SATA/SATA Expr..., SPI, Storage, Thunderbolt, USB

▼Network

Memory Slot	Size	Type	Speed	Status
▼Memory Slots				
RAM slot #0/RAM slot #0	2 GB	DRAM	0 MHz	OK
RAM slot #1/RAM slot #1	Empty	Empty	Empty	Empty
RAM slot #2/RAM slot #2	Empty	Empty	Empty	Empty
RAM slot #3/RAM slot #3	Empty	Empty	Empty	Empty
RAM slot #4/RAM slot #4	Empty	Empty	Empty	Empty
RAM slot #5/RAM slot #5	Empty	Empty	Empty	Empty
RAM slot #6/RAM slot #6	Empty	Empty	Empty	Empty
RAM slot #7/RAM slot #7	Empty	Empty	Empty	Empty
RAM slot #8/RAM slot #8	Empty	Empty	Empty	Empty
RAM slot #9/RAM slot #9	Empty	Empty	Empty	Empty
RAM slot #10/RAM slot #10	Empty	Empty	Empty	Empty

Memory Slots:

ECC: Disabled
Upgradeable Memory: Yes

RAM slot #0/RAM slot #0:

Size: 2 GB
Type: DRAM
Speed: 0 MHz
Status: OK
Manufacturer: VMware Virtual RAM
Part Number: VMW-2048MB
Serial Number: 1

Greg's Mac › Hardware › Memory › Memory Slots

Figure 3-9 Mac OS X memory information

Source: Mac OS X El Capitan

8. Close all windows, but stay logged on if you are continuing to the next project.

Project 3-6: Use Activity Monitor in Mac OS X

You can also use a feature called Activity Monitor to find information about the processor and memory in a Mac OS X computer.

1. Log on to your Mac OS X computer, if necessary.
2. Ensure that Finder is active by clicking **Finder** in the Dock, if necessary.
3. Click **Go** in the menu bar and click **Utilities**.
4. Double-click **Activity Monitor** in the Utilities window.
5. Make sure the **CPU** button is selected to display CPU activity. A small CPU meter is displayed at the bottom of the Activity Monitor window so that you can follow the current CPU usage. Also, as you learned in Chapter 1, the upper portion of the window shows the amount of CPU used (under the % CPU column) by each active program or process.
6. Click the **Memory** button in the Activity Monitor window (see Figure 3-10). The Memory column gives you information about the amount of RAM used by each program or process, and the bottom portion of the window provides statistics about memory use.

Activity Monitor (My Processes)

CPU | Memory | Energy | Disk | Network | Search

Process Name	Memory	Bytes Written	Bytes Read	Threads	Ports	PID	User
photolibraryd	5.9 MB	3.5 MB	4.0 MB	2	57	365	gtomsho
com.apple.geod	5.5 MB	1.8 MB	2.0 MB	6	87	348	gtomsho
gamed	5.2 MB	100 KB	2.9 MB	4	113	346	gtomsho
com.apple.dock.extra	5.1 MB	0 bytes	3.9 MB	3	145	301	gtomsho
storeuid	5.0 MB	725 KB	60 KB	3	134	388	gtomsho
suggestd	4.8 MB	108 KB	2.6 MB	3	80	296	gtomsho
identityservicesd	4.6 MB	2.5 MB	3.2 MB	6	200	276	gtomsho
vmware-tools-daemon	4.6 MB	0 bytes	7.0 MB	4	130	342	gtomsho
storeassetd	4.5 MB	132 KB	680 KB	4	124	286	gtomsho
akd	4.5 MB	60 KB	353 KB	4	89	307	gtomsho
com.apple.photomoments	4.2 MB	0 bytes	253 KB	5	86	367	gtomsho
soagent	4.2 MB	4 KB	2.4 MB	2	99	304	gtomsho
callservicesd	4.0 MB	4 KB	1.5 MB	2	107	303	gtomsho
fontd	3.9 MB	32 KB	1.4 MB	2	73	271	gtomsho

MEMORY PRESSURE

Physical Memory: 2.00 GB
Memory Used: 1.21 GB
Cached Files: 758.8 MB
Swap Used: 0 bytes

App Memory: 686.0 MB
Wired Memory: 542.8 MB
Compressed: 0 bytes

Figure 3-10 Activity Monitor in Mac OS X

Source: Mac OS X El Capitan

7. Right-click any of the column headers, such as User. You can choose which columns should be displayed. Click **Bytes Written**, right-click a column again, and click **Bytes Read**. These columns show you the amount of data read from and written to disk; you'll also find these columns if you click the Disk button at the top of the window. You can click and drag the columns to put them in any order you want.
8. Close Activity Monitor and any open windows.
9. Log off or shut down your Mac OS X computer.

Critical Thinking

The following activities give you critical thinking challenges. Challenge Labs give you an opportunity to use the skills you have learned to perform a task without step-by-step instructions. Case projects offer a practical problem for which you supply a written solution. Not all chapters contain Challenge Labs. There is not always a specific right or wrong answer to these critical thinking exercises. They are intended to encourage you to review the chapter material and delve deeper into the topics you have learned.

Challenge Labs

Challenge Lab 3-1: Work with Task Manager in Windows

In this challenge lab, you explore Task Manager in more depth. You may have to research how to perform some of the tasks. Once you are finished, you will answer some questions.

On your Windows computer, start Task Manager and be sure you see the Processes, Performance, and other tabs. From the Processes tab, right-click any process and click **Go to details**. You see more information about the process in the Details tab. Sort the list of processes by name and then by status. In the Details tab, add columns that report the total CPU time used by the process and the number of threads in the process.

Questions:

1. What did you do to sort the list of processes?
2. How did you add columns to the Details tab?
3. What process used the most CPU time? What do you think is the purpose of this process?

Case Projects

Mile High University has a network of servers and desktop computers that were installed in 2000. The hardware consists of the following components:

- 25 PowerPC Macintosh computers
- Four Dell Pentium 4 servers
- Two HP servers running on the Alpha CPU
- 160 desktop computers running on the AMD Duron CPU
- 25 desktop computers running on the Intel Core Duo CPU
- 45 desktop computers running on the Pentium 4 CPU

Using the information you learned in this chapter and previous chapters, you will be able to make informed recommendations in the following case projects.

Case Project 3-1: Server Upgrades

The new Director of Information Technology has asked you to recommend a strategy to upgrade the servers on their network. Recommendations on server hardware, CPU chip set, speed, and caching are needed. You should also recommend which servers to upgrade first and determine whether any servers are still appropriate to keep.

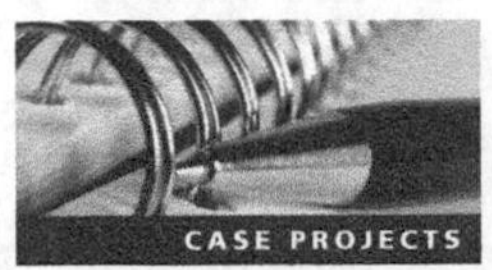

Case Project 3-2: Desktop Computing

The director has evaluated your server recommendations and asks you to design a strategy for upgrading the desktop hardware. He feels that most of the university's desktop computers need to be replaced. You should explain your strategy.

Case Project 3-3: Hardware Overheating

The university is having some problems with the desktop computer that runs the Intel Core Duo CPU. The computers will suddenly scramble the display screens and freeze. Because of this, the university wants to stay away from having desktops running any of the Intel CPUs. What would you recommend to address the problem? Research some of the causes of overheating hardware and suggest possible remedies. In addition, what desktop CPUs would you recommend for replacing their older hardware? Provide an explanation for your recommendation and what the university should do in the future.

chapter 4

File Systems

After reading this chapter and completing the exercises, you will be able to:

- List the basic functions common to all file systems
- Use and describe the file systems used by Windows OSs
- Use and describe the file systems used by UNIX and Linux systems, including ufs and ext
- Use and describe the Mac OS X Extended (HFS+) file system

In this chapter, you learn the general characteristics and functions of file systems, including their organization and specific features. You then explore the file systems used by Windows, UNIX/Linux, and Macintosh operating systems. You also learn about the tools available for file systems, such as tools for locating files and fixing damaged files.

Understanding File System Functions

One of the basic functions of an operating system is to enable you to store and access information on a computer or other digital device. This information might be letters, a report, spreadsheet files, your favorite music, or pictures of your family. All of this vital information is managed, stored, and retrieved through a **file system**. In one sense, a file system is like your personal assistant, properly saving and keeping track of the location of your important data. The file system allocates locations on a disk for storage and keeps a record of where specific information is kept. When you need the information, the file system consults its records to determine the location and then retrieves the information. Some file systems also implement recovery procedures when a disk area is damaged or when the operating system unexpectedly goes down, such as during a power failure.

To fulfill all these functions, the file systems used by computer operating systems perform the following general tasks:

- Provide a convenient interface for users and applications to open and save files
- Provide a hierarchical structure to organize files
- Store file metadata to provide detailed information about files
- Organize space on a storage device

User Interface

When a user double-clicks a file to open it, the user interface calls the file system with a request to open the file. The file type determines exactly how the file is opened. If the file is an application, the application is loaded into memory and run by the CPU. If the file is a document, the application associated with the document type is loaded into memory and opens the file. For example, on Windows computers, if you double-click the Budget.xls file, the Excel application is loaded into memory and then opens the file. If a user creates a file or changes an existing file and wants to save it, the application calls the file system to store the new or changed file on the disk. Most users of an OS interact with the file system by using a file manager program, such as File Explorer in Windows or Files in the GNOME desktop in Linux. As a future computer or network professional, you need to have a deeper understanding of how a file system works so that you can make informed choices when you need to install a file system or troubleshoot file system-related problems.

Hierarchical Structure

The overall purpose of a file system is to create a structure for filing data. The analogy that is typically used for a file system is that of file cabinets, file drawers, and file folders. For example, the computer could be considered the file cabinet and the disk drives the drawers. Within each drawer (drive), information is organized into hanging folders, manila folders, and individual documents (files), as shown in Figure 4-1.

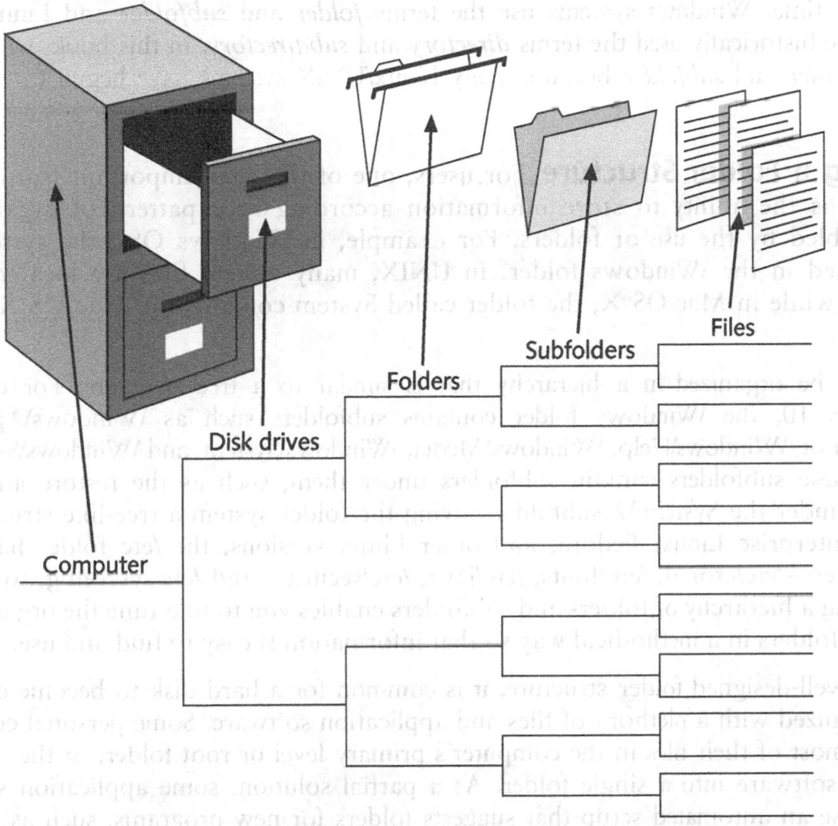

Figure 4-1 A file system metaphor

A file is a set of data that is grouped in some logical manner, assigned a name, and stored on the disk. As the file is stored, the file system records where the file is located on the disk so that it has a way to later retrieve that file. Whenever the file is needed, the operating system is given the filename, and it retrieves the data in the file from the disk.

The data contained in files can be text, images, music and sounds, video, or Web pages. But no matter what kind of data is stored in the file system, it must be converted into digital format—a series of 1s and 0s—that the computer understands. The operating system, along with the applications you use for word processing, graphics, and so on, performs this function of converting data into digital format for the computer, and back into the end-user format as text or pictures, for example.

Moreover, there must be a way to write digital information to disk, track it, update it when necessary, and call it back when the user or a user-controlled program wants it. To achieve all this, the operating system typically groups file data in some logical way, creates a record of this structure, and builds a folder or directory to track the type of data stored in each file. A **folder** or **directory** is an organizational structure that contains files and may additionally contain subfolders (or subdirectories) under it. The folder connects names to the files that are stored on the disk, which makes it easy for users and programs to obtain the right data at the right time. Windows systems use the terms *folder* and *subfolder* and Linux/UNIX systems have historically used the terms *directory* and *subdirectory*. In this book, we will use the terms *folder* and *subfolder* because many Linux/UNIX systems have begun to use those terms.

Designing a Folder Structure For users, one of the most important features of a file system is the ability to store information according to a pattern of organization that is enabled by the use of folders. For example, in Windows OSs, the system files are organized in the \Windows folder. In UNIX, many system files are located in the /etc folder, while in Mac OS X, the folder called System contains the Mac OS X critical system files.

Folders can be organized in a hierarchy that is similar to a tree structure. For example, in Windows 10, the \Windows folder contains subfolders such as \Windows\AppPatch, \Windows\Boot, \Windows\Help, \Windows\Media, \Windows\System, and \Windows\System32. Many of these subfolders contain subfolders under them, such as the restore and spool subfolders under the System32 subfolder, giving the folder system a tree-like structure. In Red Hat Enterprise Linux, Fedora, and other Linux versions, the /etc folder has many subdirectories—/etc/cron.d, /etc/fonts, /etc/java, /etc/security, and /etc/sysconfig, to name a few. Building a hierarchy of folders and subfolders enables you to fine-tune the organization of files and folders in a methodical way so that information is easy to find and use.

Without a well-designed folder structure, it is common for a hard disk to become cluttered and disorganized with a plethora of files and application software. Some personal computer users keep most of their files in the computer's primary level or **root folder**, or they load all application software into a single folder. As a partial solution, some application software programs use an automated setup that suggests folders for new programs, such as creating new subfolders under the Program Files folder in many Windows systems—but some users still have difficulty organizing files. A chaotic file structure makes it difficult to run or remove programs or determine the most current versions. It also makes users spend unproductive time looking for specific files.

In Windows 7 and later versions, a library is a collection of folders whose contents can be located anywhere on the local computer or its network, but it appears to the user as if it is in a single location. A library is a convenient way to access folders in different locations from one central location.

To avoid confusion, carefully design the file and folder structure from the start, particularly on servers that are accessed by many users. Plan to design a folder structure that complements the one already set up by the operating system, and then implement access controls that prevent unauthorized users from bypassing the structure. The default operating system structure, along with the structure that you add, might consist of folders for the following:

- Operating system files (typically set up by the operating system)
- Software applications (often set up both by the operating system, the software applications that you install, and decisions you make about how to install those applications)
- Work files, such as word-processing, graphics, spreadsheet, and database files (set up by you and by applications such as Microsoft Word)
- Public files that you share over the network (set up by you)
- Utilities files (set up by the operating system, the utilities applications, and your decisions about how to install specific utilities)
- Temporary files (set up by the operating system, applications that use temporary files, and your decisions about where to store temporary files)

Keeping temporary files for an extended period is a security risk. Temporary files should be purged as soon as they are no longer needed.

In deciding how to allocate folders for specific types of files, consider following some general practices. For instance, the root folder should not be cluttered with files or too many directories or folders. Each software application should have its own folder or subfolder so updates and software removal are easy to administer. For easy access control, similar information should be grouped, such as accounting systems or office productivity software. Operating system files should be kept separate and protected so important files are not accidentally deleted by a user. On Windows systems, some critical files are hidden from casual users and marked as system files so they cannot be easily deleted. In addition, most OS files are protected by access controls. Directories and folders should have names that clearly reflect their purposes. For example, consider a law office administrator who uses legal time-accounting software, legal forms software, Microsoft Office, confidential and shared spreadsheets, and Word documents—all on a computer running Windows 10. The same office administrator also maintains specialized Web pages for the law firm's Web site. The folder structure from the root might be as follows:

- *Windows* for the system files (the default folder set up by the operating system)
- *Program Files* for general software and utilities (the default folder set up by the operating system)
- *Documents and Settings* for work files such as Word documents and confidential spreadsheets (the default folder set up by the operating system)
- *Shared* for spreadsheets that are shared over the network (a sample folder the user could set up, or the user could employ the default Public Documents folder set up by the operating system, as noted below)

- *Forms* for specific types of forms used by the legal forms software (a sample folder the user might set up)
- *Inetpub* for Web pages (a sample folder the user might set up in conjunction with the installation of Web design software)

By default, Windows Vista and later versions create a \Users\Public\Public Documents folder for sharing. Some users choose to use this folder for sharing files over a network. However, make sure that you know what security is set on shared folders so you do not host unwelcome guests. In server environments, the IT administrator typically disables the use of Public folders. You will learn about file system security later in this chapter.

Each major folder has subfolders to keep grouped files or application software separate. For example, the Program Files folder contains subfolders for each different software package, such as \Program Files\Microsoft Office for the Microsoft Office software, and \Program Files\Time Accounting for the legal time-accounting software folder. The Users *username* folder would have a Documents subfolder to contain confidential spreadsheets and Word documents, while shared spreadsheets would be in the Public Documents folder. Figure 4-2 illustrates this folder structure.

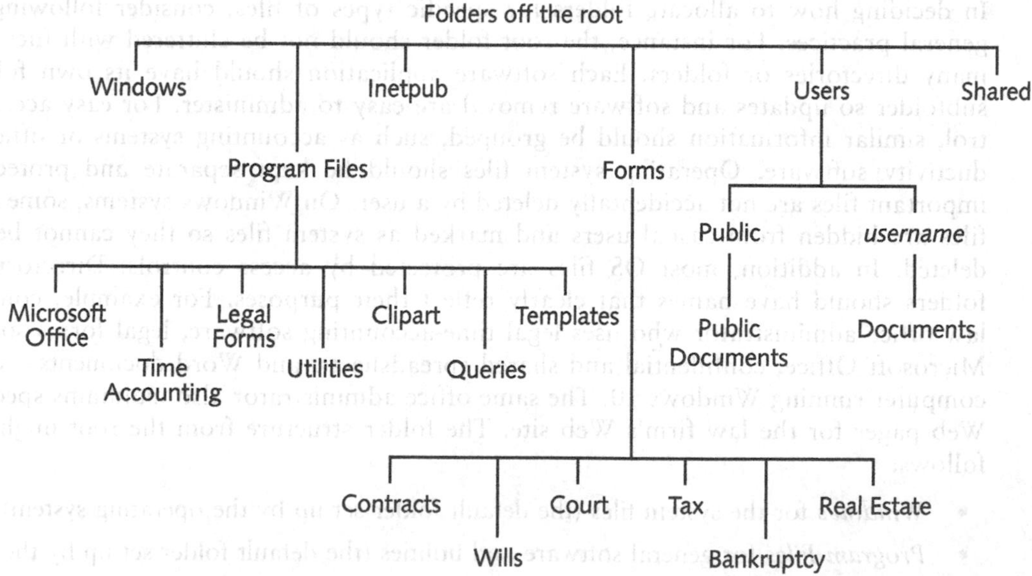

Figure 4-2 Sample folder structure for a Windows-based system

For Linux systems, such as Red Hat Enterprise Linux or Fedora, a typical folder structure already provided by the operating system is as follows:

- *bin* for user programs and utilities (binary files)
- *sbin* for system administration utilities (system binary files)

- *lib* for runtime library files needed by programs stored in the /bin and /sbin directories
- *usr* for user files and programs
- *var* for files in which content often varies or for files that are used only temporarily
- *tmp* for files used only temporarily
- *dev* for devices
- *mnt* for DVD/CD-ROM drives, flash drives, and other removable media
- *etc* for system and configuration files
- *root* for files used by the root account
- *home* for users' home directories (or folders) and typically stored in subfolders named for each user
- *proc* for system resource tracking

Figure 4-3 shows Fedora root folders in the GNOME Files tool. In Linux, the term *root folder* is used in two ways. One way is to refer to the root or main level from which all folders are created. All of the folders in the previous list are in the root, which is designated as /. The other *root folder* is the folder named /root, which is used as the home folder by the root account. Recall that the root account has complete permission to all files and applications on a Linux system.

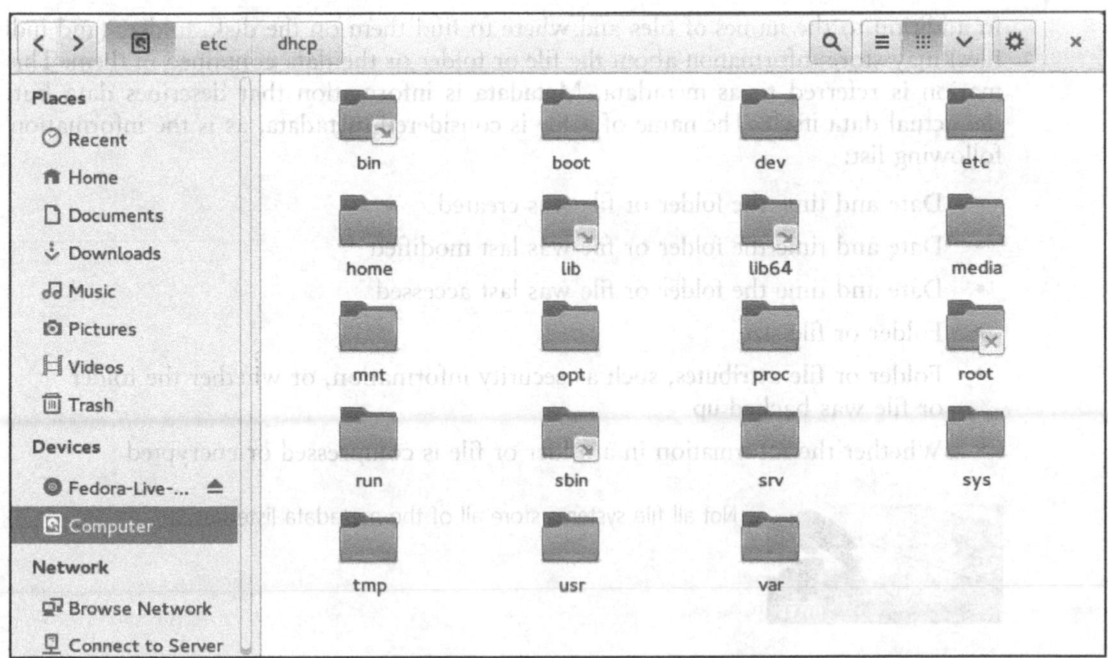

Figure 4-3 Fedora root folders in the GNOME Files tool

Source: Fedora Linux

Windows operating systems use backslashes to designate a folder, but UNIX and Linux use a forward slash. For example, the main level root is / and the bin folder is denoted as /bin.

You can view folders in Linux from the command line—for example, by using a terminal window—and from the Files tool, as demonstrated in Hands-On Project 4-7.

In Mac OS X, the default folder structure created by the operating system from the root level includes:

- *Applications* for Mac OS X software applications
- *System* for Mac OS X system files
- *Library* for library files (such as fonts)
- *Users* for user accounts, with subfolders for each user account to store files
- *Documents* for documents

Do Hands-On Projects 4-2, 4-4, and 4-6 to practice making folders in different operating systems.

File Metadata

In addition to the names of files and where to find them on the disk, folders (and individual files) may store information about the file or folder or the data contained in them. This information is referred to as metadata. **Metadata** is information that describes data but is not the actual data itself. The name of a file is considered metadata, as is the information in the following list:

- Date and time the folder or file was created
- Date and time the folder or file was last modified
- Date and time the folder or file was last accessed
- Folder or file size
- Folder or **file attributes,** such as security information, or whether the folder or file was backed up
- Whether the information in a folder or file is compressed or encrypted

Not all file systems store all of the metadata listed above.

Figure 4-4 illustrates some of the metadata that is stored for a file in Windows 10; this metadata can be displayed using File Explorer. As you learn later in this chapter, the way in which this information is stored depends on the design of the file system.

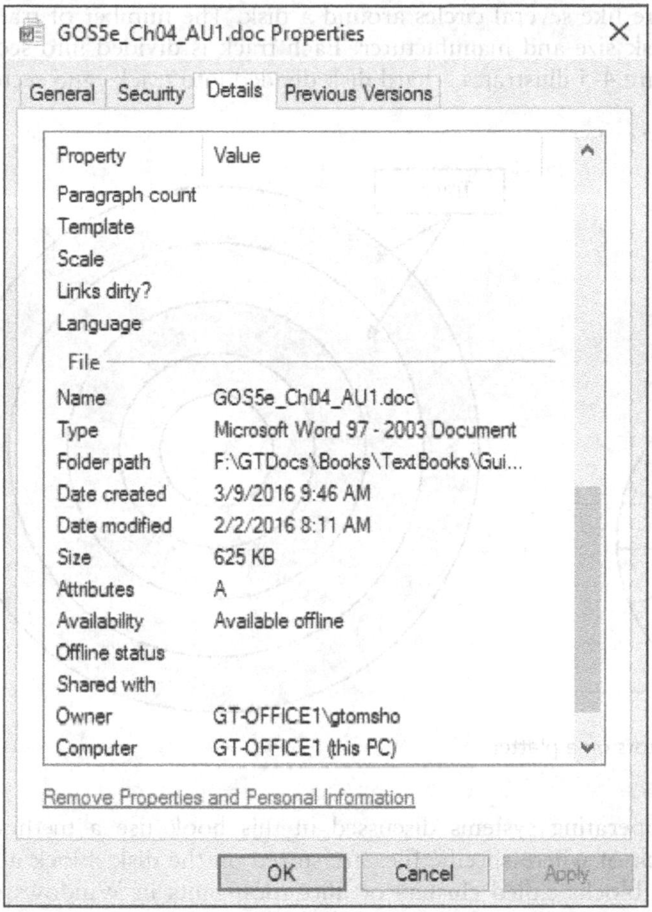

Figure 4-4 Windows file metadata

In Hands-On Project 4-2, you view folder and file information in File Explorer. Also, Hands-On Projects 4-7 and 4-8 give you experience viewing folders and files using the Files tool in Linux and the Macintosh HD desktop icon in Mac OS X.

Storage Device Space Organization

This section discusses storage in the context of mechanical hard disk drives (HDDs); however, the concepts and procedures are the same for solid-state drives (SSDs). The differences are primarily in their physical characteristics. For example, HDDs have platters and read/write heads, but SSDs do not.

When a hard disk is delivered from the manufacturer, it is low-level formatted. A **low-level format** is a software process that marks the location of disk tracks and sectors. Every disk is divided into **tracks**, which are like several circles around a disk. The number of tracks on a hard disk depends on the disk size and manufacturer. Each track is divided into sections of equal size called **sectors**. Figure 4-5 illustrates a hard disk divided into tracks and sectors on a platter.

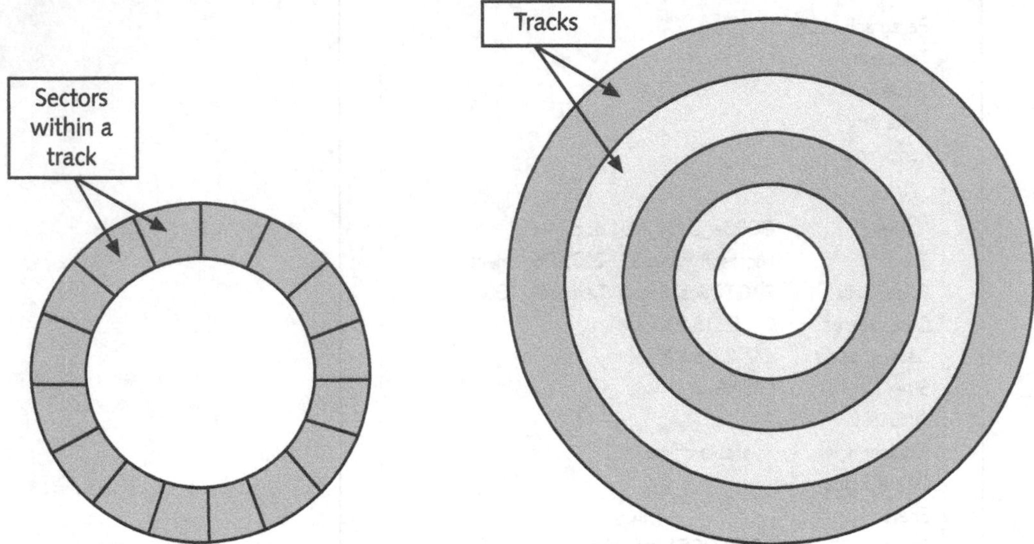

Figure 4-5 Disk tracks and sectors on a platter

Block Allocation The operating systems discussed in this book use a method called **block allocation** to keep track of where specific files are stored on the disk. Block allocation divides the disk into logical blocks called **clusters** or allocation units in Windows systems, which in turn correlate to a group of sectors on the disk.

Block allocation data is stored on the disk itself using one of two techniques. One technique uses a fixed portion of the disk to store this data—for example, the **file allocation table** (FAT) file system initially implemented in MS-DOS and supported by all versions of Windows and most other OSs. The other technique uses various locations on the disk to store a special type of file that is used for folder and file allocation information; examples include the **New Technology File System** (NTFS) and the UNIX/Linux file systems. On NTFS-formatted disks, the allocation table is called the Master File Table (MFT), which is discussed later in the chapter. As you can imagine, the areas of the disk in which allocation information and folder information are stored are very important; without this data, it would be impossible to access any of the files on the system without using specialized disk repair tools.

If a system uses a specific area or set of areas on the disk to store this file allocation data, obviously that disk area is accessed frequently. This is why many problems in accessing disk files arise as problems in file allocation tables and folder information. Because this data is also stored in a location separate from the actual file, you can see that when there is a problem with the disk, some of the folder or allocation data may not match the data actually stored on the disk. These occurrences are less common today, but it is very important to exercise proper care of disks to minimize such problems.

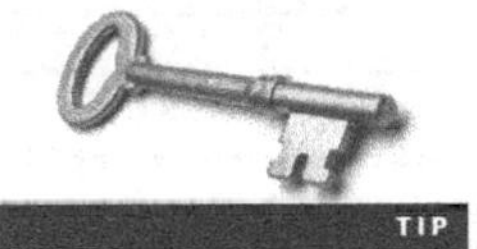

Proper disk care includes regularly maintaining a Windows disk through defragmenting (discussed later in this chapter), periodically deleting unused files (see Chapter 11), maintaining good security (see Chapter 10), implementing protection from viruses and malicious software, and providing stable power (such as through an uninterruptible power supply or UPS).

All operating systems have special tools that let you check, and sometimes repair, common file system and disk problems. Some operating systems can perform checks on the file system on an ongoing basis. These tools are discussed in more detail later in this chapter.

Partitions Before a file system can be placed on a hard disk, the disk must be partitioned and formatted. **Partitioning** is the process of blocking a group of tracks and sectors to be used by a particular file system, such as FAT or NTFS. After a disk is partitioned, it must be **high-level formatted** (or simply formatted) so that the partition contains the disk divisions and patterns needed by a particular operating system to store files. With today's technology creating disks of greater capacity, and as disks are used in more diverse applications, sometimes it is desirable to have more than one file system on a single disk, which is accomplished by having a partition for each file system. You might need multiple file systems to allow the installation of Windows 10 alongside Windows 7, or to install Red Hat Enterprise Linux and Windows 10 on the same computer, for example. Multiple operating systems may be required on a single system to accommodate certain applications designed for Linux and other applications designed for Windows 10.

The use of virtualization can provide some of the same benefits, and more, of installing multiple OSs on a computer system. Its use is generally preferred over installing multiple OSs on separate disk partitions. Virtualization is discussed in Chapter 8.

When you want to have multiple file systems on one disk, you can partition the disk so that different file systems can be installed on different disk partitions. You can also create partitions in one operating system to segment a single **physical drive**, the hard disk in a computer, into multiple logical volumes to which you can assign distinct drive letters. This technique of dividing a hard disk into multiple **logical drives** is very useful for organizing file storage, and was necessary with older operating systems, such as MS-DOS and Windows 3.1, which did not recognize very large hard drives.

Figure 4-6 illustrates a Windows 10 system that has multiple partitions (FAT32, NTFS, and **Universal Disk Format or UDF**, a format used for DVDs and other optical media) used for segmenting data on a hard disk.

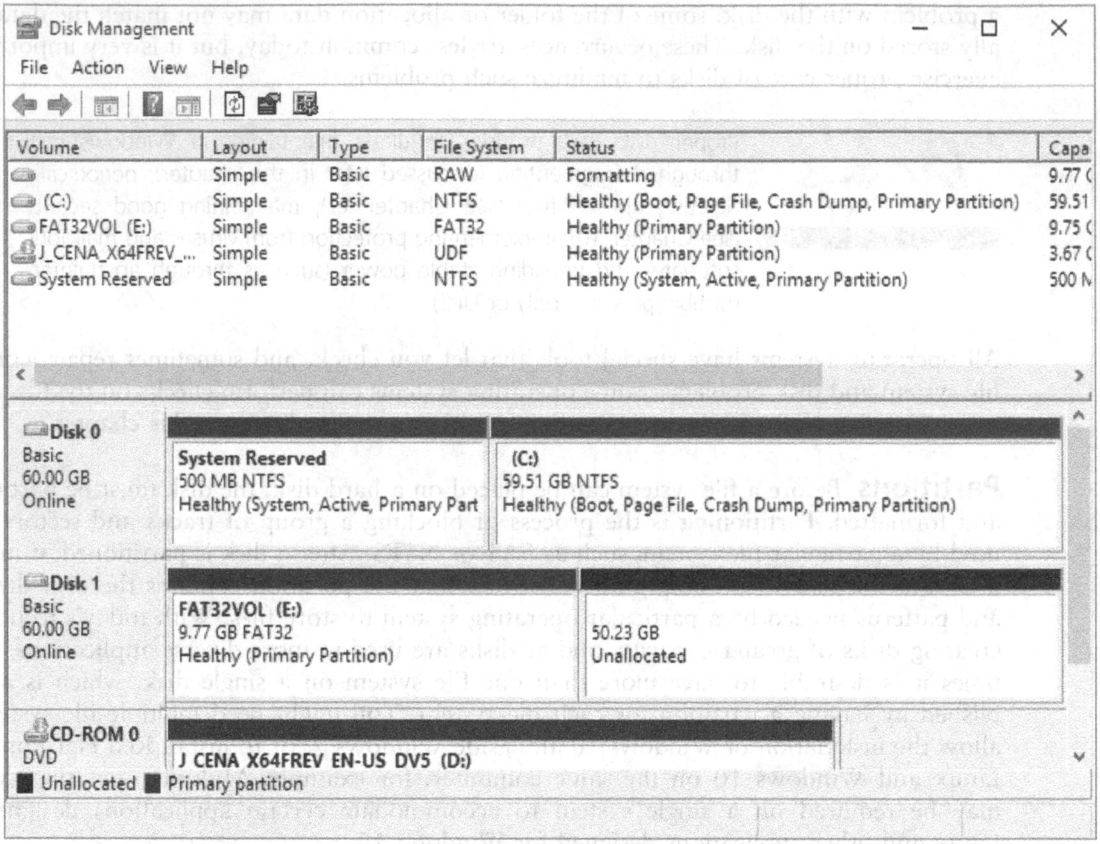

Disk Management

File Action View Help

Volume	Layout	Type	File System	Status	Capa
	Simple	Basic	RAW	Formatting	9.77 (
(C:)	Simple	Basic	NTFS	Healthy (Boot, Page File, Crash Dump, Primary Partition)	59.51
FAT32VOL (E:)	Simple	Basic	FAT32	Healthy (Primary Partition)	9.75 (
J_CENA_X64FREV_...	Simple	Basic	UDF	Healthy (Primary Partition)	3.67 (
System Reserved	Simple	Basic	NTFS	Healthy (System, Active, Primary Partition)	500 N

Disk 0
Basic
60.00 GB
Online

System Reserved
500 MB NTFS
Healthy (System, Active, Primary Part

(C:)
59.51 GB NTFS
Healthy (Boot, Page File, Crash Dump, Primary Partition)

Disk 1
Basic
60.00 GB
Online

FAT32VOL (E:)
9.77 GB FAT32
Healthy (Primary Partition)

50.23 GB
Unallocated

CD-ROM 0
DVD

J CENA X64FREV EN-US DV5 (D:)

Unallocated Primary partition

Figure 4-6 Multiple partitions used in one Windows 10 system

Partitioning can typically be done only on hard disks, SSDs, or large removable disks. Low-capacity media do not support partitioning because there simply is not enough room on these low-capacity disks to make partitioning practical. Also, some larger-capacity media, such as DVDs, CDs, and tapes, are not partitioned by the user.

The logical programming that creates disk partitions resides at an even lower level than the actual file system, and it lets you divide the disk into "slices." The slices are done at the low-level format portion of the disk, and are stored in special sections of the hard drive itself, separate from the operating system. Obviously, the partitioning scheme must be communicated to the operating system and file system. On most disks, there is a separate area that stores the partition information. This area has room to hold information about a set number of partitions. Whenever you create a partition, information about it is stored in this special area of the disk. On systems in the IBM/Intel PC hardware architecture, for example, there is typically room to store information for up to four partitions on each disk. This area is known as the **partition table** in MS-DOS, Mac OS, and Windows, and the **disk label** in UNIX/Linux. In addition to the disk label and partition table, another piece of disk is reserved, known as the **boot block** in UNIX/Linux and Mac OS X, or the **Master Boot Record (MBR)** in MS-DOS and Windows. In Windows systems, the MBR can be up to 512 bytes long and consists of four elements:

- The *boot program*, which examines the partition table to determine the partition from which to boot (the **active partition**) and enables the program code in the active partition's start area to execute and then point to the code that starts the operating system
- The *disk signature*, which stores information about the disk and is used by management software such as the Windows registry
- The *partition table* for the active partition
- The *end-of-MBR marker*, which signifies where the MBR contents end on the disk

Hands-On Project 4-3 shows you how to repair an MBR or a damaged boot sector in Windows 10.

Not all operating systems support partitions in the same way, which you will discover in the following sections on file systems for individual operating systems. Each operating system also uses specific utilities to create partitions. When a disk partition is created, the file system is stored inside the partition. The folder structures are then built inside the file system. When files are stored on the disks, they are given some space inside the partition, and data about the files is written in the folder area.

Windows supports two types of drive partitioning: basic and dynamic. Basic disks are the default type and have been around since the early 1980s, starting with the original IBM PC. Basic disks support up to four partitions per hard drive: four primary partitions or three primary partitions and one extended partition. The extended partition may then be divided further into logical drives (see Figure 4-7). Each of these logical drives can hold an individual FAT16, FAT32, or NTFS file system. Under control of the operating system, up to 26 logical drives (pointers to separate file systems), each with its own file system, can be active at one time. In Figure 4-7, the disk is divided into three primary partitions, one with FAT32 and two with NTFS, and the extended partition is divided into two logical drives, one with FAT (FAT16) and one with NTFS. Free space is also still available on the extended partition to create additional logical drives.

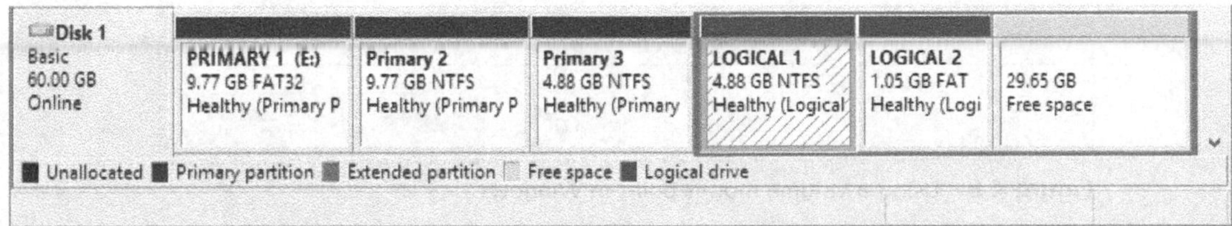

Figure 4-7 A disk with primary and extended partitions

Microsoft generally refers to a partition that has a file system installed as a **volume**. In most cases, this book will do the same.

Each volume is usually assigned a letter followed by a colon: A:, B:, C:, and so on through Z:. This design lets you easily address the individual file systems by specifying a drive letter. Letters A: and B: were traditionally reserved for two removable file systems on floppy disk drives. Because floppy drives are no longer found on modern systems, the A: and B: drive letters can be used for any storage medium. Typically, C: is reserved for the first volume, and is normally the system that contains the Windows OS. All other file systems located on fixed disks and controlled by the hard disk drivers in the operating system follow in sequential order. So, a machine with two hard disks of two partitions each will have the drive letters C: for the first volume on the first disk, D: for the second volume on the first disk, E: for the first volume on the second disk, and F: for the second volume on the second disk. Disks that require special drivers, such as DVD/CD-ROM drives or removable disks, can be assigned any unused drive letter. By default, they will be assigned the next letter after the drive letter used by the last hard disk. In the previous example, a DVD/CD-ROM drive would be drive G:.

Since Windows XP, you can access a volume as a folder on another NTFS volume. This means that instead of assigning a drive letter to a volume, you mount the volume in an empty folder on an NTFS volume that is assigned a drive letter. When you format a disk using the Windows Disk Management utility, you have the option to **mount** the disk instead of assigning a drive letter (see Figure 4-8). The empty folder into which a volume is mounted is called a **volume mount point**.

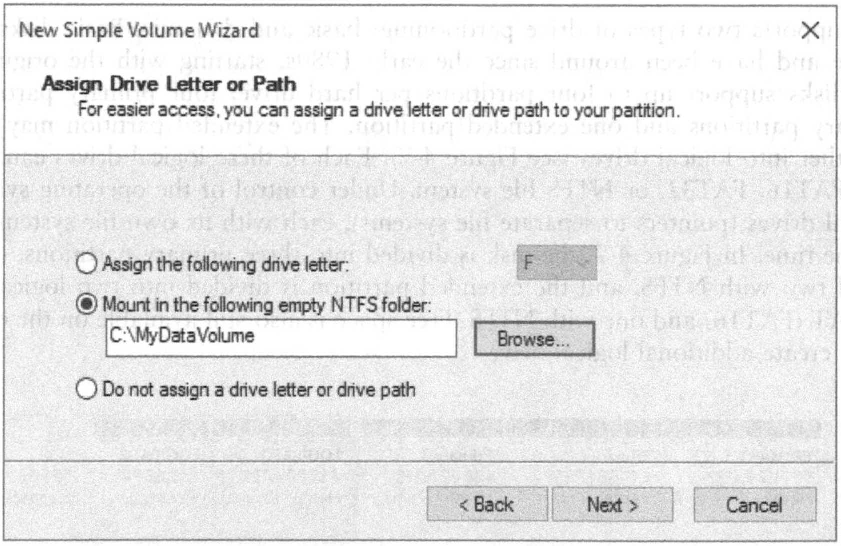

Figure 4-8 Using a volume mount point in Windows

In earlier versions of Windows, it was common to use the *fdisk* utility to partition hard disks. However, in versions of Windows starting with Windows 2000, you typically partition disks during the installation of the operating system and can add or reconfigure partitions after the operating system is installed. During the installation, it is necessary to partition at least the area on which the operating system is loaded. If your disks are currently unpartitioned, Windows will provide the option to automatically create the necessary volumes: one called System Reserved that is active and holds the boot configuration data and another that will be assigned the C: drive and hold the Windows OS. The System Reserved volume is about 500 MB and is not assigned a drive letter.

After the operating system is loaded, you can use the Disk Management tool to partition additional free space and disks. Refer to Figure 4-6 for an example of the Disk Management tool in Windows 10. The fastest way to access the Disk Management tool in Windows 8.1 and later versions is to right-click Start and then click Disk Management in the menu. The tool can also be accessed from the Control Panel and the Computer Management console. You learn more about managing disks with this tool in Chapter 7.

Formatting After you partition a disk, it is time to place the file system on the partition using the process called **formatting**. When you first install a Windows operating system, Windows will automatically create and format the necessary partitions, as mentioned, or you can create and format the partitions manually. The installation process then creates the folder structure and writes the OS files to the disk. After the operating system is installed, you can use the Disk Management tool to create additional volumes. Another option for formatting a hard disk is to use the *format* command from the Command Prompt window. This command writes all of the file system structure to the disk. As with many system-level commands, *format* includes several additional switches that modify precise program operation. You can view a list of these switches by typing *format /?* in the Command Prompt window. See Table 4-1 for a list of *format* switches.

Commands frequently use switches. A **switch** in a command changes the way a particular command operates. In many operating systems, these extra commands follow a forward slash and take the form of a letter or combination of letters, such as the *dir* command in Windows systems, which shows the contents of one or more directories and can take several switches or arguments, including */p* (pause when the screen is full) and */s* (include subdirectories). In UNIX/Linux systems, the command switches frequently begin with one (-) or two (--) dashes.

Formatting a disk removes all data that was on the disk. On disks that have never been formatted, the *format* command writes new sector and track markers on the disk. On disks used previously, you can use the */q* (quick format) option. This tells *format* to dispense with the disk check and simply write a new root folder and FAT or MFT. Using the */q* switch makes the format operation a lot faster, but it also skips the detailed checking of the disk, which can cause trouble later if an application tries to write information to a bad disk location.

Table 4-1 ***Format*** **command switches**

Switch	Function
/v:label	Specifies the volume label
/q	Uses a quick format technique that does not check the disk for damaged clusters or bad spots
/f:size	Specifies the size of the floppy disk to format (such as 160, 180, 320, 360, 720, 1.2, 1.44, or 2.88, where the file sizes are in KB or MB)
/fs:filesystem	Specifies whether to format for FAT16, FAT32, or NTFS

(continues)

Table 4-1 ***Format* command switches (*continued*)**

Switch	Function
/t:tracks	Designates the number of tracks on a side (disks can be formatted on both sides)
/n:sectors	Designates how many sectors are in a track
/c	NTFS only: this causes files created on the volume to be compressed
/p:count	Write zeros in all sectors for the number of times specified in the count parameter. This option causes all data on the disk to be overwritten with 0 bits for security reasons to ensure that no data is recoverable. This is not valid with the */q* switch.
/X	Forces the volume to dismount first, if necessary
/R:revision	UDF only: forces a specific UDF format revision
/L	NTFS only: use large file records
/A:size	Overrides the default allocation unit (cluster) size
/N:sectors	Specifies the number of sectors per track.
/S:state	Specifies support for short filenames. The state is either "enable" or "disable." Short names are disabled by default.
/I:state	ReFS only: Specifies whether integrity should be enabled on the new volume. The state is either "enable" or "disable." Integrity is enabled on storage that supports data redundancy by default.

It is possible to run Windows operating systems and UNIX/Linux systems on one machine. For example, if you only format a portion of a partitioned hard disk for Windows, you can format another portion for UNIX/Linux if you save the room required by the operating system—but it is advised that you use the appropriate disk formatting utility for your UNIX/Linux operating system or let the UNIX/ Linux installation program do the formatting.

The boot block is placed in the first sector on the disk, which also contains the root folder (the highest-level folder). The root folder is also where the system stores file information, such as name, start cluster, file size, file modification date and time, and file attributes (file characteristics such as Hidden, Read-only, Archive, and so on). The root folder on every partition has a fixed size that can contain a maximum of 512 entries in FAT16 and unlimited entries in FAT32 and NTFS. Each entry corresponds with a cluster address or sector on the disk. When the file system performs its format operation, it divides the disk into clusters that are sequentially numbered. Each of the two copies of the FAT has exactly one entry for each cluster.

When a file is stored to disk, its data is written in the clusters on the disk. The filename is stored in the folder, along with the number of the first cluster in which the data is stored. When the operating system fills the first cluster, data is written to the next free cluster on the disk. The FAT entry corresponding with the first cluster is filled with the number of the second cluster in the file. When the second cluster is full, the operating system continues to write in the next free cluster. The FAT entry for the second cluster is set to point to the cluster number for the third cluster, and so on. When a file is completely written to the disk, the FAT entry for the final cluster is filled with all 1s, which means the end of the file. At this time, the folder entry for the file is updated with the total file size. This is commonly referred to as the **linked-list** method.

Clusters are of a fixed length, and if a file does not exactly match the space available in the clusters it uses, you can end up with some unused space at the end of a cluster. This is a little wasteful, and it also explains why a file's folder entry must include the exact file size. The operating system sets all FAT entries to 0s when it formats the disk, indicating that none of the clusters is being used. When you write a file to disk, the operating system finds free space on the disk simply by looking for the next FAT entry that contains all 0s. In most cases, the *format* command reads every address on the disk to make sure they are usable. Unusable spots are marked in the FAT as **bad clusters**, and these areas are never used for file storage. The *format* command then writes a new root folder and file allocation table, and the disk is ready for use.

When formatting a hard disk, the size of each entry in the FAT16 table is 16 bits long on any disk larger than 16 MB. On a hard disk, several sectors are combined into a cluster; exactly how many sectors per cluster depends on the size of the hard disk.

Recall that the largest possible partition in a FAT16 file system is 4 GB. Keep in mind that the smallest allocation unit is one cluster. If you store a file that is 300 bytes long on a file system that has clusters of 64 KB, you will waste a lot of space. For this reason, smaller cluster sizes are generally considered desirable. As a result, Windows systems using FAT with large hard disks frequently have many hard disk partitions.

Each partition stores an extra copy of the FAT in case the first copy gets damaged. However, there is only one copy of the root folder on each partition. This concept is shown in Figure 4-9.

Partition boot record (1 sector)
Main FAT table (size is up to two clusters, for either FAT16 or FAT32—clusters can be 512 bytes to 64 KB in size).
Backup FAT table (same size as main FAT).
Root directory, room for 512 entries in FAT16—unlimited in FAT32.
Data area (size varies). Here all other files and directories are stored. Site measured in clusters, which are composed of groups of sectors.

Figure 4-9 Typical FAT directory structure

The FATs and root folder are found at the beginning of each partition, and they are always at the same location. This makes it possible for the boot program to easily find the files needed to start the operating system. Other directories in the file system are specialized files. They are identical to any other file in the operating system, with the exception of having the folder attribute set in their own folder entry. There can be a virtually unlimited number of directories, with a virtually unlimited number of files in each (limited only by the amount of storage space on the disk).

The FAT folder structure is simple. In each folder entry, information about the file is stored, including the filename, the file revision date and time, the file size, and the file attributes. The filename consists of two parts: the name and the extension, which contains up to three characters. Extensions can have a special meaning. For example, files with a .sys extension are generally device drivers; files with .com or .exe extensions are program files the operating system can execute; and files with the .bat extension are batch files of commands that can be executed as if they were typed in a command prompt window. The filename and extension are separated by a period.

Apart from the filename, each folder entry also contains some **status bits** that identify the type of filename contained in each entry. The status bits in use are Volume, Folder, System, Hidden, Read-only, and Archive. The Volume bit indicates a file system **volume label**, or a nickname for the file system. The volume name can be set with the */v* option of the *format* command, or by using the *volume* command. The volume name appears at the top of folder listings (using the *dir* command). The Folder bit is used to signify that a file contains folder data and should be treated as a folder by the file system. Folders may in turn contain subfolders, as long as the names of all subfolders in a path do not exceed 80 characters. You will see a folder marked with a <DIR> label when you use the *dir* command in the Command Prompt window, or it will be designated with a file folder icon in File Explorer. The four remaining attributes indicate additional information about a file. Files that are part of the operating system and should not be touched by programs or users are marked with a System or S flag. Files that should not be visible to the user are known as Hidden files and are marked with the H bit. Files that should not be written to are known as Read-only files and are marked with the R flag. Lastly, files that should be backed up the next time a backup is made are said to have the Archive, or A flag, set.

Overall, there are four optional flags—H, S, R, and A. You can use the *attrib* command at the Command Prompt to look at or set these attributes. Typing *attrib* followed by a folder name shows all of the attribute settings for all the files, whereas typing *attrib* followed by a filename shows only attributes specific to that file. The *attrib* command can also be used to set file attributes. To do this, you follow the *attrib* command with the attribute letter, then the + sign to set the attribute or the – sign to unset it, and then the filename in question. To make a file named test.txt hidden, for example, you would type *attrib +h test.txt*. If you then typed *dir*, you would not see the test.txt file, but if you typed *attrib test.txt*, you would once again see test.txt, with the letter *H* in front of it, letting you know it is a Hidden file. A file with the S attribute set is also not displayed in *dir* listings, but you can view it with the *attrib* command, and you can remove the System attribute with *attrib* as well. Table 4-2 shows the various arguments and switches you can use with the *attrib* command.

Table 4-2 Attribute command (*attrib*) arguments and switches

Argument/switch	Description
r	Read-only file attribute
a	Archive file attribute
s	System file attribute
h	Hidden file attribute
i	Not a content-indexed file attribute; the contents of the file will not be included in the search index
x	No scrub file attribute; only supported on ReFS file systems
v	Integrity attribute; only supported on ReFS file systems
/s	Processes files in all folders in the specified path
/d	Processes folders as well as files

Windows File Systems

Windows XP through Windows Server 2008 R2 support three file systems: extended FAT16, FAT32, and NTFS. Windows 8, Windows Server 2012, and later versions also support ReFS. All of these operating systems also support file systems for DVD/CD-ROM drives and USB devices like flash drives.

FAT16 and Extended FAT16

The extended FAT16 file system under Windows evolved from the FAT16 system used in early versions of MS-DOS and Windows (3.x/95/98/Me). An extended file system can be divided into multiple logical file systems. FAT uses a file allocation table to store folder information about files, such as filenames, file attributes, and file location. The "16" in FAT16 means that this file system uses 16-bit entries in the file allocation table and uses 2^{16} clusters. Remember that clusters are blocks of space containing one or more sectors into which the disk is divided.

In extended FAT16, the maximum size of a volume is 4 GB, and the maximum size of a file is 2 GB. One advantage to using the extended FAT16 file system is that it has been around for a long time, and even non-Windows operating systems, such as UNIX/Linux, can read disks written in FAT16 format. Further, because the file system is simple, relatively little can go wrong, which makes it a stable file system.

Originally, FAT16 used "8.3" filenames, which can be up to eight characters long followed by a period and an extension of three characters, such as Filename.ext. Examples of extensions are .txt for text files, .doc or .docx for word-processing files, .xls or .xlsx for Excel spreadsheets, and so on. The limitations of this naming convention contributed to the development and use of **long filenames (LFNs)** in extended FAT16. An LFN:

- Can contain as many as 255 characters
- Is not case sensitive
- Cannot include characters such as " / \ [ ] : ; =, (this applies both to 8.3 filenames and LFNs)

Because LFN characters are stored in **Unicode**, a coding system that allows for representation of any character in any language, it is possible to use most legitimate characters in Windows in a filename (see the previous bulleted list for some exceptions). The advantage of LFNs and Unicode is that LFNs can be read by other operating systems, including Mac OS and UNIX/Linux systems (such as on a Windows 2008 server that has file services installed for Mac OS and UNIX/Linux clients).

Until fairly recently, letters and digits were represented by ASCII (American Standard Code for Information Interchange, pronounced *as-key*) values. The problem with this standard is that it uses an entire byte to represent each character, which limits the number of characters that can be represented to 255. This is not enough to handle all the characters needed to represent world languages, which use several different alphabets (Greek, Russian, Japanese, and Hindi, for example). ASCII deals with this problem by employing many different character sets, depending on the characters you're trying to represent. The Unicode Consortium, a not-for-profit organization, represents an alternative in which there is a single, unique code for each possible character in any language. The first 128 characters in Unicode are the 128 ASCII characters. Unicode allows over a million characters to be defined. It includes distinct character codes for all modern languages and many historic scripts like Egyptian hieroglyphs. To the user who communicates primarily in English, Unicode will not make a big difference, but in this age of worldwide communication, it is a necessity.

FAT32

Starting with Windows 95 Release 2, all Windows versions support FAT32. FAT32 is designed to accommodate larger-capacity disks than FAT16 and avoid the problem of cluster size limitations. A file allocation table entry in FAT32 is 32 bits in length and FAT32 supports up to 2^{28} clusters (this figure is not to the 32nd power because some extra space is reserved for the operating system). In FAT32, the root folder does not have to be at the beginning of a volume; it can be located anywhere. Also, FAT32 can use disk space more efficiently than FAT16 because it can use smaller cluster sizes. FAT32 partitions have a theoretical size of 2 terabytes (TB); however, the largest volume that can be formatted is 32 GB (still much larger than FAT16). The maximum file size in FAT32 is raised to 4 GB.

FAT32 shares characteristics of extended FAT16, such as the double FAT structure at the beginning of a partition for fault tolerance and the use of LFNs and Unicode.

Sometimes users choose to employ extended FAT16 or FAT32 because they are familiar with these file systems or they have dual-boot systems, such as a system with Windows XP and the older Windows 98. Another reason for using extended FAT16 or FAT32 is that these file systems offer fast response on small, 1 or 2 GB partitions.

Windows file systems can be converted from FAT16 or FAT32 to NTFS, either during installation or at a later date. If you convert at a later date, use the *convert* command in the Command Prompt window. However, you cannot convert from NTFS to FAT16 or FAT32, except by reformatting to use FAT16 or FAT32 and then performing a full restore. You can use the Windows Backup tool to perform a backup or a restore from a previous backup.

If a partition is set up for FAT and is 2 GB or smaller, Windows will format it as FAT16 during installation (if the option to use FAT is selected). Partitions that are over 2 GB are formatted as FAT32.

FAT64

FAT64, also known as exFAT, is a proprietary file system. Microsoft introduced it for mobile personal storage needs to handle large files. As the size of pictures, videos, and other media files grows, the file size limits of FAT16 and FAT32 are an important consideration. The size limit for FAT16 is 2 GB minus one byte, and for FAT32 it is 4 GB minus one byte. FAT64 with a limit of 16 EB is a good choice for USB flash devices when you will be storing very large files.

FAT64 is available starting in Service Pack 1 for Windows Vista. It is also available for Linux from a third party. Apple added support in Mac OS X Snow Leopard in late 2010.

NTFS

NTFS is the primary Windows file system for all Windows operating systems starting with Windows NT 3.1. It is a modern system designed for the needs of a networked environment.

The way NTFS keeps track of files and clusters is a little different from that of FAT file systems. Rather than using a structure of FATs and directories, NTFS uses a **Master File Table (MFT)**. Like the FATs and directories, this table is located at the beginning of the partition. The boot sector is located ahead of the MFT. Following the MFT, there are several system files that the file system uses to make all the features of NTFS work. Note that the MFT in itself is nothing more than a file on the file system, as are all other system files. The second file on the disk is a copy of the first three records of the MFT. This ensures that if the MFT is damaged, it can be re-created. File number five, known as $, contains the entries in the root folder, whereas file number six, known as $Bitmap, contains data about which clusters on the disk are in use. Normally, the MFT and related files take up about 1 MB of disk space when the disk is initially formatted.

When a file is created in NTFS, a record for that file is added to the MFT. This record contains all standard information, such as filename, size, dates, and times. It also contains additional attributes, such as security settings, ownership, and permissions. If there is not enough room in an MFT record to store security settings, the settings that don't fit are put on another cluster somewhere on the disk, and the MFT record points to this information. If a file is very small, there is sometimes enough room in the MFT record to store the file data. If there is not enough room, the system allocates clusters elsewhere on the disk. The

MFT record reflects the sequence of clusters that a file uses. The attributes can generally be repeated; it is possible to have a whole series of different security attributes for different users. It is also possible to have multiple filenames that refer to the same file, a technique known as **hard linking.** This is a feature, also available in UNIX/Linux file systems, that is sometimes used to make the same file appear in multiple directories without having to allocate disk space for the file more than once.

NTFS is referred to in two ways. The first is by the actual release numbering and the second is the more accepted way, which very roughly refers to a Windows operating system. Table 4-3 shows the five versions of NTFS, the operating system they correspond to, and the generally accepted version number for NTFS.

Table 4-3 NTFS versions

Official version number	Generally accepted version number	Windows operating system
1.0	NTFS	
1.1	NTFS	
1.2	NTFS 4	Windows NT 3.51 and NT 4.0
3.0	NTFS 5.0	Windows 2000
3.1	NTFS 5.1/5.2	Windows XP/Windows Server 2003/Windows Server 2008/Vista
3.1	NTFS 6.0	Windows Server 2008 R2/Windows 7 and later

Some of the basic features incorporated into NTFS include:

- Long filenames
- Built-in security features
- Better file compression than FAT
- Ability to use larger disks and files than FAT
- File activity tracking for better recovery and stability than FAT
- **Portable Operating System Interface for UNIX (POSIX)** support
- Volume striping and volume extensions
- Less disk fragmentation than FAT

As a full-featured network file system, NTFS is equipped with security features that meet the U.S. government's C2 security specifications. C2 security refers to high-level, "top-secret" standards for data protection, system auditing, and system access, which are required by some government agencies. One security feature is the ability to establish the type of access allowed for users of folders and files within folders. The file and folder access can be tailored to the particular requirements of an organization. For example, the system files on a server can be protected so only the server administrator has access. A folder of databases can be protected with read access, but no access to change data; also, a public folder can give users in a designated group access to read and update files, but not to delete files.

File compression is a process that significantly reduces the size of a file by removing unused space within it or using compression algorithms. Some files can be compressed by more than 40 percent, saving important disk space for other storage needs. This is particularly useful for files that are accessed infrequently. NTFS provides the ability to compress files as needed. Try Hands-On Project 4-4 to compress files in Windows.

4

NTFS can be scaled to accommodate very large files, particularly for database applications. A Microsoft SQL Server database file might be 20 GB or larger, for example. This means an organization can store pictures, scanned images, and sound clips in a single database. The NTFS system can support files up to 2^{64} bytes (in theory).

Another NTFS feature is **journaling**, the ability to keep a log or journal of file system activity. This is a critical process if there is a power outage or hard disk failure. Important information can be retrieved and restored in these situations. FAT does not offer this capability.

NTFS supports POSIX standards to enable portability of applications from one computer system to another. POSIX was initially developed as a UNIX standard designed to ensure portability of applications among various versions of UNIX, but now POSIX is used by other file systems and operating systems as well. NTFS follows the POSIX 1 standard, which includes case-sensitive filenames and use of multiple filenames (called *hard links*, a concept discussed later in this chapter). For example, the files Myfile.doc and MYFile.doc are considered different files (except when using File Explorer or the Command Prompt window).

An important volume-handling feature of NTFS is the ability to create extensions on an existing volume, such as when new disk storage is added. Another feature is volume striping, which is a process that equally divides the contents of each file across two or more volumes to extend disk life, enable fault tolerance features, and balance the disk load for better performance.

Last, NTFS is less prone to file corruption than FAT in part because it has a **hot fix** capability, which means that if a bad disk area is detected, NTFS automatically copies the information from the bad area to another disk area that is not damaged.

In addition to the NTFS 4 features already described, NTFS 5 adds several new features:

- Ability to encrypt files
- No system reboot required after creating an extended volume
- Ability to reduce drive designations
- Indexing for fast access

- Ability to retain shortcuts and other file information when files and folders are placed on other volumes (In Windows systems, a shortcut is a link or icon that can start software in the same location or in a different location through a simple mouse click or double-click.)
- Ability to establish disk quotas

With NTFS 5, files can be encrypted so that their contents are available only to those granted access. Also, volume extensions can be set up without the need to reboot the system. (In NTFS 4, you must reboot after adding an extension to an existing volume.) Volume mount points, as previously discussed, can be created as a way to reduce the number of drive designations for multiple volumes, instead of designating a new drive for each new volume. In Windows, a mount point appears to the user as a folder, but it is really a link to a hard drive, DVD/CD-ROM drive, or other storage medium. NTFS 5 incorporates fast indexing in conjunction with Active Folder to make file searching and retrieval faster than in NTFS 4. A new technique called **Distributed Link Tracking** is available in NTFS 5 so that shortcuts you have created are not lost when you move files to another volume. Finally, NTFS 5 enables you to set up **disk quotas** to control how much disk space users can occupy. Disk quotas are a vital tool for disk capacity planning to ensure that there is enough disk space for all server operations and critical files.

The latest version of NTFS, referred to as NTFS 6, adds several new features:

- Transactional NTFS
- Partition resizing
- Self-healing

Transactional NTFS is used to perform operations on an NTFS volume in transaction mode; that is, all specified file system transactions take place or none of them takes place. You can package registry and file system operations in a transaction so that all of the operations take place or none of them succeed. If one of the file system operations does not work, then everything is aborted and nothing takes place. Transactional NTFS is used heavily in Windows Server 2008.

Beginning with Windows Vista, Microsoft allowed for the expanding and shrinking of partitions, so you could adjust the amount of space used by a volume without having to delete the partition and reformat the disk. The capability is still very limited and there are third-party products that are more capable and robust.

In the past, if you had problems with NTFS volumes on your disk, you used *chkdsk.exe* to fix the problem. This meant taking down the volume to run the utility. With self-healing NTFS, the utility runs in the background to correct hard disk problems. The availability of the file system is far greater than the previous way using the *chkdsk.exe* utility, data is preserved as much as possible, and better reports are provided to describe modifications made to the volume. Table 4-4 compares FAT16, FAT32, FAT64, and NTFS.

Table 4-4 FAT16, FAT32, FAT64, and NTFS compared

Feature	FAT16	FAT32	FAT64 (exFAT)	NTFS
Total volume size	2–4 GB	2 TB to 16 TB	512 TB	2 TB
Maximum file size	4 GB	4 GB	16 EB (exabytes); 1 EB equals a billion gigabytes	Theoretical limit of 264 bytes
Compatible with floppy disks	Yes	No	No	No
Security	Limited security based on attributes and shares	Limited security based on attributes and shares	Limited security based on attributes and shares	Extensive security and auditing options
File compression	Supported with extra utilities	Supported with extra utilities	Supported with extra utilities	Supported as part of NTFS
File activity tracking	None	None	None	Tracking via a log
POSIX support	None	Limited	Limited	POSIX 1 support
Hot fix	Limited	Limited	Yes	Yes
Large database support	Limited	Yes	Yes	Yes
Multiple disk drives in one volume	No	No	No	Yes

When you copy a file from an NTFS system to a FAT16 or FAT32 system, the security permissions of the file are lost because permissions are not supported in FAT16 or FAT32.

Basic and Dynamic Disks Basic disks use traditional disk partitioning techniques, meaning they are limited to four primary partitions or three primary partitions and one extended partition. Windows 2000 Server introduced dynamic disks, which do not use traditional partitioning techniques. Dynamic disks make it possible to set up a large number of volumes on one disk and provide the ability to extend volumes onto additional physical disks. You can convert basic disks to dynamic disks using the Disk Management tool.

NTFS File System and Disk Utilities Sometimes disk performance is affected by corrupted files, or when the file allocation table loses pointers to certain files. You can correct these problems and maintain the integrity of the data by periodically running the "Check disk" utility, called *chkdsk*. All versions of Windows starting with Windows 2000 come with *chkdsk*, which is run from the Command Prompt window or by clicking Start, clicking Run, entering *chkdsk*, and pressing OK. The *chkdsk* utility can detect and fix an extensive set of file system problems in FAT and NTFS systems. Table 4-5 presents a list of the switches that are available for this utility and Figure 4-10 illustrates *chkdsk* results for a computer running Windows 10.

Table 4-5 ***Chkdsk* switch options**

Switch/parameter	Purpose
[volume] (such as C:)	Specifies that *chkdsk* check only the designated volume
[filename] (such as *.dll)	Enables a check of the specified file or files only
/c	For NTFS only, *chkdsk* uses an abbreviated check of the folder structure
/f	Instructs *chkdsk* to fix errors that it finds and locks the disk while checking
/i	For NTFS only, *chkdsk* uses an abbreviated check of indexes
/L:size	For NTFS only, enables you to specify the size of the log file created by the disk check
/r	Searches for bad sectors, fixes problems, and recovers information (if possible, or use the *recover* command afterward)
/v	On FAT, shows the entire path name of files; on NTFS, shows clean-up messages associated with errors
/b	In NTFS only, clears the list of bad clusters stored on the volume and rescans everything. This feature was added in Vista.
/x	Dismounts or locks a volume before starting (*/f* also dismounts or locks a volume)

In Hands-On Project 4-5, you run *chkdsk* in Windows.

In Windows versions starting with Windows 2000, *chkdsk* runs automatically at bootup if it detects that the operating system was previously shut down with a file system problem, or shut down before the operating system had the opportunity to clean up temporary files on the disk.

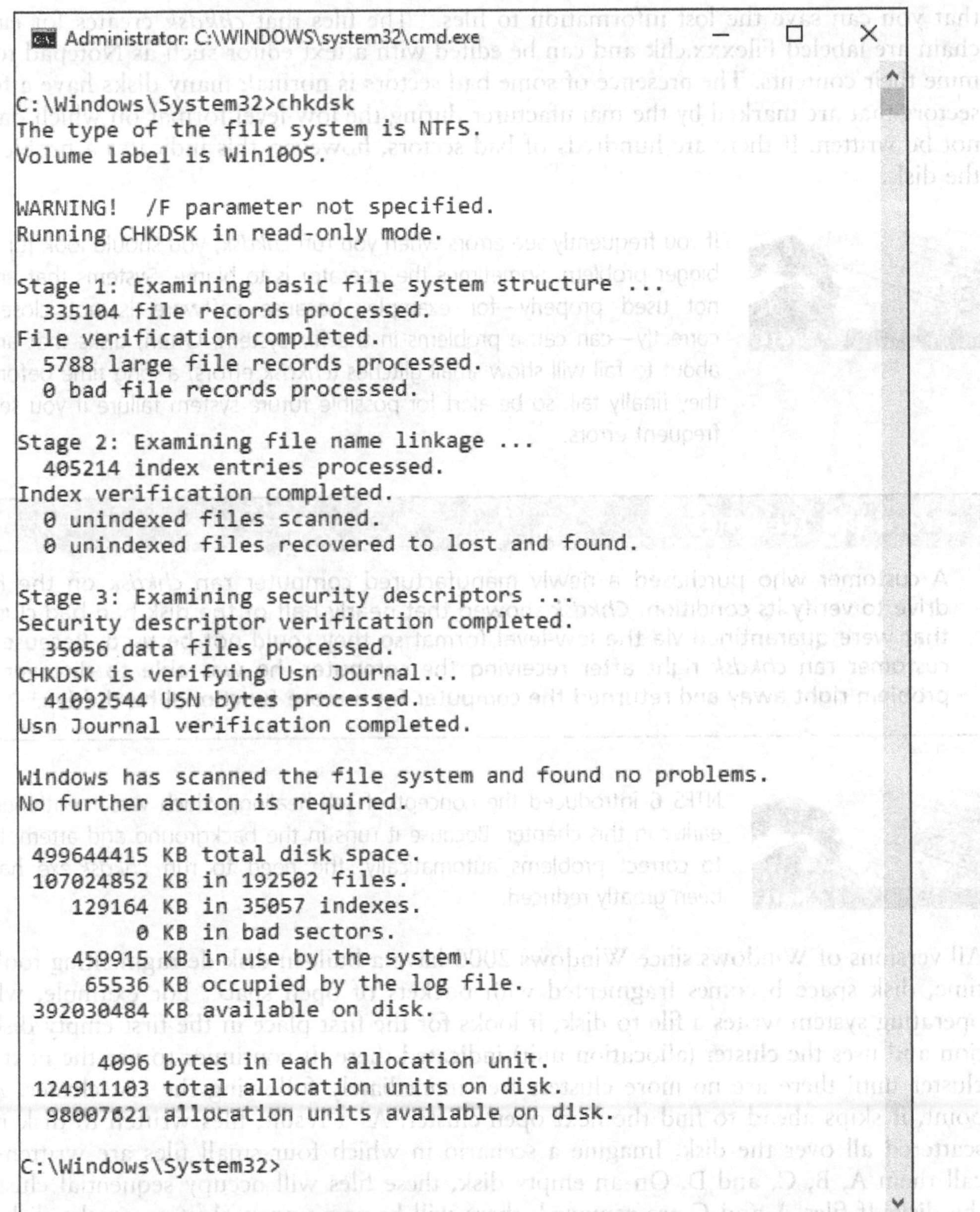

Administrator: C:\WINDOWS\system32\cmd.exe
C:\Windows\System32>chkdsk
The type of the file system is NTFS.
Volume label is Win10OS.
WARNING! /F parameter not specified.
Running CHKDSK in read-only mode.
Stage 1: Examining basic file system structure ...
335104 file records processed.
File verification completed.
5788 large file records processed.
0 bad file records processed.
Stage 2: Examining file name linkage ...
405214 index entries processed.
Index verification completed.
0 unindexed files scanned.
0 unindexed files recovered to lost and found.
Stage 3: Examining security descriptors ...
Security descriptor verification completed.
35056 data files processed.
CHKDSK is verifying Usn Journal...
41092544 USN bytes processed.
Usn Journal verification completed.
Windows has scanned the file system and found no problems.
No further action is required.
499644415 KB total disk space.
107024852 KB in 192502 files.
129164 KB in 35057 indexes.
0 KB in bad sectors.
459915 KB in use by the system.
65536 KB occupied by the log file.
392030484 KB available on disk.
4096 bytes in each allocation unit.
124911103 total allocation units on disk.
98007621 allocation units available on disk.
C:\Windows\System32>

Figure 4-10 Results of the *chkdsk* command

If *chkdsk* finds any problems, it either fixes them (depending on the error) or displays an error message. Or, you have the option of letting it fix all problems automatically by using the /f or Fix option. The most common problems are files with sizes of 0, which is caused when a file is not properly closed, or chains of clusters (file allocation units) that have no folder entries attached. When *chkdsk* finds lost allocation units or chains, it prompts you with a yes-or-no question: "Convert lost chains to files? Answer 'yes' to the question so that you can save the lost information to files." The files that *chkdsk* creates for each lost chain are labeled Filexxx.chk and can be edited with a text editor such as Notepad to determine their contents. The presence of some bad sectors is normal; many disks have a few bad sectors that are marked by the manufacturer during the low-level format on which data cannot be written. If there are hundreds of bad sectors, however, this indicates a problem with the disk.

If you frequently see errors when you run *chkdsk*, you should look for a bigger problem. Sometimes the operator is to blame. Systems that are not used properly—for example, because software is not closed correctly—can cause problems in the file system. Often, disks that are about to fail will show small glitches (*chkdsk* errors) a long time before they finally fail, so be alert for possible future system failure if you see frequent errors.

From the Trenches ...

A customer who purchased a newly manufactured computer ran *chkdsk* on the hard drive to verify its condition. *Chkdsk* showed that nearly half of the disk had bad clusters that were quarantined via the low-level format so they could not be used. Because the customer ran *chkdsk* right after receiving the computer, he was able to discover the problem right away and returned the computer for a more functional hard drive.

NTFS 6 introduced the concept of self-healing, which was mentioned earlier in this chapter. Because it runs in the background and attempts to correct problems automatically, the need to run *chkdsk.exe* has been greatly reduced.

All versions of Windows since Windows 2000 have a built-in disk defragmenting tool. Over time, disk space becomes fragmented with pockets of open space. For example, when an operating system writes a file to disk, it looks for the first place in the first empty disk location and uses the cluster (allocation unit) indicated there. It continues to use the next empty cluster until there are no more clusters free immediately following the last cluster. At that point, it skips ahead to find the next open cluster. As a result, files written to disk may be scattered all over the disk. Imagine a scenario in which four small files are written—we'll call them A, B, C, and D. On an empty disk, these files will occupy sequential clusters on the disk. If files A and C are removed, there will be some open clusters on the disk. If file E, which is larger than A and C combined, is written to the disk, it will start using the clusters formerly occupied by A, then use those formerly used by C, and then continue beyond the clusters occupied by D. When a disk is highly fragmented, the read heads have to work harder to obtain data, wasting time and creating more wear. For this reason, it is wise to periodically defragment your disks. A **defragmenter** is a tool that rearranges data on the disk in a continuous fashion, ridding the disk of scattered open clusters.

Windows versions since Windows 2000 all have Disk Defragmenter (see Figure 4-11). Disk Defragmenter can be used on volumes formatted for FAT16, FAT32, FAT64, and NTFS.

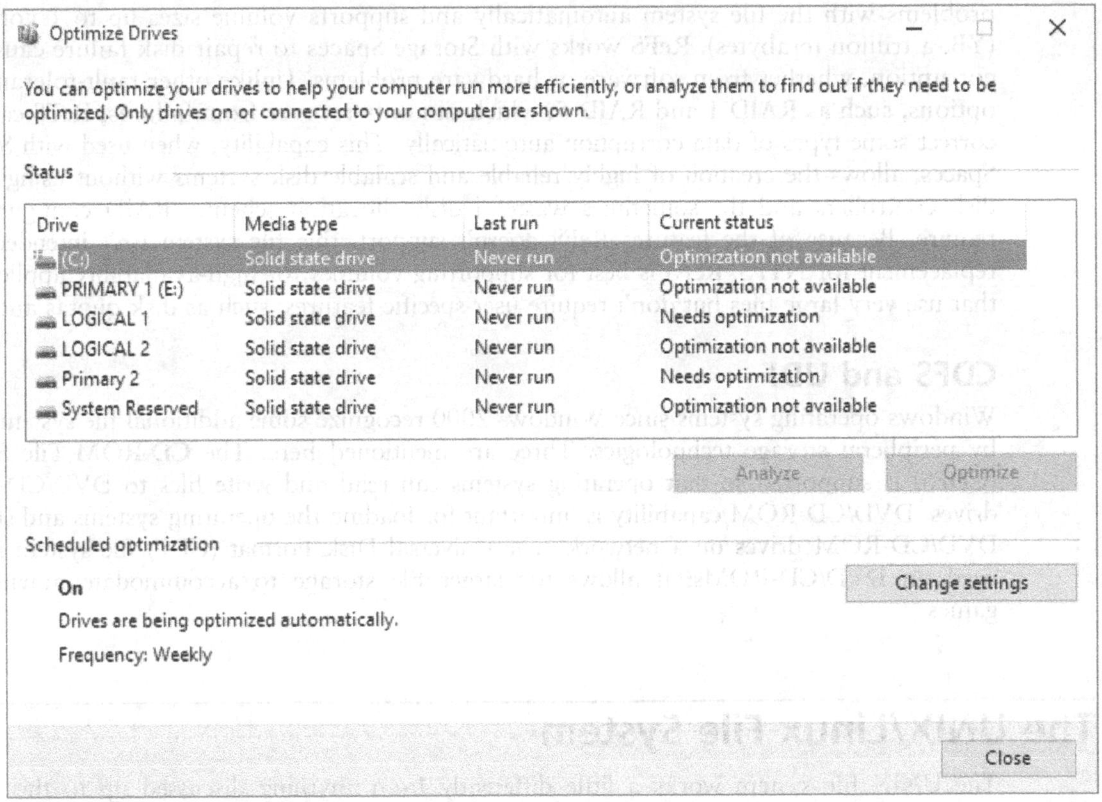

Optimize Drives

You can optimize your drives to help your computer run more efficiently, or analyze them to find out if they need to be optimized. Only drives on or connected to your computer are shown.

Status

Drive	Media type	Last run	Current status
(C:)	Solid state drive	Never run	Optimization not available
PRIMARY 1 (E:)	Solid state drive	Never run	Optimization not available
LOGICAL 1	Solid state drive	Never run	Needs optimization
LOGICAL 2	Solid state drive	Never run	Optimization not available
Primary 2	Solid state drive	Never run	Needs optimization
System Reserved	Solid state drive	Never run	Optimization not available

Analyze Optimize

Scheduled optimization

On

Drives are being optimized automatically.

Frequency: Weekly

Change settings

Close

Figure 4-11 Disk Defragmenter in Windows 10

Windows versions after XP come with a Disk Cleanup utility that deletes temporary Internet files, temporary program files, program files that are not used, and files in the Recycle Bin. To start this utility from File Explorer, right-click the disk and click Properties. From the General tab, click Disk Cleanup.

Care should be taken to use only utilities designed to work with NTFS; serious damage can occur if other utilities are used. If utilities designed for MS-DOS or Windows 95/98/Me are used on NTFS file systems, they may reach incorrect conclusions regarding file system layout. This can result in loss of data, damaged files, or even destruction of the complete file system and all of its contents.

Resilient File System (ReFS)

ReFS became available starting with Windows Server 2012. The main use of Resilient File System (ReFS) is in large file-sharing applications where volumes are managed by Storage Spaces (which was introduced in Chapter 2). Although ReFS is mostly backward-compatible with NTFS, it doesn't support file compression, disk quotas, and EFS (Encrypting File System). Also, Windows can't be booted from an ReFS volume. ReFS can repair minor problems with the file system automatically and supports volume sizes up to 1 yottabyte (YB, a trillion terabytes). ReFS works with Storage Spaces to repair disk failure caused by corruption, whether from software or hardware problems. Unlike other fault-tolerant disk options, such as RAID 1 and RAID 5, which can only recover from failures, ReFS can also correct some types of data corruption automatically. This capability, when used with Storage Spaces, allows the creation of highly reliable and scalable disk systems without using RAID disk controllers and the sometimes wasteful disk allocation schemes RAID configurations require. Because of the features ReFS doesn't support, this file system isn't intended as a replacement for NTFS. ReFS is best for supporting volumes for high-availability applications that use very large files but don't require user-specific features, such as disk quotas and EFS.

CDFS and UDF

Windows operating systems since Windows 2000 recognize some additional file systems used by peripheral storage technologies. Three are mentioned here. The **CD-ROM File System (CDFS)** is supported so that operating systems can read and write files to DVD/CD-ROM drives. DVD/CD-ROM capability is important for loading the operating systems and sharing DVD/CD-ROM drives on a network. The Universal Disk Format (UDF) file system is also used on DVD/CD-ROMs; it allows for larger file storage to accommodate movies and games.

The UNIX/Linux File System

The UNIX file system works a little differently from anything discussed up to this point. "UNIX file system" is really a misnomer. In reality, many different file systems can be used, but some are more "native" to specific UNIX operating systems than others. Most versions of UNIX and Linux support the **UNIX file system (ufs)**, which is the original native UNIX file system. Ufs is a hierarchical (tree structure) file system that is expandable, supports large storage, provides file and folder security, and is reliable. In fact, many qualities of NTFS are modeled after ufs. Ufs supports journaling so that if a system crashes unexpectedly, it is possible to reconstruct files or to roll back recent changes, resulting in minimal or no damage to the integrity of the files or data. Ufs also supports hot fixes to automatically move data on damaged portions of disks to areas that are not damaged.

In Linux, the native file system is called the **extended file system (ext or ext fs)**, which is installed by default. Ext is modeled after ufs, but the first version contained some bugs, supported files to only 2 GB, and did not offer journaling. However, in Linux, ext provides an advantage over all other file systems because it enables the full range of built-in Linux commands, file manipulation, and security. Newer versions of Linux use either the second (ext2), third (ext3), or fourth (ext4) versions of the extended file system. Ext2 is a reliable file system that handles large disk storage. Ext3 has enhancements of ext2 with the addition of journaling. Ext4 supports file sizes up to 16 TB.

TIP

If you are not sure what file systems are incorporated in UNIX/Linux, you can determine them by viewing the contents of the /proc/filesystems file, or by using the *mount* command to display the mounted file systems. Table 4-6 lists a sampling of file systems that are compatible with UNIX/Linux systems.

Table 4-6 Typical file systems supported by UNIX/Linux

File system	Description
Extended file system (ext or ext fs) and the newer versions, second extended file system (ext2 or ext2 fs), third extended file system (ext3 or ext3 fs), and fourth extended file system (ext4 or ext4 fs)	File system that comes with Linux by default (compatible with Linux and FreeBSD)
High-performance file system (hpfs)	File system developed for use with the OS/2 operating system
msdos	File system that offers compatibility with FAT12 and FAT16 (does not support long filenames); typically installed to enable UNIX to read floppy disks made in MS-DOS or Windows
International Standard Operating system (iso9660 in Linux, hsfs in Solaris, cd9660 in FreeBSD)	File system developed for DVD/CD-ROM use; does not support long filenames
Proc file system	File system that presents information about the kernel status and the use of memory (not truly a physical file system, but a logical file system)
Network file system (nfs)	File system developed by Sun Microsystems for UNIX systems to support network access and sharing of files (such as uploading and downloading files) and supported on virtually all UNIX/Linux versions as well as by many other operating systems
Swap file system	File system for the swap space; swap space is disk space used exclusively to store spillover information from memory, when memory is full (called *virtual memory*), and is used by virtually all UNIX/Linux systems
UNIX file system (ufs; also called the Berkeley Fast File System)	Original file system for UNIX that is compatible with virtually all UNIX systems and most Linux systems
umsdos	File system that is compatible with extended FAT16 as used by Windows NT, 2000, XP, Server 2003, Vista, 7, and Server 2008, but it also supports security permissions, file ownership, and long filenames
vfat	File system that is compatible with FAT32 and supports long filenames
ntfs	File system used by Windows starting with Windows NT 3.1
Global File System (GFS and GFS2)	File system used by Linux computer clusters
XFS	64-bit high-performance journaling file system that is excellent at handling large files

The main difference between native UNIX file systems, such as ufs and ext, and those covered earlier in the chapter lies in the way information is physically stored on the disk. Because ufs and ext are the most popular file systems across UNIX platforms, we detail them here and lump them under the heading of "The UNIX/Linux file system." Both file systems use the same structure, which is built on the concept of information nodes, or **inodes.** Each file has an inode and is identified by an inode number. Inode 0 contains the root of the folder structure (/) and is the jumping-off point for all other inodes. This concept is shown in Figure 4-12.

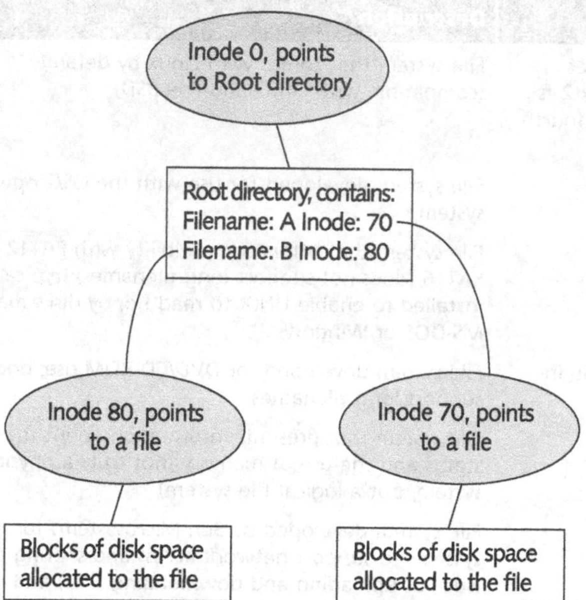

Figure 4-12 UNIX/Linux information nodes (inodes) design

You can display inode information for directories and files by using the *ls -i* command. Also, note that in most UNIX/Linux systems (commonly referred to as *nix*), a folder is technically just a file that can hold other files.

An inode contains the name of a file and general information about that file. In terms of general information, each inode indicates user and group ownership, access mode (read, write, and execute security permissions), the size and type of the file, the date the file was created, and the date the file was last modified and read.

The pointer information is based on logical blocks. Each disk is divided into logical blocks ranging in size from 512 to 8192 bytes or more, depending on the version of UNIX/Linux, but blocks can also be divided into multiple sub-blocks or fractions as needed by the file system. The inode for a file contains a pointer (number) that tells the operating system how to locate the first in a set of one or more logical blocks that contain the specific file contents. The inode can also specify the number of blocks or links to the first block used by the folder or file. In short, the inode tells the operating system where to find a file on the hard disk.

The file system itself is identified by the superblock. The **superblock** contains information about the layout of blocks, sectors, and cylinder groups on the file system. This information is the key to finding anything on the file system, and it should never change. Without the superblock, the file system cannot be accessed. For this reason, many copies of the superblock are written into the file system at the time of file system creation. If the superblock is damaged, you can copy one of the superblock copies over the damaged superblock to restore access to the file system.

Note that the inode does not contain a filename; the filename is stored in a folder, which in itself is no more than a file. In it is stored the names of the files and the inode to which they are connected.

4

Several folder entries can point to the same inode; this is called a hard link. Hard links make it possible to have one file appear in several folders, or in the same folder under several names, without using extra disk space. In Figure 4-13, there are two folders: Marketing and Sales. In the Marketing folder is a file named ClientsFile that points to inode 20301, and in the Sales folder a file named CustomerFile points to the same inode. ClientsFile and CustomerFile are the exact same file.

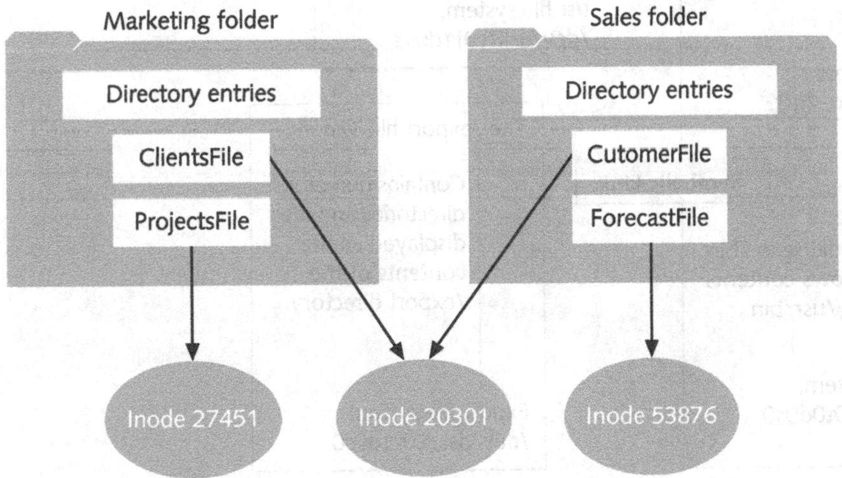

Figure 4-13 Hard links—multiple folder entries point to the same inode

The inode keeps a counter that tells how many folder entries point to a file. Deleting a file is achieved by deleting the last folder entry, which brings the inode link count down to 0, meaning the file has effectively been removed.

A UNIX/Linux system can have many file systems. Unlike the Windows environment, where drive letters are often used to access each file system, UNIX/Linux uses only mount points, in which each file system is a subfolder of the root of the file system, which is always designated as /.

In UNIX/Linux, all file systems are referred to by a path (see Figure 4-14). The path starts with root (/). If other file systems are to be used, a folder is created on the root file system—for example, a folder named "usr." Then, using the *mount* command, the UNIX/Linux operating system is told to associate the root inode of another file system to the empty folder. This process can be repeated many times, and there is no hard limit to the number of file systems that can be mounted this way, short of the number of inodes in the root file system. Every file in every file system on a computer is thus referred to by a long folder path, and jumping from one file system to another is seamless.

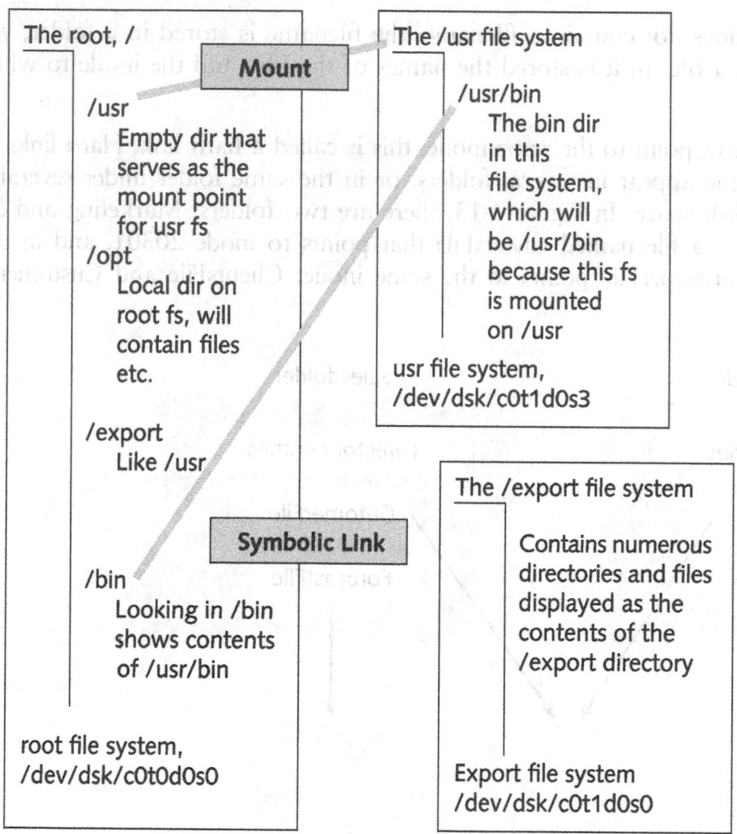

Figure 4-14 UNIX/Linux file system paths

The *mount* command has several options; typing it without parameters results in a display of the disks (and file systems) that are currently mounted. For each disk, you will see the name of the partition and the path on which it was mounted.

The UNIX/Linux operating system and file system treat uppercase and lowercase characters as different characters; a file named HELLO is different from a file named hello, which is in turn different from one named Hello. Therefore, it is extremely important to type UNIX/Linux filenames exactly as they appear.

As mentioned, a folder is nothing more than a special file. There are several other special files in the UNIX/Linux file system. For example, disks themselves are referenced by a special inode called a device. There are two types of devices: raw devices and block devices. A **raw device** has no logical division in blocks, whereas a **block device** does. Every device the UNIX/Linux computer uses must be represented by a device inode, whether it is a disk, a serial port, or an Ethernet (network) card. These devices have special parameters in the inode that enable the OS to figure out how to get to them. All partitions of all disks appear as devices. For example, an ext3 partition on a hard disk may be represented as /dev/hda1. Devices are normally kept in the /dev or /devices folder. When you look at the output of the *mount* command, you will see your disks referenced this way.

4

The **symbolic link** is another special feature of the UNIX/Linux file system we should mention here. As previously indicated, it is possible to link multiple folder entries to one inode. For this to work, the inode and the folder entry must be on the same disk partition. If you want to link a folder entry to a file that is on a different partition, you must use a symbolic link. This is a special file that has a flag set in the inode to identify it as a symbolic link. The content of the file is a path that, when followed, leads to another file. Note that a hard link, when created, must point to a valid inode and will therefore always be valid. A symbolic link is merely a pointer to a file. It is possible to create symbolic links that point to files that do not exist, or to remove the file to which a symbolic link points without removing the link. In such cases, you might end up with a symbolic link that appears to be a valid file when viewed in a folder, but when opened returns a "no such file" error. Another interesting effect of using symbolic links is that it is possible to create loops. You can make a Folder A, which contains a Folder B, which contains a link back to Folder A. However, this can become extremely confusing. Hard links and symbolic links are made with the *ln* command. The *ln* command used with no options makes a hard link, and with the *-s* option makes a symbolic link. The first option is the name of the existing file, followed by the name of the link you want to create.

One way to save time in typing is to create a link to a folder that has a long path. For example, assume that you store many files in the /user/bus/inventory folder. Each time you want to see a listing of that folder, you must type *ls /user/bus/inventory*. If you enter *ln / user/bus/inventory* to create a link to that folder, in the future you only have to type *ls inventory* to see its contents. To learn more about the *ln* command, type *man ln* in a terminal or command prompt window, and then press Enter. *Man* is the command for displaying the contents of the online manual pages for a specific command, such as *ls*.

As with all other operating systems discussed so far, you first have to partition a disk to use the UNIX/Linux file system. The command used to partition the disk differs slightly from one version of UNIX to another. In most UNIX systems, either *fdisk* or *format* does the job. Typing *man fdisk* or *man format* and pressing Enter at the command prompt gives you an overview of available command options. Figure 4-15 shows the man page for the *fdisk* command in Fedora Linux.

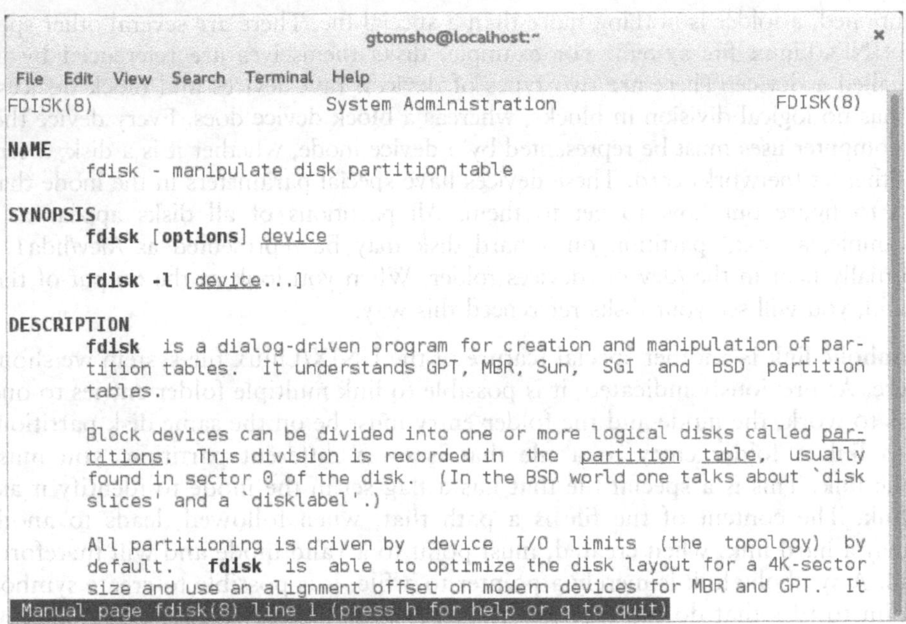

gtomsho@localhost:~
File Edit View Search Terminal Help
FDISK(8) System Administration FDISK(8)
NAME
fdisk - manipulate disk partition table
SYNOPSIS
fdisk [options] device
fdisk -l [device...]
DESCRIPTION
fdisk is a dialog-driven program for creation and manipulation of partition tables. It understands GPT, MBR, Sun, SGI and BSD partition tables.
Block devices can be divided into one or more logical disks called partitions. This division is recorded in the partition table, usually found in sector 0 of the disk. (In the BSD world one talks about `disk slices' and a `disklabel'.)
All partitioning is driven by device I/O limits (the topology) by default. fdisk is able to optimize the disk layout for a 4K-sector size and use an alignment offset on modern devices for MBR and GPT. It
Manual page fdisk(8) line 1 (press h for help or q to quit)

Figure 4-15 The man page for the *fdisk* command
Source: Fedora Linux

Once a partition is made, it is time to create the file system. To do this, you must know the device name of the partition on which you want to create the file system. This name can be obtained from the *print partition table* command in *fdisk* or *format*. The most convenient way to create a new file system is with the *newfs* command. Simply type *newfs*, followed by the name of the device. After you confirm that you want to create a new file system, you will see a progress report that shows you where copies of the superblocks are written, as well as some information about the cylinder group and the number of inodes. When *newfs* is completed, you can make a mount point for the new file system using the *mkdir* command. (Note that a mount point in UNIX/Linux is nothing more than an empty folder—the disk location in which the file system contents will appear.) If, for example, you created a file system on */dev/sdb1* and you want to mount it in the /test mount point, you type *mkdir /test*. Next, you mount the file system by typing *mount /dev/sdb1 /test*, and now you are ready to use the new file system. *Newfs* is available in many versions of UNIX, such as in Solaris UNIX, but it is not available in all versions of Linux, including Red Hat Enterprise Linux and Fedora. In UNIX/Linux varieties where *newfs* is not available, *mkfs* should be used instead. (*Mkfs* is available in Red Hat Enterprise Linux and Fedora.) The use of *mkfs* is less desirable because it requires the user to specify many parameters, such as the size of the file system, the block size, number of inodes, number of superblock copies and their locations, and a few others, depending on the version of UNIX/Linux. The *newfs* utility takes care of all these details automatically.

UNIX/Linux is very picky when it comes to file system consistency. If it finds problems on the file system in the inodes, superblock, or folder structures, it will shut down. When you save a file to disk, the system first stores part of the data in memory, until it has time to write the file to disk. If for some reason your computer stops working before the data is written to disk, you can end up with a damaged file system. This is why UNIX/Linux machines should always be shut down using the proper commands, which ensure that all data is stored on disk before the machine is brought down. In normal operation, all data waiting to be saved to disk in memory is written to disk every 30 seconds. You can manually force a write of all data in memory by using the *sync* command. When the system is properly shut down, the file systems are unmounted. Whenever the machine starts up, UNIX/Linux checks the file systems to make sure they are all working properly. To do this, the operating system verifies the integrity of the superblock, the inodes, all cluster groups, and all folder entries. The program that performs this operation is the file system checker, also known as *fsck*.

You can manually run *fsck* at any time to perform file system checks after the system is up, but take great care when doing this. If data on the disk is changed while an *fsck* is in progress, the results may be disastrous. The most common problems found when *fsck* is run are unlinked inodes, folder entries with no associated inodes, and wrong free block counts. All of these can be a result of a system that was not properly shut down. If these errors occur frequently, hardware failure may be imminent.

Table 4-7 presents a summary of useful commands for managing UNIX/Linux file systems.

Table 4-7 UNIX/Linux file system commands

Command	Description
cat	Displays the contents of a file to the screen
cd	Changes to another folder
cp	Copies a file to another folder (and you can rename the file at the same time)
fdisk	Formats and partitions a disk in some UNIX systems, such as Linux
format	Formats and partitions a disk in some UNIX systems, such as Solaris
ls	Lists contents of a folder
mkdir	Creates a folder
mkfs	Creates a file system (but requires more parameters than *newfs*)
mount	Lists the disk currently mounted; also mounts file systems and devices (such as a DVD/CD-ROM)
mv	Moves a file to a different folder
newfs	Creates a new file system in some versions of UNIX/Linux
rm	Removes a file or folder
sync	Forces information in memory to be written to disk
touch	Creates an empty file
umount	Unmounts a file system

The Macintosh File System

The original **Macintosh Filing System** (MFS) of 1984 was limited to keeping track of 128 documents, applications, or folders. This was a reasonable limit when the only storage device was a 400 KB floppy disk drive. As larger disks became available, however, the need for folders and subfolders became obvious, and Apple responded with the **Hierarchical Filing System** (HFS) in 1986.

Like FAT16, HFS divides a volume into, at most, 2^{16} (65,536) units. (*Volume* is the Mac term for a disk or disk partition.) On PC systems, these units are called *clusters* or *allocation units*. On the Mac, they are called **allocation blocks**, but the principle is the same. Interestingly, while UNIX/Linux and Windows operating systems report file sizes in terms of their actual size, the Macintosh operating system sometimes reports file sizes in terms of logical size, based on the number of allocation blocks occupied by the file. The best way to view the actual size of a file is to use the Mac's Get Info option, which shows many other types of information about a file.

In 1998, Apple released Mac OS 8.1, which introduced a new disk format, Hierarchical Filing System Extended Format. This format was variously referred to as Mac OS HFS+, Mac OS Extended, or Mac OS **Extended (HFS+)**, which is used today in Mac OS X. The newer HFS+ format increases the number of allocation blocks per volume to 2^{32}. This format creates smaller allocation blocks (clusters) and more efficient disk utilization. Systems that use Mac OS 8.1 or later can format disks in either the Mac OS Standard (HFS) or Mac OS Extended (HFS+) format. However, Macintoshes with pre-8.1 versions of the OS can't read disks in Extended format. Volumes that are smaller than 32 MB must also continue to use Standard format.

In Mac OS X version 3.0, Mac OS Extended (HFS+) includes several new features:

- An optional case-sensitive format to make the file system more compatible with other UNIX/Linux systems
- Journaling, which is turned on by default (see Figure 4-16) so that data can be recovered from a journal file if a disk or system problem occurs while data is being updated or modified
- The ability to store up to 16 TB of data, which is particularly important for the Mac OS X Server version

4

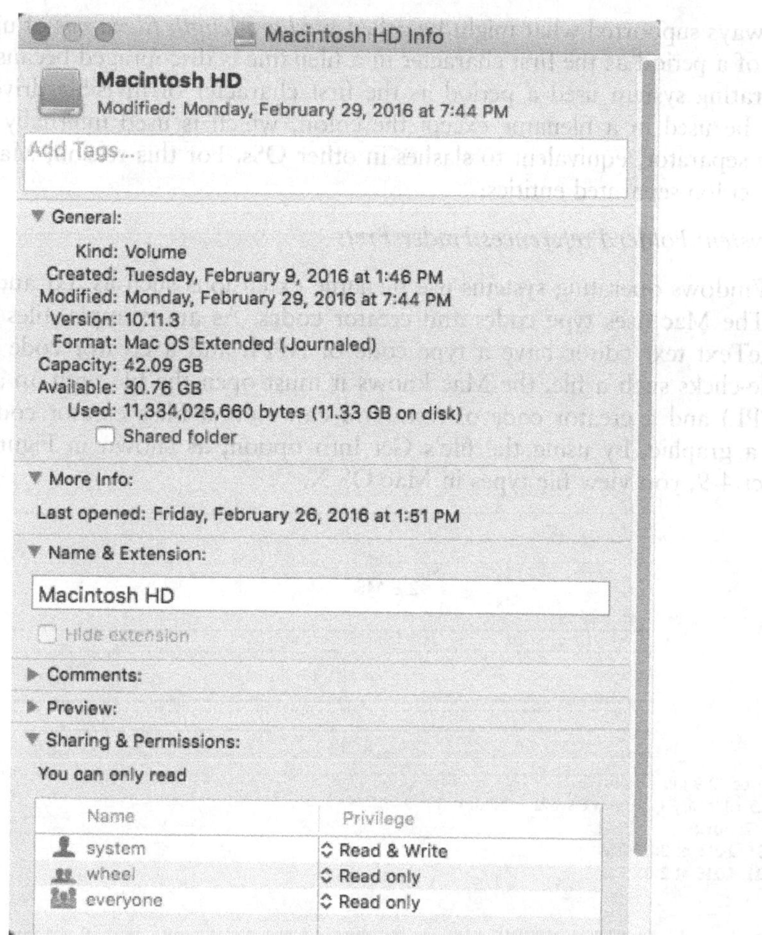

Figure 4-16 Mac OS X using the Mac OS Extended (HFS+) file system

Source: Mac OS X

The first two sectors of a Mac-formatted disk are the boot sectors, or boot blocks in Macintosh terminology. The boot blocks identify the filing system, the names of important system files, and other important information. The boot blocks are followed by the **volume information block**, which points to other important areas of information, such as the location of the system files and the catalog and extents b-trees.

The **catalog b-tree** is the list of all files on the volume. It keeps track of a file's name, its logical location in the folder structure, its physical location on the disk surface, and the locations and sizes of the file's data fork and resource forks (as discussed later in the chapter). The **extents b-tree** keeps track of the location of file fragments, or extents.

Macintoshes can read and write to disks from other operating systems. For instance, Macs can read iso9660 DVD/CD-ROMs using a dedicated driver. Macs can also read all manner of MS-DOS- and Windows-formatted disks, thanks to pre-Mac OS X tools such as the PC Exchange control panel, and thanks to various Mac OS X tools, such as those offered through System Preferences and as disk utilities.

The Mac OS has always supported what might be called *medium-length filenames* of up to 31 characters. The use of a period as the first character in a filename is discouraged because older versions of the operating system used a period as the first character of invisible driver files. Any character may be used in a filename except the colon, which is used internally by the Mac OS as a folder separator, equivalent to slashes in other OSs. For this reason, Macintosh paths are written as colon-separated entities:

Hard Drive:System Folder:Preferences:Finder Prefs

UNIX/Linux and Windows operating systems use filename extensions such as .txt and .gif to identify file types. The Mac uses **type codes** and **creator codes.** As an example, files created with Apple's SimpleText text editor have a type code of APPL and a creator code of ttxt. When a user double-clicks such a file, the Mac knows it must open the file with an application (type code APPL) and a creator code of ttxt. You can view a file's creator code, such as a JPEG file for a graphic, by using the file's Get Info option, as shown in Figure 4-17. In Hands-On Project 4-9, you view file types in Mac OS X.

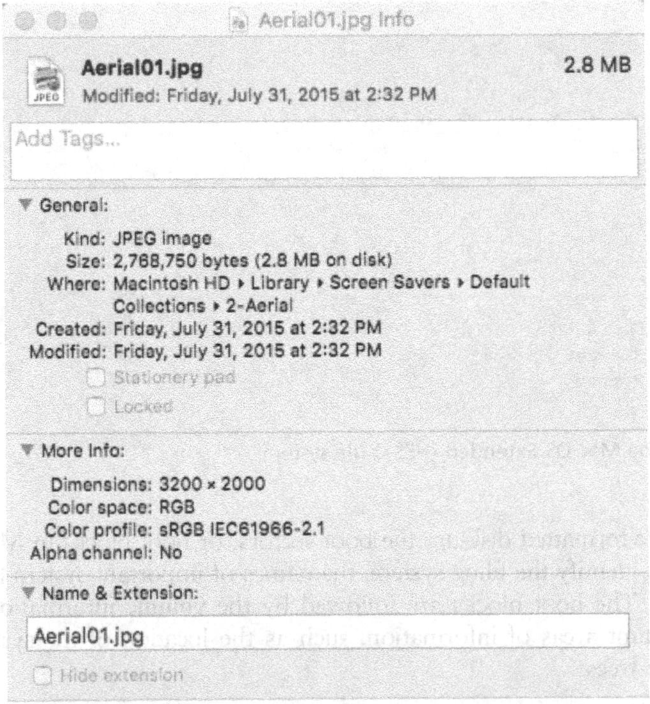

Figure 4-17 Using the Get Info option for a JPEG file
Source: Mac OS X

The type and creator codes facilitate the Mac's use of icons. Documents do not store their own icons; instead, the Mac gets the icon from the creating application. Instead of accessing the application each time the icon must be displayed, the Mac stores the icons and file associations in invisible files called the *desktop databases*. Each disk or volume has its own desktop databases. "Rebuilding the desktop" on a Macintosh means rebuilding these database files, and is a common troubleshooting step when icons appear incorrectly. You can rebuild the desktop on a disk at startup by holding down the command and option keys. For removable media, hold down the command and option keys before inserting the disk.

One way in which Macintosh files are unique is that they can contain two parts, or forks: the data fork and the resource fork. The **data fork** contains frequently changing information, such as word-processing data, while the **resource fork** contains fixed information, including a program's icons, menu resources, and splash screens. One advantage of resource forks for programmers is that they modularize the program. For instance, it becomes very easy to change the text of a warning dialog or the name of a menu item without having to change the underlying code, so customization and internationalization are easier.

Folders can be created using the New Folder option in the Finder's File menu and in the Save and Save As dialog boxes in most applications. All volumes have two special, invisible folders: Trash and Desktop. If you move a file's icon from a USB drive to the desktop, the file still resides in the USB drive's Desktop folder. Likewise, you can move the file's icon to the Trash can without deleting it, and it will still reside in the USB drive's Trash folder. You can prove this to yourself by ejecting the USB drive and inserting it in another Macintosh. The files will appear on the desktop, and the Trash can will bulge.

Apple's equivalent of the UNIX/Linux symbolic link and Windows shortcut is the **alias**, which was introduced in System 7.0 in 1991. Files, folders, applications, and disks can be aliased. The system-level Alias Manager keeps track of the original item, even if it is moved or renamed. The word *alias* is added to the filename when the alias is created, and the filename is presented in italicized text. Beginning in OS 8.5, aliases also have small arrows on their icons, similar to shortcuts in Windows-based operating systems. In Hands-On Project 4-9, you create an alias.

Mac OS X comes with two important disk utilities: Disk Utility for managing disk drives and Disk First Aid for repairing disk problems. Figure 4-18 shows Disk Utility after running First Aid on Macintosh HD.

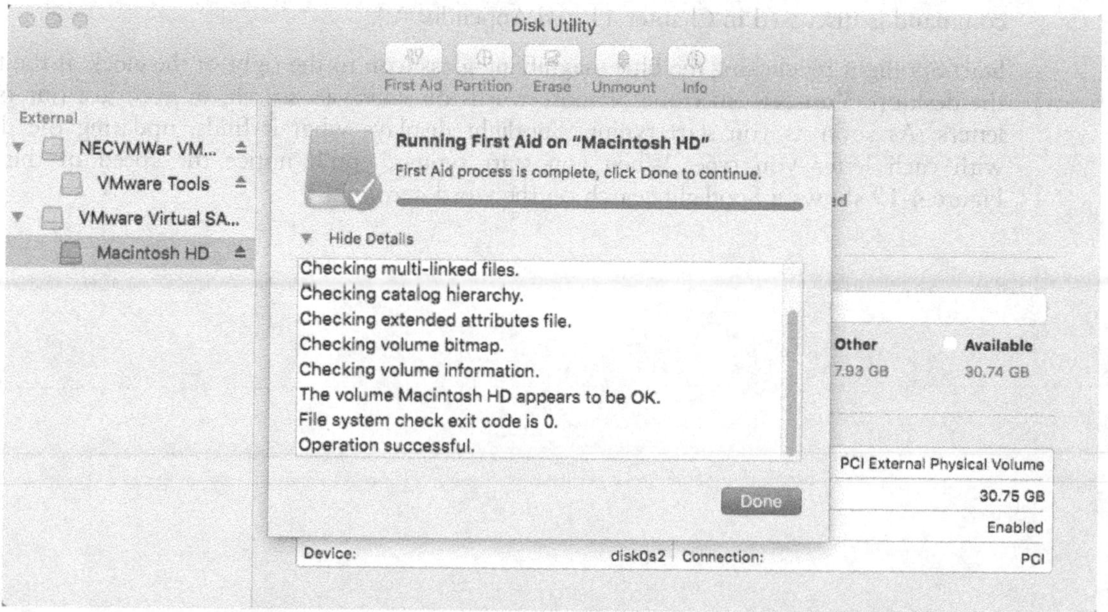

Figure 4-18 Mac OS X Disk Utility running First Aid

Source: Mac OS X

Older versions of Mac OS X came with the Sherlock program, which can search disks for filenames and text within files. These operations are extremely fast because Sherlock pre-indexes local disks, just as search engines index Web pages. Because indexing takes significant processor time, it can be scheduled for times when the computer is not heavily used. Sherlock also functions as a program for querying multiple Internet search engines or the site search engines available on many Web sites.

Spotlight replaced Sherlock in Mac OS X 10.4 Tiger, although Sherlock continued to ship with Mac OS until it was officially retired with the release of Mac OS X 10.5 Leopard. Mac OS X users have always faced the same problems as Windows users when it comes to organizing and finding files. Nothing is more frustrating than knowing you have created and saved a document, spreadsheet, song, or photo and being unable to find it. Spotlight does the following for you:

- Indexes files so you can find them faster
- Enables you to search for something just by typing a few letters of the name
- Quickly searches the computer's nooks and crannies for what you want, even if you're not sure how to spell it exactly
- Works in conjunction with the smart folders capability so you can organize files you've found according to different characteristics you choose

One reason for Spotlight's speed is that it indexes not only by filenames, but by metadata associated with documents, such as the author, creation, date, and lots of other information. It also indexes based on individual words inside regular text files, word-processing files, and even PDF files used by Adobe. Spotlight does not work on files in the UNIX system and kernel. For these files you have to use UNIX commands, such as *find* or *locate*. (The *find* command is discussed in Chapter 11 and Appendix A.)

Start Spotlight by clicking the blue magnifying-glass icon to the right of the clock at the top of the desktop. You can enter one or more words on which to search, or even just one or two letters. As soon as you start typing, Spotlight displays what it finds, updating the display with each letter you type. When you start typing, you'll notice the speed of this tool. Figure 4-19 shows a Spotlight search on the word *account*.

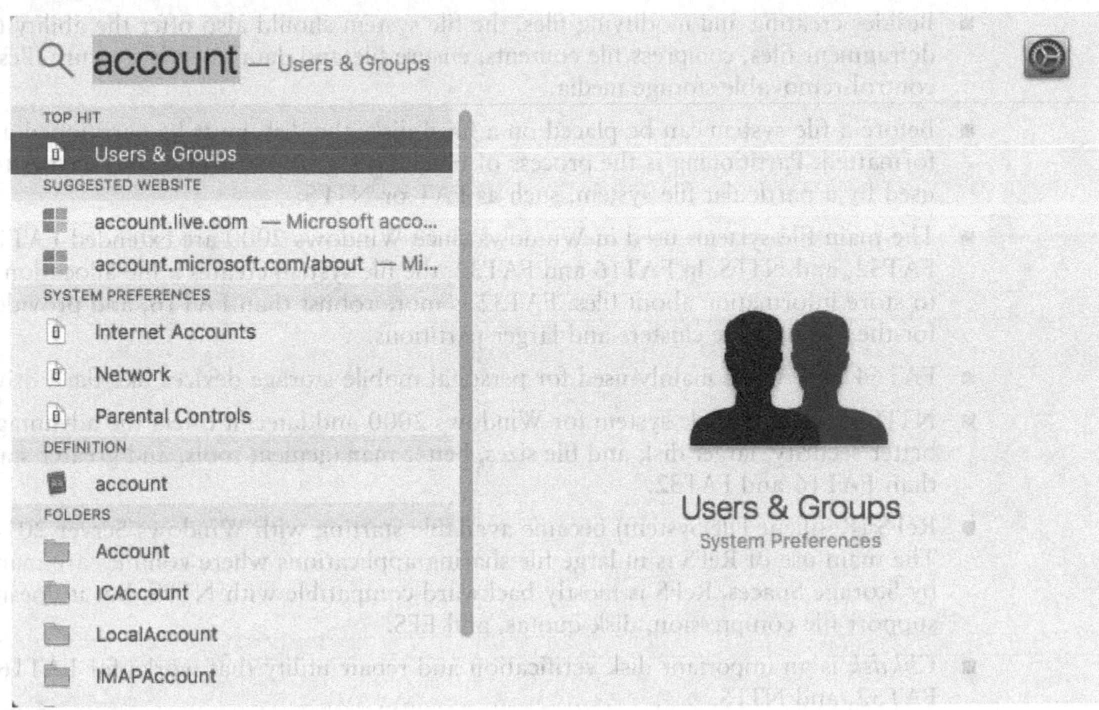

Figure 4-19 A Spotlight search in Mac OS X

Source: Mac OS X

When the Mac is shut down normally using the Apple menu's Shut Down option, a flag is set on the hard drive. In the event of a crash or forced reboot, this flag is not set. If the flag is not set, the Mac will see during the next startup that the computer was not shut down properly and run a disk integrity check.

The Mac is extremely versatile at booting from different devices. Like other operating systems, the Mac will boot from a DVD/CD-ROM inserted during the boot sequence. If the disk does not contain a valid System Folder, the Mac will eject the disk and continue searching for a bootable device, such as a SCSI device. Since the early 1990s, Macs have been able to boot from a DVD/CD-ROM drive—simply press the C key while booting up. Pressing the Shift-Option-Delete-Apple (SODA) keys during the boot sequence will bypass the internal hard drive and boot from the next drive in the SCSI chain.

Chapter Summary

- One of the basic functions of an operating system is to enable you to store and access information on a computer or other digital device. This information is managed, stored, and retrieved through a file system.
- Some of the tasks performed by a file system include providing a convenient interface, providing a hierarchical structure, storing file metadata, organizing space on a storage device, and providing utilities to maintain and manage the file system.

- Besides creating and modifying files, the file system should also offer the ability to defragment files, compress file contents, ensure file and data integrity, secure files, and control removable storage media.
- Before a file system can be placed on a hard disk, the disk must be partitioned and formatted. Partitioning is the process of blocking a group of tracks and sectors to be used by a particular file system, such as FAT or NTFS.
- The main file systems used in Windows since Windows 2000 are extended FAT16, FAT32, and NTFS. In FAT16 and FAT32, the file system creates a file allocation table to store information about files. FAT32 is more robust than FAT16, and provides for the use of more clusters and larger partitions.
- FAT64 (exFAT) is mainly used for personal mobile storage devices like flash drives.
- NTFS is the native file system for Windows 2000 and later; it offers the advantages of better security, larger disk and file sizes, better management tools, and greater stability than FAT16 and FAT32.
- ReFS (Resilient File System) became available starting with Windows Server 2012. The main use of ReFS is in large file-sharing applications where volumes are managed by Storage Spaces. ReFS is mostly backward-compatible with NTFS, but it doesn't support file compression, disk quotas, and EFS.
- *Chkdsk* is an important disk verification and repair utility that works for FAT16, FAT32, and NTFS.
- UNIX and Linux support many different file systems, but typically they employ ufs or ext.
- Ufs and ext use information nodes (inodes) to organize information about files. Also, a UNIX/Linux system can have many file systems mounted as subfolders of the root.
- Different varieties of UNIX/Linux use different file system utilities, such as *fdisk* and *format*, to partition and format disks. The *fsck* (file system checker) utility is used to verify the integrity of UNIX/Linux file systems.
- Mac OS X uses the Mac OS Extended (HFS+) file system, which is an enhancement of HFS and was introduced in 1998 with Mac OS 8.1. Like NTFS, the Mac OS Extended file system makes more efficient utilization of disk space and supports larger disk sizes, and in Mac OS X version 10.3 and higher, it offers a case-sensitive capability, journaling, and support for 8 EB disk storage.
- Two important Mac OS X disk tools include the Disk Utility and Disk First Aid.

Key Terms

8.3 filenames An older filename format in which the name of the file can be up to eight characters long, followed by a period and an extension of three characters. See also *extension*.

active partition The logical portion of a hard disk drive that is currently being used to store data. In a PC system, the partition that contains the bootable operating system.

alias In the Macintosh file system, a feature that presents an icon representing an executable file. Equivalent to the UNIX/Linux link and the Windows shortcut.

allocation block In the Macintosh file system, a division of hard disk data, equivalent to the Windows disk cluster. Each Macintosh volume is divided into 2^{16} (65,535) individual units.

bad clusters On a hard disk drive, areas of the surface that cannot be used to safely store data. Bad clusters are usually identified by the *format* command or one of the hard drive utilities, such as *chkdsk* or *fsck*.

block allocation A hard disk configuration scheme in which the disk is divided into logical blocks, which in turn are mapped to sectors, heads, and tracks.

4

block device In the UNIX/Linux file system, a device that is divided or configured into logical blocks. See also *raw device*.

boot block The UNIX/Linux and Mac OS X equivalent of the Windows Master Boot Record (MBR), the area of the hard disk that stores partition information for the disk. For example, on a Mac-formatted disk, the first two sectors are boot blocks that identify the filing system, the names of important system files, and other important information. See also *volume information block*.

catalog b-tree In the Macintosh file system, a list of all files on a given volume. Similar to a folder in the Windows file system.

CD-ROM File System (CDFS) A 32-bit file system used on CD-ROMs and DVDs.

cluster In Windows-based file systems, a logical block of information on a disk containing one or more sectors. Also called an *allocation unit*.

creator codes Hidden file characteristics in the Macintosh file system that indicate the program (software application) that created the file. See *type code*.

data fork The portion of a file in the Macintosh file system that stores the variable data associated with the file. Data fork information might include word-processing data, spreadsheet information, and so on.

defragmenter A tool that rearranges data on a disk in a continuous fashion, ridding the disk of scattered open clusters.

directory An organizational structure that contains files and may additionally contain subdirectories under it. A directory contains information about files, such as filenames, file sizes, date of creation, and file type. More commonly referred to as a *folder* in modern OSs.

disk label The UNIX/Linux equivalent of a partition table in MS-DOS or Windows systems. The disk label is a table containing information about each partition on a disk, such as the type of partition, size, and location.

disk quota Allocation of a specific amount of disk space to a user or application with the ability to ensure that the user or application cannot use more disk space than is specified in the allocation.

Distributed Link Tracking A technique introduced in NTFS 5 so that shortcuts, such as those on the desktop, are not lost when files are moved to another volume.

extended file system (ext or ext fs) The file system designed for Linux that is installed by default in Linux operating systems.

Extended (HFS+) A file system released in 1998 with Mac OS 8.1 and the file system used in Mac OS X.

extension In MS-DOS and Windows-based systems, the part of a filename that typically identifies the type of file associated with the name. File extensions are typically three characters long and include standard notations such as .sys, .exe, .bat, and so on.

extents b-tree A file system component that keeps track of the location of file fragments, or extents, in the Mac OS HFS file system.

file A set of data that is grouped in some logical manner, assigned a name, and stored on the disk.

file allocation table (FAT) A file management system that defines the way data is stored on a disk drive. The FAT stores information about a file's size and physical location on the disk.

file attributes File characteristics stored with the filename in the disk folder; attributes specify certain storage and operational parameters associated with the file, such as hidden, read-only, archive, and so on.

file system A design for storing and managing files on a disk drive.

folder See *directory*.

formatting The process of installing a file system on a disk partition.

hard link In Windows versions starting with Windows 2000 and UNIX/Linux, a file management technique that permits multiple folder entries to point to the same file.

Hierarchical Filing System (HFS) An early Apple Macintosh file system storage method that uses a hierarchical folder structure.

high-level formatting A process that prepares a disk partition (or removable media) for a specific file system.

hot fix A procedure used by a file system that can detect a damaged disk area and then automatically copy information from that area to another disk area that is not damaged.

inode Short for "information node." In UNIX/Linux, a system for storing key information about files.

journaling The ability of a file system or software (such as database software) to track file changes so that if a system crashes unexpectedly, it is possible to reconstruct files or to roll back changes with minimal or no damage.

linked list Used in FAT file systems so that when a file is written to disk, each cluster containing that file's data has a pointer to the location of the next cluster of data.

logical drive A software definition that divides a physical hard drive into multiple drives for file storage.

long filename (LFN) A name for a file, folder, or folder in a file system in which the name can be up to 255 characters in length. Long filenames in Windows, UNIX/Linux, and Mac OS systems are also POSIX compliant in that they honor uppercase and lowercase characters.

low-level format A software process that marks tracks and sectors on a disk. A low-level format is necessary before a disk can be partitioned and formatted.

Macintosh Filing System (MFS) The original Macintosh filing system, introduced in 1984. MFS was limited to keeping track of 128 documents, applications, or folders.

Master Boot Record (MBR) An area of a hard disk in MS-DOS and Windows that stores partition information about the disk. MBRs are not found on disks that do not support multiple partitions.

Master File Table (MFT) A storage organization system used with the NTFS file system. The MFT is located at the beginning of the partition.

metadata Information that describes data but is not the actual data.

mount A process that makes a disk partition or volume available for use by the operating system.

New Technology File System (NTFS) The file storage system that is the native system in Windows versions starting with Windows NT.

partitioning Blocking a group of tracks and sectors to be used by a particular file system, such as FAT or NTFS. Partitioning is a hard disk management technique that permits the installation of multiple file systems on a single disk or the configuration of multiple logical hard drives that use the same file system on a single physical hard drive.

partition table A table containing information about each partition on a disk, such as the type of partition, size, and location. Also, the partition table provides information to the computer about how to access the disk.

physical drive A hard drive in a computer that you can physically touch and that can be divided into one or more logical drives.

Portable Operating System Interface for UNIX (POSIX) A UNIX standard designed to ensure portability of applications among various versions of UNIX.

raw device In the UNIX/Linux file system, a device that has not been divided into logical blocks. See also *block device.*

Resilient File System (ReFS) A file system in Windows Server 2012 and later that is used in large file-sharing applications and that can correct some types of data corruption automatically.

resource fork In the Macintosh file system, the portion of a file that contains fixed information, such as a program's icons, menu resources, and splash screens.

root folder The highest-level folder in the structure of files and folders in a file system.

sectors Equally sized portions of a disk track. See *tracks*.

Spotlight The new way to search in Mac OS X, starting with version 10.4 Tiger. Spotlight stores a virtual index of everything on the system.

status bits Bits used as part of a folder entry to identify the type of file contained in each entry. The status bits in use are Volume, Folder, System, Hidden, Read-only, and Archive.

superblock In the UNIX/Linux file system, a special data block that contains information about the layout of blocks, sectors, and cylinder groups on the file system. This information is the key to finding anything on the file system, and it should never change.

switch An operating system command option that changes the way certain commands function. Command options, or switches, are usually entered as one or more letters, separated from the main command by a forward slash (/) in Windows and by a dash (-) in UNIX/Linux.

symbolic link A special file in the UNIX/Linux file system that permits a folder link to a file that is on a different partition.

tracks Concentric rings that cover an entire disk like grooves on a phonograph record. Each ring is divided into sectors in which to store data.

type code In the Macintosh file system, embedded file information that denotes which applications were used to create the files. Mac OS type codes are used in much the same way as Windows file extensions that identify file types with .txt, .doc, and other extensions. See *creator codes*.

Unicode A 16-bit character code that allows for the definition of up to 65,536 characters.

Universal Disk Format (UDF) A removable disk formatting standard used for large-capacity CD-ROMs and DVD-ROMs.

UNIX file system (ufs) A file system supported in most versions of UNIX/Linux; ufs is a hierarchical (tree structure) file system that is expandable, supports large storage, provides excellent security, and is reliable. Ufs employs information nodes (inodes).

volume A portion of a disk that has a file system installed and is ready to be accessed for data storage and retrieval.

volume information block On a Mac-formatted disk, the sector after the boot blocks. See also *boot block*. The volume information block points to other important areas of information, such as the location of the system files and the catalog and extents trees.

volume label A series of characters, commonly used as a nickname, that identify a volume.

volume mount point An empty folder into which a volume is mounted. See *mount*.

Review Questions

1. As you are using some files on a workstation running Linux, you determine that a few of the files seem to be corrupted. What should you do?
   a. Close all files and applications and run *fsck*.
   b. Start DiskScan to check for file links.
   c. Reformat your disk using the *format* command.
   d. Use the Disk Check utility, which can be run at any time.
2. You are installing Windows 10 on a new disk that has only been low-level formatted. What is the first thing you need to do to prepare the disk?
   a. Use Disk Scrub to ensure there are no bad spots on the disk.
   b. Format the disk for NTFS.
   c. Partition the disk.
   d. Initialize the disk with the root folder.

3. You need to create a new folder in a Linux system and you choose to do so from a terminal window. Which of the following commands enables you to create a folder?
   a. *fdisk*
   b. *mkdir*
   c. *mkfs*
   d. *mkfsdir*
4. What file system is used on a hard disk in a computer running Mac OS X?
   a. Macintosh Filing System (MFS)
   b. Macintosh Network File System (MNFS)
   c. Extended file system (ext)
   d. Mac OS Extended (HFS+) file system
5. Your assistant has documentation that shows how to modify a device file in Linux, but the documentation does not mention which folder to find the file in. Which folder should you suggest?
   a. /mnt
   b. /var
   c. /dev
   d. /proc
6. On a Windows-based system, which of the following are contained in the Master Boot Record? (Choose all that apply.)
   a. disk signature
   b. boot program
   c. boot block
   d. partition table for the active partition
7. You developed a proposal for the president of your company several months ago. You know you saved it, but you are not sure where. You created the proposal on your Mac OS X El Capitan computer. Which of the following is the easiest option for finding the document? (Choose all that apply.)
   a. Use Get Info on each of the folders that you think the document might be in. Check the creation date. When you find dates that look promising, open the folder and check the documents.
   b. Use the search tool Sherlock to search for text within files.
   c. Use the UNIX command-line prompt to search your Mac for the proposal using *find* or *locate*.
   d. Use Spotlight to search for the document on your Mac.

4

8. You need to find the date and time a file was created and the file's size. Where should you look?
   a. in the volume label
   b. in the Master File Table
   c. in the file metadata
   d. in the file allocation table
9. You need to find out more about the *fdisk* utility and the commands associated with it before you set up a new Linux system in addition to the one you are already using. What command can you use on your present system to find out more about *fdisk*?
   a. *man fdisk*
   b. *fdisk /?*
   c. *fdisk /help*
   d. *find fdisk*
10. Mac OS X files can contain which of the following? (Choose all that apply.)
    a. application generator
    b. data fork
    c. extension marker
    d. resource fork
11. Users on your organization's Windows Server 2012 R2 server are beginning to take up excessive disk space on the NTFS volumes. You have plenty of disk space now, but you're concerned about this situation in the future. What can you do?
    a. Enforce stronger security so it is harder for users to write files to their home directories.
    b. Establish disk quotas.
    c. Encrypt portions of the users' home directories so they can only be used by the Administrator account.
    d. Use bigger blocks for the partition.
12. In which file system would you find the Master File Table?
    a. FAT12
    b. NFS
    c. NTFS
    d. ufs
13. What command in Windows Server 2012 can you use to format a disk for FAT32?
    a. *fdisk:FAT32*
    b. *format /fs:FAT32*
    c. *part /FAT32*
    d. *mkdisk FAT32*

14. You are installing a file-sharing application on a Windows Server 2012 R2 server in which the volumes are managed by Storage Spaces and fault tolerance is a major consideration. Which file system should you use?
    a. FAT64
    b. ReFS
    c. NTFS
    d. ext4
15. In what file system(s) would you find inodes? (Choose all that apply.)
    a. FAT16
    b. ufs
    c. ext3
    d. NTFS
16. The president of your company uses Mac OS X and wants to find out more about a file, such as whether the file is a TIFF document. What tool should she use?
    a. the Get Info option for the file
    b. Explorer
    c. Files
    d. the Window options for the file
17. Which of the following is a process that marks the location of tracks and sectors on a disk?
    a. disk tracking
    b. a low-level format
    c. a high-level format
    d. etching
18. In FAT32, file characteristics such as Hidden and Read-only are examples of ______________.
    a. cluster designations
    b. formatting properties
    c. file attributes
    d. properties applied only to files and folders in the root
19. You run a computer support business and one of your customers calls to say he formatted his hard drive because it seemed to contain lots of bad clusters. The problem is that now the operating system won't start. What might be the problem?
    a. He performed a quick format that does not fix bad clusters.
    b. A hard disk can only be formatted once.
    c. He formatted using the wrong driver.
    d. Formatting the disk destroyed all the files on it, including the operating system files.

20. Which of the following holds information about the layout of blocks and sectors in the UNIX file system?
    a. root
    b. file allocation table
    c. superblock
    d. folder flag

Hands-On Projects

Project 4-1: Explore the File System in Windows

File systems store and manage files, like a personal assistant to the file system user. In this project, you employ File Explorer to view folders and files in Windows. Also, you view the information that is stored for files.

1. Start your Windows 10 computer and log on. Right-click **Start** and click **File Explorer.**
2. In the left pane, click to expand **This PC,** if necessary. Double-click **Local Disk (C:)** to view folders and files on the hard drive.
3. In the right pane, double-click **Windows** to view more folders and files.
4. Click the **View** menu and then click **Content** in the Layout section of the Ribbon to change the view of the folders and files.
5. Click to select the **File name extensions** and **Hidden items** check boxes, if they are not already checked. You'll see additional folders and file extensions.
6. Close File Explorer.
7. Stay logged on if you are continuing to the next project.

Project 4-2: Create Folders in Windows

When you use an operating system, you will often need to create a new folder. In this project, you learn how to create a new folder in Windows.

1. Start your Windows 10 computer and log on, if necessary. Right-click **Start** and click **File Explorer.**
2. In the left pane, click to expand **This PC,** if necessary. Double-click **Local Disk (C:)** to view folders and files on the hard drive.
3. In the right pane, double-click the **Users** folder and then double-click the folder that has the same name as the account you used to log on.
4. Click the **Home** tab on the Ribbon and click **New folder.**

5. Type your initials and then the word **folder**. For example, the user entered "GTfolder" as the folder name in Figure 4-20. Press **Enter**. (Don't delete this folder because you will use it again in Hands-On Project 4-3.)

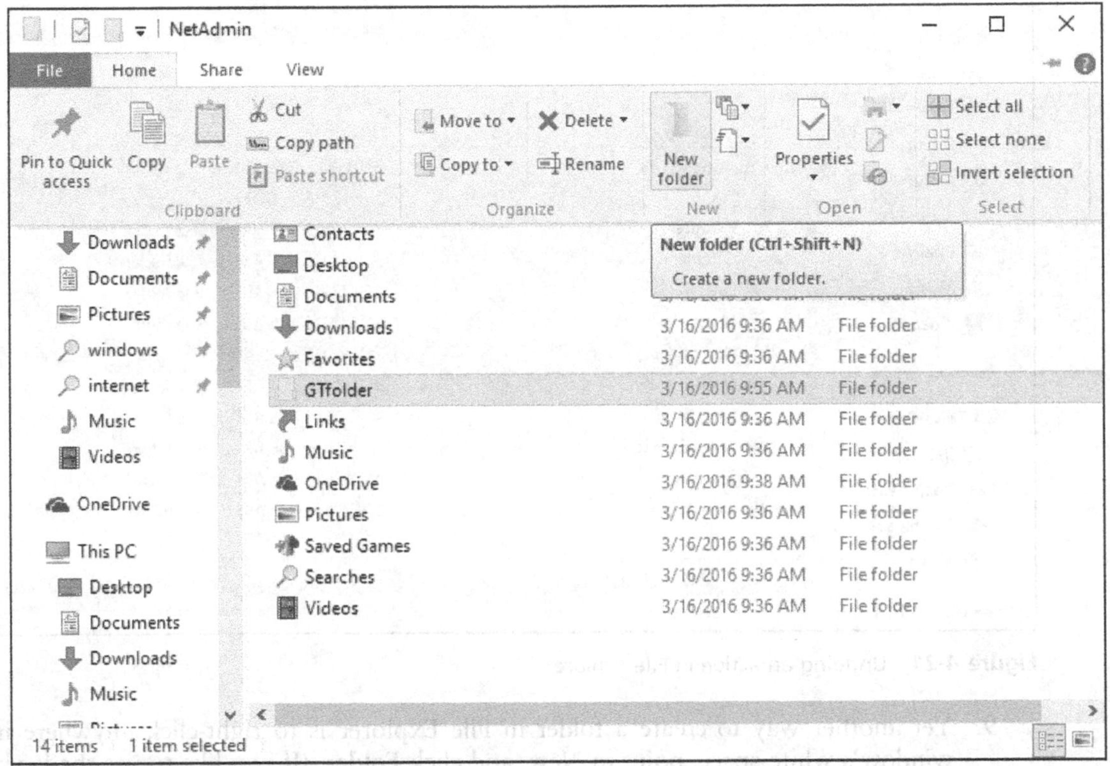

Figure 4-20 Creating a folder in Windows 10

6. Right-click the folder you just created and click **Properties** to view its associated properties. Click each tab to quickly get an overview of the kinds of properties you can configure for the folder.
7. Click **Cancel**.
8. Another method for creating a folder is available in File Explorer. Open File Explorer, and then click the **Folder** icon in the Quick access menu, next to the name of the folder you are viewing. (In Figure 4-20, it is the Folder icon next to NetAdmin on the upper-left side of the window.) You see a new folder, ready to be named. Click the down arrow next to the folder icon you just clicked, and click **Undo** to remove the folder you just created (see Figure 4-21). Close **File Explorer**.

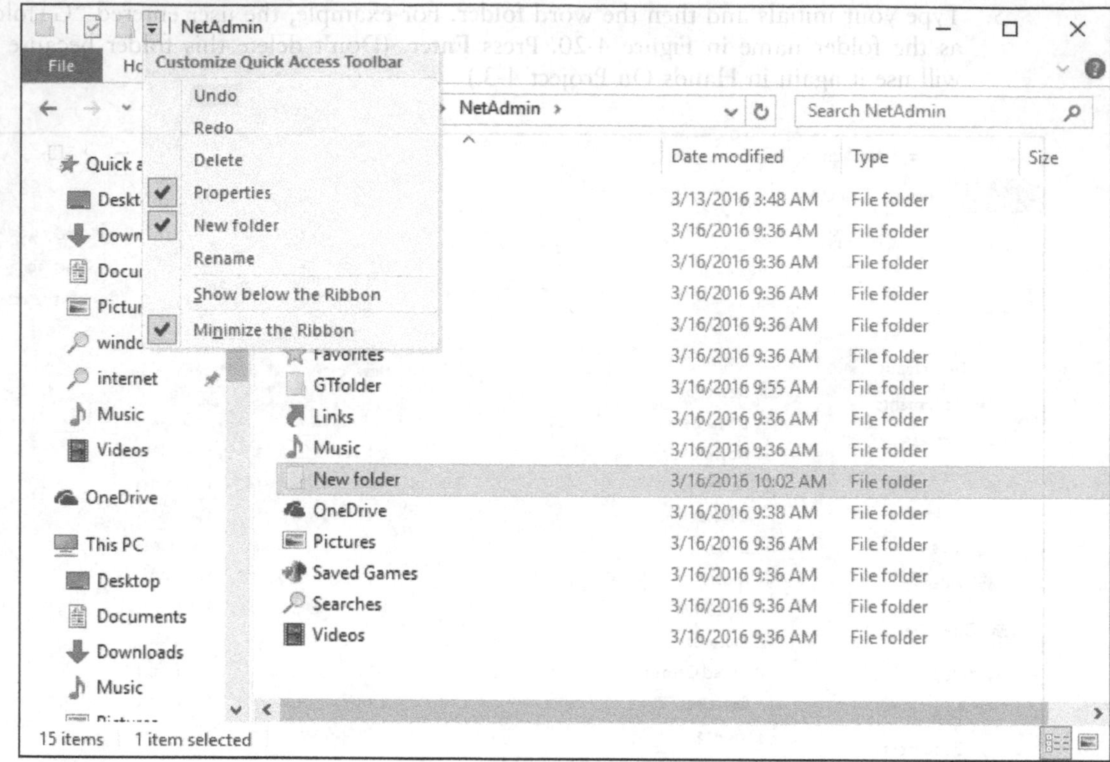

Figure 4-21 Undoing an action in File Explorer

9. Yet another way to create a folder in File Explorer is to right-click anywhere in the window's white space, point to **New**, and click **Folder**. (If you like to use the keyboard rather than the mouse, click Ctrl+Shift+N to create a new folder.) Undo the creation of this new folder.

10. To create a folder at the Windows Command Prompt, right-click **Start** and click **Command Prompt**. The prompt shows the path in the file hierarchy where any file system command you enter will be applied by default. The Command Prompt opens in C:\Users*CurrentUser*, where CurrentUser is the currently logged-on user.

11. Type **dir** and press **Enter**. Notice the folder you created earlier. To create a new folder named MyDocs, type **mkdir MyDocs** and press **Enter**. To verify that the folder was created, type **dir** and press **Enter**.

12. Type **cd mydocs** and press **Enter**. (Remember that Windows folder names and filenames are not case sensitive, so you don't have to capitalize these names in commands.) Notice that the prompt changes by adding MyDocs to the path. Type **dir** and press **Enter**.

13. The *dir* command shows two folders named "." and "..". These are more like placeholders than actual folders. The "." folder simply refers to the current folder and the ".." folder refers to the parent folder. Type **cd .** and press **Enter**; you'll see that your

prompt doesn't change because the command basically tells the operating system to "go to the current folder." Type cd .. and press **Enter** to return to the C:\Users*Current User* folder.

14. Navigate to the root of the drive by typing **cd ** and pressing **Enter**. The prompt changes to C:\> to indicate that you are in the C:\ folder, which is the root of C:. Close the command prompt. Figure 4-22 shows the commands you entered and their output, although some of the *dir* output has been omitted to save space.

15. Shut down your Windows computer in preparation for the next project.

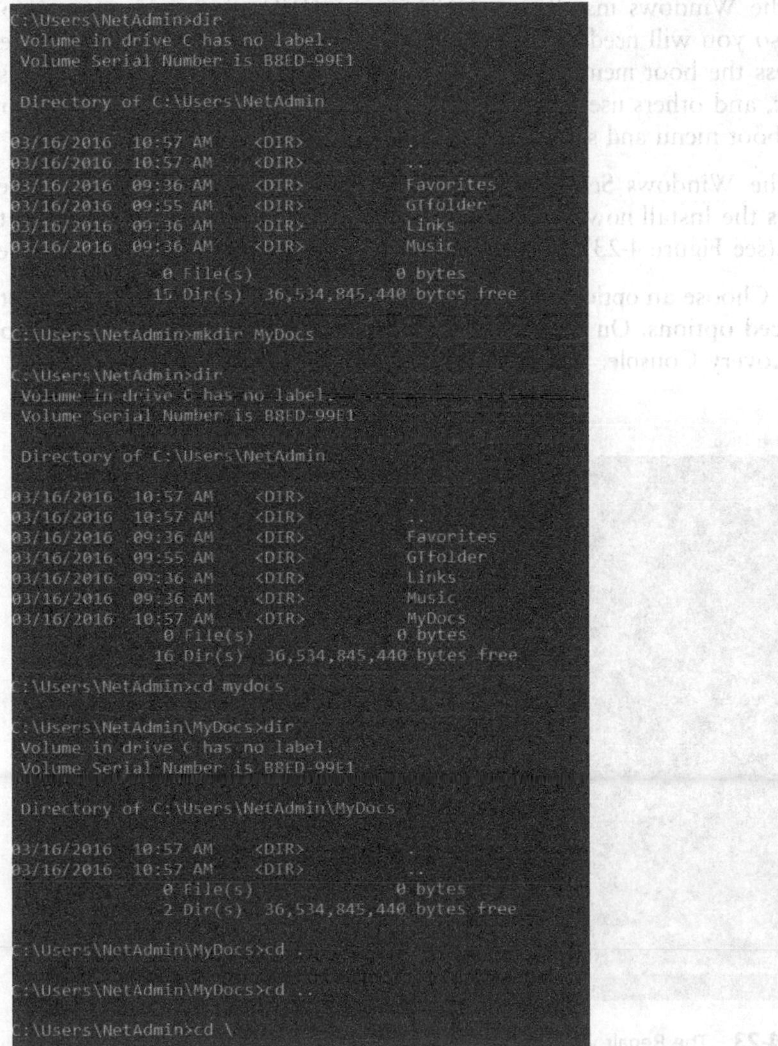
C:\Users\NetAdmin>dir
Volume in drive C has no label.
Volume Serial Number is B8ED-99E1
Directory of C:\Users\NetAdmin
03/16/2016 10:57 AM <DIR> .
03/16/2016 10:57 AM <DIR> ..
03/16/2016 09:36 AM <DIR> Favorites
03/16/2016 09:55 AM <DIR> GTfolder
03/16/2016 09:36 AM <DIR> Links
03/16/2016 09:36 AM <DIR> Music
0 File(s) 0 bytes
15 Dir(s) 36,534,845,440 bytes free
C:\Users\NetAdmin>mkdir MyDocs
C:\Users\NetAdmin>dir
Volume in drive C has no label.
Volume Serial Number is B8ED-99E1
Directory of C:\Users\NetAdmin
03/16/2016 10:57 AM <DIR> .
03/16/2016 10:57 AM <DIR> ..
03/16/2016 09:36 AM <DIR> Favorites
03/16/2016 09:55 AM <DIR> GTfolder
03/16/2016 09:36 AM <DIR> Links
03/16/2016 09:36 AM <DIR> Music
03/16/2016 10:57 AM <DIR> MyDocs
0 File(s) 0 bytes
16 Dir(s) 36,534,845,440 bytes free
C:\Users\NetAdmin>cd mydocs
C:\Users\NetAdmin\MyDocs>dir
Volume in drive C has no label.
Volume Serial Number is B8ED-99E1
Directory of C:\Users\NetAdmin\MyDocs
03/16/2016 10:57 AM <DIR> .
03/16/2016 10:57 AM <DIR> ..
0 File(s) 0 bytes
2 Dir(s) 36,534,845,440 bytes free
C:\Users\NetAdmin\MyDocs>cd .
C:\Users\NetAdmin\MyDocs>cd ..
C:\Users\NetAdmin>cd \

Figure 4-22 A series of file system commands at a Windows command prompt

Project 4-3: Fix a Corrupted MBR in Windows

A sudden power failure or a bad spot on a disk can corrupt the Master Boot Record and prevent a computer from booting. In Windows, you can fix the Master Boot Record using the Recovery Console. This project shows you how to start the Recovery Console and fix the Master Boot Record in Windows. For this project, you'll need the installation DVD/CD-ROM for the operating system. Also, you need to make sure all files are saved and that all users are logged off the server. Insert the DVD/CD-ROM for your operating system, but take no action if you see an installation start-up window. Shut down the operating system and computer.

1. Place the Windows installation DVD in the DVD player. You want to boot to the DVD, so you will need to enter the appropriate keystroke while the system is booting to access the boot menu. Ask your instructor to identify this keystroke; some systems use Esc, and others use F2 or another function key. Turn on your Windows computer to the boot menu and select the DVD as the boot device.
2. After the Windows Setup program starts, click **Next** until you see the screen that displays the Install now prompt and the Repair your computer option in the lower-left corner (see Figure 4-23). Press **R** (for repair) to open the Windows Recovery Menu.
3. On the Choose an option screen, click **Troubleshoot.** On the Troubleshoot screen, click **Advanced options.** On the Advanced options screen, click **Command prompt** to enter the Recovery Console.

Figure 4-23 The Repair your computer option in the Windows setup screen

4. The *bootrec /fixmbr* command is used to fix the Master Boot Record from the command line. Type **bootrec /?** and press **Enter** to view the help information for this command.

Read the description for each option. As you can see, *bootrec* can solve more problems than just a bad MBR.

5. If you have permission from your instructor, type **bootrec /fixmbr** and press **Enter**. Because nothing is wrong with the MBR, this command should not cause any problems, but be sure you have permission if you are not using your own computer. The command should output a message that "The operation completed successfully."

6. Type **exit** and press **Enter** to close the Recovery Console. Click **Continue** to boot to Windows.

Enter
HANDS-ON PROJECTS

Project 4-4: Compress Files in Windows

In this project, you learn how to compress files in Windows. You need a computer with a drive formatted for NTFS.

1. Start your Windows computer and log on, if necessary. Open **File Explorer**.
2. Navigate to the folder you created in Project 4-2 (C:\Users*CurrentUser**YY* folder), where *CurrentUser* is the logged-on user account and *YY* represents your initials. Double-click the folder to open it. The right pane should be empty.
3. Create a new folder named **SubFolder** using one of the methods described in Project 4-2.
4. Right-click **SubFolder** and click **Properties**.
5. Click the **Advanced** button to view a dialog box similar to Figure 4-24. Notice the advanced attributes you can configure.

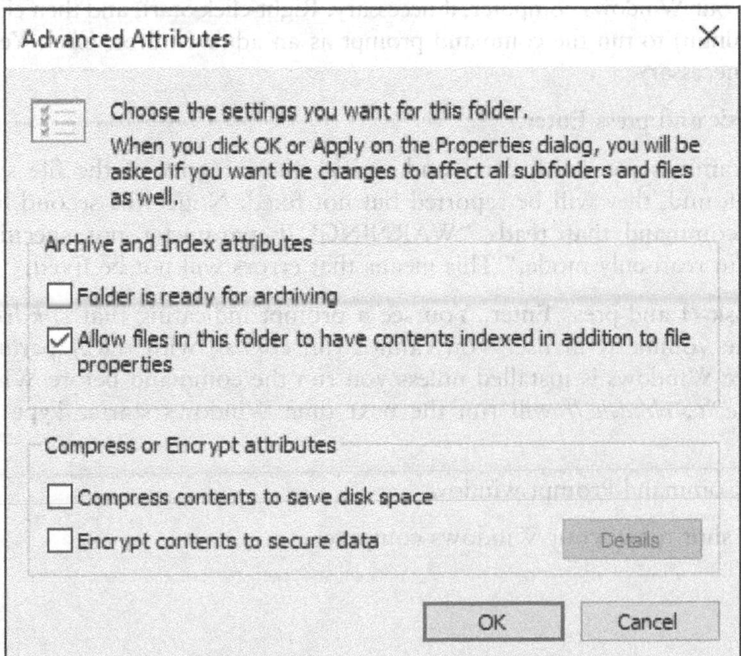
Advanced Attributes
Choose the settings you want for this folder.
When you click OK or Apply on the Properties dialog, you will be asked if you want the changes to affect all subfolders and files as well.
Archive and Index attributes
Folder is ready for archiving
Allow files in this folder to have contents indexed in addition to file properties
Compress or Encrypt attributes
Compress contents to save disk space
Encrypt contents to secure data
Details
OK
Cancel

Figure 4-24 The Advanced Attributes dialog box

6. Click **Compress contents to save disk space** and click **OK**.
7. Click **OK** to exit the folder's Properties dialog box.
8. Notice the change to the SubFolder icon. It now displays two blue arrows pointing toward each other in the upper-right corner, indicating that the folder and its contents are compressed.
9. Double-click **SubFolder** to open it. Right-click in the right pane, point to **New**, click **Text Document**, and press **Enter** to keep the default name. Notice that the file displays the two blue arrows to indicate it is compressed. All files that are placed in a compressed folder are automatically compressed.
10. Close File Explorer.
11. Stay logged on if you are continuing to the next project.

You cannot compress a folder that is encrypted.

Project 4-5: Run *chkdsk* in Windows

Chkdsk is an important utility included in Windows that verifies the integrity of a disk and its file system. It also can fix problems that it encounters. In this project, you run *chkdsk* to see how it works.

1. Log on to your Windows computer, if necessary. Right-click **Start**, and then click **Command Prompt (Admin)** to run the command prompt as an administrator. Click **Yes** at the UAC prompt, if necessary.
2. Type **chkdsk** and press **Enter**.
3. *Chkdsk* examines your disk drive and verifies the integrity of the file system. If any errors are found, they will be reported but not fixed. Notice the second line of output from the command that reads "WARNING! /F parameter not specified. Running CHKDSK in read-only mode." This means that errors will not be fixed.
4. Type **chkdsk /f** and press **Enter**. You see a prompt indicating that *chkdsk* cannot run because the volume is in use. You cannot run *chkdsk* with the */f* parameter on the drive where Windows is installed unless you run the command before Windows starts. If you type Y, *chkdsk /f* will run the next time Windows starts. Type **N** and press **Enter**.
5. Close the Command Prompt window.
6. Log off or shut down your Windows computer.

Another way to have *chkdsk* start is to save all your work and simply turn off the computer without properly shutting it down. When you reboot, the system will run *chkdsk* if it detects a problem with the way the computer was shut down. In most cases, this is a safe test because you will most likely not cause damage to files or the file system if your work is saved and all programs are closed.

Project 4-6: Navigate the Linux Folder Structure from the Shell Prompt

There are two common ways to view and manage folders and files in Linux: from the shell prompt and from the GNOME Files tool. In this project, you use the shell prompt in Fedora, although the steps are similar in many UNIX/Linux systems.

1. Start and log on to your Linux computer. Open a terminal window.
2. Type **ls -a** and press **Enter** to view the folders and files in your home folder, including those that are hidden. (Hidden files are represented by a period in front of the filename.)
3. Type **ls -l /** and press **Enter** to view the main folder structure in the system (see Figure 4-25).

```
gtomsho@localhost:~
File Edit View Search Terminal Help
[gtomsho@localhost ~]$ ls -l /
total 62
lrwxrwxrwx.   1 root root     7 Dec 11  2013 bin -> usr/bin
dr-xr-xr-x.   6 root root  1024 Feb 11 01:52 boot
drwxr-xr-x.  20 root root  3300 Mar  8 10:50 dev
drwxr-xr-x. 127 root root 12288 Mar 16 13:20 etc
drwxr-xr-x.   3 root root  4096 Feb 10 08:28 home
lrwxrwxrwx.   1 root root     7 Dec 11  2013 lib -> usr/lib
lrwxrwxrwx.   1 root root     9 Dec 11  2013 lib64 -> usr/lib64
drwx------.   2 root root 16384 Dec 11  2013 lost+found
drwxr-xr-x.   2 root root  4096 Aug  7  2013 media
drwxr-xr-x.   3 root root  4096 Feb 10 08:28 mnt
drwxr-xr-x.   2 root root  4096 Aug  7  2013 opt
dr-xr-xr-x. 181 root root     0 Mar  8 10:49 proc
dr-xr-x---.   6 root root  4096 Feb 10 16:01 root
drwxr-xr-x.  35 root root   960 Mar 16 13:20 run
lrwxrwxrwx.   1 root root     8 Dec 11  2013 sbin -> usr/sbin
drwxr-xr-x.   2 root root  4096 Aug  7  2013 srv
dr-xr-xr-x.  13 root root     0 Mar  8 10:50 sys
drwxrwxrwt.  12 root root   300 Mar 16 13:21 tmp
drwxr-xr-x.  12 root root  4096 Dec 11  2013 usr
drwxr-xr-x.  20 root root  4096 Mar  8 10:50 var
[gtomsho@localhost ~]$
```

Figure 4-25 The Linux folder structure
Source: Fedora Linux

4. At the Linux shell prompt, you see a "~" character, which indicates you are in your home folder. Type **cd /** and press **Enter** to move to the root; notice how the prompt changes.
5. Type **cd** and press **Enter** to go back to your home folder. Notice the prompt again. Type **cd /** and press **Enter**. You can also go to your home folder by typing **cd ~** and pressing **Enter**.
6. Type **cd /home** and press **Enter**. Type **ls** and press **Enter**. You see a list of all the home folders. You might see folders other than your own, depending on how many users are on your Linux computer.
7. Type **cd *username***, where ***username*** is the account you used to log on. If you are in the correct folder, the prompt again changes to ~.
8. Type **mkdir Folder1** and press **Enter** to create a new folder in your home folder. Type **cd folder1** and press **Enter**. If you used the folder capitalization specified in both commands, you will receive an error because Linux considers Folder1 and folder1 to be different names.
9. Type **cd Folder1** and press **Enter**. Your prompt changes to indicate you are in the Folder1 folder.
10. Type **ls** and press **Enter**. There is no output because the folder is empty, or at least it seems that way. Like Windows, Linux has two folders named "." and "..", but they are hidden files. Type **ls –a** and press **Enter** to see all files, including hidden files.
11. Type **touch newfile1** and press **Enter**. The *touch* command creates a new file or updates the time stamp on an existing file. Type **ls -l** and press **Enter**.
12. Close the terminal window but stay logged on if you are continuing to the next project.

Project 4-7: Navigate the Linux Folder Structure in Files

As mentioned in the previous project, there are two common ways to view and manage folders and files in Linux: from the shell prompt and from the GNOME Files tool. In this project, you use the Files tool in Fedora, although the steps are similar in many UNIX/Linux systems.

1. Log on to your Linux computer, if necessary.
2. To open the Files tool, click **Activities** and then click the **Files** icon.
3. Files places you in the Home folder by default. You see the Folder1 folder you created using the *mkdir* command in the preceding project. Double-click **Folder1**.
4. You see the file you created using the *touch* command in the preceding project.

5. In the left pane, double-click **Computer** to go to the root of the file system. (The Computer entry should be listed under the Devices category in the left pane of Files—you may need to scroll the left pane to see it.) Double-click the **home** folder.

6. Double-click the folder that represents your home folder. Right-click **Folder1**, view the options, and then click **Compress**.

7. The compression function is different in Linux than in Windows. In Linux a new file is created from the folder and its contents are called a compressed tar file by default. See Figure 4-26. Notice also that the system creates the compressed tar file in your home directory. Click **Create**, and then click **Close**. You see a new file named Folder1.tar.gz in your home directory.

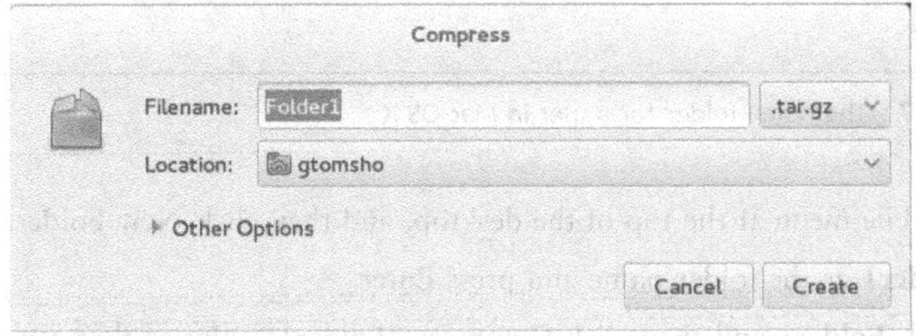

Figure 4-26 Creating a compressed file in Linux

Source: Fedora Linux

8. Close Files and log off or shut down your Linux computer.

Project 4-8: Navigate the Mac OS X Folder Structure

In this project, you learn to use the Macintosh HD desktop icon in Mac OS X to access files and folders.

1. Start and log on to your Mac OS X computer. Double-click the **Macintosh HD** icon on the desktop.

2. Double-click the **Users** folder. You should see a folder for each user account on the system, and a Shared folder.

3. Double-click your account's home folder, which looks like a house.

4. Your home folder contains a combination of folders and files. Typically, documents that you create using this account are placed in the Documents folder. There are also folders in which to store Downloads, Movies, Music, Pictures, and so on, as shown in Figure 4-27.

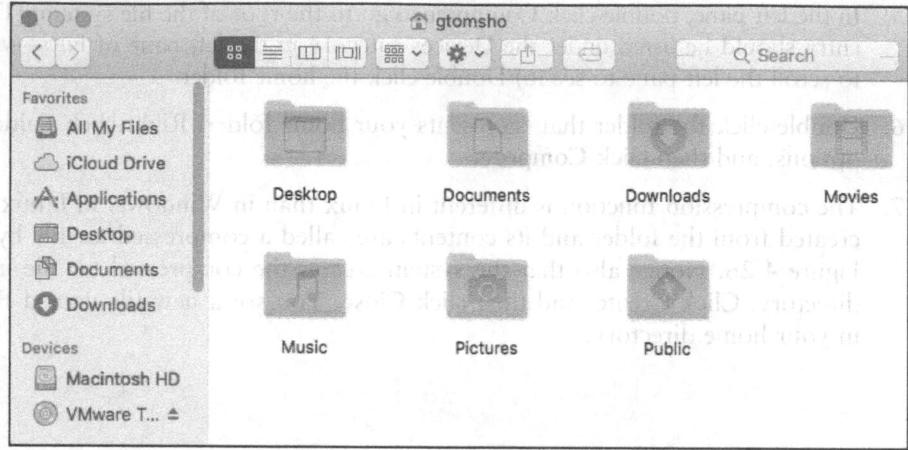

Figure 4-27 The home folder for a user in Mac OS X

Source: Mac OS X

5. Click the **File** menu at the top of the desktop, and then click **New Folder**.
6. Type **Folder1** as the folder name and press **Enter**.
7. Right-click **Folder1** and then click **Compress "Folder1"**. Notice that a new file named Folder1.zip is created in your home folder.
8. Click the **Go** menu at the top of the desktop, and then click **Utilities**.
9. Double-click **Terminal** in the Utilities window.
10. Type **ls** and press **Enter** to view the contents of your home folder. You see the folder you created in Step 6.
11. Type **mkdir Folder2** and press **Enter**.
12. Type **ls** and press **Enter** to verify that your folder was created. Note that you also used the *ls* and *mkdir* commands in Linux to work with files.
13. Click the **Terminal** menu at the top of the desktop, and then click **Quit Terminal**.
14. Close the Utilities window, but stay logged on if you are continuing to the next project.

Project 4-9: Create Aliases with Mac OS X

Mac OS X includes the Get Info option to allow you to view file types. Also, aliases are a useful feature in Macintosh file systems. Like shortcuts in Windows, aliases let you create custom icons and names to place on your desktop, menus, or elsewhere to point to other applications. Aliases give you multiple ways to access the same application and let you easily place these access points in various convenient locations. In this project, you view the file type of an application and create an alias.

1. From your Mac OS X desktop, click **Go** in the menu bar at the top of the desktop and then click **Applications**.
2. Click **Contacts**. (Don't double-click, because you do not want to open the application.)

3. Click the **File** menu and then click **Get Info**. Review the information you see. Close the Contacts Info window.
4. Make sure **Contacts** is still selected, and then click the **File** menu and click **Make Alias**.
5. If necessary, click to move the cursor to the box under the Contacts icon and change the text to insert your initials before Contacts. For example, the user entered GT Contacts as the alias in Figure 4-28.

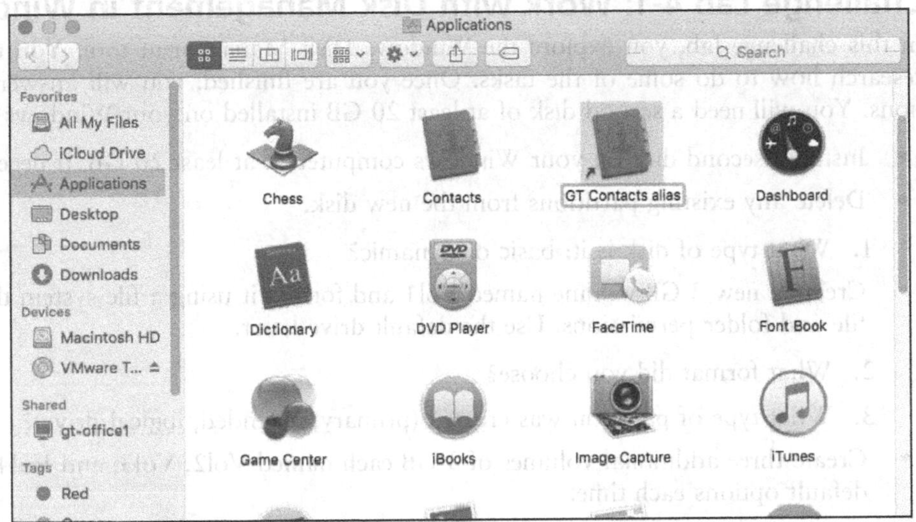

Figure 4-28 Creating a new alias in Mac OS X

Source: Mac OS X

6. Right-click the new alias and click **Copy**. Right-click the desktop and click **Paste Item**. The new alias is copied to the right side of the desktop.
7. Double-click the alias on the desktop to see that it opens the Contacts application.
8. Log off or shut down your Mac OS X computer.

Although an alias only points to the actual application, you can treat an alias like an application. For example, you can drag a file onto an alias icon to open the file with the application to which the alias points. You can also create an alias for a folder instead of an application, which lets you save files into a folder by choosing its alias. Further, you can create an alias from a network connection so you can open the server it represents simply by double-clicking the alias icon.

Critical Thinking

The following activities give you critical thinking challenges. Challenge Labs give you an opportunity to use the skills you have learned to perform a task without step-by-step instructions. Case projects offer a practical problem for which you supply a written solution. Not all chapters contain Challenge Labs. There is not always a specific right or wrong answer to these critical thinking exercises. They are intended to encourage you to review the chapter material and delve deeper into the topics you have learned.

Challenge Labs

Challenge Lab 4-1: Work with Disk Management in Windows

In this challenge lab, you explore the Windows Disk Management tool. You may have to research how to do some of the tasks. Once you are finished, you will answer some questions. You will need a second disk of at least 20 GB installed on your Windows computer.

- Install a second disk on your Windows computer of at least 20 GB, if necessary.
- Delete any existing partitions from the new disk.

1. What type of disk is it: basic or dynamic?

- Create a new 3 GB volume named Vol1 and format it using a file system that supports file and folder permissions. Use the default drive letter.

2. What format did you choose?
3. What type of partition was created (primary, extended, logical drive)?

- Create three additional volumes of 3 GB each named Vol2, Vol3, and Vol4. Accept the default options each time.

4. For each partition, what was the partition type you created?
5. Explain what happened when you created the fourth volume.

- Convert the disk to a dynamic disk. (Convert only the new disk you installed; do not convert Disk 0, which is the Windows boot disk.)

6. How did this change the way the volumes and partitions are labeled?

- Close Disk Management.

Case Projects

GT Yummy Ice Cream is a company that produces ice cream and sells it to distributors in North America. The company's headquarters are in a large building in downtown Chicago. All of the senior management—the president and all vice presidents—use Macintosh computers with the Mac OS X operating system. The Marketing Department uses Windows 10, as does the Accounting Department. The Manufacturing and Operations Department uses workstations running Linux, which have specialized software for their area, including a complex inventory and distribution client/server system. The servers used by the company include a combination of Windows Server 2008 R2 and Windows Server 2012 R2. There has been some turnover in the company's Computer Support area, so you have been hired as a consultant to provide help.

Case Project 4-1: Train a New Vice President in Using Mac OS X Folders

A new vice president has just been hired, and she is not familiar with Macintosh computers. You have been asked to provide her with a set of simple written instructions for how to access the documents in the home folder, which were left by her predecessor. Also, provide instructions for how to create a new folder in Mac OS X. Note that both the predecessor and the new vice president have the same user account name, which is VP Financials. Finally, the vice president needs your advice for creating a folder structure under her home folder. She wants a separate location for each of the following:

- Rulings by the board of directors
- Financial spreadsheets
- Word-processed documents that pertain to her division
- Word-processed documents that relate to senior management activities
- Marketing reports

Explain how you would set up the folder structure and what you would name the folders.

Case Project 4-2: Determine Whether a File System is Mounted for a DVD/CD-ROM Drive

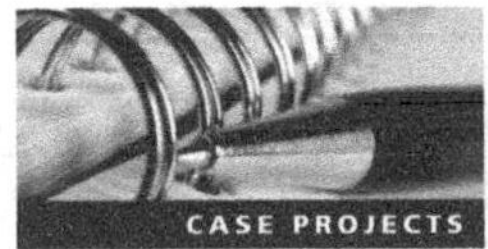

An inventory specialist in the Manufacturing and Operations Department needs to determine what file systems are mounted on his Linux computer because he is not sure that the DVD/CD-ROM drive is properly mounted. Explain the steps he should use to determine the mounted file systems, and note which file system should be mounted for the DVD/CD-ROM drive.

Case Project 4-3: Choose a File System for Windows 10

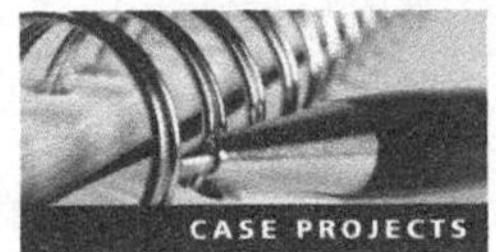

A new computer has just been purchased for the accounting manager. The company purchased the computer without an operating system because they already have extra licensed copies of Windows 10. You need to set up the computer. What Windows 10 file system do you implement, recognizing that the accounting manager needs a secure system? Explain your decision and briefly discuss the advantages of this file system. Also, the accounting manager asks you to set up a preliminary folder structure to contain:

- Accounting reports
- Word-processed documents
- Department memos
- Personnel evaluations

Explain where you would set up this folder structure and show how you would name the new folders.

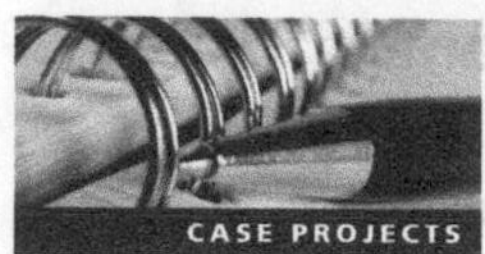

Case Project 4-4: The Advantages of the Windows Server 2012 File System

GT Yummy Ice Cream has just hired a new person who is training to be a Windows Server administrator. She has worked with computers in many capacities, but has never managed a Windows Server 2012 server. You are asked to train her, and as part of the orientation to Windows Server 2012, you decide to explain the advantages of its file system. Create a short report that summarizes the advantages you will discuss in your training.

Case Project 4-5: Repair a File Problem

The copywriter in the Marketing Department uses a Windows 10 computer that has some problems. Each time the copywriter accesses certain files, he sees an error message. He is concerned because the files will be used for an upcoming catalog that will go into print soon. Explain the steps needed to fix these files. The files are on the D: drive and the Windows OS is installed on the C: drive.

chapter 5

Installing and Upgrading Operating Systems

After reading this chapter and completing the exercises, you will be able to:

- Explain the overall process of installing and upgrading operating systems
- Prepare to install an operating system and understand the factors involved in an upgrade
- Install and upgrade the following operating systems and understand the various options:
  - Windows 7 and Windows 10
  - Windows Server 2008 and Windows Server 2012
  - Linux using the Fedora 23 distribution
  - Mac OS X El Capitan
- Obtain operating system patches and minor upgrades via the Internet

For many, the installation or upgrade of an operating system (OS) sounds like a daunting task. This chapter takes the mystery out of the process by showing you, step by step, how to install or upgrade modern OSs. First you learn some of the basic tasks and planning you must do before installing or upgrading an OS, and then you step through actual installations and upgrades in the Hands-On Projects at the end of the chapter. When you are finished, you will know how to prepare for an OS installation or upgrade; what to expect, what to watch for, and what to avoid during the process; and how to update your OS once it is installed. It is beyond the scope of this book to cover all possible options and settings, so only typical installations and upgrades are presented. For easier reading, the chapter is divided into two parts:

- Part 1: Introduction and Initial Preparations
- Part 2: OS Installations and Upgrades

Part 1: Introduction and Initial Preparations

In Part 1, you learn general concepts about OS installations and upgrades. You also learn how to make advance preparations to help maximize the success of an installation, such as by verifying hardware and hardware drivers, backing up OSs before starting, and conducting a test upgrade.

Introduction to Installing an OS

There are two basic types of OS installations: clean installations and upgrade installations. A **clean installation** is performed in one of the following scenarios:

- The installation is performed on a computer that has no OS installed (a new hard drive or one that has been formatted)
- The computer has an OS already installed; it is deleted and replaced by the new OS
- The computer has an OS installed and the new OS is installed on another volume, making it possible to boot either to the old OS or the new one

An **upgrade installation** occurs on a computer that already contains an earlier version of the OS. The upgrade replaces the earlier version with a new version, and usually retains some or all of the original settings, user accounts, applications, data files, and other existing user files.

The process of installing an OS varies from one OS to another, but certain features are common to all installations. OS installation can be divided into three general stages: preparation, the installation itself, and the configuration tasks performed following the installation.

Preparing for installation involves the following:

- Choosing a computer configuration that meets or exceeds the minimum requirements for the OS you are installing
- Ensuring that all computer hardware is operating correctly
- Having the OS installation media available (DVDs, ISO files, setup programs) and any license or activation codes

- Understanding the general features of the OS you are installing so you can decide which modules to install and which to omit
- Having device drivers that might not be included with the OS installation files. This preparation is particularly important for disk controllers. (During the Windows installation process, you will be prompted to add drivers for any disks that are not recognized by the setup program.)
- Having accurate information available about your computer and peripheral devices
- Being aware of the network environment in which you are installing the OS; this preparation may involve having information about how and where the computer should be connected to the network or having Wi-Fi access information, knowing how IP addressing is done on the network, and knowing what to name the computer

During the installation, you may need to provide some or all of the following information:

- Where (in which drive, folder, or path) to install the OS and what to name the folder that contains the OS
- Whether you want to perform a clean installation or an upgrade and the name(s) the OS uses for these different installation types (for example, Windows uses the term *Custom install* for a clean installation)
- Information about you, your company, and your computer; this information might include your name, company name, computer name, or workgroup name
- A license or activation code that verifies your right to install the OS
- Which components of the OS you want to install

After you complete an installation, keep the product key, ID number, or activation code in a safe place so you can reinstall the OS in the event that your computer or hard drive fails. Also, always keep the installation DVDs and other media in a safe place after completing the installation.

Modern OSs can automatically detect and configure devices such as monitors, keyboards, printers, mice, network cards, video cards, and sound cards, as long as the OS has the appropriate device driver as part of the installation media. However, automatic detection may also misidentify a device, and you might need to reinstall the correct driver.

Some installation programs are primarily GUI-based or use a combination of GUI- and text-based screens. Modern versions of Windows, Linux, and Mac OS X primarily use GUI screens during an installation, and they use automated "wizards" to step you through the process. OSs can usually be installed from DVDs, and in many cases over a network. (Network installations are not covered in this book.)

The installation itself consists of some or all of the following general functions:

- Running the installation program
- Gathering system information
- Determining which elements of the OS will be installed
- Copying OS files to your computer

- Configuring devices and drivers
- Restarting the system and finalizing configuration of devices

For most OSs, device and driver configuration is part of the installation process. The Plug and Play (PnP) feature automatically configures internal and external devices as part of the installation and at startup whenever a new device is added.

Windows 95 was the first OS to be compatible with PnP. Besides Windows, UNIX/Linux distributions and Mac OS X are also PnP compatible.

Even with a PnP-capable OS, you may have to configure devices to work optimally with the OS. For example, your computer may detect a video card in the system and a monitor, but it may not have the correct or newest driver for the card. Also, the monitor settings may need to be configured for optimal performance. In some cases, the OS may search for and download the correct driver automatically, or you might have to supply a disc or flash drive that contains the driver or download it manually.

Preparing for Installation

Before you can install any OS, you must make a few advance preparations. Naturally, you must select a computer on which you will install the OS. You might have an existing computer or a new computer that was purchased specifically for the OS. The "computer" may also be a virtual machine in which the "hardware" is virtual hardware emulated by virtual machine software, such as VMware or Microsoft Hyper-V. (Virtualization is discussed in more detail in Chapter 8.) In any case, the computer must meet the minimum specifications for the OS you are installing. Most commonly, the minimum specifications cover the speed and type of CPU, the amount of memory, and the amount of free disk space.

Checking the Hardware

First, and most important, the machine must be working correctly. If you have defective hardware, such as a bad disk drive, a bad DVD/CD-ROM drive, or a bad memory chip, the OS installation can be extremely difficult or impossible. Most OSs interface with the hardware on many levels.

Before you begin an installation, you should be sure that all hardware needed for the installation is turned on and ready for use, including the computer, monitor, and any external peripheral devices, such as USB devices and external disk drives.

You should remove or disconnect any removable media that contain important data or that are not necessary for the installation. In general, an OS installation will not destroy data on removable media, unless it is specifically instructed to do so. However, if important data is backed up and removable media are taken out of their drives or disconnected, there is no chance of losing anything.

You should also have available information about your hardware, including how many hard disks you have, their size, and their type, such as SAS or SATA disks. (You learn about these disks in Chapter 7, "Using and Configuring Storage Devices.") You should also know how much memory you have in your machine. For any expansion cards, such as your video card, network card, sound card, and disk controllers, you should know the make and model. If you have a printer, modem, scanner, or other device, you should keep the device driver disks handy and know their types. Table 5-1 is an example of how you might organize this information for installation.

Table 5-1 Hardware component information

Component	Description/setting
CPU (type and bit size)	The computer's basic input/output system (BIOS) knows the CPU information, and the OS should automatically make all required adjustments. One caveat, however, is that the bit size (32-bit or 64-bit) of the CPU must match the bit size of the OS you are installing.
Amount of RAM	Your OS should automatically detect the amount of random access memory (RAM) in your computer. However, guidelines supplied with your OS tell you how much RAM is recommended. You should know how much you have to ensure that minimum requirements are met.
Type of buses	Before you install the OS, you might want to install any expansion cards you want to use. You'll need to know what expansion buses your computer supports and how many slots are available before you purchase the expansion cards. Examples of expansion bus slot types include PCI Express, PCI-X, and PCI.
Hard disk(s)	You need to know the type and size of your hard disks and whether they are empty or have a file system installed. If you are doing an upgrade or installing alongside an existing OS, you need to know how much free space is available. Most new hardware includes BIOS routines to automatically detect the type of hard drive installed, as well as critical drive settings.
Keyboard	Unless your keyboard has special features that require custom drivers, the type of keyboard you have should not be a factor during OS installation.
Mouse	The type of mouse or pointing device can be important; there can be differences between a wired mouse and a wireless mouse. In some cases, a custom driver may be needed for a mouse that has extra features.
Video card	Most modern OSs will detect your video card and automatically include required drivers. However, special features of your video card may become available only with the use of a special driver provided by the manufacturer. This is particularly true of video cards that support multiple monitors.
DVD/CD-ROM type	Your OS automatically detects this information.
Sound card	Some OSs include drivers for common sound card hardware. If your card isn't one of the popular models, make sure you have the required drivers supplied by the card's manufacturer.
Network interface card (NIC)	Most OSs will automatically detect your NIC. However, it may still be a good idea to use the manufacturer's custom drivers for best performance.
Printer	You should have custom drivers from your printer manufacturer.
Other input/output (I/O) devices	If your OS doesn't detect other hardware during the installation, you must understand hardware basics and have access to any custom drivers required to make it function properly with your OS. Most motherboards come with a DVD that contains drivers for all the on-board devices, but it's a good idea to check the motherboard manufacturer's Web site and see if there are updated drivers for the OS you are installing.

5

Chapter 6, "Configuring Input and Output Devices," and Chapter 7, "Using and Configuring Storage Devices," provide more detailed information on devices and device drivers.

Some cards installed in the computer include their own settings. In the Intel PC architecture, these cards must often be configured to interface with the computer in a certain way. Modern OSs use the PnP capability to do this. If you install an OS that supports PnP, card configuration is usually automatic. If you do not use an OS that supports PnP, or if you install a component that does not support PnP, you may be in for a few surprises. Many PnP cards come with a utility that lets you configure them to work in non-PnP mode; this utility is usually included on the manufacturer's disk with the drivers.

All modern Windows OSs support PnP. Most Linux distributions also support PnP, but the use of drivers in Linux can be more complex than in Windows systems, so there can be occasional problems in detecting PnP cards and devices in Linux. If a detection problem occurs, contact the card or device manufacturer. Interface cards in the Apple Mac architecture don't usually need any special configuration for the hardware to work properly because Mac OS X is specifically designed for Mac hardware.

Newer hardware may have BIOS settings that can turn PnP compatibility on or off. PnP should be enabled by default. If it isn't, check your computer's BIOS documentation to find out how to turn it on before installing a new OS. USB devices, such as flash or removable hard drives, can be hot-plugged into a computer and recognized because they are equipped with PnP capability. A hot-plug device can be installed and removed from the computer while the computer is on and the OS is running.

Checking Drivers

Many devices, such as DVD drives, SCSI drives, network interface cards, printers, and scanners, require special drivers to work correctly. In general, drivers are included on the disks that come with the devices, but often these disks do not include drivers for all possible OSs or the most up-to-date drivers. Also, your device may not be on the list of drivers that come with the OS, which can result in some installation problems.

If you install drivers that came with your hardware, the hardware should operate properly. However, in some cases, you may get significantly better performance by installing later drivers that you secure from the manufacturer. The easiest way to access the latest drivers is to go to the hardware manufacturer's Web site for drivers and support information, or contact the manufacturer and ask for the latest driver disks for your device.

Even though you may have driver disks on hand, it is best to obtain recent drivers because driver updates often fix bugs or performance problems in older versions. In some cases, your strategy may involve reading forums about manufacturers' devices so you are aware of any problems with the newest drivers. For example, a new driver that is relatively untested in the market may have some problems, in which case you want to use the driver issued just prior to the newest driver.

You should also check the documentation that came with any hardware you want to use with your new OS. In many cases, the manufacturer includes a disclaimer indicating which OSs are certified for use with particular hardware.

Ensuring Hardware Compatibility

Because of the wide range of hardware available today, you will find that many OSs have certain hardware requirements. These are usually listed on the vendor's Web site or in the OS's documentation. Some OSs enable you to look up compatible hardware online. For example, you can find compatibility information for Windows servers on Microsoft's Windows Server Catalog Web site, at *www.windowsservercatalog.com/*. For client OSs such as Windows 10, go to the Windows Compatibility Products List Web site: *https://sysdev.microsoft.com/en-us/hardware/lpl/*. Red Hat has a certified products catalog that combines Red Hat hardware, software, and plug-in compatibility information into a single publication (*https://access.redhat.com/ecosystem/*). For Mac OS X, use Apple Macintosh hardware such as the iMac to ensure compatibility.

If you are installing the OS on a virtual machine, the virtual machine software allows you to select the OS you are installing and the virtual machine is configured appropriately to ensure the virtual hardware is compatible.

Migrating to a New OS

No matter how comfortable you are with an OS, there comes a time when you must upgrade or migrate to the next version. In this context, an upgrade refers to an installation in which the original settings and user files are retained; we use **migration** to more broadly refer to moving from one OS to another, which may or may not involve implementing a new computer.

For instance, a migration may be necessary when you find that your current OS version does not support new software or certain devices you want to use. Also, older versions of OSs don't have the new security features required for safer network and Internet access, or to protect e-mail systems. Whether it is a small upgrade to fix bugs or a larger upgrade or migration, many of the procedures are similar to those required for an initial installation. In this section, you'll learn about general upgrade and migration considerations, backup and safety recommendations, and the specific steps and possible pitfalls involved in upgrading or migrating computer OSs.

Deciding Whether to Perform an Upgrade or Clean Installation

When you consider migrating to a newer OS version, decide whether you can perform an upgrade installation or whether you need to do a clean installation. An upgrade installation can be an advantage in that it typically costs less to purchase an upgrade license than a new license for an OS. In many cases, you can also elect to retain your existing settings, data files, and applications, which can save time and money.

Alternatively, the advantage of a clean installation is that you can start fresh by reformatting the hard disk used by the OS, which enables disk problems to be identified and remedied before they become a headache later. In some cases, reformatting may also help your system to run faster. The downside of a clean installation is that it takes extra time to configure the OS, restore data files, and reinstall applications.

Although it takes time to reinstall applications, the reinstallation may solve problems with applications that don't work properly or that have become sluggish. When you reinstall applications, also plan to apply application updates that manufacturers often distribute through the Internet.

In some cases, you need to perform a clean installation because the new OS version does not support your old hardware. For example, organizations that were using Windows XP may need to upgrade to Windows 10 because Windows XP is no longer supported; the computers running Windows XP will probably not meet the minimum requirements of Windows 10, so clean installations on new hardware are required.

Preparing for an Upgrade or Migration

Before you upgrade or migrate, the first thing to consider is whether this step is truly necessary. For example, will it enable you or your organization to perform tasks or use software you can't use now? Will it save money in the long run by increasing productivity or enabling new services? Is your current OS no longer supported, or does it have security vulnerabilities that a new OS resolves?

If you are certain that an upgrade or migration is necessary and desirable, then you must make sure you have the necessary hardware and software (including device drivers) for the new OS version, as well as information about your computer that may be needed. You should also make a complete backup of your current system and data before starting. If you are upgrading or migrating more than two or three computers at once, consider performing a test upgrade or migration on one or two computers to identify and solve possible problems. These types of considerations are discussed in the following sections.

If you are upgrading or migrating a large number of desktop or server OSs, investigate automated installation methods, such as Microsoft's unattended installation option, or large-scale installation options such as Windows Deployment Services (available in Windows Server). There is not room in this chapter to discuss these automated techniques, but it is important to be aware they are available.

Deciding to Upgrade or Migrate When new versions of OSs are released that promise new features, bug fixes, enhanced capabilities, and more speed, it is tempting to jump immediately on the upgrade bandwagon. However, before taking such a step, especially in a large production environment, you should carefully consider whether you need to upgrade or migrate and whether the time is right. Although newer versions of OSs promise great new features, you should ask yourself whether you actually need the new functionality. Objective analysis of the situation may show that an upgrade or migration may not be cost effective. In other cases, the result might significantly lower the total cost of ownership (TCO) if the OS you are upgrading to can be more easily managed. For example, Group Policy is a feature that works in Windows domains to manage security, configuration, settings, and other configurable features on Windows client computers. Generally speaking, Microsoft enhances the capabilities of Group Policy with each release of its server and client OS versions, making newer OSs easier to manage while improving security in an enterprise network.

In some cases, moving to a new OS has little immediate effect on the functions performed by the computers and users for which you are responsible. However, you may want to upgrade to newer hardware for warranty, performance, and reliability reasons. In this case, your old OS may not support the new hardware features, making your decision to upgrade to a newer version an easy and necessary one.

Sometimes OS vendors publish a list of the applications tested on the new OS. These tests may not be comprehensive enough to ensure that all features of the applications work properly, or that they work on all types of computers. Install the new OS and the applications your organization uses on a test computer so that you can verify them before implementing them on a large scale.

Experience has also shown that it is best not to upgrade or migrate shortly after a new OS is released. If you can put off moving to a new OS for several months, or maybe even a year, you benefit from the experiences of many other users solving problems that might have been yours. If you wait, you will have access to many patches and bug fixes that are not available for early releases. If you feel you must upgrade or migrate soon after a new version is released, consider using the test strategy covered later in this chapter.

The OS Version Development Cycle Some OS vendors offer prerelease or beta software for you to try. Microsoft, for example, typically offers prereleases in the form of **alpha software, beta versions,** and **release candidate (RC) versions. Alpha software** is an early development version of software in which there are likely to be bugs, and not all of the anticipated software functionality is present. **Beta software** has successfully passed the alpha test stage. Beta testing may involve dozens, hundreds, or even thousands of people, and may be conducted in multiple stages, such as beta 1, beta 2, and so on. Beta software likely still has bugs, but is at a more tested stage. A **release candidate (RC)** is software at the final stage of testing by vendors and users before the official release that is sold commercially. A release candidate is usually tested by a very large audience of customers.

When an OS has been well tested and contains all of the new features, it is ready to go to market. At this stage Microsoft calls the software a **release to manufacturing (RTM)** version. Never install anything other than an official release or RTM version of an OS on **production computers** because preliminary versions can have bugs, security vulnerabilities, and reliability problems. In addition, some OS vendors put a time limit on preliminary releases so that they stop working or receiving updates after a specified date.

A production computer is any computer used to perform real work. If it were to become unusable for any reason, it would cause an inconvenience, hinder workflow, or cause data to be lost.

If you plan to implement a new OS for an organization, consider obtaining an alpha or beta version, and put it on a machine used specifically for testing. Use this computer for training and investigation to learn about the new features of the OS and how they will affect your work environment, particularly your existing software. Virtual machines are excellent choices for testing preliminary software releases because they can be quickly built and just as quickly removed when you are finished with them.

Checking Hardware and Software Before you decide to upgrade or migrate, you should carefully check the affected computers against the requirements of the new OS. As already noted, newer OSs often require more advanced hardware, including increased memory, disk space, CPU speed, and sometimes even improved display properties. Take special note of the hardware installed in the computer, such as network cards, scanners, sound cards, and other devices that require special drivers. If your organization supports many computers, consider obtaining network software that can automatically inventory the hardware components of the computers on your network. Or, you can inventory the hardware yourself, as illustrated in the example hardware inventory list in Table 5-2.

Table 5-2 Sample hardware inventory for multiple computers

Computer ID	CPU/clock speed	RAM	Disk capacity	DVD/CD-ROM	Video	Special devices
CFNP9012	2.8 GHz	4 GB	750 GB	DVD/CD-ROM	On board	None
D3FX1931	3.2 GHz	8 GB	1 TB	Blu-ray disc and DVD/CD-ROM	VisionTEK PCIe	Tablet
...	...	...	...	...	...	...

Also, before you migrate to a new OS, make sure that the current drivers for I/O devices and storage media work with the new version, or that drivers are available for these devices on the new OS. It is a good idea to contact hardware vendors and get some assurance that their devices will continue to work properly after the upgrade. Do not leave this to chance; older or discontinued hardware may not be supported in newer OS versions.

The issue of drivers is another reason to delay your migration until an OS has been on the market for several months. Sometimes OS vendors release a system before hardware manufacturers have had time to develop and test new drivers. Waiting to migrate usually means there will be more drivers—and hardware—available to use with an OS.

Make sure that you have all the device drivers needed for the hardware available on a DVD, flash drive, or removable hard drive. If there are drivers that exist only on the hard disk of the computer, copy them to a flash drive, removable hard drive, or some other safe place. Otherwise, if the installation fails, you will not have the drivers you need to get the computer back to work. If there are new drivers for the new version of the OS, keep them handy, as well as copies of your current drivers. You will then be able to reinstall the old OS if you cannot complete the upgrade for some reason.

It is also a good idea to keep detailed records of custom software settings—changes in the default settings for the OS and other software—so that these custom settings can be restored if necessary after any OS or other software upgrade. For example, it is not uncommon for users to modify display or other settings after they run an OS for a while; they may use an automated backup program, run special disk tools on a regular basis, or have customized network settings. Upgrade installations may reset some settings to their defaults, which may not be what you want.

5

Determine what software is used on systems prior to an upgrade or migration so that you can check to see if there are any compatibility problems. Windows 10 has a Program Compatibility Troubleshooter that can help you configure an application that will run on an older Windows version but won't run on Windows 10.

Another way to run older applications on new operating systems is to use virtualization. Using a virtualization program such as VMware Player, Hyper-V, or VirtualBox, you can run the old OS as a virtual machine in the new OS. In addition, some virtualization programs let you create a virtual machine from your physical computer, a process called *physical to virtual (P2V)*. Using this procedure, the OS and applications on your old computer are put into virtual disks that are attached to a virtual machine you can run in your new OS.

Making Backups Before Migrating to a New OS

A **backup** involves copying files from a computer system to another medium, such as tape, a DVD, another hard drive, or a removable drive. It is essential to have a complete backup of your old OS, software, and data before beginning a migration. Making backups of software and data is also a very important part of day-to-day computer operation because unexpected things happen, such as hard disk crashes or unintentional file deletions. As OSs and computers get more complicated, failures can even happen for unexplainable reasons during normal computer operation. If you use computers long enough, eventually you will lose critical information. Backups are essential to recovering from such a loss.

Most OSs have a backup utility, and software vendors offer many other choices that provide plenty of additional backup options.

If a program is lost, you may be able to simply reinstall it, but when data files are lost, the damage may take hours or days to repair. For this reason, regular backup of your system during normal operations and full backup prior to an upgrade are necessities.

Consider the following points when backing up your information:

- Close all open windows and save all files before starting a backup because many backup tools do not back up open files.
- Make sure that you have the software needed to restore the backups under both the old and new OSs. There is nothing more frustrating than having a backup but not being able to restore it. Even though you probably tested the backup and restore software with the old OS, there is no guarantee it will work properly with the new one. Before you perform an upgrade, you should test the restore software, preferably by making a backup and restoring it to the computer you set up to test the new OS.
- Make sure that you make a full backup of the system. You should make a backup of the entire contents of all disks connected to the computer, not just the disk the OS is installed on.

When you perform a backup, make sure that you back up critical system files, such as the system state data in Windows desktop and server OSs, which includes the registry. In the backup utility that comes with these OSs, and for some third-party utilities, you can manually select a system state backup. Another way to make sure that you have a backup of all files, including system files, is to perform an image (binary) backup by using tools in the OS's backup software or third-party software. Disk imaging software vendors include Paragon, Acronis, and Symantec.

Some computers you upgrade will not have a built-in drive, such as a tape drive or dedicated backup drive, that is suitable to make a full backup. In this situation, consider using a removable external hard drive or a network drive. Another option is to back up to another computer on the network that is equipped with an appropriate backup device. Keep in mind that almost all OSs support easily removable external drives that connect to the USB, FireWire, or eSATA port on a computer. It is worth the money to have one of these devices handy to make full backups before an upgrade installation. Chapter 7 and Chapter 11 provide more information about backups.

Upgrading an OS can be very simple; it may take only 20 minutes, and you may never need the backup media you created or the test system you used to verify the restore would work properly. However, if the upgrade does not go as planned, you will be very happy to have the backup. The time spent backing up, including testing the backup, can prevent many headaches and problems with your system upgrade.

From the Trenches ...

A small credit union was migrating from an older UNIX server to a new Linux server. They used third-party backup software that was advertised as supporting both OSs, so they did not run a test to ensure the software worked with both OSs. After upgrading to the Linux server, the information on the tapes made from the old UNIX system could not be read by the new Linux server. In fact, the backup could not be read even by the old UNIX system. Fortunately, the credit union staff had not dismantled the old UNIX system before discovering this problem.

Conducting a Test Migration

You should plan to test an upgrade or migration before you apply it to a production computer. If you have only one or two computers to upgrade or migrate, this may not be an option, but when you have five or more computers to upgrade or migrate, it can be beneficial to perform a test on one or more.

The purpose of a test is to simulate what would happen in a real upgrade or migration and discover any problems that might occur. To run the test, you need a working computer that closely resembles the computers you will be upgrading or migrating. Choose a computer that resembles the "lowest common denominator" of the computers you are upgrading or migrating, in terms of their amount of memory, CPU speed, size of the hard disk, and any connected devices. You should also install all software that is typically found on a production computer in your situation. If you are in a network environment, connect the computer to the network and make sure everything is fully functional. You should be able to use this machine as if it were a production computer. At the beginning of the test, this computer will run the old version of the OS, the version you currently run on your production computers. Part of the test is to practice upgrading or migrating this OS.

Consider using virtual machines as part of your upgrade test. Virtual machines don't test hardware compatibility, but you can at least install the applications in the new OS on a virtual machine to verify that the applications will work correctly.

When the test computer is fully functional, you can perform the upgrade or migration. It is helpful to take specific notes describing the steps of the installation, any problems that arose, and what you did about them. Also note any questions you had about the installation, and any information you had to look up to complete the installation. Write down the names of any drivers that you needed. These notes will serve as a guide in later installations.

When there are many computers to upgrade or migrate, it is common to do so over a period of several weeks or months, so having notes on the exact steps of the process will help you remember the information you need and the problems you found. Another approach is to create a written checklist that documents the upgrade or migration process step by step, including how to handle problems as well as special driver and software installations and configurations.

Once you complete the upgrade or migration on the test computer and immediately deal with any software issues that arise, test the computer for a couple of days. Perform tasks that you would normally perform, and take note of any changes in the computer and the user interface.

If you find no apparent problems, you may want to ask an experienced user whose computer is on the list to be upgraded or migrated to use the test computer for work for a few days. Keep in close communication with this person, taking note of any problems and anything that does not work properly. After moving to a new OS, one of the first things to check is whether all application software functions normally. Sometimes after upgrades or migrations, particular functions in software packages do not work, or work differently. If there are problems, chances are they will not surface until a user tries to access a certain function you never thought to test.

During the testing phase for an upgrade installation, ensure that the upgrade did not change any settings or move or remove files or programs. If you encounter significant problems with hardware or software, delay the upgrade or migration until they are resolved. Just as a prerelease test will uncover major and minor problems with a new OS design, an upgrade or migration test can uncover conflicts between the new OS and your particular system configuration.

After resolving any problems, repeat the test installation process. Install the old OS, then all software, then upgrade or migrate the OS, and make the changes you think will resolve the issues you encountered earlier. Test the computer yourself for a couple of days, and then let a user test the computer. In this way, you have another chance to test the upgrade or migration and your installation notes.

These tests can be time consuming; you may need a week or longer to get through them. In some cases, you may perform many test installations before you get every detail worked out. Or, you may decide after repeated tries that the upgrade or migration will not work and cancel the plan. Either way, the test results, when carefully documented, will tell you what to expect. Obviously it is better to find out in a test situation that an OS upgrade or migration won't work for you. Your test results can also be used to explain to employees and management why an upgrade or migration should or should not be carried out. If you decide that the plan should proceed, you will know the steps, you will know what to expect, and you will be efficient in performing the upgrade or migration.

Training

In small to large organizations that migrate to a new desktop OS, it is important to arrange for user training. This training might be in the form of classes, training videos, training DVDs, or other means. The important thing is to ensure that users have the opportunity to learn the new OS. There is an initial expense for training, but the return on investment (ROI) can be worth it in terms of user productivity as well as user morale.

Also, training for server administrators on new server systems is important. Training the server administrators will help them understand the new features of the server and how to best use those features to improve reliability, security, and productivity.

Part 2: OS Installations and Upgrades

The second half of this chapter focuses on the practical steps to install and upgrade the OSs discussed in this book. For each OS you learn:

- Information about OS versions
- Minimum and recommended hardware configurations
- Installation steps
- Upgrade steps
- How to install minor upgrades or patches (minor enhancements or fixes are often made available through the Internet on a weekly, monthly, or as-needed basis)

5

Installing and Upgrading Windows 7

Mainstream support for Windows 7 ended in January 2015, but it's still widely used in business and at home. Extended support for Windows 7 is scheduled to end in January 2020. The editions available in Windows 7 include:

- *Starter edition*—A stripped-down version of Windows 7 that offers limited functions, including fewer desktop display options. It is often preinstalled on **netbook computers**, which are small portable or laptop computers that have limited computing capabilities and are designed for lightweight portability. Netbook computers are generally used for Web access, e-mail, and basic document creation. Starter edition could originally handle only three simultaneously open applications, but this restriction no longer applies.
- *Home basic edition*—Just a step above Starter edition, the Home Basic edition is intended for Web surfing, e-mail, photos, music, and basic document handling. It has only limited support for the Aero desktop feature.
- *Home premium edition*—Offers more digital capabilities than Home Basic edition for expanding home entertainment, use of photos, and more capable document handling. Home Premium is particularly well suited to entertainment activities involving games, TV, music, and multimedia. Home Premium edition provides full support for the Aero desktop.
- *Professional edition*—A platform for accomplishing professional activities on the computer in a home, small office, or larger office work environment. Windows Professional is well suited to setting up projectors, networks, printers, and other shared resources. It enables the user to set up automatic backups in a home or work context.
- *Business edition*—Intended for business users to enable the use of business applications, network mobility throughout an office, and for remote access, document collaboration, versatile backup and shadow copy capabilities, and strong security. Business edition is also well adapted for membership in a Windows Server domain.
- *Ultimate edition*—A union of the home entertainment and business productivity capabilities of the Home Premium and Business editions. Ultimate edition also offers advanced battery management for portable computers and the most advanced security protection, including BitLocker Drive Encryption. BitLocker is a whole-disk encryption system that can prevent the system from booting without the necessary key.

- *Enterprise edition*—Contains the same features as Ultimate edition except that it is sold to large companies using volume licensing instead of to individual users.

All Windows 7 editions, except Starter edition (32-bit only), come in 32- and 64-bit versions. The user's direct experience of security in Windows 7 is toned down from Windows Vista, in that it requires less user intervention. However, the actual security is strengthened to meet new security threats.

Hardware Requirements For satisfactory performance, users should consider purchasing a computer that has a 1.2 GHz dual-core or better CPU, 2 GB or more of RAM, and 100 GB or more of storage. These aren't the minimum requirements (see Table 5-3), but they are recommended for satisfactory performance.

Windows 7 offers visual features that can take full advantage of the high resolution and display capabilities of systems with advanced graphics features. When you use a computer with an advanced graphics processor, Windows 7 can display high-quality results for multimedia and gaming applications.

The hardware requirements for Windows 7 are summarized in Table 5-3.

Table 5-3 Windows 7 hardware requirements

Hardware	Minimum	Recommended
CPU	1 GHz 32- or 64-bit processor	Multicore processor or multiple processors for better performance; also, an Intel-VT or AMD-V capable processor for handling virtual desktop software to run multiple OSs
RAM	1 GB (32-bit) 2 GB (64-bit)	2 GB or more for 32-bit systems (2 GB is required to run Windows Virtual PC) 3 GB or more for 64-bit systems
Storage	16 GB (32-bit) 20 GB (64-bit)	50 GB or much more depending on the applications to be used
Video card	DirectX 9 graphics device with WDDM 1.0 or higher	Video capabilities appropriate for the applications to be used; gaming and multimedia applications may require specialized video capabilities

Installing Windows 7 The Windows installation process is simple and straightforward. With the installation DVD inserted in the drive, start the computer. The system boots from the DVD and the setup program begins. You are prompted for the language and locale settings, as shown in Figure 5-1.

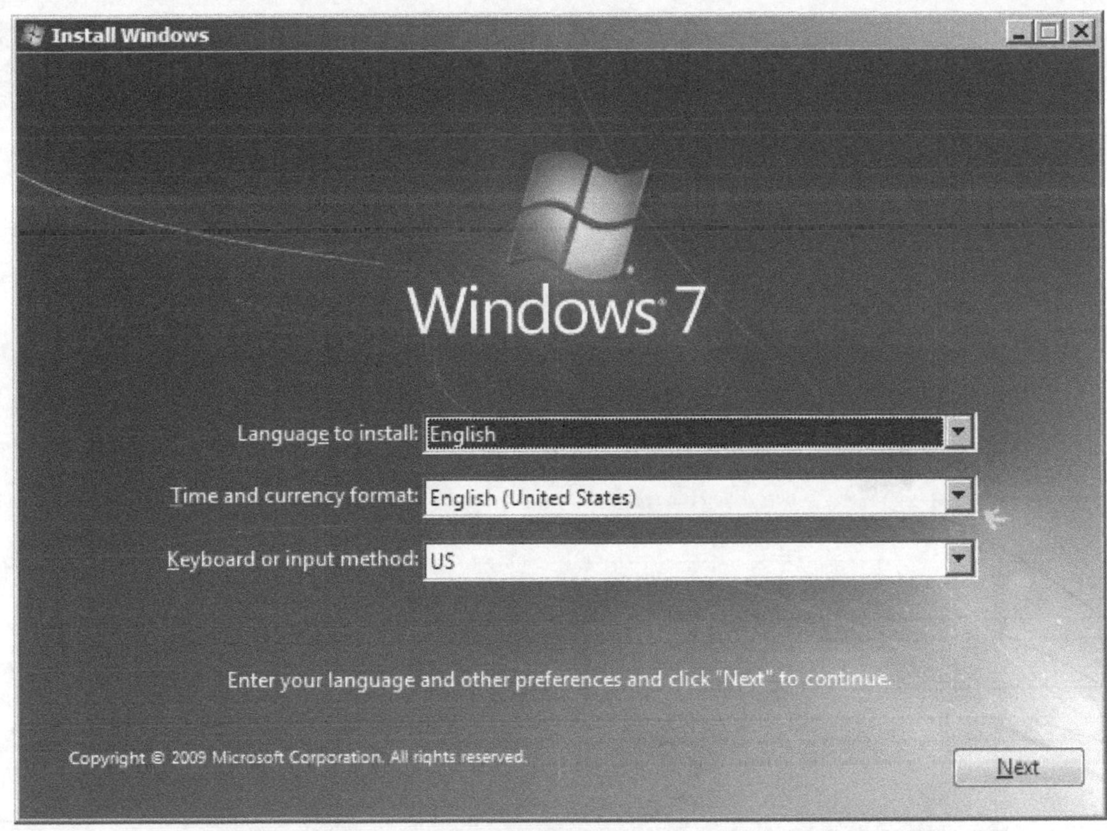

Figure 5-1 Choosing language and locale settings in Windows 7 setup

After clicking Next, you click Install now and setup continues. You must accept the license terms and then choose the type of installation you want (see Figure 5-2).

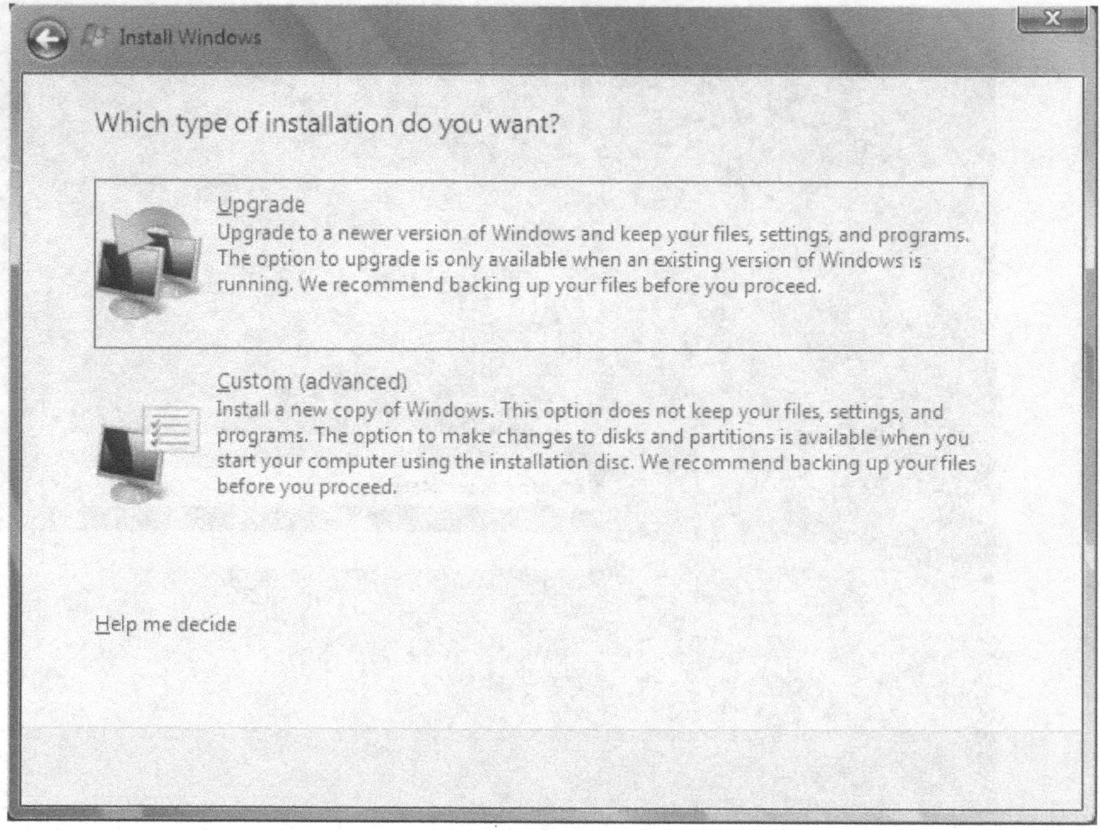

Figure 5-2 Choosing an Upgrade or Custom installation in Windows 7

Your choices are Upgrade and Custom (advanced). For a clean installation, choose Custom (advanced). An upgrade installation can only be started if you boot the system to an existing OS. Next, you choose where to install Windows. If your disk is empty, as in Figure 5-3, you can accept the default option, and Windows will create a 300 MB System Reserved partition for the boot files and assign the remaining disk space to the C: drive where Windows is installed. Optionally, you can create your own partitions or delete existing partitions by clicking Drive options.

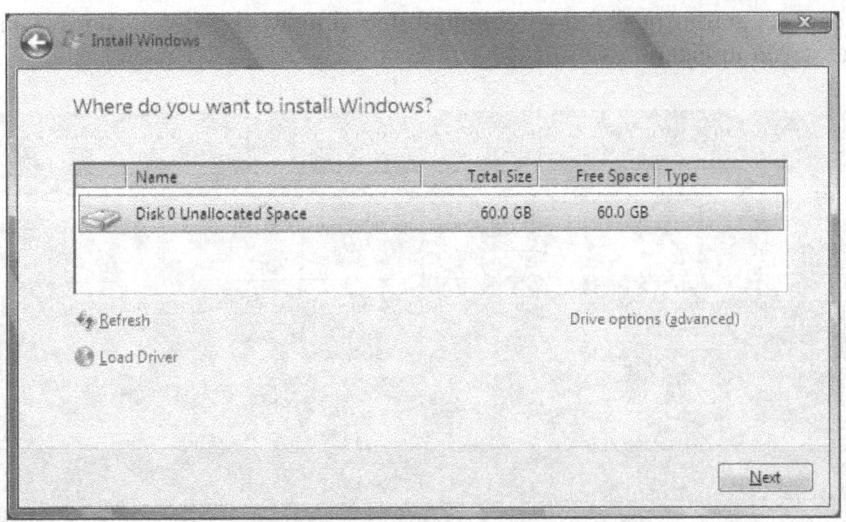

Figure 5-3 Choosing where to install Windows

Next, Windows copies files needed for installation and the installation continues. Your computer will restart once or twice during installation; when it is complete, you are prompted to create a user and a name for your computer and then create a password. You are then prompted to configure Windows Updates, set the time and time zone, and select your network location (Home, Work, or Public). Windows finalizes settings, the desktop appears, and installation is complete.

Most editions of Windows 7 require you to enter the activation code during installation. An exception is the Enterprise edition, which allows centralized activation for volume license holders.

Upgrading to Windows 7 There are two approaches to upgrading to Windows 7. One upgrade path is to go from one edition of Windows 7 to a more full-featured edition. You can perform this type of upgrade by purchasing the Windows Anytime Upgrade for Windows 7. Another path is to upgrade from Windows XP or Windows Vista to Windows 7. We'll forego the details of the upgrade paths because at this point in the Windows 7 life-cycle, most updates will be to a more current version of Windows, such as Windows 10.

Installing and Upgrading Windows 10

The actual installation process for Windows seems to become more streamlined and hands-off with each successive version. The installation process for Windows 10 doesn't differ substantially from that of Windows 7 or Windows 8/8.1 until the initial installation is over and you are asked whether you want to customize settings or use express settings. If you customize settings, you can specify how much information your computer should send to Microsoft for personalizing your experience, whether you want your location and browsing information shared with Windows and apps, whether to send diagnostics to Windows, and whether you should connect automatically to wireless and shared networks. If you choose Customize, you'll see the screen in Figure 5-4.

Customize settings

Personalization

Personalize your speech, typing, and inking input by sending contacts and calendar details, along with other associated input data to Microsoft.

On

Send typing and inking data to Microsoft to improve the recognition and suggestion platform.

On

Let apps use your advertising ID for experiences across apps.

On

Location

Let Windows and apps request your location, including location history, and send Microsoft and trusted partners some location data to improve location services.

On

Back Next

Figure 5-4 Customizing settings in Windows 10

After you customize settings or accept the express settings, you'll be asked how you want to connect to your organization's network if you're using the Enterprise or Education edition. For all other editions, you'll be asked to sign in to your PC using a Microsoft account. You can create a new Microsoft account or use an existing account by entering your e-mail address. If you want to sign in with a local user account, you are given that option as well. After you log on, Windows finishes installing and configuring your system and displays the Windows desktop. You will have an opportunity to install Windows 10 in a Hands-On Project at the end of the chapter.

All Windows 10 editions except Enterprise require you to enter an activation key during the installation process.

Upgrading to Windows 10 If you want to upgrade to Windows 10 on a computer with an existing OS installed, you have a number of options. Free in-place upgrades to Windows 10 are supported for Windows 7 and Windows 8/8.1. An **in-place upgrade** essentially overwrites your current OS installation and maintains your applications, settings, and data.

Windows 10 is a free upgrade for qualified editions unless you are running the Enterprise edition of Windows 7 or 8/8.1. If you are running the Enterprise edition, you must upgrade to an Enterprise edition of Windows 10 using your company's volume licensing agreement.

The easiest way to upgrade to Windows 10 is to download the Windows upgrade program. The Windows upgrade program will detect your edition of Windows 7 or 8/8.1 and will install the correct edition of Windows 10. Just open Internet Explorer from the computer you want to upgrade, and go to *www.microsoft.com*. You will be prompted to upgrade to Windows 10, which includes downloading and running the upgrade program. Once started, the upgrade program downloads and then installs the appropriate upgrade version of Windows 10. You can also upgrade by performing a custom installation from the Windows 10 installation DVD. Simply insert the Windows 10 installation media in the DVD drive, navigate to the DVD drive, and double-click Setup. Once the installation is started, there is very little for the user to do except accept the license agreement and let Setup to do the rest. If you do use the installation DVD, you should know which versions of Windows 7 and Windows 8/8.1 can be upgraded to Windows 10, as shown in Table 5-4.

5

Table 5-4 Windows 10 upgrade paths

Current OS	Edition	Windows 10 edition
Windows 7	Starter	Home
	Home Basic	Home
	Home Premium	Home
	Professional	Pro
	Ultimate	Pro
Windows 8/8.1		Home
	Pro	Pro
	Pro Student	Pro

If you are running Windows 7 or Windows 8.1, Windows Update will automatically install the Get Windows 10 app, which you can run to verify that your system is compatible with Windows 10.

If you are running a 32-bit version of Windows 7/8/8.1, you must upgrade to the 32-bit version of Windows 10. If you are running a 64-bit version of Windows 7/8/8.1, you must upgrade to the 64-bit version of Windows 10. In addition, upgrading to Windows 10 Enterprise requires a Windows 7/8/8.1 Enterprise edition.

Installing and Upgrading Windows Server 2008/R2

As with Windows 7, mainstream support for Windows Server 2008 and Windows Server 2008 R2 ended in January 2015 and extended support is scheduled to end in January 2020.

Windows Server 2008/R2 was widely adopted by IT departments. This section will lump together Windows Server 2008 and Windows Server 2008 R2 using the /R2 nomenclature to refer to both versions, while pointing out differences between the two releases as necessary. Most of the new features of Windows Server 2008/R2 were discussed in Chapter 2, but because Windows Server 2008 came five years after Windows Server 2003, there were many significant changes, most of which were carried over to Windows Server 2012. Some of the new features are:

- Centralized server management through the Server Manager tool
- Improved security
- Enhanced Web hosting services
- Hyper-V to create a virtual server environment
- Windows Server Core for running a server strictly through a command-line interface with a smaller network footprint
- Windows PowerShell, which provides a command-line and shell-based environment for creating time-saving computer management scripts

The following list shows some of the enhancements made with Windows Server 2008 R2.

- Active Directory enhancements, such as the Active Directory Administrative Center tool for centralizing tasks related to Active Directory and the Active Directory Recycle Bin that allows administrators to easily restore deleted objects
- File classification and file management tasks to improve file and folder organization
- Hyper-V (virtualization) enhancements, including better processor and networking support, and **live migration**, which allows administrators to move a virtual machine from one server to another with little to no downtime
- Windows AppLocker to better manage how clients access applications and server scripts
- New PowerShell commands to provide better script-based management of Windows servers

The main editions of Windows Server 2008/R2 are:

- *Standard edition*—Designed for basic everyday server needs for small to large businesses, such as file and printer sharing, basic network services including **Domain Name Service (DNS)**, and general management of network access. (DNS is an application protocol that resolves domain and computer names to IP addresses or IP addresses to domain and computer names.)
- *Enterprise edition*—Meets the needs of organizations that deploy networks with applications and Web services requiring high-end servers and a high level of productivity. This edition helps facilitate scaling server services upward as an organization grows, and it provides full clustering services for joining multiple servers in a fail-safe environment.
- *Datacenter edition*—Targeted for organizations that have mission-critical applications that use large databases of information.
- *Web Server edition*—Intended for hosting and deploying Web services and Web applications. This edition is optimized for Microsoft Internet Information Services for Web servers.

- *Itanium edition*—Designed for servers that use the Intel Itanium 64-bit processor but can still run both 32- and 64-bit applications. This OS enables resource-intense applications, such as the accounting system for a large corporation.
- *Windows Server 2008 R2 Foundation edition*—A less full-featured edition intended for small businesses as a file and print server, terminal server, or domain controller (to manage a Windows Server domain). This edition was new to R2.

Microsoft also offers Windows High-Performance Computing (HPC) Server 2008, which is a specialized edition used to cluster high-performance computers to simulate supercomputing capabilities, with support for thousands of CPU cores.

5

The Standard, Enterprise, and Datacenter editions of the original release of Windows Server 2008 come in 32-bit and 64-bit versions. Starting with Windows Server 2008 R2, only a 64-bit version is available. Also, you can purchase these editions with Microsoft Hyper-V to create a virtual server. A **virtual server** is a computer that can be configured to run multiple virtual machines. A **virtual machine** is a discrete OS running inside virtual server software, such as Hyper-V, on one computer. Multiple virtual machines can run on one virtual server. For example, one virtual server might house three virtual machines, each running its own copy of Windows Server 2008/R2, and two virtual machines, each running a Linux server distribution. In this example, one computer is performing as five servers. Using a virtual server consolidates server management and space and reduces expenses for electricity, resulting in financial savings and increased server manager productivity. As mentioned, virtualization is discussed in more detail in Chapter 8.

Hardware Requirements The hardware requirements for Windows Server 2008/R2 are pretty standard for all the primary editions, with the exception of the Itanium edition because it requires a specific CPU. Table 5-5 lists the hardware requirements. Also, be aware that the requirement for the 32-bit version of Windows only applies to the original release, not R2.

Table 5-5 Windows Server 2008/R2 minimum and recommended system requirements (all editions unless noted)

Component	Requirement
Processor	Minimum: 1 GHz for x86 CPU or 1.4 GHz for x64 CPU Recommended: 2 GHz or faster (Itanium CPU required for Itanium edition)
Memory	Minimum: 512 MB RAM Recommended: 2 GB RAM or more
Available disk space	Minimum: 10 GB Recommended: 40 GB or more
Additional drives	DVD-ROM
Display and peripherals	Super VGA or higher Keyboard and mouse

In Table 5-5, x86 means 32-bit and x64 means 64-bit.

Installing Windows Server 2008/R2 There are several ways to install Windows Server 2008. These methods include:

- Traditional DVD clean installation
- Unattended installation that uses specialized files for automating the installation of one or more servers without server administrator intervention
- Installation into a virtual machine, such as in Hyper-V
- Windows Deployment Services, which is a Windows Server 2008 application feature that enables multiple OSs to be installed from a master server over a network

The details of each installation method vary and are too complex to cover in this book. However, the installation steps used for a traditional DVD clean installation are the main steps used for any installation, and are almost identical to a Windows 7 installation.

Upgrading to Windows Server 2008/R2 Microsoft recommends that you perform a clean installation of Windows Server 2008/R2 rather than perform an upgrade. A server installation affects many more people than a workstation installation. Also, a server is likely to have more critical applications, databases, and other mission-critical information vital to an organization. In an upgrade, there is a greater possibility that compatibility problems or unexpected problems may result with applications and data. It is generally safer to fully back up data, perform a clean installation, reinstall applications, restore data, and spend several weeks testing the new system before releasing it live to users. Because mainstream support for Windows Server 2008/R2 has ended, this book will forego the details of upgrading to Windows Server 2008/R2, as most upgrades should probably be focused on Windows Server 2012 or newer versions.

When testing a new server installation, plan to involve users in the testing so they can help to find problems with the applications and data that are important to them.

Performing an upgrade to Windows Server 2008 is similar to performing a clean installation, but existing applications and data are retained.

Installing and Upgrading Windows Server 2012/R2

Windows Server 2012 was released to manufacturing in August 2012 with Windows 8, and Windows Server 2012 R2 was released in August 2013 with Windows 8.1. Most of the new features and the various editions were discussed in Chapter 2, but some of the other notable changes from Windows Server 2008/R2 included dropping support for the Itanium processor, dropping Enterprise edition, and the adoption of the Metro-style user interface from Windows

8/8.1. As with Windows 7 and Windows Server 2008/R2, there is very little for the user to do during installation. In fact, all the user really needs to do is select the language and locale settings, enter the activation code, accept the license agreement, and assign a password for the Administrator user. Most of the server configuration comes after the installation. Tasks such as assigning a name to the computer, setting the time zone, configuring the IP address, configuring updates, and installing server roles are all very important, and define how the server will operate in the network. Windows Server 2012/R2 has a convenient configuration panel called Local Server Properties that gives you access to most of these tasks, as shown in Figure 5-5.

PROPERTIES
For Server1 TASKS

Computer name	Server1	Last installed updates	Never
Workgroup	WORKGROUP	Windows Update	Download updates only, using Windows Update
		Last checked for updates	8/3/2015 12:08 AM
Windows Firewall	Public: On	Windows Error Reporting	Off
Remote management	Enabled	Customer Experience Improvement Program	Not participating
Remote Desktop	Disabled	IE Enhanced Security Configuration	On
NIC Teaming	Disabled	Time zone	(UTC-08:00) Pacific Time (US & Canada)
Ethernet0	IPv4 address assigned by DHCP, IPv6 enabled	Product ID	Not activated
Operating system version	Microsoft Windows Server 2012 R2 Standard Evaluation	Processors	Intel(R) Core(TM) i7-2600 CPU @ 3.40GHz
Hardware information	VMware, Inc. VMware Virtual Platform	Installed memory (RAM)	2 GB
		Total disk space	59.66 GB

Figure 5-5 Windows Server 2012 R2 Local Server Properties

Hardware Requirements The minimum and recommended hardware requirements for Windows Server 2012/R2 are shown in Table 5-6. The requirements apply to all editions unless noted. (The editions of Windows Server 2012/R2 were discussed in Chapter 2.)

Table 5-6 Windows Server 2012/R2 minimum and recommended system requirements (all editions unless noted)

Component	Requirement
Processor	Minimum: 1.4 GHz 64-bit CPU Recommended: 3.1 GHz or faster 64-bit multicore
Memory	Minimum: 512 MB RAM (2 GB for Essentials) Recommended: 2 GB RAM or more (8 GB for Essentials)
Available disk space	Minimum: 32 GB (90 GB for Essentials) Recommended: 60 GB or more for the system partition
Additional drives	DVD drive
Network interface card	Gigabit (10/100/1000 BaseT) Ethernet Adapter
Display and peripherals	Super VGA or higher Keyboard and mouse Internet access

The minimum requirements for Essentials are greater than for the other editions because Essentials installs several network services automatically.

Installing Windows Server 2012/R2 The Windows Server 2012/R2 installation routine is similar to that of Windows Server 2008/R2. You have the same option of installing the OS with a GUI or installing the Server Core version. The only substantial difference is that Microsoft now recommends installing Server Core, so it is the default choice (see Figure 5-6).

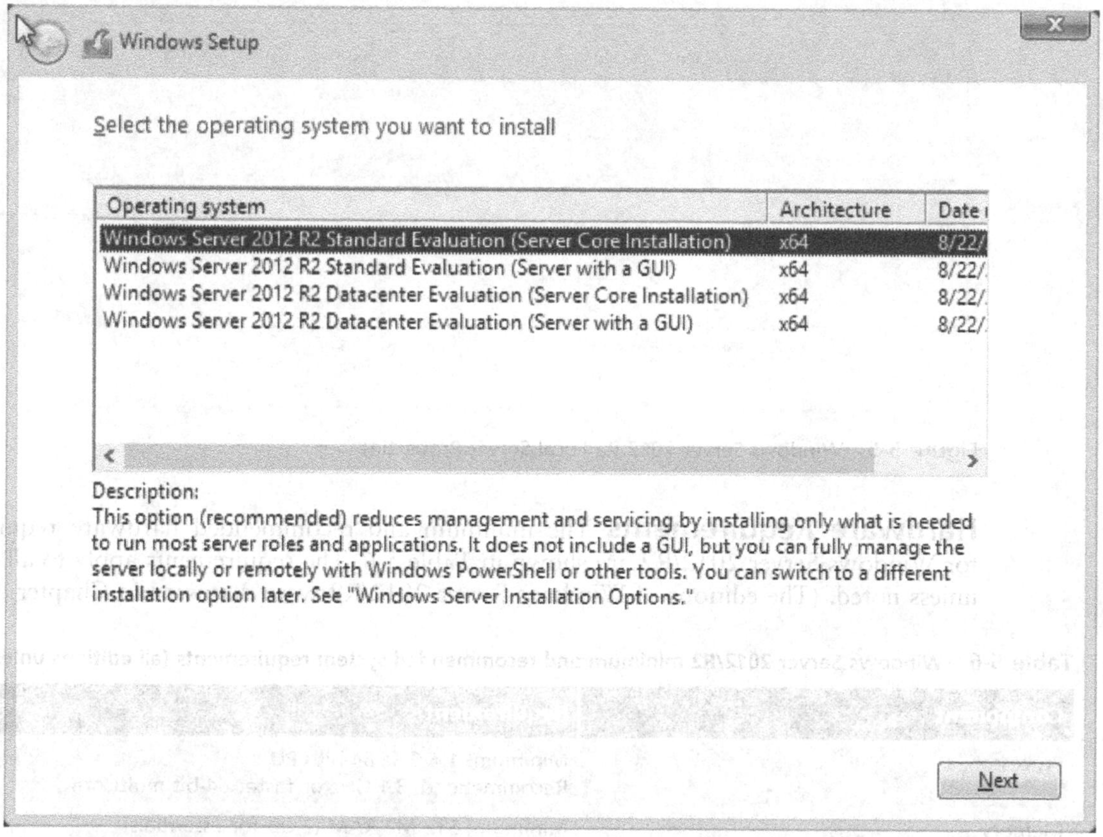

Windows Setup

Select the operating system you want to install

Operating system	Architecture	Date
Windows Server 2012 R2 Standard Evaluation (Server Core Installation)	x64	8/22/
Windows Server 2012 R2 Standard Evaluation (Server with a GUI)	x64	8/22/
Windows Server 2012 R2 Datacenter Evaluation (Server Core Installation)	x64	8/22/
Windows Server 2012 R2 Datacenter Evaluation (Server with a GUI)	x64	8/22/

Description:
This option (recommended) reduces management and servicing by installing only what is needed to run most server roles and applications. It does not include a GUI, but you can fully manage the server locally or remotely with Windows PowerShell or other tools. You can switch to a different installation option later. See "Windows Server Installation Options."

Next

Figure 5-6 Selecting Server Core or Server with a GUI

Upgrading Windows Server 2012/R2 When you upgrade to Windows Server 2012/R2, you can use one of two main methods: an in-place upgrade or server role migration. With an in-place upgrade, you boot to the existing OS and run setup.exe from the Windows Server 2012/R2 installation medium. With **server role migration**, you perform a clean installation of Windows Server 2012/R2 and migrate the server roles the old OS version performed. Here's an overview of in-place upgrade considerations, followed by available upgrade paths in Table 5-7:

- The only previous Windows versions supported for upgrade are Windows Server 2008 and Windows Server 2008/R2.
- If you're running Server Core, you can upgrade only to Windows Server 2012/R2 Server Core, but you can install the GUI afterward.
- All Windows Server 2012/R2 versions are 64-bit, and cross-platform upgrades aren't supported, so you can only upgrade the Windows Server 2008 64-bit version to Windows Server 2012/R2. A Windows Server 2008 32-bit version requires a clean installation.
- You can't upgrade to a different language.

Table 5-7 Windows Server 2012/R2 upgrade paths

Current edition	Server 2012/R2 upgrade path
Windows Server 2012 Datacenter	Windows Server 2012 R2 Datacenter
Windows Server 2012 Standard	Windows Server 2012 R2 Standard or Datacenter
Windows Server 2008 Standard or Enterprise	Windows Server 2012/R2 Standard or Datacenter
Windows Server 2008 Datacenter	Windows Server 2012/R2 Datacenter
Windows Server 2008 R2 Standard or Enterprise	Windows Server 2012/R2 Standard or Datacenter
Windows Server 2008 R2 Datacenter	Windows Server 2012/R2 Datacenter
Windows Web Server 2008 or Windows Web Server 2008 R2	Windows Server 2012/R2 Standard

If you're considering an in-place upgrade, Microsoft recommends removing any third-party software the manufacturer doesn't specifically support for a Windows Server 2012/R2 upgrade before you begin. In addition, make sure your system meets the minimum CPU, RAM, and disk requirements for Windows Server 2012/R2.

An upgrade is similar to a clean installation with a few exceptions. First, you must boot the existing OS and log on. Then you can start the setup.exe program from the installation medium. Next, you're asked whether Windows should go online to get the latest updates for installation. This option is recommended. You aren't prompted for the language, time, currency format, or keyboard layout; they must match the settings for the Windows Server 2012/R2 edition being installed. In addition, you aren't prompted during an upgrade for the location to install Windows. It's installed on the same disk partition as the OS you booted to.

Before an upgrade begins, Windows runs a compatibility check and produces a compatibility report. Any application, hardware, or driver issues discovered during the check are noted; you can't continue the installation until you address issues known to prevent a successful upgrade.

Migrating from an Earlier Version As you can see, in-place upgrades are somewhat limiting, and you can run into software incompatibility problems. In addition, upgrading isn't always possible if the specified upgrade path isn't available. For these reasons, Microsoft recommends a clean installation followed by server role migration, when possible.

Windows Server 2012/R2 has a number of tools to help with this process, which avoids most of the upgrade path restrictions. For example, migration allows you to do the following:

- Migrate from a 32-bit Windows server installation to Windows Server 2012/R2.
- Migrate from Windows Server 2003 SP2 and later.
- Migrate from a Windows Server 2008 R2 Server Core installation to a GUI installation and vice versa.

Migrating Windows server roles and features isn't an all-or-nothing proposition. You can migrate roles and features from a server running an earlier version to a Windows Server 2012/R2 server, move a role or feature from one Windows Server 2012/R2 server to another, or move a role or feature from a virtual machine to a physical machine or vice versa. However, language migration isn't supported; both server versions must be running the same language package.

Installing and Upgrading Linux

In general, installing and upgrading Linux isn't so much different from installing and upgrading Windows. However, there are many distributions of Linux, and details will differ depending on the distribution. This section discusses installing one Linux distribution version—Fedora 23—on the AMD/Intel PC platform. There are numerous other distributions of Linux designed for different hardware platforms. If you understand how Linux installs on the AMD/Intel platform, you should have no problem installing other distributions of Linux.

Hardware Requirements As with any OS, the optimal hardware requirements of Linux depend on how the computer will be used. This section only discusses the recommended minimum requirements for Fedora 23, which are shown in Table 5-8.

Table 5-8 Fedora 23 hardware requirements

Hardware	Recommended minimum
CPU	1 GHz or faster processor
RAM	1 GB or more
Storage (server)	10 GB free space
Video card	Minimum 800×600 resolution for a GUI installation
Removable storage	DVD drive or USB connection for installation or capability to run the OS from external media

Installing Linux Linux is available in free open source and commercial distributions. There is not room in this chapter to cover the installations of all distributions. Fedora 23, the free open source distribution on which the popular commercial Red Hat Enterprise Linux is based, provides a good starting point from which to learn about a Linux installation.

Fedora 23 Live Media can be booted and run from a DVD or Fedora 23 can be loaded as a permanent OS that boots from a computer's hard drive.

In one sense, the Fedora 23 installation from the Live Media DVD is not fully representative because you first start Fedora 23 from the DVD (and load it into memory), boot into the OS's GNOME desktop, and click an icon on the desktop to install Fedora 23 on the hard drive. In many other Linux distributions, including the non-Live Media Fedora 23 distribution, you boot from the DVD and can install Linux without first starting the OS. However, once you get started with the installation using either method, the installation steps are very similar to those of any Linux distribution.

Linux comes with the complete source code for the kernel, all the drivers, and most of the utilities. In particular, it comes with many program development tools, such as compilers for creating executable files that users can run on the computer. Linux distributions also often come with many appealing applications, such as OpenOffice.org, which is a free office suite distribution that is compatible with Microsoft Office.

5

When you run the live media version of Fedora 23 from the DVD, there are typically fewer applications available than when you install Linux onto the hard drive and simultaneously load a full range of open source applications, such as program language compilers.

Although most Linux distributions can be used as desktop or server OSs, some distributions have a specific version for the desktop and another version for a server. Server versions usually work the same way as desktop versions, but come with software intended for server environments, such as DNS and DHCP server software, Web server software, e-mail server software, account management software, and so on.

Upgrading Linux In Linux, the upgrade process works like the installation process. You start the installation in the normal way, and then choose to perform an upgrade. The installer asks for some basic system information, such as which language and keyboard to use. Also, it checks to determine what hard disks to use for the installation. It then gets most of the system information previously stored on the hard disk by the old OS. The appropriate system files are replaced, and the installer asks if you want to customize the package installation. If you select Yes, you can choose specific elements to install or update for each previously installed package. Note that many libraries and programs will be replaced, and if you add software to the computer, you should check carefully to ensure that everything still works as expected after installation.

An important caveat in Linux upgrades is that many configuration files are overwritten during the upgrade. The e-mail system, printing system, window system, and network services may be reconfigured. You should make sure you have backups of these files before you begin an upgrade, and double-check configuration files on these services to make sure they did not change.

Installing and Upgrading Mac OS X

The installation of Mac OS X uses a graphical interface and a Setup Assistant that functions like the Windows setup wizards. Early versions of Mac OS X up through Mac OS X Leopard can be installed on a computer with a PowerPC processor chip. Mac OS X Leopard can also be installed on a computer that has an Intel processor. Mac OS X Snow Leopard and later versions can only be installed on an Intel-based computer.

Besides the desktop editions of Mac OS X such as Mac OS X El Capitan, there are also server editions of Mac OS X Server. Mac OS X Server was released as a separate product with every desktop version of Mac OS X through Snow Leopard. Starting with Mac OS X Lion, Apple no longer produces a separate server version; rather, users can install an OS X Server add-on package through the Mac App Store for about $20 U.S. The server add-on package includes a number of server applications:

- *File sharing*—Allows more powerful file sharing between Macs, PCs, iPads, and iPhones
- *Caching server*—Speeds downloads and uploads between devices on the network and with cloud-based applications such as App Store, iTunes Store, and iBooks Store
- *Profile manager*—Simplifies the deployment and configuration of Apple devices by centralizing the management of user accounts, mail, calendar, contacts, and so forth
- *Time machine*—Makes any Mac act as a Time Machine backup location for all Macs on the network
- *Xcode server*—Provides team software development tools
- *Wiki server*—Provides a Web server with the capability for users to collaborate on Web pages, including blogs, uploads, and collaboration histories
- *Calendar, contacts, and mail servers*—Allows you to share calendars and contacts, and to manage e-mail with Mac e-mail clients on the Mac, iPad, iPhone, and PCs
- *Xsan 4*—Provides a scalable storage solution for centralized data

Hardware Requirements for Mac OS X Server Add-On The Mac OS X Server add-on requirements are shown in Table 5-9. The current version, as of this writing, requires the Mac to run Mac OS X El Capitan.

Table 5-9 Mac OS X Server hardware requirements and recommendations

Requirement
Mac computer running Mac OS X El Capitan
2 GB RAM
10 GB available disk space
Some features require a valid Apple ID
Some features require an Internet connection

Installing Mac OS X Installations of recent versions of Mac OS X are geared toward upgrades because it is assumed that you are already running some version of Mac OS X. You upgrade your current version of Mac OS X by downloading an installer from the App Store and then running the installer app, which installs the most current version of the OS on your system. Upgrading to Mac OS X El Capitan using this method is a safe bet for most Mac models from 2008 onward and for Macs running Snow Leopard or newer versions. In addition, you should make sure your current Mac OS X and the installed apps are up to date before performing the upgrade.

While using the downloadable installer is the easiest way to install the newest Mac OS X on your Mac, you may want to perform a DVD installation—for example, if you must replace your disk. You can create a bootable DVD and perform a clean installation of the OS if you want. To create a bootable DVD, follow these general steps:

- Download the installer for the current version from the Mac App Store.
- Open a terminal window.
- Run the *createinstallmedia* command, which is located in the installer program. The *createinstallmedia* command requires a series of complex options that will be different depending on the Mac you use, so it is not detailed here. To learn more about creating a bootable DVD, do an Internet search for "make a bootable Mac OS X installer disk."
- Boot from the DVD and start the installation, as described next.

A number of third-party DVD creators for Mac OS X will create a bootable DVD you can use to install Mac OS X.

5

Performing a Clean Installation from a DVD A Macintosh will boot from the DVD drive only if instructed to do so. Simply hold down the option key when you turn on the computer and then select the option to boot from the Mac OS X Installation DVD.

Here are the general steps for installing Mac OS X from scratch:

1. Insert the Mac OS X Installation DVD.
2. Turn on the Macintosh and hold down the option key as it boots.
3. In the OS X Startup Manager, choose the installer drive, and then click the arrow to continue.
4. Click Agree to accept the license agreement.
5. In the Install Mac OS X window, click the drive on which to install the OS.

Before you click Install in the window, notice the Customize button that you can click to customize components that will be installed. Also, you can choose to erase and reformat the drive before you click Install. You might do this, for example, if you suspect the drive has some bad spots or you want to be certain to overwrite any existing data on the drive and start fresh. To do so, click Utilities in the Mac OS X Installer menu bar and then click Disk Utility. Select the drive in the left pane and use the Disk Utility to erase and then format the drive.

6. Click Install. You will be prompted for the administrator password.
7. Wait for the installation process to finish; the computer will restart at least once.
8. In the Welcome window, select the country or region and click Continue.

9. Select the keyboard layout, such as U.S., in the Select Your Keyboard window. Click Continue.
10. In the Do You Already Own a Mac window, select the appropriate option to transfer information to the new Mac, and then click Continue. The options include:
    - From another Mac
    - From another volume on this Mac
    - From a Time Machine backup
    - Do not transfer my information now

    At this point you may need to take appropriate steps for the option you selected. For example, if you have a Time Machine backup on a USB removable hard drive, you need to connect the drive. Time Machine is the software used to back up a Mac.
11. If you see the Select a Wireless Service window, which is likely if you have a modern Mac, select your wireless service from the list. Also, enter the wireless service password if needed, such as that for WPA2 (Wi-Fi Protected Access 2) wireless security. Click Continue.
12. In the Sign in with Your Apple ID window, enter your ID, if applicable, for access to the iTunes store, iCloud, and the Apple Store. If you don't have an Apple ID for these services, leave this information blank. Click Continue.
13. Provide your personal information, including your first and last name, address, and e-mail address, in the Registration Information window. Click Continue.
14. In the A Few More Questions window, enter your answers in the appropriate boxes, including where you will primarily use the computer and what you do for a living. Click Continue.
15. In the Create Your Account window, enter your account name, a short name, the account password, a confirmation of the password, and a password hint. Click Continue.
16. In the Select a Picture For This Account window, select the source for the picture, such as the picture library. Click Continue.
17. In the Thank You window, you see a summary of what the Mac is set up to do, such as organizing your work and e-mail. Click Go to access the Mac.

Mac OS X comes with Migration Assistant to help you transfer user accounts, files, applications, and computer settings from another Macintosh computer. To run Migration Assistant, make sure Finder is running, click Go in the menu bar, click Utilities, and double-click Migration Assistant.

Regular Updates for OSs

Every OS vendor has a mechanism to provide bug fixes, security patches for threats such as worms and viruses, and interim upgrades between major releases of their OS. You've already been introduced to the Windows Update feature, which should be used following a Windows installation or upgrade. This section briefly reviews the update features of the OSs covered in this book.

Windows Updates Beginning with the Windows 98 release, Microsoft includes Windows Update, a Web-based function that allows you to download and install fixes, updates, and enhancements to your Windows OS.

An easy way to start Windows Update in Windows Vista/7, Windows Server 2008, or Windows Server 2008/R2 is to connect to the Internet, click Start, type Windows Update in the Start Search or "Search programs and files" box, and then click Windows Update. When you click Check (or Scan) for updates, Windows Update will automatically scan your computer to determine your OS and check on the installed updates. It then provides you with a list of updates that you can download and install on your computer.

You should download and install any Critical Updates and Service Packs (SPs) listed for your system. These updates will fix known bugs, security issues, and other problems that should be addressed as soon as possible.

Linux Updates Fedora and other Linux systems come with an update module for obtaining the latest updates. In Fedora 23 with the GNOME desktop, you can manually obtain and install updates by clicking Activities, Show Applications, and then Software. Click the Updates tab to list any new updates. You have the option to install the updates or not. To configure automatic updates, open a shell prompt, type *dnf install dnf-automatic*, and press Enter. Next, you must edit the /etc/dnf/automatic.conf file to specify the schedule. Finally, enable and run the update timers using systemctl:

systemctl enable dnf-automatic.timer && systemctl start dnf-automatic.timer

Mac Updates Mac OS X El Capitan provides updates through the App Store. Check to see if updates are available by clicking the Apple icon in the menu bar and looking for the App Store. If updates are available, you will be informed how many there are (see Figure 5-7). Click the button next to App Store to have Mac OS X download and install the updates. OS X will also display a notification when updates are available; you can choose to install them immediately or wait until later.

About This Mac
System Preferences...
App Store... 1 update
Recent Items ▶
Force Quit... ⌥⌘⎋
Sleep
Restart...
Shut Down...
Log Out Greg Tomsho... ⇧⌘Q

Figure 5-7 Checking for updates in Mac OS X

Source: Mac OS X El Capitan

Chapter Summary

- There are two basic types of installations: a clean installation on a computer with no OS installed or one that completely overwrites an existing installation on a computer, and an upgrade installation on a computer that already has an OS installed and where existing settings, applications, data, and other user files are often retained. The process of installing OSs varies from one OS to another, but all installations can be divided into three general stages: preparation, the installation itself, and any required or optional steps following installation.
- Before installing an OS or upgrading to a new OS, make sure that it is necessary. Also, when you decide to migrate or upgrade, check that your hardware meets the requirements for the new OS, and make sure you have the correct, most up-to-date drivers for the various devices on your system. Gather and document information about your system.
- Before you upgrade, make sure that you have a working backup of the current OS and data. Check your backup after it is made to make sure you can perform a restore from it if the installation or upgrade is unsuccessful, or if you need to retrieve data that was overwritten by the installation.
- Installations and upgrades to Windows, Linux, and Mac OS X are overviewed in the chapter text. Some of these installations are described step by step in the Hands-On Projects.
- After installation, and at regular intervals thereafter, it is a good idea to check for and download OS updates. All of the Windows versions described in this chapter provide the Windows Update tool. Linux provides an update module, and Mac OS X Leopard and Snow Leopard offer the Software Update tool.

Key Terms

alpha software An early development version of software in which there are likely to be bugs, and not all of the anticipated functionality is present. Alpha software is usually tested only by a select few users to identify major problems and the need for new or different features before the software is tested by a broader audience in the beta stage.

backup A process of copying files from a computer system to another medium, such as a tape, another hard drive, a removable drive, or a DVD/CD-ROM.

beta software During software development, software that has successfully passed the alpha test stage. Beta testing may involve dozens, hundreds, or even thousands of people, and may be conducted in multiple stages: beta 1, beta 2, beta 3, and so on.

clean installation An OS installation on a computer that either has no existing OS or an OS that is overwritten by the installation.

Domain Name Service (DNS) An application protocol that resolves domain and computer names to IP addresses, or that resolves IP addresses to domain and computer names.

in-place upgrade An OS upgrade that overwrites your current OS and maintains your applications, settings, and data.

live migration A feature of virtualization that allows a virtual machine to be moved from one server to another with little or no downtime.

migration Moving from one OS to another OS, which may or may not involve implementing a new computer as well.

netbook computers Small portable or laptop computers that have limited computing capabilities and are designed to be lightweight and portable. Netbook computers are generally used for Web access, e-mail, and basic document creation.

production computer Any computer used to perform real work; it should be protected from problems that might cause an interruption in workflow or loss of data.

release candidate (RC) The final stage of software testing by vendors before cutting an official release that is sold commercially. A release candidate is usually tested by a very large audience of customers. Some vendors may issue more than one release candidate if problems are discovered in the first RC.

release to manufacturing (RTM) A version of a Microsoft OS that is officially released to be sold and has gone through the alpha, beta, and release candidate phases prior to official release.

server role migration An alternative to a Windows server OS upgrade in which you perform a clean installation of Windows Server 2012/R2 and migrate the server roles the old OS version performed.

upgrade installation An OS installation on a computer that already has an earlier version of the OS; the upgrade replaces the earlier version with a new version, often with the option to retain some or all of the original settings, user accounts, applications, data files, and other existing user files.

virtual machine A discrete OS running inside virtual server or virtual desktop software, such as Hyper-V, on one computer. Multiple virtual machines can run on one virtual server. See *virtual server*.

virtual server A server computer that can be configured to run multiple virtual machines with multiple server or desktop OSs. See *virtual machine*.

Review Questions

1. Your manager is very interested in having a new version of an OS, and wants you to install a beta version to use on a server so that your company can be one of the first to take advantage of the new features. What is your advice?
   a. Beta versions are usually very stable and this is a good decision to help stay ahead of the competition.
   b. Beta versions are often sold at a lower cost, which would offer savings to the company.
   c. OS vendors often provide extensive onsite help to users of beta systems in a production environment.
   d. A safer path is to wait for an official release and to avoid using a beta system in a production environment.

2. Under which conditions should you consider a clean installation? (Choose all that apply.)
    a. The installation is performed on a computer that has no OS installed.
    b. You want to replace the current OS but maintain all your settings.
    c. You don't want to have to reinstall applications.
    d. You want to be able to boot to your old OS and the new OS.
3. Which of the following should you do prior to creating a backup in preparation for an OS upgrade? (Choose all that apply.)
    a. Be sure you have the software needed to perform a restore on old and new OSs.
    b. Unmount the disk being backed up.
    c. Close active windows and programs.
    d. Mount all volumes in a volume mount point.
4. You are in a committee meeting in which the members are debating whether the Windows XP Professional computers in a laboratory can be directly upgraded to Windows 10 for free. What is your recommendation?
    a. Check Windows Help on each computer.
    b. Purchase all new computers because Windows 10 can rarely run on computers suited for Windows XP.
    c. Configure the XP computers for the Enterprise edition first.
    d. You will need to perform a clean installation of Windows 10.
5. Which of the following is true about Windows Server 2012?
    a. You can upgrade from Windows Server 2003/R2 SP2.
    b. You can upgrade from Windows Server 2008 x86.
    c. You can upgrade from Server Core to Server with a GUI.
    d. You can't upgrade to a different language.
6. You are running Windows Server 2008 x86 on a 32-bit CPU. You want to upgrade to Windows Server 2012/R2. What can you do?
    a. Run the Windows Server Upgrade program and insert the Windows Server 2012/R2 installation DVD.
    b. First, upgrade to Windows Server 2008/R2, and then upgrade to Windows Server 2012/R2.
    c. Install Windows Server 2012/R2 on a new computer and migrate server roles.
    d. Back up the computer and perform a clean installation of Windows Server 2012/R2, then restore the data and applications.

7. You need to perform a backup in Windows that includes the registry. Which type of backup should you perform?
   a. system state backup
   b. data drive backup
   c. scheduled backup
   d. incremental backup

8. When you install an OS on a computer with a hard drive that has been formatted and does not contain a previous OS, you perform a ______________ installation.
   a. clean
   b. update
   c. upgrade
   d. new

9. Which key should you press to boot a Macintosh computer from an installation DVD?
   a. Esc
   b. Option
   c. Ctrl
   d. Apple

10. Choosing the Customize button during a Mac OS X installation allows you to ______________.
   a. select which OS to install
   b. choose the installation location
   c. choose various OS components you want to install
   d. repartition the hard drive for a different file system

11. Which of the following are possible ways to install Windows Server 2008? (Choose all that apply.)
   a. from a set of floppy disks combined with a CD-ROM
   b. using an unattended installation
   c. into a virtual machine
   d. through Windows Deployment Services

12. You have a Windows Server 2008 server with a 2 GHz, 32-bit processor and 4 GB of memory. You plan to upgrade it to Windows Server 2012/R2. When you attempt the upgrade, the Setup program stops with a message that it cannot continue. Which of the following might be the problem?
   a. There is not enough memory for the upgrade.
   b. You must have a quad-core processor.
   c. You didn't run the setup routine from Windows Server 2008.
   d. Windows Server 2012/R2 requires a 64-bit processor.

13. Mac OS X El Capitan can run on which of the following processors?
    a. PowerPC G3
    b. PowerPC G5
    c. AMD M4
    d. Intel
14. Each OS upgrade is different, but which of the following are general steps you should conduct with every upgrade? (Choose all that apply.)
    a. Test the upgrade on a non-production computer.
    b. Don't upgrade as soon as the new OS is released; wait a few months.
    c. Back up all data and applications before starting the upgrade.
    d. Format the installation disk before starting the upgrade.
15. You have purchased a computer that is loaded with Windows 7 Home Premium. After using the computer for several months, you decide you want to upgrade to Windows 10. Which of the following Windows 10 editions can be upgraded from Windows 7 Home Premium?
    a. Enterprise
    b. Home
    c. Pro
    d. Starter
16. Which of the following is true about the Enterprise edition of Windows 10?
    a. It's only available if it's pre-installed by a computer vendor.
    b. You can upgrade to it from Windows Home Premium.
    c. You don't need to enter an activation key during installation.
    d. It's only available in a 64-bit version.

Hands-On Projects

Project 5-1: Change BIOS Settings to Boot to a DVD

Your hardware system BIOS controls many basic functions of your computer. This chapter discusses the need to be able to boot from a DVD. You can find out how your system BIOS handles DVD booting by displaying the BIOS Setup or Configuration screen on your computer.

1. Start your Windows or Linux computer. You must watch carefully for a message that tells you which key to press to enter the BIOS setup. You may also consult the system documentation or ask an instructor. The F1, F2, Esc, and Del keys are commonly used to access BIOS setup. Another way to enter BIOS setup is to hold down a key on the keyboard while booting. The BIOS sometimes generates a keyboard error message and gives you the option to go into setup.

2. Once you are in the BIOS setup, look for settings for boot order or boot sequence. For example, Figure 5-8 displays the PhoenixBIOS Setup Utility with the Boot tab selected. Some BIOS setup routines require you to use the keyboard rather than the mouse to navigate; the navigation keys are often shown on the bottom of the screen, as in Figure 5-8.

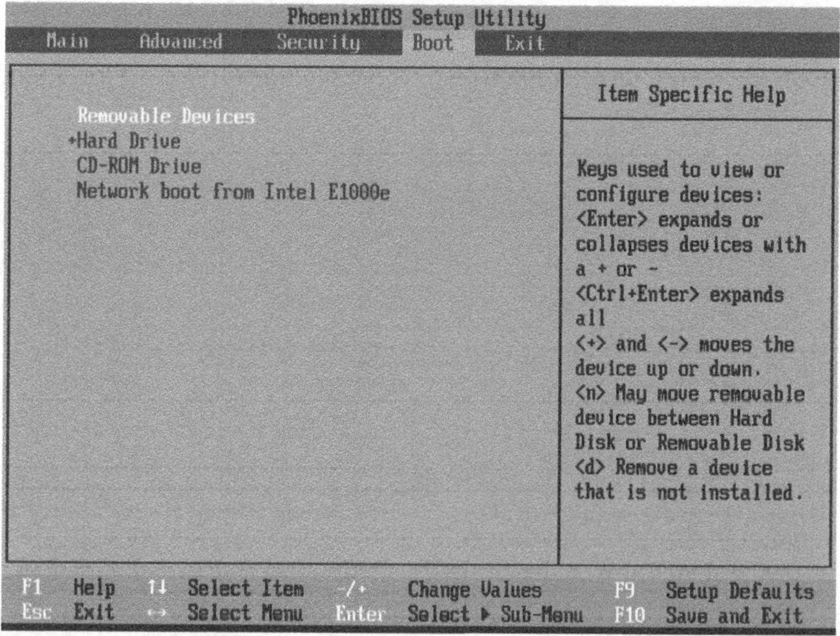

Figure 5-8 BIOS setup program showing boot options

3. Use the appropriate keys to change the order of boot devices.
4. If available (and with your instructor's permission), choose a DVD or CD-ROM drive, and then save and exit the Setup or Configuration screen.
5. Insert a Windows or Linux OS installation disk and reboot the computer. You may see a message that says, "Press any key to boot to the DVD/CD." Your computer should boot to the installation disk. Do not install the OS now.
6. Restart the computer, change the boot order back to the hard drive, and remove the installation disk. Save the configuration and exit.

Project 5-2: Document Installed Software in Windows

Before performing a clean installation or upgrading an OS, it is important to know what software is currently installed in the current OS. If you have to do a clean installation or the update doesn't correctly recognize the installed software, you need to have an accurate inventory of all your applications (not those that come with the OS, but those you install after the OS installation) so they can be reinstalled in the new OS, if necessary. This project shows you where to look for installed applications in Windows 10.

1. Start your Windows computer and log on if necessary.
2. Right-click **Start** and click **Control Panel**.
3. In Control Panel, click **Programs** and then click **Programs and Features**. You will see a list of installed programs, as shown in Figure 5-9.

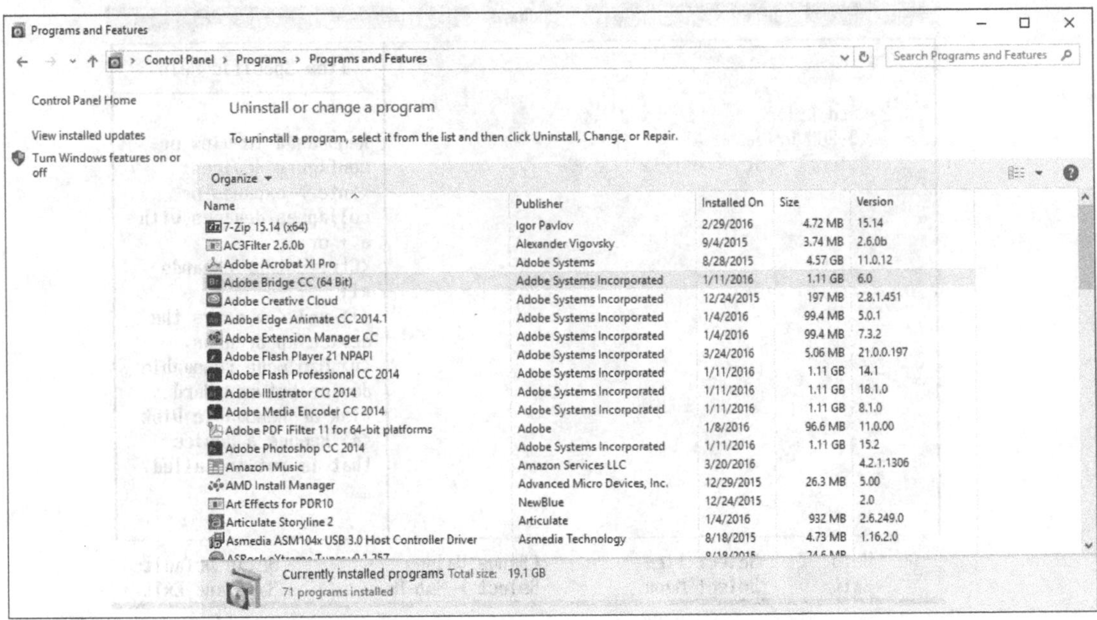

Figure 5-9 A list of installed programs in Windows

4. Taking a screen shot is probably the easiest way to record the list. In Windows 10, you click in the search box next to Start and type **snip**. In the search results, click **Snipping Tool**.
5. In Snipping Tool, click **New**. Position the mouse in the upper-left corner of the Control Panel window and click and drag until the window is highlighted. When you release the mouse button, the Snipping Tool will open with your screen shot. If you have more programs than will fit on one screen, scroll down and create another screen shot. You can print or save the screen shots.
6. Verify that you have the necessary installation media or setup programs and license codes for all your installed applications before you begin an OS update. If you only have setup files for downloaded applications, be sure to save them on external media before you begin the installation.
7. Close all open windows.
8. Log off or shut down your Windows computer.

Project 5-3: Document Installed Software in Mac OS X

This project helps you document the installed applications in Mac OS X.

1. Start your Mac OS X computer and log on if necessary. Click **Go** and click **Applications.**
2. The Applications folder displays all installed applications on your Mac, including those that came with the OS and those you installed manually. Scroll through the applications. Take a screen shot of the Applications folder by pressing **Shift+Command+4** and then dragging over the area you want to capture. If you are using a PC keyboard, you can use **Shift+Windows+4**. The screen shot is saved to your Mac desktop.
3. Close the Applications window.
4. If you only want to view the list of applications you installed from the App Store, click the **Apple** icon, and then click **App Store.** Click **Purchased** in the menu bar and sign in with your Apple ID, if necessary. You will see a list of purchased apps.
5. If you only installed apps from the App Store, you probably don't need to document your installed apps. When you install the upgrade, you can connect to the App Store and download any software you previously purchased. Close all open windows and then log off or shut down your Mac.

5

Project 5-4: Document Installed Software in Linux

This project helps you document the installed applications in Linux Fedora 23 with GNOME.

1. Start your Linux computer and log on, if necessary. Click **Activities** and **Show Applications.**
2. You will see applications that came installed with Linux and those you installed after Linux was installed. To take a screen shot, press **Shift+PrtScn** on your keyboard. Click and drag the cursor over the area you want to capture. The screen shot is saved to the Pictures folder.
3. You can also use the ScreenShot utility by clicking the search box at the top of the screen and typing **screen**. In the search results, click **Screenshot.** You can take a screen shot of the whole screen, the current window, or a specific area (see Figure 5-10). When you finish, close the Take Screenshot window.

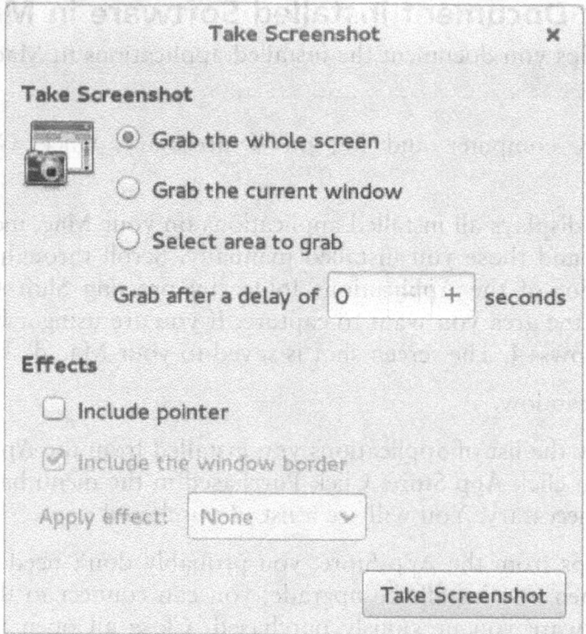

Figure 5-10 The Linux Screenshot application

Source: Fedora Linux

4. To see a list of installed applications using the command line, open a terminal window, type **rpm –qa,** and press **Enter**. You will see a more complete list of applications than you were able to obtain simply by using the Applications menu in the GNOME desktop.
5. You can view each screen of output. Type **rpm –qa | more** and press **Enter**. Press **Space** to scroll through each page of output. Press **q** to quit before viewing all pages.
6. To redirect the output to a file, type **rpm –qa > softwarelist.txt** and press **Enter**. Type **cat softwarelist.txt** and press **Enter** to see the created file. Close the terminal window.

The command to view installed software packages is different in various UNIX systems. For example, you enter *pkginfo* in Solaris, *swlist* in HP UNIX, *pkg_info -a* in FreeBSD, and *lslpp -L all* in IBM's AIX.

It is highly recommended that you use virtualization software to perform the Hands-On Projects that walk you through the installation of various OSs. If you use virtualization software such as VMware Player, VirtualBox, or Hyper-V, you will not need physical installation media. You can connect the virtual DVD drive to the installation media ISO file, and your virtual machine will boot from the ISO file. If you are using virtualization, do not burn a DVD and insert it into the DVD drive, as instructed in the following projects; connect the virtual DVD drive to the ISO file instead.

Project 5-5: Install Windows 10

In this project, you install Windows 10 using the DVD installation method. Before you start, you will need the Windows 10 installation DVD. You can get a 90-day evaluation of Windows 10 Enterprise Edition from the Technet Evaluation Center at *www.microsoft.com/en-us/evalcenter/evaluate-windows-10-enterprise*. You will be asked to sign in using your Microsoft account; you can create an account if you don't already have one. After you download the ISO file, burn it to a DVD.

5

1. Insert the Windows 10 installation DVD in the DVD drive of a computer that meets the minimum requirements for Windows 10.
2. Start your computer if you are sure it will boot to the DVD. (Refer to Hands-On Project 5-1 for details on booting via a DVD.)
3. After the Windows logo is displayed, Windows Setup begins. The screen prompts you to choose your language and location preferences (see Figure 5-1 earlier in this chapter). Click **Next.**
4. On the next screen, you have the option to repair your computer or install the OS. Click **Install now.**
5. If you are using an edition that requires an activation key, enter it on the next screen and click **Next;** otherwise, read the Windows 10 Licensing terms, click **I accept the license terms,** and click **Next.**
6. The next screen asks, "Which type of installation do you want?" (see Figure 5-2 earlier in this chapter). Click **Custom: Install Windows only (advanced)** to perform a clean installation.
7. If you already have an OS installed, your disks will be partitioned like they are in Figure 5-11; otherwise, your screen will look like Figure 5-3 (shown earlier). If you already have an OS installed and you want to keep it on your computer, you will need another partition or disk on which to install Windows 10. To delete the old OS, click each partition and click **Delete.** This project assumes that you have a blank disk on which to install Windows 10. (The name of the disk will include the words "Unallocated Space.").

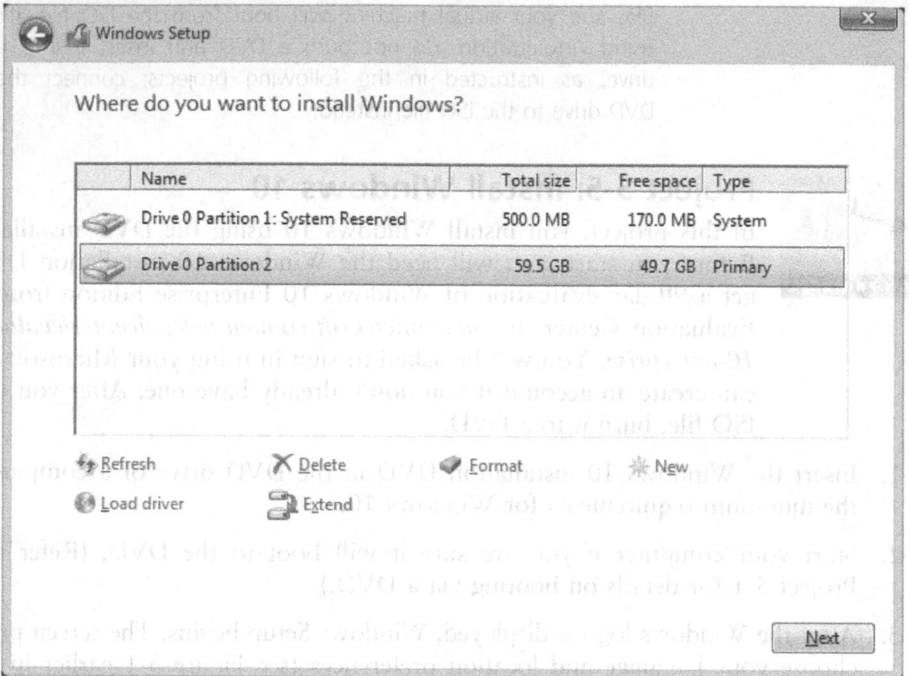

Figure 5-11 A system with a Windows OS already installed

8. Click the disk on which to install Windows 10, and then click **Next.** The setup program copies files and installs Windows 10. The computer will restart at least once. When the computer restarts, be sure to remove the installation DVD, or the computer might boot to the DVD and start the installation process from the beginning.
9. After the computer restarts, you are prompted to use Express settings or Customize settings. Click **Use Express settings.** The system restarts.
10. If you are using the Enterprise evaluation edition or the Education edition, you are prompted to choose how you'll connect to the network (see Figure 5-12). Click **Join a domain** and then click **Next.**

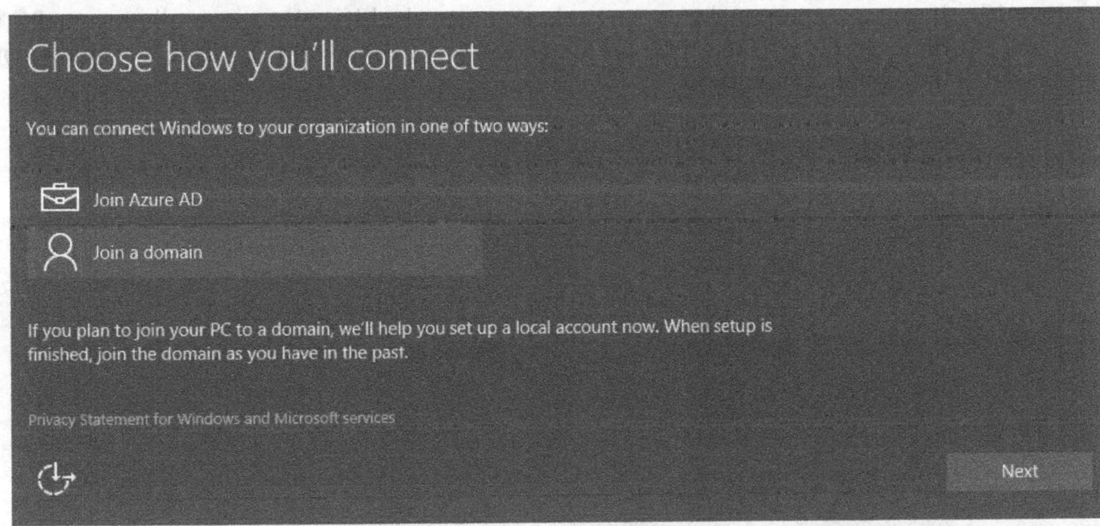
Choose how you'll connect
You can connect Windows to your organization in one of two ways:
Join Azure AD
Join a domain
If you plan to join your PC to a domain, we'll help you set up a local account now. When setup is finished, join the domain as you have in the past.
Privacy Statement for Windows and Microsoft services
Next

Figure 5-12 Choose how you'll connect

11. On the "Create an account for this PC" screen (see Figure 5-13), type a user name, a password, and a password hint, and then click **Next**.

Create an account for this PC
If you want to use a password, choose something that will be easy for you to remember but hard for others to guess.
Who's going to use this PC?
gtomsho
Make it secure.
••••••••
••••••••
my hint
Back
Next

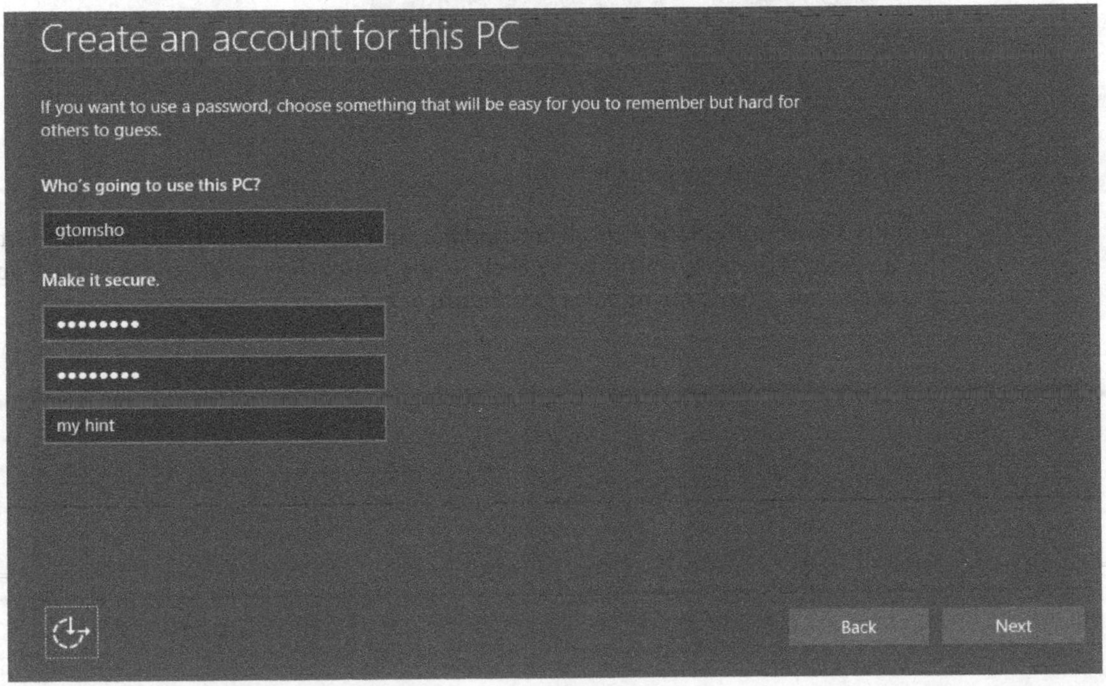

Figure 5-13 Create an account for this PC

12. Windows 10 completes the setup process and you are logged in.

13. If you are connected to a network, you are asked if you want to allow your PC to be discoverable by other PCs on the network (see Figure 5-14). Click **Yes** unless you are on a public network.

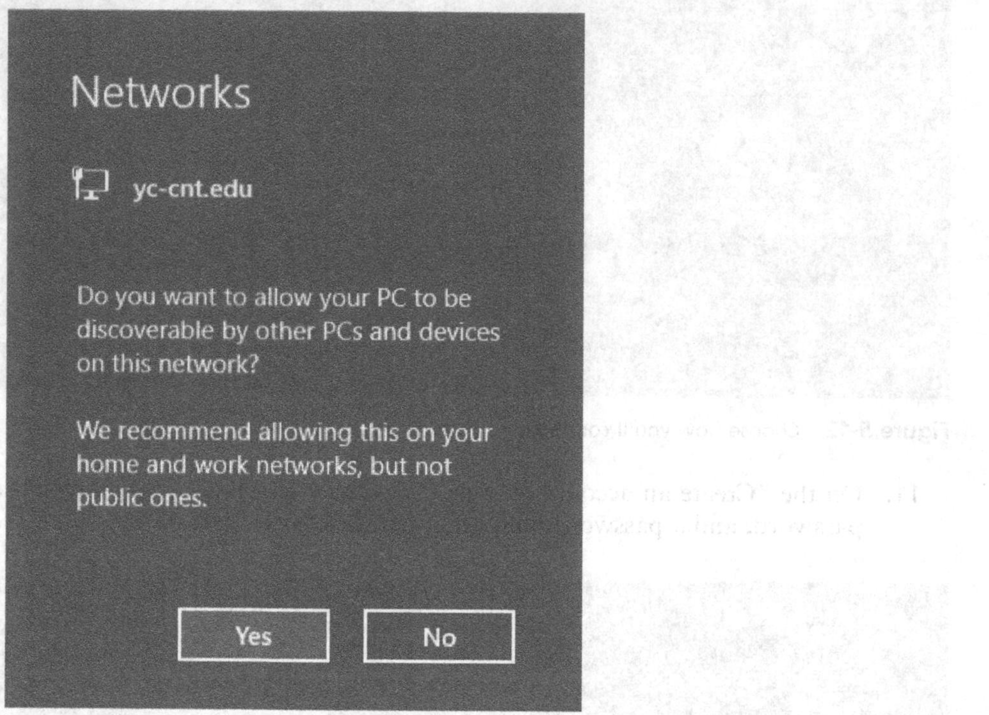

Figure 5-14 Choosing network behavior

14. Windows will immediately check for updates and install them if you are connected to the Internet. To check on updates, click in the search box next to **Start,** type **update,** and then click **Check for updates** (see Figure 5-15).

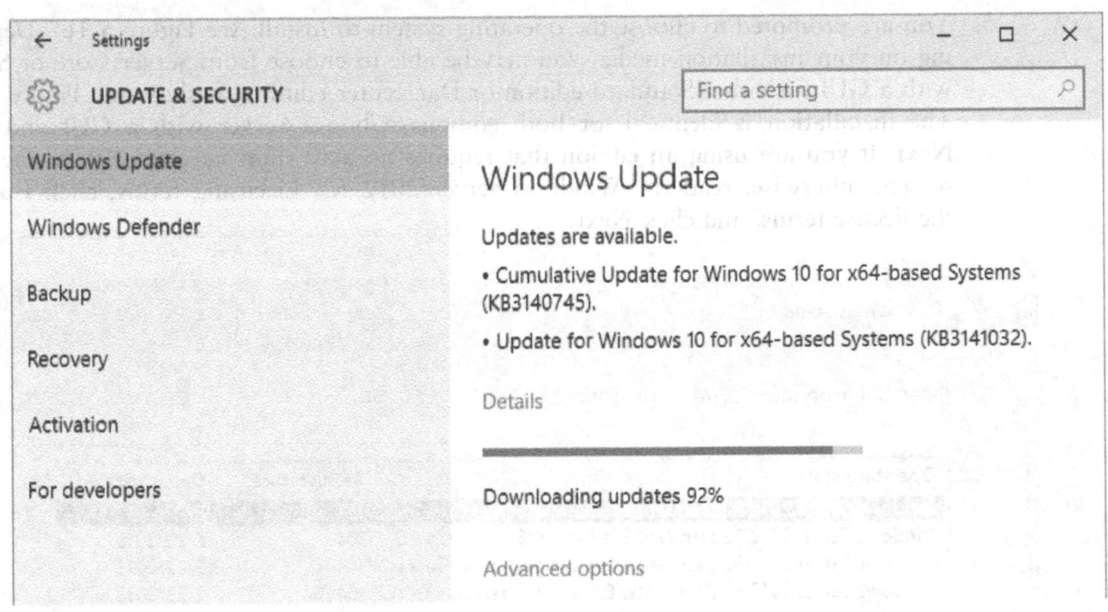

Figure 5-15 Windows Update

15. Log off or shut down your computer.

Project 5-6: Install Windows Server 2012 R2

In this project, you install Windows Server 2012 R2. You need the installation DVD for either the Windows Server 2012 R2 Standard or Datacenter edition. You can download a 180-day evaluation of Windows Server 2012 R2 from *www.microsoft.com/en-us/evalcenter/evaluate-windows-server-2012-r2*. You will be asked to sign in using your Microsoft account, which you can create if you don't already have one. After you download the ISO file, burn it to a DVD.

The installation procedure for Windows Server 2012 R2 is nearly identical to that of Windows 10 until the system restarts. Only screens that are substantially different are shown in this project. This installation procedure assumes that no other OS is installed on the computer and that the disk is unpartitioned.

1. Insert the Windows Server 2012 R2 installation DVD in the DVD drive of a computer that meets the minimum requirements for Windows Server 2012 R2.
2. Start your computer if you are sure it will boot to the DVD.
3. After the Windows logo is displayed, Windows Setup begins. The screen prompts you to choose your language and location preferences. Click **Next**.
4. On the next screen, you have the option to repair your computer or install the OS. Click **Install now**.

5. You are prompted to choose the operating system to install (see Figure 5-16). Depending on your installation media, you may be able to choose from Server Core or Server with a GUI for either Standard edition or Datacenter edition, as shown in Figure 5-16. The installation is identical for both editions. Choose **Server with a GUI** and click **Next**. If you are using an edition that requires an activation key, enter it on the next screen; otherwise, read the Windows Server 2012 R2 Licensing terms, click **I accept the license terms**, and click **Next**.

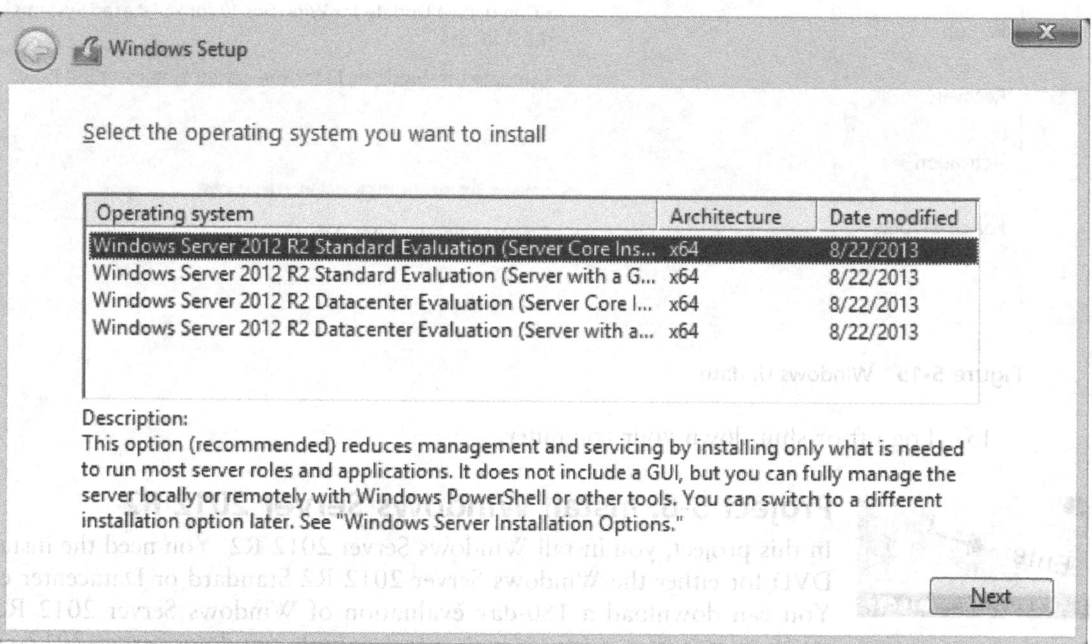

Figure 5-16 Choosing the edition and interface for Windows Server 2012 R2

6. The next screen asks, "Which type of installation do you want?" Click **Custom** to perform a clean installation.
7. Click the disk on which to install Windows Server 2012 R2, and then click **Next**. The setup program copies files and installs Windows Server 2012 R2. The computer will restart at least once. When the computer restarts, be sure to remove the installation DVD, or the computer might boot to the DVD and start the installation process from the beginning.
8. After the computer restarts, you are prompted to enter a password for the Administrator account. You must use a password that meets minimum requirements. Type **Password01** in the Password and Reenter Password boxes and click **Finish**.
9. To log on to Windows Server 2012 R2, press **Ctrl+Alt+Delete**, enter the password for Administrator, and press Enter.

10. If you are connected to a network, you are asked if you want to allow your PC to be discoverable by other PCs on the network. Click Yes unless you are on a public network.
11. Windows Server Manager automatically starts and displays the Windows Server 2012 R2 Server Manager Dashboard (see Figure 5-17).

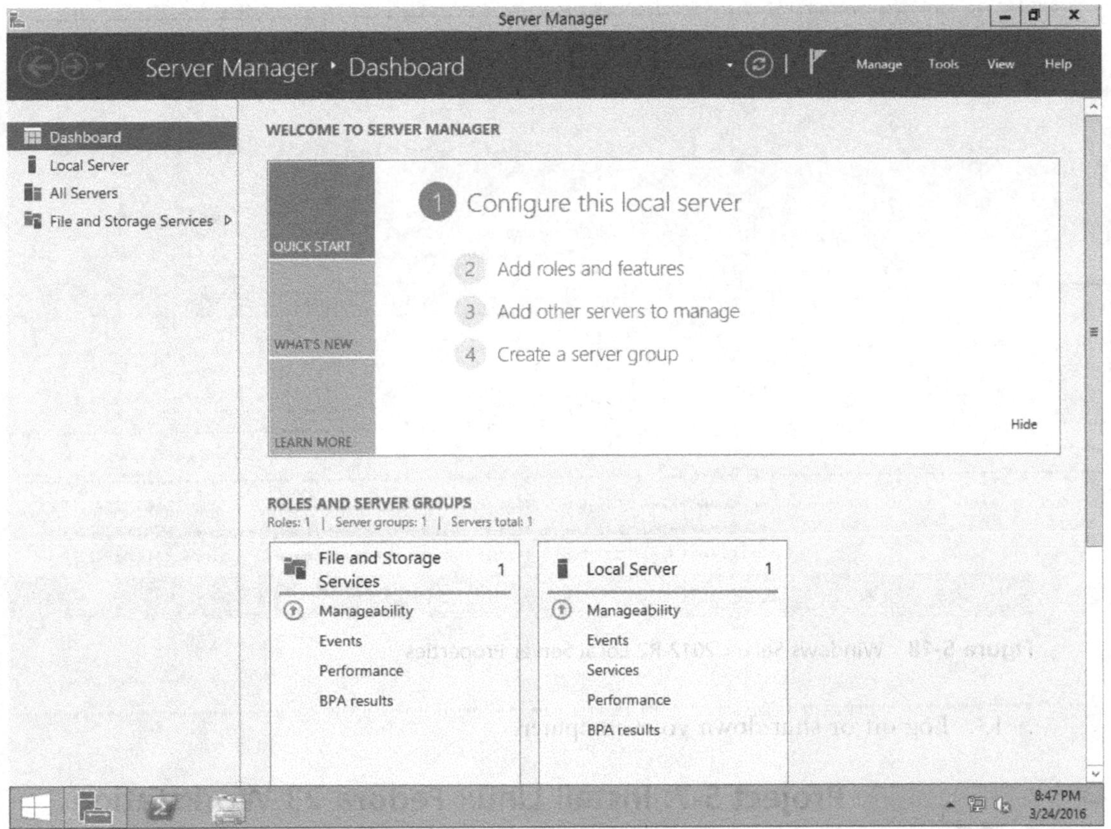

Figure 5-17 Windows Server 2012 R2 Server Manager Dashboard

12. Click **Local Server** in the left pane to see and change basic settings. On this screen (see Figure 5-18), you can change the computer name, join a workgroup or domain, change IP address settings, configure Windows Update, and so on.

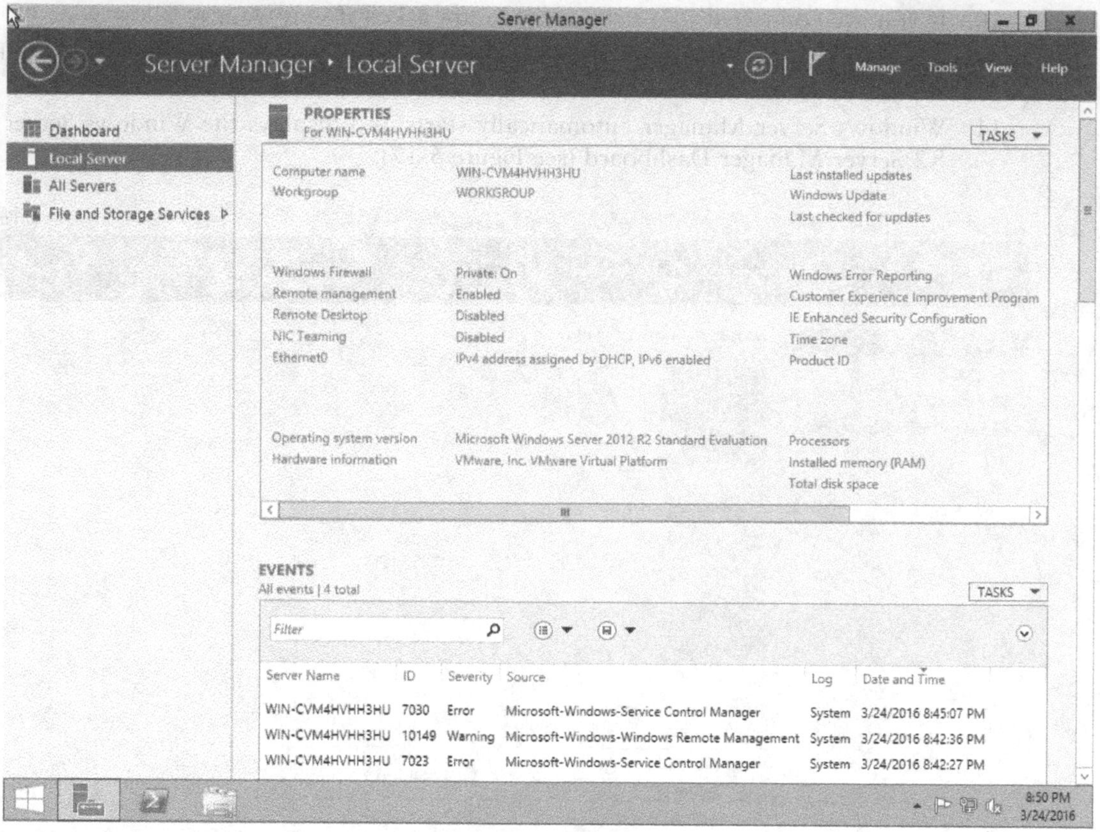

Figure 5-18 Windows Server 2012 R2 Local Server Properties

13. Log off or shut down your computer.

Project 5-7: Install Linux Fedora 23 Workstation

In this project, you practice installing Fedora 23 Workstation onto a hard drive. You need the Fedora 23 Workstation installation DVD, which can be downloaded from *https://getfedora.org/en/workstation/download/*. This project assumes you have a blank disk on which to install Fedora 23.

1. Insert the Fedora 23 installation DVD in the DVD drive of a computer that meets the minimum requirements for Fedora 23.

2. Start your computer if you are sure it will boot to the DVD.

3. Fedora Live will start automatically. When Fedora starts, click **Install to Hard Drive** on the Welcome to Fedora screen (see Figure 5-19).

4. On the Welcome to Fedora screen, you are prompted to select the language you want to use. Click the appropriate language and click **Continue**.

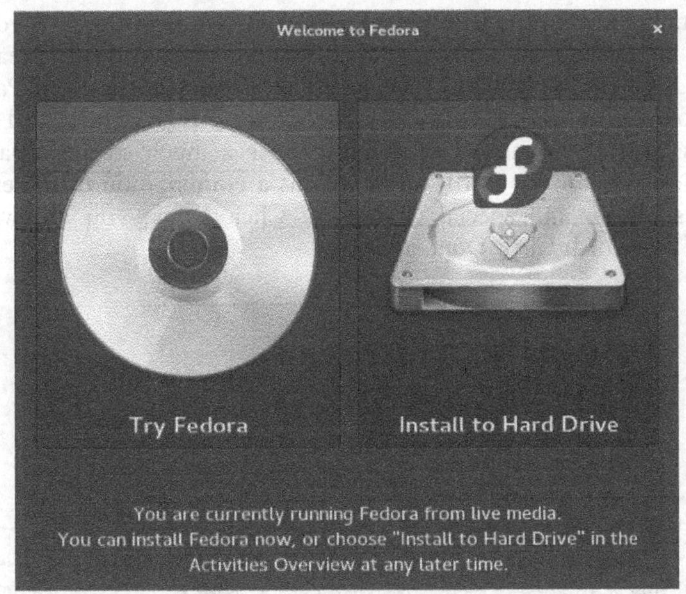

Figure 5-19 Welcome to Fedora screen

Source: Fedora Linux

5. On the Installation Summary screen (see Figure 5-20), review the choices. Click **INSTALLATION DESTINATION** and review the options. Notice that you have the option to encrypt the data on the disk. Click the hard disk you want to use, if necessary, and click **Done.**

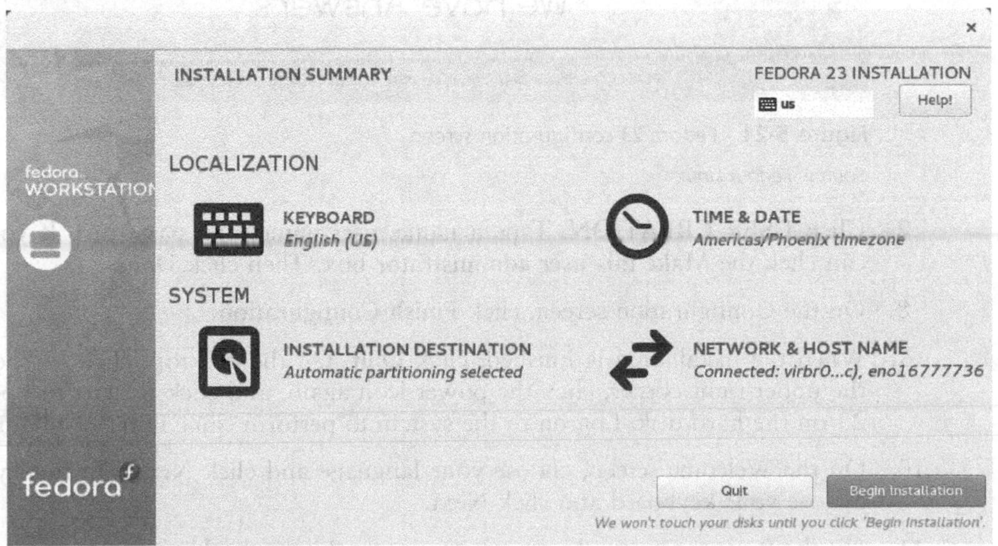

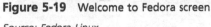

Figure 5-20 Installation Summary screen in Fedora 23

Source: Fedora Linux

5

6. Click **Begin Installation.** On the Configuration screen (see Figure 5-21), you must perform two tasks before you can continue: create a root password and create a regular user. Click **ROOT PASSWORD** and then type **Password01** in the Root Password box and Confirm box. Linux does a dictionary check on your password and reports that the password is weak. Normally, you would choose a much stronger password that doesn't contain any dictionary words and contains a combination of uppercase letters, lowercase letters, digits, and special characters. Click **Done**; you are warned again about the weak password. Click **Done** again.

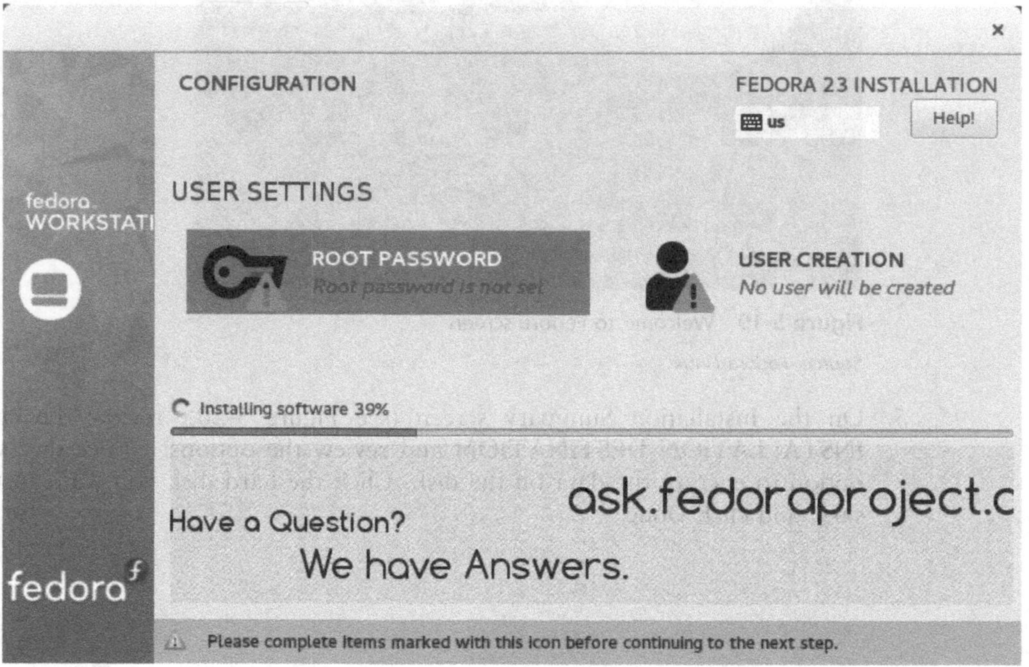

Figure 5-21 Fedora 23 configuration screen

Source: Fedora Linux

7. Click **USER CREATION.** Type a name, user name, and password. If you want, you can click the **Make this user administrator** box. Then click **Done.**
8. On the Configuration screen, click **Finish Configuration.**
9. When the installation is finished, click **Quit.** On the desktop, click the power icon in the upper-right corner, click the power icon again, and click **Restart** to boot to Fedora 23 on the hard disk. Log on to the system to perform some initial configuration tasks.
10. On the Welcome screen, choose your language and click **Next.** On the Typing screen, choose your keyboard and click **Next.**
11. On the Privacy screen, choose whether to enable or disable location services and automatic problem reporting. Click **Next.**
12. On the Online Accounts screen, you can choose any online accounts you want to connect to the Fedora 23 installation. Click **Skip.**

13. On the Ready to Go screen, click **Start using Fedora.** You see a Getting Started (GNOME Help) window that provides tutorials for using GNOME.
14. Log off and shut down the computer.

Critical Thinking

The following activities give you critical thinking challenges. Challenge Labs give you an opportunity to use the skills you have learned to perform a task without step-by-step instructions. Case projects offer a practical problem for which you supply a written solution. Not all chapters contain Challenge Labs. There is not always a specific right or wrong answer to these critical thinking exercises. They are intended to encourage you to review the chapter material and delve deeper into the topics you have learned.

Challenge Labs

Challenge Lab 5-1: Perform a Windows 7/Windows 10 Dual Boot

In this challenge lab, you start from a Windows 7 computer and install Windows 10 while maintaining your Windows 7 installation. Answer the following questions in preparation for this installation:

- What hardware considerations must you take into account before performing the installation? Think about CPU requirements, disk requirements, and memory requirements, plus anything else you can think of.
- What will you need to have on hand before starting the installation?
- What tasks should you perform before beginning the installation?
- What are some of the critical choices you must make during the installation from the time you power on your Windows 7 computer to the time that file copying begins?

Case Projects

Merlinos Mills is a company that produces flours and grains for grocery stores. It owns mills and distribution centers in the northwestern and midwestern United States. The headquarters in Bend, Oregon employs more than 400 people, most of whom use computers. Also, the headquarters has 28 servers, all running Microsoft Windows Server 2008 Enterprise Edition. The company employees use a full range of OSs, including Windows Vista, Windows 7, Windows 8.1, and Mac OS X Mavericks.

The management of Merlinos Mills wants each department to upgrade to newer OSs. Also, they are very concerned about network security, and they want to install new servers and upgrade their current servers to OS versions that take better advantage of security features. Your role in the process is to work with each department to help ensure that the installations and upgrades go smoothly.

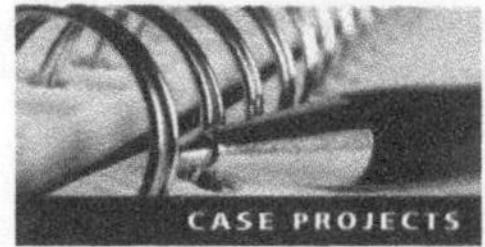

Case Project 5-1: Determine Preliminary Steps

The master distribution center in Bend, Oregon includes 42 people, including nine Windows Vista users, 22 people using Windows 7 Professional, and 11 people using Windows 8.1. The distribution center is slated to upgrade its computers to Windows 10 Pro. What preliminary steps should be taken before starting the upgrades on these computers? In general, are there any problems involved in upgrading to Windows 10 from each of these OSs?

Case Project 5-2: Decide to Upgrade or Not

The distribution center's nine Windows Vista users are all certain they need to upgrade to Windows 10 Pro to perform their work. However, the 33 people in the distribution center who are running Windows 8.1 and Windows 7 Professional are currently able to use all software, such as office software, customized distribution software, and inventory software that is integrated with the distribution software. They are resisting the upgrade to Windows 10 Pro, and the distribution manager asks for your opinion about whether to upgrade these computers. Should they upgrade from Windows 8.1 and Windows 7 to Windows 10?

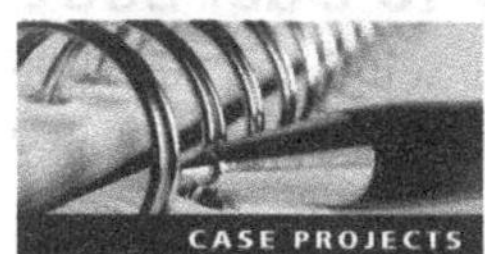

Case Project 5-3: Install Windows 10 Pro

After considering the issues in Case Project 5-2, management has decided that the distribution center will replace the computers running Windows Vista and Windows 7, and purchase new machines with Windows 10 Pro. The Windows 8.1 users already have computers that can run Windows 10 for a possible upgrade. The user support person for the distribution center has not performed an installation for Windows 10. Tell her generally what to expect when performing this installation.

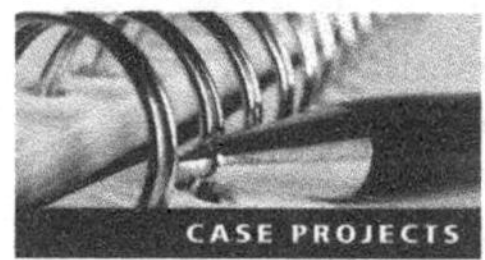

Case Project 5-4: Move to Windows Server 2012 R2

The IT Department has already been testing Windows Server 2012 R2, and some time ago purchased licenses to convert all of its Windows Server 2008 Enterprise Edition servers to Windows Server 2012 R2 Enterprise Edition. Two of the servers are running the Server Core installation of Windows Server 2008. Two other servers are running the 32-bit edition of Windows Server 2008. Management wants all servers to run the Server with a GUI installation. Explain the general process the department must follow to convert to Windows Server 2012 R2. Include any caveats or problems they might encounter.

Case Project 5-5: Upgrade to Mac OS X El Capitan

The Marketing Department strictly uses computers that run Mac OS X Mountain Lion and plans to upgrade to Mac OS X El Capitan. What steps should it follow for the upgrade?

chapter 6

Configuring Input and Output Devices

After reading this chapter and completing the exercises, you will be able to:

- Understand how OSs interface with input and output devices
- Explain the need for device drivers and install devices and drivers
- Describe popular input device technologies
- Discuss the types of printers and install printers
- Explain display adapter technologies
- Install circuit boards for new devices

Input and output devices enable people to communicate with the computer and enable the computer to communicate with people. The keyboard is an example of an input device through which you issue commands and enter text. A computer monitor is an output device that enables the computer to communicate back, showing the results of your work in text or rendering eye-catching graphics. A printer lets you output your work on the printed page.

This chapter describes how OSs interface with input and output devices, such as through device drivers. You learn general techniques for installing devices and device drivers for each OS. You also learn about many types of input and output devices, such as keyboards, mice, monitors, scanners, and printers. Further, you learn how to install printers in a variety of OSs.

OSs and Devices: An Overview

As you learned in Chapter 1, a primary function of any OS is to provide basic input/output (I/O) support for application software—that is, to translate requests from application software into commands that the hardware can understand and carry out. For example, the OS must:

- Handle input from the keyboard, mouse, and other input devices
- Handle output to the screen, printer, and other output devices
- Control information storage and retrieval using various types of disk and optical drives
- Support communications with remote computers through a network

An OS accomplishes these tasks in two ways: through software—device driver code within the OS itself, as well as accessing third-party device driver software—and through hardware controlled by the OS. Specifically, the OS controls chips and circuits inside a computer that communicate with specific input or output devices. Device drivers perform the actual communication between the physical device and the OS. The particular configuration of device drivers and adapters varies, but they function in the same way in each OS.

Likewise, setting up or installing input, output, or storage devices involves three general steps across OSs:

1. Install the device drivers that are required.
2. Connect the input, output, or storage device.
3. Turn on the device, if necessary, and follow any configuration instructions.

Installing and configuring storage devices is covered in Chapter 7.

Using Device Drivers

A device driver is software that enables the OS and application software to access specific computer hardware, such as a monitor or disk drive. A separate device driver is usually needed for each input or output device used on the computer. The OS provides the basic I/O support for your printer and other hardware, but it doesn't support specific features of individual devices. For that, you need a driver, which may be supplied by the hardware manufacturer or the producer of the OS. (See the discussion of driver software in Chapter 1.)

Computer monitors, flash drives, printers, and disk drives are so much a part of using a computer that it might be surprising that a device driver is necessary for each. However, when you consider that there are thousands of devices and device manufacturers, it makes sense. If all computer OS vendors attempted to incorporate code for all of the possible devices, the OS code would be huge and probably slow. Also, the OS would have to be updated each time a new device or manufacturer came on the market. The advantages of using device drivers are:

- Only essential code is necessary to build into the OS kernel for maximum performance.
- Use of specific devices does not have to be linked to a single OS.
- In a competitive marketplace, the number of I/O devices can expand in virtually unlimited directions to offer computer users a broad range of device selections, functions, and features.
- New devices can come on the market without requiring extensive updates to OSs.

Many hardware manufacturers make drivers for current OSs available as a free download from the Internet or supply a DVD/CD-ROM with the device. While OS vendors supply drivers for many devices as part of the OS installation package, you should generally use the manufacturer's driver, if available, instead of the driver supplied with the OS. Although many OS drivers for specific hardware were developed by the hardware manufacturer in cooperation with the OS producer, they may be generic—designed to support a range of hardware models—or they may be older than the specific hardware you are installing. Using the driver available on the Internet gives you a better chance of having the latest version, and it often provides bug fixes and performance optimizations as well.

Even if your hardware is brand new, it is good practice to check the manufacturer's Web site for newer driver software. Drivers are usually designated by version number, and sometimes with a date. Drivers with later version numbers and dates may contain fixes for problems identified with earlier releases, and they sometimes enable or improve the performance of some hardware features.

For example, to find drivers for a broad range of Epson hardware products, go to *www.epson.com,* click Support, and then pick your device from the list or search for it by name. Most manufacturers have Web sites that contain support for their products, including troubleshooting tips and downloadable drivers.

Remember that you can usually guess the home page for major companies. Simply type *www.companyname.com* in the address line of your browser, where *companyname* is the name of the manufacturer of your hardware product. If this doesn't work, use a Web search engine to search for information about a particular company or product.

The procedure for installing drivers varies slightly with the source of the driver and the OS you are using. If you download a new driver from a manufacturer's Web site, you'll probably have to uncompress the file before you can use it.

For example, Microsoft has included built-in zip support in its OSs since the late 1990s. PC users can also use the PKZIP or WinZip compression and decompression utilities. Many software producers distribute software that is bundled and compressed with the PKZIP/WinZip format. Compression software not only reduces the size of the supplied files by removing redundant information, it also groups multiple files into a single distribution file. Distribution files may be supplied in self-extraction format, an executable file that decompresses the archive and expands individual files. PC-executable files normally use an .exe file extension. If you download a driver archive that includes this extension, it is a self-extracting file. If the file includes a .zip extension, you can open it directly within the OS; Windows File Explorer supports zip files and can open them just like a normal folder. You can also use a stand-alone program such as PKZIP or WinZip to expand the archive before installing the driver software.

If your OS does not include built-in zip support or you want the PKZIP or WinZip software, you can download it from a variety of Web sites. Other programs perform similar functions. One resource for a wide variety of shareware, freeware, and inexpensive software is *www.tucows.com/downloads.*

Since version 10.3 Tiger, Mac OS X has had built-in zip support. Mac OS X users can use ZIP-format archives, but a more common format is StuffIt, a utility similar to PKZIP, which also bundles multiple files into a single distribution archive. StuffIt products are available for Windows, Linux, and Mac OS X OSs, and for some versions of UNIX. StuffIt files can be self-extracting, or you can use StuffIt Expander or another utility to expand the archive into its individual components. To obtain this utility, visit *my.smithmicro.com.* StuffIt also supports ZIP format, and it lets you retrieve compressed or archived files from Macintosh users. The basic StuffIt Expander is a free download, and you can purchase the full-blown StuffIt Deluxe so you can create archives for Mac and Windows environments. The third-party ZIP utilities available for the Mac don't always produce files that are compatible with Windows systems. The StuffIt Expander software, on the other hand, works both ways quite well.

UNIX/Linux system users may retrieve drivers and other software in a *tar* format. Tar files are also archives that group multiple files into a single distribution file. *Tar* doesn't compress the files; it merely groups files to make it easier to copy and distribute multiple files together. You may find that a *tar* archive is also zipped. UNIX/Linux systems also have a *zip* command that is compatible with the PKZIP software. You can use StuffIt or a UNIX/Linux version of *unzip* to expand the compressed *tar* archive into an uncompressed file, and then you can issue a UNIX/Linux *tar* command to extract individual files from the archive.

Once you locate the driver you want to use, you generally have three choices for installation, depending on the source of the driver: you can use your OS's installation utility, the Plug and Play (PnP) feature, or the installation utility provided by the hardware manufacturer. Procedures are slightly different among OSs, and precise steps differ depending on the equipment (a printer installs differently from a sound card, for example), but the general process is very similar. The following sections discuss manufacturer driver installation and specific steps for installing devices in OSs.

From the Trenches ...

An IT professional was called to help a company president's administrative assistant with a printer problem during a board of director's meeting. She tried all types of troubleshooting steps, from turning the printer off and on to testing the network and looking for a paper jam in the printer. After working on the problem for quite some time (and delaying the meeting), the IT professional realized that the printer driver had been removed from the OS used to print the documents. After a quick download and installation from the manufacturer's Web site, the printer was back up and printing correctly.

6

Manufacturer Driver Installation

When you use a hardware manufacturer's installation utility, the process is usually fully automatic and well documented. In fact, newer printers, plotters, and other devices frequently come with extensive support material on a DVD or CD-ROM. You might be presented with video or animated training material to teach you how to install or use the device. You shouldn't have to know much about the way your OS installs drivers or interfaces with the device you're installing because the manufacturer's installation routine handles it all for you.

Because each manufacturer has a different procedure with different devices and different OSs, it is difficult to document each system and device type. In general, however, the procedure is to double-click an installation program or insert a DVD/CD-ROM into a drive and either wait for a program to start automatically or run a setup or install utility. Then, simply follow on-screen prompts. If you run into problems, look for a disk-based tutorial or go to the manufacturer's Web site to search for more information. Some software suppliers also include .txt files on installation disks to present new information or tips for the installer. You can use Notepad or any text editor to look for these files and read them.

Windows Driver Installation

There are several ways to install drivers in Windows. The easiest way to install a driver for a new system is to use the PnP capability to automatically detect the new hardware and install drivers. Another way to install new devices and drivers is to use the Add a device wizard in Windows. You can also use Device Manager to install a new driver, update an existing one, or roll back a driver to a previous version. Each of these methods is explained in the following sections.

Using PnP to Install a Device and Driver You can quickly install a new printer, for example, by following these general steps:

1. Install any software drivers that are required.
2. Connect the printer to the computer.
3. Plug the printer into a power outlet and turn it on.
4. Follow any configuration instructions.

When the printer is turned on, the OS recognizes that a new piece of hardware is attached and tries to locate the drivers for it. If Windows already has a built-in driver for this device, the OS finds the driver on the Windows distribution disk or DVD/CD-ROM. Otherwise, you must insert the manufacturer's DVD/CD-ROM into an appropriate drive when the OS asks for it.

Using a Windows Wizard to Install a Device and Driver If Windows doesn't recognize newly installed hardware, or if you want to conduct an installation manually or start automatic procedures to detect a hardware device because PnP did not work initially, use the Add a device wizard. In Windows 7 and later versions, open Control Panel and click Add a device under the Hardware and Sound category. Windows will search for the device you are trying to install.

If you have a driver from the device manufacturer, you should probably use it to ensure that the latest driver is installed. When you use the wizard, the drivers may not be the most current ones because Windows uses the drivers from its installation media.

Using Device Manager to Install or Update a Driver If you need to install a device driver, update one for a device that is already installed, or roll back a driver to an earlier version, Device Manager (see Figure 6-1) offers a convenient way to accomplish the task. You can also use Device Manager to:

- Determine the location of device driver files
- Check to make sure a device is working properly
- Determine if there is a resource conflict for a device

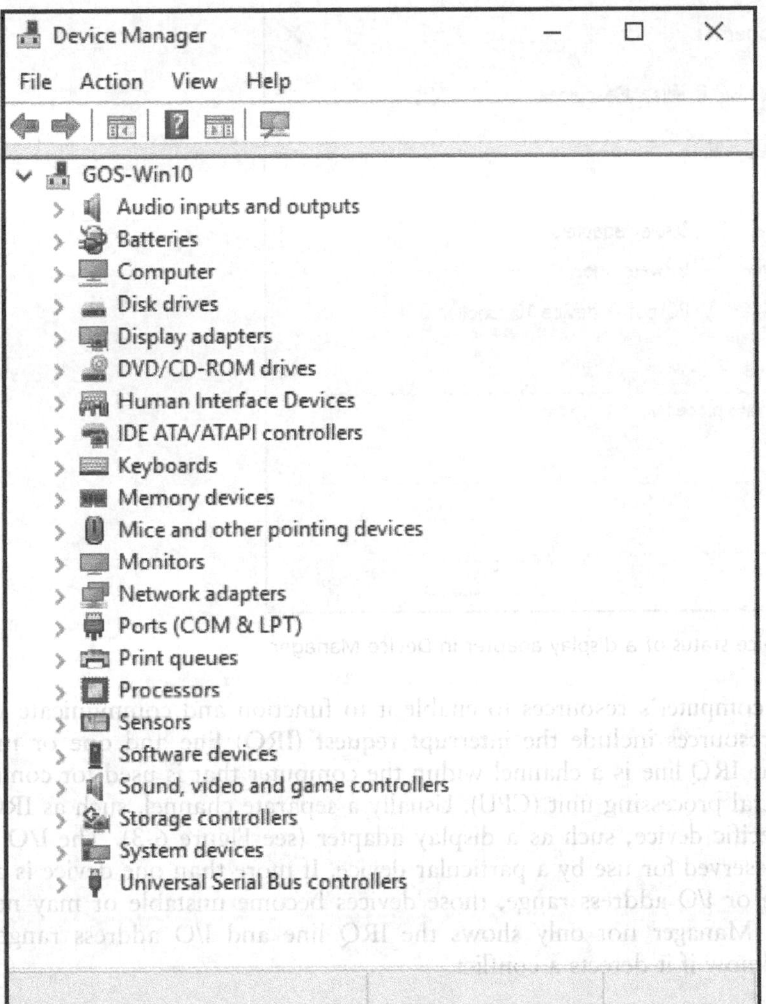

Figure 6-1 Device Manager in Windows 10

The advantage of determining the location of a device file is that you not only verify that the driver is installed, you can also check the version of the device driver. For example, if you suspect that you have an old driver, check with the manufacturer for the version level or date of the most current driver and then use Device Manager to compare it with the version you have installed.

When you access a device through Device Manager, you can determine if the device is installed in two ways. First, Device Manager places a question mark on the device if there is a problem with the installation or if the driver is not installed. Also, when you use Device Manager to access a device that has a driver set up, the utility checks to verify that the device is working properly. Figure 6-2 shows an example of a display driver in Windows 10 that is working properly.

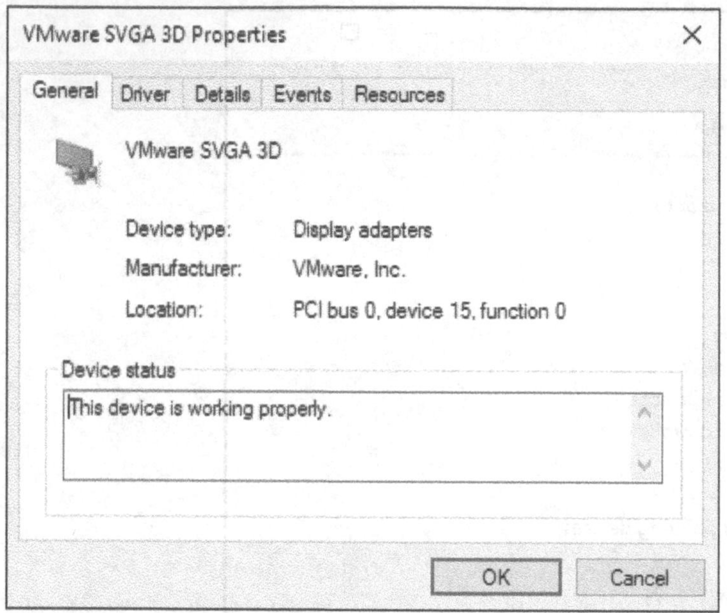

Figure 6-2 The device status of a display adapter in Device Manager

A device uses the computer's resources to enable it to function and communicate with the computer. These resources include the **interrupt request (IRQ) line** and one or more I/O address ranges. The IRQ line is a channel within the computer that is used for communications with the central processing unit (CPU). Usually a separate channel, such as IRQ 16, is allocated for a specific device, such as a display adapter (see Figure 6-3). The **I/O address range** is memory reserved for use by a particular device. If more than one device is assigned the same IRQ line or I/O address range, those devices become unstable or may not work altogether. Device Manager not only shows the IRQ line and I/O address ranges for a device, it lets you know if it detects a conflict.

You rarely run into resource conflicts on modern PCs. I/O addresses are dynamically configured in cooperation with the BIOS to ensure there are no conflicts. Many devices, such as those that use the PCI Express bus, don't use hardware interrupts (IRQs) at all; instead, a process called *message signaled interrupts* (MSI) uses the data bus to signal a virtual interrupt of sorts.

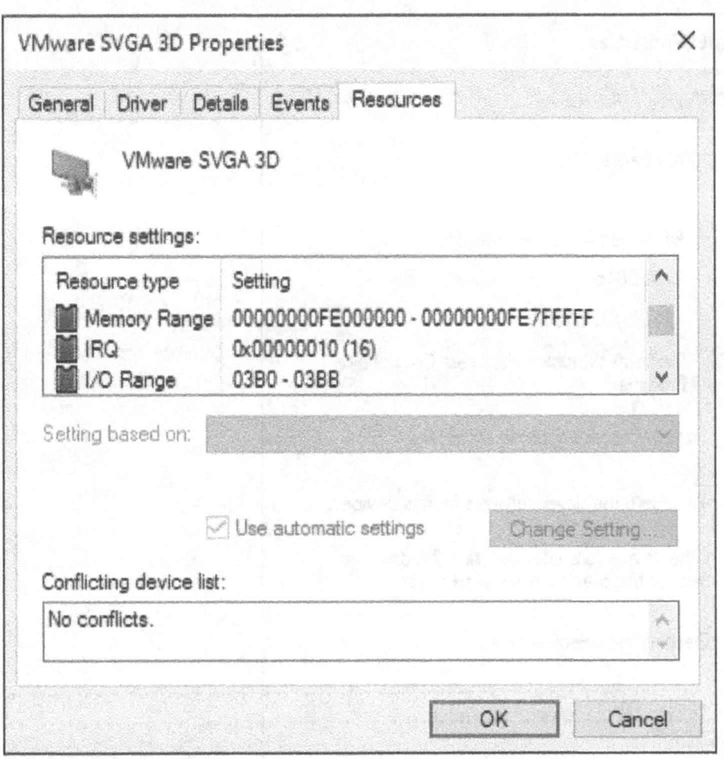

Figure 6-3 Viewing the resources used by a device

Updating and Rolling Back Drivers Aside from checking on the status and resources of a device, Device Manager lets you update a driver or roll it back to an earlier version. You might update a driver if the device is not performing well or is causing system instability. To update a driver from Device Manager, double-click the device and click the Driver tab (see Figure 6-4). When you click the Update Driver button, Windows gives you the option to search your computer and the Internet for an updated driver or to manually browse to the driver file location. If you have recently updated a driver and it is causing system instability or performance problems, you can roll back the driver to an earlier version by clicking the Roll Back Driver button, which is on the same tab as the Update Driver button shown in Figure 6-4. Windows will uninstall the current driver and install the previous version, if available.

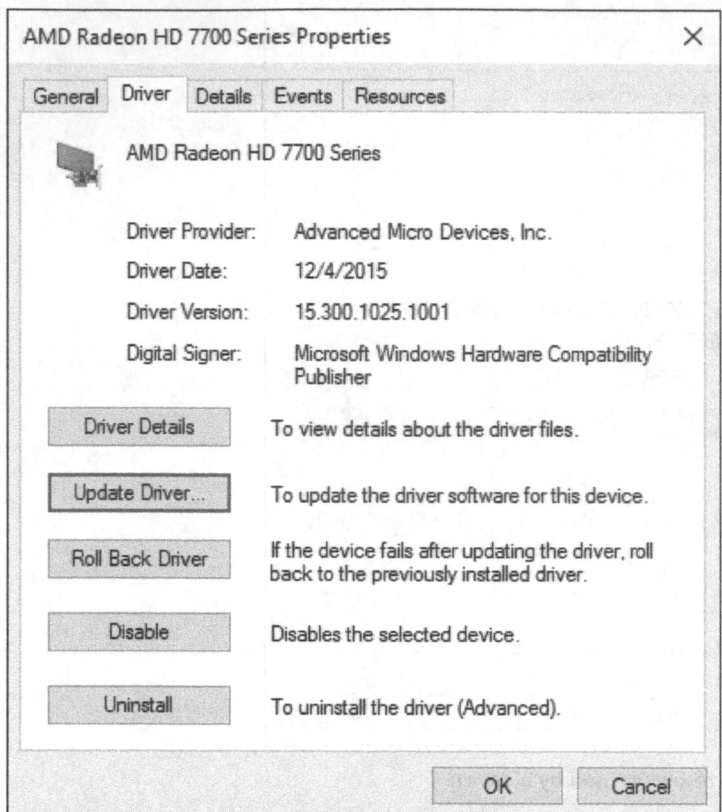

Figure 6-4 Updating or rolling back a driver

Configuring Driver Signing When you install a Windows I/O device, such as a pointing device or a new sound card, Windows makes sure that the device driver has been verified by Microsoft. A unique digital signature is incorporated into the verified driver in a process called **driver signing**. In Windows 10 and newer versions, unsigned drivers are not permitted. Developers of device drivers must use a test signing procedure to test drivers they are developing.

On older Windows versions, you can choose to be warned that a driver is not signed, ignore whether or not a driver is signed, or have the OS prevent you from installing an unsigned driver. The warning level is assigned by default so that you are warned before you install an unsigned driver, but you can still choose to install it. Using driver signing helps to ensure that the driver works properly with the device and in conjunction with other devices. It is also a security feature to ensure that no one has tampered with the driver, such as by incorporating malicious code or a virus.

UNIX/Linux Driver Installation

The concept of drivers in UNIX/Linux is slightly different from that in other OSs. The central portion of the UNIX/Linux OS, the kernel, is where most of the UNIX/Linux device drivers are loaded. Device drivers are either in the form of kernel modules, which are pieces of code that must be linked into the kernel, or loadable modules, similar pieces of code that are not linked into the kernel but are loaded when the OS is started. Device support in most UNIX/Linux versions is limited when compared to other OSs; manufacturers of devices often provide drivers for special hardware, which are then linked or loaded into the kernel.

UNIX/Linux devices are managed through the use of **device special files**, which contain information about I/O devices that is used by the OS kernel when a device is accessed. In many UNIX/Linux systems, there are three types of device special files:

- **Block special files**, which are used to manage random access devices that handle blocks of data, including DVD/CD-ROM drives, hard disk drives, tape drives, and other storage devices.
- **Character special files**, which handle byte-by-byte streams of data, such as through USB connections. USB is the most common interface for mice, keyboards, external disk drives, and other external hardware such as printers and digital cameras.
- **Named pipes** for handling internal communications, such as redirecting file output to a monitor.

6

When you install a UNIX/Linux OS, device special files are created for the devices already installed on the system. On many UNIX/Linux distributions, these files are stored in the /dev directory. Table 6-1 provides a sampling of device special files.

Table 6-1 UNIX/Linux device special files

File	Description
/dev/console	For the console components, such as the monitor and keyboard attached to the computer (/dev/tty0 is also used at the same time on many systems)
/dev/hd*xn*	For Integrated Drive Electronics (IDE) and Enhanced Integrated Drive Electronics (EIDE) hard drives, where *x* is a letter representing the disk and *n* represents the partition number—for example, hda1 for the first disk and partition
/dev/modem	Symbolic link to the device special file (typically linked to /dev/ttys1) for a modem
/dev/mouse	Symbolic link to the device special file (typically linked to /dev/ttys0) for a mouse or pointing device
/dev/sd*xn*	For a hard drive connected to a SCSI or SATA interface, where *x* is a letter representing the disk and *n* represents the partition—for example, sda1 for the first SATA drive and first partition on that drive
/dev/st*n*	For a SCSI tape drive, where *n* is the number of the drive—for example, st0 for the first tape drive. The USB devices appear as a SCSI device.
/dev/sr*x*	For an IDE CD/DVD drive

If you need to create a device special file for a new device, use the *mknod* command, as explained in the following general steps:

1. Log in with superuser permissions.
2. Access a terminal window or the command prompt.
3. Type *cd/ dev* and press Enter to switch to the /dev folder.

4. Use the ***mknod*** command, and then enter the device special file name, such as ttys42. Next, enter the file type, such as character (c) or block (b), and a major and minor node value used by the kernel. (Check with the device manufacturer for these values.) For example, you might type ***mknod ttys20 c 8 68***, and press Enter for a new device.

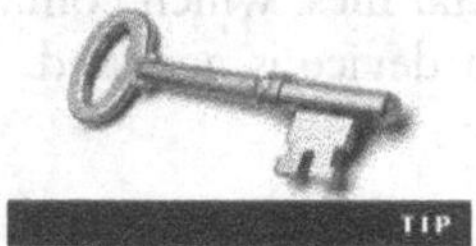

TIP

Some versions of UNIX/Linux also support the *makedev* command for creating a device special file. To determine which commands are supported in your UNIX/Linux version and learn the syntax, use the *man mknod* or *man makedev* command to view the documentation.

To view the I/O device special files that are already on your system, use the *ls* command to see all of the files in the /dev folder. You can view all the PCI (and PCI Express) devices installed on a Fedora Linux system using *lspci*. Another command, *lshw*, provides detailed system information, including installed devices and disks.

Mac OS X Driver Installation

Mac OS X systems come with device drivers for most hardware that connects to these systems. When you obtain new hardware, make sure that you have an installation DVD/CD-ROM from the hardware manufacturer. The general steps for installing new hardware on a Mac OS X system are:

1. Shut down the OS and turn off the computer.
2. Attach the new hardware.
3. Restart the computer and OS.
4. Insert the DVD/CD-ROM for the hardware.
5. Run the installer program on the DVD/CD-ROM for that hardware.

TIP

If you are having problems with hardware in Mac OS X, it may be necessary to reinstall the OS. In earlier versions of Mac OS X, you can insert the Mac OS X Install Disk 1 DVD/CD-ROM, select the Mac OS X disk as the destination, click Options, and select Archive and Install. In Mac OS X v10.3 and later versions, insert the installation disk and double-click Install Mac OS X; the installation will retain your previous settings and software.

Now that you're familiar with device drivers and the basic process of installing devices and drivers in various OSs, it's time to survey the types of input and output devices and get a more in-depth look into how they relate to OSs.

Standard Input Devices

There are several standard and universal computer input devices: the keyboard, the mouse, and the touch pad. The keyboard is the most important input device; other important devices include the mouse and touch pad as well as the mouse alternatives, such as a trackball, stylus, and pointing stick. Touch input has become popular; iPads, smartphones, book readers, and tablet touch screens are part of the daily routine for many people.

Mouse and Keyboard Drivers

Because the I/O routines for the mouse and keyboard are highly standardized across OSs, it is unlikely that you will need to interact with the OS to set up these devices. Although mice and keyboards do use device drivers, unlike printers and other output devices, these drivers are standard and are usually included as part of the OS. The OS provides only general support for output devices like printers; it includes routines to send data out through a USB port, for example, and to receive data sent to the computer from a device connected to this port, but it has no intrinsic routines to support specific printer brands, models, or capabilities. For keyboards and mice, however, most OSs contain intrinsic routines to handle them.

Wireless mice and keyboards are available from computer manufacturers and third-party vendors. You may purchase them as a package or separately. Each device requires batteries to operate, along with a USB receiver for communication between the device and computer. Wireless mice and keyboard packages normally have one USB receiver that both the mouse and keyboard use. Bluetooth mice and keyboards are also available; some come with a USB option and others are Bluetooth only. Almost all mice are now optical. They use either an LED or a laser to illuminate the surface on which they are used, and they contain an optical sensor (a very small camera) that takes thousands of pictures per second. The pictures are compared to calculate the direction and speed of the optical mouse.

Some older mice use a ball on the underside that rotates as you move them across a desk or mouse pad. They are becoming rare as the optical mouse has become the preferred device.

A wired mouse or keyboard uses a USB port, similar to the way a printer uses a USB port. (A wireless mouse uses a receiver.) Like a printer or other output device, a wired keyboard or mouse can also come with drivers and additional software on DVD/CD-ROM. Some OSs include a custom keyboard configuration utility, such as the one from Windows 10, shown in Figure 6-5.

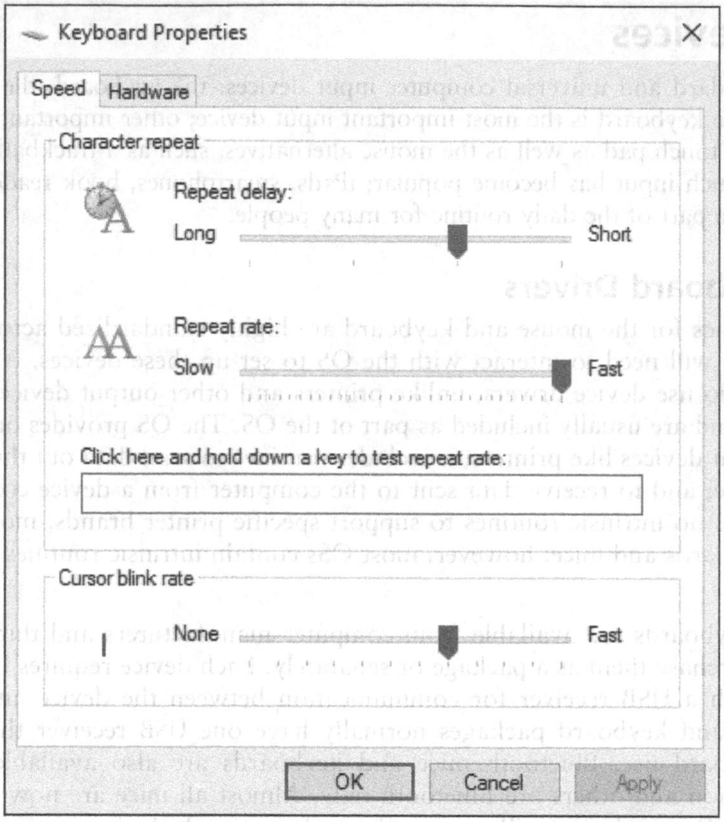

Figure 6-5 Keyboard settings in Windows 10

As you can see from this figure, the degree of configuration is minimal, which points out the standard nature of the keyboard itself and the drivers that support it. Earlier OSs—particularly non-Windows systems—may have even more limited keyboard configuration options. You plug it in and it either works or not.

As with the keyboard, the intrinsic OS mouse drivers may offer customization options to the user. Mouse preferences in Mac OS X El Capitan are shown in Figure 6-6.

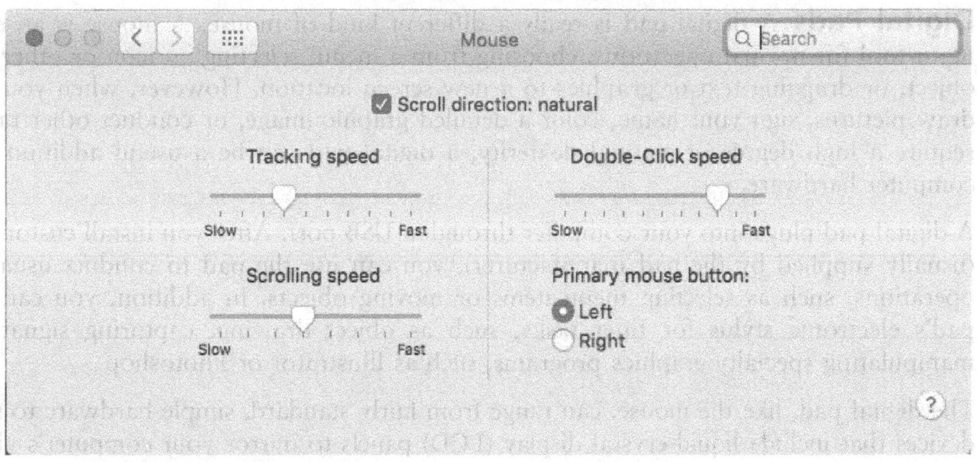

Figure 6-6 Mac OS X mouse settings

Source: Mac OS X El Capitan

Typically, the configuration routines let you set the double-click speed, calibrate mouse movement and direction based on how you hold the mouse as you roll it around the desk, customize the pointer graphic, and a variety of other features. In addition to having special features to enhance the function of the mouse itself, manufacturers' drivers usually provide additional levels of user configuration, such as options to help you quickly find the cursor on the screen or to select a window just by pointing to the title bar.

Touch Input Drivers

Touch input devices also use device drivers. In most cases, the drivers are included in the OS or preloaded by the computer manufacturer. With a touch screen, you can open files, select items on the screen, and move items with the touch of your finger. Multi-touch technology allows you to use multiple fingers to resize a window, scroll through documents, or page forward or back in your Web browser. To use multi-touch, you need a laptop or monitor equipped with multi-touch technology. Windows 7 and newer versions as well as Linux/Fedora support multi-touch capabilities. Apple has incorporated the touch technology used in the iPad and iPhone into Mac OS X.

A touch pad is another type of touch input. Touch pads are usually found below the keyboard on laptops, but they are also available as a peripheral for desktop computers. A touch pad is a surface that converts finger motion and position to a point on your screen.

Other Input Devices

The keyboard and mouse are ubiquitous and standard. If your computing needs stop with fairly common business applications such as word processing, spreadsheets, and databases, you probably won't need anything more. On the other hand, if you need your computer for graphics design, Web page development, playing games, making video calls, digital photography, or movie or sound editing, you will use one or more specialty input devices, such as digital pads, scanners, joysticks and gamepads, digital sound input, and digital picture and video input/output. The following sections introduce these devices.

Digital Pads A digital pad is really a different kind of mouse. A mouse is an excellent input tool for normal operations: choosing from a menu, selecting an icon or other graphic object, or dragging text or graphics to a new screen location. However, when you need to draw pictures, sign your name, color a detailed graphic image, or conduct other tasks that require a high degree of manual dexterity, a digital pad can be a useful addition to your computer hardware.

A digital pad plugs into your computer through a USB port. After you install custom drivers (usually supplied by the pad manufacturer), you can use the pad to conduct usual mouse operations, such as selecting menu items or moving objects. In addition, you can use the pad's electronic stylus for finer tasks, such as object drawing, capturing signatures, or manipulating specialty graphics programs, such as Illustrator or Photoshop.

The digital pad, like the mouse, can range from fairly standard, simple hardware to specialty devices that include liquid crystal display (LCD) panels to mirror your computer's video display. Even the simplest pads require some custom software and a unique installation process.

Scanners A scanner scans text and images to be manipulated by software on your computer. Once in the computer, the digital image from the scanner can be saved in a variety of graphics image formats, edited, merged with other images or text, transmitted over the Internet or other network connection, and printed.

Scanners may also be used with optical character recognition (OCR) software. Instead of scanning text into a digital graphic image, which does not allow for text manipulation, imaging software scans each character on the page as a distinct image. You can then import the scanned results into a word-processing document to work with the text.

If you're using a USB scanner with Windows, installation and configuration should be automatic through PnP. Figure 6-7 shows the Windows Fax and Scan application in Windows 10.

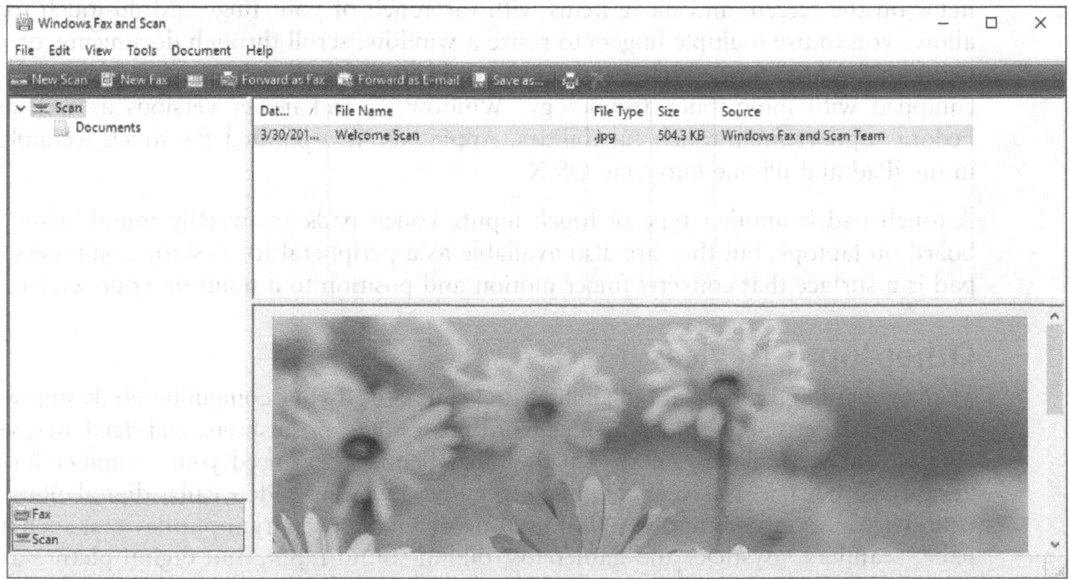

Figure 6-7 Windows Fax and Scan window

If the built-in Windows Fax and Scan application doesn't suit your needs, you can usually install custom drivers and custom scanning software supplied by the scanner manufacturer. In most cases, the driver software—usually a driver with user interface and scanner control—automatically links with a variety of graphics software. If you're using Photoshop, for example, the scanner may show up as an add-in; if you're using a Microsoft product such as Publisher or Picture Manager, you'll see a scanner icon on your toolbar. When you click the icon, the scanner software will load so you can use the scanner. These drivers and the user interface interact with the OS to control the USB port and capture data supplied by the scanner.

Joysticks, Gamepads, and Other Controllers If you run computer simulations, are involved in game development, or enjoy playing games on your computer, you'll most likely have a need for alternative input devices. Some of these may include **joysticks** and **gamepads** along with flight yoke systems and other devices.

A joystick is more like a mouse than a digital pad. Like a mouse, the joystick uses a mechanical or optical device to rotate one or more potentiometers. Changing resistance tells the joystick driver what value to feed to the OS and any associated application software. You use the joystick for three-dimensional movement of an on-screen cursor or other object, such as a car, airplane, or cartoon character. Just as the digital pad makes it easier to input handwriting, picture retouching, and the like, the joystick offers much more control than a mouse when it comes to detailed movements of graphical screen objects. Although games are the primary application for joysticks, Mac users sometimes use them to supplement mouse functionality. Joysticks can be used for virtually any application input task, given the proper driver.

In addition to the three-dimensional movements of the vertical joystick, it usually includes one or more push-button switches that can be associated with gun firings, boxing swings, menu selection, and so on. Like the digital pad, the joystick uses the PC and Mac's USB port. Potentiometer settings or switch closures are sent through the USB port as positive/negative pulses or as variable values on a scale. The OS's basic port I/O routines grab this data, and then it is up to the associated application—a game, for example—to interpret this data in a meaningful way.

Joysticks continue their development to keep up with the games that are being created. There are flight yoke systems, 3D joysticks, attack joysticks, and much more. Logitech and Saitek are just a couple of the vendors that are very active in this arena.

Gamepads come in a wide variety of designs. As the name suggests, they are primarily designed for interaction with games, and include multiple buttons, wheels, or balls to effect movement of a variety of on-screen objects. As with the joystick, the gamepad sends standard signals to the USB port, where the OS I/O routines take the data and pass it off to an application program or custom driver for interpretation. Gamepads from Logitech, Microsoft, and Saitek have become very sophisticated. Some are wireless, some are programmable, and some have LCD displays. There are even vendors that allow your Wii Remote and PS3 controllers to connect to your computer not only to play games, but to control your computer. Apple supports gamepads and sells third-party models on its Web site.

Digital Sound Input Every Mac, PC, and workstation computer is supplied with some kind of digital sound card for sound input and output. It may be built into the motherboard or be a separate card. You can connect a microphone to your computer's USB port and record voice mail that you can include with electronic mail, for example, or for narration of slide presentations. Along with your webcam, you can use the microphone to make audio and video calls with Skype and other VoIP (Voice over Internet Protocol) applications. Skype is application software that allows you to make calls with or without video over the Internet. It can also be used for instant messaging and video conferencing (connecting multiple locations via video).

You can download custom sounds or music from Internet sites, such as iTunes, for use within software applications. Voice input to word-processing and other programs is important for people who are unable to use a keyboard or mouse. You can capture digital sound from a digital recorder or digital camera directly into your computer without having to do any conversion in the process. You can also copy digital audio directly from a recorder to your hard drive in much the same way you would copy digital information from one hard drive to another.

There are multiple professional audio I/O standards, but most devices come with a USB port. All you need is a USB cable. Whether you use audio I/O ports or a USB port depends on the external hardware you will interface with your computer. Some high-end digital cameras include more than one digital I/O port, so you can choose which format to use based on personal preference, your need to interface with other users, or which interface you can find. Even high-end digital cameras include a USB port, and most require custom driver software. Also, like scanners, they can usually be controlled and accessed from inside application software, such as digital audio or video editing packages. Once the driver is installed, you can transfer audio information through the USB port from the application you are using to manipulate the audio files.

Digital Picture and Video Input/Output Digital picture and video I/O works similarly to digital audio I/O. You need a digital I/O interface and drivers to allow your OS to recognize and use the USB device. As with digital audio, you import digital images into whatever application software you are using for picture or video editing. In some cases, you use a utility supplied by the interface manufacturer to import the digital image, then launch another application, such as Adobe Premier or Photoshop, to conduct the actual editing. On the other hand, some manufacturers include the ability to link their hardware drivers directly into editing software so you can import and export digital files from an external camera and edit the video or still images from the same application.

USB ports are the standard way to connect most devices to a computer. USB 1.0 (version 1.0) had a data transfer rate of 1.5 Mbps. USB 2.0 increased that rate significantly to 480 Mbps and was referred to as Hi-Speed. With SuperSpeed USB 3.0, the data transfer rate has increased to up to 5.0 Gbps, and the newer SuperSpeed+ USB 3.1 standard ups that rate to 10 Gbps.

1394 Technology IEEE 1394 (or 1394a) is the original specification for a high-speed digital interface that supports data communication at 100, 200, or 400 megabits per second (Mbps). The newer 1394b specification enables communications at 800 Mbps, 1.6 Gbps, and 3.2 Gbps.

IEEE 1394a and 1394b are technologies currently targeted at multimedia peripherals, which include digital camcorders, music systems, DVDs, digital cameras, and digital TVs. The IEEE 1394b standard also enables data transfer over regular twisted-pair (copper wire) network cable and glass and plastic fiber-optic cable.

FireWire, an IEEE 1394 implementation for bus communications, was developed by Apple Computer and Texas Instruments and is used in computers built by those companies. IEEE 1394 is also known as i.Link (Sony), Lynx (Texas Instruments), and the High Performance Serial Bus (HPSB). The 1394 Trade Association reports that over 2 billion FireWire ports have shipped worldwide. While there is a considerable installed base of 1394 devices, the increases in speed realized by USB 3.0 and USB 3.1 have substantially reduced the popularity and growth of the 1394 standard.

The **Institute of Electrical and Electronics Engineers (IEEE)** is an international organization of scientists, engineers, technicians, and educators that plays a leading role in developing standards for computers, network cabling, and data transmissions, and for other electronics areas, such as consumer electronics and electrical power. Also, visit *www.1394ta.org* for links to information and vendors that support 1394 technologies.

6

Printers

A printer is an important part of nearly every computer installation. The following sections outline the most popular types of printers and printer connections. You also learn how to install printers.

Printer Types

The following types of printers are the most popular today:

- **Inkjet printers** create characters by squirting tiny droplets of ink directly onto the page. Full color—even photographic quality—printing with inkjets is quite common today. Small, quiet, and inexpensive, these printers are popular personal printers in many offices, and dominate the market for schools and homes. Models that deliver color and high resolution are used for proofing by graphics designers and printers, as well as home and office users. With the popularity of digital electronic cameras, high-resolution inkjet printers are used to produce photograph-like output on heavy, slick paper, much like photographic paper stock.
- **Laser printers** use an imaging technology similar to copiers to produce computer output, and are probably the most popular printer for business text and graphics. A typical laser printer contains its own CPU and memory because printed pages are first produced electronically within the printer. Laser printer prices, including those for color printers, have declined sharply over the years so that even small businesses, home offices, and individuals can now afford them.
- **Multifunction printers** combine color inkjet or laser printing, scanning, copying, and faxing into one physical device. Multifunction printers are good for locations that do not

have a lot of desktop space, and can be purchased for as little as $100. The downside to a multifunction printer is that if it breaks, you lose all functions rather than just one.

The cost of printing is more than just the expense of the printer. Ink and laser cartridges add to printing costs. Depending on the cost of the cartridges and the number of pages you can print with each one, many people find that a less expensive printer may cost more in the long run. For example, if you print a high volume of documents, it can be cheaper to use a laser printer than an inkjet printer because one laser cartridge can print tens of thousands of sheets, while one inkjet cartridge may only print hundreds.

In addition to traditional printers, another printer-like device called a **plotter** is popular in engineering, architecture, and other fields where hard copy output (such as blueprints) won't fit on standard paper sizes or can't be produced by standard character or graphics printers. Plotter design is more complex than that of printers, and uses pen and control mechanisms. As with printers, plotters require special drivers to enhance the OS's intrinsic capabilities, but the process of installing plotter hardware and software is similar to that for printers. Likewise, plotters can be installed on a company's network or your computer's USB port in much the same way as printers. (See the next section, "Printer Connections.")

Aside from the three major printer types, other printer designs are used in specialized arenas.

- **3D printers** use an additive process to create one layer of the object at a time. They build the parts from drawings that are cross-sectioned into thousands of layers. There are companies that will create your 3D object from the computer file you send them.
- **Label printers** produce labels and are useful for an eBay seller or shipping business. They only produce labels and do not interfere with other printers attached to your computer.
- **Dot-matrix (impact) printers** produce characters by slamming a group of wires (dots) from a rectangular grid onto a ribbon and then to paper. Although dot-matrix printers have declined in popularity, you'll still find them behind sales counters to support point-of-sale (POS) computers in some businesses. They are also still used when a computer fills out forms or when multiple copies of the same document are needed simultaneously.
- **Line printers** are generally used on older mainframes. These impact printers print an entire line at a time rather than a character at a time. Line printers are fast but extremely noisy because the "line" is usually a metal chain. They use some form of tractor feed or pin feed. Line printers are rare these days; you may see them in government agencies, colleges, universities, or other venues that require large amounts of paper output, particularly output with multiple copies.

Vestiges of the line printer still remain: the main printer port on a PC is designated **LPT1**, which stands for *line print terminal 1*. It is doubtful that many PCs were ever connected to a true line printer, but this big machine terminology stays with us.

- **Thermal-wax transfer printers** exist in two basic designs. One uses rolls of plastic film coated with colored wax, which is melted onto the page one primary color at a time. A second type, known as phase change, melts wax stored in individual colored sticks and sprays the molten, colored wax onto the page. These printers generally produce high-quality color output, but they are also relatively slow. In addition, these printers frequently require special paper, which adds to the cost of the printed output. Thermal-wax transfer and dye sublimation printers are used in many graphics applications when high-quality, color printed output is required.
- **Dye sublimation** (sometimes shortened to *dye sub*) printers have a design that takes the concept of atomizing waxy colors onto paper a step further. Dye sub printers don't just melt pigments and spray them onto the paper, they vaporize them. Colored gas penetrates the surface of the paper to create an image on the page. Dye sub printers produce high-quality output. Moreover, they can mix and blend colors to produce output at near-photographic quality.

High-speed copiers, printers, and most other printing devices found in a printing shop are now connected to a network, which allows the device to receive materials electronically from any computer connected to the network. The operator of these printing devices schedules printing in accordance with the instructions submitted electronically with the materials.

Printer Connections

Most printers today come standard with a USB port. However, wireless printing provides freedom for computer users and allows printing from handheld devices such as tablets and smartphones. You can print from anywhere in your home, office, or around the world.

Many printers have a direct network connection option that lets you place the printer on a local area network (LAN), where it can be shared by all the computers attached to the LAN. If a particular printer doesn't include a networked option, you can purchase a network printer interface from a third party. These interfaces have one or more network ports plus one or more printer ports. You connect the network on one side and plug in the printer on the other.

It is generally more efficient to use a direct network-attached printer rather than a printer attached to a computer and configured for sharing on the network. Using a printer attached to a computer can be a drain on the computer's resources when others are using the printer, and a network interface is always on, making the printer always available to network users.

Installing Printers

OSs provide one or more ways to install printers because printing is vital to outputting documents from word processors, spreadsheets, graphics programs, and other software. In the following sections, you learn how to install a printer in the OSs that are the focus of this book.

Installing Windows Printers In Windows, many printers can be installed by connecting them to the computer and then letting PnP initiate the installation, as discussed earlier in this chapter. Another option is to connect the printer and use the Add a device wizard, which was also discussed earlier. However, if an installation DVD/CD-ROM comes with the printer, the best approach is to insert the DVD/CD-ROM and follow the instructions. You should not connect the printer until you are instructed to do so. Finally, if you need to perform a manual installation or initiate automatic detection and setup of a new printer, you can use the Add a printer option in Control Panel, as shown in Figure 6-8. Windows will attempt to find a printer connected to your computer or on the network. If no printer is detected, you will be prompted to install one manually.

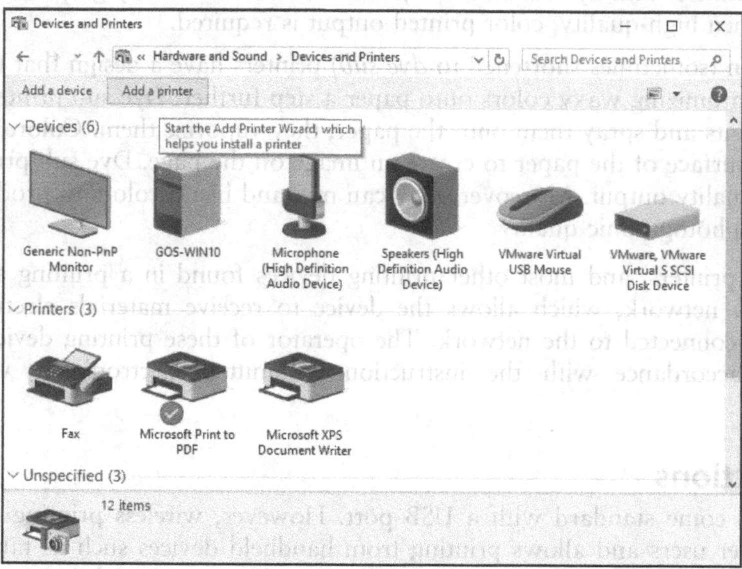

Figure 6-8 Add a printer option in Windows 10

Installing UNIX/Linux Printers When a **print job** is sent from an application, a **print spooler** accepts the job and stores it in a **print queue**, a temporary file used to store jobs until they can be sent to the printer. When the printer is ready, the print spooler sends the job from the queue to the printer. The most common Linux printing system is the Common UNIX Printing System (CUPS). With CUPS, the print spooler is called the *CUPS daemon*, a service that runs on Linux.

Windows also uses a print queue, but users do not have to configure the print queue on a Windows system when installing a new printer.

Older Linux distributions might use the Line Printer Daemon (LPD) printing system. LPD works in a similar manner to CUPS, but CUPS is used in more contemporary distributions and has more features than LPD.

Most of the CUPS configuration files are in /etc/cups. For example, the configuration file for the CUPS daemon is /etc/cups/cupsd.conf, and installed printer configurations are found in /etc/cups/printers.conf. If you have a printer that is directly connected to the computer, the CUPS daemon will usually detect and install it automatically, placing an entry in the printers.conf file. For printers that are not detected, or for network printers, you can edit the printers.conf file directly, but it is better to run the Printers tool in Fedora Linux, as shown in Figure 6-9. The figure shows a network-attached HP LaserJet printer. To access the Printers tool, click Activities, Show Applications, Settings, and then double-click Printers. To add a new printer, click the plus sign on the lower-left side of the Printers tool, or if no printers are currently installed, click the Add New Printer button. Another option is to use the CUPS Web administration tool by opening a Web browser to *http://localhost:631*.

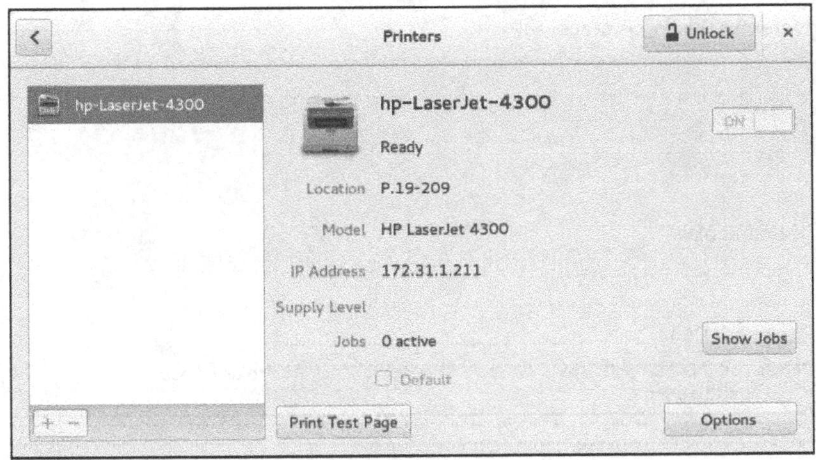

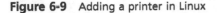

Figure 6-9 Adding a printer in Linux

Source: Linux

A printer connected to one computer can be used to print jobs from another computer. Every computer that wants to use a printer, whether remotely or locally, must first create a print queue for that printer. If one computer has the printer connected and three other Linux computers want to use the printer, a print queue for that printer must be created on all four computers. When a print job is submitted, it is queued in the local print queue. From there, it is submitted to the print queue of the computer to which the printer is connected, and then it spools to the printer.

Installing Mac OS X Printers In Mac OS X, most printer drivers are already installed when you install the OS. If not, make sure that the printer you buy has a DVD/CD-ROM to install the new printer driver. To set up a printer, use the Printers & Scanners utility in System Preferences and click the plus sign to add the new printer.

Depending on the setup of your computer, you can add or configure the following types of printers (see Figure 6-10).

- Default
- IP
- Windows

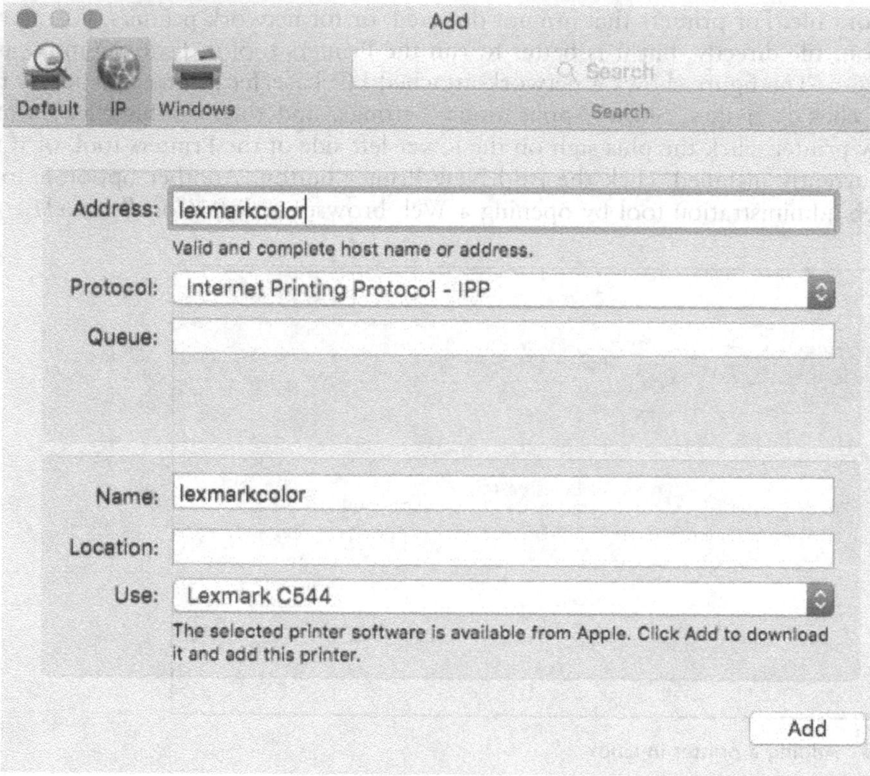

Add
Default IP Windows
Search
Address: lexmarkcolor
Valid and complete host name or address.
Protocol: Internet Printing Protocol - IPP
Queue:
Name: lexmarkcolor
Location:
Use: Lexmark C544
The selected printer software is available from Apple. Click Add to download it and add this printer.
Add

Figure 6-10 Adding a printer in Mac OS X

Source: Mac OS X

Printers listed under Default are those that OS X detects on your local network. Select a listed printer to have OS X install the printer driver. An IP printer is a **network-attached printer** that uses the Internet Printing Protocol (IPP). If OS X doesn't automatically detect a network printer, click IP, and then type the IP address or name of the printer. If Mac OS X finds the printer on the network, click Add to install the necessary driver. The Windows option is for connecting to a shared printer on a Windows computer. If your Mac is on a network that includes Windows computers that are sharing printers, you can use this option to access those printers.

Display Adapters

Once wildly diverse in design and features, display adapters today have reached a common ground across OSs and hardware platforms. The general industry acceptance of the **Peripheral Component Interconnect** (**PCI**) bus, then the **Accelerated Graphics Port** (**AGP**) bus, and finally the **Peripheral Component Interconnect Express** (**PCIe**) bus standard, has enabled adapter manufacturers to supply one hardware product or a line of hardware products to a variety of hardware platforms. The PCIe bus enables high-performance graphics capabilities and is the current standard for most types of add-on cards, such as display adapters and disk controllers.

Basic Display Adapter Technology

If you are using a PC with a monitor, you have a display adapter card already installed in your computer. The display adapter is part of a standard computer package. No matter what computer platform you are using, the basic display consists of a number of pixels horizontally and a number of pixels vertically. A **pixel**, remember, is a picture element—actually a small dot of light—that represents one small portion of your overall screen display.

In general, as you display more pixels on the screen, you'll need a larger monitor to comfortably read the displayed data. For a given size of screen, higher-resolution displays can present more data at a time, but this data is presented in a smaller format. Most monitors today offer an optimal resolution setting that you should use. However, most OSs allow you to change the resolution if you want.

Current OSs support devices with the full range of resolution, so the major considerations in choosing an adapter are its resolution capabilities, the amount of memory included with the adapter, the type of video processor, and cost. More memory on the adapter generally means faster performance when rendering screen images; also, when it comes to processors, display adapters may have their own CPU or accelerator to speed things up. As noted previously, you should also consider what kind of monitor you need as you decide on the screen resolution.

6

Another aspect of screen resolution isn't often discussed: the density of the displayed image, or bit density. A resolution of 1024×768 simply means that images are displayed with 1024 dots of light from left to right and 768 dots of light from top to bottom. However, there is a third consideration to the display, the bit density—the number of dots of light that can be crammed into an inch of display. When you consider graphics programs such as Photoshop or CorelDRAW, or choose a digital camera or other image source, this aspect of resolution becomes important.

These dots are referred to in terms of **dots per inch (dpi)** for printers and **pixels per inch (ppi)** for monitors. These two terms have been used interchangeably, but they are specific to the device you are using.

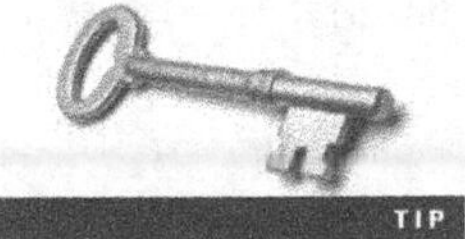

TIP

When you view graphics on your computer monitor, its bit density will be less than that of your printer. Your printer may be able to reproduce 600, 1200, 1440, or 2880 dpi, or more for some applications. It is important to know this third dimension when you specify printers, plotters, scanners, digital cameras, video editing software, and graphics programs. Print resolution, for example, may be more precise than the resolution of the monitor. The printer may show imperfections that the monitor does not display.

Standard video adapters have color depth capabilities that depend on the OS, software drivers, and video adapter memory. They range from 16 colors at the very low end to 64-bit color. Most computers are set to run at 24-bit or 32-bit color.

Larger monitors are also the norm. For example, a 19-inch display or larger is now common. With a 19-inch monitor, you can routinely set a resolution of 1280×1024 and still see everything you need to see.

Digital Visual Interface (DVI) was developed as a high-quality visual standard for flat-panel LCD displays and digital projectors. A resolution of 1920×1200 is the standard for a single cable, and a dual cable can display 3840×2400 at 33 Hz. DVI is mostly compatible with the **High-Definition Multimedia Interface (HDMI)**, which is a way to connect digital audio/video devices in televisions, but it is also a popular way to connect devices and computers. **DisplayPort** is a digital interface standard that is projected to replace DVI and HDMI for computers. Both DVI and HDMI signals will run over the DisplayPort interface.

Installing Display Adapters

There are good reasons for upgrading display hardware. Changes in technology, software, and our personal needs can all require upgrades. Another reason for upgrading or adding a display adapter is to take advantage of multiple monitors. Most OSs support two, three, four, or even more monitors, and you can buy a single display adapter that has up to four outputs to connect multiple monitors. Figure 6-11 shows the Advanced Display Settings control panel in Windows 10 on a system with four monitors.

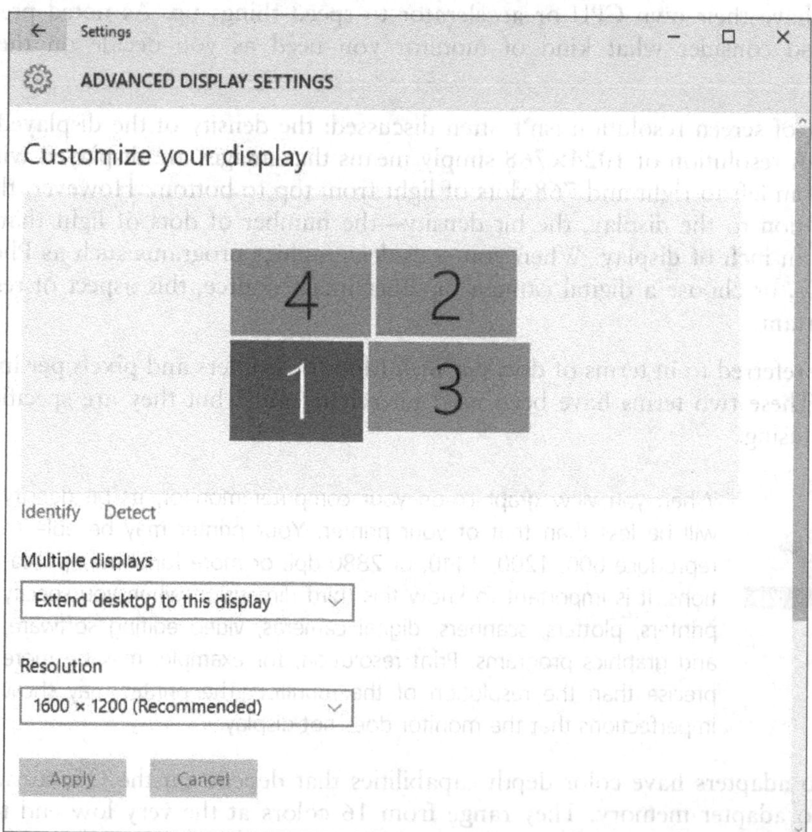

Figure 6-11 Advanced Display Settings with four monitors

By far, the majority of display adapters are supplied as cards that plug into the PCIe slot on the motherboard. The PCIe bus is the most common expansion bus standard among computer hardware manufacturers, including Intel-based computers, Macintosh computers, and workstations designed for UNIX, Oracle, and other systems. As with printers and other hardware, display adapters are installed in two phases: hardware and software.

Installing any display adapter card is similar to installing circuit boards, as detailed in the last section of this chapter. Thanks to the industry's adoption of the PCIe bus standard and similarities among computer case designs, the installation procedure should be the same across platforms.

Sound Cards

High-quality sound output and even high-quality recording capabilities have become more important to a broader range of computer users. Businesses use sound as part of documentation or training, sales presentations, and even for music and motion video productions.

The sound card comes preinstalled, and the OS includes integral support for sound input and output on newer computers. However, drivers for individual pieces of sound hardware must be installed, as described earlier in the chapter.

Sound devices are of two general types: hardware integrated with the motherboard and bus cards, which are installed into a bus slot in the same way as a display adapter (see the last section of this chapter). Increasingly you will see sound cards built into the motherboard. This approach provides the easiest installation because the hardware is always there, and all you might need to do is install or configure drivers. The downside to motherboard sound hardware, as with built-in disk controllers, video adapters, and other devices, is that it may be harder to update or change the hardware.

Other Output Devices

Today's computer marketplace offers so many output options that it would be impossible to cover them all here. Digital video, for example, is a popular consumer and professional feature in computers. Adapter cards are available that let you capture and output digital video to a camera or DVR, and are coupled with capable, low-cost video editing software to help you use them.

Enhanced sound output is also now reasonably priced. Multiport sound cards are available that permit a computer to serve as a fully digital, multichannel recorder for sound studio applications.

As you interact with a variety of computer systems and read specifications for products from a variety of industries, be aware of what hardware and software may be driving the features you are using or reading about. Also, be aware that specialty software is probably required to make everything work properly.

The next section outlines the general steps for installing all types of cards.

Installing Circuit Boards

Today's computer hardware is pretty rugged. Still, perhaps the biggest enemy of the devices supplied on circuit boards or cards is static electricity—high-voltage, low-current charges that can exist between any two devices, including human bodies. Static discharges are obvious when the voltage is great enough to cause a spark to jump between objects, or from an object to your finger. However, you can damage delicate computer parts with voltages below this sparking level.

To avoid damage to circuit boards during installation, follow these simple guidelines:

- Leave the card inside its protective cover until you are ready to install it.
- Disconnect all power to the computer.
- Prepare the computer by removing the case and any slot covers for the slots you will use.
- Touch a grounded part of the computer to discharge any static. The computer case is a good choice. Then, without removing your hand from the computer, open the bag and remove the card you are about to install. Once you have the card in your hands, you can stop touching the case.

Electrostatic discharge (ESD) straps can be used to prevent damage to your computer and cards. An ESD strap usually consists of a wrist strap with a grounding cord to clip to the computer's metal frame.

- Insert the card carefully into the chosen slot and press it firmly into place. It is helpful to wiggle the card into position, pressing first one end, then the other, until it is firmly seated. You'll quickly get the hang of it as you work with more cards. Just remember that the card itself is quite rugged. Except for static discharge, it isn't likely that you'll hurt a modern computer card during installation.

Chapter Summary

- An OS handles input and output device communications through device drivers (software) and through hardware such as controller and adapter boards.
- Device drivers are often provided with an OS, but the most up-to-date device drivers come directly from each device manufacturer.
- Manufacturer device and device driver installations are typically performed from a manufacturer's DVD/CD-ROM. Up-to-date drivers can usually be downloaded from the manufacturer's Web site.
- You can install devices and drivers in Windows using PnP, the Add a device wizard, Control Panel options, and Device Manager. Also, plan to configure driver signing to ensure successful and secure device driver installations.
- UNIX/Linux systems use device special files for managing input and output devices.
- For Mac OS X devices, most drivers come with the OS or can be installed from an installation DVD/CD-ROM provided by the device manufacturer.
- Common input devices include mice, keyboards, touch inputs, digital pads, scanners, joysticks, gamepads, digital sound devices, digital picture devices, and a variety of devices that use USB or 1394 technology.

- Printers are common output devices. The most common types are inkjet and laser printers.
- Most OSs include tools for installing printers, such as the Add a device wizard in Windows, Printers in Fedora Linux, and the Printers & Scanners Utility in Mac OS X.
- Besides printers, other examples of common output devices include display adapters and sound cards. Today, many other output devices are available for high-end audio and video processing.

Key Terms

3D printer A printer that uses an additive process to create one layer at a time of a three-dimensional object.

Accelerated Graphics Port (AGP) A bus standard that has been replaced by the PCI Express or PCIe standard.

block special file In UNIX/Linux, a file used to manage random access devices that handle blocks of data, including DVD/CD-ROM drives, hard disk drives, tape drives, and other storage devices.

character special file An I/O management file in UNIX/Linux used to handle byte-by-byte streams of data, such as through a USB connection, including printers and network communications.

device special file A file used in UNIX and Linux for managing I/O devices. The file can be one of two types: a *block special file* or a *character special file*.

digital pad An alternative input device frequently used by graphic artists and others who need accurate control over drawing and other data input.

Digital Visual Interface (DVI) A high-quality visual standard for connecting flat-panel LCD displays and digital projectors.

DisplayPort A digital interface standard that is projected to replace DVI and HDMI for computers.

dot-matrix (impact) printer An impact character printer that produces characters by arranging a matrix of dots.

dots per inch (dpi) Used to measure the resolution of a printer; the number of dots contained in an inch.

driver signing A digital signature that Microsoft incorporates into driver and system files as a way to verify the files and to ensure that they are not inappropriately overwritten.

dye sublimation A printer technology that produces high-quality color output by creating "sublimated" color mists that penetrate paper to form characters or graphic output.

gamepad An input device primarily designed for interaction with games. It includes multiple buttons, wheels, or balls to effect movement of a variety of on-screen objects.

High-Definition Multimedia Interface (HDMI) A high-quality visual standard for connecting digital audio and video devices.

inkjet printer A printer that forms characters and images by spraying droplets of ink from a nozzle print head onto the paper.

Institute of Electrical and Electronics Engineers (IEEE) An international organization of scientists, engineers, technicians, and educators that plays a leading role in developing standards for computers, network cabling, and data transmissions, and for other electronics areas, such as consumer electronics and electrical power.

interrupt request (IRQ) line A channel within the computer that is used for communications with the CPU.

I/O address range A range of memory addresses used to temporarily store data that is transferred between a computer device or component and the CPU.

joystick An input device shaped like a stick that allows for three-dimensional movement of an on-screen cursor or other object, such as a car, airplane, or cartoon character.

label printers Special-purpose printers that produce labels only.

laser printer A high-quality page printer design that is popular in office and other professional applications.

line printer A printer design that prints a full line of character output at a time; it is used for high-speed output requirements.

LPT1 The primary printer port designation on many desktop computers; also designated as line print terminal 1.

multifunction printers Printers that combine printing, scanning, and faxing in one physical device. They can be color inkjet or laser printers.

named pipe In UNIX/Linux, a device special file for handling internal communications, such as redirecting file output to a monitor.

network-attached printer A printer that has a network interface, is connected to the network, and can be accessed by computers on the network via a host name or IP address.

optical character recognition (OCR) Imaging software that scans each character on the page as a distinct image and is able to recognize the character.

Peripheral Component Interconnect (PCI) A bus standard that has been replaced by the PCI Express or PCIe standard.

Peripheral Component Interconnect Express (PCIe) A bus standard that has enabled adapter manufacturers to supply one hardware product to a variety of hardware platforms.

pixel Short for *picture element*; the small dots that make up a computer screen display.

pixels per inch (ppi) A unit used to measure the resolution of a display screen; the number of dots (pixels) contained in an inch.

plotter Computer hardware that produces high-quality printed output, often in color, by moving ink pens over the surface of paper. Plotters are often used with computer-aided design (CAD) and other graphics applications.

print job The data or document sent from an application to a printer and accepted by the print spooler.

print queue A temporary file used to store a print job until it can be sent to the printer.

print spooler A process that accepts print jobs from applications, stores them in the print queue, and then sends them to the printer when the print device is ready.

scanner A digital image created from a hard copy that is then transmitted to the computer.

tar A UNIX file archive utility.

thermal-wax transfer printer A printer that creates high-quality color printed output by melting colored wax elements and transferring them to the printed page.

Review Questions

1. The *tar* format for retrieving drivers is used in which of the following?
   a. Windows 10
   b. Windows Server 2012
   c. UNIX/Linux
   d. Windows 7
2. What communicates between the OS and computer devices?
   a. device driver
   b. OS kernel
   c. applications
   d. user interface
3. You need to check a printer parameter for a Linux printer. In what directory should you look for information about the printer configuration?
   a. /dev/printers
   b. /bin/ptr
   c. /usr/printer
   d. /etc/cups
4. When a Linux application prints a document, what accepts the document and stores it in a temporary location before it is sent to the printer?
   a. print device
   b. print spooler
   c. printer service
   d. printer process
5. You support the Windows 10 computers in your organization. A new network interface driver has been issued to plug a security hole. Which tool would you use to quickly install this driver update?
   a. Device Manager
   b. Add Network Interface Wizard
   c. PnP
   d. Registry editor

6. On a Mac OS X computer, what is the name for a 1394 port?
   a. Centronics
   b. FireWire
   c. RS232
   d. USB
7. The Accounting Department needs to purchase a printer that prints receipts for customers. The department also needs three-part carbonless paper. What type of printer would you recommend? (Choose all that apply.)
   a. inkjet printer
   b. laser printer
   c. thermal-wax printer
   d. dot-matrix impact printer
8. Which of the following might be attached to a computer through a USB port? (Choose all that apply.)
   a. mouse
   b. keyboard
   c. printer
   d. video display adapter
9. What type of port is typically used for a scanner?
   a. DVI
   b. AGP
   c. USB
   d. SCSI
10. You installed a new printer in Red Hat Enterprise Linux, but when you print the test page, several characters are not printing correctly. Which of the following should you do first?
    a. Use a different printer cable.
    b. Obtain the latest printer drivers from the printer manufacturer's Web site.
    c. Reconfigure the speed of the printer port.
    d. Return the printer for a refund.
11. Your organization often receives long paper forms to complete and return. Which of the following tools can you use to convert these forms to digital format for faster completion using a word processor? (Choose two.)
    a. SCSI interpreter
    b. scanner
    c. digital picture I/O
    d. OCR software

12. After you install a new sound card and its related device drivers, your monitor frequently pauses or stops working until you reboot. Which of the following is most likely to be the problem?
    a. You need a new monitor.
    b. You need a new display adapter.
    c. There is an I/O address range conflict.
    d. You need to update the driver.
13. You are the computer support person in your small company. One of the employees has installed an off-brand network interface card (NIC) and its drivers on his Windows 10 computer. Now the OS will not run several network-related programs, such as e-mail, a calendar scheduling program, and programs used for remote database access. You suspect a driver problem, so you uninstall the NIC driver and the NIC, and then install a NIC that is known to be Windows 10 compatible. How can you prevent this problem from happening the next time the user installs a device?
    a. Configure driver signing.
    b. Disable Control Panel.
    c. Set up a device block.
    d. Configure a firewall.
14. Which command in Linux enables you to create a device special file?
    a. *tty*
    b. *mknod*
    c. *mkspc*
    d. *devmake*
15. When you create a device special file in Linux, in what folder should it be stored?
    a. /etc
    b. /dev
    c. /sbin
    d. /tmp
16. Where are print jobs stored before being sent to the print device?
    a. spooler
    b. job file
    c. print queue
    d. printer cache
17. What is the most common printing system used in contemporary Linux distributions?
    a. Print Management
    b. IPP
    c. LPD
    d. CUPS

18. A friend was installing a circuit board and damaged it by creating a static discharge at the time of installation. How can this be avoided?
    a. Remove all batteries from circuit boards prior to installation.
    b. Scrape the contacts on the circuit board before you install it.
    c. Turn the computer off, then ground yourself by touching the computer case.
    d. Only purchase self-grounding circuit boards.
19. In UNIX and Linux, which of the following is true about device drivers? (Choose all that apply.)
    a. They must be written in C or Pascal.
    b. They can be loadable modules.
    c. They can be NLMs.
    d. They must never be kernel modules.
20. Which is the most common expansion bus used in personal computers?
    a. PCIe
    b. PCI-X
    c. ISA
    d. AGP

Hands-On Projects

Project 6-1: Use the Add a Device Wizard in Windows 10

The Add a device wizard is a valuable tool for installing all types of devices and drivers. In this project, you use the wizard in Windows 10. You need an account that has Administrator privileges; also, your computer should not have newly installed hardware, so that you can manually practice the full range of steps. You do not need to have a connected printer to complete these steps.

1. Start your Windows 10 computer and log on.
2. Right-click **Start,** and click **Control Panel.** Make sure the **Category** View by option is selected. Click **Hardware and Sound,** and then click the **Add a device** link (see Figure 6-12).

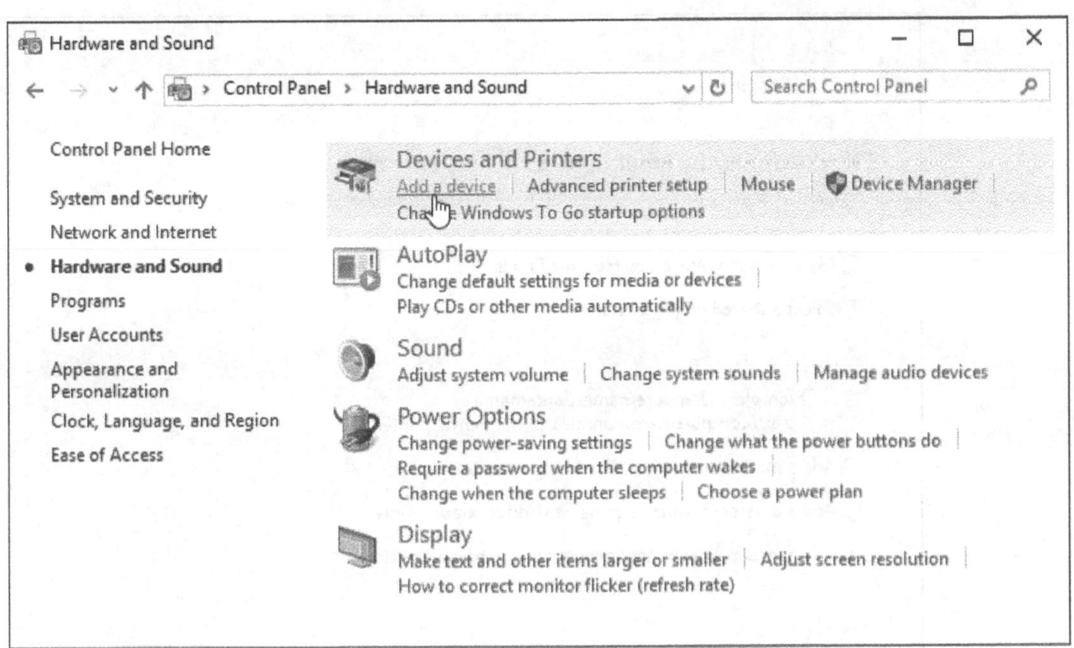

Figure 6-12 Starting the Add a device wizard

3. Windows looks for a device to add. If Windows can't find one, you must use a different method. For example, to add a printer, click **Advanced printer setup** from the Devices and Printers section of Control Panel. To add other devices, you can try Device Manager. Click **Cancel**.
4. To add a printer, click the **Advanced printer setup** link. Windows looks for a printer to install.
5. When Windows stops looking for the printer, click **The printer that I want isn't listed**.
6. From the Add Printer dialog box (see Figure 6-13), you have several choices, including the option to add a shared, network, or Bluetooth printer.

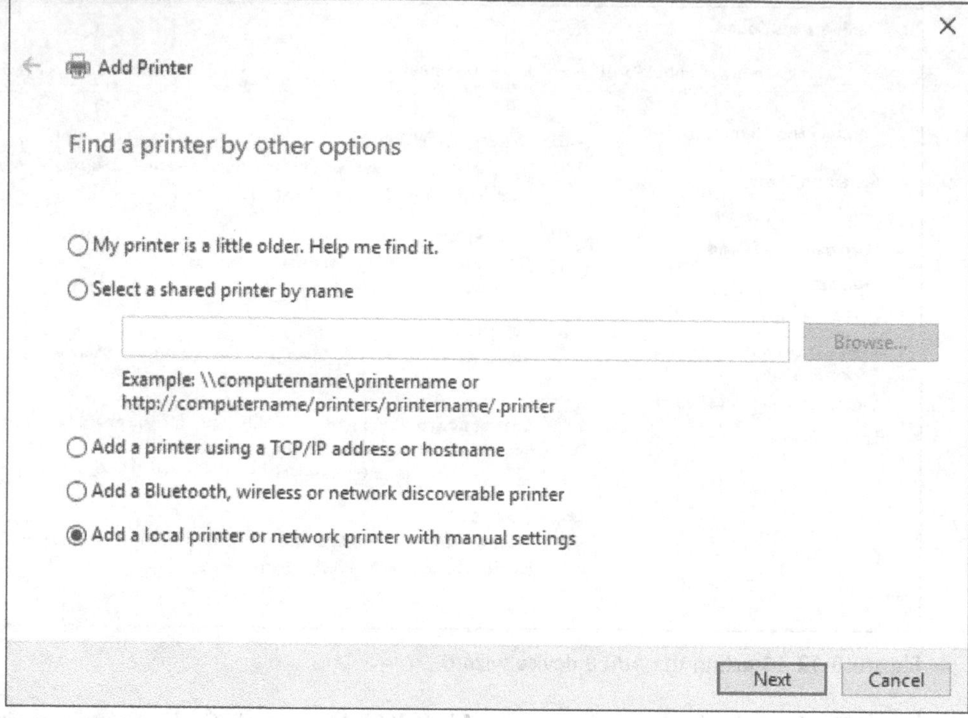

Figure 6-13 Adding a printer manually

7. Click **Add a local printer or network printer with manual settings.** Click **Next.**
8. Use the default port selection, which is LPT1 (Printer Port), and click **Next.**
9. In the Manufacturer box, click **HP,** and in the Printers box, click **HP Color LaserJet 1600 Class Driver.** On this screen, you also have the option to supply a disk or get the driver via Windows Update. Click **Next.**
10. You can leave the default name for the printer on the next screen. Click **Next.**
11. On the next screen, click **Do not share this printer,** and then click **Next.**
12. Windows installs the printer driver and gives you the option to print a test page. Because you aren't installing an actual printer, click **Finish.**
13. Close all open windows, but stay logged on if you are continuing to the next project.

Project 6-2: Install a Network Printer in Windows 10

In this project, you install a network-attached printer in Windows 10. Your instructor will have to give you the name or address of the network printer.

1. Log on to your Windows 10 computer, if necessary.
2. Right-click **Start,** and click **Control Panel.** Make sure the **Category** View by option is selected. Click **Hardware and Sound,** and click the **Advanced printer setup** link.

3. Windows looks for a printer. If Windows can't find it, click **The printer that I want isn't listed.**
4. To add a network printer, click **Add a printer using a TCP/IP address or hostname.** Click **Next.**
5. In the next window, type the name or IP address of the printer in the Hostname or IP address text box. Click **Next.**
6. Windows connects to the printer and installs the drivers. In the Printer name text box, type a descriptive name or accept the default name. Click **Next.**
7. In the Printer Sharing window, click **Do not share this printer**, and then click **Next.** (You can share the printer later by accessing the printer properties.)
8. Click **Print a test page** if desired, and click **Finish.**
9. Close all open windows, but stay logged on if you are continuing to the next project.

Project 6-3: Use Device Manager in Windows 10

In this project, you use Device Manager to view where to install or update a driver in Windows 10. You also use this utility to determine if a device is working properly and to view other information about the device.

1. Log on to your Windows 10 computer, if necessary. Right-click **Start** and click **Device Manager.**
2. Click to expand **Display adapters.**
3. Double-click the specific adapter under Display adapters.
4. Make sure that the **General** tab is displayed. You see the device status, which tells you the device is working properly.
5. Click the **Driver** tab (see Figure 6-14). Notice that you can click the Update Driver button to obtain an updated driver or install a driver if one is not already installed. Also, click the Roll Back Driver button to revert to a previously installed driver if there is a problem with an updated driver. (This button is disabled if you are installing the first driver.) You can click Disable to disable a device without actually installing it, and you can click the Uninstall button to remove a driver.

Figure 6-14 The Driver tab

6. Click the **Driver Details** button.
7. Display drivers usually have a number of associated files. The Driver File Details dialog box lets you view the name and location of the driver files. Click **OK**.
8. Click the **Resources** tab to see the resource settings for the display adapter. Notice there are one or more I/O ranges, one or more memory ranges, and an IRQ setting. A message at the bottom of the dialog box tells you if any conflicts are detected.
9. Click **Cancel** and then close Device Manager.
10. Stay logged on if you are continuing to the next project.

Project 6-4: Configure Mouse Settings in Windows 10

In this project, you view the settings available for your mouse in Windows 10.

1. Log on to your Windows 10 computer, if necessary.
2. Right-click **Start,** and click **Control Panel.** Click the selection arrow next to **View by** and click **Small icons.**

3. Click **Mouse** to open the Mouse Properties window (see Figure 6-15). Review the options available for changing the behavior of the mouse.

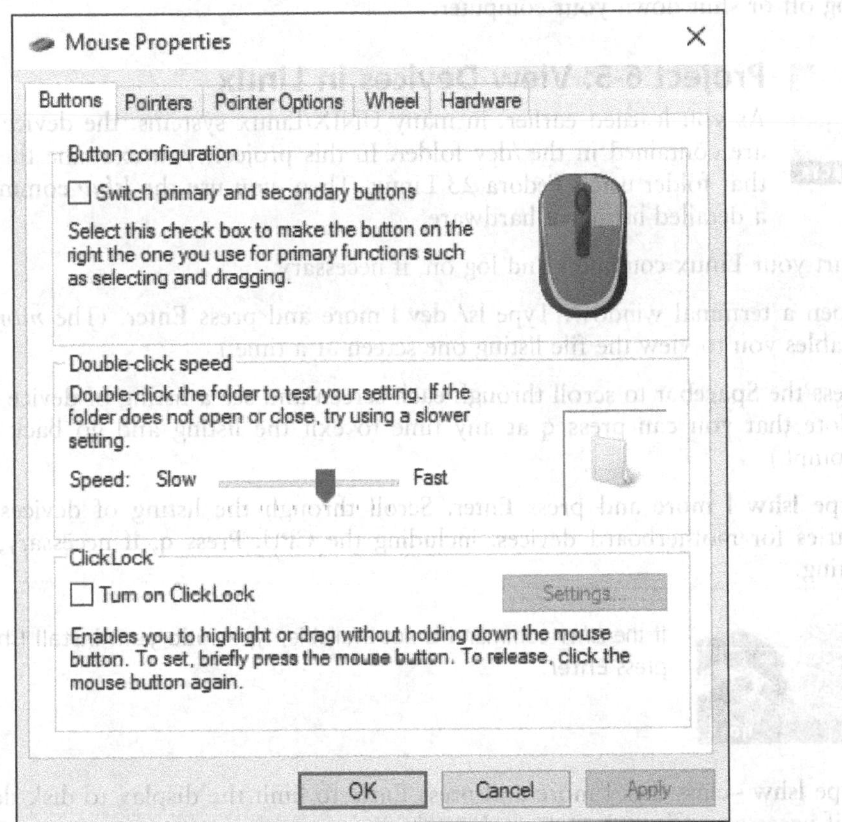

Figure 6-15 Mouse Properties window

4. Click the **Pointers** tab. Click the selection arrow under Scheme and click **Windows Inverted (extra large) (system scheme)**. Click **OK**.
5. Move your mouse around the screen to see how it changes when you are inside a window. In Control Panel, click **Mouse** again.
6. Click the **Pointers** tab and select **Windows Default (system scheme)** to set the mouse pointer back to its original settings.
7. Click the **Pointer Options** tab, and review the options available. Click the **Show location of pointer when I press the CTRL key** check box. Click **OK**.
8. Press **Ctrl**. Notice the concentric circles displayed around the mouse pointer, which help you locate the mouse pointer easily. The circles are very helpful when you are using multiple monitors.

6

9. In Control Panel, click **Mouse** again. Click the remaining tabs to see the other mouse configuration options. Click **Cancel** when you are finished.
10. Log off or shut down your computer.

Project 6-5: View Devices in Linux

As you learned earlier, in many UNIX/Linux systems, the device special files are contained in the /dev folder. In this project, you examine the contents of that folder using Fedora 23 Linux. Then, you use the *lshw* command to view a detailed listing of hardware.

1. Start your Linux computer and log on, if necessary.
2. Open a terminal window. Type **ls/ dev | more** and press **Enter**. (The *more* command enables you to view the file listing one screen at a time.)
3. Press the **Spacebar** to scroll through each screen and see a listing of device special files. (Note that you can press **q** at any time to exit the listing and go back to the shell prompt.)
4. Type **lshw | more** and press **Enter**. Scroll through the listing of devices. You'll see entries for motherboard devices, including the CPU. Press **q**, if necessary, to exit the listing.

If the *lshw* command is not available, type **sudo yum install lshw** and press **Enter**.

5. Type **lshw –class disk | more** and press **Enter** to limit the display to disk devices. Press **q**, if necessary. Close the terminal window.
6. Stay logged on if you are continuing to the next project.

Project 6-6: Use the Settings Menu in Linux

In Fedora 23 Linux with the GNOME desktop, you can configure devices using the Settings menu. This menu enables you to configure Bluetooth devices, desktop effects, the keyboard, monitor, mouse, and other devices and settings. In this project, you use the Settings menu to review settings for one or more monitors connected to the computer, and to review mouse settings.

1. Log on to your Linux computer, if necessary.
2. Click **Activities**, click **Show Applications**, and then click **Settings**. Notice the many devices and settings that can be configured (see Figure 6-16).

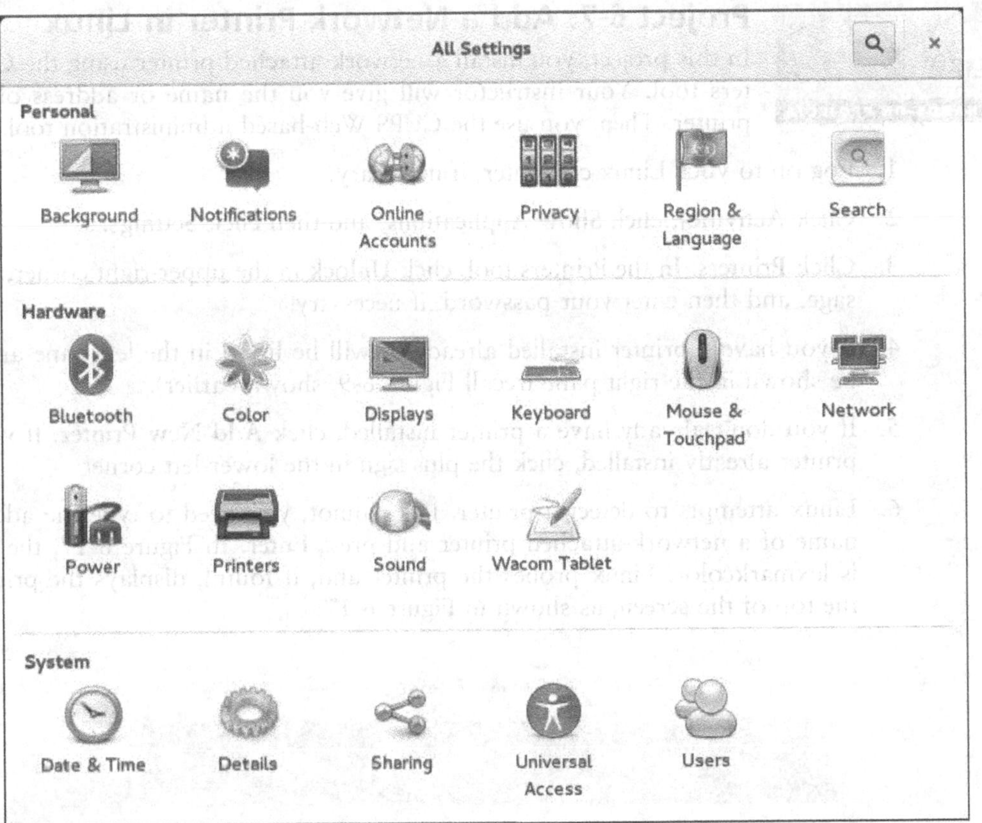

Figure 6-16 The Linux All Settings window

Source: Linux

3. Click **Displays.** Click the monitor icon; it may display a name or it may be labeled Unknown Display. If more than one monitor is attached, you will see a monitor icon for each.

4. You can change the resolution on most monitors, and some allow you to change other settings, such as the refresh rate.

5. Click **Cancel** and then click the arrow in the upper-left corner of the Displays window to return to the All Settings window.

6. Click **Mouse & Touchpad.**

7. Review the available settings and then click the arrow in the upper-left corner of the Mouse & Touchpad window to return to the All Settings window.

8. Click **Sound.** Click each tab to review the available sound options, and then click the arrow in the upper-left corner of the Sound window to return to the All Settings window. Close the All Settings window.

9. Stay logged on if you are continuing to the next project.

Project 6-7: Add a Network Printer in Linux

In this project, you install a network-attached printer using the GNOME Printers tool. Your instructor will give you the name or address of the network printer. Then, you use the CUPS Web-based administration tool.

1. Log on to your Linux computer, if necessary.
2. Click **Activities,** click **Show Applications,** and then click **Settings.**
3. Click **Printers.** In the Printers tool, click **Unlock** in the upper-right corner, read the message, and then enter your password, if necessary.
4. If you have a printer installed already, it will be listed in the left pane and details will be shown in the right pane (recall Figure 6-9, shown earlier).
5. If you don't already have a printer installed, click **Add New Printer.** If you do have a printer already installed, click the plus sign in the lower-left corner.
6. Linux attempts to detect a printer. If it cannot, you need to type the address or DNS name of a network-attached printer and press **Enter.** In Figure 6-17, the printer name is lexmarkcolor. Linux probes the printer and, if found, displays the printer model at the top of the screen, as shown in Figure 6-17.

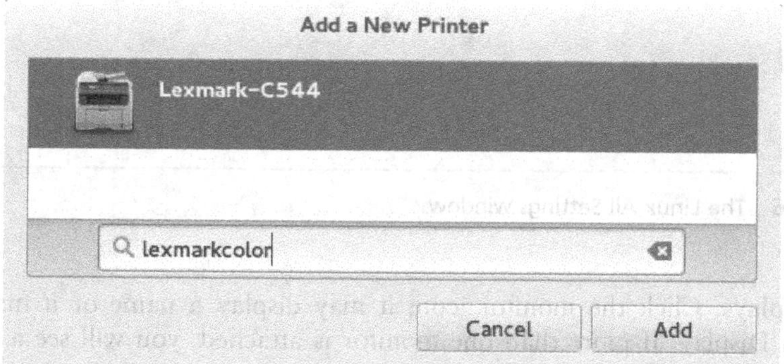

Figure 6-17 Adding a printer in Linux
Source: Linux

7. When the printer is found, click **Add** to install the printer driver. If allowed by the instructor, click **Print Test Page** to verify that the printer is working.
8. Close the Printers window.
9. Open a Web browser. In the address bar, type ***http://localhost:631*** and press Enter. The CUPS administration page opens.
10. Click each tab and review the tasks that you can perform. The Administration page is where you add printers and manage printers. Use the Jobs tab to manage print jobs and the Printers tab to view the status of installed printers (see Figure 6-18). Close the Web browser.

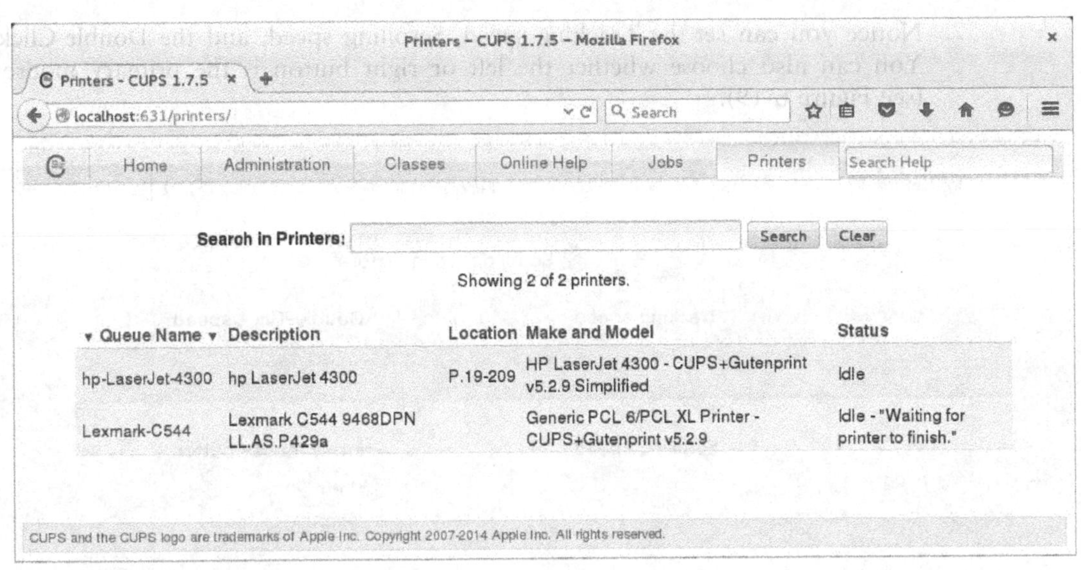

Figure 6-18 The CUPS Web-based administration page

Source: Linux

11. One of the command-line tools for managing CUPS is *lpstat*. Open a terminal window, type **lpstat –p**, and then press **Enter** to see the status of your printers. Type **lpstat –v** and press **Enter** to see the printers and their attached devices. In the case of network printers, you will see the IP address of the printer. Type **man lpstat** and press **Enter** to view the manual pages for *lpstat*. Press q after looking at the manual pages.
12. Close the terminal window.
13. Log off or shut down your computer.

Project 6-8: Use System Preferences in Mac OS X

In this project, you learn how to use the System Preferences tool in Mac OS X and see where to configure the keyboard and mouse. You will need to have a mouse plugged into your computer, and the account you use must have Administrator privileges.

1. Start your Mac computer and log on, if necessary.
2. Click the **Apple** icon and then click **System Preferences.**
3. Click **Keyboard** in the System Preferences window.
4. Ensure that the **Keyboard** tab is selected.
5. Notice that you can set the Key Repeat Rate and Delay Until Repeat parameters.
6. Click the **Back** arrow at the top of the Keyboard window to return to System Preferences. Click **Mouse.**

7. Notice you can set the Tracking speed, Scrolling speed, and the Double-Click speed. You can also choose whether the left or right button is the primary mouse button (see Figure 6-19).

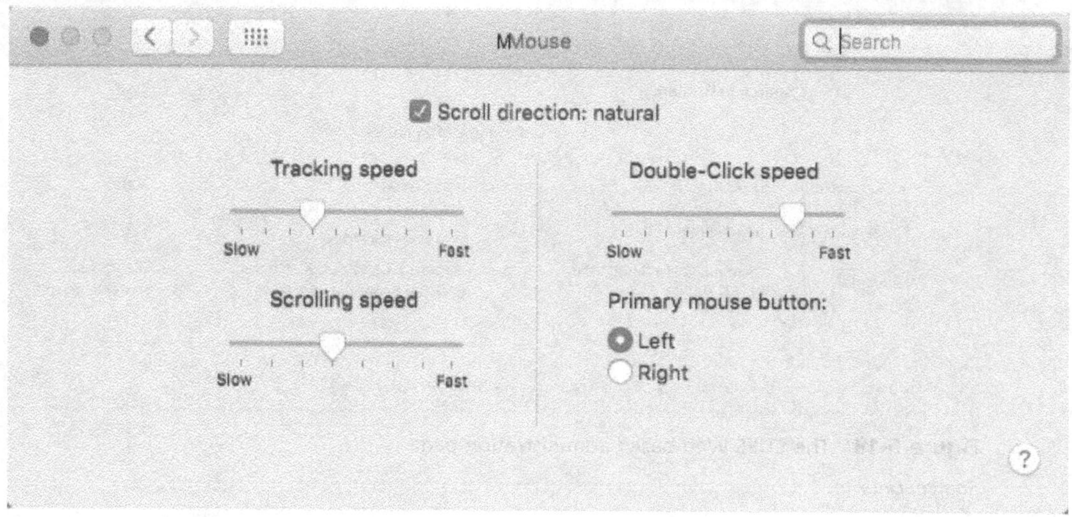

Figure 6-19 Configuring mouse settings in Mac OS X

Source: Mac OS X

8. Click the **Back** arrow at the top of the Mouse window to return to System Preferences.
9. Click **Displays.** Mac OS X will choose the default resolution for the connected monitor. You can configure the resolution by clicking **Scaled** if more than one resolution is available. If you have a compatible AirPlay device, you can select the device for AirPlay Mirroring. AirPlay mirroring allows you to display your Mac screen on an Apple TV device.
10. Click the **Back** arrow at the top of the Display window to return to System Preferences.
11. Leave the System Preferences window open for the next project.

Project 6-9: Install a Network Printer in Mac OS X

In this project, you install a network-attached printer in Mac OS X. Your instructor will give you the name or address of the network printer.

1. Log on to your Mac and open **System Preferences**, if necessary.
2. Click **Printers & Scanners** in the System Preferences window. The Printers & Scanners dialog box shows currently installed printers (see Figure 6-20).

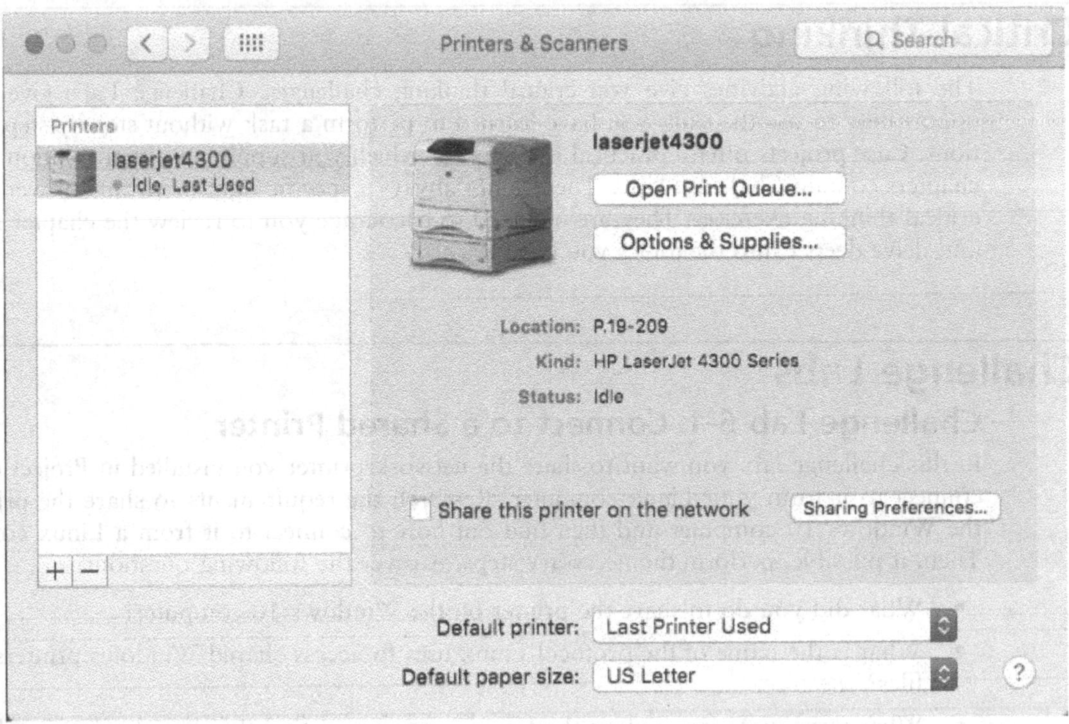

Figure 6-20 Printers & Scanners dialog box in OS X

Source: Mac OS X

3. To add a new printer, click the plus sign (+) in the Printers & Scanners window.
4. You see the Add window. To add a printer already detected by OS X, select it from the list of printers and click the **Add** button. However, for a network printer that is not detected, click **IP**.
5. In the Address text box, type the IP address or name of a printer that is connected to the network (see Figure 6-10 earlier).
6. If OS X finds the printer, click **Add** to install the printer driver.
7. On the Printers & Scanners dialog box, click the printer you just installed and click **Open Print Queue**. The print queue shows any current or pending print jobs. Close the print queue.
8. Close the Printers & Scanners dialog box.
9. Log off or shut down the computer.

Critical Thinking

The following activities give you critical thinking challenges. Challenge Labs give you an opportunity to use the skills you have learned to perform a task without step-by-step instructions. Case projects offer a practical problem for which you supply a written solution. Not all chapters contain Challenge Labs. There is not always a specific right or wrong answer to these critical thinking exercises. They are intended to encourage you to review the chapter material and delve deeper into the topics you have learned.

Challenge Labs

Challenge Lab 6-1: Connect to a Shared Printer

In this challenge lab, you want to share the network printer you installed in Project 6-2 and connect to it from your Linux computer. Research the requirements to share the printer on the Windows 10 computer and then find out how to connect to it from a Linux computer. Then, if possible, perform the necessary steps. Answer the following questions:

- What did you do to share the printer on the Windows 10 computer?
- What is the name of the protocol Linux uses to access shared Windows printers and files?
- What steps were required on the Linux computer to find the shared printer and install the printer driver to access the shared printer?

Case Projects

Hard Rock makes hard candies that are sold worldwide. One of its specialties is fruit-flavored candies, such as papaya, guava, grapefruit, kiwi, orange, banana, and watermelon. Hard Rock employs 328 people and makes extensive use of computers and networks in the business. Users in the business office have Windows 10. The candy kitchen staff all use Mac OS X, while the shipping unit prefers Fedora Linux. The IT unit uses Fedora Linux for its own desktop computing needs and supports eight Windows Server 2012 R2 servers.

Case Project 6-1: Install Printers

The business office has just received three new laser printers for installation and wants you to train the printer support coordinator to install printers for the Windows 10 computers. The laser printers have network interfaces and are connected to the network. The printers are named Laser1, Laser2, and Laser3. The business office has three rooms with a network-attached printer in each room. Describe the steps required to install the printers in each room.

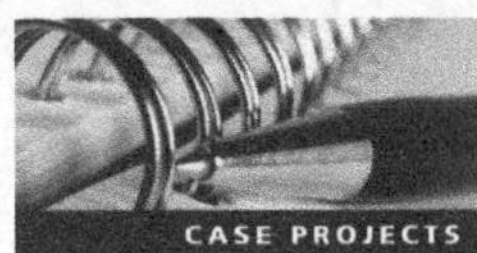

Case Project 6-2: Check the Printer Status for Troubleshooting in Fedora 23 Linux

The shipping unit has a Fedora 23 Linux computer to which it has connected three printers for different uses. One is a color laser printer, one is an inkjet printer, and a third is a dot-matrix printer. The shipping unit is having trouble with the laser printer and wants to check its status. What tools might be useful for this purpose in troubleshooting the problem?

Case Project 6-3: Solve a Driver Problem in Windows 10

A user downloaded and installed a new driver for her video card on her Windows 10 computer. Now, the user complains that the monitor occasionally flickers and goes black for a few seconds. The system has restarted twice. What should be done to solve this problem?

chapter 7

Using and Configuring Storage Devices

After reading this chapter and completing the exercises, you will be able to:

- Describe computer storage
- Configure local disks
- Work with different types of volumes and virtual disks
- Describe cloud storage
- Describe tape drive technologies
- Work with storage management tools

Configuring storage is usually one of the first tasks you need to perform on a new computer; this is particularly true of servers. In the past, computer storage was simply a disk controller and one or two hard drives, but advanced storage solutions are now available to provide fault tolerance and high performance. This chapter covers the basics of computer storage, and then explains how to configure local disks. With virtualization becoming such an important part of computer environments, it's no surprise that more OSs support creating and mounting virtual disks. This chapter describes the basic steps to work with virtual disks. A major enhancement to configuring storage in Windows is Storage Spaces, a new storage model.

An Overview of Computer Storage

One of the main reasons people use computers is to create, receive, and download files and documents of every type. Everything is stored on digital media now—documents, e-mail, music, photographs, videos—and this trend is continuing. In addition, people want instant access to whatever they store. Just about every large Internet company has its own version of cloud storage, from Dropbox to iCloud to OneDrive. Dozens of cloud storage services are competing to store your files, and although these services are convenient and seemingly work by magic, they all start with a computer and some hard drives. The following sections cover some basics of computer storage: what it is, why you need it, and the common methods for accessing storage.

What Is Storage?

Generally speaking, storage is any digital medium that data can be written to and later retrieved. Technically, this definition includes random access memory (RAM), but the term *computer storage* generally means long-term storage in which data is maintained without a power source. For example, RAM only holds data when it has electrical power—this is referred to as *volatile storage*. Long-term storage maintains data when the power is turned off, and is referred to as *nonvolatile storage*. Long-term storage includes the following types of media:

- USB memory sticks (flash drives)
- Secure Digital (SD) cards and Compact Flash (CF) cards
- CDs and DVDs
- Magnetic tape
- Solid-state drives
- Hard disk drives

This discussion centers on internal computer storage, which is based on hard disk drives (HDDs), although **solid-state drives (SSDs)** are rapidly closing the price and performance gap with HDDs. SSDs are very popular for applications requiring greater speed, smaller size, and lower power requirements. An SSD uses flash memory and the same type of high-speed interfaces (usually SATA or the newer SATA Express) as traditional hard disks. An SSD has no moving parts, requires less power, and is faster and more resistant to shock than an

HDD, but the cost is higher per gigabyte than an HDD. Also, SSDs don't yet have the capacity of HDDs, so discussions of computer storage are mainly about traditional HDD storage. Nonetheless, most of the discussion of HDD storage applies to SSDs as well, and as technology progresses and prices drop, SSDs will continue to replace HDDs in devices that require high speed and smaller sizes.

Reasons for Storage

Every computer needs some amount of storage, and servers generally require more than client computers because one of the server's main purposes is to store and serve files when they're requested. The following list isn't exhaustive, but it covers most uses of computer storage:

- *Operating system files*—The OS itself requires substantial storage. The files that make up the OS include boot files, the kernel, device drivers, user interface files, and all the files for additional features you can install. Together, they add up to around 20 GB for a typical Windows 10 and Mac OS X installation, and 8 to 10 GB for Windows Server 2012 and Fedora 23, depending on installed options.
- *User applications*—On client computers, user applications often use the most storage space, especially if users are running entire office suites and multimedia applications like photo editing programs.
- *User documents*—User documents might take up the most space if pictures, videos, and audio files are being stored on the computer. If a server is being used to store the files of dozens or hundreds of users, their documents might be the largest use of disk space on servers. Using disk quotas on servers that store user files is a good idea so that a single user can't monopolize disk space—for example, by storing an entire collection of movies on a network server.
- *Virtual memory*—Most OSs use **virtual memory** to supplement physical RAM. Virtual memory is disk space that is used to store the least recently used pages of memory when more physical RAM is needed but not available. For example, if you have five applications open but you haven't used three for several minutes, and then you open another application, the ones that haven't been used recently may be written to virtual memory if there is not enough free physical RAM. In Windows, virtual memory is stored as a file called **pagefile.sys**, which is usually located at the root of the C: drive. In Linux/UNIX OSs, virtual memory is implemented as a **swap partition**, a separate partition on the disk set aside exclusively for virtual memory. The size of virtual memory varies depending on how much RAM is installed, memory use patterns, and other factors, but it is usually 1 GB or larger on modern systems.
- *Log files*—Most OSs maintain log files to which various system components and applications can write when an event occurs. Log files can be used to track down system or security problems. Log files can slowly eat up disk space unless you keep an eye on their size and delete or archive them periodically.
- *Virtual machines*—If a server is a virtualization server, you need plenty of space to store files for virtual hard disks. Because it is so widely used, virtualization is one of the largest uses of disk space on servers.
- *Database storage*—If a server is running one or more databases, disk storage requirements vary depending on the size of the databases. Because databases can grow

dynamically, it's a good idea to store them on a drive separate from the drive where the OS is installed, preferably on a volume that can have its capacity expanded if needed.

When deciding how much disk space you need for a computer, you should take all the preceding uses into account. Remember that certain storage benefits from being on separate disks from the one where the OS is stored. This advice is particularly true of virtual memory, but ideally, the volume on which the OS is stored should be a separate drive from most other storage uses.

Storage Access Methods

This discussion of storage access methods revolves around where storage is located in relation to the server. There are four broad categories of storage access methods:

- Local storage
- Direct-attached storage (DAS)
- Network-attached storage (NAS)
- Storage area network (SAN)

Local Storage Local storage has been around as long as computers, but the interfaces to storage media have improved as speed and capacity requirements have grown. Local storage is the focus of this chapter; disk interface technologies are discussed later in the "Configuring Local Disks" section.

Local storage can be defined as storage media with a direct, exclusive connection to the computer's system board through a disk controller. Local storage is almost always inside the computer's case, and is attached to the disk controller via internal cables and powered by the computer's internal power supply. The term *local storage* usually refers to HDDs or SSDs instead of CD/DVDs or other types of media. Local storage provides rapid and exclusive access to storage media through ever-faster bus technologies. The downside of local storage is that only the system where it's installed has direct access to the storage medium. Data on disks can be shared through network file sharing, but the system with the installed storage must fulfill requests for shared data.

Direct-Attached Storage Direct-attached storage (DAS) is similar to local storage in that it's connected directly to the server using it. In fact, local storage is a type of DAS because DAS includes hard drives mounted inside the server case. However, DAS can also refer to one or more HDDs in an enclosure with its own power supply. In this case, the DAS device is connected to a server through an external bus interface, such as eSATA, SCSI, USB, FireWire, or Fibre Channel.

A DAS device with its own enclosure and power supply can usually be configured as a disk array, such as a RAID configuration (discussed later in the "Types of Volumes" section). Although most DAS devices provide exclusive use to a single computer, some have multiple interfaces so that more than one computer can access the storage medium simultaneously. Most of the related discussion later in this chapter also applies to DAS devices because the computer usually sees an externally attached DAS device as local storage.

The term *DAS* was created to distinguish it from storage connected to a network, such as NAS and SAN.

Network-Attached Storage Network-attached storage (NAS), sometimes referred to as a **storage appliance,** has an enclosure, a power supply, slots for multiple HDDs, a network interface, and a built-in OS tailored for managing shared storage. An NAS is designed to make access to shared files easy to set up and easy for users to access. Because an NAS is typically dedicated to file sharing, it can be faster than a traditional server in performing this task because a server often shares its computing and networking resources among several duties. An NAS shares files through standard network protocols, such as Server Message Block (SMB), Network File System (NFS), and File Transfer Protocol (FTP). Some NAS devices can also be used as DAS devices because they often have USB, eSATA, or other interfaces that can be attached directly to a computer.

Storage Area Network The most complex type of storage is a **storage area network** (SAN), which uses high-speed networking technologies to give servers fast access to large amounts of shared disk storage. To the server OS, the storage a SAN manages appears to be physically attached to the server. However, it's connected to a high-speed network technology and can be shared by multiple servers. The most common network technologies used in SANs are Fibre Channel and iSCSI. These technologies are designed to connect large arrays of hard drive storage that servers can access and share. Client computers access shared data by contacting servers via the usual method, and the servers retrieve the requested data from the SAN devices and pass it along to the client computer. Figure 7-1 shows a SAN using Fibre Channel, in which disk arrays are connected to a Fibre Channel switch and servers are connected to the Fibre Channel network as well as a traditional network. In this arrangement, all servers have access to the storage medium, which can be shared and allocated as needed.

SANs use the concept of a **logical unit number (LUN)** to identify a unit of storage. A LUN is a logical reference point to a unit of storage that could refer to an entire array of disks, a single disk, or just part of a disk. To the server using the SAN, the LUN is easier to work with because the server doesn't have to know how the storage is provided; it only needs to know how much storage is available.

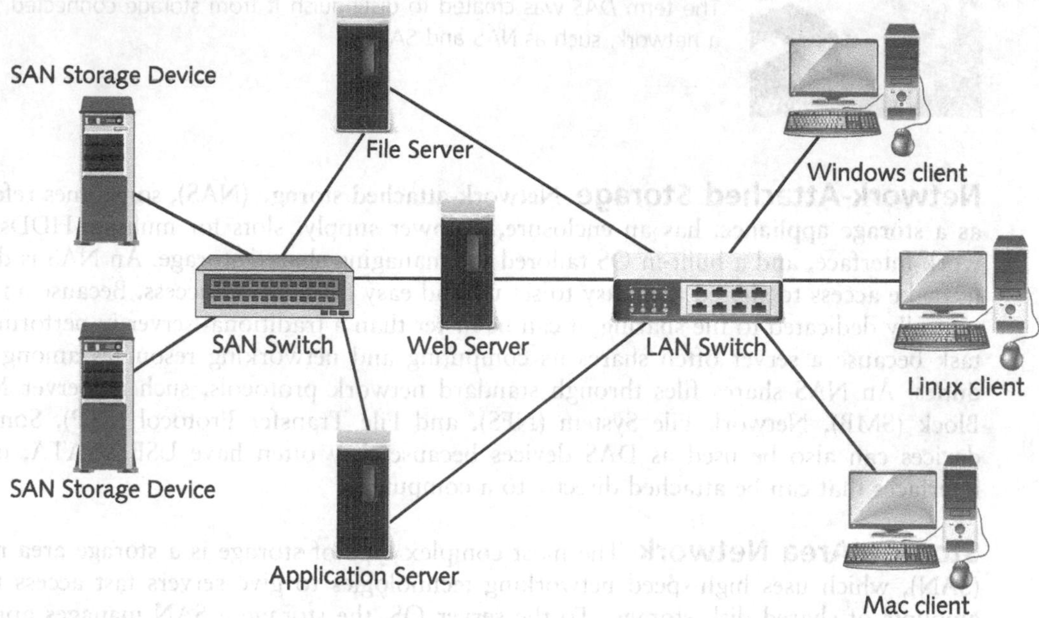

Figure 7-1 A storage area network

SANs are often used by server clusters so that all cluster members have access to shared storage for the purposes of load balancing and fault tolerance.

Configuring Local Disks

Configuration of local disks can be divided into two broad categories: physical disk properties and logical properties. Physical disk properties, which must be considered before purchasing disk drives for a server, include disk capacity, physical speed, and the interface for attaching a disk to the system. Logical disk properties include its format and the partitions or volumes created on it. Before you get too far into these properties, however, let's review some disk-storage terms, most of which were introduced in Chapter 4:

- *Disk drive*—A **disk drive** is a physical component with a disk interface connector (such as SATA or SCSI) and a power connector. A mechanical disk drive (usually called an *HDD*) has one or more circular magnetic platters that store the data's actual bits and one or more read/write heads—one for each side of the magnetic platters. The platters spin at high speed, and the read/write heads move from the inside of the platter to the outside to read data on the disk. An SSD has a disk interface and power connector but has flash memory chips instead of magnetic platters, and there are no read/write heads or other moving parts.
- *Volume*—Before an OS can use a disk drive, a volume must be created on the drive. A **volume** is a logical unit of storage that can be formatted with a file system. A disk drive can contain one or more volumes of different sizes. Disk drive space that hasn't been assigned to a volume is said to be unallocated. Volumes can also span two or more

disks in an arrangement called RAID. Volumes, including RAID volumes, are discussed in more detail later in the "Types of Volumes" section.

- *Partition*—This older term means the same thing as ***volume***, but is used with basic disks. The term **partition** is still used at times, but in Windows it has largely been replaced by *volume*.
- *Formatting*—Before an OS can use a volume, the volume must be formatted. As you learned in Chapter 4, formatting prepares a disk with a file system that is used to organize and store files. There are different format standards; the format you choose for a disk depends on how the disk will be used. Disk formats were discussed in Chapter 4.

Disk Capacity and Speed

The disk capacity you need depends entirely on how the disk will be used. Will it be a system disk for storing the OS and related files, a disk for storing documents and other files, a file-sharing disk, a disk storing a database, or maybe one that stores virtual machines? Perhaps you plan to have a combination of uses, but in general, distinct types of data should be kept on separate disks so that you can optimize some of the disk's logical properties for the type of data it will store. Before we talk more about disk capacities, review Table 7-1 for a list of storage capacity units.

7

Table 7-1 Storage unit equivalents

Storage measurement	Bytes	Base 2 (binary) equivalents
Kilobyte (KB)	1,024	2^{10}
Megabyte (MB)	1,048,576	2^{20}
Gigabyte (GB)	1,073,741,824	2^{30}
Terabyte (TB)	1,099,511,627,776	2^{40}
Petabyte (PB)	1,125,899,906,842,624	2^{50}
Exabyte (EB)	1,152,921,504,606,846,976	2^{60}
Zettabyte (ZB)	1,180,591,620,717,411,303,424	2^{70}

One byte is 8 bits; bytes are represented by a capital *B*, while bits are represented by a small *b*.

Keep in mind that you might not be basing disk capacity decisions on a single disk because you could be configuring an array of disks in a RAID. HDD capacities are now measured in hundreds of gigabytes, with two, four, and eight terabyte disks being common. (Remember that one terabyte equals 1000 gigabytes.) Disk capacity is fairly inexpensive, and having more than you need is better than having less. Here are some considerations for deciding how much disk capacity to buy and how many disks to use in a server:

- On servers or high-performance workstations, the OS installation should be on a separate disk from the data and applications to get the best performance. An SSD is a good candidate for the OS installation disk.
- Virtual memory should be on its own disk, if possible (pagefile.sys on Windows systems or the swap partition on Linux/UNIX systems). An SSD is also a good candidate for virtual memory. If a separate disk is impractical, at least try to put virtual memory on its own volume.
- Take fault tolerance into account by using a RAID, which combines multiple disks to make a single volume so that data stored on the volume is maintained even if a disk fails. However, overall storage capacity is diminished.

The speed of HDDs is affected by a number of factors. For example, the disk interface technology is an important performance factor, as you will learn in the next section. Other factors include rotation speed and the amount of cache memory installed. The rotation speed of disk platters in HDDs ranges from about 5400 revolutions per minute (rpm) to 15,000 rpm, with speeds of 7200 and 10,000 rpm in between. A server should be outfitted with an HDD that rotates at a minimum of 7200 rpm, but for high-performance applications, look for 10,000 or 15,000 rpm drives.

Even for desktop computers, you should look for HDDs with a rotation speed of 7200 rpm or faster. You can still purchase 5400 rpm HDDs, but they are low-end models that will likely become obsolete in the coming years.

The amount of cache in an HDD allows the drive to buffer read and write data locally, which speeds overall disk access. Cache sizes of 32 and 64 MB are common for server-class drives, but some very fast drives might have as little as 16 MB. The key factor for disk performance is how fast data can be read from and written to the disk—the data rate. When researching disks for performance factors, look for the sustained data rate the manufacturer claims, which tells you how fast the drive can transfer data for an extended period.

Disk Interface Technologies

The disk interface connects a disk to a computer system, usually with some type of cable. The cable acts as a bus that carries data and commands between the disk and computer. The faster the bus, the faster the system can read from and write to the disk. The most common types of disk interfaces for locally attached disks are SATA, SAS, and SCSI. Each technology has advantages and disadvantages, as you will learn in the following sections.

You might also find a few parallel ATA (PATA) or Integrated Drive Electronics (IDE) drives on the low end and Fibre Channel drives on the high end, but for locally attached drives, the most common by far are SATA, SAS, and SCSI. IDE drives are nearly obsolete, and Fibre Channel drives are most likely to be used in SANs.

Serial ATA Drives Serial ATA (SATA) drives have mostly replaced PATA drives and have several advantages over this older technology, including faster transfer times and smaller cable size. Whereas the older PATA interface is limited to about 167 megabytes per second (MB/s), SATA drives boast transfer times of up to 6 gigabits per second (Gb/s; 600 MB/s) and higher. SATA drives are inexpensive, fast, and fairly reliable. They're a good fit both for client computers and lower-end servers. The SATA standard has evolved from SATA 1.0, which supports transfer speeds of 1.5 Gb/s (150 MB/s), to the current SATA 3.2, which supports speeds of up to 16 Gb/s (or 1.6 gigabytes per second, GB/s). However, most readily available devices support SATA 2.0 (3 Gb/s) or SATA 3.0 (6 Gb/s). Even with their high transfer rates, however, SATA drives take a back seat to SCSI and SAS drives in the enterprise server realm.

SCSI and SAS Drives Small computer system interface (SCSI) drives have been a mainstay in enterprise-class servers for decades, and this drive technology has endured through more than a half-dozen upgrades. The most recent SCSI variation, developed in 2003, is Ultra-640, with up to 640 MB/s transfer rates. SCSI is a parallel technology, like PATA, and has probably reached its performance limits. SCSI, however, has always provided high reliability and enterprise-level command features, such as error recovery and reporting. Its successor is **serial attached SCSI (SAS)**, which maintains the high reliability and advanced commands of SCSI and improves performance, with transfer rates of up to 6 Gb/s and higher speeds under way. SAS enjoys the benefit of having bus compatibility with SATA, so SATA drives can be connected to SAS backplanes. A **backplane** is a connection system that uses a printed circuit board instead of traditional cables to carry signals.

7

The SAS standard offers higher-end features than SATA drives. SAS drives usually have higher rotation speeds and use higher signaling voltages, which allow their use in server backplanes. Overall, SAS is considered the more enterprise-ready disk interface technology, but enterprise features come with a price—SAS drives are more expensive than SATA drives. As with many other things, disk technologies have a trade-off between performance and reliability versus price.

Partitioning Methods Most OSs, including Windows, Mac OS X, and Linux/UNIX, offer two methods for partitioning disks. The most common method, **Master Boot Record (MBR)**, has been around since DOS. MBR partitions support volume sizes of up to 2 TB. MBR-based disks have the advantage of being compatible with most OSs, old and new.

The second and newer method is **GUID Partitioning Table (GPT)**. GPT disks became an option when HDDs larger than 2 TB started becoming common. GPT-partitioned disks support volume sizes of up to 18 exabytes (EB, which is one million terabytes); however, most file systems are only able to support a fraction of that size. For example, Windows file systems currently support volume sizes only up to 256 TB. You can convert an MBR disk to GPT and vice versa, but you must delete existing partitions first, which erases all data, so if you choose to convert, be sure to have a current backup. In addition to larger volume sizes, GPT partitions offer improved reliability in the form of partition table replication (a backup copy of the partition table) and Cyclic Redundancy Check (CRC) protection of the partition table.

GPT partitions contain an area on the disk called the "protective MBR," which is maintained for backward compatibility with disk utilities that work only with MBR disks.

Types of Volumes

When you create a volume, most OSs have provisions for creating a variety of volume types, from simple single-disk volumes to fault-tolerant multi-disk RAID volumes. **Redundant array of independent disks (RAID)** is a disk configuration that uses space on multiple disks to form a single logical volume. Most RAID configurations offer fault tolerance, and some enhance performance. RAID is commonly configured in one of two ways: by the storage controller in hardware and via the OS storage system in software. Hardware RAID provides better performance by offloading the OS from having to perform the processes involved in RAID, and hardware RAID controllers usually have more options for RAID configurations. Many OSs support at least the three most common configurations: RAID 0, RAID 1, and RAID 5. The following are some of the most common volume types supported by most OSs.

- *Simple volume*—A **simple volume** resides on a single disk. Simple volumes can be extended (made larger) using the OS's disk utilities if unallocated space is available on the disk. A simple volume can also be shrunk. On some OSs, a simple volume can be extended on the same disk or to multiple disks as long as they have unallocated space.
- *Spanned volume*—A **spanned volume** extends across two or more physical disks. For example, a simple volume that has been extended to a second disk is a spanned volume. When the first disk has filled up, subsequent disks are used to store data. Spanned volumes don't offer fault tolerance; if any disk fails, data on all disks is lost. There's also no performance advantage in using a spanned volume compared to a volume that resides on a single disk.
- *RAID 0 volume*—A **RAID 0 volume** extends across two or more disks, but data is written to all disks in the volume equally. For example, if a 10 MB file is written to a RAID 0 volume with two disks, 5 MB is written to each disk. A RAID 0 volume must use at least two disks but can use many more than that; for example, Windows supports RAID 0 volumes with up to 32 disks. RAID 0 volumes don't offer fault tolerance, but they do have a read and write performance advantage over spanned and simple volumes because multiple disks can be accessed simultaneously to read and write files. A RAID 0 volume is also referred to as a *striped volume* because data is said to be striped across each disk. The Windows system and boot volumes can't be on a striped volume. Figure 7-2 shows a RAID 0 volume with two files, F1 and F2. F1 has two parts, F1-a and F1-b, striped across the two disks, and F2 has four parts that are striped across the two disks.

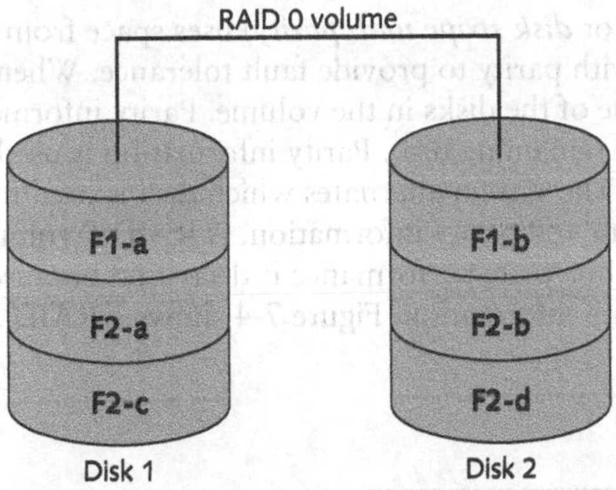

Figure 7-2 A RAID 0 volume

- *RAID 1 volume*—A RAID 1 volume (or *mirrored volume*) uses space from two disks and provides fault tolerance. Data written to one disk is duplicated, or mirrored, to the second disk. If one disk fails, the other disk has a good copy of the data, and the system can continue to operate until the failed disk is replaced. The space used on both disks in a mirrored volume is the same. Mirrored volumes might have a disk read performance advantage, but they don't have a disk write performance advantage. Figure 7-3 shows a RAID 1 volume with the same two files; however, instead of being spread across the disks, they are duplicated so that the contents of disk 1 are also on disk 2.

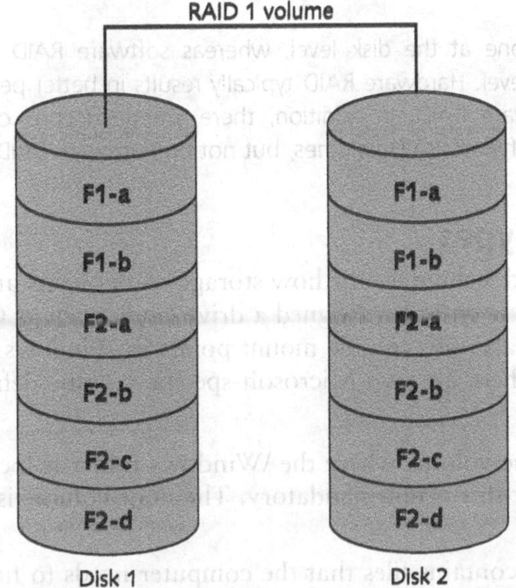

Figure 7-3 A RAID 1 volume

- *RAID 5 volume*—A **RAID 5 volume** (or *disk stripe with parity*) uses space from three or more disks and uses disk striping with parity to provide fault tolerance. When data is written, it's striped across all but one of the disks in the volume. Parity information derived from the data is written to the remaining disk. Parity information is used to re-create lost data after a disk failure. The system alternates which disk is used for parity information, so each disk has both data and parity information. A RAID 5 volume provides increased read performance, but write performance is decreased because the volume has to calculate and write parity information. Figure 7-4 shows a RAID 5 volume.

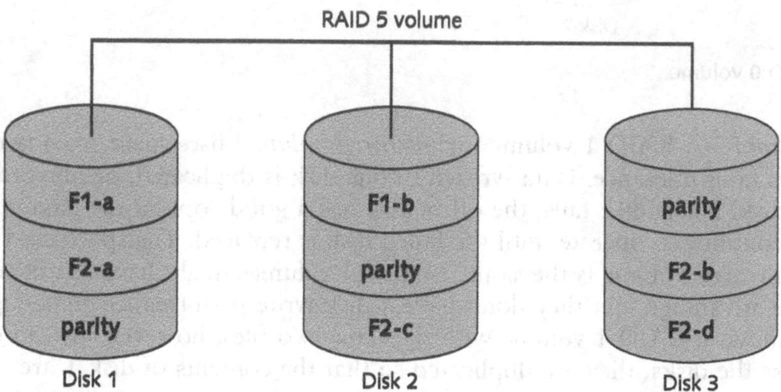

Figure 7-4 A RAID 5 volume

Hardware RAID is done at the disk level, whereas software RAID is done at the volume level. Hardware RAID typically results in better performance than software RAID. In addition, there are restrictions on placing OS files on software RAID volumes, but not on hardware RAID.

Windows Volumes and Disk Types

Different OSs use different terminology and techniques for how storage components are identified. On a Windows system, each volume is typically assigned a drive letter, such as C or D, although you learned earlier that you can also use volume mount points in Windows so you can access a volume with a drive letter. There are two Microsoft-specific volume definitions you need to know:

- *Boot volume*—The **boot volume** is the volume where the \Windows folder is located. The usual location is the C drive, but this is not mandatory. The boot volume is also called the *boot partition.*
- *System volume*—The **system volume** contains files that the computer needs to find and load the Windows OS. In Windows 2008 and later versions, it's created automatically during installation if you're installing an OS for the first time on the system. Also, the system volume is not assigned a drive letter, so you can't see it in File Explorer. You can, however, see it in Disk Management (see Figure 7-5). In earlier Windows versions,

the system volume was usually the C drive. In Figure 7-5, it's labeled *Active*, which tells the BIOS to try booting from that volume. The system volume is also called the *system partition.*

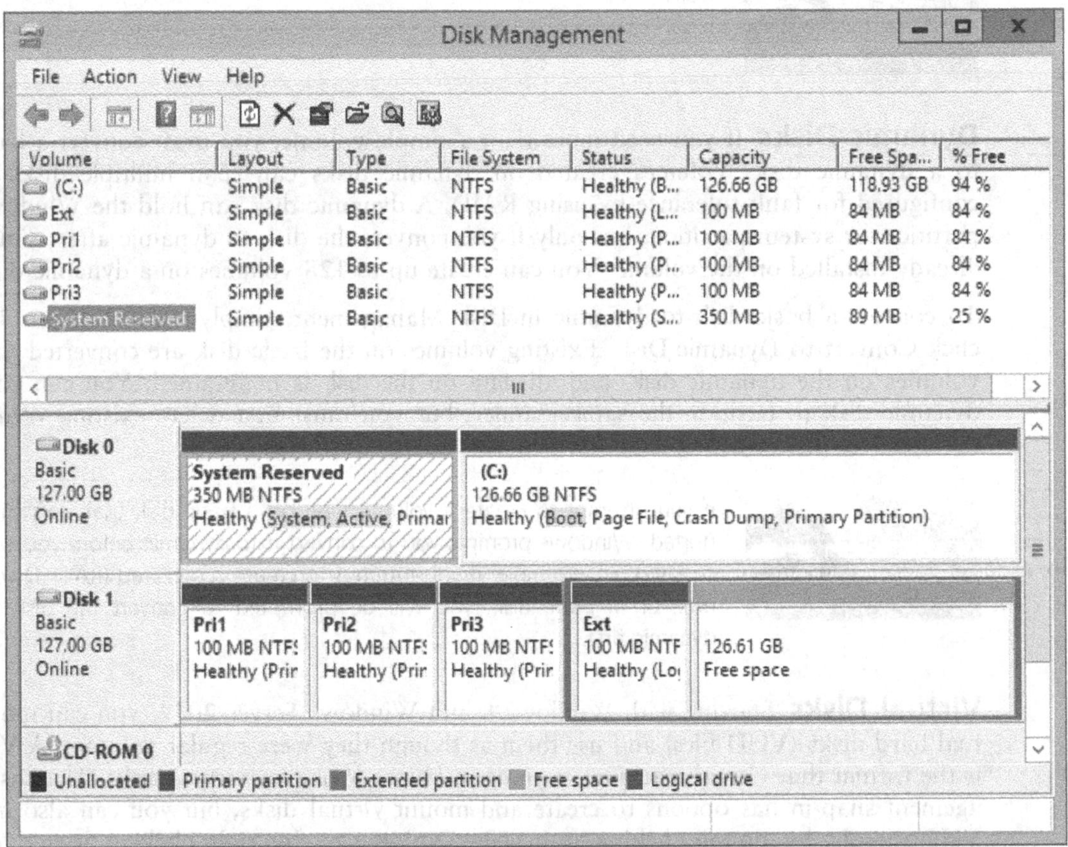

Figure 7-5 Boot and system volumes in Disk Management

In Windows, the types of volumes you can create on a disk depend on how the disk is categorized. Windows defines two disk categories, which are discussed next: basic and dynamic.

Basic Disks As the name implies, a **basic disk** can accommodate only simple volumes. The volumes on a basic disk are also called *partitions*. The Windows Disk Management tool uses both terms in its interface, but the term *partition* is more accurate and distinguishes it from a volume created on a dynamic disk. When Windows detects a new disk drive, it's initialized as a basic disk by default.

As discussed in Chapter 4, you can create a maximum of four partitions on a basic disk. The first three you create with Disk Management are primary partitions. A **primary partition** can be an active partition and can be the Windows system volume. It's usually assigned a drive letter but doesn't have to be, as with the Windows system partition. If you create a fourth partition, it's called an **extended partition**, which can be divided into one or more logical drives, each assigned a drive letter. A logical drive on an extended partition can hold the boot volume, but it can't hold the system volume because it can't be marked as active.

The Windows boot and system volumes can only be created on basic disks.

Dynamic Disks If you need more than a simple volume, you must convert a basic disk to a dynamic disk. Volumes created on dynamic disks can span multiple disks and be configured for fault tolerance by using RAID. A dynamic disk can hold the Windows boot partition or system partition, but only if you convert the disk to dynamic after Windows is already installed on the volume. You can create up to 128 volumes on a dynamic disk.

To convert a basic disk to dynamic in Disk Management, simply right-click the disk and click Convert to Dynamic Disk. Existing volumes on the basic disk are converted to simple volumes on the dynamic disk, and all data on the disk is maintained. You can convert a dynamic disk to basic in the same manner, but you must first delete existing volumes on the dynamic disk; existing data will be lost.

If you attempt to create a volume type on a basic disk that isn't supported, Windows prompts you to convert it to dynamic before you can proceed. For example, if you attempt to create a mirrored (RAID 1) volume on a basic disk, you will be prompted to convert the disk to dynamic first.

Virtual Disks Starting with Windows 8 and Windows Server 2012, you can mount virtual hard disks (VHD files) and use them as though they were regular volumes. A **VHD file** is the format that virtual machines running in Hyper-V use for virtual disks. The Disk Management snap-in has options to create and mount virtual disks, but you can also mount a VHD simply by double-clicking it in File Explorer or by right-clicking it and clicking Mount.

You might want to use virtual disks instead of physical volumes to store data. Virtual disks have the advantage of being very portable. Because a virtual disk is just a file on an existing physical volume, you can copy it to any location quickly and easily for the purposes of backing up data on the virtual disk or allowing it to be used by another computer.

Virtual disks can have a .vhd or .vhdx extension. Windows Server 2012/R2 can mount either file type. The VHDX format, introduced in Windows Server 2012 Hyper-V, has more capacity (up to 64 TB), protection from corruption, and performance improvements than the VHD format.

Storage Spaces **Storage Spaces**, a new feature starting with Windows Server 2012, provides flexible provisioning of virtual storage. It uses the flexibility available with virtual disks to create volumes from storage pools. A **storage pool** is a collection of physical disks from which virtual disks and volumes are created and assigned dynamically. Volumes created from storage pools can be simple volumes, striped volumes, or fault-tolerant RAID volumes.

Unlike traditional physical disks and volumes created in Disk Management, Storage Spaces can allocate storage by using thin provisioning. **Thin provisioning** uses dynamically expanding disks so that you can provision a large volume, even if you have the physical storage for a volume only half the size. Later, you can add physical disks, and Storage Spaces expands into the additional storage as needed. If the disk pool becomes full, Windows takes it offline to alert you that you need to add physical storage to the pool.

Storage Spaces uses the concept of **just a bunch of disks (JBOD)**, in which two or more disks are abstracted to appear as a single disk to the OS but aren't arranged in a specific RAID configuration. JBOD gives you more flexibility because you can simply add a physical disk to a storage pool, and existing volumes can grow into the new space as needed. You can even add external disks to a pool via an external bus architecture, such as SAS or eSATA.

Storage Spaces brings storage flexibility to a Windows server for a fraction of the cost of a traditional SAN, which before Storage Spaces was the best way to achieve similar storage features and performance. Storage Spaces offers the following features that are usually found only in traditional SAN-based storage arrays:

- *Disk pooling*—A collection of physical disks viewed as a single storage space from which volumes can be provisioned for the server's use.
- *Data deduplication*—A new feature in Windows Server 2012 that finds data duplicated on a volume multiple times and reduces it to a single instance, thereby reducing space used on the volume. Data deduplication is a role service that can be installed and then enabled on volumes separately.
- *Flexible storage layouts*—Storage Spaces has three storage options, called **storage layouts**: simple space, which can be a simple volume or RAID 0 volume; mirror space, which is the same as a RAID 1 volume; and parity space, which is the same as a RAID 5 volume.
- *Storage tiering*—A new feature in Windows Server 2012 R2, **storage tiering** combines the speed of SSDs with the low cost and high capacity of HDDs. You can add SSDs to a storage pool with HDDs, and Windows keeps the most frequently accessed data on the faster SSD disks and moves less frequently accessed data to HDDs. This scheme improves performance substantially without the expense of moving all storage to costly SSDs.

Storage Spaces is managed in Windows 10 using the Storage Spaces control panel under System and Security (see Figure 7-6). In Windows Server 2012, open Server Manager, click File and Storage Services, and then click Storage Pools. To use Storage Spaces, you need at least one hard disk that is unallocated—in other words, a disk that has not been partitioned.

Figure 7-6 Storage Spaces in Windows 10

> **From the Trenches ...**
>
> The network technicians for a small department in a community college operate six Windows Server 2012 R2 servers. Because the department teaches computer and networking technology, the staff feel it is important to build their own servers and maintain their own network. The servers maintain the department domain, and provide DNS, DHCP, Web services, VPN services, virtual machine access, and a host of other services for the faculty and students. A continual problem is maintaining reliable fault tolerance with the disk system. The staff use RAID 1 and RAID 5 disk configurations implemented in hardware, but every time they need to update the OS, they run into problems finding reliable drivers for the RAID controller. Furthermore, when a disk drive fails, they sometimes find it difficult to get a compatible replacement disk because disk models change so often. Enter Storage Spaces on Windows Server 2012. The technicians did away with their hardware RAID controllers and used the RAID 1 and RAID 5 capabilities of Storage Spaces, including tiered storage, to increase the performance of their storage system in a cost-effective manner. Now, they have far fewer worries when a disk drive fails because Storage Spaces doesn't have specific requirements for matching drives, and standard disk controller drivers are less of a problem when OS upgrades occur.

Volume Types in Linux/UNIX and Mac OS X

Linux/UNIX and Mac OS X share most terminology for managing storage. In fact, if you open a terminal prompt on Mac OS X, you can use most of the same tools that are used in Linux/UNIX. This section will refer to Linux, but most concepts also apply to UNIX and Mac OS X.

Linux volumes can be created using two methods: basic partitions and the **logical volume manager** (LVM). This concept is not so different from using basic disks and dynamic disks in the Windows environment. Using basic partitions, you have the same restriction as with basic disks in Windows: you can have up to four primary partitions or three primary partitions and one extended partition. Using LVM, you can create as many partitions as there is space.

Linux requires only one partition, which is used to hold the root folder (/). However, most Linux systems use separate partitions for various folders such as /home, /usr, and /var, each of which is mounted into the root folder—from a user's point of view, it looks like a single partition.

Basic partitions have substantial limitations; for example, you can't resize them, so if you run out of space, you need to copy all the data on that partition to a new, larger partition, which is inconvenient and inefficient. Using LVM provides more flexibility, and most Linux systems use this method for creating and accessing volumes.

LVM uses physical disk partitions called *volume groups*. From volume groups, logical volumes are created and assigned space. A logical volume can be expanded while the volume is still in use by simply adding more space from the volume group. Volume groups can also be expanded by adding more physical disks or by replacing a smaller disk with a larger disk, all without having to take the volume offline.

In addition, LVMs support RAID configurations like disk mirroring.

Virtual Disks in Linux You can work with virtual disks in Linux by creating an image file, installing a file system on it, and mounting it into the file system. Here are the general steps and commands to create and mount a 500 MB virtual disk named mydisk from a Fedora 23 Linux shell prompt:

1. Create a new file using the *fallocate* command: *fallocate -l 500M mydisk.img*
2. Install the ext4 file system: *mkfs -t ext4 mydisk.img*
3. Create a folder to mount the virtual disk: *mkdir /mnt/vdisk*
4. Mount the virtual disk: *mount mydisk.img /mnt/vdisk*

After you have completed the preceding steps, you can use the virtual disk as you would any physical disk that's mounted into the file system. You can also use the Disks utility in GNOME to create a disk image from a hard disk or CD/DVD and attach a disk image. In Mac OS X, you can use the Disk Utility to create an image from an existing device or folder, or you can create a blank disk image, as shown in Figure 7-7. Once the disk image is created, Mac OS X automatically mounts it and places an icon on your desktop. Notice in Figure 7-7 that you have the option to encrypt the disk, which can be useful for storing sensitive documents.

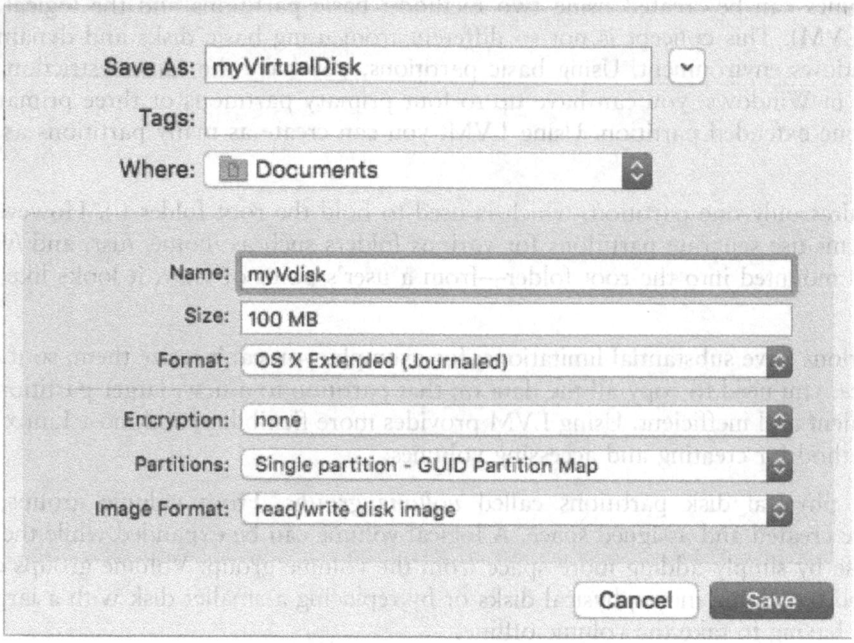

Figure 7-7 Creating a new disk image in Mac OS X

Source: Mac OS X

Cloud Storage

When a company's storage needs have outgrown its storage capabilities, whether because of physical capacity limits or the lack of personnel to maintain in-house storage, the company can turn to the cloud. With **cloud storage**, some or all of an organization's data is stored on servers located offsite and maintained by a storage hosting company. The customer can manage storage by assigning permissions for user access and allocating storage for network applications without having to physically maintain the servers. If more storage is needed, the customer simply pays the storage hosting company for the additional space. The advantage of this approach is that the details of managing and backing up storage on local servers are offloaded to a third party, which enables a company to focus its monetary and personnel resources on business rather than IT tasks. However, cloud-based storage isn't for everyone. The data a company maintains might be too sensitive to trust to a third party or the data access speed might not be sufficient, for example.

You are probably already familiar with some popular types of public cloud storage. For example, YouTube hosts millions of video files loaded by users. Google Docs enables users to store document files and spreadsheets that can be accessed and manipulated on Google Internet servers. Such files can also be published so that others can access the files through the Internet. Dropbox, Microsoft OneDrive, and Google Drive are popular cloud storage services for individuals and small businesses. For larger applications, there is Google Cloud Storage, Microsoft's OneDrive for Business, Microsoft Azure, and Amazon Web Services, to name just a few of the services in this fast-growing market.

Cloud storage is a comparatively new model in data storage. As you learned in Chapter 1, many services are being offered in the cloud, but the companies that provide cloud storage services use many of the technologies discussed in this chapter.

Tapes and Tape Drives

Tape backup systems are a relatively inexpensive and traditional choice for backing up large amounts of data. Tapes use magnetic storage and record data in sequential order. The disadvantage of sequential access is that in order to find a file recorded near the end of the tape, the tape drive has to first go through all of the preceding data. This means access to data is typically much slower than that for a removable hard drive, which uses direct access. Tapes, however, are reliable and the technology is well tested because it has been around a long time.

Tapes are most popular for long-term storage, such as backups, or for archiving data that will be stored off-site. With the capacity of disk drives growing into terabytes, a constant need exists to develop tape technologies that can store more and more data on a single tape. The following sections briefly describe several types of tape storage systems. For most tape systems, the actual tape capacity is stated in terms of whether the stored data is compressed. Compressing the data on the tape typically doubles the noncompressed capacity. Table 7-2 lists tape media and their capacities.

Table 7-2 Tape media capacities

Tape medium	Capacity (compressed)
Digital audio tape (DAT)	Up to 72 GB
Digital linear tape (DLT)	Up to 1.6 TB
Super digital linear tape (SDLT)	Up to 2.4 TB
Advanced intelligent tape (AIT) and super advanced intelligent tape (S-AIT)	Up to 1.3 TB
Linear tape open (LTO)	Up to 1.6 TB

DAT Drives

Digital audio tape (DAT) drives use a 4-mm tape. The most common use is the digital data storage (DDS) format. The first DDS (DDS-1) standard has a capacity of 2 GB (4 GB compressed). The current standard is DDS-5, which has a storage capacity of 36 GB (72 GB compressed). The DDS format standard is backward-compatible; for example, you can upgrade to a DDS-5 tape drive and still read DDS-4 tapes. DAT tapes are typically rated to have an archival life of about 10 years. DAT is still used for audio recordings, but its use for data storage has mostly been replaced by other tape technologies.

DLT and SDLT Drives

Digital linear tape (DLT) drives use half-inch-wide magnetic tapes to record data. These tapes record data in tracks that run the whole length of the tape. Each tape contains 128, 168, 208, 240, 352, or 488 tracks, and the data is recorded on the first track from the beginning to the end of the tape. Then, the tape is reversed and the data is written from the end to the beginning. This continues until all the tracks are full. Using this track system with high-speed search capability, a file can often be found in a few seconds, although the search might take a little over a minute, depending on the file's location on the tape. DLT tape drives are used in many automated tape backup systems.

Super digital linear tape (SDLT) drives use both magnetic and optical recording methods. This method, along with laser technology, more accurately writes data to the tape and allows for greater density of information—up to 2.4 TB compressed. DLT and SDLT tapes have an archival life of up to 30 years, and some tape manufacturers rate their tapes at up to 500,000 tape passes.

AIT and S-AIT Drives

Advanced intelligent tape (AIT) drives were introduced in 1996 and are used mainly in mid-range servers. The tapes for this drive have an erasable memory chip inside the cartridge that stores the information normally written at the beginning of a tape. This provides the information necessary to fast forward and pinpoint the desired information. AIT drives started with a capacity of 35/90 GB (native/compressed) of recorded data. Today, the **super advanced intelligent tape (S-AIT)** has a capacity of 500 GB/1.3 TB (native/compressed). AIT and S-AIT tapes can sustain up to 30,000 tape passes and have an archival life of around 30 years.

LTO Drives

The **linear tape open (LTO)** drive is most widely accepted in the high-end server market because of its high-speed performance. LTO is an open standards tape technology, which means that the standards are open to the public and are nonproprietary. The LTO Ultrium format was developed so that LTO tapes could be used in existing DLT tape drives for faster conversion to LTO Ultrium tape technology.

LTO Ultrium tape drives offer fast data transfer speeds of up to 240 MB/s for noncompressed data and 120 MB/s for compressed data. LTO tapes can sustain up to 260 tape passes and have an archival life of 15 to 30 years.

Storage Management Tools

This section covers some of the operating system tools and commands used to manage storage devices. Also, you will find step-by-step instructions for using some of these tools in the Hands-On Projects at the end of the chapter.

Windows Storage Management Tools

All modern Windows OSs offer the Windows Disk Management tool for hard drives as well as removable storage. For a hard drive, this tool enables you to create and delete partitions, format partitions for a file system, and generally manage partitions. The tool also recognizes and enables you to manage removable storage, including removable hard drives, DVD/CD-ROM drives, and flash drives. In Windows 10, you can access the Disk Management tool by right-clicking Start or from the Computer Management console. On Windows Server 2012/R2 and newer versions, you can also use the File and Storage Services tool from Server Manager (see Figure 7-8) to manage volumes and Storage Spaces.

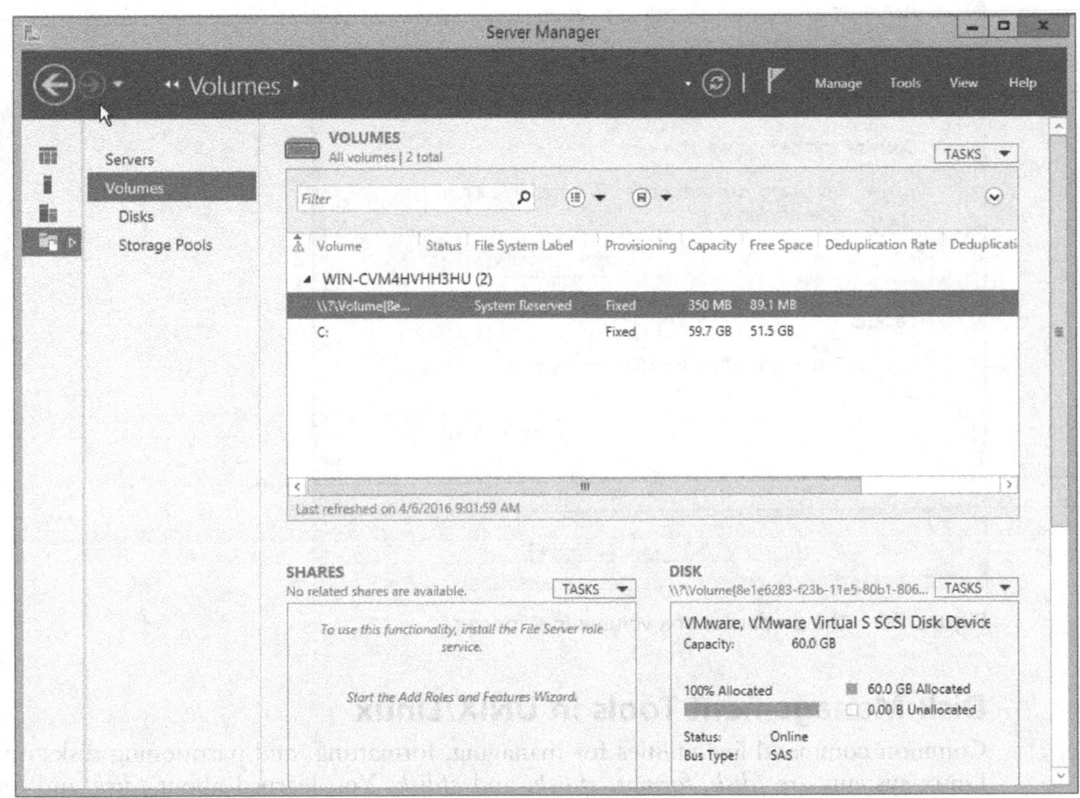

Figure 7-8 File and Storage Services on Windows Server 2012 R2

One of the easiest ways to manage an existing storage volume is to access its properties. In File Explorer, right-click the volume and click Properties. From the Properties dialog box (see Figure 7-9), you can access several management options, such as viewing free space on the disk, defragmenting or backing up the drive, checking the drive for errors, limiting users' disk space through quotas, and setting permissions.

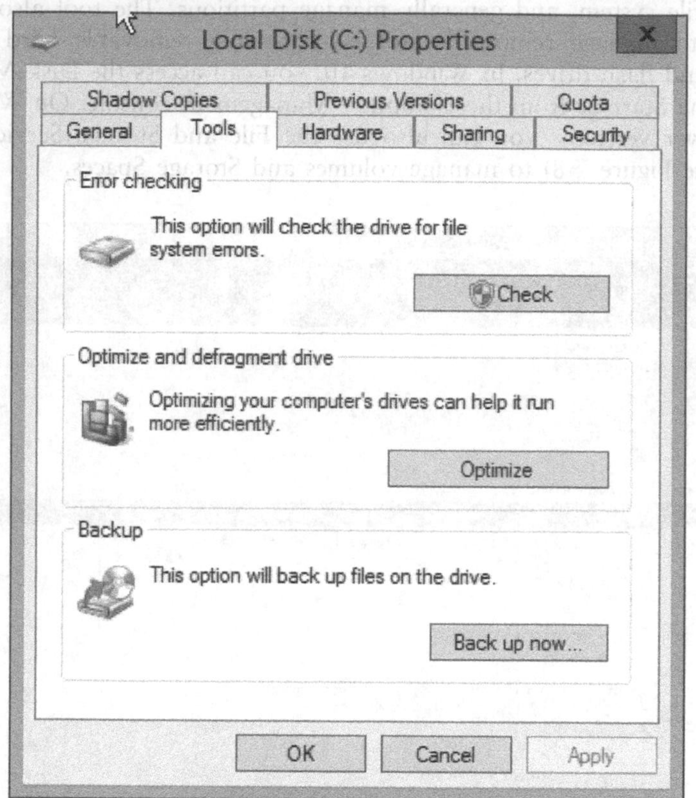

Figure 7-9 The properties of a volume in Windows

Disk Management Tools in UNIX/Linux

Common command-line utilities for managing, formatting, and partitioning disks on UNIX/Linux systems are *fdisk*, *format*, *sfdisk*, and *cfdisk*. You learned about *fdisk* and *format* in Chapter 4. The *sfdisk* and *cfdisk* utilities enable you to verify partitions, list information about partitions, such as their size, and repartition a disk. Linux operating systems offer *fdisk*, *sfdisk*, and *cfdisk*, but not *format*, which is used on some UNIX systems.

Further, UNIX/Linux systems offer the *mount* command-line utility, introduced in Chapter 4, to mount a file system so that you can use a disk partition, virtual disk, DVD/CD-ROM drive, or flash drive. Normally, when you boot UNIX/Linux, the main file systems are mounted as part of the boot process—for example, the ext4 file system in Linux. However, you may need to manually mount file systems for DVD/CD-ROM or flash drives (although these are automatically detected and mounted in modern Linux operating systems). For example, to mount a DVD/CD-ROM drive, you would use the following command:

mount -t iso9660 /dev/cdrom /mnt/cdrom or *mount -t iso9660 /dev/cdrom /cdrom*

For a DVD formatted for the udf file system, use:

mount -t udf /dev/cdrom /mnt/cdrom or mount -t udf /dev/cdrom /cdrom

The *-t iso9660* portion of the first command mounts the iso9660 (CD-ROM) file system. The *-t udf* portion of the second command is for the Universal Disk Format file system, which is a file system that supplants iso9660 for DVDs and other optical media. Further, these commands mount the device, /dev/cdrom, to the mount point, /mnt/cdrom or /cdrom, so that after the DVD or CD-ROM file system is mounted, you can view its files by viewing the contents of /mnt/cdrom or /cdrom.

Use the *umount* command to unmount a file system. For example, you would enter *umount /mnt/cdrom* or *umount /cdrom* to unmount the file system for a DVD/CD-ROM drive. Table 7-3 summarizes UNIX/Linux commands for disk management. These commands typically have many different options, which are documented in the online manual pages. For example, to learn more about the *mount* command, use the command *man mount* to read the documentation.

Table 7-3 Summary of UNIX/Linux disk management commands

Command	Explanation
cfdisk	Partitions and verifies a hard disk
cpio	Copies and backs up files to archive them on tape or disk
dump	Backs up particular files or an entire file system and offers levels to specify the degree to which to back up files; use the *restore* command to restore files backed up by *dump*
fdisk	Maintains disk partitions, including creating and deleting partitions and flagging the active partition
format	Partitions and formats a disk in some UNIX distributions, but not in Linux
mount	Connects or mounts a file system for access in the directory tree
restore	Restores an entire file system or only specific files backed up by the *dump* command
tar	Copies files to an archive medium and can restore files; this command is traditionally popular with server administrators
sfdisk	Provides information about a partition and can be used to create a partition (Caution: This command does not work with PC systems that use a GUID Partitioning Table)
umount	Disconnects or unmounts a file system partition from access in the directory tree
xfsdump	Backs up files in the XFS file system; the ext file system is the default option in Linux, but Linux also supports XFS
xfsrestore	Restores files backed up by *xfsdump*

If you use Linux with the GNOME desktop, you can use the Disks tool to manage disk storage. For example, to unmount a DVD from the Disks utility, click the CD/DVD drive in the left pane and click the Eject button in the right pane (see Figure 7-10).

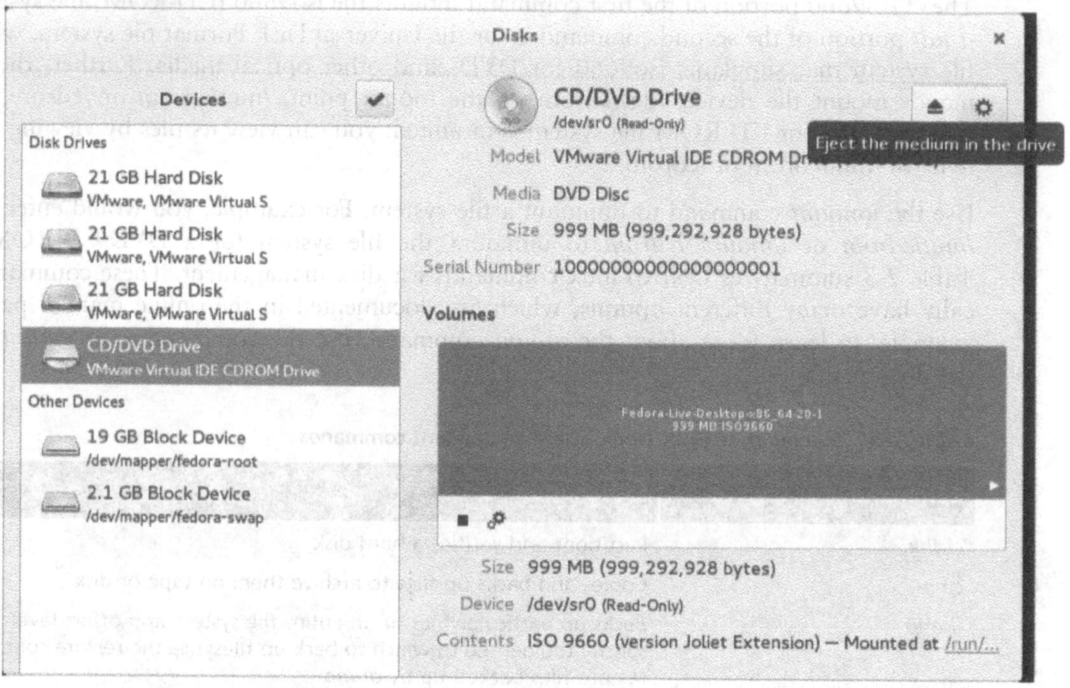

Figure 7-10 The Disks utility in Linux

Source: Fedora Linux

Mac OS X Disk Utility

The Mac OS X Disk Utility can partition, format, and manage hard drives. It can also manage DVD/CD-ROM drives, removable hard drives, flash drives, and other storage. When you select a storage medium in the left pane, the Disk Utility displays appropriate tabs for the actions you can perform on that storage medium. For example, for a hard disk you can:

- Repair the disk using the First Aid option.
- Erase the contents.
- Partition and format the disk.
- Set up RAID on the disk.
- Restore a disk image or volume.

For removable media, you can use the Disk Utility to mount media, eject media, burn a CD or DVD, and perform other actions. Because Mac OS X is a UNIX-based system, you can also open a terminal window and use the *mount* command to manage storage media. To learn the *mount* command options, type *man mount* and press Enter at the command line.

Chapter Summary

- Storage is any digital medium that data can be written to and later retrieved. Long-term storage includes USB drives, SD cards, CDs/DVDs, magnetic tape, SSDs, and HDDs.
- All computers require at least some storage, but servers usually require more than client computers. Storage is needed for OS files, page files, log files, virtual machines, database files, and user documents, among others.
- The main methods of storage access are local, DAS, NAS, and SAN. Local and DAS are similar methods, but DAS can also be a separate unit attached through an external interface. NAS is a stand-alone storage device with a network interface. A SAN is the most complex storage device; it uses high-speed networking technologies to provide shared storage.
- Configuration of local disks can be divided into two broad categories: physical disk properties and logical properties. Physical properties include disk capacity, rotation speed, and the disk interface technology. SATA and SAS are the most common disk interfaces.
- Disk types include basic disks, dynamic disks, and virtual disks. Partitioning types include MBR and GPT. Volume types include simple, spanned, RAID 0, RAID 1, and RAID 5.
- Storage Spaces, a new feature starting with Windows 8/8.1 and Windows Server 2012/R2, provides flexible provisioning of virtualized storage by using storage pools. A storage pool is a collection of physical disks from which virtual disks and volumes are created and assigned dynamically.
- Storage Spaces uses the concept of just a bunch of disks (JBOD), in which two or more disks are abstracted to appear as a single disk to the OS but aren't arranged in a specific RAID configuration.
- With cloud storage, some or all of an organization's data is stored on servers located offsite and maintained by a storage hosting company.
- Tape backup systems are a relatively inexpensive and traditional choice for backing up large amounts of data. Tapes use magnetic storage and record data in sequential order. There are several types of tape devices, including DAT, DLT, SDLT, AIT, and LTO.
- Storage management tools in Windows include Disk Management and File and Storage Services. Linux has a number of command-line tools, such as *fdisk*, *format*, and *mount*, plus the Disks GUI tool. Mac OS X includes many of the same Linux command-line tools, plus the Disk Utility tool.

Key Terms

advanced intelligent tape (AIT) A tape drive that has an erasable memory chip and a capacity of up to 1.3 TB.

backplane A connection system that uses a printed circuit board instead of traditional cables to carry signals.

7

basic disk A traditional Windows or DOS disk arrangement in which the disk is partitioned into primary and extended partitions. A basic disk can't hold volumes spanning multiple disks or be part of a RAID.

boot volume The volume where the \Windows folder is located—usually the C drive, but this location is not mandatory. The boot volume is also referred to as the *boot partition*.

cloud storage A storage paradigm in which an individual's or company's storage is hosted by a third party and accessed over the Internet.

digital audio tape (DAT) A tape system that uses 4-mm tape and has a capacity of up to 72 GB.

digital linear tape (DLT) A tape system that uses half-inch magnetic tapes and has a capacity of up to 1.6 TB.

direct-attached storage (DAS) A storage medium directly connected to the server using it. DAS differs from local storage in that it includes externally connected HDDs in an enclosure with a power supply.

disk drive A physical component with a disk interface connector (such as SATA or SCSI) and a power connector.

dynamic disk A disk arrangement that can hold up to 128 volumes, including spanned volumes, striped volumes, and RAID volumes.

extended partition A division of disk space on a basic disk that must be separated into logical drives; it can't be marked active and can't hold the Windows system volume.

GUID Partitioning Table (GPT) A disk-partitioning method that supports volume sizes of up to 18 exabytes.

just a bunch of disks (JBOD) A disk arrangement in which two or more disks are abstracted to appear as a single disk to the OS but aren't arranged in a specific RAID configuration.

linear tape open (LTO) A tape drive used in the high-end server market; it has a storage capacity of up to 1.6 TB.

local storage Storage media with a direct and exclusive connection to the computer's system board through a disk controller.

logical unit number (LUN) A logical reference point to a unit of storage that could refer to an entire array of disks, a single disk, or just part of a disk.

logical volume manager (LVM) A method of creating volumes in Linux that uses physical disk partitions called *volume groups* to create logical volumes.

Master Boot Record (MBR) A disk-partitioning method that supports volume sizes of up to 2 TB.

network-attached storage (NAS) A storage device that has an enclosure, a power supply, slots for multiple HDDs, a network interface, and a built-in OS tailored for managing shared files and folders.

pagefile.sys A system file in Windows used as virtual memory; it is also used to store data produced when the system crashes (dump data), which is used for troubleshooting.

partition A logical unit of storage that can be formatted with a file system; it is similar to a volume but used with basic disks.

primary partition A division of disk space on a basic disk used to create a volume. It can be assigned a drive letter, be marked as active, and contain the Windows system volume.

RAID 0 volume A volume that extends across two or more dynamic disks, but data is written to all disks in the volume equally; it provides no fault tolerance but does provide a performance advantage over simple or spanned volumes.

RAID 1 volume A volume that uses space from two dynamic disks and provides fault tolerance. Data written to one disk is duplicated, or mirrored, to the second disk. If one disk fails, the other disk has a good copy of the data, and the system can continue to operate until the failed disk is replaced. This volume is also called a *mirrored volume*.

RAID 5 volume A volume that uses space from three or more dynamic disks and uses disk striping with parity to provide fault tolerance. When data is written, it's striped across all but one of the disks in the volume. Parity information derived from the data is written to the remaining disk, which is used to re-create lost data after a disk failure. This volume is also called a *disk stripe with parity*.

redundant array of independent disks (RAID) A disk configuration that uses space on multiple disks to form a single logical volume. Most RAID configurations provide fault tolerance, and some enhance performance.

7

Serial ATA (SATA) A common disk interface technology that's inexpensive, fast, and fairly reliable, with transfer speeds up to 6 Gb/s; it is used both in client computers and low-end servers and replaces the older parallel ATA (PATA) technology.

serial attached SCSI (SAS) A newer, serial form of SCSI with transfer rates of up to 6 Gb/s and higher; the disk technology of choice for servers and high-end workstations. See also *small computer system interface (SCSI)*.

simple volume A volume that usually resides on a single basic or dynamic disk.

small computer system interface (SCSI) An older parallel bus disk technology still used on some servers, although it has reached its performance limits at 640 MB/s transfer rates.

solid-state drive (SSD) A type of storage medium that uses flash memory, has no moving parts, and requires less power than a traditional HDD. It is faster and more shock resistant than a traditional HDD, but it costs more per gigabyte and doesn't have as much capacity as an HDD.

spanned volume A volume that extends across two or more physical disks; for example, a simple volume that has been extended to a second disk is a spanned volume.

storage appliance See *network-attached storage (NAS)*.

storage area network (SAN) A storage device that uses high-speed networking technologies to give servers fast access to large amounts of shared disk storage. To the server OS, the storage a SAN manages appears to be physically attached to the server.

storage layout The method used to create a virtual disk with Storage Spaces; the three methods include simple, mirror, and parity. See also *Storage Spaces*.

storage pool A collection of physical disks from which virtual disks and volumes are created and assigned dynamically.

Storage Spaces A new feature in Windows 8/8.1 and Windows Server 2012/R2 and later versions that provides flexible provisioning of virtualized storage.

storage tiering A feature of Storage Spaces that combines the speed of SSDs with the low cost and high capacity of HDDs to create high-performance volumes.

super advanced intelligent tape (S-AIT) A tape system technology that has an erasable memory chip and a capacity of up to 1.3 TB.

super digital linear tape (SDLT) A tape system that uses both magnetic and optical recording and has a tape capacity of up to 2.4 TB.

swap partition In Linux/UNIX OSs, a separate partition on the disk set aside exclusively for virtual memory.

system volume A volume that contains the files a computer needs to find and load the Windows OS. See also *volume*.

thin provisioning A method for creating virtual disks in which the virtual disk expands dynamically and uses space from the storage pool as needed until it reaches the specified maximum size.

VHD file The format that virtual machines running in Hyper-V use for their virtual disks. VHD files can also be created and mounted with Disk Management and used like physical disks.

virtual memory Disk space that stores the least recently used pages of memory when more physical RAM is needed, but not available.

volume A logical unit of storage that can be formatted with a file system.

Review Questions

1. Which of the following is an example of long-term storage? (Choose all that apply.)
   a. magnetic tape
   b. CPU cache
   c. SSD
   d. RAM
2. Which of the following is true about an SSD?
   a. It uses magnetic platters.
   b. It has no moving parts.
   c. It uses a proprietary interface.
   d. It uses EPROM.
3. Which of the following is an example of what a computer stores? (Choose all that apply.)
   a. virtual memory
   b. log files
   c. working memory
   d. documents

4. Which of the following is true about a page file?
   a. It should be stored on a separate disk from the Windows folder.
   b. It's usually stored in fast random access memory.
   c. Windows stores frequently accessed drivers in it.
   d. It is usually smaller than 50 MB.
5. Local storage is rarely direct-attached storage. True or False?
6. You want shared network storage that's easy to set up and geared toward file sharing with several file-sharing protocols, but you don't want the device to be dedicated to file sharing. What should you consider buying?
   a. SAN
   b. DAS
   c. NAS
   d. LAS
7. What type of interface are you likely to find that connects a DAS device to the server that uses it?
   a. SATA
   b. IDE
   c. PATA
   d. eSATA
8. You have four servers that need access to shared storage because you're configuring them in a cluster. Which storage solution should you consider for this application?
   a. NAS
   b. SAN
   c. SCSI
   d. DAS
9. Which of the following is defined as a physical component with a disk interface connector?
   a. format
   b. partition
   c. volume
   d. disk drive
10. You have installed a new disk and created a volume on it. What should you do before you can store files on it?
   a. Format it.
   b. Partition it.
   c. Initialize it.
   d. Erase it.

11. On your Windows server, you're planning to install a new database application that uses an enormous amount of disk space. You need this application to be highly available, so you need a disk system with the capability to auto-correct from disk errors and data corruption. You also want a flexible storage solution that makes it easy to add space and supports deduplication. Which of the following is the best option?
    a. MBR disk with *chkdsk*
    b. NTFS format with EFS
    c. ReFS format and Storage Spaces
    d. GPT disk with shadow copies
12. Which of the following commands can verify a new partition you have configured in Linux? (Choose all that apply.)
    a. *chkdsk*
    b. *vdisk*
    c. *fdisk*
    d. *sfdisk*
13. Which disk interface technology transfers data over a parallel bus?
    a. SATA
    b. USB
    c. SAS
    d. SCSI
14. What is created automatically when you install Windows Server 2012 R2 on a system with a disk drive that has never had an OS installed on it before?
    a. system volume
    b. dynamic disk
    c. GPT
    d. extended partition
15. What type of volumes or partitions can be created on a basic disk? (Choose all that apply.)
    a. spanned volume
    b. striped partition
    c. extended partition
    d. simple volume
16. Which of the following is true about GPT disks?
    a. They support a maximum volume size of 2 TB.
    b. GPT is the default option when initializing a disk in Disk Management.
    c. They use CRC protection for the partition table.
    d. You can't convert a GPT disk to MBR.

17. You have a server with Windows Server 2012 R2 installed on Disk 0, a basic disk. You use the server to store users' documents. You have two more disks that you can install in the server. What should you do if you want to provide fault tolerance for users' documents?
    a. Convert Disk 0 to dynamic. Create a striped volume using Disk 0, Disk 1, and Disk 2.
    b. Create a RAID 1 volume from Disk 1 and Disk 2.
    c. Convert the new disks to GPT. Create a spanned volume using Disk 1 and Disk 2.
    d. Create a RAID 5 volume from Disk 0, Disk 1, and Disk 2.
18. You need a disk system that provides the best performance for a new application that frequently reads and writes data to the disk. You aren't concerned about disk fault tolerance because the data will be backed up each day; performance is the main concern. What type of volume arrangement should you use?
    a. spanned volume
    b. RAID 1 volume
    c. RAID 0 volume
    d. RAID 5 volume
19. You are ordering eight new desktop computers for your small business. Which of the following hard drive technologies is likely to be used in the new computers?
    a. SATA
    b. PATA
    c. SCSI
    d. SAS
20. You come across a file with a .vhd extension on your Windows 10 computer's hard disk. What should you do to see this file's contents?
    a. Right-click the file and click Open.
    b. Open the file in Notepad.
    c. Burn the file to a DVD.
    d. Mount the file.

Hands-On Projects

Project 7-1: Use the Windows Disk Management Tool

In this project, you use the Windows Disk Management tool to view existing volumes and create a new volume.

If your Windows 10 computer is configured according to instructions in the "Before You Begin" section of the Introduction, you should have three physical disks. Disk 0 has the Windows OS installed, and Disk 1 and Disk 2 are empty and offline. If you only have two disks in your system, you can still perform this activity. If you only have one disk in your system but have some unallocated space, you can perform this activity with minor changes (see your instructor). If you have no additional disks and no unallocated space, you cannot perform this activity.

1. Start your Windows 10 computer and log on.
2. Right-click **Start** and click **Disk Management**.
3. If you see a message about initializing a disk, click **OK**. There are two panes in Disk Management: The upper pane shows a summary of configured volumes and basic information about each volume. The lower pane shows installed disks and how each disk is being used.
4. Right-click the (C:) volume in the upper pane and note some of the options you have.
5. In the lower pane, find Disk 1. If its status is online and initialized, skip to the next step; otherwise, right-click **Disk 1** and click **Online**. Right-click it again and click **Initialize Disk** to open the dialog box shown in Figure 7-11. Leave the default option **MBR** selected, and click **OK**.

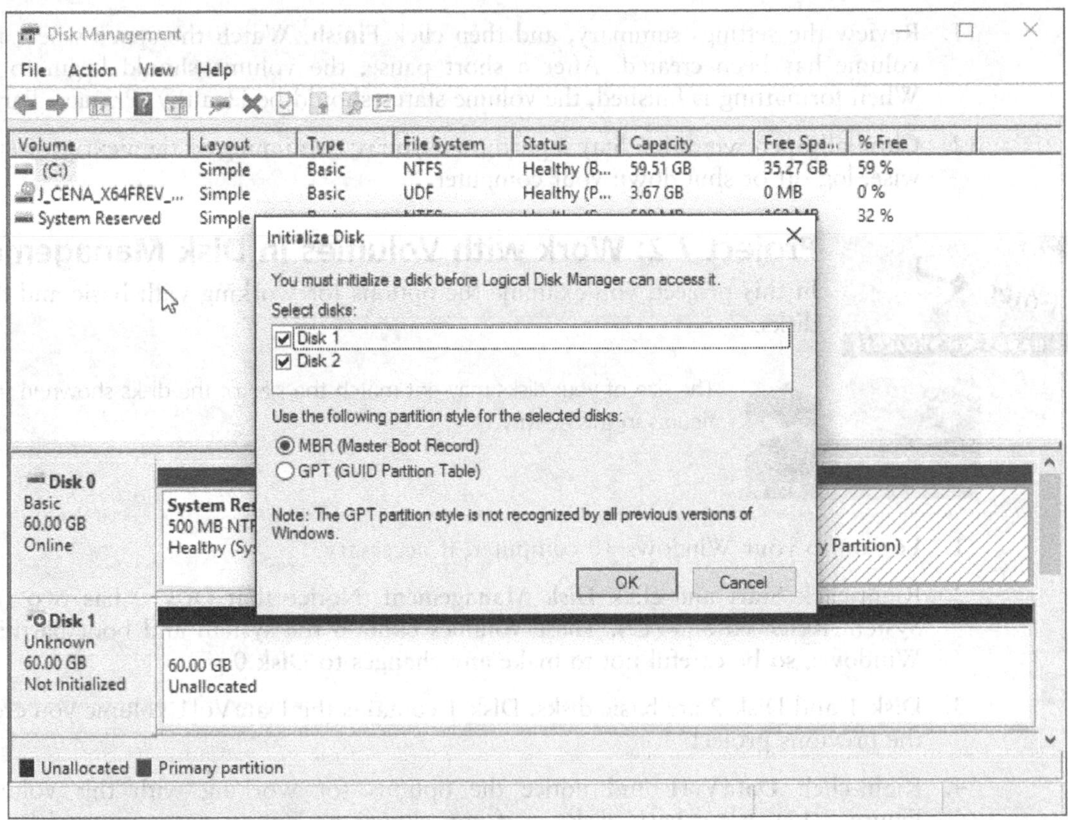

Figure 7-11 Initializing a disk in Disk Management

6. Right-click the unallocated space of **Disk 1**, and notice the options for making the unallocated space into a new volume. In Windows XP and Windows Server 2003, the term *partition* was used instead of *volume*. In Windows Vista and Windows Server 2008 and newer versions, the term *volume* is often used instead when preparing disks for use.

7. Click **New Simple Volume** to start the New Simple Volume Wizard. In the welcome window, click **Next.**

8. In the Specify Volume Size window, type **500** to make a 500 MB volume, and then click **Next.**

9. In the Assign Drive Letter or Path window, you have the option to assign a drive letter or mount the new volume into a folder on another volume. From the drop-down menu next to "Assign the following drive letter," click drive letter **S**, and then click **Next.** (If the S drive isn't available, ask your instructor which drive letter to select.)

10. In the Format Partition window, click the **File system** list arrow, and note the available options. Click **NTFS** to select it as the file system. In the Volume label text box, type **DataVol1**, and then click **Next.**

11. Review the settings summary, and then click **Finish**. Watch the space where the new volume has been created. After a short pause, the volume should begin to format. When formatting is finished, the volume status should be Healthy (Primary Partition).
12. Close all open windows. Stay logged on if you're continuing to the next project; otherwise, log off or shut down your computer.

Project 7-2: Work with Volumes in Disk Management

In this project, you examine the options for working with basic and dynamic disks.

The size of your disks may not match the size of the disks shown in the figures in this activity.

1. Log on to your Windows 10 computer, if necessary.
2. Right-click **Start** and click **Disk Management**. Notice that Disk 0 has two volumes: System Reserved and (C:). These volumes contain the system and boot partitions for Windows, so be careful not to make any changes to Disk 0.
3. Disk 1 and Disk 2 are basic disks. Disk 1 contains the DataVol1 volume you created in the previous project.
4. Right-click **DataVol1** and notice the options for working with this volume (see Figure 7-12). It's a basic disk, so if you choose an option not supported by a basic disk, you're prompted to convert the disk to dynamic. If you were working with a FAT/FAT32 volume, you would not have the option to extend, shrink, or add a mirror.

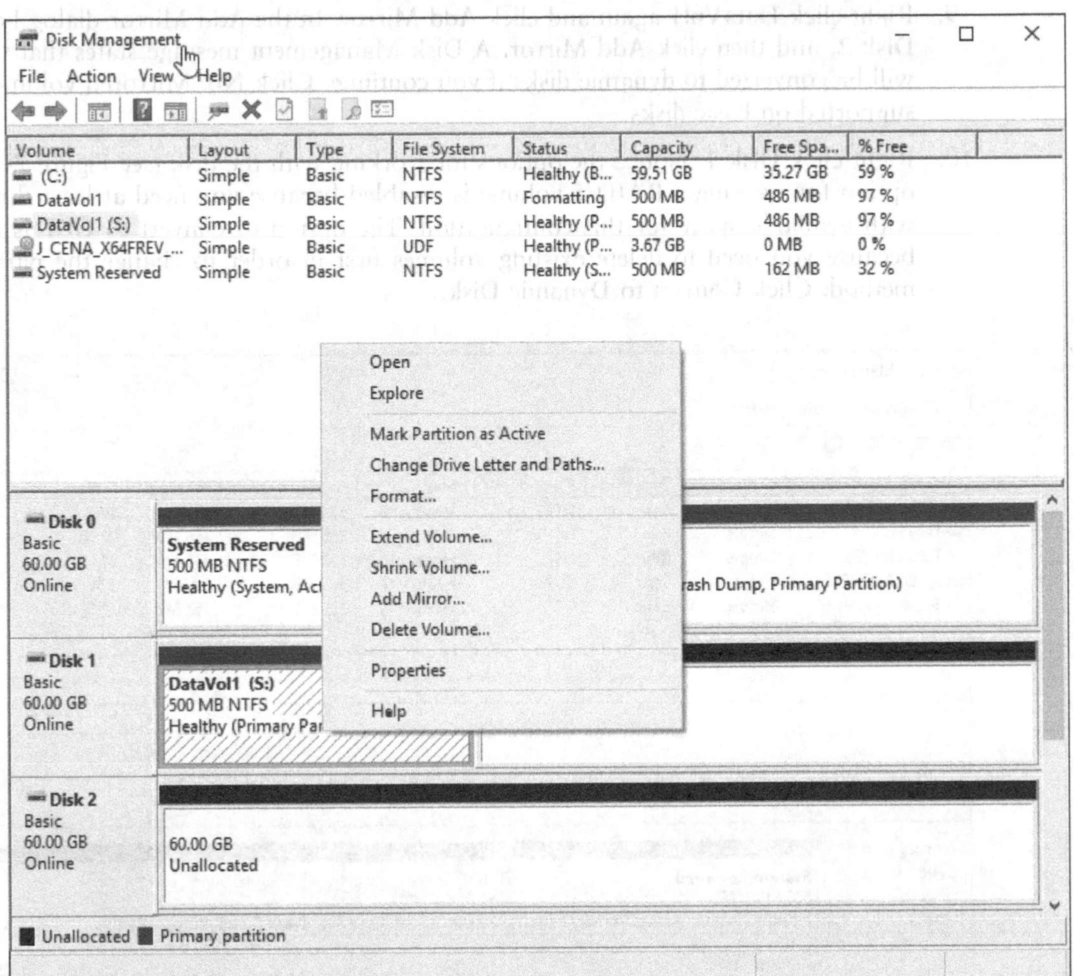

Figure 7-12 Options for NTFS volumes

5. Right-click **DataVol1** again, if necessary, and click **Extend Volume.** In the Extend Volume Wizard welcome window, click **Next.**

6. In the Select Disks window, you have the option of adding disks to which to extend. If you do so, you're prompted to convert the disk to dynamic because basic disks don't support extending to other disks (disk spanning). In the "Select the amount of space in MB" text box, type **500**, which makes the volume 1 GB. Click **Next.**

7. In the Completing the Extend Volume Wizard window, click **Finish**. The disk is extended to about 1000 MB.

8. In Disk Management, right-click **DataVol1** and then click **Shrink Volume** to open the Shrink S: dialog box. In the "Enter the amount of space to shrink in MB" text box, type **500** and click **Shrink**. The volume is back to 500 MB.

9. **Right-click DataVol1** again and click **Add Mirror**. In the Add Mirror dialog box, click **Disk 2**, and then click **Add Mirror**. A Disk Management message states that the disks will be converted to dynamic disks if you continue. Click **No**. Mirrored volumes aren't supported on basic disks.

10. Right-click **Disk 1**. Notice the options for working with the disk (see Figure 7-13). The option for creating a RAID 5 volume is disabled because you need at least three disks with available space for this configuration. The option to convert to GPT is disabled because you need to delete existing volumes first in order to change the partitioning method. Click **Convert to Dynamic Disk**.

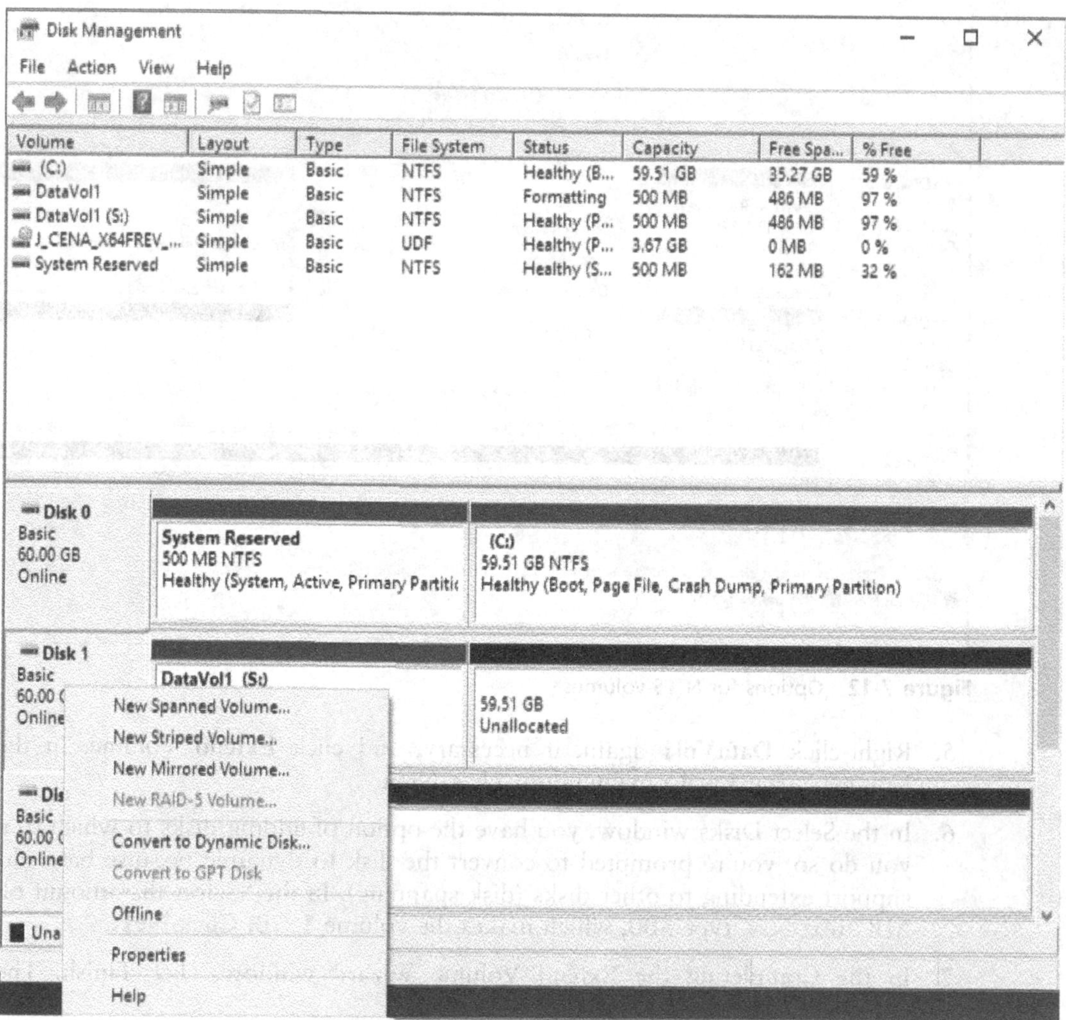

Figure 7-13 Options for working with Disk 1

11. In the Convert to Dynamic Disk dialog box, you have the option to convert more than one disk to dynamic. Leave the **Disk 1** check box selected and click **OK**. Click **Convert**,

and then click **Yes**. The color of the volume label changes from blue to yellow-green to indicate it's now a simple volume rather than a primary partition.

12. Right-click **DataVol1** and click **Add Mirror**. Click **Disk 2** and then **Add Mirror**. Click **Yes** to confirm that Disk 2 will be converted to a dynamic disk.

13. The volume label changes color to red, indicating a mirrored volume (see Figure 7-14). A status message shows that the volume is resyncing (copying information from the primary disk to the mirrored disk). Disk 2 now has a volume named DataVol1 and assigned the letter S. Close Disk Management.

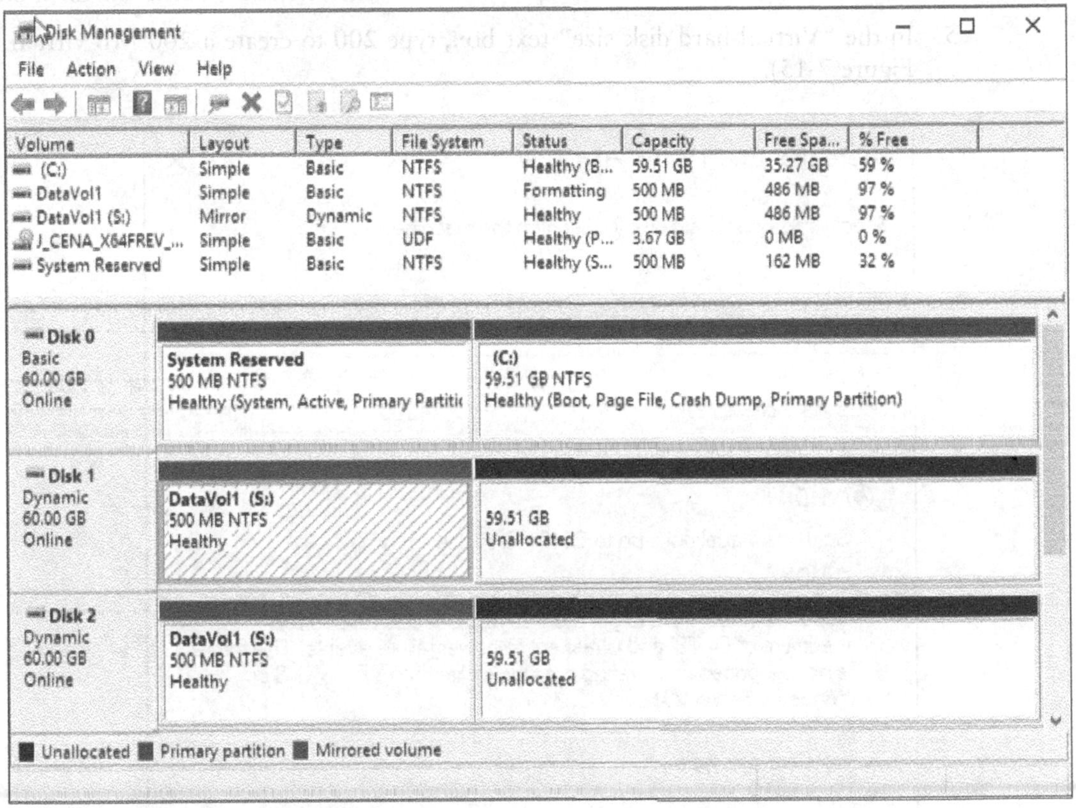

Figure 7-14 A mirrored volume

14. If you're continuing to the next activity, stay logged on; otherwise, log off or shut down the server.

Disk 1 is an MBR disk and Disk 2 is a GPT disk. You can use disks of different types in RAID configurations.

Enter
HANDS-ON PROJECTS

Project 7-3: Work with Virtual Disks in Windows

In this project, you create and mount a virtual disk, and then view it in Disk Management and File Explorer.

1. Log on to your Windows 10 computer, if necessary.
2. Open Disk Management. Click the **Action** menu, and then click **Create VHD.**
3. In the Create and Attach Virtual Hard Disk dialog box, click **Browse.**
4. Click **DataVol1** (S:) and then type **Virtual1** in the File name text box. Click **Save.**
5. In the "Virtual hard disk size" text box, type **200** to create a 200 MB virtual disk (see Figure 7-15).

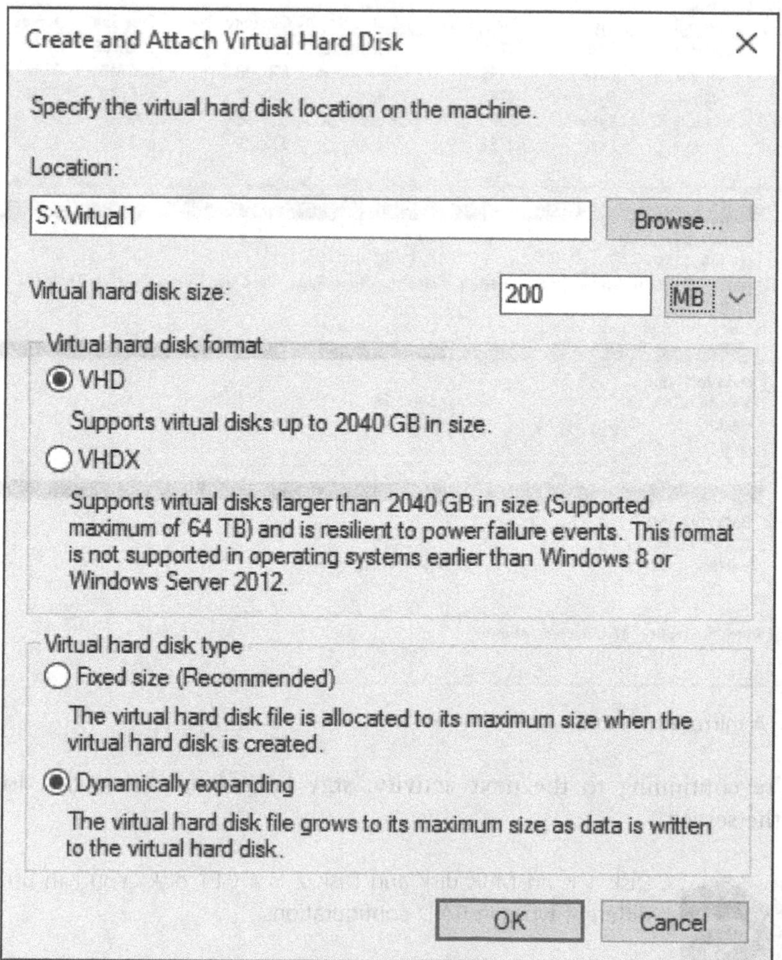
Create and Attach Virtual Hard Disk
Specify the virtual hard disk location on the machine.
Location:
S:\Virtual1
Browse...
Virtual hard disk size:
200
MB
Virtual hard disk format
VHD
Supports virtual disks up to 2040 GB in size.
VHDX
Supports virtual disks larger than 2040 GB in size (Supported maximum of 64 TB) and is resilient to power failure events. This format is not supported in operating systems earlier than Windows 8 or Windows Server 2012.
Virtual hard disk type
Fixed size (Recommended)
The virtual hard disk file is allocated to its maximum size when the virtual hard disk is created.
Dynamically expanding
The virtual hard disk file grows to its maximum size as data is written to the virtual hard disk.
OK
Cancel

Figure 7-15 Configuring a virtual hard disk

6. The virtual hard disk format is VHD by default. Because you're creating a small volume, you can accept this default setting. Click the **Dynamically expanding** option button so that the disk's file size is very small at first and then expands as you add data, up to the 200 MB you specified. (Recall that this concept is called *thin provisioning*.) Click **OK**.

7. When you create a VHD file in Disk Management, it's mounted automatically. The disk should be listed as Disk 3, and its status is Not Initialized (see Figure 7-16). Right-click **Disk 3** and notice the Detach VHD option in the menu. Click **Initialize Disk**.

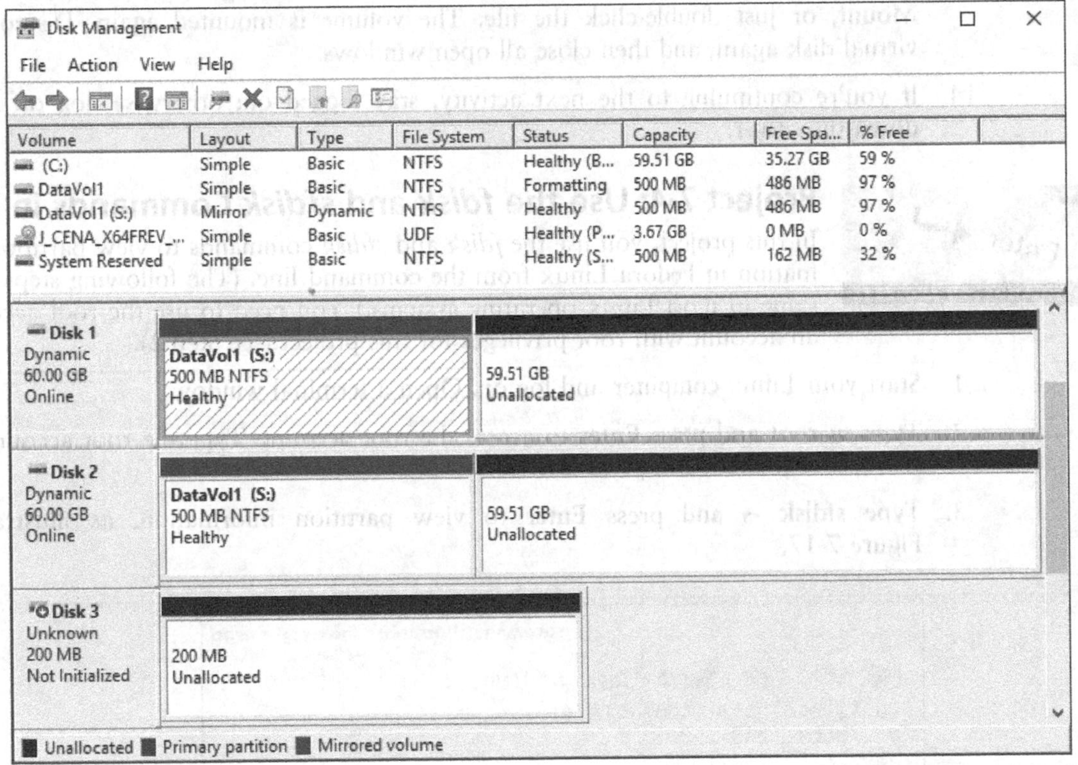

Figure 7-16 A virtual disk in Disk Management

8. In the Initialize Disk dialog box, click **OK**. Your new virtual disk is initialized and ready to have a volume created on it.

9. Right-click the unallocated space of Disk 3 and click **New Simple Volume**. Follow the New Simple Volume Wizard to select the following settings:

   - Volume size: Use the maximum size.
   - Drive letter: Assign drive letter V:.
   - Format: Use the default settings, but make the volume label **Virtual1**.

10. When the volume has finished formatting, you can access it. The icon color of Disk 3 changes to light blue, indicating a virtual disk. Right-click the volume and click **Explore**.
11. File Explorer treats the virtual disk and volumes in it like any other disk and volume. In File Explorer, click the **S** drive. You should see a file named Virtual1 with an adjacent icon indicating a virtual disk.
12. Right-click **Virtual1 (V:)** in the left pane of File Explorer and then click **Eject**. The disk is no longer shown in File Explorer or Disk Management.
13. In File Explorer, click the **S** drive. Notice that the virtual disk's file size is only about 10 MB. That size expands if you add data to the file. Right-click **Virtual1** and click **Mount**, or just double-click the file. The volume is mounted again. Dismount the virtual disk again, and then close all open windows.
14. If you're continuing to the next activity, stay logged on; otherwise, log off or shut down the server.

Project 7-4: Use the *fdisk* and *sfdisk* Commands in Linux

In this project, you use the *fdisk* and *sfdisk* commands to view partition information in Fedora Linux from the command line. (The following steps are the same in most Linux operating systems.) You need to use the root account or an account with root privileges for this project (see Step 2).

1. Start your Linux computer and log on. Open a terminal window.
2. Type **su root** and press **Enter** to access the root account. Type the root account password, if requested, and press **Enter**.
3. Type **sfdisk -s** and press **Enter** to view partition information, as illustrated in Figure 7-17.

```
gtomsho@localhost:/home/gtomsho
File  Edit  View  Search  Terminal  Help
[root@localhost gtomsho]# sfdisk -s
/dev/sdb:  20971520
/dev/sda:  20971520
/dev/sdc:  20971520
/dev/mapper/fedora-root:  18358272
/dev/mapper/fedora-swap:   2097152
total: 83369984 blocks
[root@localhost gtomsho]# █
```

Figure 7-17 The output from the *sfdisk -s* command

Source: Fedora Linux

4. Next, type **fdisk -l** and press **Enter**. Compare the information from the *fdisk* command to the information displayed for the *sfdisk* command.
5. Close the terminal window.

Project 7-5: Use the Disks Utility in Linux

In this project, you use the Disks utility in Linux to work with a newly installed disk.

If your Linux computer is configured according to instructions in the "Before You Begin" section of the Introduction, you should have two physical disks installed. The first disk will have the Linux OS installed and the second disk will be blank. If you don't have more than one disk installed, you can't do this project.

1. Start your Linux computer, and log on.
2. Click **Activities** and click **Show Applications**.
3. Click **Utilities** and then click **Disks** to open the Disks utility (see Figure 7-18). Depending on your system configuration, your Disks utility may look different. In Figure 7-18, there are two hard disks; the Linux system in the figure is running on VMware, so the disks are labeled as VMware disks. 7

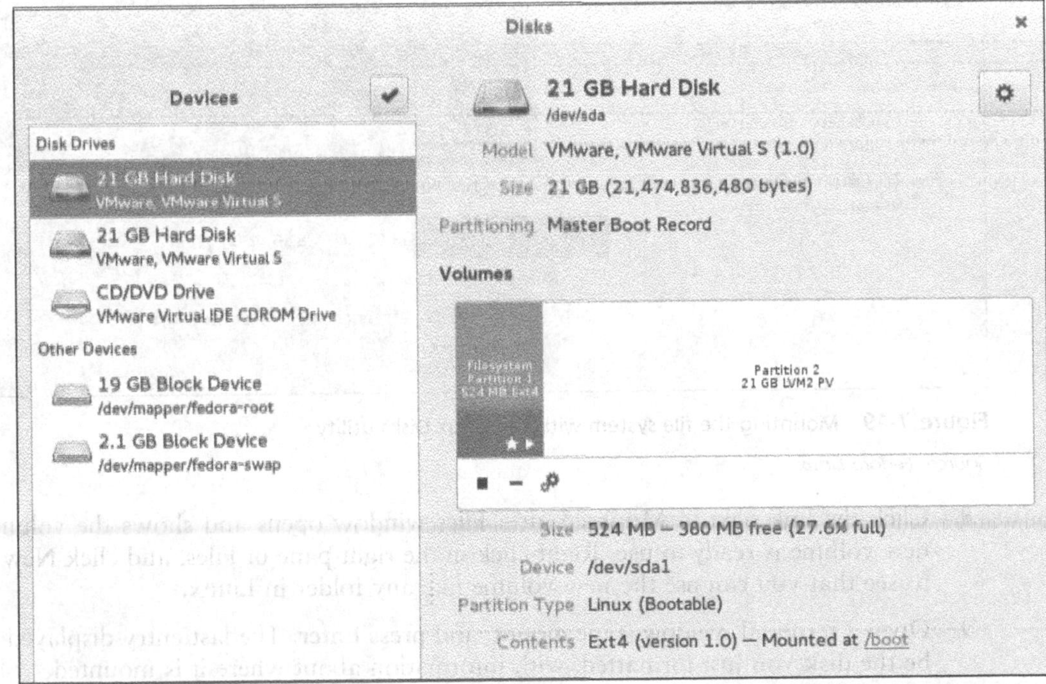

Figure 7-18 Linux Disks utility

Source: Fedora Linux

4. Click the second disk in the left pane. In the right pane, you see that the volume is listed as Unknown.

5. Right-click the **More actions** button under the volume and click **Format.** In the Format Volume dialog box, accept the default Erase and Type options, and type **Vol1** in the Name text box. Click **Format.**

6. The next dialog box asks if you are sure you want to format the volume. Click **Format.** If you are prompted for your password, enter it and click **Authenticate.**

7. Click the **Mount the filesystem** arrow under the volume (see Figure 7-19). If you are prompted for your password, enter it and click **Authenticate.** By default, the volume is mounted in /run/media/*user*/Vol1, where *user* is the logon name of the current user.

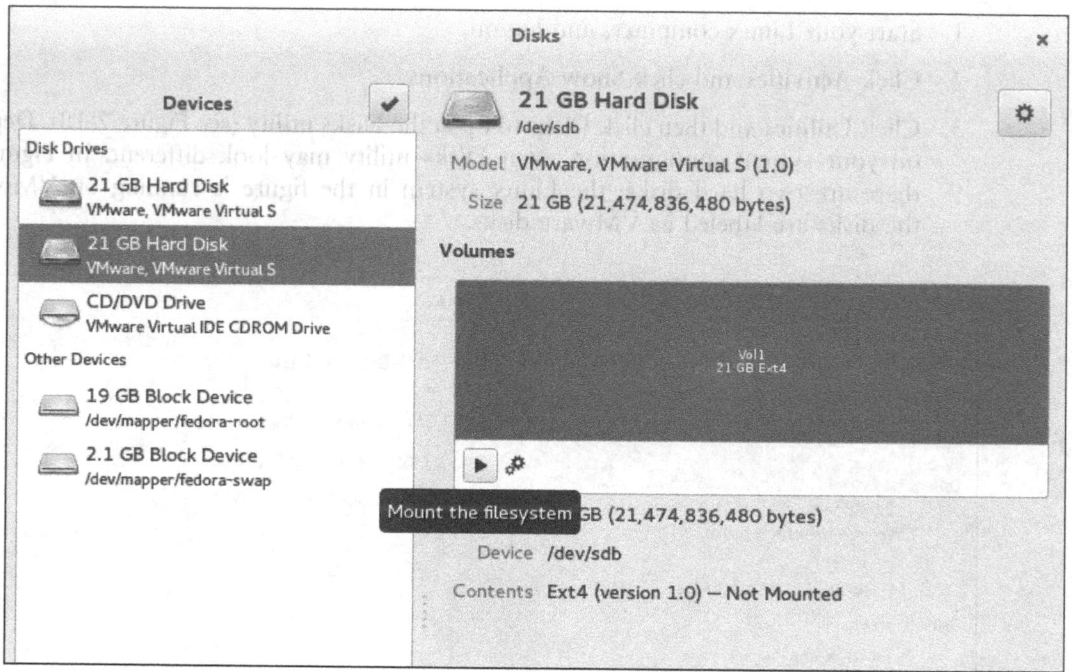

Figure 7-19 Mounting the file system with the Linux Disks utility

Source: Fedora Linux

8. Click the link next to Mounted at; a Files window opens and shows the volume. The new volume is ready to use. Right-click in the right pane of Files, and click **New Folder** to see that you can use the new volume like any folder in Linux.

9. Open a terminal window, type **mount,** and press **Enter.** The last entry displayed should be the disk you just formatted, with information about where it is mounted.

10. To unmount the disk, type **umount /dev/sdb** and press **Enter.** The disk is no longer mounted.

11. Close all windows and log off or shut down your computer.

Project 7-6: Use the Disk Utility in Mac OS X

Mac OS X provides the Disk Utility for working with storage. In this project, you use the Disk Utility to view information about a disk and see how to partition a disk. You need Administrator privileges to perform this activity.

1. Start your Mac and log on. Make sure that Finder is open (if not, click **Finder** in the Dock). Click the **Go** menu and click **Utilities**.
2. Double-click **Disk Utility**.
3. Click **Macintosh HD** in the left pane.
4. Click the **Info** icon in the menu bar to view information about the disk (see Figure 7-20).

Macintosh HD

Volume name	Macintosh HD
Volume type	Physical Volume
BSD device node	disk0s2
Mount point	/
File system	OS X Extended
Connection	PCI
Device tree path	IODeviceTree:/PCI0@0/P2P0@11/S5I
Writable	Yes
Is case-sensitive	No
File system UUID	1EE7D8A2-A046-3225-A623-5D45
Volume capacity	42,089,914,368
Available space	24,025,808,896
Free space	24,025,808,896

Figure 7-20 Information about Macintosh HD
Source: Mac OS X

5. Close the Information window.
6. In the left pane, click the disk drive above Macintosh HD. Click the **Partition** icon in the menu bar. Read the information displayed about the partition. Notice that the partition scheme is GUID Partition Map, which is the same as GPT, and the format is OS X Extended (Journaled), which is the same as HFS Plus. Click **Cancel**.
7. Close the Disk Utility window and any other open windows.
8. Shut down your computer.

Critical Thinking

The following activities give you critical thinking challenges. Challenge Labs give you an opportunity to use the skills you have learned to perform a task without step-by-step instructions. Case projects offer a practical problem for which you supply a written solution. Not all chapters contain Challenge Labs. There is not always a specific right or wrong answer to these critical thinking exercises. They are intended to encourage you to review the chapter material and delve deeper into the topics you have learned.

Case Projects

Case Project 7-1: Deal with a Disk Crash

Last week, a disk on a Windows Server 2012 system that contained CSM Tech Publishing's current project manuscripts crashed. Fortunately, there was a backup, but all files that had been added or changed that day were lost. No RAID configurations were in use. A new disk had to be purchased for overnight delivery, and the data had to be restored. A couple days of work were lost. The owner of CSM Tech wants to know what can be done to prevent the loss of data and time if a disk crashes in the future. The server currently has two disks installed: one for the Windows boot and system volumes and one for manuscript files. The disk used for manuscript files is about one-third full. There's enough money in the budget to purchase up to two new drives if needed. What solution do you recommend, and why?

Case Project 7-2: Create Flexible Storage

It's been six months since the disk crash at CSM Tech Publishing, and the owner is breathing a little easier because of the solution you implemented in Case Project 7-1. Business is good, and the current solution is starting to run low on disk space—less than 20 percent of free space remains. In addition, the owner has some other needs that might require more disk space, and he wants to keep the data on separate volumes (what he calls *drives*). He wants a flexible solution in which drives and volumes aren't restricted in their configuration. He also wants to be able to add storage space to existing volumes easily without having to reconfigure existing drives. He has the budget to add a disk storage system that can contain up to 10 HDDs. Which Windows feature can accommodate these needs, and how does it work?

chapter 8

Virtualization and Cloud Computing Fundamentals

After reading this chapter and completing the exercises, you will be able to:

- Describe the components of virtualization
- Use and describe hosted virtualization
- Use and describe bare-metal virtualization
- Describe cloud computing

OS virtualization has become a mainstream technology in both small and large networks. Large companies use it to consolidate server hardware and make efficient use of server processing power and network bandwidth. Individuals use virtualization to quickly try a new operating system without having to install the OS to their hard disk. IT professionals use virtualization to perform testing and what-if scenarios. Software developers can test their applications on multiple OSs and multiple versions of an OS without having to configure multiple physical computers. The ability to work at one physical Windows, Mac, or Linux workstation while using one, two, three, or even a dozen other OSs running on virtual machines opens up a world of possibilities. Users and IT professionals can become proficient on multiple OSs while owning just a single physical computer and data center administrators benefit from the ease in which virtual servers can be deployed and managed compared to their physical counterparts.

This chapter introduces you to virtualization, its terminology, and some of the popular virtualization products that can be used on the OSs this book has discussed.

Virtualization Fundamentals

Virtualization is a process that creates a software environment to emulate a computer's hardware and BIOS, allowing multiple OSs to run on the same physical computer at the same time. This environment can be installed on most current OSs, including Windows, Linux, and Mac OS. In this case, a picture is worth a thousand words, so examine Figure 8-1. It shows a Windows 10 client running a Windows Server 2016 (technical preview) virtual machine that uses VMware Workstation virtualization software. Notice the two Start buttons: one on the host desktop and one on the virtual machine.

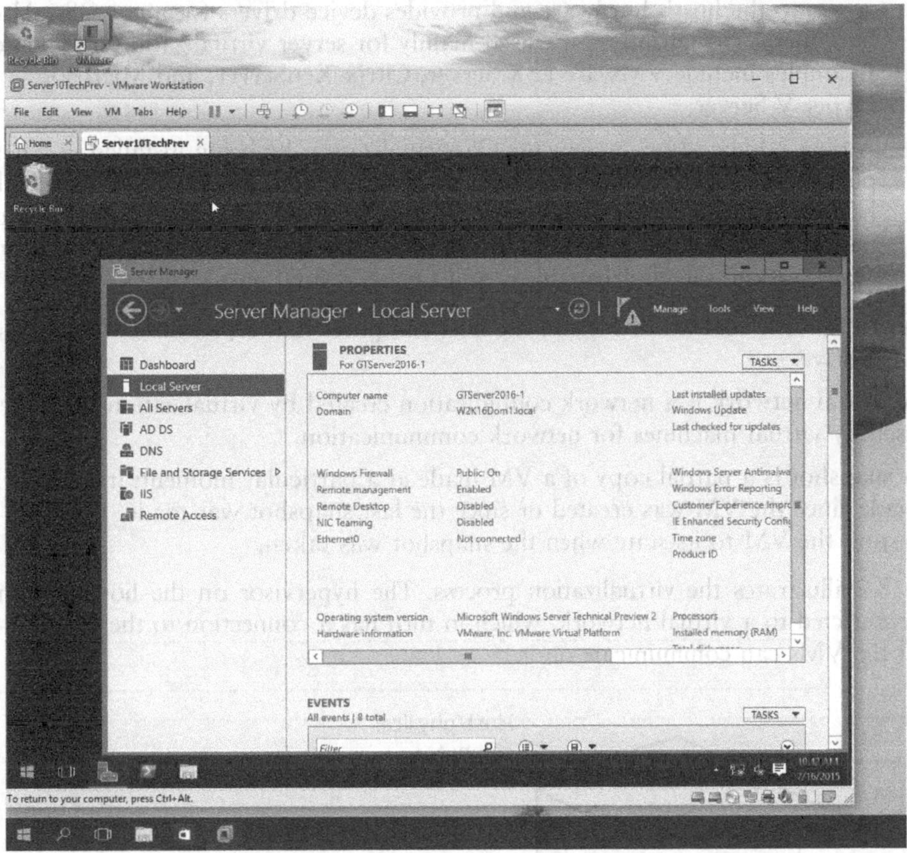

Figure 8-1 Windows Server 2016 running as a virtual machine in Windows 10

Like all technologies, virtualization comes with a collection of terms that define its operation and components:

- A **virtual machine** (VM) is the virtual environment that emulates a physical computer's hardware and BIOS. A **guest OS** is the operating system installed on a VM.
- A **host computer** is the physical computer on which VM software is installed and VMs run.
- Virtualization software is used for creating and managing VMs and creating the virtual environment in which a guest OS is installed. Examples of this software are VMware Workstation, Oracle VirtualBox, and Microsoft Hyper-V.
- The **hypervisor** is the part of virtualization software that creates and monitors the virtual hardware environment, which allows multiple VMs to share physical hardware resources. On a host computer, the hypervisor acts somewhat like an OS kernel, but instead of scheduling processes for access to the CPU and other devices, it schedules VMs. It's sometimes called the *virtual machine monitor (VMM)*. There are two types of hypervisors:
    - A type 1 hypervisor implements OS virtualization by running directly on the host computer's hardware and controls and monitors guest OSs. It also controls

access to the host's hardware and provides device drivers for guest OSs. Also called **bare-metal virtualization,** it's used mainly for server virtualization in data centers. Examples include VMware ESX Server, Citrix XenServer, and Microsoft Hyper-V Server.

- A type 2 hypervisor implements OS virtualization by being installed in a general-purpose host OS, such as Windows 10 or Linux, and the host OS accesses host hardware on behalf of the guest OS. Also called **hosted virtualization,** it's used mostly for desktop virtualization solutions. Examples include VMware Player and Workstation, Oracle VirtualBox, and OpenVZ for Linux.

- A **virtual disk** consists of files on the host computer that represent a virtual machine's hard drive.
- A **virtual network** is a network configuration created by virtualization software and used by virtual machines for network communication.
- A **snapshot** is a partial copy of a VM made at a particular moment; it contains changes made since the VM was created or since the last snapshot was made. It is used to restore the VM to its state when the snapshot was taken.

Figure 8-2 illustrates the virtualization process. The hypervisor on the host is running two VMs connected to a virtual network, which in turn has a connection to the physical network so that the VMs can communicate on it.

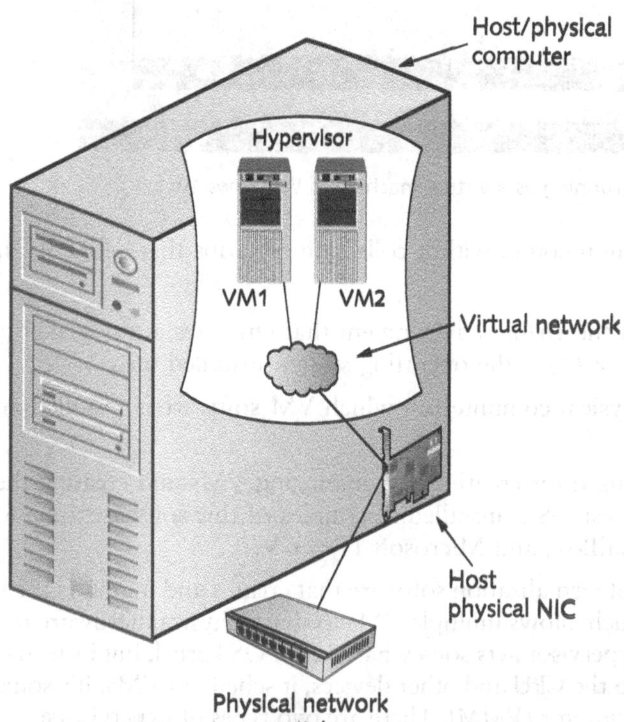

Figure 8-2 How virtualization works

One of the best ways to understand a technology is to understand why it's used. The reasons to use virtualization are many and varied. They are best discussed by splitting the topic into the two main types of virtualization: hosted and bare-metal.

Hosted Virtualization

As mentioned, hosted virtualization uses a type 2 hypervisor, which is installed on a standard desktop or server OS. It has the advantage of supporting a wider variety of guest OSs than bare-metal virtualization, mostly because the guest OS uses the host OS to access host hardware, so there are few incompatibility problems between the guest OS and hardware. For example, you can run a distribution of Linux in a virtual machine on a host computer, even if you can't install Linux directly on the physical machine because of driver incompatibilities.

Another advantage of hosted virtualization is that it's easy and straightforward to use. With hosted virtualization, you install the virtualization software on your computer and begin creating virtual machines. There are few hardware requirements, and most products run on Windows versions starting with Windows XP as well as Mac OS X and most Linux distributions. All you need are enough memory to support the host and guest OSs, adequate CPU power, and enough free disk space to store the virtual disk. A system running Windows 10 with 4 GB of RAM, a 2.0 GHz CPU, and a hard drive with 40 GB of free space can run Linux and Windows Server 2016 virtual machines at the same time. Performance might not be stellar, but the virtual machines should work well enough for experimenting or training, which are among the main reasons for using hosted virtualization.

Hosted Virtualization Applications

Hosted virtualization is flexible and easy to use, so its applications continue to grow as people find different uses for it. Some common applications include the following:

- *OS training*—In the classroom and at home, learning multiple OSs has often been a problem of not having enough computers or a lack of compatibility between the OS and available computers. With virtualization, a computer can have a host OS installed, such as Windows 10, and have virtual machines for numerous Linux distributions, Windows 7, Windows Server 2016, and even Novell NetWare. If you want to learn about past OSs, you can install Windows 3.11, DOS, or OS/2, assuming you can find installation media for them. In addition, you can run multiple VMs at the same time by using a virtual network, which enables you to work with both client and server OSs in situations that would normally take two or more physical computers.
- *Software training*—Students and employees can be trained on new software packages by giving them VMs with preinstalled software.
- *Application isolation*—Not all software plays well together, so if an application conflicts with other installed software, it can be installed in its own VM, effectively isolating it from the host machine's installed software.
- *Network isolation*—Installing certain networking services, such as DHCP, can wreak havoc with an existing network. Virtual networks can be isolated from the rest of the network, however, so you can experiment with these services without causing conflicts.

8

- *Software development*—Software developers often need to design software that works on multiple OSs and OS versions. Testing on VMs makes this process easier than using a physical computer for each OS to be tested.
- *What-if scenarios*—If you want to try out a software package or see whether a configuration option you read about will actually improve performance, you might not want to risk destabilizing your computer. You can install software and make configuration changes safely on a VM before making the commitment on your production computer.
- *Use of legacy applications*—If you have a favorite application that won't run on a newer OS, you don't have to forego the latest software technology because of one application. You can install the old OS in a VM and run your legacy application on it.
- *Physical-to-virtual conversion*—Your six-year-old machine is getting slow and unreliable, so you bought a new desktop computer. However, you have several applications on your old computer and no longer have the installation media. You can convert your old computer to a virtual machine, and then keep all the software and run it on your new desktop computer as a VM. You'll probably even see a speed boost.

As you can see, virtualization can bring plenty of benefits to your computing experience. You have many choices of products, and the good news is that many are free. The following section describes some products for hosted virtualization.

Hosted Virtualization Products

Several hosted virtualization products are available. The following are the most well known:

- *VMware Workstation Pro*—VMware, the virtualization pioneer in the PC world, released VMware Workstation in 1999. Of the hosted virtualization products, it offers the most features, including multiple snapshots, extensive guest OS support, and nested virtualization (the capability to run a virtual machine inside another virtual machine).
- *VMware Workstation Player*—This version of VMware Workstation has a streamlined user interface and fewer advanced features than Workstation Pro, but it maintains excellent guest OS support. The current version (Workstation 12 Player) is free for personal, noncommercial use, but it costs about $150 for business or commercial use as of this writing.
- *Microsoft Virtual PC*—This free download from Microsoft enables you to create and run virtual machines. XP mode is a feature available only in Windows 7 Professional or Ultimate that integrates Windows XP virtual machine applications with the Windows 7 desktop. Virtual PC is no longer available in Windows 8 and later versions.
- *VirtualBox*—Originally developed by Innotek, VirtualBox is now developed by Oracle Corporation. Two versions are available: a proprietary version that's free for home users and can be purchased for enterprise use, and a free open-source version with a reduced feature set. VirtualBox runs on Linux, Mac OS X, or Windows hosts. The proprietary version has features similar to VMware Workstation.

For more information on virtualization products, the platforms they run on, and supported guest OSs, review the article at *http://en.wikipedia.org/wiki/Comparison_of_platform_virtual_machines*.

The preceding products have their strengths and weaknesses; the best approach is to work with different products to see which best serves your needs. The following sections discuss the use of these products.

Using VMware Workstation

VMware Workstation isn't free, but you can download a free trial version and try it for 30 days. Nonprofit educational institutions can join the VMware Academic program to give students and faculty free downloads of VMware Workstation and other VMware products.

After VMware Workstation is installed, a wizard takes you through the steps of creating a virtual machine. You can choose the size of the virtual disk and set other hardware options or just accept the default settings.

One convenience of installing a guest OS in a VM is being able to boot to the installation program with an ISO file rather than a DVD disk. This way, if you download the ISO file, burning a DVD to install the OS is unnecessary. In addition, the ISO file can be stored on a server and used by multiple users for VM installations.

8

An advanced feature of VMware Workstation is its flexible networking options. You can configure the network interface card (NIC) on your VM to use one of the five virtual network options or you can create your own custom virtual network. VMware Workstation supports VMs with multiple NICs, and each NIC can be connected to a different virtual network. The five options are as follows (see Figure 8-3):

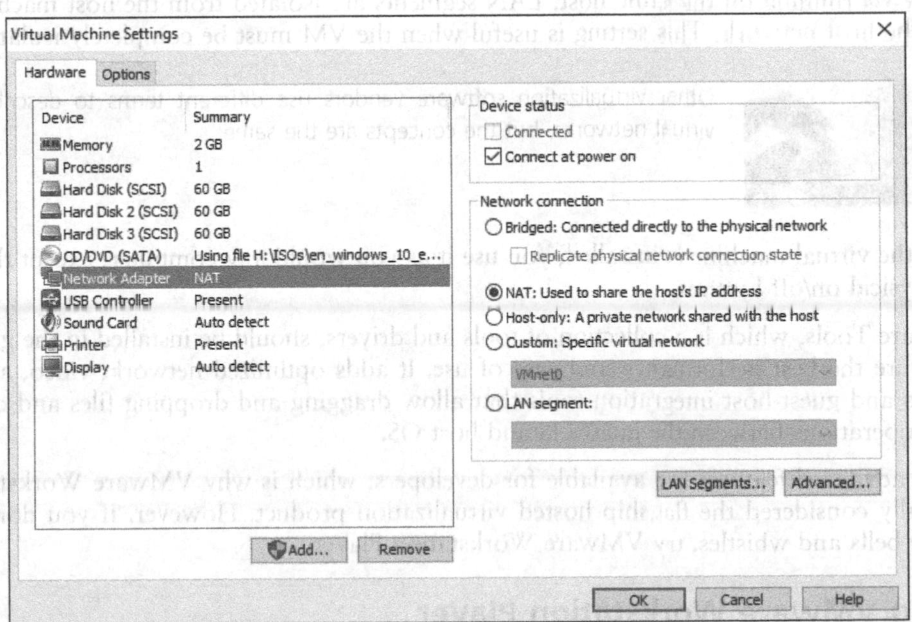

Figure 8-3 VMware virtual network options

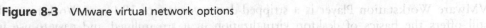

Source: VMware, Inc., www.vmware.com

- *Bridged*—This option connects the VM's virtual network to the physical network, and the VM acts like any other computer on the physical network, including having an IP address on the physical network. This option was illustrated in Figure 8-2, which showed that the virtual network has a (virtual) connection to the host's physical NIC.
- *NAT*—Using this default option, the host computer's IP address is shared with the VM by using Network Address Translation (NAT). The main difference between the NAT and Bridged options is that VMs are assigned an IP address from the host computer rather than the physical network, and the host translates the address for incoming and outgoing packets. This option is more secure than the Bridged option because the VM isn't directly accessible on the network. However, it's not a viable option for a VM that provides server functions to the host network.
- *Host-only*—This option isolates the VM from the host network and only allows network communication between VMs running on the host and the host computer. It's the most secure configuration and has the lowest risk that the VM will cause problems with the host network. This configuration works well when you have multiple VMs that must communicate with one another but you don't need to access computers or devices outside the host.
- *Custom*—You can use this option to connect the VM to a virtual network created with the virtual network editor, a tool accessible from the Edit menu in VMware Workstation. With a custom network, you assign a subnet to the network, and you have the option of using DHCP to assign IP addresses to connected VMs. With the virtual network editor, you can make the custom virtual network bridged, NAT, or host-only.
- *LAN segment*—LAN segments are private networks that can be shared with other VMs running on the same host. LAN segments are isolated from the host machine and the host network. This setting is useful when the VM must be completely isolated.

Other virtualization software vendors use different terms to describe virtual networks, but the concepts are the same.

After the virtual machine is installed, you use it as you would any computer, except there are no physical on/off buttons.

VMware Tools, which is a collection of tools and drivers, should be installed in the guest OS to ensure the best performance and ease of use. It adds optimized network, video, and disk drivers and guest-host integration tools that allow dragging and dropping files and cut-and-paste operations between the guest OS and host OS.

Other advanced features are available for developers, which is why VMware Workstation is generally considered the flagship hosted virtualization product. However, if you don't need all the bells and whistles, try VMware Workstation Player.

Using VMware Workstation Player

VMware Workstation Player is a stripped-down version of VMware Workstation Pro that still offers the basics of desktop virtualization in a streamlined and easy-to-use interface.

You can download a free trial from the VMware Web site, and it's also included with the VMware Workstation package. The opening window of VMware Workstation Player gives you an idea of its clean interface (see Figure 8-4).

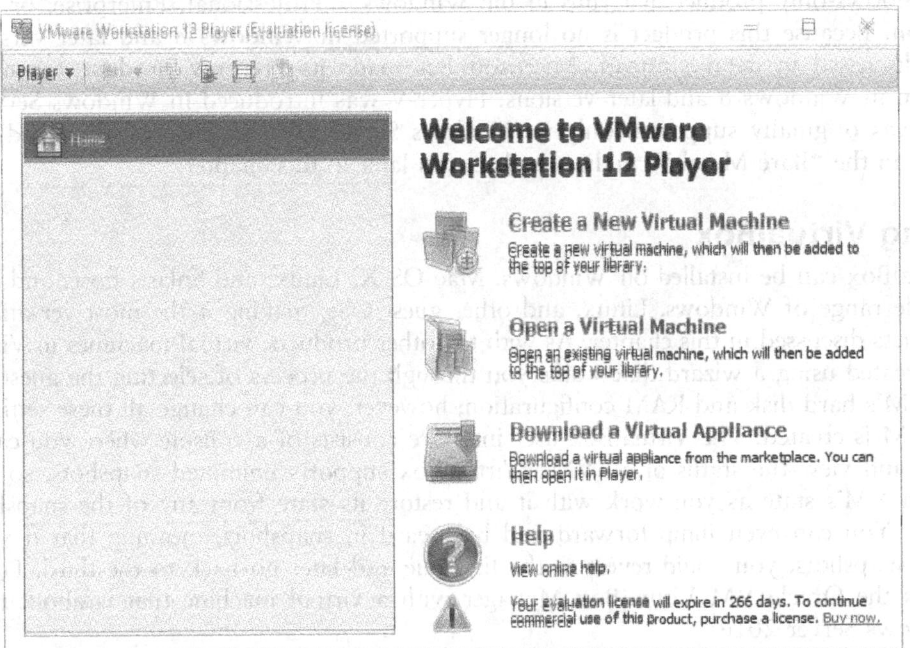

Figure 8-4 The VMware Workstation Player Welcome window

Source: VMware, Inc., www.vmware.com

VMware Workstation 12 Player is now a paid product for business and commercial use. As of this writing, you may still be able to download and install version 7 of the VMware Player, which was the last version that VMware offered as a totally free product. You can download most of VMware's products for a 30-day trial.

To create a VM in VMware Workstation Player, you use a wizard that is nearly identical to the one in VMware Workstation. Notice in Figure 8-4 that you have the option to download a virtual appliance. Virtual appliances are ready-to-use VMs from OS and software vendors that contain a guest OS with preconfigured applications or network services. In some cases, a virtual appliance is just a preinstalled guest OS. A virtual appliance is an easy way to use and evaluate a product or configuration without having to install it yourself. Virtual appliances can be run by VMware Workstation Player or VMware Workstation Pro and sometimes by VMware's bare-metal virtualization products.

VMware Player offers many of the same features as VMware Workstation, with the exception of snapshots, customized virtual networks (although the three preconfigured network options are available), and some advanced network and virtual hardware settings. It's a good choice for new virtualization users and for classroom and training centers where the interface's simplicity is an advantage.

8

Using Microsoft Virtual PC

The VMware products just discussed can be installed on both Windows and Linux OSs; another desktop product called VMware Fusion runs in Mac OS X. However, Virtual PC is a Windows-only product that runs in the Windows 7 Professional, Enterprise, or Ultimate edition. Because this product is no longer supported in Windows 8 and later versions, it's not discussed in detail. Instead, Microsoft has made its Hyper-V product a configurable option in Windows 8 and later versions. Hyper-V was introduced in Windows Server 2008 and was originally supported only in Windows Server OSs. Hyper-V is discussed in more detail in the "Bare-Metal Virtualization" section later in this chapter.

Using VirtualBox

VirtualBox can be installed on Windows, Mac OS X, Linux, and Solaris hosts and supports a wide range of Windows, Linux, and other guest OSs, making it the most versatile of the products discussed in this chapter. As with the other products, virtual machines in VirtualBox are created using a wizard that walks you through the process of selecting the guest OS and the VM's hard disk and RAM configuration; however, you can change all these settings after the VM is created. The VirtualBox user interface consists of a console where you can create VMs and view the status of all VMs. VirtualBox supports unlimited snapshots, so you can save a VM's state as you work with it and restore its state from any of the snapshots you make. You can even jump forward and backward in snapshots, meaning that if you have three snapshots, you could revert to the first one and later go back to the third. Figure 8-5 shows the Oracle VM VirtualBox Manager with a virtual machine that is about to install Windows Server 2016.

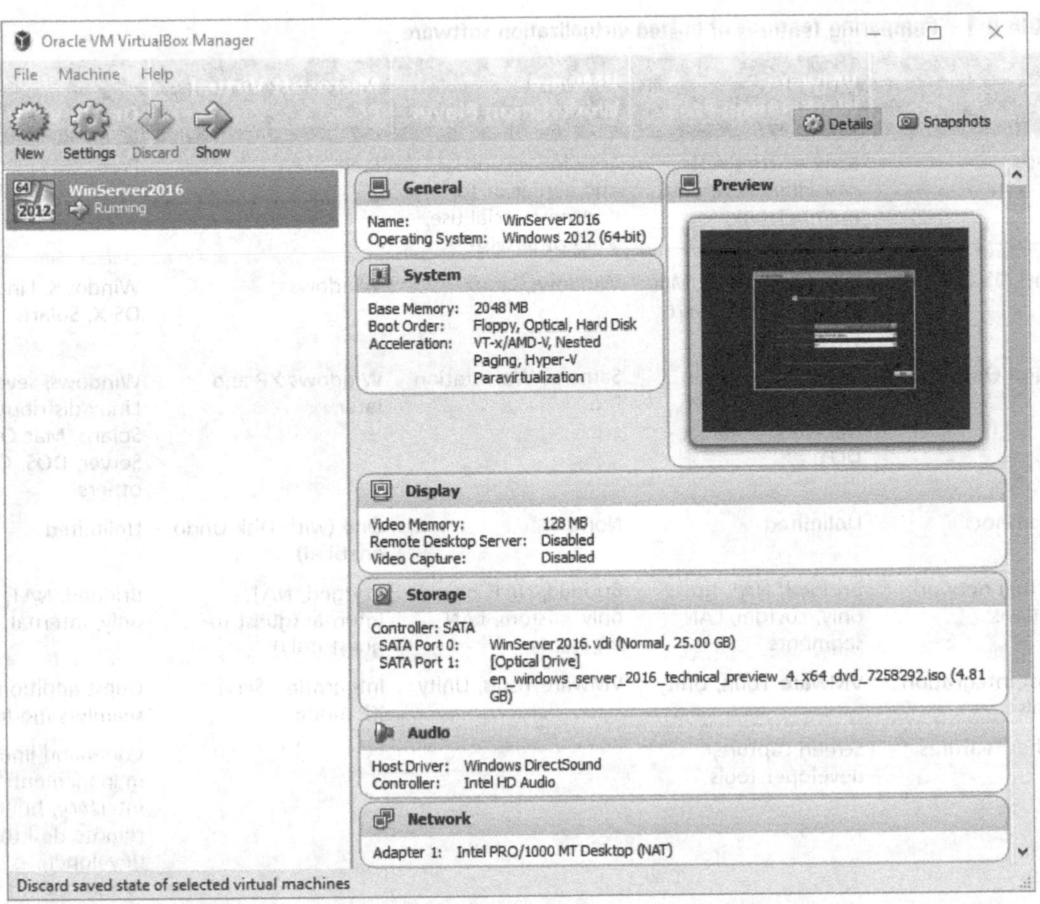

Figure 8-5 Oracle VM VirtualBox Manager

Virtualization Software Summary

All the virtualization products discussed so far provide a type 2 hypervisor for hosted virtualization. Table 8-1 summarizes some major features and differences in these products. A benefit is that you can install all of these products and run them at the same time on a single host computer, so you can download and install each one and evaluate it for yourself.

8

Table 8-1 Comparing features of hosted virtualization software

	VMware Workstation Pro	VMware Workstation Player	Microsoft Virtual PC	Oracle VirtualBox
Price	$249 or free with Academic Program membership	Free for versions 7 and earlier or for noncommercial use, $149 otherwise	Free	Free
Host OS support	Windows, Linux, Mac OS X (with VMware Fusion)	Windows, Linux	Windows	Windows, Linux, Mac OS X, Solaris
Guest OS support	Windows, several Linux distributions, NetWare, Solaris, DOS	Same as Workstation Pro	Windows XP and later	Windows, several Linux distributions, Solaris, Mac OS X Server, DOS, OS/2, others
Snapshots	Unlimited	None	One (with Disk Undo enabled)	Unlimited
Virtual network options	Bridged, NAT, host-only, custom, LAN segments	Bridged, NAT, host-only, custom, LAN segments	Bridged, NAT, internal (guest-to-guest only)	Bridged, NAT, host-only, internal
Host integration tools	VMware Tools, Unity	VMware Tools, Unity	Integration Services, XP mode	Guest additions, seamless mode
Other features	Screen capture, developer tools			Command-line management interface, built-in remote desktop, developer programming interface, open-source edition

Bare-Metal Virtualization

Bare-metal virtualization products (type 1 hypervisors) are targeted mainly for production virtualization in data centers. These products are installed directly on hardware and have more stringent host machine requirements than hosted products. Because they're targeted for IT departments, they have more features for managing VMs and have a performance advantage over hosted virtualization products. Their installation and use tend to require more sophisticated, knowledgeable users. Before learning about specific products, take a look at some applications for bare-metal virtualization products.

Bare-Metal Virtualization Applications

Bare-metal virtualization products come with a price tag for the virtualization software, the hardware to run it, or both. When considering whether to use virtualization in an IT data center, most IT managers look for a return on their investment in real money or in productivity gains. The following applications show that bare-metal virtualization can deliver both:

- *Consolidate servers*—Server consolidation is probably the original reason for using bare-metal virtualization. It has the following benefits:
    - Retire old or unreliable hardware: Converting physical machines to VMs and running them on the latest hardware means you can get rid of old hardware, thereby gaining a reliability advantage and avoiding the tedious task of reinstalling and reconfiguring a server OS on new hardware. You might also improve performance.
    - Make optimal use of multicore, high-performance servers: Some server roles, such as Active Directory, should be the only major network service running on a server. With multicore server CPUs, you're likely to waste a lot of the server's power if you install a single-role OS. Instead, run two, three, or more VMs on the server, making optimal use of the available performance.
    - Maintain application separation: Some applications and services run best when they're the only major application installed on an OS. You avoid OS resource conflicts and gain stability and reliability.
    - Reclaim rack or floor space: By consolidating a dozen physical servers into three or four host servers, you're no longer tripping over a plethora of towers or wondering whether your rack can handle one more server. You can even clear enough room for an easy chair and a reading lamp so that you can catch up on the latest technical journals in comfort!
    - Reduce cooling and power requirements: By reducing the number of servers (even with higher-performance machines), you usually save money on the costs of cooling and powering a data center, especially when you reduce hundreds of servers down to dozens of virtualization servers.
- *Test installations and upgrades*—Before you install a major software package or upgrade on your server, create a copy of the VM (referred to as *cloning* in some products), and go through a test run to iron out any potential problems or conflicts. If something goes wrong on the production VM, you can revert to a snapshot.
- *Test a preconfigured application*—Are you unsure whether the application the vendor wants to sell you is right for your company? Some vendors offer virtual appliances you can use to evaluate the application without having to install it.
- *Test what-if scenarios*—You can create a virtual network and run clones of your production VMs to test ideas for improving your network's performance, functionality, and reliability. This type of testing on live production systems is never a good idea, but it's ideal on virtual machines.
- *Live migration*—Virtual machines can be migrated to new hardware while they're running for performance or reliability improvements with practically no downtime. Live migration features also ensure VM fault tolerance in clustered server environments.
- *Dynamic provisioning*—Advanced VM management systems can deploy VMs and storage dynamically to meet application requirements. This advanced feature has uses in clustered computing and cloud computing.

VMs that run distributed server applications, such as Active Directory, in which multiple servers synchronize a common database with one another, shouldn't be backed up or moved by copying the virtual hard disk because it might result in database inconsistencies. Use only backup and migration tools approved for the virtualization software.

Bare-Metal Virtualization Products

VMware dominated the type 1 hypervisor category for years, but now you have a choice of products. The following are the most common bare-metal virtualization products:

- *Microsoft Hyper-V*—Hyper-V was introduced with Windows Server 2008 and can be installed as a server role, in which case the hypervisor is installed as a layer of software between Windows Server and the server hardware. Windows Server acts as a parent or management OS for VMs installed with Hyper-V. Hyper-V is included with Windows Server at no additional cost, or you can download the stand-alone Hyper-V Server free from the Microsoft Web site. (You can install Hyper-V Server directly on the server, with only a command-line interface available for rudimentary management tasks; it's managed remotely by another Windows Server computer.) Hyper-V supports advanced features, such as host server clustering and live migration, and requires a 64-bit CPU with virtualization extensions enabled on the host system. Virtualization extensions offload some virtualization work to the CPU and are present on most current CPUs.

  A big advantage of using Hyper-V is that Microsoft provides virtual instances of the OS with no additional licensing fees. For example, Windows Server 2012 Standard Edition allows you to run two virtual instances (or two VMs) of the OS at no additional cost. Datacenter Edition allows an unlimited number of virtual instances. Hyper-V has guest OS support for Windows Server OSs (Windows 2000 Server and later), SUSE and Red Hat Enterprise Linux distributions, Windows client OSs (Windows XP and later), and more.

  Microsoft has made Hyper-V available with Windows client OSs, too. You can enable Hyper-V in Windows 8 and later versions by opening Programs and Features in Control Panel and clicking "Turn Windows features on or off." After Hyper-V is installed, you need to restart your computer and open Hyper-V Manager (see Figure 8-6) from Administrative Tools in Control Panel.

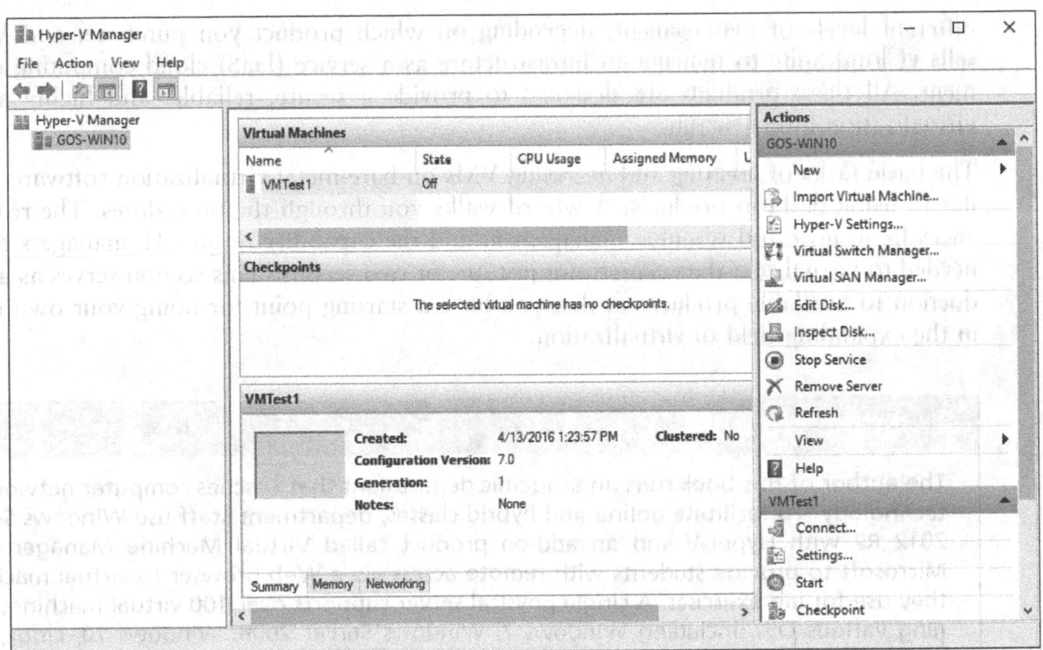

Figure 8-6 The Hyper-V Manager console

- *Citrix XenServer*—This open-source hypervisor uses Linux as a management OS on the host. It's available free or as a commercial edition that adds enterprise-level features, such as fault tolerance, performance management, and host power management. A number of modified Linux versions and Solaris can run as the management OS, and like Hyper-V, a XenServer host computer requires a 64-bit CPU with virtualization extensions to run Windows guest OSs. Guest OS support includes most Windows OSs, starting with Windows XP, and SUSE, Red Hat, and CentOS Linux distributions. To manage your host and VMs, you download and install XenCenter on a Windows computer or use a command-line interface on the host computer. XenCenter provides virtual machine management, monitoring, and administration from any Windows OS.
- *VMware vSphere*—vSphere includes VMware ESX Server, which is installed directly on the physical server without a management OS. After ESX Server is installed, a basic command-line console based on Linux is available for simple configuration tasks, such as IP address configuration. Most configuration tasks are performed from a remote client OS using vSphere Client, which is downloaded and installed on a Windows or Linux OS. You can also create, manage, and access VMs via a Web browser. ESX Server has the broadest guest OS support of the type 1 hypervisors, including Windows versions back to Windows 3.1, more than a dozen Linux distributions, Novell NetWare, and Solaris.

All these products have extensive management tools for managing up to hundreds of hosts and a wide array of storage resources. These tools are available for a fee from virtualization software vendors. For example, Microsoft offers System Center Virtual Machine Manager (SCVMM) for managing Hyper-V and ESX Server hosts. XenServer offers versions with different levels of management, depending on which product you purchase, and VMware sells vCloud Suite to manage an infrastructure as a service (IaaS) cloud computing environment. All these products are designed to provide a secure, reliable, and highly available virtualization infrastructure.

The basic tasks of creating and accessing VMs on bare-metal virtualization software are similar to using desktop products: A wizard walks you through the procedures. The real differences lie in host and resource management and the capability to give IT managers the tools needed to virtualize a data center, not just one or two servers. This section serves as an introduction to available products so that you have a starting point for doing your own research in the expanding field of virtualization.

From the Trenches ...

The author of this book runs an academic department that teaches computer networking technology. To facilitate online and hybrid classes, department staff use Windows Server 2012 R2 with Hyper-V and an add-on product called Virtual Machine Manager from Microsoft to provide students with remote access via a Web browser to virtual machines they use for lab exercises. A single physical server supports over 100 virtual machines running various OSs, including Windows 7, Windows Server 2008, Windows 10, Linux, and Windows Server 2012/R2. The server has two quad-core Xeon CPUs, 64 GB of RAM, two terabytes of disk space, and four 1000BaseT Ethernet ports. To access a virtual machine, students point their Web browser to the server's address and log on. Their logon ID is paired with one or more VMs to which they are assigned. The students can start, log on, and use their VM to complete lab activities. The server can efficiently run about 30 VMs simultaneously, and if students forget to shut down their VM, a PowerShell script runs every 10 minutes automatically and shuts down any VMs that have been running longer than four hours. This is an example of virtualization and private cloud computing.

Cloud Computing

Many people rely on the Internet's services for communication, research, and entertainment. This trend has continued to the point that many functions once handled in a company's IT center are now handled by servers on the Internet—what's referred to as *cloud computing*. Cloud computing is a networking model in which data, applications, and processing power are managed by servers on the Internet; users of these resources pay for what they use rather than for the equipment and software needed to provide resources. It's like paying only for cell phone minutes you use instead of paying for the towers and switching equipment needed to make your phone work.

The word *cloud* is used to obscure the details of equipment and software that actually provide resources. For the most part, customers don't care whether equipment consists of Windows or Linux servers, large tower computers, or rack-mounted computers, as long as it works.

For many companies, cloud computing's allure is based on the following benefits:

- *Reduced physical plant costs*—Having fewer servers means less space is needed to house them, and less electricity and cooling are required to keep servers running.
- *Reduced upfront costs*—Paying only for services and software that are used means a company can avoid the startup costs of purchasing a lot of expensive hardware and software.
- *Reduced personnel costs*—Having fewer servers and applications to support means fewer IT employees are needed to support hardware and applications.

Although cloud computing has seemingly limitless applications, three main categories of cloud computing have taken center stage:

- Software as a service
- Platform as a service
- Infrastructure as a service

The phrase *as a service* simply means that the resource resides on another server or network than the one using the resource, and customers use it as a paid service. You might also hear the term *SPI model*, which is based on the combination of the three aforementioned "as a service" terms (*S*oftware, *P*latform, *I*nfrastructure).

8

Software as a Service

Software as a service (SaaS) is also called *hosted applications* or *on-demand applications* because the customer doesn't actually buy any software that's installed on its own equipment. Instead, the customer pays for the use of applications that run on a service provider's network. The most well-known examples are Google Apps and Microsoft Office 365, which a business or a home user can use to run hosted applications, such as e-mail, calendar, word-processing, and spreadsheet programs. More complex applications involve large database systems, such as payroll services from ADP and customer relationship management software offered by companies such as Salesforce.com.

SaaS is usually offered as a subscription based on the number of people using the application. It takes the burden of installation and maintenance off the customer so that companies can focus on maintaining their LANs and Internet access instead of maintaining hundreds of copies of an installed application. In addition, customers can take advantage of new software editions much faster than with the standard deployment times of traditional application upgrades. Some application upgrades require client computer or OS upgrades, but with SaaS, the vendor handles infrastructure upgrades when needed.

In addition, SaaS is available anywhere the customer has a connection to the Internet. Mobile users and telecommuters have access to the same applications they use in the office without having to install the software on their laptops or home computers. Some applications can't even be installed on home computers, but with SaaS, the software runs on remote servers, so local installations aren't necessary.

Platform as a Service

Platform as a service (PaaS)—also called *hosted platform*—is similar to SaaS, but the customer develops applications with the service provider's tools and infrastructure. After applications are developed, they can be delivered to the customer's users from the provider's servers. This setup differs from SaaS, in which the service provider owns the applications delivered to users; with PaaS, the customer develops and owns the application and then delivers it to a third party.

Developers who use PaaS can take advantage of many of the same benefits enjoyed by SaaS users. In addition, after an application is developed with PaaS, the developer can usually deploy the application immediately to customers who access it as a hosted application. The same operating environment used to develop the application is used to run it, which bypasses the sometimes complex and problem-prone process of migrating from a traditional development environment to a production environment.

The most common PaaS products are Salesforce.com's Apex, Azure for Windows, Google's App Engine for Python and Java, WaveMaker for Ajax, and Engine Yard for Ruby on Rails. Others are available, but details on these development platforms are beyond the scope of this book. PaaS is still an evolving model for application development, and platforms will come and go as developers weed out what works and what doesn't. Developing in the cloud is likely here to stay because it offers benefits that aren't usually available in a locally managed environment. In addition, because small businesses and individual developers have access to expensive, full-featured development environments, entrepreneurs can be on an equal footing with the big boys, which increases competition and innovation—and that's always a good thing.

Infrastructure as a Service

Infrastructure as a service (IaaS), or *hosted infrastructure*, allows companies to use a vendor's storage or even entire virtual servers as needed. Traditionally, if a company needs another 100 GB of storage to house a new database, it has to buy a new hard drive—assuming the server can accommodate a new hard drive. By using IaaS, the company simply pays for another 100 GB of space without worrying about how that space is actually provided. In addition, if a customer needs another server to handle its application workload, it simply pays for the amount of processing and storage the additional server actually requires instead of paying for the physical device. In most cases, IaaS servers run as virtual machines on more powerful physical servers.

IaaS differs from other hosted services because customers mostly rent the resources they're using but are still responsible for application installations and upgrades. Although IT staff can be reduced because the IaaS vendor handles physical device upkeep, customers still need IT staff to configure and manage applications and server OSs.

IaaS isn't just for server infrastructure. Companies can "upgrade" to the latest OSs and desktop applications by using virtualized desktops through their IaaS providers. By accessing desktops remotely, IaaS customers can use thin clients (client computers with minimal hardware resources) or computers with older OSs to make use of the latest desktop OSs and applications. This IaaS feature, virtual desktop infrastructure (VDI), is becoming a popular way for companies to deliver desktop OSs and applications rather than use traditional methods of installing OSs and applications locally.

Examples of IaaS include Amazon Web Services (AWS), Rackspace Cloud, and Microsoft Azure, but many more companies and products are getting into this burgeoning market.

You may hear the term *anything as a service*, which is abbreviated as XaaS. There are also variations on the preceding services, such as storage as a service (SaaS), database as a service (DaaS), and network as a service (NaaS). Other "as a service" functions will undoubtedly be created.

Cloud computing relies heavily on virtualization, which allows a cloud service provider to offer a flexible computing environment to its customers and get the most out of its physical computing devices. With virtualization, a provider can quickly deploy additional computing power for a customer simply by clicking a configuration check box to add more virtual CPUs. Entire virtual servers can be deployed within seconds; using virtual disks, customers can get access to more storage quickly and easily.

Cloud computing isn't for every company or situation, but it offers a flexible array of services that can complement an IT department's existing resources and sometimes replace them. The trend toward cloud computing is growing with no abatement in site.

Private Cloud Versus Public Cloud

The preceding cloud technologies have been discussed in the context of a third party providing services to customers via the Internet—a **public cloud** solution. In a public cloud, computing resources and their management are the responsibility of the cloud service provider. This arrangement allows a company to focus on its primary business rather than a large IT infrastructure. However, because the cloud resources are in someone else's hands, you must depend on the provider to ensure the reliability and security of the provided service and your data. In addition, you are depending on Internet providers to connect your location with the cloud service provider. If the Internet goes down anywhere in that path, you will be unable to access the cloud service.

Many companies deliver cloud services to their own employees through the use of virtualization technologies, such as VMware and Microsoft Hyper-V—a **private cloud**. VDI, cloud storage, and SaaS are commonly accessed as private cloud services deployed from the company's own data center instead of using a public cloud service. This setup gives a company more control and more security, yet provides its employees many of the benefits of cloud computing. The drawback is the up-front and ongoing costs of maintaining a large IT infrastructure.

Chapter Summary

- Virtualization is a process that creates a software environment to emulate a computer's hardware and BIOS, allowing multiple OSs to run on the same physical computer at the same time.
- Virtualization can be divided into two categories: hosted virtualization and bare-metal virtualization. Hosted virtualization uses a type 2 hypervisor and bare-metal virtualization uses a type 1 hypervisor.

- Hosted virtualization products are installed on a desktop OS and include VMware Workstation, Virtual PC, and VirtualBox.
- Bare-metal virtualization products are targeted mainly for production virtualization in data centers. These products are installed directly on hardware and have more stringent host machine requirements than hosted products. Bare-metal virtualization software is used in data centers, is installed on servers, and includes products such as Microsoft Hyper-V, VMware vSphere, and Citrix XenServer.
- Cloud computing is a networking model in which data, applications, and processing power are managed by servers on the Internet. Users of these resources pay for what they use rather than for the equipment and software needed to provide resources. Cloud computing models include SaaS, PaaS, and IaaS.

Key Terms

bare-metal virtualization A system in which the hypervisor implements OS virtualization by running directly on the host computer's hardware and controls and monitors guest OSs. See also *virtualization*.

cloud computing A networking model in which data, applications, and processing power are managed by servers on the Internet; users of these resources pay for what they use rather than for the equipment and software needed to provide resources.

guest OS The operating system installed on a virtual machine.

host computer The physical computer on which virtual machine software is installed and virtual machines run.

hosted virtualization A system in which the hypervisor implements OS virtualization by being installed in a general-purpose host OS, such as Windows 10 or Linux, and the host OS accesses host hardware on behalf of the guest OS. See also *virtualization*.

hypervisor The component of virtualization software that creates and monitors the virtual hardware environment, which allows multiple VMs to share physical hardware resources.

infrastructure as a service (IaaS) A category of cloud computing in which a company can use a provider's storage or virtual servers as its needs demand; IaaS is also called *hosted infrastructure*.

platform as a service (PaaS) A category of cloud computing in which a customer develops applications with the service provider's development tools and infrastructure. After applications are developed, they can be delivered to the customer's users from the provider's servers. PaaS is also called *hosted platform*.

private cloud Cloud services that a company delivers to its own employees.

public cloud Cloud services delivered by a third-party provider.

snapshot A partial copy of a virtual machine made at a particular moment; it can be used to restore the virtual machine to its state when the snapshot was taken. See also *virtual machine (VM)*.

software as a service (SaaS) A category of cloud computing in which a customer pays for the use of applications that run on a service provider's network; SaaS is also called *hosted applications*.

virtual disk Files stored on the host computer that represent a virtual machine's hard disk.

virtual machine (VM) A software environment that emulates a physical computer's hardware and BIOS.

virtual network A network configuration created by virtualization software and used by virtual machines for network communication.

virtualization A process that creates a software environment to emulate a computer's hardware and BIOS, allowing multiple OSs to run on the same physical computer at the same time.

8

Review Questions

1. Which of the following can best be described as developing applications by using a service provider's development tools and infrastructure?
   a. hosted applications
   b. hosted networking
   c. hosted platforms
   d. hosted infrastructure
2. Which of the following is a partial copy of a VM made at a particular moment that enables you to restore the VM's state?
   a. incremental backup
   b. virtual disk
   c. load balancing
   d. snapshot
3. What can be defined as software that creates and monitors the virtual hardware environment?
   a. host computer
   b. hypervisor
   c. snapshot
   d. guest OS
4. Bare-metal virtualization is best for desktop virtualization. True or False?
5. If you want your virtual machine to have direct access to the physical network, which virtual network option should you configure?
   a. bridged
   b. NAT
   c. host-only
   d. internal

6. Which of the following is the virtual environment that emulates a physical computer's hardware and BIOS?
   a. virtual machine
   b. guest OS
   c. host computer
   d. snapshot
7. Which component of virtualization allows multiple VMs to share physical hardware resources?
   a. virtual machine
   b. snapshot
   c. host computer
   d. hypervisor
8. Which of the following is true about bare-metal virtualization?
   a. It supports a wider variety of guest OSs.
   b. It uses the host OS to access hardware.
   c. It uses a type 1 hypervisor.
   d. VMware Workstation Player is an example.
9. Which virtual network configuration shares an IP address with the host computer?
   a. bridged
   b. NAT
   c. host-only
   d. LAN segment
10. Which virtual network configuration is isolated from the host computer?
    a. bridged
    b. NAT
    c. host-only
    d. LAN segment
11. On which host OS can you run Hyper-V?
    a. Mac OS X
    b. Windows 10
    c. Ubuntu Linux
    d. Solaris

12. Which feature provided by some virtualization products allows you to move a VM to a new host computer while the VM is running?
    a. live migration
    b. snapshots
    c. VM cloning
    d. dynamic provisioning
13. Which of the following are reasons to use bare-metal virtualization?
    a. retiring old hardware
    b. reusing older computers
    c. reducing cooling
    d. reclaiming floor space
14. Which feature of some virtualization products allows you to deploy VMs and storage as needed and has uses in cloud computing?
    a. live migration
    b. snapshots
    c. VM cloning
    d. dynamic provisioning
15. When did Microsoft introduce the Hyper-V product?
    a. with Windows Server 2012
    b. with Windows Server 2008
    c. with Windows Vista
    d. with Windows 7
16. In which cloud computing model does Google Apps best fit?
    a. IaaS
    b. PaaS
    c. SaaS
    d. DaaS

Hands-On Projects

Project 8-1: Enable Hyper-V for Windows 10

In this project, you enable Hyper-V on a Windows 10 computer.

1. Start and log on to your Windows 10 computer.
2. Right-click **Start** and click **Control Panel**. In Control Panel, click **Programs**.
3. Under Programs and Features, click **Turn Windows features on or off**.

4. Click **Hyper-V** to select it. Click the plus sign to see the options under Hyper-V. You will enable the management tools and the Hyper-V platform. Click **OK**.
5. When prompted, click **Restart now** to finish the installation.
6. When Windows restarts, log on, click in the search box next to the Start button, and type **admin**. In the search results, click **Administrative Tools**.
7. In Administrative Tools, double-click **Hyper-V Manager**. In the next project, you will create a virtual machine and explore the settings. Leave Hyper-V Manager open if you are continuing to the next project.

Project 8-2: Create a VM in Hyper-V

You have installed the Hyper-V role on Windows 10 and are ready to create a virtual machine.

1. Log on to your Windows 10 computer and open Hyper-V Manager, if necessary. If your Windows 10 computer is not selected in the left pane, click **Connect to Server** in the Actions pane, click **Local computer**, and then click **OK**.
2. In the Actions pane, click **New**, and then click **Virtual Machine**.
3. Read the information in the Before You Begin window. You can create a default virtual machine simply by clicking Finish in this window, but for this activity, click **Next**.
4. In the Name text box, type **VMTest1**. You can choose a location to store the virtual machine configuration, but for this activity, accept the default location of C:\ProgramData\Microsoft\Windows\Hyper-V by clicking **Next**.
5. In the Specify Generation window, you choose whether to create a generation 1 or generation 2 virtual machine. Leave the default selection, **Generation 1**, and click **Next**.
6. In the Assign Memory window, type **512** in the Startup memory text box, and then click **Next**.
7. In the Configure Networking window, leave the default option, **Not Connected**. Click **Next**.
8. In the Connect Virtual Hard Disk window, you can enter the virtual hard disk's name, size, and location. By default, the size is 127 GB, and Hyper-V assigns the hard disk the same name as the VM, with the extension .vhdx. You can also use an existing virtual disk or attach one later. Write down the location where Hyper-V stores the virtual hard disk by default, in case you want to access the virtual disk later. Click **Next** to accept the default settings.
9. In the Installation Options window, click the **Install an operating system later** option button, if necessary. Click **Next**.
10. The Completing the New Virtual Machine Wizard window displays a summary of your virtual machine configuration. Click **Finish**. After the virtual machine is created,

you return to Hyper-V Manager and see your new VM in the Virtual Machines pane of Hyper-V Manager (see Figure 8-7).

11. Leave Hyper-V Manager open if you're continuing to the next activity.

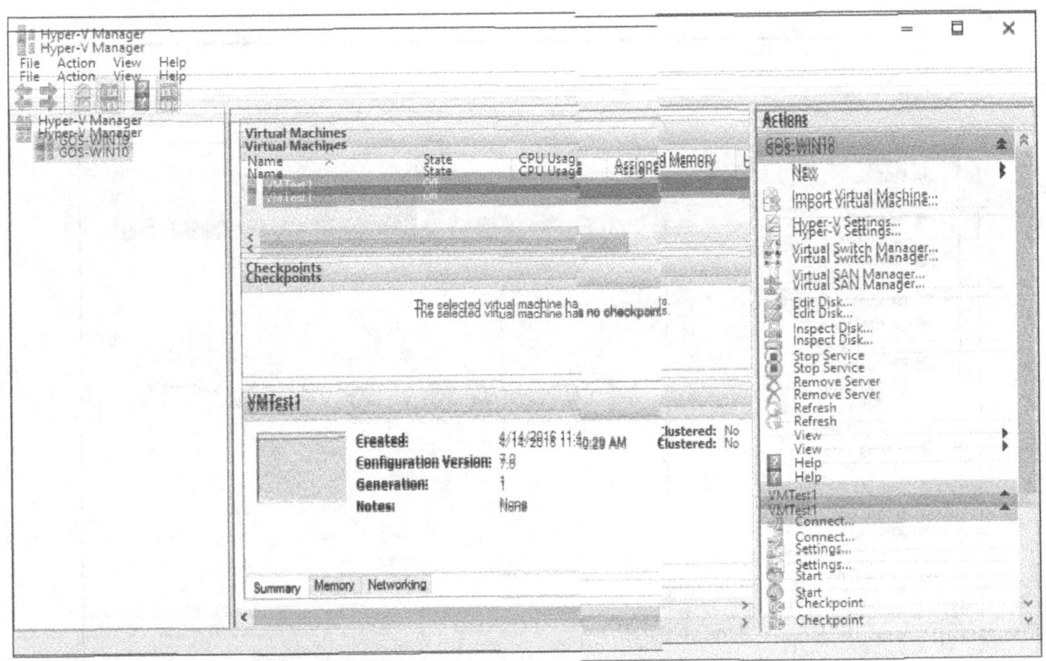

Figure 8-7 Hyper-V Manager with a VM

Project 8-3: Install Windows Server 2012 R2 in a VM

You have created a virtual machine and are ready to install Windows Server 2012 R2 as a guest OS using the installation DVD. You need the installation media for Windows Server 2012 R2.

You can download an ISO file for a trial version of Windows Server 2012 R2 from *https://www.microsoft.com/en-us/evalcenter/evaluate-windows-server-2012-r2*. Once downloaded, you can burn a DVD or attach the ISO file to the virtual DVD drive on your virtual machine. These steps assume you have an ISO file that you will attach to the VM's virtual DVD.

You can also use Windows Server 2016, if it's available, for this project. Only the preview was available at the time of this writing, so Windows Server 2012 was used.

1. Log on to your Windows 10 computer and open Hyper-V Manager, if necessary.
2. Click **VMTest1** in the Virtual Machines pane of Hyper-V Manager. In the Actions pane, click **Settings** under VMTest1 to open the Settings for VMTest1 window (see Figure 8-8).

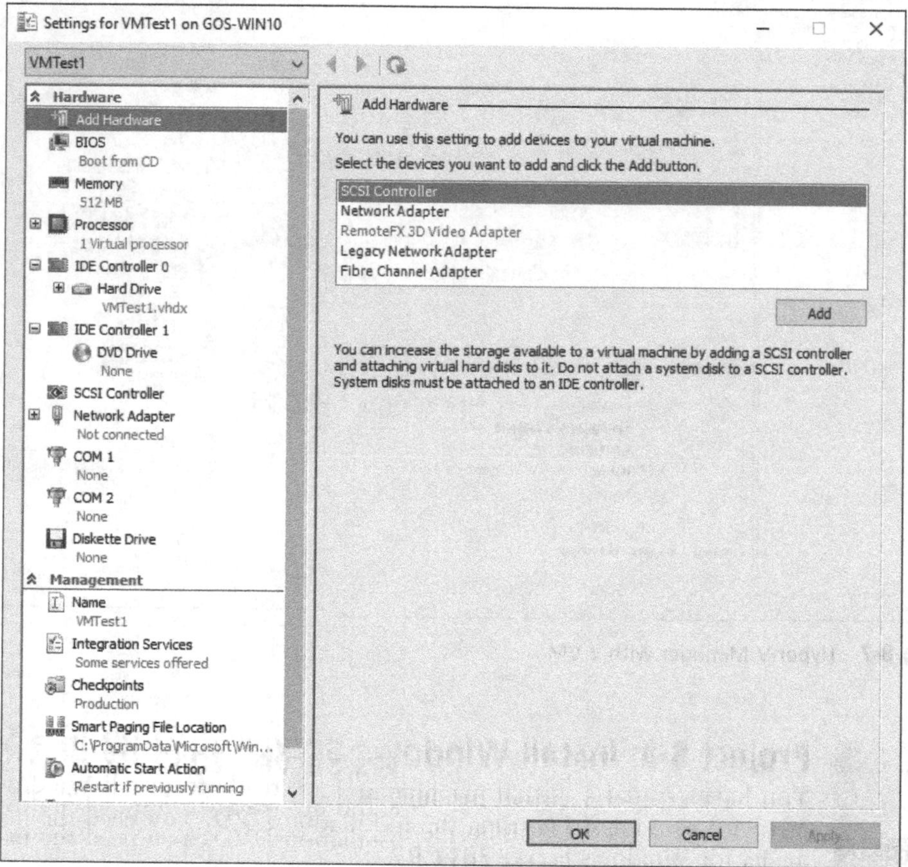

Figure 8-8 Settings for a Hyper-V VM

3. If you are using a physical DVD, skip to Step 4. Click **DVD Drive** in the left pane. In the right pane, click **Image file** and then click **Browse.** Locate and then click the Windows Server 2012 R2 ISO file. Click **Open.** Click **OK.**
4. Right-click the **VMTest1** virtual machine you created and click **Connect.**
5. Power on VMTest1 by clicking the **Start** toolbar icon or by clicking **Action** and then **Start** from the menu. While the computer is booting, close the Virtual Machine Connection console. Notice that in Hyper-V Manager, the VM's CPU use changes as the Windows installation starts, and the VM screen in the bottom pane changes periodically.

To see a description of any toolbar icon, hover your mouse pointer over it.

6. Double-click the VM screen at the bottom of Hyper-V Manager to open the Virtual Machine Connection console. Begin the installation of Windows Server 2012 R2 by clicking **Next** on the Windows Setup window. From here, the installation steps are the same as installing in a physical computer. As a reminder, review Project 5-6, which walked you through the process of installing Windows Server 2012 R2.
7. After Windows Server 2012 R2 is installed, close the Virtual Machine Connection console and shut down the virtual machine by right-clicking **VMTest1** and clicking **Shut Down.** Click **Shut Down** again to confirm, if necessary.
8. Leave Hyper-V Manager open if you're continuing to the next activity.

Project 8-4: Work with Virtual Machines in Hyper-V Manager

You have installed a test VM that you can use to become familiar with managing virtual machines in Windows Server 2012 R2. In the following steps, you create a checkpoint, make some changes to the OS, and revert to the checkpoint.

1. Log on to your Windows 10 computer and open Hyper-V Manager, if necessary.
2. Right-click **VMTest1** and click **Connect.**
3. Power on VMTest1 by clicking the **Start** toolbar icon.
4. After Windows Server 2012 R2 boots, log on and open Notepad, and then type your name in a new text document. Don't close Notepad or save the file yet. Click the **Save** toolbar icon or click **Action** and then **Save** from the menu of the Virtual Machine Connection console.
5. Close the Virtual Machine Connection console. In Hyper-V Manager, notice that the State column for the VM displays *Saved* or *Saving*. After the state has been saved, open the Virtual Machine Connection console by double-clicking **VMTest1.** Start the VM by clicking the **Start** toolbar icon. You're right where you left off in Notepad.
6. Save the Notepad file to your desktop as **file1.txt,** and then exit Notepad.
7. Click the **Checkpoint** toolbar icon or click **Action** and then **Checkpoint** from the menu. When prompted to enter a name for the checkpoint, type **BeforeDeletingFile1,** and then click **Yes.** In the status bar of the Virtual Machine Connection console, you see a progress bar that reads *Taking checkpoint.*
8. After the checkpoint is finished, minimize the VM, and note that the checkpoint is listed in the Checkpoints section of Hyper-V Manager. Maximize the VM, and delete the Notepad file you created. Empty the Recycle Bin to make sure the file is deleted.
9. Click the **Revert** toolbar icon or click **Action** and then **Revert** from the menu.

8

10. Click **Revert** when prompted. The VM displays a message that it's reverting. When the desktop is displayed again, you should see the Notepad file back on the desktop. Close the Virtual Machine Connection console.

11. In Hyper-V Manager, right-click **VMTest1** and click **Shut Down**. When prompted, click the **Shut Down** button. The Status column displays *Shutting Down Virtual Machine*.

12. After the VM state changes to Off, delete the checkpoint by right-clicking BeforeDeletingFile1 in the Checkpoints section and clicking **Delete Checkpoint**. Click Delete to confirm.

13. Close Hyper-V Manager, but stay logged on to Windows 10 if you are continuing to the next project.

Project 8-5: Download and Install VirtualBox

In this project, you download and install VirtualBox.

1. Log on to your Windows 10 computer, if necessary.
2. Start a Web browser, and go to www.virtualbox.org. In the left pane, click **Downloads**. Under VirtualBox binaries, click **VirtualBox *version* for Windows hosts**, where *version* is the current VirtualBox version.
3. After downloading the file, start the installation of VirtualBox. Follow the prompts and leave the default options selected.
4. When the installation is finished, VirtualBox should automatically start. If not, double-click the **Oracle VM VirtualBox** shortcut on your desktop to start Oracle VM VirtualBox Manager.
5. You're ready to create a virtual machine. Leave Oracle VM VirtualBox Manager running for the next project.

Project 8-6: Create a Virtual Machine in VirtualBox

In this project, you create a virtual machine in VirtualBox.

1. If necessary, start Oracle VM VirtualBox Manager.
2. Click **New** to start the Create Virtual Machine wizard.
3. In the "Name and operating system" window, type **VMTest2** in the Name text box.
4. Click the selection arrow next to the Type box, and review the guest OSs that are supported. Click **Microsoft Windows**.
5. Click the selection arrow next to the Version box and click the name of any OS. Click **Next**.
6. In the Memory size window, accept the default setting and click **Next**. In the Hard Disk window, accept the default setting and then click **Create**.

7. In the "Hard disk file type" window, accept the default setting and click **Next**. In the "Storage on physical disk" window, click **Next** to accept the default setting of Dynamically allocated.

8. Click **Create** in the "File location and size" window. The VM is created and you are returned to Oracle VM VirtualBox Manager.

9. Review the information displayed on the details screen (see Figure 8-9).

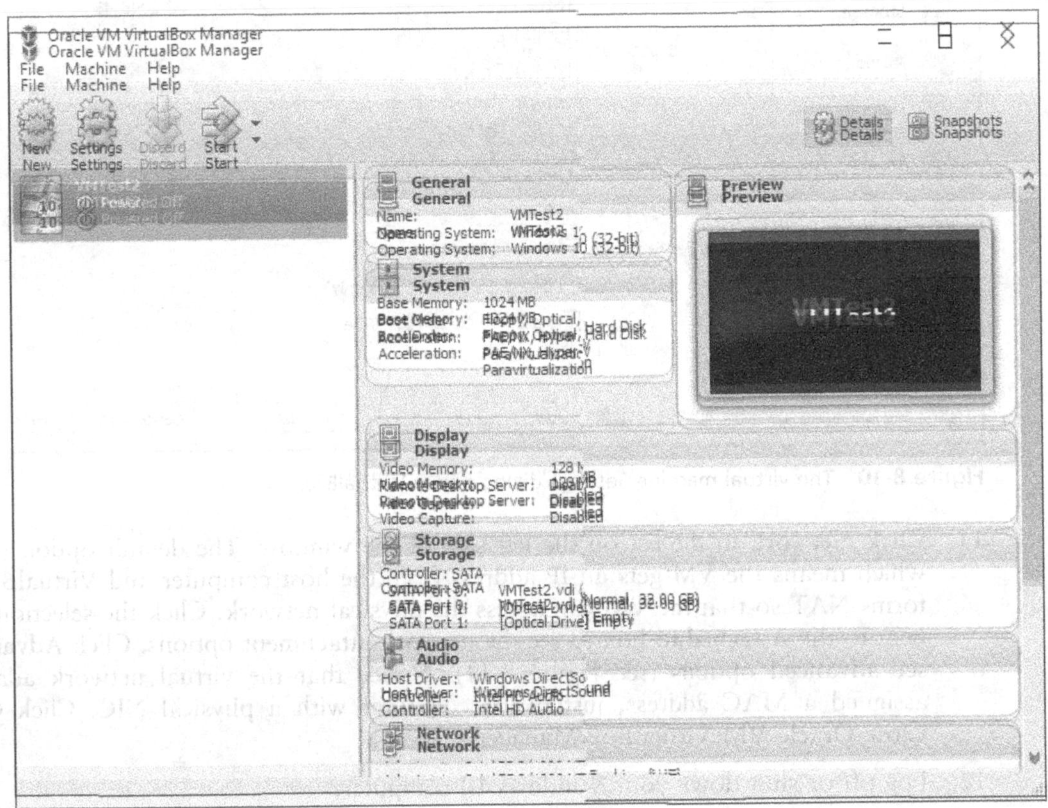

Figure 8-9 The VirtualBox details screen

10. Installing and working with a VM in VirtualBox is similar to the process in Hyper-V. You can connect the virtual DVD drive to an ISO file or boot from a physical DVD placed in the host. To see and change the VM's settings, right-click **VMTest2** in the left pane and click **Settings**. Select each setting in the left pane to see the configuration options for the VM (see Figure 8-10). In this dialog box, you can change the amount of memory allocated to the VM, change processor options, configure storage, change the virtual network settings, and configure many more settings. You can also add virtual hardware, such as hard disks and network adapters.

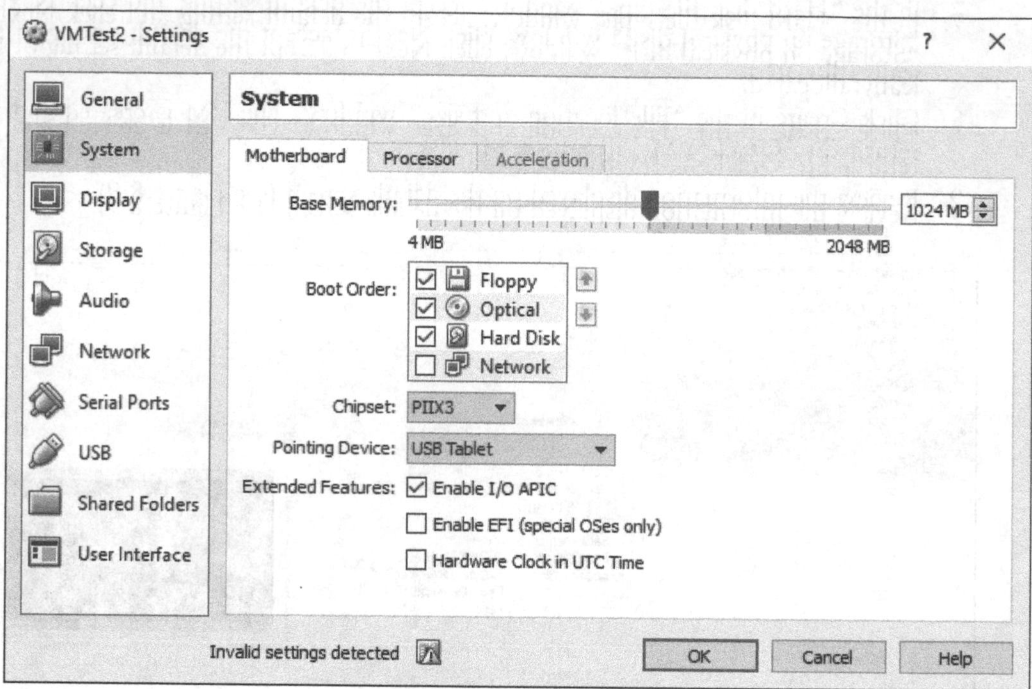

Figure 8-10 The virtual machine Settings dialog box in VirtualBox

11. Click **Network** in the list on the left side of the window. The default option is NAT, which means the VM gets an IP address from the host computer and VirtualBox performs NAT so that the VM can access the physical network. Click the selection arrow next to the **Attached to** box to see the network attachment options. Click **Advanced** to see advanced options (see Figure 8-11). Notice that the virtual network adapter is assigned a MAC address, just like a computer with a physical NIC. Click **Cancel.** Close Oracle VM VirtualBox Manager.

12. Log off or shut down your Windows 10 computer.

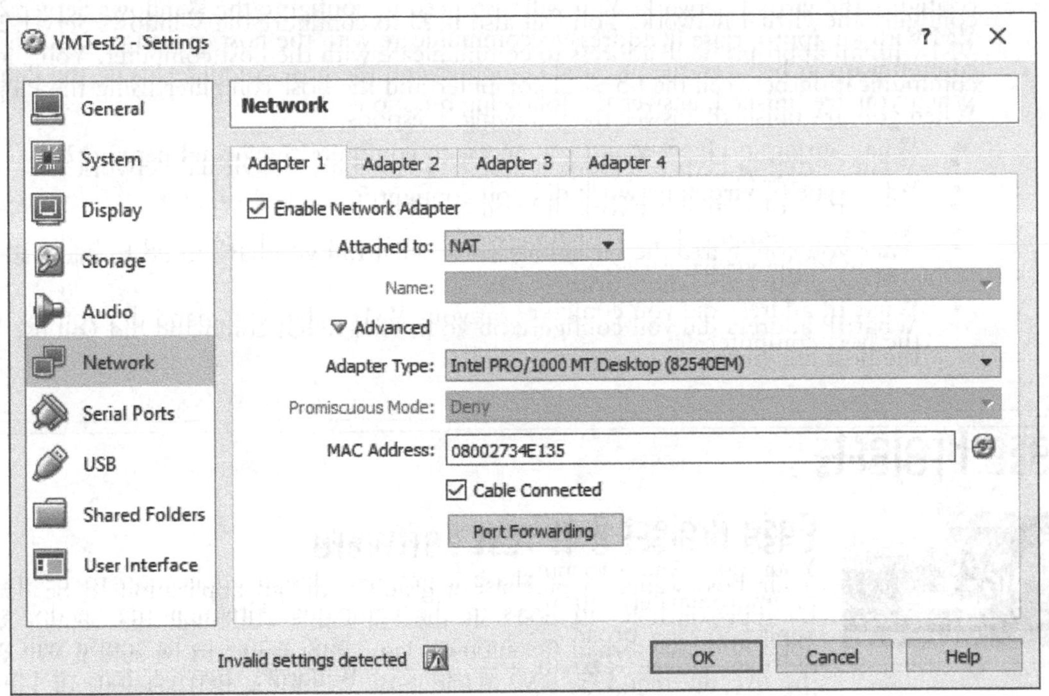

Figure 8-11 Advanced settings for network adapters in VirtualBox

Critical Thinking

The following activities give you critical thinking challenges. Challenge Labs give you an opportunity to use the skills you have learned to perform a task without step-by-step instructions. Case projects offer a practical problem for which you supply a written solution. Not all chapters contain Challenge Labs. There is not always a specific right or wrong answer to these critical thinking exercises. They are intended to encourage you to review the chapter material and delve deeper into the topics you have learned.

Challenge Labs

Challenge Lab 8-1: Configure Network Settings in Hyper-V

Your Windows Server 2012 R2 server is installed in a VM named VMTest1 that you created in the Hands-On Projects. You are ready to perform postinstallation tasks. One of the things you will need to do is configure the virtual network. Do a little research on configuring the virtual network in Hyper-V. Open Hyper-V Manager and study the configuration tasks you can perform in the Actions pane.

You should configure the virtual network so that VMs you are running in Hyper-V can communicate with each other and with the host computer. You will need to perform two steps to configure the virtual network. You will also need to configure the Windows Server 2012 R2 VM with an appropriate IP address to communicate with the host computer. You should test communication between the physical computer and the host computer using the Ping utility. When you are finished, answer the following questions:

- What setting in Hyper-V did you access to configure the virtual network?
- What type of virtual network did you configure?
- After you configured the virtual network, what did you have to do to make sure your VM used the virtual network?
- What IP address did you configure on your VM? What command did you use to ping the host computer?

Case Projects

Case Project 8-1: Test Software

Your boss wants to purchase a graphics design application to be distributed to approximately 40 users in the company. Although the vendor says the application has broad OS support, your boss wants to be sure it will work on the five different OSs (two versions of Windows, two versions of Linux, and the latest Mac OS X) running on the company's user workstations. He wants you to verify compatibility by using evaluation copies of the software without disrupting users or their computers. You have the installation disks for all five OSs your company uses, but you don't have a lot of computers available to install the OSs. What's your plan?

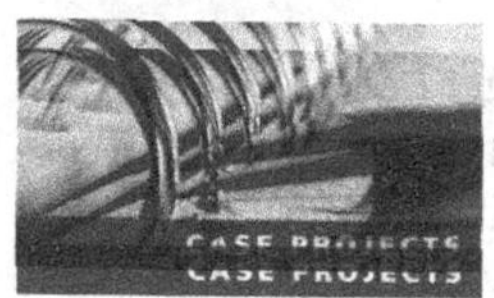

Case Project 8-2: A Small Business Startup IT Solution

You've been called in to consult with a small startup company that needs advice on how to set up its computer systems and network. The startup company does not have a lot of money to invest in the necessary IT infrastructure, but it will have 30 employees that use computers to run a variety of applications, many of which are server-based. The company wants to run Windows 10 and Mac OS X client stations, and it will need Windows Server and Red Hat Enterprise server. The company already has cabling and switches in place to connect its computers to a LAN, and it has a 50 Mbps Internet connection. What do you advise for this small business to satisfy its IT needs?

chapter 9

Configuring a Network Connection

After reading this chapter and completing the exercises, you will be able to:

- Explain the fundamentals of network communication
- Define common networking terms
- Compare and describe network device types
- Configure and describe network protocols
- Describe the OSI model of networking
- Configure networking in an operating system

In only a few decades, computer networks have evolved from a complex technology accessible to only the most tech-savvy users to being part of most people's everyday lives. Computer networks can be found in almost every business, school, and home. Their use is available to anyone with a computer and a network connection, but installation and upkeep of all but the smallest networks still require considerable know-how. This chapter starts you on the path toward acquiring the skills you need to work with network devices and configure an operating system to work in a network. Proper configuration of an operating system in a network is paramount to your overall understanding of operating systems. You cannot properly configure and troubleshoot the operation of a client or server computer in a network unless you have a solid understanding of the technologies and protocols used in building a network and connecting devices to a network.

This chapter begins by discussing the fundamentals of network communication. Many new terms are introduced and defined, and you will learn the fundamentals of the TCP/IP protocol and the OSI model of networking.

The Fundamentals of Network Communication

A computer **network** consists of two or more computers connected by some kind of transmission medium, such as a cable or airwaves. After they're connected, correctly configured computers can communicate with one another. The primary motivations for networking are to share resources, such as printers and hard drives; to share information, such as word-processing files; and to communicate by using applications such as e-mail. These motivations are important, especially for businesses, but another motivating factor for both businesses and home users is to "get online"—to access the Internet. The Internet, with its wealth of information, disinformation, fun, and games, has had a tremendous impact on how and why networks are used. Indeed, many of the networking technologies described in this book were developed as a result of the Internet explosion.

You might know how to use a network already; in particular, you probably know how to use programs that access the Internet, such as Web browsers and e-mail programs. To understand *how* networks work, however, you need to learn about the underlying technologies and processes used when you open a Web browser or an e-mail program. A good place to start is with the components that help turn a stand-alone computer into a networked computer.

Network Components

Imagine a computer with no networking hardware or software. It's hard to imagine now, but a computer's main purpose once was to run applications such as word processors and spreadsheets, not Web browsers and e-mail. Such computers had neither the hardware nor software needed to run networked programs, which is why they were called **stand-alone computers**. If you wanted to network a computer, you had to add these required components:

- *Network interface card (NIC)*—A NIC (pronounced *nick*) is an add-on card that's plugged into a motherboard expansion slot and provides a connection between the computer and the network. Most computers have a NIC built into the motherboard, so an additional card is not necessary.

- *Network medium*—This cable plugs into the NIC and makes the connection between a computer and the rest of the network. In networks with just two computers, the other end of the cable can plug into the second computer's NIC. More likely, the other end of the cable plugs into an interconnecting device that accommodates several computer connections. Network media can also be airwaves, as in wireless networks. In this case, the connection is made between the antenna on the NIC and the antenna on another NIC or interconnecting device.
- *Interconnecting device*—Although this component isn't always necessary because two computers can be connected directly with a cable and small wireless networks can be configured without an interconnecting device, most networks include one or several of these components. They allow computers to communicate on a network without being connected directly. Interconnecting devices include switches, hubs, routers, and wireless access points. A small network connected to a switch is shown in Figure 9-1.

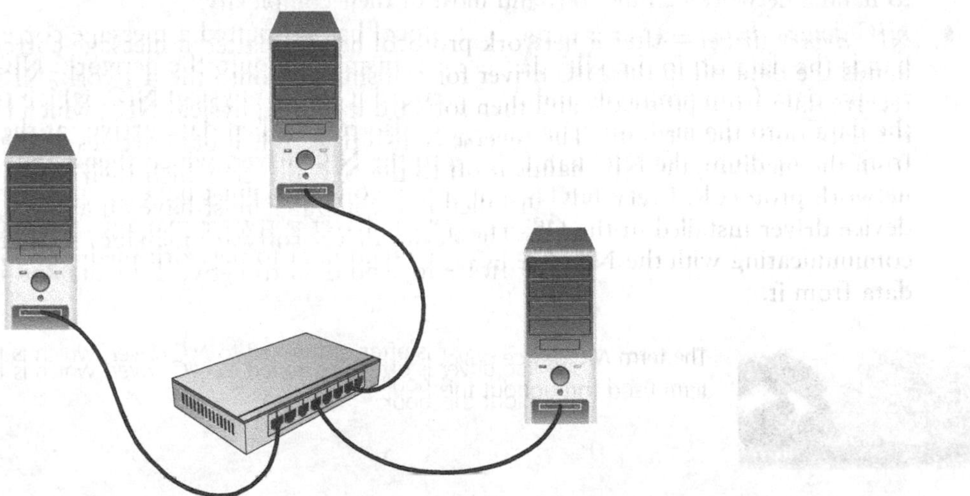

Figure 9-1 A network of computers connected to a switch

The preceding hardware components make a stand-alone computer into a networked computer, but software is also needed to interact with network hardware and communicate with other computers on the network. Network software transforms a stand-alone OS into a network OS. It's the software that allows a word-processing program to open a document on a server and knows how to request a Web page or send an e-mail. It's also the software that communicates between the OS and network hardware. Network software can be divided into the following categories:

- *Network clients and servers*—**Network client software** requests information that's stored on another network computer or device. **Network server software** allows a computer to share its resources by responding to resource requests generated by network clients. Network client software can be an integral part of well-known applications, such as Web browsers and e-mail programs. A Web browser, for example, sends a request for a Web page to a Web server. Network client software can also run in the background, usually when installed as a networking service. In such cases, it enables programs without built-in client software to access shared network resources on other computers. For example, Client for Microsoft Networks, which is installed automatically in Windows, allows a word-processing program to open a file that's shared on another Windows computer or print to a printer attached to another Windows computer. In this setup, server software called File and Printer Sharing for Microsoft Networks receives the request from the client and provides access to the shared file or printer.

- *Protocols*—When clients and servers need to send information on the network, they must pass it to network protocols, which define the rules and formats a computer must use when sending information across the network. A network protocol can be likened to a human language: Just as two people communicate by speaking the same language, two computers communicate by using the same protocol. An example of a network protocol is TCP/IP. Network protocols perform all the behind-the-scenes tasks required to handle networking functions and most of their complexity.
- *NIC device driver*—After a network protocol has formatted a message correctly, it hands the data off to the NIC driver for transmission onto the network. NIC drivers receive data from protocols and then forward it to the physical NIC, which transmits the data onto the medium. The reverse is also true. When data arrives at the NIC from the medium, the NIC hands it off to the NIC driver, which then hands it off to network protocols. Every NIC installed in a computer must have an associated device driver installed in the OS. The device driver software manages the details of communicating with the NIC hardware to send data to network media and receive data from it.

The term *NIC device driver* is often shortened to *NIC driver*, which is the term used throughout this book.

Each of these software components plays a role in the steps of network communication, as described in the next section.

Steps of Network Communication

Most network communication starts with a user who needs to access a resource on another computer, such as a Web server or file server. A user's attempt to access network resources is summarized in these basic steps:

1. An application tries to access a network resource by attempting to send a message to it.
2. Network client software detects the attempt to access the network. Client software formats the message generated by the application and passes the message on to the network protocol.
3. The protocol packages the message in a format suitable for the network and sends it to the NIC driver.
4. The NIC driver sends the data in the request to the NIC, which converts it into the necessary signals to be transmitted across the network medium.

Remember that there are two sides to a communication session—a client tries to access network resources and a server provides those resources. The steps taken on the server side are essentially the reverse of those on the client side:

1. The NIC on the server receives signals from the network medium and converts them into message data, which is read by the NIC driver.
2. The NIC driver passes the message to the network protocol.
3. The network protocol determines which server software the message is targeting and passes the message to the designated software. Remember that a computer can have many clients and servers running at the same time. For example, a computer running Windows Server 2016 might be acting both as a mail server and as a file server. Each server function requires different server software.
4. The server software receives the message and responds by sending the requested data to the client computer, using the steps outlined previously.

Layers of the Network Communication Process

Each step a client takes to access network resources is often referred to as a *layer* in the network communication process. Each layer has a specific function, and all the layers work together. Figure 9-2 and Table 9-1 depict this process. Keep in mind that the previous steps simplified the communication process, which is one reason the layered approach is so effective: Complex concepts can be described in simple steps.

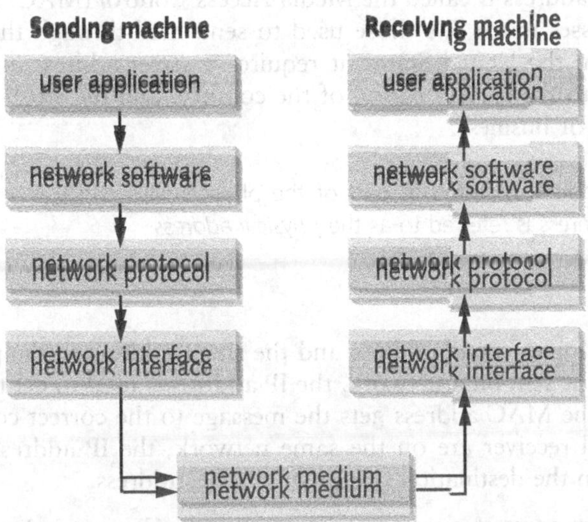

Figure 9-2 Layers of the network communication process

Table 9-1 Layers of the network communication process

Step	Description	Layer
1	An application tries to access a network resource.	User application
2	Client software detects the attempt to access the network and passes the message on to the network protocol.	Network client or server software
3	The protocol packages the message in a format suitable for the network and sends it to the NIC driver.	Network protocol
4	The NIC driver sends the data in the request to the NIC, which converts it into the necessary signals to be transmitted across the network medium.	Network interface

The four steps outlined in Table 9-1 give you a basic understanding of the layered approach to networking. A more detailed model for network communication—a universal standard for teaching and designing network communication called the *OSI model*—is discussed later in this chapter.

How Two Computers Communicate on a LAN

The layers of the network communication process provide an overview of how network communication works. However, there are few details on what each layer accomplishes. This discussion focuses on computer addresses and how they're used during network communication.

In a network that uses a protocol such as TCP/IP (the most common network protocol), computers have two addresses: a logical address and a physical address. The logical address is the IP address, and the physical address is called the Media Access Control (MAC) address. You can look at these two addresses much like those used to send mail through the postal system. When a letter is mailed in the United States, it requires a street address and a zip code. The zip code gets the letter to the correct region of the country, and the street address gets the letter to the correct home or business.

The MAC address is stored as part of the physical NIC, which is why the MAC address is referred to as the *physical address*.

You can liken the zip code to the logical or IP address and the street address to the physical or MAC address. When a message is sent on a network, the IP address is used to get the message to the correct network, and the MAC address gets the message to the correct computer on the network. If the sender and receiver are on the same network, the IP address in the message is used mainly to ascertain the destination computer's MAC address.

For example, Figure 9-3 shows two computers connected to a switch. Computer A wants to communicate with Computer B. One of the simplest forms of communication is a *ping* command, which sends a message from one computer to another, essentially asking the other computer whether it's listening on the network. If a computer receives a ping, it replies so that the sending computer knows the message was received. It's like the cell phone commercial in which the caller asks, "Can you hear me now?" Here are the steps of this communication process:

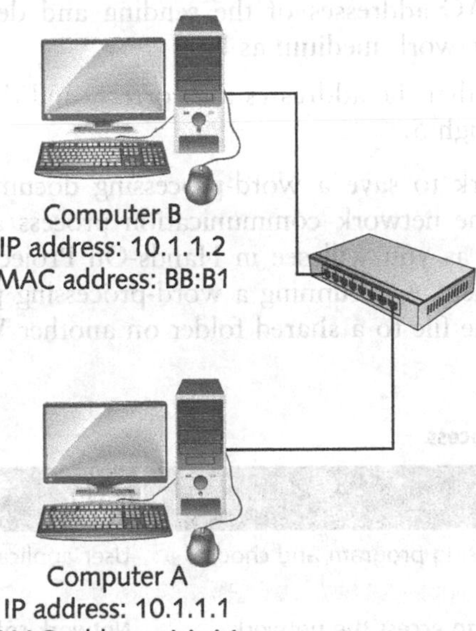

Figure 9-3 Communication between two computers

1. A user at Computer A types *ping 10.1.1.2* (the IP address of Computer B) at a command prompt.
2. The network software creates a ping message.
3. The network protocol packages the message by adding IP addresses of the sending and destination computers and acquires the destination computer's MAC address.
4. The network interface software adds MAC addresses of the sending and destination computers and sends the message to the network medium as bits.
5. Computer B receives the message, verifies that the addresses are correct, and then sends a reply to Computer A using Steps 2 through 4.

Users don't usually initiate network communication by using a computer's IP address; instead, they use the computer name. However, just as you can't mail a letter with only the recipient's name, you can't communicate over a network with only the computer's name. You certainly know the name of the person you're writing to, but you might have to look up his or her address before you can address the envelope. Similarly, computers use an address book of sorts, called a **name server**, to get a computer's IP address when the name is known. TCP/IP provides name server functions through its Domain Name System (DNS). With this information in mind, the preceding steps can be expanded as follows:

1. A user at Computer A types *ping Computer B* at a command prompt.
2. A name lookup is done to retrieve Computer B's IP address.

3. The network software creates a ping message.
4. The network protocol packages the message by adding IP addresses of the sending and destination computers and acquires the destination computer's MAC address.
5. The network interface software adds MAC addresses of the sending and destination computers and sends the message to the network medium as bits.
6. Computer B receives the message, verifies that the addresses are correct, and then sends a reply to Computer A using Steps 3 through 5.

Next, examine an example of using a network to save a word-processing document to a Windows server and see how the layers of the network communication process are used. Several components are involved in this task, as you will see in Hands-On Project 9-3. In the example shown in Table 9-2, a user at Client A is running a word-processing program, such as Microsoft Word, and wants to save the file to a shared folder on another Windows computer named Server X.

Table 9-2 Saving a file with the network communication process

Step	Description	Layer
1	The user on Client A clicks Save in the word-processing program and chooses a shared folder on Server X to save the file.	User application
2	Client for Microsoft Networks detects the attempt to access the network, formats the message, and passes the message to the network protocol.	Network software
3	The network protocol (in this case, TCP/IPv4) packages the message in a format suitable for the network interface and sends it to the NIC driver.	Network protocol
4	The NIC driver sends the data in the request to the NIC (in this case, Ethernet0), which converts it into signals to be transmitted across the network medium.	Network interface
5	Server X's NIC receives the message from the network medium, processes it, and sends the data to TCP/IPv4.	Network interface
6	TCP/IPv4 on Server X receives the message from the NIC, processes it, and sends the data to the network software (in this case, File and Printer Sharing for Microsoft Networks).	Network protocol
7	File and Printer Sharing for Microsoft Networks formats the message and requests that the OS save the file to the disk.	Network software

In Table 9-2, there's no "User application" step on the server. When a server is involved, the last step is typically handled by network software, such as File and Printer Sharing for Microsoft Networks, a Web server, or other server software.

Now that you have an idea of how network communication occurs, you can learn some common terms for describing networks and network components in the next section. Along the way, you see more illustrations of different types of networks.

Network Terminology

Every profession has its own language with its own terms and acronyms. Learning this language is half the battle of becoming proficient in a profession, and it's no different in computer and networking technology. The following sections explain some common terms used in discussing computer networks. Because some of these terms are associated with network diagrams, a number of figures are included to show different ways of depicting networks.

LANs, Internetworks, WANs, and MANs

A small network that is limited to a single collection of machines and connected by one or more interconnecting devices in a small geographic area is called a **local area network (LAN)**. LANs also form the building blocks for larger networks called *internetworks*. In Figure 9-4, the computers in a LAN are interconnected by a switch; Figure 9-5 shows a wireless LAN.

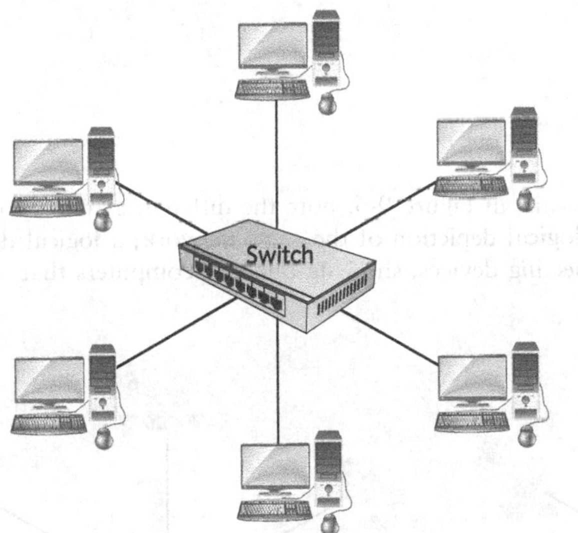

Figure 9-4 A LAN with computers interconnected by a switch

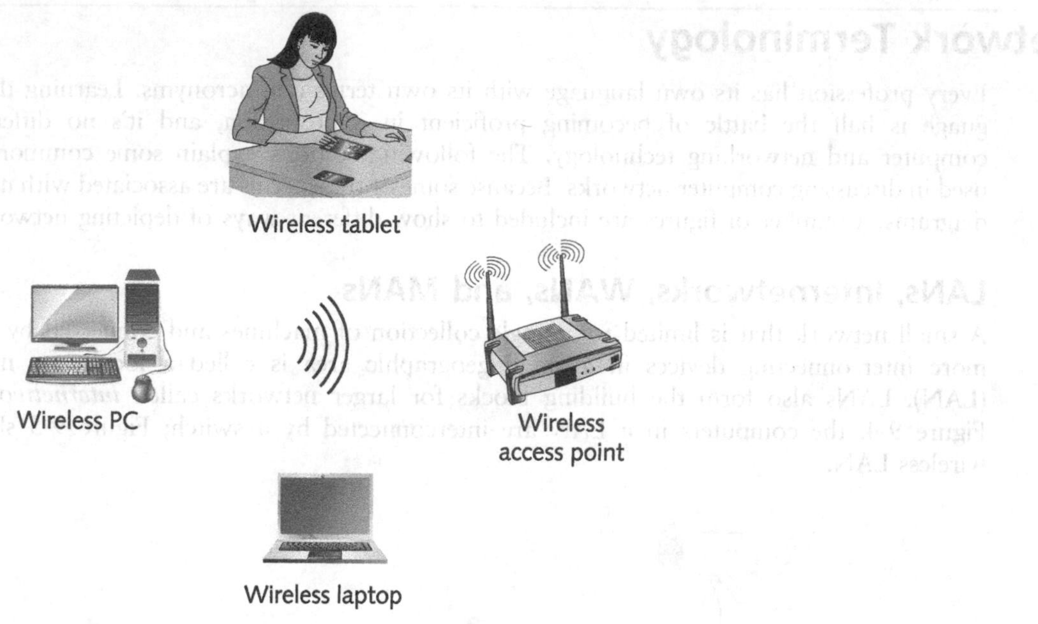

Figure 9-5 A wireless LAN

LANs are represented in other ways, as in Figure 9-6; note the different symbols for a hub and a switch. Figure 9-7 shows a logical depiction of the same network; a logical depiction leaves out details such as interconnecting devices, showing only the computers that make up the network.

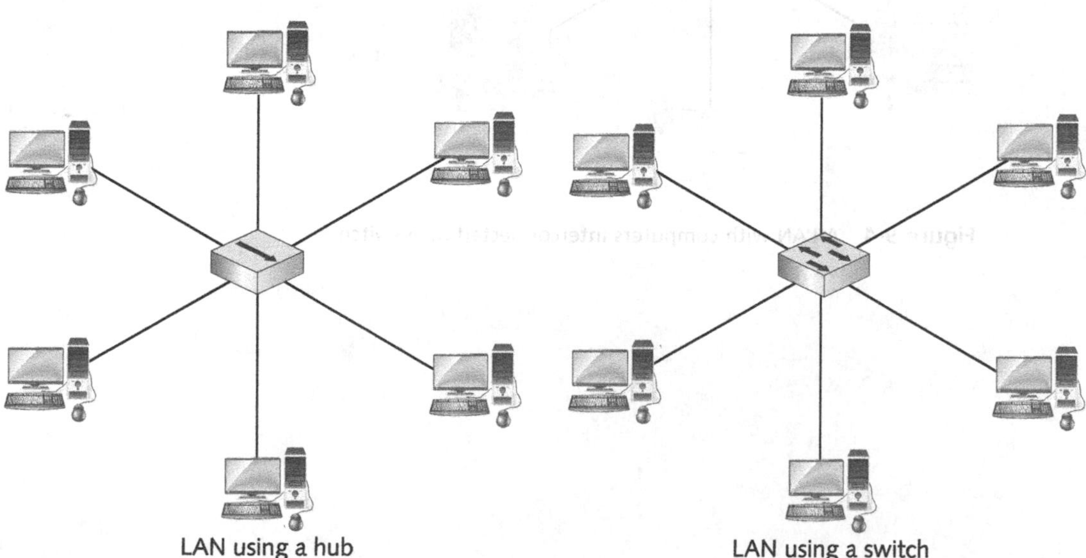

Figure 9-6 A LAN with a symbolic hub (left) and a symbolic switch (right)

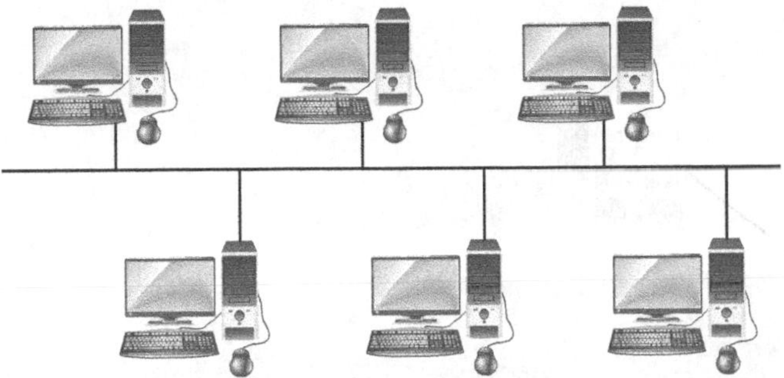

Figure 9-7 A logical depiction of a LAN

An **internetwork** is a networked collection of LANs tied together by devices such as routers, as discussed later in this chapter. Figure 9-8 shows two LANs interconnected by a router, which is represented by the standard symbol. Internetworks are usually created for the following reasons:

- Two or more groups of users and their computers should be logically separated on the network, yet the groups should be able to communicate. For example, in a school, you might want to logically separate the LAN that contains student computers from the LAN that contains faculty computers. Routers provide this logical separation but still allow communication between groups.
- The number of computers in a single LAN has grown to the point that network communication is no longer efficient. The nature of certain network protocols and devices makes network communication increasingly less efficient as the number of computers on a LAN grows. Routers can be used to separate the computers into two or more smaller LANs, thereby increasing communication efficiency.
- The distance between two groups of computers exceeds the capabilities of most LAN devices, such as switches. This problem can occur, for example, when a company occupies multiple buildings or multiple floors in a building. Routers are often used to communicate between groups of computers that are separated geographically.

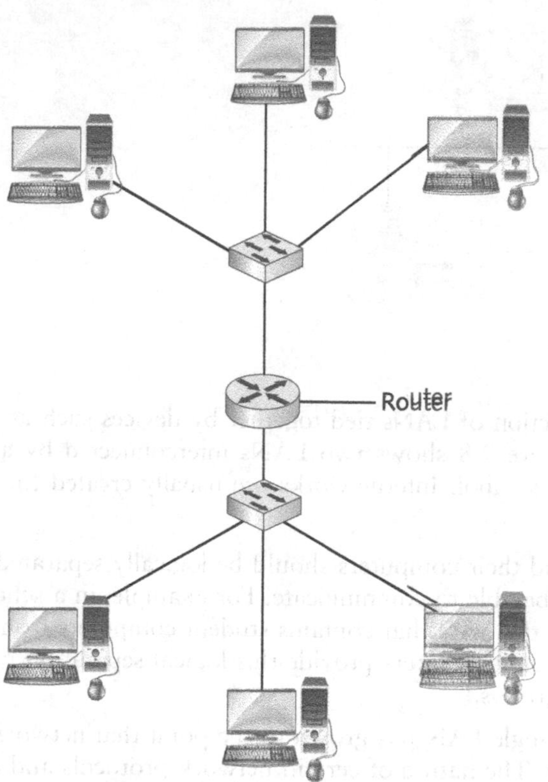

Figure 9-8 An internetwork with two LANs connected by a router

You might not realize it, but your home computer is probably part of an internetwork. Every time you go online to browse the Web or check your e-mail, your computer or LAN becomes part of the world's largest internetwork: the Internet.

As a network's scope expands to encompass LANs in geographically dispersed locations, internetworks become classified as **wide area networks (WANs)**. A WAN spans distances measured in miles and links separate LANs. WANs use the services of third-party communication providers, such as phone companies, to carry network traffic from one location to another. So, although both internetworks and WANs connect LANs, the difference lies mainly in the LANs' proximity to each other and the technologies used to communicate between LANs. Therefore, the Internet is both an internetwork and, because it spans the globe, a very large WAN.

Occasionally, you might encounter a network type called a **metropolitan area network** (MAN). MANs use WAN technologies to interconnect LANs in a specific geographic region, such as a county or city. It's not uncommon to find large, complex networks that use all four network types: LANs and internetworks for purely local access, MANs for regional or city-wide access, and WANs for access to remote sites elsewhere in the country or around the world. For example, consider a nationwide bank. The main branch in a large city has a building with multiple floors and hundreds of computers. Each floor constitutes a LAN, and these LANs are connected to form an internetwork. The internetwork at the main branch is connected to other branches throughout the city to form a MAN. In addition, the main branch is connected to other branches in other cities and states to form a WAN.

In network drawings, WANs are often shown with a jagged or thunderbolt-shaped line to represent the connection between two devices, usually routers, and the Internet is usually represented as a cloud. A cloud is used to obscure the details of a large network, as if to say "There's some collection of networks and network devices, but the details aren't important." Figure 9-9 shows a WAN connection between two routers and with a connection to the Internet. A grouping of three computers is often used to represent multiple computers on a LAN when the exact number doesn't matter.

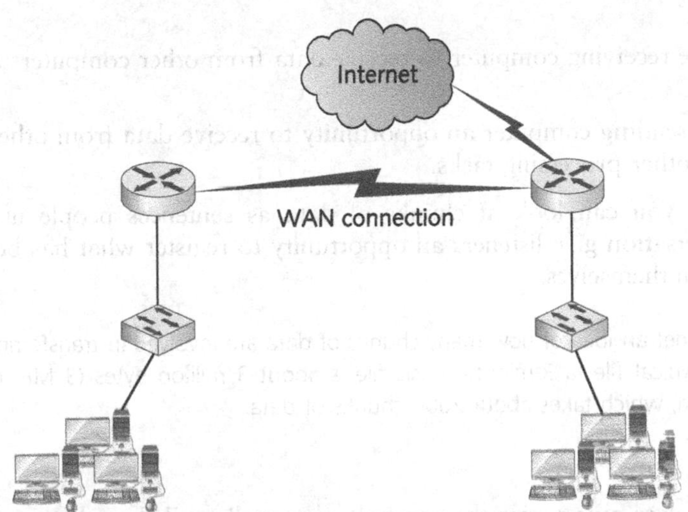

Figure 9-9 A WAN with a connection to the Internet

Internet, Intranet, and Extranet

The Internet is a worldwide public internetwork that uses standard protocols, such as TCP/IP, DNS, and HTTP, to transfer and view information. It's a public network because devices such as routers and Web servers that make up much of the network are accessible directly through an IP address. An intranet, on the other hand, is a private network, such as a school or company network, in which the devices and servers are available only to users connected to the internal network. Many of the same protocols and technologies used on the Internet are used to access information on an intranet. An extranet sits somewhere between the Internet and an intranet. It allows limited and controlled access to internal network resources by outside users. It's used when two organizations need to share resources, so controls are put in place to allow the organizations to access resources without making them available to the wider Internet.

Packets and Frames

When computers transfer information across a network, they do so in short bursts of about 1500 bytes of data. Each burst, or chunk, of data has the same basic structure; specifically, each chunk of data contains the MAC addresses and IP addresses of both the sending (source) and receiving (destination) computers. So, to transfer a small word-processing file, only one burst of data transfer might be needed, but large photo or music files are first divided into several hundred or even thousands of chunks before they're transferred. After each chunk of data is sent, the computer pauses momentarily. Data is transferred in this way for a number of reasons:

- If an error occurs during transmission of a large file, only the chunks of data involved in the error have to be sent again, not the entire file.
- The pause between bursts might be necessary to allow other computers to transfer data during pauses.
- The pause allows the receiving computer to process received data, such as writing it to disk.
- The pause allows the receiving computer to receive data from other computers at the same time.
- The pause gives the sending computer an opportunity to receive data from other computers and perform other processing tasks.

To use another analogy, you can look at chunks of data as sentences people use when speaking. Pauses in conversation give listeners an opportunity to register what has been said and possibly get a word in themselves.

To get an idea of how many chunks of data are involved in transferring a typical file, a 3-minute music file is about 3 million bytes (3 MB) of data, which takes about 2000 chunks of data.

Packets The chunks of data sent across the network are usually called *packets* or *frames*. Packet, the more well-known term, is often used generically, but it does have a particular meaning: It's a chunk of data with source and destination IP addresses (as well as other IP protocol information) added to it. Figure 9-10 shows a representation of data to be transferred, and Figure 9-11 shows the packets created after the data has been broken into chunks and IP addresses added.

Lorem ipsum dolor sit amet, consectetuer adipiscing elit. Maecenas porttitor congue massa. Fusce posuere, magna sed pulvinar ultricies, purus lectus malesuada libero, sit amet commodo magna eros quis urna.

Nunc viverra imperdiet enim. Fusce est. Vivamus a tellus.

Pellentesque habitant morbi tristique senectus et netus et malesuada fames ac turpis egestas.

Proin pharetra nonummy pede. Mauris et orci.

Lorem ipsum dolor sit amet, consectetuer adipiscing elit. Maecenas porttitor congue massa. Fusce posuere, magna sed pulvinar ultricies, purus lectus malesuada libero, sit amet commodo magna eros quis urna.

Nunc viverra imperdiet enim. Fusce est. Vivamus a tellus.

Pellentesque habitant morbi tristique senectus et netus et malesuada fames ac turpis egestas.

Proin pharetra nonummy pede. Mauris et orci.

Lorem ipsum dolor sit amet, consectetuer adipiscing elit. Maecenas porttitor congue massa. Fusce posuere, magna sed pulvinar ultricies, purus lectus malesuada libero, sit amet commodo magna eros quis urna.

Nunc viverra imperdiet enim. Fusce est. Vivamus a tellus.

Pellentesque habitant morbi tristique senectus et netus et malesuada fames ac turpis egestas. Proin pharetra nonummy pede. Mauris et orci.

Figure 9-10 Original data

Dest: IP: 172.16.1.2, Source IP: 172.16.1.1	Lorem ipsum dolor sit amet, consectetuer adipiscing elit. Maecenas porttitor congue massa. Fusce posuere, magna sed pulvinar ultricies.
Dest: IP: 172.16.1.2, Source IP: 172.16.1.1	purus lectus malesuada libero, sit amet commodo magna eros quis urna. Nunc viverra imperdiet enim. Fusce est. Vivamus a tellus.
Dest: IP: 172.16.1.2, Source IP: 172.16.1.1	Pellentesque habitant morbi tristique senectus et netus et malesuada fames ac turpis egestas. Proin pharetra nonummy pede. Mauris et orci
Dest: IP: 172.16.1.2, Source IP: 172.16.1.1	Lorem ipsum dolor sit amet, consectetuer adipiscing elit. Maecenas porttitor congue massa. Fusce posuere, magna sed pulvinar ultricies
Dest: IP: 172.16.1.2, Source IP: 172.16.1.1	Pellentesque habitant tristique senectus et netus et malesuada fames ac turpis egestas. Proin pharetra nonummy pede. Mauris et orci.

Figure 9-11 Data divided into several packets

Using the U.S. mail analogy, you can look at a packet as an envelope with the zip code added but not the street address. In relation to the layers of the network communication process, packets are generated and processed by the network protocol.

Frames A frame is a packet with the source and destination MAC addresses added to it. In addition, frames have an error-checking code added to the back end of the packet, so the packet is "framed" by MAC addresses (and other network interface information) on one end and an error-checking code on the other. A frame is like a letter that's addressed, stamped, and ready to deliver.

Frames are essentially the final state of data before it's placed on the network medium as bits. The network interface is the layer of the network communication process that works with frames. Figure 9-12 shows what the packets from Figure 9-11 look like after the frame information is added.

Dest MAC, Source MAC	Dest IP, Source IP	Lorem ipsum dolor sit amet, consectetuer adipiscing elit. Maecenas porttitor congue massa. Fusce posuere, magna sed pulvinar ultricies,	Error check
Dest MAC, Source MAC	Dest IP, Source IP	purus lectus malesuada libero, sit amet commodo magna eros quis urna. Nunc viverra imperdiet enim. Fusce est. Vivamus a tellus.	Error check
Dest MAC, Source MAC	Dest IP, Source IP	Pellentesque habitant morbi tristique senectus et netus et malesuada fames ac turpis egestas. Proin pharetra nonummy pede. Mauris et orci	Error check
Dest MAC, Source MAC	Dest IP, Source IP	Lorem ipsum dolor sit amet, consectetuer adipiscing elit. Maecenas porttitor congue massa. Fusce posuere, magna sed pulvinar ultricies	Error check
Dest MAC, Source MAC	Dest IP, Source IP	Pellentesque habitant tristique senectus et netus et malesuada fames ac turpis egestas. Proin pharetra nonummy pede. Mauris et orci.	Error check

Figure 9-12 The packets are now frames and ready for delivery

The error-checking code at the end of a frame is called a *cyclical redundancy check* (CRC).

The process of adding IP addresses and then MAC addresses to chunks of data is called encapsulation. Information added at the front of data is called a header, and information added at the end of data is called a trailer. Data is encapsulated several times as it works its way down from the sending application and makes it to the network interface as a frame. When the destination computer receives the frame, the process is reversed as the network interface de-encapsulates the frame (has the header and trailer removed) so that it becomes a packet again. This process continues until the packet arrives at the receiving application or service as the original data. This process is all part of the layered approach to networking.

Clients and Servers

You've already learned about the role of client network software and server network software. Unfortunately, the world of networking sometimes uses the same terms to discuss two different things. The following sections clarify what these terms mean and how their meanings can differ depending on how they're used.

Client A client, in networking terms, can be a workstation running a client OS, such as Windows 10, or the network software on a computer that requests network resources from a server. In addition, you can refer to a physical computer as a client computer. The meaning of *client*, therefore, depends on the context in which it's used. To clarify, it's typically used in the following three contexts:

- *Client operating system*—The OS installed on a computer is designed mainly to access network resources, even though it might be capable of sharing its own resources. Windows 10 and Mac OS X fit this description, for example, as do certain distributions of Linux. A client OS is also often referred to as a *desktop OS*.
- *Client computer*—This computer's primary role in a network is to run user applications and access network resources. Most computers in a network fit this description.
- *Client software*—This software requests network resources from server software running on another computer. For example, a Web browser, an e-mail client (such as Microsoft Outlook), and Client for Microsoft Networks fit into this category.

Server When most people hear the word *server*, they conjure up visions of a large tower computer with lots of hard drives and memory. This image is merely a computer hardware configuration that may or may not be used as a server, however. In short, a computer becomes a server when software is installed on it that provides a network service to client computers. In other words, you can install certain software on an inexpensive laptop computer and make it act as a server. By the same token, a huge tower computer with six hard drives and 128 GB of RAM can be used as a workstation for a single user. So, although some hardware configurations are packaged to function as a server, and others are packaged as client or desktop computers, what makes a computer a server is the software installed on it. Just as there are three contexts in which the term *client* is used, so it is with the term *server*:

- *Server operating system*—This term is used when the OS installed on a computer is designed mainly to share network resources and provide other network services. A server OS is tuned to be able to share files efficiently and perform network operations in response to client requests, even though the OS might also be able to run user applications and client software. Windows Server 2012, Mac OS X Server, UNIX, and many Linux distributions fit this description.
- *Server computer*—This term is used when a computer's primary role in the network is to give client computers access to network resources and services. The computers that most often fit this description are usually in the IT room or locked away in a closet.
- *Server software*—This software responds to requests for network resources from client software running on another computer. A Web server (such as Internet Information Services), an e-mail server (such as Microsoft Exchange), and File and Printer Sharing for Microsoft Networks fit into this category.

Microsoft refers to server software components as *services*. Other OSs use other terms; for example, in Linux/UNIX, server software components are referred to as *daemons*.

As you can see, the lines between a client computer and a server computer are often blurred because OSs are designed as network operating systems, and most can take on the roles of both server and client. As you're learning, however, the language of networking is often imprecise, and you must pay attention to the context in which networking terms are used to grasp their meaning. As you get more comfortable with all the terms and better understand how networks work, the nuances of the terminology will fall into place.

Peer-to-Peer and Client/Server Networks

Network models, which define how and where resources are shared and how access to these resources is regulated, fall into two major types: peer-to-peer and client/server. Client/server networks are the most common in business settings, but understanding both types is essential, especially as they compare with one another.

Peer-to-peer networks running Windows OSs are referred to as *workgroup networks*, and client/server networks running Windows Server are called *domain-based networks*.

In a **peer-to-peer network**, most computers function as clients or servers as circumstances dictate. For example, a computer can act as a server by sharing a printer it's connected to and simultaneously act as a client by accessing a file shared by another computer on the network. In this type of network, there's no centralized control over who has access to network resources; each user maintains control over his or her own shared resources. The computers in peer-to-peer networks usually run desktop or client OSs.

In a peer-to-peer network, every user must act as the administrator of his or her computer's resources. Users can give everyone unlimited access to their resources or grant restricted (or no) access to other users on the network. To grant this access, users must create user accounts and passwords for each user who will access shared resources on their computers. The username and password for accessing a computer are called **credentials**. If you have five computers in a peer-to-peer network, each user might have to remember as many as five different sets of credentials. Because of the lack of centralized authority over resources, controlled chaos is the norm for all but the smallest peer-to-peer networks, and security can be a major concern because not all users might be educated in creating secure passwords.

Another issue that affects peer-to-peer networks is data organization. If every machine can be a server, how can users keep track of what information is stored on which machine? If five users are responsible for a collection of documents, any of those users might have to search through files on all five machines to find a document. The decentralized nature of peer-to-peer networks makes locating resources more difficult as the number of peers increases.

In a **server-based network**, certain computers take on specialized roles and function mainly as servers, and ordinary users' machines tend to function mainly as clients. Windows Server

2012, Red Hat Enterprise Linux, and UNIX are OSs designed primarily for server use. In these networks, servers have centralized authority over who has access to network resources, mainly by providing an environment in which users log on to the network with a single set of credentials maintained by one or more servers running a server OS. Server OSs are designed to handle many simultaneous user logons and requests for shared resources efficiently. In most cases, servers are dedicated to running network services and shouldn't be used to run user applications. You want to reserve servers' CPU power, memory, and network performance for user access to network services.

When you're using Windows server OSs in a server-based network with centralized logons, you're running a Windows domain. A **domain** is a collection of users and computers whose accounts are managed by Windows servers called **domain controllers**. Users and computers in a domain are subject to network access and security policies defined by a network administrator and enforced by domain controllers. The software that manages centralized access and security is a **directory service**. On Windows servers, the directory service software is **Active Directory**; this software is what makes a Windows server a domain controller.

The Linux OS supports a centralized logon service called Network Information Service (NIS), but more often Linux administrators use a service compatible with Active Directory, called Lightweight Directory Access Protocol (LDAP), if they want to use a directory service. A directory service is one of several network services usually found only on server OSs running in a server-based network. Other services include the following:

- *Naming services*—Translate computer names to their addresses.
- *E-mail services*—Manage incoming and outgoing e-mail from client e-mail programs.
- *Application services*—Grant client computers access to complex applications that run on the server.
- *Communication services*—Give remote users access to an organization's network.
- *Web services*—Provide comprehensive Web-based application services.

Unlike peer-to-peer networks, server-based networks are easier to expand. Peer-to-peer networks should be limited to 10 or fewer users, but server-based networks can handle anywhere from a handful to thousands of users. In addition, multiple servers can be configured to work together, which enables administrators to add more servers to share the load when an application's performance wanes or to provide fault tolerance if a server's hardware malfunctions.

Table 9-3 summarizes the strengths and weaknesses of peer-to-peer/workgroup and server/domain-based networks.

9

Table 9-3 Peer-to-peer versus server-based networks

Network attribute	Peer-to-peer network	Server-based network
Resource access	Distributed among many desktop/client computers; makes access to resources more complex	Centralized on one or more servers; streamlines access to resources
Security	Users control their own shared resources and might have several sets of credentials to access resources; not ideal when tight security is essential	Security is managed centrally, and users have a single set of credentials for all shared resources; best when a secure environment is necessary
Performance	Desktop OS not tuned for resource sharing; access to shared resources can be hindered by users running applications	Server OS tuned for resource sharing; servers are usually dedicated to providing network services
Cost	No dedicated hardware or server OS required, making initial costs lower; lost productivity caused by increasing complexity can raise costs in the long run	Higher upfront costs because of dedicated hardware and server OSs; additional ongoing costs for administrative support

Peer-to-peer networks and server-based networks each have advantages. For this reason, using a combination of the two models isn't uncommon. For example, a user might want to share a printer with a group of users in close proximity or a document folder with a department colleague. With this arrangement, a user is in control of a shared resource, yet can still assign permissions to this resource by using accounts from the central user database on the server. Although sharing the resource is decentralized, the logon credentials to access the resource are still centralized.

Network Device Fundamentals

LANs, WANs, MANs, and internetworks are built with a variety of network hardware. Your understanding of how the most common network hardware works is crucial to your success in building reliable, high-performance networks. This section begins by discussing the simplest of network devices: the hub, a device that's nearly obsolete but is still found in older installations, or for special purposes. Switches have supplanted hubs in networks large and small and are the main network building block today. Wireless access points are the foundation of wireless networks; you will learn about their operation and basic configuration. Network interface cards have become such an essential component of computers that they're now built into most motherboards. Your understanding of NIC configuration options and properties will help you build a better network. The last topic of this section covers the most complex network devices: routers, the gateway to the Internet that makes it possible for large companies to build vast internetworks and WANs.

Network Hubs

A hub, also called a *multiport repeater*, is the simplest of the network devices. A hub has the rather straightforward job of receiving bit signals generated by NICs and other devices, strengthening them, and then sending them along (repeating them) to other devices connected to its ports (see Figure 9-13). Think of a hub as a microphone for network signals. When people speak, their voices carry only so far until people in the back of the room can no longer hear what's being said. Network signals, too, carry only so far on their medium before receiving computers can no longer interpret them correctly. A hub enables you to connect computers whose distance from one another would otherwise make communication impossible. Its function is as follows:

- Receives bit signals generated from a connected computer on any one of its ports
- Cleans the signal by filtering out electrical noise
- Regenerates the signal to full strength
- Transmits the regenerated signal to all other ports a computer (or other network device) is connected to

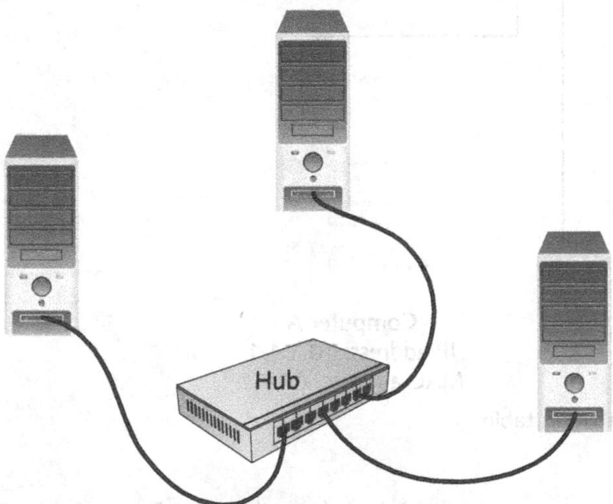

Figure 9-13 A multiport repeater, or hub

9

Network Switches

A network switch, like a hub, is used to interconnect multiple computers so that they can communicate with one another. A switch looks just like a hub, with several ports for plugging in network cables. However, instead of simply regenerating incoming bit signals and repeating them to all other ports, a switch actually reads data in the message, determines which port the destination device is connected to, and forwards the message only to that port. So, the first important difference between hubs and switches is that hubs work only with electrical signals and the bits these signals represent, whereas switches work with the actual information these bits compose, to make frames.

By reading the destination MAC address of each frame, the switch can forward the frame to the port the destination computer is on. A switch maintains a **switching table** (see Figure 9-14) of MAC addresses that have been learned and their associated port numbers.

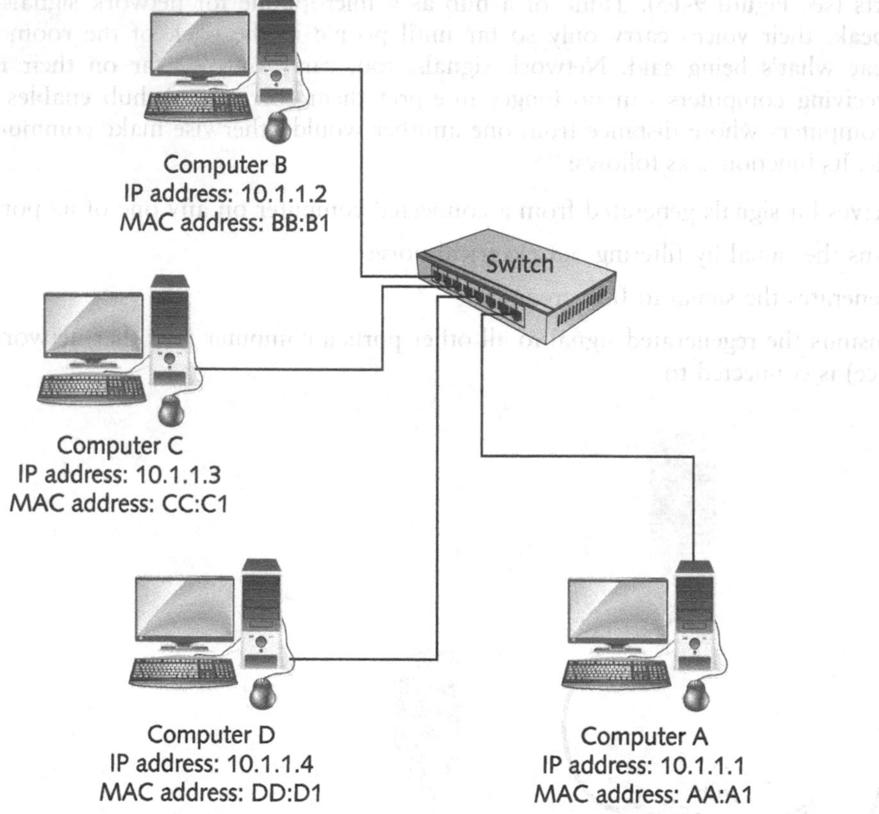

Figure 9-14 Switches maintain a switching table

MAC addresses consist of 12 hexadecimal digits. Figure 9-14 uses shorter addresses only as an example.

A switch's operation can be summarized in these steps:

1. The switch receives a frame.
2. The switch reads the source and destination MAC addresses.
3. The switch looks up the destination MAC address in its switching table.
4. The switch forwards the frame to the switch port to which the computer that owns the MAC address is connected.
5. The switching table is updated with the source MAC address and port information.

Wireless Access Points

Not all networks require a cable to tether the computer to a switch or hub. Wireless networks have become ubiquitous on college and corporate campuses and in many public locations, such as airports and libraries. At the heart of a wireless LAN is the wireless **access point (AP)**. An AP is a lot like a hub, in that all computers send signals through it to communicate with other computers. The obvious difference is that signals don't travel through a physical medium; they travel through the airwaves as radio signals.

Again, an AP is much like a wired hub—all stations hear all network data transmitted by all other wireless devices in the network. All communication goes to the AP, which then retransmits or repeats the transmission to the destination station. However, unlike hubs, communication between two stations requires an extra step. The destination device sends an acknowledgement back to the sending device to indicate that the frame was received. When the sending device receives the acknowledgement, it knows that no error has occurred.

Network Interface Cards

Attaching a computer to a network requires a NIC to create and mediate the connection between the computer and the networking medium. The networking medium might be copper wire, fiber-optic cable, or the airwaves, but in all cases, data is represented as bit signals that the NIC transmits or receives.

9

For incoming data, the NIC must be able to interpret the signals used for the network medium, which are electrical for copper wire, light for fiber-optic cable, or radio waves for wireless networks. These signals are then converted to bits and assembled into frames. For outgoing data, the NIC converts frame data into bits and transmits them to the medium in the correct signal format. The following list summarizes the tasks a NIC and its driver perform:

- Provide a connection from the computer to the network medium.
- For incoming messages, receive bit signals and assemble them into frames, verify the frame's destination address, remove the frame header and trailer, and transfer the packet to the network protocol.
- For outgoing messages, receive packets from the network protocol and create frames by adding source and destination MAC addresses and error-checking data.
- Convert the frame data into bit signals in a format suitable for the network medium and transmit the signals.

Figure 9-15 shows a NIC handling incoming data, and Figure 9-16 shows a NIC handling outgoing data.

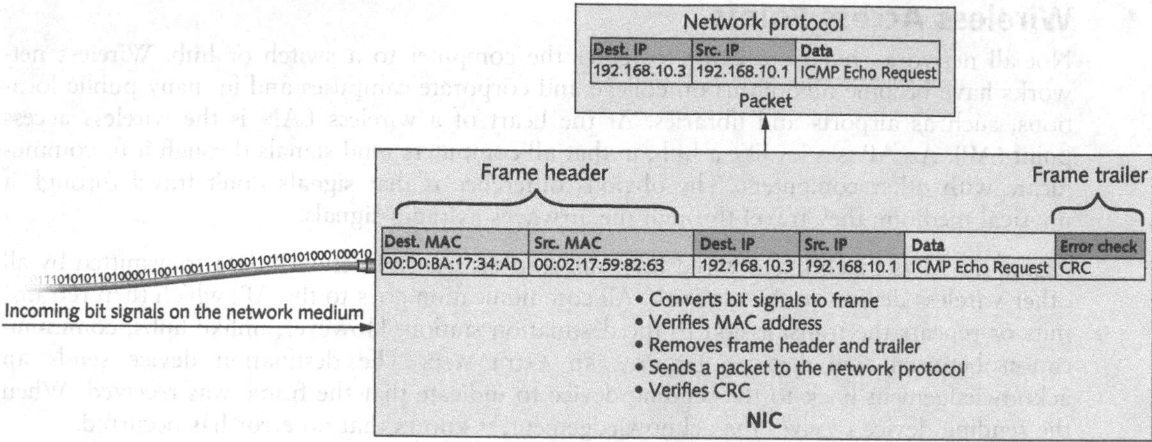

Figure 9-15 A NIC handles incoming data from the network medium

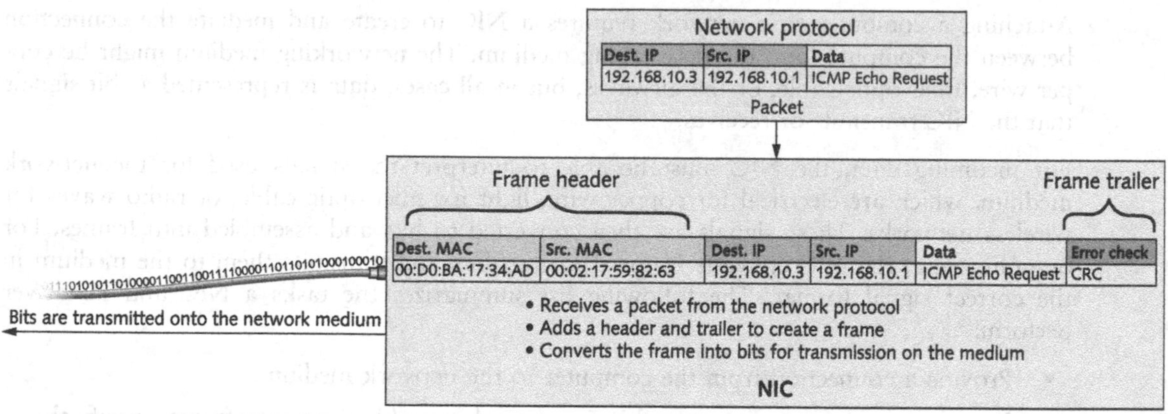

Figure 9-16 A NIC handles outgoing data to be sent to the network medium

Routers

Routers are the most complex devices discussed in this chapter. Hubs and switches connect computers to the LAN; routers connect LANs to one another. Routers typically have two or more network ports to which switches are connected to form an internetwork. Figure 9-17 is a diagram of an internetwork, with two LANs connected via a router. Each LAN in this example uses switches to connect workstations and a router port to the LAN. LAN 2 has two switches that are connected.

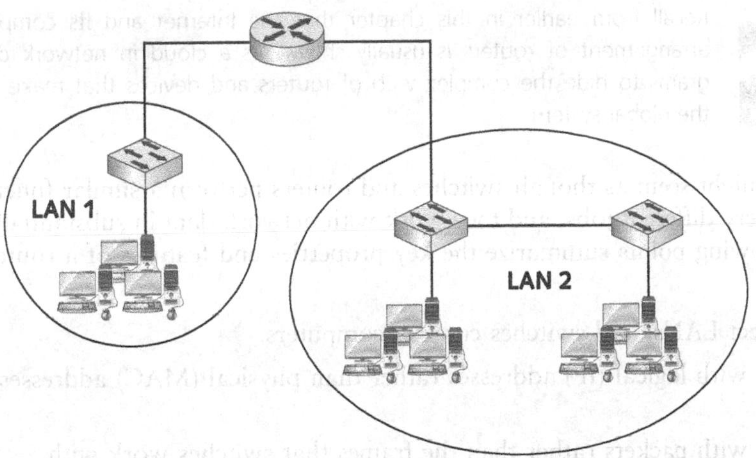

Figure 9-17 Two LANs connected by a router to make an internetwork

A router enables multiple LANs to communicate by forwarding packets from one LAN to another. It also forwards packets from one router to another when LANs are separated by multiple routers. The Internet is built on a vast collection of LANs, all interconnected via routers. Figure 9-18 shows a small business network connected to its Internet service provider (ISP), then to several other Internet routers, and ultimately to a Web server on the Cengage.com network.

9

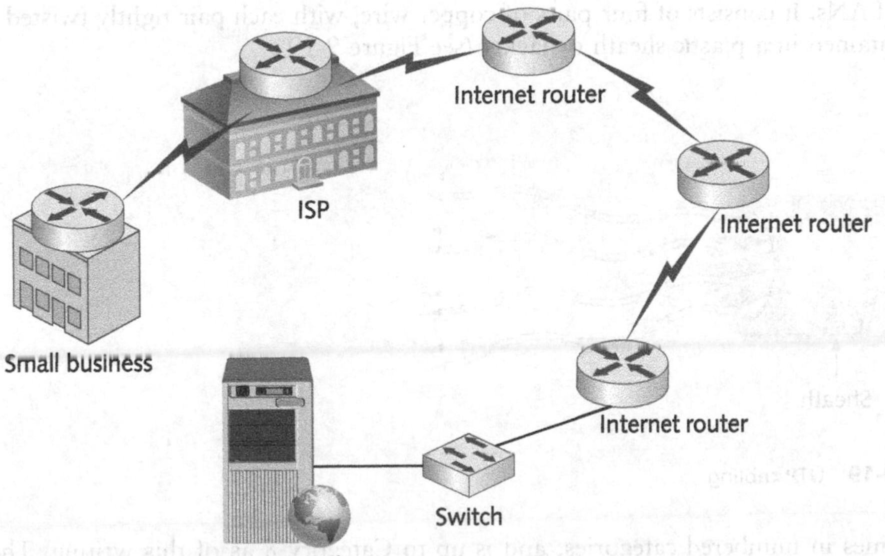

Figure 9-18 Routers interconnect LANs to form the Internet

Recall from earlier in this chapter that the Internet and its complex arrangement of routers is usually shown as a cloud in network diagrams to hide the complex web of routers and devices that make up the global system.

On the surface, it might seem as though switches and routers perform a similar function, but in reality they do very different jobs, and they work with network data in substantially different ways. The following points summarize the key properties and features of a router versus a switch:

- Routers connect LANs, and switches connect computers.
- Routers work with logical (IP) addresses rather than physical (MAC) addresses, as switches do.
- Routers work with packets rather than the frames that switches work with.
- Routers don't forward broadcast packets, but switches do.
- Routers use routing tables, and switches use switching tables.

Network Media

Certain network technologies specify the types of media they require to operate. The following sections summarize the most common media types.

Unshielded Twisted Pair Unshielded twisted pair (UTP) is the most common media type in LANs. It consists of four pairs of copper wire, with each pair tightly twisted together and contained in a plastic sheath or jacket (see Figure 9-19).

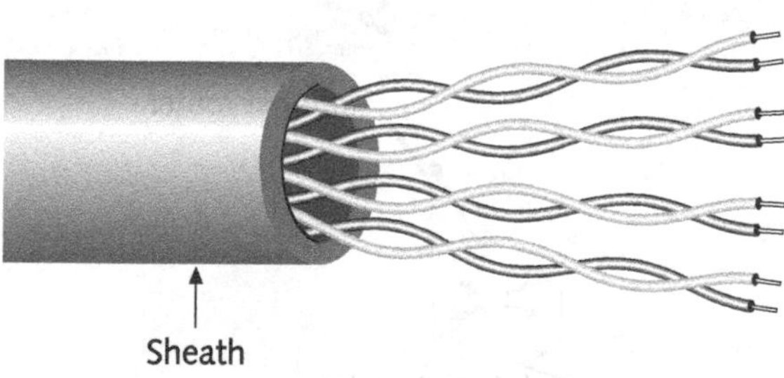

Figure 9-19 UTP cabling

UTP comes in numbered categories, and is up to Category 8 as of this writing. The higher the category is, the higher the cable's bandwidth potential. Category 5 Enhanced (Cat 5E) and Category 6 (Cat 6) are the most common in wired LANs; they allow speeds of up to 10 Gbps. UTP cabling is used in physical star networks, and the maximum cable length from NIC to switch is 100 meters in LAN applications. UTP cabling is susceptible to electrical interference, which can cause data corruption, so it shouldn't be used in electrically noisy environments.

Fiber-Optic Cabling Fiber-optic cabling (see Figure 9-20) uses extremely thin strands of glass to carry pulses of light long distances and at high data rates. It's typically used in large internetworks to connect switches and routers and sometimes to connect high-speed servers to the network. Because of its capability to carry data over long distances (several hundred to several thousand meters), it's also used frequently in WAN applications. Fiber-optic cabling isn't susceptible to electrical interference, so unlike UTP, it can be used in electrically noisy environments. It requires two strands of fiber to make a network connection: one for transmitting and one for receiving.

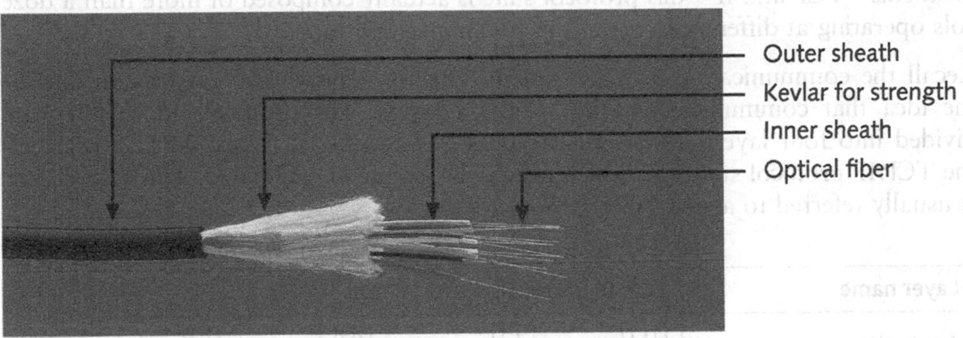

Figure 9-20 Fiber-optic cabling

Coaxial Cable Best known for its use in cable TV, coaxial cable is obsolete as a LAN medium, but it's used as the network medium for Internet access via cable modem. Coaxial cable was the original medium used by Ethernet in physical bus topologies, but its limitation of 10 Mbps half-duplex communication made it obsolete for LAN applications after 100 Mbps Ethernet became the dominant standard.

Network Protocol Fundamentals

For effective communication across a network, computers must be capable of transmitting data reliably and efficiently. Network protocols are designed to accomplish this goal; some protocols emphasize reliability, others efficiency. Network protocols often work together at different layers of the network communication process to provide both reliability and efficiency. This section discusses network protocols in general but focuses on the most common suite of protocols used in networks: TCP/IP.

The term *protocol* isn't specific to the field of networking. In general, a **protocol** consists of rules and procedures for communication and behavior. Just as two people must share a common set of rules for verbal communication—a language—computers must also "speak" the same language and agree on the rules of communication. You use protocols in other ways as well. Texting, e-mail, and Facebook communication, for example, have their own rules of etiquette and language use.

Until fairly recently, you had a choice of network protocols you could install on your computer, depending on the computing environment. A small network in the 1990s running

Windows 3.1 or Windows 95 probably ran the Windows-specific NetBEUI protocol. A network with Novell NetWare 4.x servers typically ran IPX/SPX. Both these protocols are obsolete now and are found only in networks that haven't been upgraded in more than a decade. Today, you can focus on the TCP/IP protocol suite, the protocol of the Internet and the one all contemporary OSs run.

When a set of protocols works cooperatively, it's called a **protocol suite** (or *protocol stack*). The most common one is **Transmission Control Protocol/Internet Protocol (TCP/IP)**, the Internet protocol suite. Although you can see by its name that TCP/IP consists of at least two protocols—TCP and IP—this protocol suite is actually composed of more than a dozen protocols operating at different layers of the communication process.

Recall the communication process explained earlier. This discussion was an introduction to the idea that communication takes place in layers. The protocols in TCP/IP can also be divided into four layers, with similar names and functions. Figure 9-21 shows the layers of the TCP/IP protocol suite and which protocols operate at each layer. This layered architecture is usually referred to as the *TCP/IP model.*

Layer name	TCP/IP protocols			
Application	HTTP	FTP	DHCP	TFTP
	SMTP	POP3	DNS	SNMP
Transport	TCP		UDP	
Internetwork	ICMP	ARP	IPsec	
	IPv4 and IPv6			
Network access	Ethernet, token ring, FDDI, WAN technologies			

Figure 9-21 The TCP/IP layered architecture

The Internetwork layer is where computer professionals usually do the most network configuration. It's where the IP protocol operates, and it can be considered the heart of the TCP/IP protocol suite. IP addresses, of course, are defined here, and routing takes place in this layer, too. Without routing, the Internet and World Wide Web wouldn't exist. With all the complexity of configuring routing and managing IP addresses, this layer is also where most errors occur in network configuration. In a large internetwork, a lot of time is typically spent unraveling the intricacies of the Internetwork layer.

The Internetwork layer is responsible for four main tasks, as discussed in the following sections:

- Defines and verifies IP addresses
- Routes packets through an internetwork
- Resolves MAC addresses from IP addresses
- Delivers packets efficiently

Internet Protocol Version 4

Internet Protocol version 4 (IPv4), or just IP, is an Internetwork layer protocol that provides source and destination addressing and routing for the TCP/IP protocol suite. IPv4 is the most common IP version in networks and the first version that was in widespread use. Earlier versions never really made it out of the lab. One of IP's most important functions is the definition of a logical address, called an **IP address.** IPv4 defines a 32-bit dotted decimal address: 172.31.149.10, for example. Each grouping of numbers separated by a dot (period) is an 8-bit value called an **octet** that can range from 0 to 255. Because an IP address has 32 bits, a total of 2^{32} addresses are possible—that's approximately 4 billion addresses, which certainly seems like a lot, but many are wasted, and available addresses to assign to Internet devices are running out.

Part of an IP address specifies the network ID, and the rest of the address specifies a unique host ID in the network. For example, in the address 172.31.149.10, 172.31 is the network ID and 149.10 is the host ID. Determining which part of the IP address is the network ID and which part is the host ID depends on the **subnet mask**, another 32-bit dotted decimal number consisting of a contiguous series of binary 1 digits followed by a contiguous series of binary 0 digits. A contiguous series of eight binary 1s equals the decimal value 255. For example, a typical subnet mask is 255.0.0.0 or 255.255.0.0. In these two examples, for each 255 in the subnet mask, the corresponding octet of the IP address is part of the network ID.

For example, you might configure a computer with the following IP address and subnet mask:

IP address: 10.1.221.101

Subnet mask: 255.0.0.0

Because the first octet of the subnet mask is 255 (a series of eight binary 1s), the first octet of the IP address is the network ID, which is 10. The network ID is written as 10.0.0.0, and the host ID is 1.221.101. Understand, however, that the network ID and host ID are used together when configuring a computer's IP address, so you will always see them written as 10.1.221.101.

Now take this example:

IP address: 172.31.100.6

Subnet mask: 255.255.0.0

The first two octets of the subnet mask are 255 (a total of 16 contiguous binary 1s), so the network ID is 172.31, which is written as 172.31.0.0. The host ID is 100.6. When referring to the network ID, you always fill in the host part of the address with 0s.

Continuing with this pattern, say you have the following IP address and subnet mask:

IP address: 192.168.14.250

Subnet mask: 255.255.255.0

This combination gives you the network ID 192.168.14.0 and the host ID 250. You can't have a subnet mask like 255.0.255.0 because the network ID must be contiguous.

IPv4 Address Classes When you enter an IP address in the Internet Protocol Version 4 (TCP/IPv4) Properties dialog box in Windows, as shown in Figure 9-22, Windows fills in a subnet mask automatically. You can change this value if needed. Windows bases the suggested subnet mask on the class of the IP address you enter.

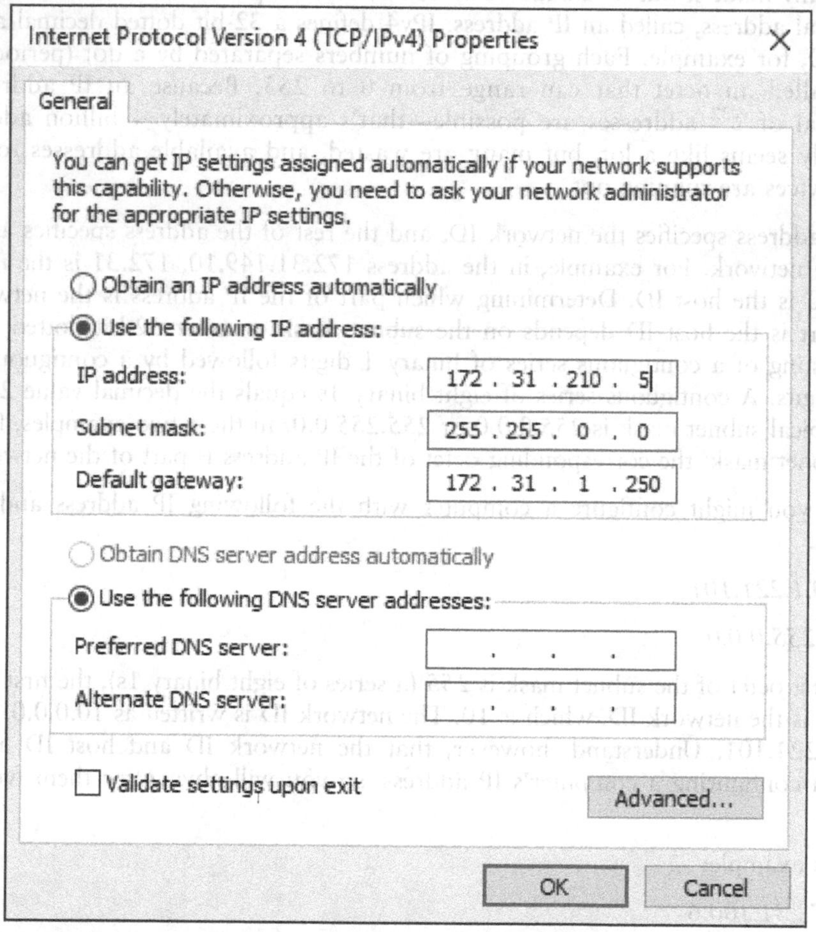

Internet Protocol Version 4 (TCP/IPv4) Properties

General

You can get IP settings assigned automatically if your network supports this capability. Otherwise, you need to ask your network administrator for the appropriate IP settings.

Obtain an IP address automatically

Use the following IP address:

IP address: 172 . 31 . 210 . 5

Subnet mask: 255 . 255 . 0 . 0

Default gateway: 172 . 31 . 1 . 250

Obtain DNS server address automatically

Use the following DNS server addresses:

Preferred DNS server: . . .

Alternate DNS server: . . .

Validate settings upon exit

Advanced...

OK Cancel

Figure 9-22 A subnet mask based on the address class

IP addresses are categorized in ranges referred to as Classes A, B, C, D, or E. Only IP addresses in the A, B, and C classes can be assigned to a network device (host). Although the IP address class system has been superseded by a more flexible way to manage IP addresses, called Classless Interdomain Routing (CIDR), the class system is a basis for determining which part of an IP address is the network ID and which part is the host ID. The first octet of an address denotes its class. Review the following facts about IP address classes:

- The value of the first octet for Class A addresses is between 1 and 127. Class A addresses were intended for use by large corporations and governments. An IP address registry assigns the first octet, leaving the last three octets for network administrators to assign to hosts. This allows 24 bits of address space, or 16,777,214 hosts per network address. In a Class A IP address such as 10.159.44.201, for example, the network address is 10.0.0.0. So, the first address in the 10.0.0.0 network is 10.0.0.1, and the last address is 10.255.255.254.

- Class B addresses begin with network IDs between 128 and 191; they were intended for use in medium-sized to large networks. An IP address registry assigns the first two octets, leaving the third and fourth octets available for administrators to assign as host addresses. In the Class B address 172.17.11.4, for example, the network address is 172.17.0.0. Having two octets in the host ID allows 65,534 hosts per network address.
- Class C addresses were intended for small networks. An IP address registry assigns the first three octets, with network IDs ranging from 192 to 223. In the Class C address 203.0.113.254, for example, the network address is 203.0.113.0. These networks are limited to 254 hosts per network.
- Class D addresses are reserved for **multicasting,** in which a packet is addressed so that more than one destination can receive it. Applications using this feature include videoconferencing and streaming media. In a Class D address, the first octet is in the range from 224 to 239. Class D addresses can't be used to assign IP addresses to host computers.
- Class E addresses have a value from 240 to 255 in the first octet. This range of addresses is reserved for experimental use and can't be used for address assignment.

Note a couple of things about the preceding list: First, if you do the math, you can see that a Class C address provides 2^8 bits of **address space,** which yields 256 addresses, not 254. An address space is the total number of addresses in an IP network number that can be assigned to hosts. The number of addresses specified for Classes A and B are also two fewer than the address space suggests. This discrepancy happens because each network has two reserved addresses: the address in which all host ID bits are binary 0s and the address in which all host ID bits are binary 1s. For example, all the host bits in address 203.0.113.0 are binary 0s; this address represents the network number and can't be assigned to a computer. The host bits in address 203.0.113.255 are binary 1s; this address is the broadcast address for the 203.0.113.0 network and can't be assigned to a computer.

The other note concerns the 127.0.0.0 network. Although technically a Class A address, it's reserved for the **loopback address,** which always refers to the local computer and is used to test the functioning of TCP/IP. A packet with a destination address starting with 127 is sent to the local device and does not reach the network medium. Likewise, the reserved name **localhost** always corresponds to the IP address 127.0.0.1, so that a local machine can always be referenced by this name.

Even though localhost and the loopback address are usually associated with the address 127.0.0.1, any address in the 127.0.0.0 network (except 127.0.0.0 and 127.255.255.255) references the local machine in most OSs.

Table 9-4 summarizes address Classes A, B, and C and the default subnet masks.

Table 9-4 IPv4 address class summary

Class	A	B	C
Value of first octet	0–127	128–191	192–223
Default subnet mask	255.0.0.0	255.255.0.0	255.255.255.0
Number of network ID bits	8	16	24
Maximum number of hosts/network	16,777,214	65,534	254
Number of host bits	24	16	8

Internet Protocol Version 6

IPv4 has been the driving force on the Internet for decades and continues to be the dominant protocol in use. However, it's showing its age as more and more IPv4 address space is used up and workarounds for security and quality of service must be put in place. IPv4 was developed more than 40 years ago, so it seems natural that as all other aspects of technology slowly get replaced, so will IPv4. This section discusses that replacement: **Internet Protocol version 6 (IPv6)**. IPv6 addresses look very different from IPv4 addresses, and unlike IPv4, IPv6 addresses have a built-in hierarchy and fields with a distinct purpose. Configuring an IPv6 address is clearly different from configuring an IPv4 address. The transition from IPv4 to IPv6 won't happen overnight, so methods have been developed to allow IPv4 and IPv6 networks to coexist and communicate with one another.

This section doesn't attempt to give you a full explanation of IPv6 and its many complexities; there are entire books on this topic. However, this section addresses the key aspects of the IPv6 protocol and what you need to know to configure and support a computer using IPv6. The Internet Engineering Task Force (IETF) started development on IPng (IP next generation) in 1994, and it was later named IPv6. IPv6 was developed to address IPv4's shortcomings. Some of the improvements of IPv6 over IPv4 include the following:

- *Larger address space*—IPv4 addresses are 32 bits, which theoretically provide four billion addresses. IPv6 addresses are 128 bits, meaning there are 340 trillion trillion trillion possible addresses. It's probably safe to say that running out of IPv6 addresses is unlikely.
- *Hierarchical address space*—Unlike IPv4, in which numbers in the address have little meaning other than the address class, network ID, and host ID, IPv6 addresses have a more defined structure. For example, the first part of an address can indicate a particular organization or site.
- *Autoconfiguration*—IPv6 can be self-configuring or autoconfigured from a router or server running IPv6 or through DHCPv6.
- *Built-in Quality of Service (QoS) support*—IPv6 includes built-in fields in packet headers to support QoS strategies without having to install additional protocol components, as IPv4 does. QoS strategies are used to prioritize data packets based on the type or urgency of information they contain.
- *Built-in support for security*—From the ground up, IPv6 is built to support secure protocols, such as Internet Protocol Security (IPsec), whereas IPv4's support for IPsec is an add-on feature.

- *Support for mobility*—With its built-in support for mobility, routing IPv6 packets generated by mobile devices over the Internet is more efficient than with IPv4.
- *Extensibility*—IPv6 uses extension headers instead of IPv4's fixed-size 40-byte header. Extension headers allow adding features to IPv6 simply by adding a new header.

IPv6 Addresses An IPv6 address is 128 bits rather than the 32 bits in an IPv4 address. This length increases the number of possible addresses from about 4 billion in IPv4 to 3.4×10^{38} addresses (that's 34 followed by 37 zeros!) in IPv6. Unless IP addresses are assigned to every star in the universe, it's safe to say enough IPv6 addresses will be available.

Unlike IPv4 addresses, which are specified in dotted decimal notation in 8-bit sections, IPv6 addresses are specified in hexadecimal format in 16-bit sections separated by a colon, as in this example: 2001:1b20:302:442a:110:2fea:ac4:2b.

If one of the 16-bit numbers doesn't require four hexadecimal digits, the leading 0s are omitted. Furthermore, some IPv6 addresses contain consecutive 0s in two or more 16-bit sections, so a shorthand notation is used to eliminate consecutive 0 values. Two colons replace two or more consecutive 0 values, as the following example shows:

- Longhand notation: 2001:DB8:0:0:0:2ed3:340:ab
- Shorthand notation: 2001:DB8::2ed3:340:ab

The host ID of an IPv6 address is typically 64 bits and uses the interface's MAC address to make up the bulk of the address. Because a MAC address is only 48 bits, the other 16 bits come from the value FF-FE inserted after the first 24 bits of the MAC address. In addition, the first two zeros that compose most MAC addresses are replaced with 02. For example, given the MAC address 00-0C-29-7C-F9-C4, the host ID of an IPv6 address is 02-0C-29-FF-FE-7C-F9-C4.

Introducing the OSI Model of Networking

The **Open Systems Interconnection (OSI) reference model** for networking explains how networks behave within an orderly, seven-layered model for networked communication. The OSI model isn't specific to a particular network protocol and can be applied to most networking protocols past and present. Many of the networking hardware and software components discussed in this chapter can be identified as working in one or more of the OSI model layers.

Although the OSI model isn't specific to one set of protocols, it's the standard model for discussing, teaching, and learning the field of computer networking. It's unlikely you'll have a course in networking that doesn't at least mention the OSI model, and some courses you take will likely cover it in more detail than this chapter.

Several networking models have sought to create an intellectual framework for clarifying network concepts and activities, but none has been as successful as the OSI model, which was originally proposed by the International Organization for Standardization (ISO). This model is sometimes called the *ISO/OSI reference model*.

ISO isn't an acronym; it comes from the Greek prefix *iso*, which means *equal* or *the same*. The ISO, based in Geneva, Switzerland, is a network of national standards institutes from 161 countries. The expanded name differs from language to language. For example, in France the organization is called the Organisation Internationale de Normalisation. The term *ISO* gives the network of institutes a common name.

The OSI reference model has become a key part of networking, in large part because it's a common framework for developers and students of networking to work with and learn from. The attempt to develop a working set of protocols and technologies based on the OSI model and put these efforts into common use never materialized, partly because existing protocols, such as TCP/IP, were already entrenched in the marketplace. However, the OSI reference model has a prominent place in networking as a model and teaching tool. This section briefly covers the model's seven-layer organization, the function of each layer, and the networking devices and components operating at each layer.

The set of protocols developed to conform to the OSI model is called *ISO*. You can view the fruits of these labors at *www.protocols.com/pbook/iso*.

Structure of the OSI Model

The OSI model divides network communication into the seven layers shown in Figure 9-23.

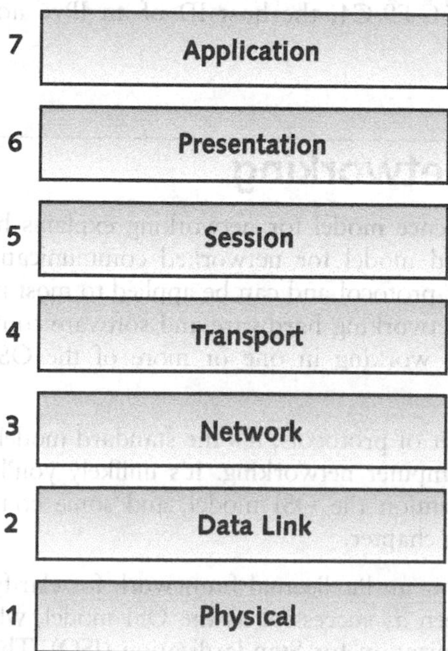

Figure 9-23 The seven layers of the OSI reference model

Here are two mnemonics to help you remember the seven layers of the OSI reference model. From the bottom up, starting with the Physical layer, the mnemonic is "People Do Not Throw Sausage Pizza Away." From the top down, starting with the Application layer, try "All People Studying This Need Drastic Psychotherapy" or "All People Seem To Need Data Processing."

At the top, the Application layer provides interfaces that enable user applications—such as File Explorer or Microsoft Word—to access network services. These user applications aren't part of the OSI model, but communicate with its top layer. On the other hand, some user applications, such as Web browsers and e-mail programs, are integrated with functions of the Application layer (as well as the Presentation and Session layers).

At the bottom of the OSI model, the Physical layer is where the network medium and the signals traversing it reside. All the activities needed to handle network communication occur between the top and bottom layers. To comprehend how a network works as a whole, you simply need to understand how each layer functions, what networking components and devices operate at each layer, and how the layers interact with one another.

Each layer in the OSI model has its own well-defined functions, and the functions of each layer communicate and interact with the layers immediately above and below it. For example, the Transport layer works with the Network layer below it and the Session layer above it. The Application layer, although not having a layer above it, interacts with user applications and network services.

When discussing devices or protocols in relation to the OSI model, the OSI layer number is often used rather than its name. For example, you hear terms such as *Layer 3 switch* or *Layer 7 gateway*.

Application Layer The Application layer (Layer 7) provides interfaces for applications to access network services, such as file sharing, message handling, and database access. It also handles error recovery for applications, as needed.

Common protocols at the Application layer include HTTP, FTP, SMB/CIFS, TFTP, and SMTP. Computers with network OSs and some security devices operate at Layer 7 because they work with these Application layer protocols.

Presentation Layer The Presentation layer (Layer 6) handles data formatting and translation. For outgoing messages, it converts data into a format specified by the Application layer, if necessary; for incoming messages, it reverses the conversion if required by the receiving application. In short, Layer 6 "presents" data in a suitable format to the Application layer. The Presentation layer handles protocol conversion, data encryption and decryption, data compression and decompression, data representation incompatibilities between OSs, and graphics commands.

An example of functionality at this level is a Web browser that connects to a secure Web server with encryption protocols that must encrypt data before it's transferred to the server and decrypt data arriving from the Web server.

9

A software component known as a *redirector* operates at this layer. It intercepts requests for service from the computer; requests that can't be handled locally are redirected across the network to a network resource that can handle the request.

Session Layer Layer 5, the **Session layer**, permits two computers to hold ongoing communications—called a *session*—across a network, so applications on either end of the session can exchange data for as long as the session lasts. The Session layer handles communication setup ahead of data transfers when necessary and session teardown when the session ends. Some common network functions this layer handles include name lookup and user logon and logoff.

Transport Layer The **Transport layer** (Layer 4) manages data transfer from one application to another across a network. It breaks long data streams into smaller chunks called *segments*. Segmenting the data is important because every network technology has a maximum frame size called the **maximum transmission unit (MTU)**. For Ethernet, the MTU is 1518 bytes, which means segments must be small enough to allow for the Network layer and Data Link layer headers and still be no larger than 1518 bytes.

The components working at this layer include TCP and UDP from the TCP/IP protocol suite, although UDP is sometimes called a *pseudo-Transport layer protocol* because it doesn't perform all the functions required of the Transport layer, such as breaking data into segments.

Network Layer Layer 3, the **Network layer**, handles logical addressing, translates logical network addresses (IP addresses) into physical addresses (MAC addresses), and performs best path selection and routing in an internetwork. A router performs best path selection when multiple pathways, or routes, are available to reach a destination network; the router attempts to choose the best, or fastest, path.

The software components working at this layer include IP, ARP, ICMP, and several routing protocols from the TCP/IP suite. Routers work at this layer, as do firewalls and certain remote access devices, such as virtual private network (VPN) servers. A switch with routing capabilities, called a *Layer 3 switch*, also works at the Network layer. Essentially, any device that works mainly with packets and their source and destination IP addresses is said to be a Network layer device or Layer 3 device.

Data Link Layer Layer 2, the **Data Link layer**, is the intermediary between the Network layer and Physical layer. It defines how computers access the network medium—a process also called *media access control*, which is why the media access control (MAC) address is defined at this layer.

The software component operating at this layer is the NIC driver, and the hardware components include NICs and switches. A NIC operates at this layer because it contains the MAC address and is responsible for media access control. Switches operate at this layer because they do their job by examining MAC addresses and using the information to switch packets from incoming ports to outgoing ports. Networking technologies such as Ethernet and Token Ring operate at this layer.

Physical Layer Last but not least, the job of the **Physical layer** (Layer 1) is to convert bits into signals for outgoing messages and signals into bits for incoming messages. The types of signals generated depend on the medium; for example, wire media, such as twisted-pair cable, use electrical pulses, fiber-optic media use pulses of light, and wireless media use radio waves. At this layer, details are specified for creating a physical network connection, such as the type of connectors used to attach the medium to the NIC. The network components working at the Physical layer include all the cables and connectors used on the medium plus repeaters and hubs.

The unit of information at each layer of the OSI model is called a *protocol data unit (PDU)*. For example, at the top three layers, the PDU is simply called *data*. At the Transport layer, the PDU is called a *segment*; at the Network layer, it is called a *packet*; and at the Data Link layer, it is called a *frame*.

Summary of the OSI Model The OSI model is a helpful way to categorize and compartmentalize networking activities, and most discussions of protocol suites and networking software use its terminology. Table 9-5 summarizes the actions occurring at each layer. Even though most protocol suites don't adhere strictly to this model (perhaps because so many of them were already implemented in some form before the model's development), they still incorporate its concepts.

Table 9-5 OSI model summary

Layer	PDU	Protocols/ software	Devices	Function
7. Application	Data	HTTP, FTP, SMTP, DHCP	Computers	Provides programs with access to network services
6. Presentation	Data	Redirectors	N/A	Handles data representation to application and data conversions, ensures that data can be read by the receiving system, and handles encryption and decryption
5. Session	Data	DNS, authentication protocols	N/A	Establishes, maintains, and coordinates communication between applications
4. Transport	Segment	TCP, UDP	N/A	Ensures reliable delivery of data, breaks data into segments, handles sequencing and acknowledgements, and provides flow control
3. Network	Packet	IP, ICMP, ARP	Routers, firewalls, Layer 3 switches	Handles packet routing, logical addressing, and access control through packet inspection
2. Data Link	Frame	Ethernet, token ring, FDDI, NIC drivers	Switches, NICs	Provides physical device addressing, device-to-device delivery of frames, media access control, and MAC addresses
1. Physical	Bits	N/A	Network media, hubs/ repeaters, connectors	Manages hardware connections, handles sending and receiving binary signals, and handles encoding of bits

9

Although not all networking protocols adhere to the OSI model, a network administrator's clear understanding of the functions at each layer is essential in troubleshooting networks and network equipment and in understanding how network devices operate.

There is a lot more to say about network devices, protocols, network models, and IPv6 and IPv4 addresses, but this book is about operating systems, so we'll turn our attention now to configuring networking in an operating system.

Configuring Networking in an Operating System

Network configuration in an operating system follows a similar pattern as the steps in the network communication process, the TCP/IP model, and the OSI model. All the functions of the network model must be accounted for, and some but not all might require some level of configuration. We'll start at the bottom, where the physical aspects of the network exist.

Configuring the Network Interface

The network interface is where the NIC and its driver lives; it comprises the Physical and Data Link layers of the OSI model. In most cases, you don't have to configure the network interface; if a NIC is installed, the OS will usually install the proper driver and the network interface is ready to go. However, it's possible you will need to install a new or different driver if an update becomes available, if the OS is unable to install a driver, or if the OS installs the wrong driver. Installing and updating device drivers was discussed in Chapter 6.

Some network interface drivers provide a number of configuration options. For example, in Figure 9-24, the properties of the Windows network connection have more than 20 configuration options. Some of the options include the speed and duplex mode of the connection, the number of buffers the connection should use, and whether packet prioritization should be enabled. The particular options for a network connection depend on the features of the NIC and its driver.

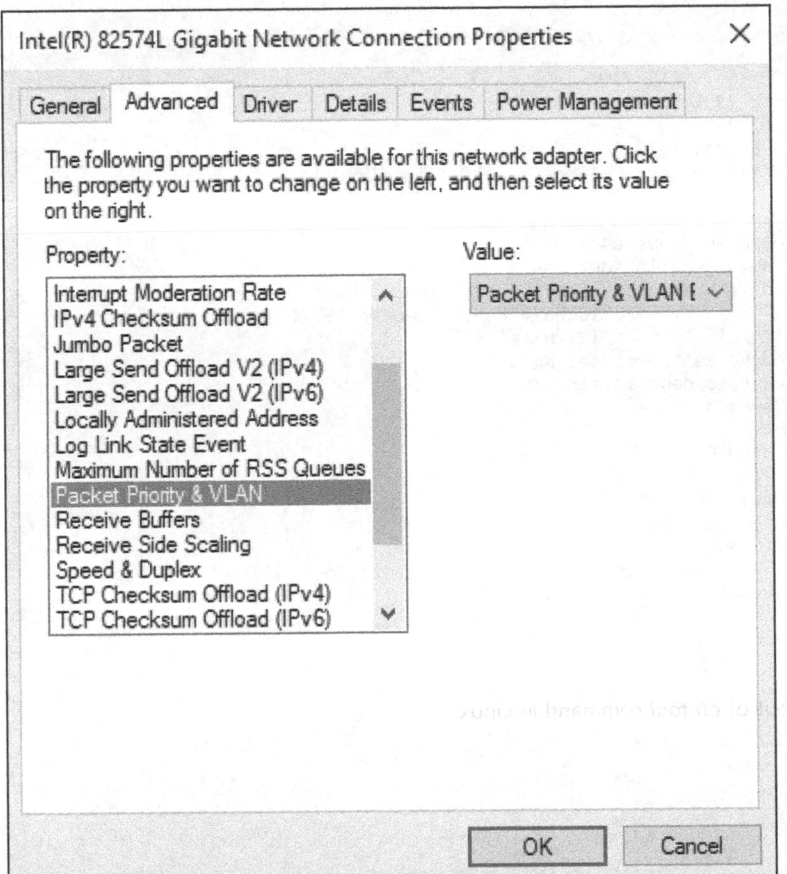

Figure 9-24 The properties of a network connection in Windows

Linux and Mac OS X also offer configuration settings for the network interface. For example, in Fedora Linux, you can use the command-line tool *ethtool* to display and change network interface settings (see Figure 9-25). In Mac OS X, use the advanced settings in the Network dialog box (see Figure 9-26).

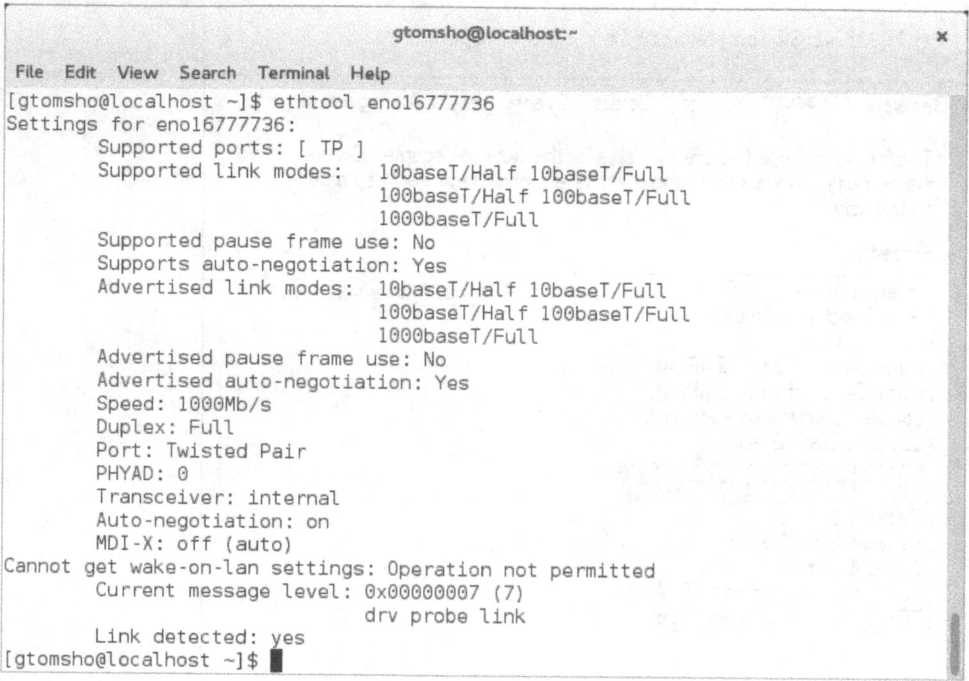

gtomsho@localhost:~
File Edit View Search Terminal Help
[gtomsho@localhost ~]$ ethtool eno16777736
Settings for eno16777736:
Supported ports: [TP]
Supported link modes: 10baseT/Half 10baseT/Full
100baseT/Half 100baseT/Full
1000baseT/Full
Supported pause frame use: No
Supports auto-negotiation: Yes
Advertised link modes: 10baseT/Half 10baseT/Full
100baseT/Half 100baseT/Full
1000baseT/Full
Advertised pause frame use: No
Advertised auto-negotiation: Yes
Speed: 1000Mb/s
Duplex: Full
Port: Twisted Pair
PHYAD: 0
Transceiver: internal
Auto-negotiation: on
MDI-X: off (auto)
Cannot get wake-on-lan settings: Operation not permitted
Current message level: 0x00000007 (7)
drv probe link
Link detected: yes
[gtomsho@localhost ~]$

Figure 9-25 Output of *ethtool* command in Linux

Source: Fedora Linux

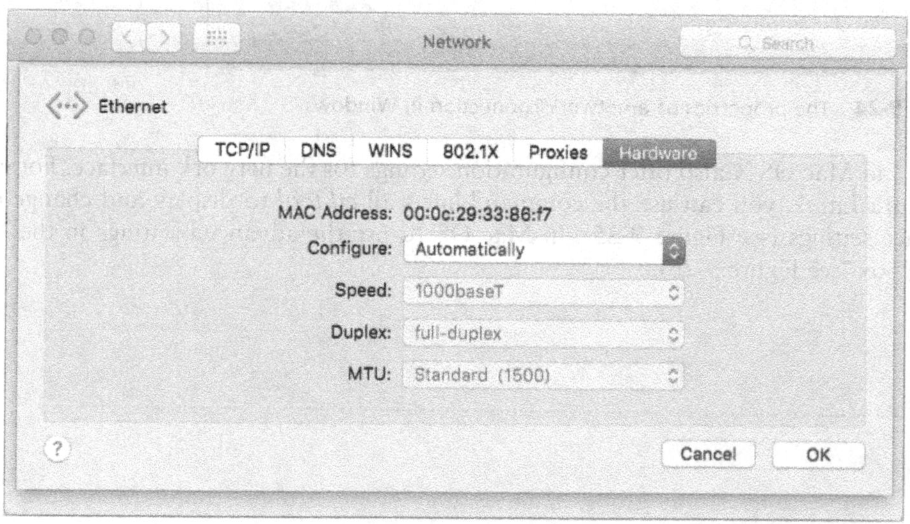

Figure 9-26 Viewing network interface settings in Mac OS X

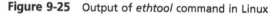

Source: Mac OS X

Configuring IPv4 Addresses

The configuration of an IPv4 address consists of the following parts (see Figure 9-27):

- *IP address*—The IP address is required and identifies the computer on the network.
- *Subnet mask*—The subnet mask is required because it determines the network and host IDs.
- *Default gateway*—The default gateway is not required, but is necessary for the computer to access other networks, including the Internet.
- *Preferred DNS server*—The preferred DNS server address is not required but is necessary to translate domain names to addresses. Without a DNS server address, communication with another computer would require you to know the computer's IP address. With a DNS server, your computer can communicate with other computers using their names, such as *server1* and *www.awebserver.com*.
- *Alternate DNS server*—The alternate DNS server address is not required. If the preferred DNS server is not available, the computer will use the alternate DNS server.

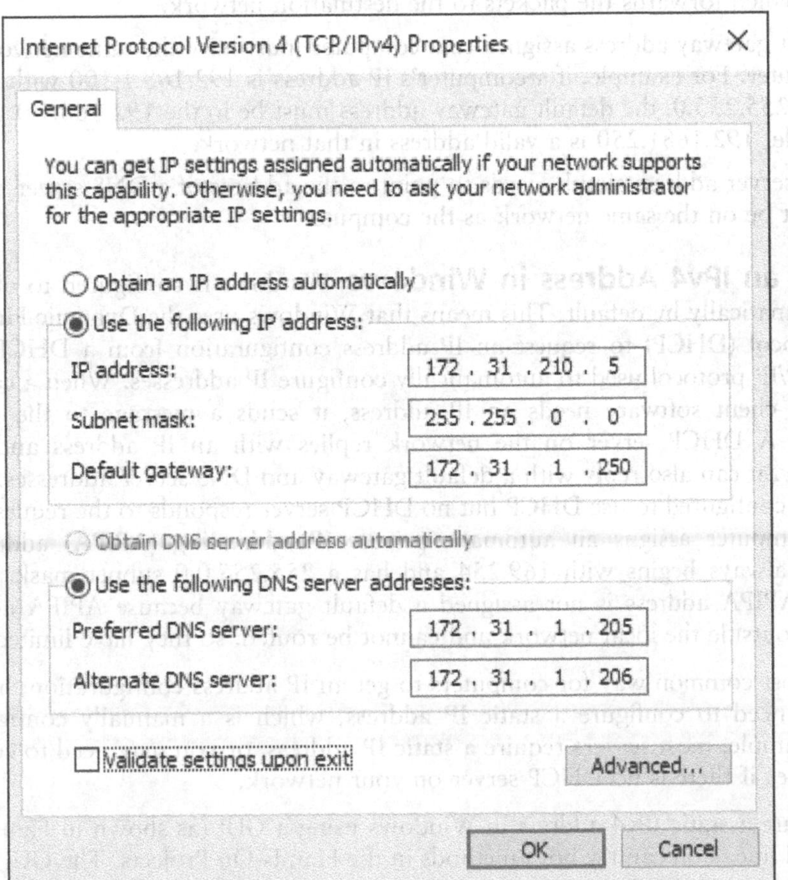

Figure 9-27 The Internet Protocol Version 4 (TCP/IPv4) Properties dialog box

9

When you assign a computer an IP address, there are some rules to remember:

- A host can be assigned an IP address only in the range of Class A, Class B, or Class C addresses.
- All hosts on the same network must have the same network ID in their IP addresses. The term *network* in this case means a group of computers connected to one or more switches (or access points), and not separated by a router.
- All host IDs on the same network must be unique.
- You can't assign an IP address in which all the host ID bits are binary 0. This type of IP address is reserved as the network ID. For example, IP address 10.1.0.0 with subnet mask 255.255.0.0 is reserved to identify network 10.1.
- You can't assign an IP address in which all the host ID bits are binary 1. This type of IP address is reserved as the network broadcast address. For example, IP address 10.1.255.255 with subnet mask 255.255.0.0 has all host ID bits set to binary 1 and is reserved as the broadcast address for the 10.1.0.0 network.
- Computers assigned different network IDs can communicate only by sending packets to a router, which forwards the packets to the destination network.
- The default gateway address assigned to a computer must have the same network ID as that computer. For example, if a computer's IP address is 192.168.1.100 with subnet mask 255.255.255.0, the default gateway address must be in the 192.168.1.0 network; for example, 192.1681.250 is a valid address in that network.
- The DNS server address simply needs to point to the address of a DNS server that may or may not be on the same network as the computer.

Configuring an IPv4 Address in Windows Windows is configured to obtain an IP address automatically by default. This means that Windows uses the **Dynamic Host Configuration Protocol (DHCP)** to request an IP address configuration from a DHCP server. DHCP is a TCP/IP protocol used to automatically configure IP addresses. When a computer running DHCP client software needs an IP address, it sends a message to the network requesting one. A DHCP server on the network replies with an IP address and subnet mask; optionally, it can also reply with a default gateway and DNS server addresses. If a client computer is configured to use DHCP but no DHCP server responds to the request for an address, the computer assigns an **automatic private IP addressing (APIPA)** address. An APIPA address always begins with 169.254 and has a 255.255.0.0 subnet mask. A computer with an APIPA address is not assigned a default gateway because APIPA addresses cannot be used outside the local network and cannot be routed, so they have limited utility.

DHCP is the most common way for computers to get an IP address configuration; however, sometimes you need to configure a **static IP address**, which is a manually configured IP address. For example, most servers require a static IP address, or you may need to configure static IP addresses if there is no DHCP server on your network.

You can configure a static IPv4 address in Windows using a GUI (as shown in Figure 9-27) or the command line. You can try both methods in the Hands-On Projects. The GUI method is accessed from the properties window of a network connection. To configure an IPv4 address from the command line, use the *netsh* command from a command prompt. You can use the *netsh* command for a wide variety of network configuration tasks. To see a list of *netsh* commands, type *netsh /?* at the command prompt. To configure the IP address of a network interface, you need to know the name of the interface. Windows names its network interfaces Ethernet0, Ethernet1, and so on. You can find the name of your interface from the Network Connections control panel, by typing *netsh interface show interface* from the command prompt, or by typing *ipconfig* from the command prompt. To configure the IP address of an interface named Ethernet0 to 10.1.1.1 with subnet mask 255.255.0.0, use this command:

netsh interface ipv4 set address "Ethernet0" static 10.1.1.1 255.255.0.0

You can include the default gateway by adding the address to the end of the command:

netsh interface ipv4 set address "Ethernet0" static 10.1.1.1 255.255.0.0 10.1.1.250

To set the primary DNS server for the computer to 10.1.1.100, use the following command:

netsh interface ipv4 set dns "Ethernet0" static 10.1.1.100 primary

To view your IP address configuration, use the *ipconfig* command. For extended IP configuration information, use *ipconfig /all*. You'll use *ipconfig* in the Hands-On Projects.

Configuring an IPv4 Address in Linux and Mac OS X As with Windows, most Linux distributions use automatically assigned IP addresses using DHCP by default. If you need to configure a static address in Linux, use the *ifconfig* command from a shell prompt. As with the Windows *netsh* command, you need to know the name of your network interface, which you can find out by typing *ifconfig* and pressing Enter to display your current interface configuration. Linux names its interfaces eno*Number*, where *Number* is an 8-digit number. You might also see Linux interface names such as eth0 and eth1. To configure an IP address on an interface named eth0, use the following command from the shell prompt: 9

ifconfig eth0 10.1.1.1 netmask 255.255.0.0

To configure a default gateway in Linux, use the *route* command:

route add default gw 10.1.1.250

To configure a DNS server in Linux, you must configure the /etc/resolv.conf file and add an entry that looks like:

nameserver 10.1.1.100

Most Linux installations that include a GUI have a GUI tool for configuring the IP address settings. For example, in Fedora 23, you can find the Network utility by clicking Activities, Show Applications, Settings, and then Network. To configure an IP address, click the settings icon and then click IPv4. If you want to use DHCP, leave the setting configured to Automatic (DHCP); otherwise, click Manual to see the dialog box in Figure 9-28.

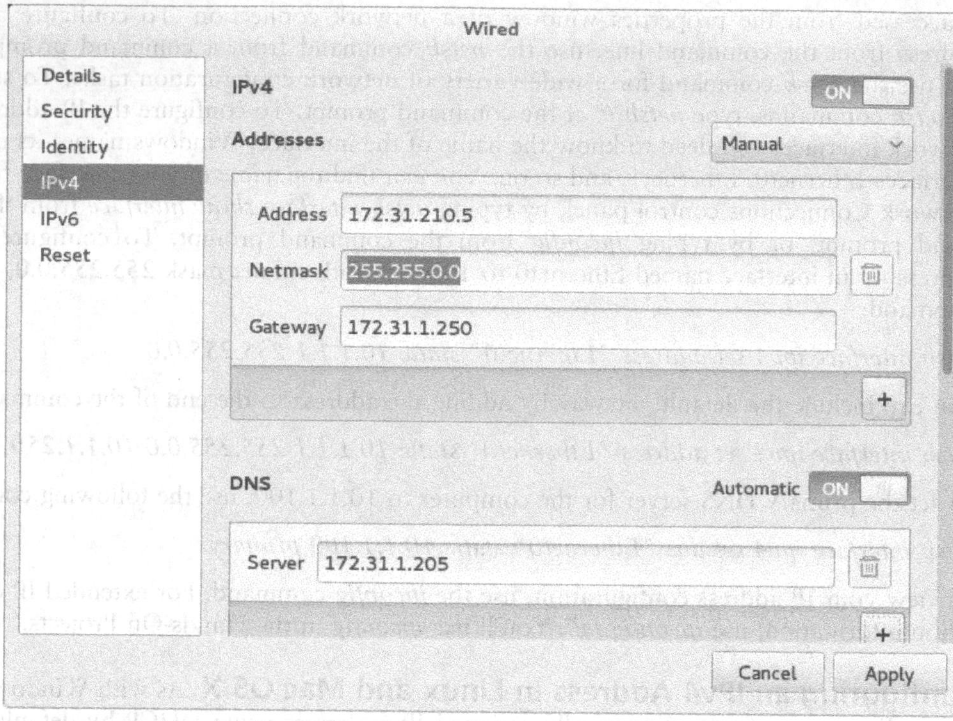

Figure 9-28 Configuring an IP address in Linux

Source: Fedora Linux

As with Linux, you can configure an IP address in Mac OS X using the *ifconfig* command at a shell prompt. To use a GUI in Mac OS X, click the Apple icon, click System Preferences, and then click Network to see the window shown in Figure 9-29.

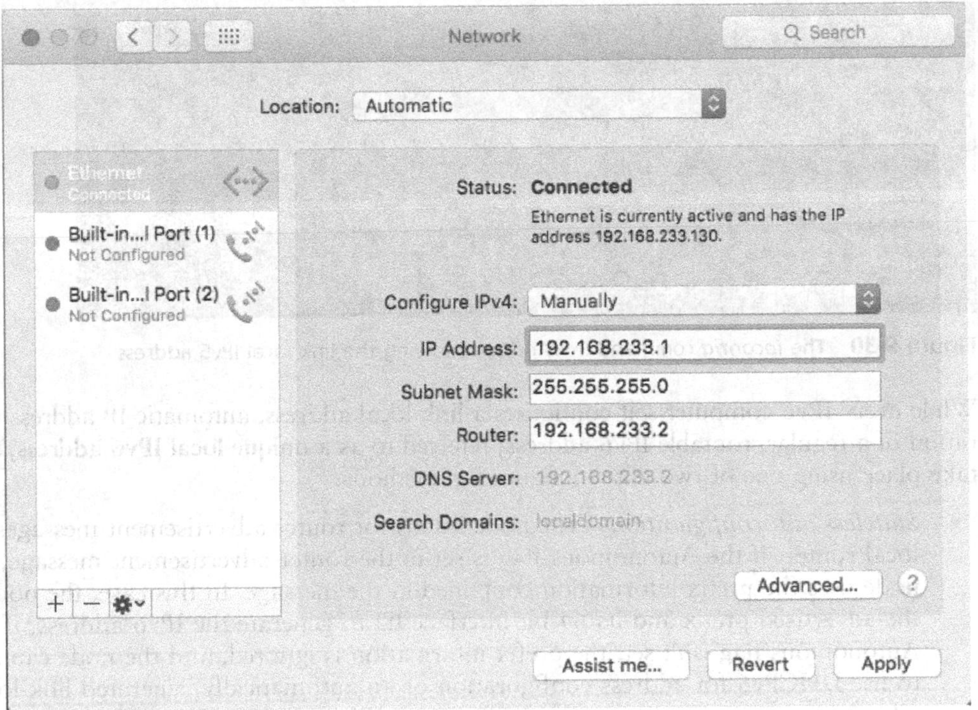

Figure 9-29 Configuring an IP address in Mac OS X
Source: Mac OS X

Configuring IPv6 Addresses

Like IPv4, IPv6 can configure itself automatically, which is the preferred method of IPv6 configuration. Static configuration is also an option, when necessary. A computer with IPv6 enabled is always automatically assigned a **link-local IPv6 address.** A link-local address always begins with *fe80* and is self-configuring, using the MAC address or a random value for the host ID. Link-local addresses can't be routed and are somewhat equivalent to APIPA addresses in IPv4. These addresses can be used for computer-to-computer communication in small networks where no routers are needed. When you display your IP configuration in Windows, Linux, or Mac OS X, you will see your link-local IPv6 address, as shown in the output of the *ipconfig* command in Figure 9-30.

```
C:\WINDOWS\system32>ipconfig

Windows IP Configuration


Ethernet adapter Ethernet 3:

   Connection-specific DNS Suffix  . :
   Link-local IPv6 Address . . . . . : fe80::2421:5ac1:6a44:b979%3
   IPv4 Address. . . . . . . . . . . : 172.31.210.1
   Subnet Mask . . . . . . . . . . . : 255.255.0.0
   Default Gateway . . . . . . . . . : 172.31.1.250
```

Figure 9-30 The *ipconfig* command in Windows showing the link-local IPv6 address

While every IPv6 computer self-configures a link-local address, automatic IP address configuration of a regular, routable IPv6 address, referred to as a **unique local IPv6 address**, can also take place using one of two autoconfiguration methods:

- *Stateless autoconfiguration*—The node listens for router advertisement messages from a local router. If the Autonomous flag is set in the router advertisement message, the node uses the prefix information contained in the message. In this case, the node uses the advertised prefix and its 64-bit interface ID to generate the IPv6 address. If the Autonomous flag isn't set, the prefix information is ignored, and the node can attempt to use DHCPv6 for address configuration or an automatically generated link-local address.
- *Stateful autoconfiguration*—The node uses an autoconfiguration protocol, such as DHCPv6, to get its IPv6 address and other configuration information. A node attempts to use DHCPv6 to get IPv6 address configuration information if no routers on the network provide router advertisements or if the Autonomous flag isn't set in router advertisements.

Static assignment of IPv6 addresses is always an option. For Windows, you can use the properties dialog box for Internet Protocol Version 6 (TCP/IPv6) or the *netsh* command. For Linux and Mac OS X, you use the *ifconfig* command or the GUI utilities described earlier in the "Configuring IPv4 Addresses" section. You will configure IP addresses in all three OSs in the Hands-On Projects.

Chapter Summary

- The components needed to make a stand-alone computer into a networked computer include a NIC, a network medium, and usually an interconnecting device. In addition, network client and server software, protocols, and the NIC driver are needed to enable a computer to communicate on a network.
- The layers of the network communication process can be summarized as user application, network software, network protocol, and network interface.
- The terms for describing networks of different scopes are *LAN*, *internetwork*, *WAN*, and *MAN*. A LAN is a single collection of devices operating in a small geographic

area. An internetwork is a collection of LANs tied together by routers, and a WAN and MAN are geographically dispersed internetworks.

- Packets and frames are the units of data handled by different network components. Packets, which are processed by the network protocol, are units of data with the source and destination IP addresses added. Frames, which are processed by the network interface, have MAC addresses and an error-checking code added to the packet.
- A client is the computer or network software that requests network data, and a server is the computer or network software that makes network data available to requesting clients.
- A peer-to-peer network model has no centralized authority over resources; a server-based network typically uses a directory service for centralized logon, security settings, and resource management.
- LANs, WANs, MANs, and internetworks are built with a variety of network hardware. Network hubs take incoming bit signals and repeat them at their original strength out of all connected ports. Network switches read the destination MAC address in the frame to determine which port the destination device is connected to and forward the frame only to that port. Access points are a central device in a wireless network and perform a function similar to hubs. Network interface cards create and mediate the connection between the computer and network medium. Routers connect LANs to one another and forward packets from one LAN to another, according to the destination IP address specified in the packet. Routers use routing tables to determine where to forward packets.
- TCP/IP is the main protocol suite used in networks. Like most facets of networking, TCP/IP takes a layered approach and is organized into four layers: Application, Transport, Internetwork, and Network access.
- The Open Systems Interconnection (OSI) reference model for networking explains how networks behave within an orderly, seven-layered model for networked communication. The OSI model isn't specific to a particular network protocol and can be applied to most networking protocols past and present.
- Network configuration in an operating system follows a similar pattern as the steps in the network communication process, the TCP/IP model, and the OSI model. All the functions of the network model must be accounted for, and some but not all might require some level of configuration.

Key Terms

access point (AP) A wireless device that serves as the central connection point of a wireless LAN and mediates communication between wireless computers.

Active Directory The directory service used by Windows servers.

address space The number of addresses available in an IP network number that can be assigned to hosts.

Application layer Layer 7 in the OSI model, which provides interfaces that enable applications to request and receive network services. See also *Open Systems Interconnection (OSI) reference model.*

automatic private IP addressing (APIPA) A private range of IP addresses assigned to an APIPA-enabled computer automatically when an IP address is requested via DHCP but no DHCP server responds to the request. See also *Dynamic Host Configuration Protocol (DHCP).*

client The term used to describe an OS designed mainly to access network resources, a computer's primary role in a network (running user applications and accessing network resources), and software that requests network resources from servers.

credentials A username and password or another form of identity used to access a computer.

Data Link layer Layer 2 in the OSI model, which is responsible for managing access to the network medium and delivery of data frames from sender to receiver or from sender to an intermediate device, such as a router. See also *Open Systems Interconnection (OSI) reference model.*

directory service The software that manages centralized access and security in a server-based network.

domain A collection of users and computers in a server-based network whose accounts are managed by Windows servers called *domain controllers*. See also *domain controller.*

domain controller A computer running Windows Server with Active Directory installed; it maintains a database of user and computer accounts as well as network access policies in a Windows domain. See also *directory service.*

Dynamic Host Configuration Protocol (DHCP) An Application layer protocol used to configure a host's IP address settings dynamically.

encapsulation The process of adding header and trailer information to chunks of data.

extranet A private network that allows limited and controlled access to internal network resources by outside users, usually in a business-to-business situation.

frame A packet with source and destination MAC addresses added and an error-checking code added to the back end. Frames are generated and processed by the network interface. See also *packet.*

header Information added to the front end of a chunk of data so it can be correctly interpreted and processed by network protocols.

Internet A worldwide public internetwork that uses standard protocols, such as TCP/IP, DNS, and HTTP, to transfer and view information.

Internet Protocol version 4 (IPv4) A connectionless Internetwork layer protocol that provides source and destination addressing and routing for the TCP/IP protocol suite; IPv4 uses 32-bit dotted decimal addresses.

Internet Protocol version 6 (IPv6) A connectionless Internetwork layer protocol that provides source and destination addressing and routing for the TCP/IP protocol suite. IPv6 uses 128-bit hexadecimal addresses and has built-in security and QoS features.

internetwork A networked collection of LANs tied together by devices such as routers. See also *local area network (LAN)*.

intranet A private network in which devices and servers are available only to users connected to the internal network.

IP address A 32-bit dotted decimal address used by IP to determine the network a host resides on and to identify hosts on the network at the Internetwork layer.

link-local IPv6 address Similar in function to IPv4 APIPA addresses, link-local IPv6 addresses begin with *fe80*, are self-configuring, and can't be routed. See also *Automatic private IP addressing (APIPA)*.

local area network (LAN) A small network limited to a single collection of machines and linked by interconnecting devices in a small geographic area.

localhost A reserved name that corresponds to the loopback address in an IP network. See also *loopback address*.

loopback address An address that always refers to the local computer; in IPv4, it's 127.0.0.1, and in IPv6, it's ::1. This address is used to test TCP/IP functionality on the local computer.

maximum transmission unit (MTU) The maximum frame size allowed to be transmitted across a network medium.

metropolitan area network (MAN) An internetwork confined to a geographic region, such as a city or county; a MAN uses third-party communication providers to supply connectivity between locations. See also *internetwork*.

multicasting A network communication in which a packet is addressed so that more than one destination can receive it.

name server A computer that provides the service of name-to-address resolution; for example, it resolves a host and domain name to an IP address.

network Two or more computers connected by a transmission medium that allows them to communicate.

network client software An application or OS service that can request information stored on another computer.

network interface card (NIC) A device that creates and mediates the connection between a computer and the network medium.

Network layer Layer 3 of the OSI model, which handles logical addressing and routing of PDUs across internetworks. See also *Open Systems Interconnection (OSI) reference model*.

network protocols The software that defines the rules and formats a computer must use when sending information across the network.

network server software The software that allows a computer to share its resources by fielding requests generated by network clients.

octet An 8-bit value; a number from 0 to 255 that's one of the four numbers in a dotted decimal IP address.

Open Systems Interconnection (OSI) reference model ISO Standard 7498 defines a frame of reference for understanding networks by dividing the process of network communication into seven layers. Each layer is defined in terms of the services and data it handles on behalf of the layer above it and the services and data it needs from the layer below it.

packet A chunk of data with source and destination IP addresses (as well as other IP information) added to it. Packets are generated and processed by network protocols.

peer-to-peer network A network model in which all computers can function as clients or servers as needed, and there's no centralized control over network resources.

Physical layer Layer 1, the bottom layer of the OSI model, transmits and receives signals and specifies the physical details of cables, NICs, connectors, and hardware behavior. See also *Open Systems Interconnection (OSI) reference model.*

Presentation layer At Layer 6 of the OSI model, data can be encrypted and/or compressed to facilitate delivery. Platform-specific application formats are translated into generic data formats for transmission or from generic data formats into platform-specific application formats for delivery to the Application layer. See also *Open Systems Interconnection (OSI) reference model.*

protocol Rules and procedures for communication and behavior. Computers must use a common protocol and agree on the rules of communication.

protocol suite A set of protocols working cooperatively to provide network communication. Protocols are "stacked" in layers, and each layer performs a unique function required for successful communication. Also called a *protocol stack.*

router A device that enables LANs to communicate by forwarding packets from one LAN to another. Routers also forward packets from one router to another when LANs are separated by multiple routers.

server The term used to describe an OS designed mainly to share network resources, a computer with the main role of giving client computers access to network resources, and the software that responds to requests for network resources from client computers.

server-based network A network model in which servers take on specialized roles to provide client computers with network services and to maintain centralized control over network resources.

Session layer Layer 5 of the OSI model, which is responsible for setting up, maintaining, and ending communication sequences (called *sessions*) across a network. See also *Open Systems Interconnection (OSI) reference model.*

stand-alone computer A computer that doesn't have the necessary hardware or software to communicate on a network.

static IP address A manually configured IP address.

subnet mask A 32-bit dotted decimal number consisting of a contiguous series of binary 1 digits followed by a contiguous series of binary 0 digits. The subnet mask determines which part of an IP address is the network ID and which part is the host ID.

switch A network device that reads the destination MAC addresses of incoming frames to determine which ports should forward the frames.

switching table A table of MAC address and port pairs that a switch uses to determine which port to forward frames it receives.

trailer Information added to the back end of a chunk of data so it can be correctly interpreted and processed by network protocols.

Transmission Control Protocol/Internet Protocol (TCP/IP) The most common protocol suite, the default protocol in contemporary OSs, and the protocol of the Internet.

Transport layer Layer 4 of the OSI model, which is responsible for reliable delivery of data streams across a network. Layer 4 protocols break large streams of data into smaller chunks and use sequence numbers and acknowledgements to provide communication and flow control. See also *Open Systems Interconnection (OSI) reference model.*

unique local IPv6 address An address for devices on a private network that can't be routed on the Internet.

wide area networks (WANs) Internetworks that are geographically dispersed and use third-party communication providers to supply connectivity between locations. See also *internetwork*.

Review Questions

1. An IPv6 address is made up of how many bits?
   a. 32
   b. 48
   c. 64
   d. 128
   e. 256
2. The subnet mask of an IP address does which of the following?
   a. provides encryption in a TCP/IP network
   b. defines network and host portions of an IP address
   c. allows automated IP address configuration
   d. allows users to use a computer's name rather than its address
3. What's the term for each grouping of 8 bits in an IP address?
   a. quartet
   b. quintet
   c. hexadecimal
   d. octet
4. Which of the following IPv6 features is an enhancement to IPv4? (Choose all that apply.)
   a. larger address space
   b. works at the Internetwork and Transport layers
   c. built-in security
   d. connectionless communication

5. Which protocol can configure a computer's IP address and subnet mask automatically?
   a. TCP
   b. IP
   c. ARP
   d. DNS
   e. DHCP
6. When a Windows computer is configured to use DHCP but no DHCP server is available, what type of address is configured automatically for it?
   a. PAT
   b. APIPA
   c. NAT
   d. static
7. Which OSI layer determines the route a packet takes from sender to receiver?
   a. 7
   b. 1
   c. 3
   d. 4
8. Which of the following best describes a MAC address?
   a. a 24-bit number expressed as 12 decimal digits
   b. an address with 12 hexadecimal digits
   c. a 48-bit number composed of 12 octal digits
   d. a dotted decimal number burned into the NIC
9. Which OSI model layer takes a large chunk of data from the Application layer and breaks it into smaller segments?
   a. Network access
   b. Internetwork
   c. Transport
   d. Application
10. You have just installed a new NIC in your PC to replace the old one that had started malfunctioning. What additional software must be installed to allow the OS to communicate with the new NIC?
    a. network application
    b. device driver
    c. BIOS
    d. protocol

11. Which of the following requests information stored on another computer?
    a. NIC
    b. network client
    c. network server
    d. network protocol
    e. device driver

12. Choose the correct order for the process of a user attempting to access network resources:
    1. network protocol
    2. application
    3. network client
    4. NIC driver
       a. 4, 2, 1, 3
       b. 3, 2, 1, 4
       c. 1, 4, 2, 3
       d. 2, 3, 1, 4
       e. 3, 1, 2, 4

13. TCP/IP is an example of which of the following?
    a. NIC
    b. network client
    c. network server
    d. network protocol
    e. device driver

14. In network communication, what address is used to deliver a frame to the correct computer on the network? (Choose all that apply.)
    a. MAC
    b. logical
    c. IP
    d. physical

15. What type of message is used to determine whether a computer is listening on the network?
    a. MAC
    b. ping
    c. IP
    d. TCP

16. What does TCP/IP use to look up a computer's IP address when its name is known?
    a. DNS
    b. ping
    c. MAC
    d. TCP
17. What is the unit of information that contains MAC addresses and an error-checking code that's processed by the network interface layer?
    a. packet
    b. ping
    c. frame
    d. chunk
18. Data is processed from the time an application creates it to the time it reaches the network medium. This process includes adding information such as addresses and is called ___________________.
    a. packetization
    b. encapsulation
    c. de-encapsulation
    d. layering
19. You're the network administrator for a company that has just expanded from one floor to two floors of a large building, and the number of workstations you need has doubled from 50 to 100. You're concerned that network performance will suffer if you add computers to the existing LAN. In addition, new users will be working in a separate business unit, and there are reasons to logically separate the two groups of computers. What type of network should you configure?
    a. WAN
    b. MAN
    c. internetwork
    d. extended LAN
20. Which of the following best describes a client?
    a. A computer's primary role in the network is to give other computers access to network resources and services.
    b. A computer's primary role in the network is to run user applications and access network resources.
    c. It's the software that responds to requests for network resources.
    d. The OS installed on a computer is designed mainly to share network resources.

21. You work for a small company with four users who need to share information on their computers. The budget is tight, so the network must be as inexpensive as possible. What type of network should you install?
    a. server-based network
    b. peer-to-peer network
    c. wide area network
    d. storage area network
22. Which of the following characteristics is associated with a peer-to-peer network? (Choose all that apply.)
    a. decentralized data storage
    b. inexpensive
    c. user-managed resources
    d. centralized control
    e. uses a directory service
23. A device interconnects five computers and a printer in a single office so users can share the printer. This configuration is an example of which of the following?
    a. LAN
    b. MAN
    c. WAN
    d. internetwork
24. A company has just made an agreement with another organization to share their two networks' resources by using TCP/IP protocols. What best describes this arrangement?
    a. MAN
    b. LAN
    c. intranet
    d. extranet
25. You have installed Windows Server 2012 on a new server and want to centralize user logons and security policies. What type of software should you install and configure on this server?
    a. naming services
    b. application services
    c. communication services
    d. directory services

Hands-On Projects

Project 9-1: Upgrade a Stand-Alone Computer to a Networked Computer

In this project, you install a NIC and connect it to an interconnecting device with a cable. This project can be done in groups or as an instructor demonstration. It's intended only to familiarize you with the hardware components needed to make a stand-alone computer into a networked computer. You will need a computer, a network interface card (NIC), a patch cable, and a switch. A USB NIC is a good option if you don't want to open the computer case. Even though most computers have a built-in NIC, you may need to add a stand-alone NIC if the built-in interface fails or you want a computer with two or more NICs, a common feature on servers.

1. Install the NIC, following the steps your instructor provides. This process might involve opening the computer case or simply plugging a USB NIC into a USB slot.
2. Turn on the computer. If necessary, insert a disk that contains the NIC driver and follow the instructions for installing it.
3. Using the supplied cable, plug one end into the NIC and the other end into the interconnecting device, which should be a hub or a switch.
4. Examine the indicator lights on the NIC and the hub or switch. There might be one or two lights on each port of the device, depending on its features. At least one indicator on the NIC and on each port of the hub or switch is usually referred to as a *link light*. The link light glows when a data connection has been made between the NIC and the hub or switch. Your instructor can supply more details about the indicator lights available on your hub or switch.
5. When the computer is finished booting, view your IP address settings by opening a command prompt and typing *ipconfig* (for a Windows computer) or *ifconfig* (for a Linux or Mac OS X computer).
6. If your classmates are plugged into the same switch, exchange IP addresses with them and then type **ping *IPaddress*** and press **Enter**, replacing *IPaddress* with the IP address of one of your classmates. You'll work more with *ping* in other Hands-On Projects in this chapter.
7. Shut down the computer, and then unplug and put away the cables.

Project 9-2: Examine NIC Properties in Windows 10

In some of the following Hands-On Projects, you will work with network settings. Note that the name of the interface referenced in these projects (for example, Ethernet0) may be different from the actual interface name on your computer. Substitute the correct interface name, if necessary.

When you describe a NIC as a component of networking, you're referring to both the hardware NIC and its driver. NIC drivers are configured in the OS in which they're installed and control certain operational aspects of the network interface as a whole. In this project, you examine the properties of your installed NIC. You also use the NIC's MAC address to look up the vendor. Not all NICs or NIC drivers have equivalent features, so your NIC might have more or fewer features than are described here.

1. Start your Windows computer and log on.
2. Right-click **Start,** and click **Network Connections.** (You can get to Network Connections in Windows 7 and earlier versions by going to Control Panel, opening Network and Sharing Center, and clicking Change adapter settings). Right-click **Ethernet0** and click **Status.** The Ethernet0 Status window shows a summary of information about your network connection. To see more information, click **Details** to open the Network Connection Details window (see Figure 9-31).

The *ipconfig /all* command shows much of the same information shown in the Network Connection Details window.

9

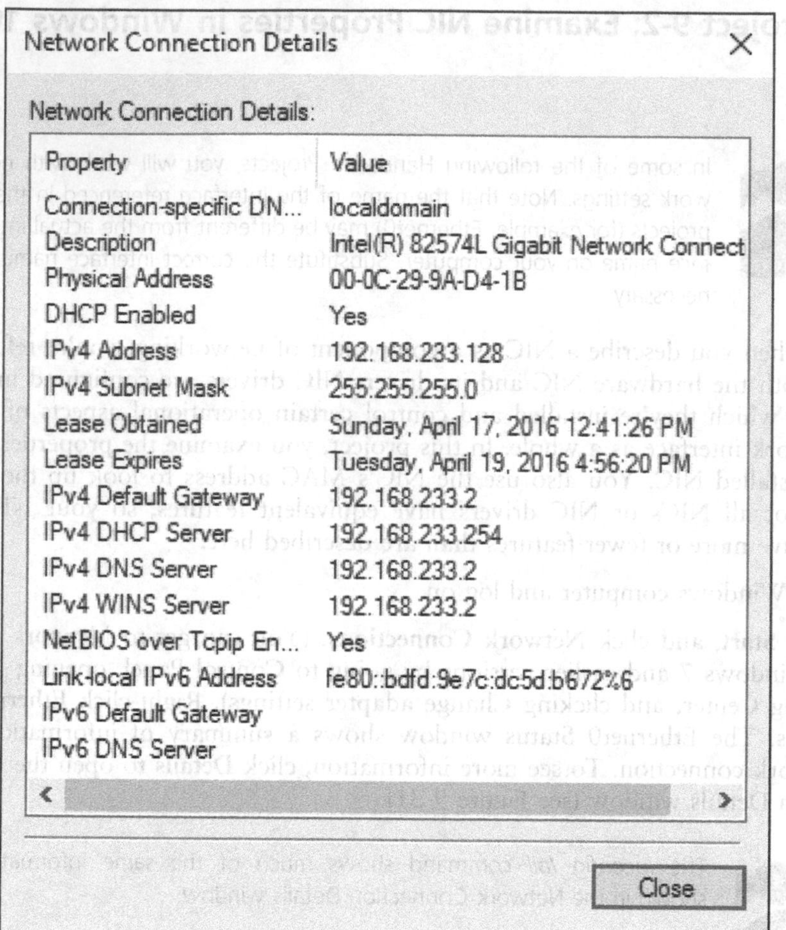

Figure 9-31 The Network Connection Details window

3. The Network Connection Details window shows information about your connection, including the NIC model, the physical (MAC) address, and your IP address configuration. Write down your MAC address, which you will use later to look up the NIC vendor. Review the remaining information, and then click **Close**.

   MAC address: ______________________________

4. In the Ethernet0 Status window, click **Properties.** In the Ethernet0 Properties dialog box, click the **Configure** button under the "Connect using" text box. In the Network Connection Properties dialog box, click the **Advanced** tab (see Figure 9-32). Your NIC might have fewer, more, or different options.

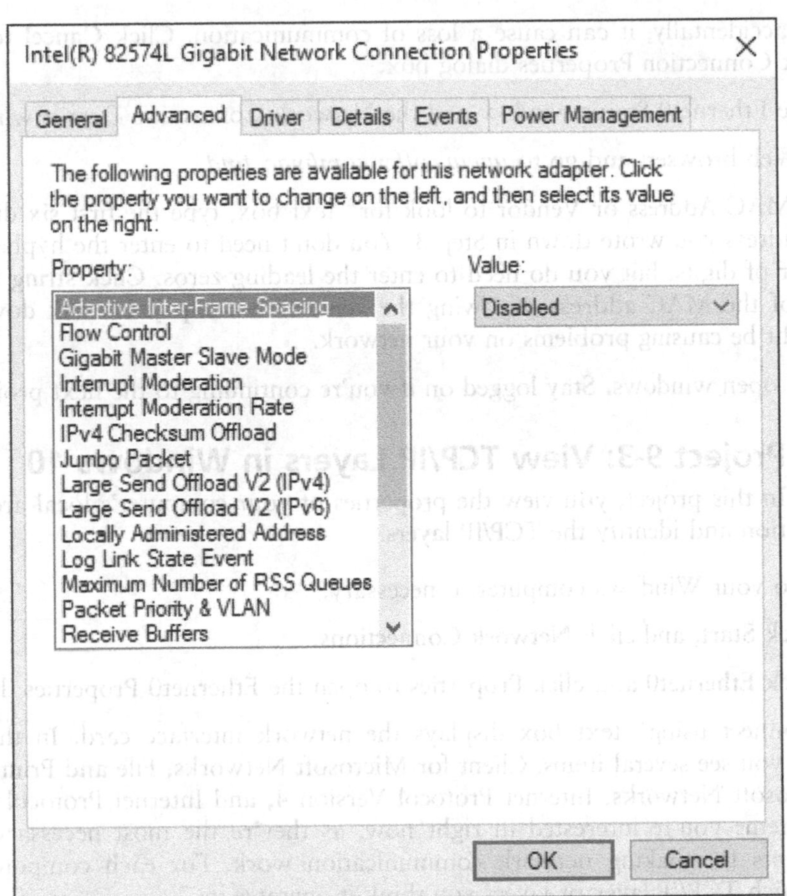

Figure 9-32 Viewing advanced settings in the Network Connection Properties dialog box

5. Review the available properties for your NIC. When you select a property, you can see its possible values in the Value drop-down list.

6. Click **Speed & Duplex** (or Link Speed and Duplex), and then click the **Value** list arrow to see the possible values. On most NICs, the default value is Auto Negotiation, which means the NIC and switch exchange signals to determine the optimum operational mode. Other modes usually include combinations of 10, 100, and 1000 Mbps, full-duplex, and half-duplex. Normally, you don't need to change these values unless auto-negotiation fails to work. If this happens, you'll probably see the link status light change from on to off repeatedly or never turn on at all.

7. Click the **Locally Administered Address** property. (It might also be listed as Network Address, Physical Address, or MAC Address.) In most cases, this property's value is set to Not Present. You can use this property to override the NIC's burned-in MAC address by entering a new address in the Value text box. Normally, however, you shouldn't override the burned-in MAC address because if you duplicate an existing

address accidentally, it can cause a loss of communication. Click **Cancel** to close the Network Connection Properties dialog box.

8. Close the Ethernet0 Status window and the Network Connection Details window.
9. Start a Web browser, and go to *www.coffer.com/mac_find*.
10. In the "MAC Address or Vendor to look for" text box, type the first six digits of the MAC address you wrote down in Step 3. You don't need to enter the hyphen between each pair of digits, but you do need to enter the leading zeros. Click **string** to find the vendor of the MAC address. Knowing the vendor can help you track down devices that might be causing problems on your network.
11. Close all open windows. Stay logged on if you're continuing to the next project.

Project 9-3: View TCP/IP Layers in Windows 10

In this project, you view the properties of your computer's local area connection and identify the TCP/IP layers.

1. Log on to your Windows computer, if necessary.
2. Right-click **Start**, and click **Network Connections.**
3. Right-click **Ethernet0** and click **Properties** to open the Ethernet0 Properties dialog box.
4. The "Connect using" text box displays the network interface card. In the list box under it, you see several items. Client for Microsoft Networks, File and Printer Sharing for Microsoft Networks, Internet Protocol Version 4, and Internet Protocol Version 6 are the items you're interested in right now, as they're the most necessary software components for making network communication work. For each component, write down which TCP/IP layer or layers you think it operates in:
   - NIC displayed in the "Connect using" text box: ____________________
   - Client for Microsoft Networks: ____________________
   - File and Printer Sharing for Microsoft Networks: ____________________
   - Internet Protocol Version 4: ____________________
   - Internet Protocol Version 6: ____________________
5. Close all open windows, but leave your computer running for the next project.

Project 9-4: Use *ipconfig, ping,* and *arp* in Windows 10

In this project, you use command-line tools to view your network configuration and test your computer's capability to communicate with other computers. The *ipconfig* command displays the IP address configuration of network interfaces. The *ping* command sends a message to a computer to verify the capability to communicate with it, and the *arp* command displays the MAC (physical) addresses your computer has discovered. You will work with one or more partners in this project.

1. Log on to your Windows computer, if necessary.
2. Right-click **Start** and click **Command Prompt** to open a command prompt window. At the command prompt, type **ipconfig** and press **Enter**. You should see a screen similar to that shown earlier in Figure 9-30, although the numbers will vary. The *ipconfig* command lists the IP address configuration for network interfaces as well as other network settings.
3. To see more details about your network configuration, type **ipconfig /all** and press **Enter**. You can scroll up the command prompt window to see all the output. Under the heading "Ethernet adapter Ethernet0," find the row labeled Physical Address (see Figure 9-33). The number in this row is the MAC address. Also, find the IP address in the IPv4 Address row. Write down these two addresses:

   ____

   ____

```
C:\Users\Administrator>ipconfig /all

Windows IP Configuration

   Host Name . . . . . . . . . . . . : WIN-CUM4HVHH3HU
   Primary Dns Suffix  . . . . . . . :
   Node Type . . . . . . . . . . . . : Hybrid
   IP Routing Enabled. . . . . . . . : No
   WINS Proxy Enabled. . . . . . . . : No
   DNS Suffix Search List. . . . . . : localdomain

Ethernet adapter Ethernet0:

   Connection-specific DNS Suffix  . : localdomain
   Description . . . . . . . . . . . : Intel(R) 82574L Gigabit Network Connectio
n
   Physical Address. . . . . . . . . : 00-0C-29-AB-7A-DD
   DHCP Enabled. . . . . . . . . . . : Yes
   Autoconfiguration Enabled . . . . : Yes
   Link-local IPv6 Address . . . . . : fe80::4c8e:49d6:cebd:c294%12(Preferred)
   IPv4 Address. . . . . . . . . . . : 192.168.233.138(Preferred)
   Subnet Mask . . . . . . . . . . . : 255.255.255.0
   Lease Obtained. . . . . . . . . . : Monday, April 18, 2016 6:55:03 PM
   Lease Expires . . . . . . . . . . : Tuesday, April 19, 2016 5:25:05 PM
   Default Gateway . . . . . . . . . : 192.168.233.2
   DHCP Server . . . . . . . . . . . : 192.168.233.254
   DHCPv6 IAID . . . . . . . . . . . : 301993001
   DHCPv6 Client DUID. . . . . . . . : 00-01-00-01-1E-86-6B-FD-00-0C-29-AB-7A-DD

   DNS Servers . . . . . . . . . . . : 192.168.233.2
   Primary WINS Server . . . . . . . : 192.168.233.2
   NetBIOS over Tcpip. . . . . . . . : Enabled
```

Figure 9-33 Using *ipconfig /all* to list physical (MAC) and IP addresses

4. Tell your partner your IP address and make a note of your partner's IP address. At the command prompt, type **ping *IPaddress*** and press **Enter** (replacing *IPaddress* with your partner's IP address). You should see output similar to that in Figure 9-34.

```
C:\Users\NetAdmin>ping 172.31.1.250

Pinging 172.31.1.250 with 32 bytes of data:
Reply from 172.31.1.250: bytes=32 time<1ms TTL=128
Reply from 172.31.1.250: bytes=32 time<1ms TTL=128
Reply from 172.31.1.250: bytes=32 time<1ms TTL=128
Reply from 172.31.1.250: bytes=32 time<1ms TTL=128

Ping statistics for 172.31.1.250:
    Packets: Sent = 4, Received = 4, Lost = 0 (0% loss),
Approximate round trip times in milli-seconds:
    Minimum = 0ms, Maximum = 0ms, Average = 0ms

C:\Users\NetAdmin>_
```

Figure 9-34 Results of the *ping* command

5. Remember that your computer needs both the destination IP address and MAC address to communicate with another computer. You supplied the IP address by typing it at the command prompt. Your computer discovered the MAC address of your partner's computer by using Address Resolution Protocol (ARP). To see this address, type **arp** -a and press Enter. The output should be similar to that in Figure 9-35. You might see more lines of output, depending on what other devices your computer has been communicating with.

```
C:\Users\Administrator>arp -a

Interface: 192.168.233.138 --- 0xc
  Internet Address      Physical Address      Type
  192.168.233.2         00-50-56-e3-8d-08     dynamic
  192.168.233.254       00-50-56-e9-23-93     dynamic
  192.168.233.255       ff-ff-ff-ff-ff-ff     static
  224.0.0.22            01-00-5e-00-00-16     static
  224.0.0.252           01-00-5e-00-00-fc     static
  255.255.255.255       ff-ff-ff-ff-ff-ff     static
```

Figure 9-35 The *arp -a* command displays MAC addresses

6. Use the **ping** command to communicate with other computers and devices on your network.
7. Close all open windows, but leave your computer running for the next project.

Project 9-5: Configure the IP Address in Windows 10

In this project, you configure your IP address in Windows 10.

1. Log on to your Windows computer, if necessary.
2. Right-click **Start** and click **Network Connections.**
3. Right-click **Ethernet0** and click **Properties** to open the Ethernet0 Properties dialog box. Click **Internet Protocol Version 4 (TCP/IPv4)** and then click **Properties.**

4. If your IP settings have the "Obtain an IP address automatically" option enabled, click **Use the following IP address.** You use this option to set a static IP address. If your address is already static, make a note of it, and skip entering the information in Step 5.
5. For the following IP address settings, enter the information shown unless your instructor tells you to use different values. Click **OK** when you're finished:
   - IP address: **192.168.100.*XX*** (replacing *XX* with a number provided by your instructor)
   - Subnet mask: **255.255.255.0**
   - Default gateway: provided by your instructor
   - Preferred DNS server: provided by your instructor
6. Click **Close.** If you're prompted to set a network location, click **Work network,** and then click **Close.**
7. Test the configuration using the *ping* command to communicate with another student's computer or with your default gateway (if provided).
8. To configure an address using the *netsh* command, open a command prompt with administrator privileges (right-click **Start** and click **Command Prompt (Admin)**). To display your current configuration using *netsh*, type **netsh interface ipv4 show addresses** and press **Enter.**
9. To configure your Ethernet0 interface with the same IP address and subnet mask shown in Step 5, type **netsh interface ipv4 set address "Ethernet0" static 192.168.100.*XX* 255.255.255.0** and press **Enter.** Be sure to replace *XX* with an appropriate number.
10. If your interface was using DHCP before you started this project, type **netsh interface ipv4 set address "Ethernet0" dhcp** and then press **Enter.** This command changes the settings back to using DHCP.
11. To configure a static IPv6 address, type **netsh interface ipv6 set address "Ethernet0" 2001:db8::*XX*** and press **Enter,** replacing *XX* with a value assigned by your instructor. The value *db8* in the address is not required, but it designates the address as one used for testing.
12. To test the configuration, type **ping -6 2001:db8::*XX*** and press **Enter,** replacing *XX* with the address of another student's computer. The -6 in the *ping* command tells *ping* to use IPv6 addresses.
13. Close all open windows and shut down your Windows 10 computer.

Project 9-6: Configure the IP Address in Linux

In this project, you configure the IP address in Linux using the *ifconfig* command. You can use *ifconfig* in Mac OS X as well.

1. Start and log on to your Linux computer.
2. Open a terminal window.

3. Type **ifconfig** and press **Enter** to view your current interface settings (see Figure 9-36). Make a note of the interface that is listed on the first line of the output. In Figure 9-36, the interface name is eno16777736. You see your IPv4 address (the number after *inet* in the output) and your IPv6 address (the number after *inet6* in the output).

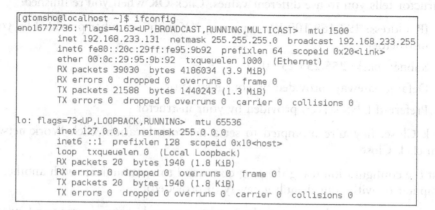

```
[gtomsho@localhost ~]$ ifconfig
eno16777736: flags=4163<UP,BROADCAST,RUNNING,MULTICAST>  mtu 1500
        inet 192.168.233.131  netmask 255.255.255.0  broadcast 192.168.233.255
        inet6 fe80::20c:29ff:fe95:9b92  prefixlen 64  scopeid 0x20<link>
        ether 00:0c:29:95:9b:92  txqueuelen 1000  (Ethernet)
        RX packets 39030  bytes 4186034 (3.9 MiB)
        RX errors 0  dropped 0  overruns 0  frame 0
        TX packets 21588  bytes 1440243 (1.3 MiB)
        TX errors 0  dropped 0 overruns 0  carrier 0  collisions 0

lo: flags=73<UP,LOOPBACK,RUNNING>  mtu 65536
        inet 127.0.0.1  netmask 255.0.0.0
        inet6 ::1  prefixlen 128  scopeid 0x10<host>
        loop  txqueuelen 0  (Local Loopback)
        RX packets 20  bytes 1940 (1.8 KiB)
        RX errors 0  dropped 0  overruns 0  frame 0
        TX packets 20  bytes 1940 (1.8 KiB)
        TX errors 0  dropped 0 overruns 0  carrier 0  collisions 0
```

Figure 9-36 Output from the *ifconfig* command
Source: Linux

4. To configure your interface with an IPv4 address of 192.168.100.XX and a subnet mask of 255.255.255.0, type **ifconfig *InterfaceName* 192.168.100.*XX* netmask 255.255.255.0** and press **Enter**, being sure to replace *InterfaceName* with the name of the interface in the output and *XX* with a number provided by your instructor. If you get an "Operation not permitted" error, you need root permissions, so type **sudo** followed by the command above and then enter your password when prompted.

5. To test the configuration, type **ping *IPAddress*** and press **Enter**, replacing *IPAddress* with the address of another computer. In Linux, the *ping* command keeps sending packets until you stop it. Press **Ctrl+C** to stop the *ping* command.

6. When you use *ifconfig* to configure the IP address, it is only temporary; it will revert to permanent settings (such as using DHCP) at the next boot. To use the GUI tool to configure an IP address, click **Activities** and then click **Show Applications.**

7. Click **Settings** and then click **Network.** Click the settings button in the lower-right corner and then click **IPv4.** To change how Linux receives its IP address, click the list box next to Addresses, then click Automatic (DHCP) to use DHCP or the Manual option to enter an address manually. Click **Cancel.** Close all open windows and shut down your Linux computer.

Project 9-7: Configure the IP Address in Mac OS X

In this project, you configure the IP address in Mac OS X using the Network preferences utility. You can also use the *ifconfig* command in Mac OS X.

1. Start and log on to your Mac OS X computer.
2. Click the **Apple** icon and then click **System Preferences.** Click **Network.**

3. Be sure that Ethernet is selected in the left pane and click the selection arrow next to **Configure IPv4** in the right pane (see Figure 9-37). Make a note of your current settings.

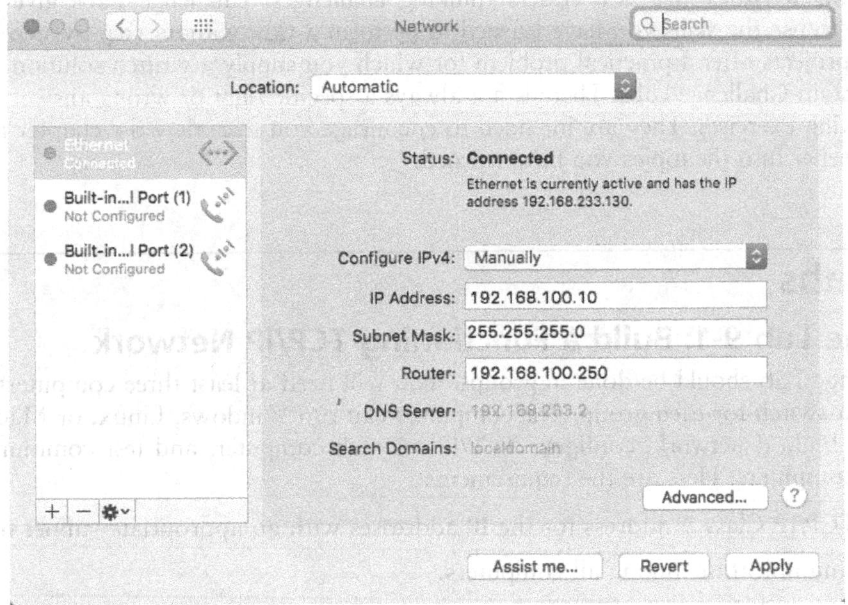

Figure 9-37 Configuring IPv4 in Mac OS X

Source: Mac OS X

4. Click **Manually**, if necessary. Then type the following values:
   - IP Address: **192.168.100.*XX*** (replacing *XX* with a number provided by your instructor)
   - Subnet Mask: **255.255.255.0**
   - Router: provided by your instructor
5. Click **Apply**.
6. To test the configuration, open a terminal window by clicking **Finder** in the Dock. Next, click **Go**, click **Utilities**, and then double-click **Terminal**. Type **ping *IPAddress*** and press **Enter**, replacing *IPAddress* with the address of another computer. As in Linux, the *ping* command keeps sending packets until you press Ctrl+C. Press **Ctrl+C**, close the terminal window, and then close the Utilities window.
7. In the Network window, click **Advanced**. Click each tab to see the options for configuring the network settings. Click the **Hardware** tab. You can use this tab to configure certain properties of the network interface, such as the speed and duplex mode.
8. Click the **TCP/IP** tab. Configure the IP address settings as they were originally set; for example, click the selection arrow next to **Configure IPv4** and click **Using DHCP** if that was the original setting. Click **OK** and click **Apply**.
9. Close all windows and log off or shut down your computer.

Critical Thinking

The following activities give you critical thinking challenges. Challenge Labs give you an opportunity to use the skills you have learned to perform a task without step-by-step instructions. Case projects offer a practical problem for which you supply a written solution. Not all chapters contain Challenge Labs. There is not always a specific right or wrong answer to these critical thinking exercises. They are intended to encourage you to review the chapter material and delve deeper into the topics you have learned.

Challenge Labs

Challenge Lab 9-1: Build a Functioning TCP/IP Network

This Challenge Lab should be done in groups. You will need at least three computers, patch cables, and a switch for each group. The computers can run Windows, Linux, or Mac OS X. You should build a network, configure TCP/IP on each computer, and test communication among the computers. Here are the requirements:

1. Use a TCP/IP Class A address for the IP addresses with an appropriate subnet mask.
2. Test communication among all computers.
3. Answer the following questions.
   - What IP network address did you use?
   - What subnet mask did you use?
   - What command did you use to test communication?
   - What would you need to add to the network to gain access to other networks, including the Internet? How would your TCP/IP configuration change?

Case Projects

Case Project 9-1: Peer-to-Peer or Server-Based Network?

Networking Gadgets, Inc. currently employs eight people but plans to hire 10 more in the next four months. Users will work on multiple projects, and only users assigned to a project should have access to the project files. You're instructed to set up the network to make it easy to manage and back up, yet still provide centralized storage for project files. Would you choose a peer-to-peer network, a server-based network, or a combination? Why?

Case Project 9-2: Peer-to-Peer or Server-Based Network?

CNT Books hired you as a productivity consultant. Currently, it employs six people who will be moving into a new office space. You are to configure a network that allows them to share files and printers. Employees must also be able to control resources on their own machines. The company wants the least expensive solution and only minimal training for employees. Would you choose a peer-to-peer network or a server-based network? Write a list of supplies you might need to purchase to perform this task. What computer configuration tasks might you need to perform?

Case Project 9-3: What Type of Network?

CNT Books has expanded considerably since you got the network up and running three years ago. The company now occupies an entire floor in the building, and its LAN has grown to include several servers and more than 60 workstations. CNT Books has recently purchased another book company and needs more space and computers. Expansion plans include leasing another floor four stories above the current offices in the same building and adding 35 workstations and at least one more server immediately, with additional equipment purchases expected. What type of network is called for—LAN, WAN, MAN, or internetwork? What additional devices might be needed to ensure efficient network communication?

Case Project 9-4: Troubleshoot an IP Configuration

You work at a help desk and have just received a call from an employee who says she can't access network resources. You want the employee to view her IP address configuration. Write an e-mail to the employee explaining what command-line program to use and how she can use it to find the information you need. After following your instructions, the employee tells you that her IP address is 169.254.14.11 with the subnet mask 255.255.0.0. What conclusion can you make from this information?

9

chapter 10

Sharing Resources and Working with Accounts

After reading this chapter and completing the exercises, you will be able to:

- Configure file and printer sharing
- Manage user and group accounts

One of the primary reasons networks were built was to facilitate the sharing of information. In this chapter, you learn about sharing files and printers in Windows, Linux, and Mac OS X. In order to secure access to shared files, you need to configure user and group accounts, then assign permissions to these accounts to determine who can access the shared resources and what type of access they have (read or write, for example). You will learn about different types of user accounts and groups, how to create them, and how to assign permissions to shared resources.

File and Printer Sharing

File and printer sharing is one reason businesses began to outfit computers with network interfaces and network software. Sharing files and printers with other computers on the network requires a file sharing client and a file sharing protocol. The dominant file sharing protocol is **Server Message Block (SMB)**, the native protocol used by Windows; it is also supported by Linux and Mac OS X. **Network File System (NFS)** is the native Linux/UNIX file sharing protocol, and it is supported by Windows and Mac OS X. The protocol you use depends on which client OS is most prevalent on your network—for most networks, it is Windows, so the SMB protocol is the focus of this chapter.

NFS support for Windows is available in Windows Server 2008 and in Windows Vista and later versions.

Printer sharing also uses the SMB protocol in Windows, Linux, and Mac OS X. The native Linux printer sharing protocols are line printer daemon/line printer remote (LPD/LPR) and Common UNIX Printing System (CUPS). CUPS has become the more popular protocol because it is based on the Internet Printing Protocol (IPP).

Sharing Files in Windows

File sharing in Windows is based on Client for Microsoft Networks on the client side and File and Printer Sharing for Microsoft Networks on the server side. To see these client/server components, view the properties of your network connection, as shown in Figure 10-1. Neither Client for Microsoft Networks nor File and Printer Sharing for Microsoft Networks has any configuration options other than the ability to disable them on a particular network connection.

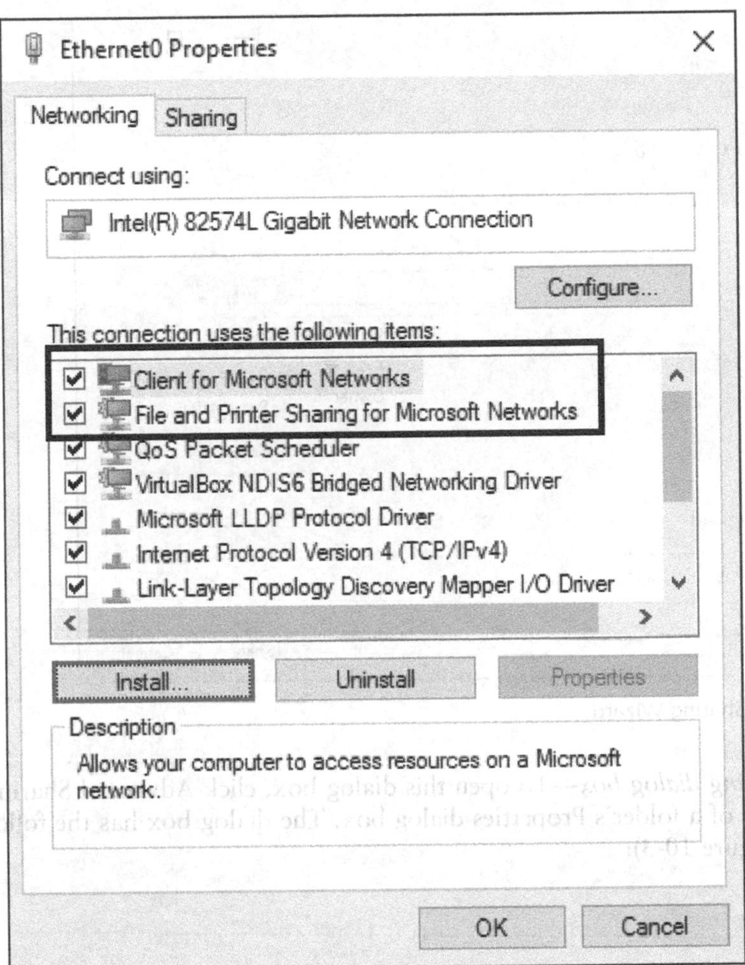

Figure 10-1 File sharing components in Windows

To share files in Windows, you share the folder in which the files are located. You can use the following methods to configure folder sharing in Windows. The procedures are similar in Windows client OSs:

- *File Sharing Wizard*—To start this wizard, right-click a folder, point to Share with, and then click Specific people. The File Sharing Wizard (see Figure 10-2) simplifies sharing for novices by simplifying the permissions settings.

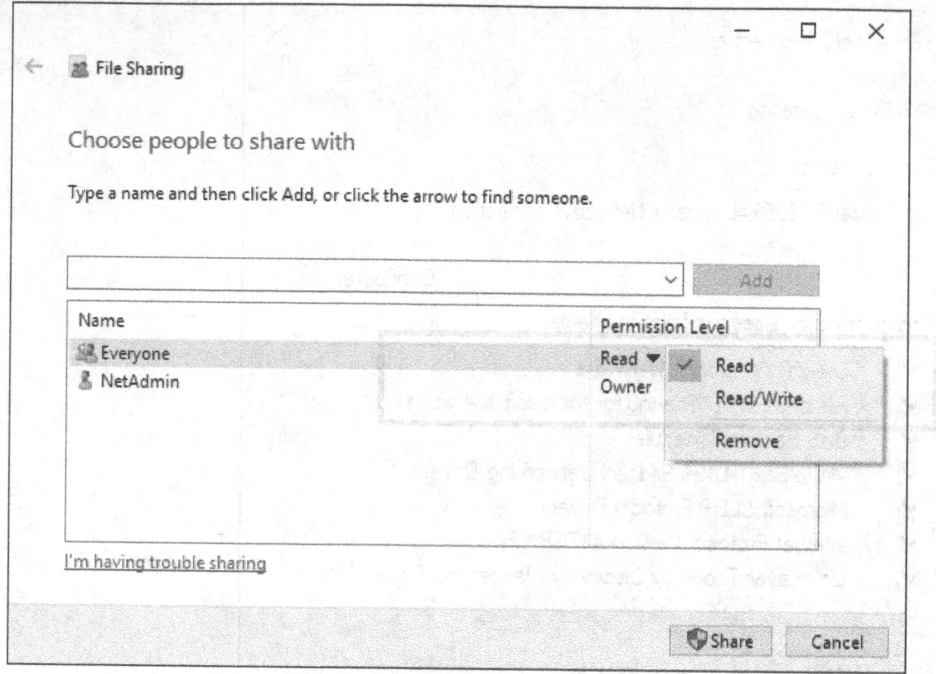

Figure 10-2 The File Sharing Wizard

- *Advanced Sharing dialog box*—To open this dialog box, click Advanced Sharing in the Sharing tab of a folder's Properties dialog box. The dialog box has the following options (see Figure 10-3):

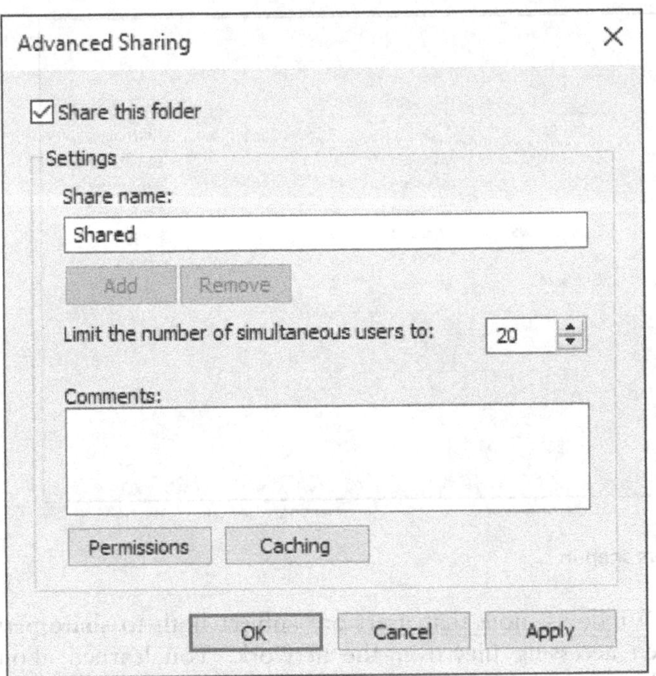

Figure 10-3 The Advanced Sharing dialog box

- *Share this folder:* To enable folder sharing, click this check box.
- *Share name:* Users see the folder share name in the Network folder of File Explorer or when using the net share command. In other words, it's the name you use to access the folder with the UNC path (\\server\share name). You can add or remove share names. A single folder can have multiple share names and different permissions, a different number of simultaneous users, and caching settings for each share name.
- *Limit the number of simultaneous users to:* In Windows Server, the default limit is 16,777,216, which is practically unlimited. In Windows client OSs, up to 20 users can access a share simultaneously.
- *Comments:* You can enter a description of the share's contents and settings in this text box.
- *Permissions:* Click this button to open the Permissions dialog box.
- *Caching:* This option controls how offline files are configured. Offline files enable users to disconnect from the network and still have access to the shared files they were using.

- *Shared Folders snap-in*—Use this component of the Computer Management console (see Figure 10-4) to monitor, change, and create shares on the local computer or a remote computer. To create a share, right-click the Shares node under the Shared Folders snap-in and click New Share. The Create A Shared Folder Wizard walks you through the processes of selecting a folder to share or creating a new folder to share, naming the share, configuring offline files, and setting permissions.

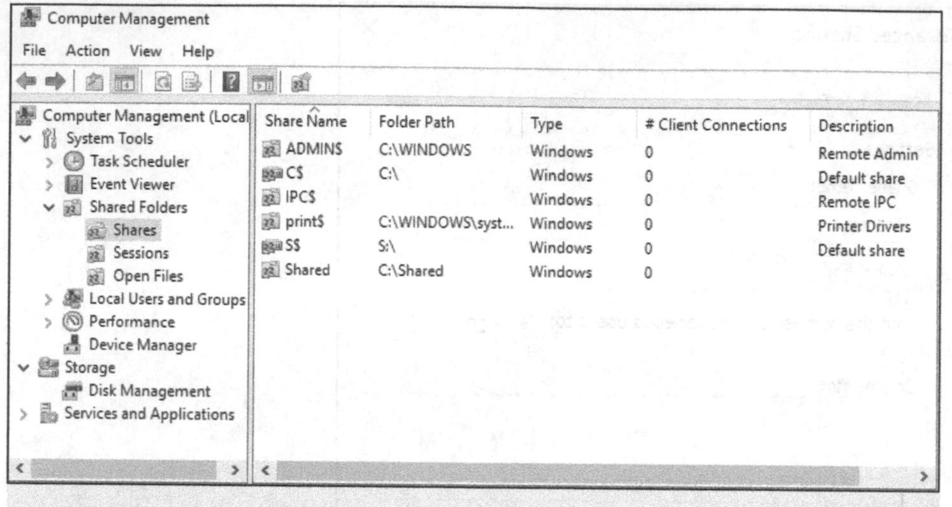

Figure 10-4 The Shared Folders snap-in

When using file sharing in Windows, note that users are subject both to share permissions and NTFS permissions when accessing files over the network. You learned about NTFS permissions in Chapter 4. Share permissions are somewhat simpler, and there are only three (see Figure 10-5):

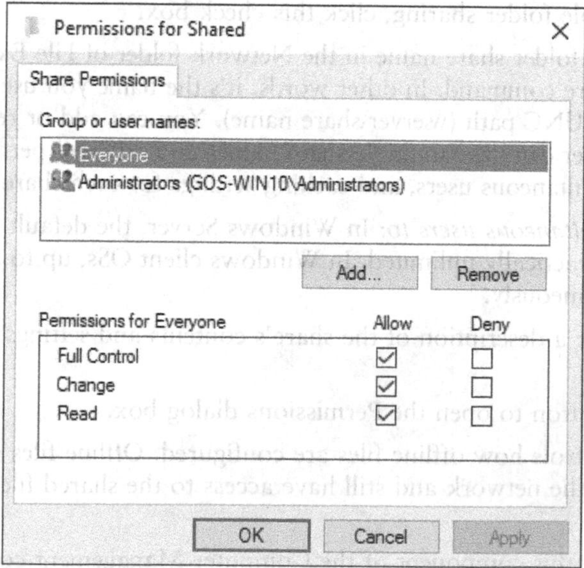

Figure 10-5 Viewing share permissions

- *Read*—Users can view contents of files, copy files, run applications and script files, open folders and subfolders, and view file attributes.

- *Change*—Users have all the permissions granted by Read, as well as the ability to create files and folders, change their contents and attributes, and delete files and folders.
- *Full Control*—Users have all the permissions granted by Change; they can also change file and folder permissions as well as take ownership of files and folders.

Windows assigns default permissions depending on how a folder is shared. Generally, the default share permission is Read for the Everyone group. On FAT/FAT32 volumes, share permissions are the only way to secure files accessed through the network because these file systems don't support local file permissions.

Sharing files on the network isn't difficult in a Windows environment. Nonetheless, you should be familiar with some techniques and options before setting up a file sharing server.

Accessing Shared Files in Windows A file sharing client requests access to shared files and printers on a network server. When a user or an application requests a resource—such as a printer or a data file—a **redirector** intercepts the request and then examines it to determine whether the resource is local (on the computer) or remote (on the network). If the resource is local, the redirector sends the request to the local software component for processing. If the resource is remote, the redirector sends the request over the network to the server hosting the resource.

With redirectors, network resources can be accessed as though they were local. For example, a user or user application doesn't distinguish between a printer connected to a local USB port and one connected to the network. In addition, with drive mapping, shared network folders are accessed just like a drive that's physically attached to the system—at least from the user's point of view. In Windows, the redirector component is part of Client for Microsoft Networks. The two most common ways to access a shared resource in Windows are by using the UNC path and mapping a drive.

The UNC path is used to access a shared folder, and has the syntax *\\server-name\sharename*. The *server-name* is the name of the computer where the shared resource resides. You can also use the server's IP address in place of its name. The *sharename* is the name given to the folder or printer when it was shared. You can directly access a subfolder or file in the share by continuing the UNC path, as in *\\server-name\sharename\subfolder\file.extension*.

Linux and Mac OS X systems also use the UNC path to access shared resources, but forward slashes are used in place of backslashes.

TIP

You can use the UNC path to access shared folders and printers, but you must type the path every time you need it or create a shortcut with the UNC path as the target. In Windows, one common method of simplifying access to shared files (particularly those that are used often) is drive mapping, which associates a drive letter with the UNC path to a shared folder. Drives are usually mapped by using File Explorer or the *net* command. To use File Explorer, simply type the server portion of the UNC path in the Search text box on the taskbar to see a list of shared folders and printers the server is hosting. Right-click a shared folder and click Map network drive, as shown in Figure 10-6. You can then pick a drive letter that's not already in use and choose to have Windows reconnect to the share with the same drive letter every time you log on.

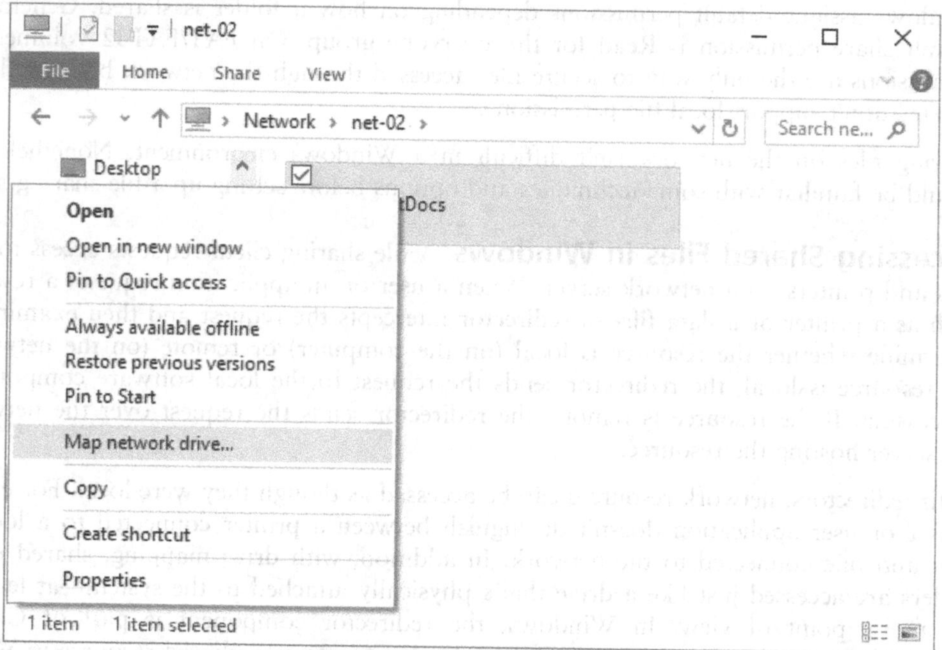

Figure 10-6 Mapping a drive in File Explorer

Another method of mapping a drive is to use the *net* command. This method is often used by administrators in a logon script, which consists of commands that run when a user logs on to a Windows domain. The command syntax to map a drive with the *net* command is *net use drive-letter: \\server-name\sharename*.

The *drive-letter* is an unused drive letter, and it must be followed by a colon (:). The command can be entered at the command prompt or placed in a batch file. A **batch file** is a text file with a .bat or .cmd extension that contains a list of commands you ordinarily type at the command prompt. To run a batch file, enter its name at the command prompt or double-click the file in File Explorer. Batch files are useful for storing long, complex commands that are used often or a series of commands that are always used together.

As you've learned, Linux and Mac OS X don't use drive letters at all. Instead, their file systems are based on the concept of a file system root designator, which is simply the / character. All local and network drives and folders are accessed from the root as folders. A drive or network share is mounted into an empty directory so that it becomes part of the file system hierarchy. To access a shared folder in Linux or Mac OS X, you create a new directory at the root of the file system or in a subdirectory, and then mount the shared folder in the new directory.

Sharing Printers in Windows To understand how to work with and share printers in a Windows environment, first you need to know the terminology for defining the components of a shared printer:

- *Print device*—The physical printer to which print jobs are sent. There are two basic types of print devices:
    - *Local print device:* A printer connected to a port on a computer with a parallel or USB cable or through a TCP/IP port, which is used to access a printer attached directly to the network through the printer's NIC
    - *Network print device:* A printer attached to and shared by another computer
- *Printer*—The icon in the Printers folder that represents print devices. Windows programs use a printer driver to format the print job and send it to the print device or print server. A printer can be a local printer, which prints directly to a local or network print device, or a network printer, which prints to a print server.
- *Print server*—A Windows computer that shares a printer. It accepts print jobs from computers on the network and sends jobs to the printer.
- *Print queue*—A storage location for pending print jobs. In Windows, the print queue is implemented as a folder (by default, C:\Windows\System32\Spool\Printers) where files are stored until they're sent to the print device or print server.

A configured print server can perform a host of functions that aren't possible when users' computers print directly to a print device:

- *Access control*—Using permissions, administrators can control who may print to a printer and manage print jobs and printers.
- *Printer pooling*—A single printer represents two or more print devices. The print server sends the job to the print device that's least busy.
- *Printer priority*—Two or more printers can represent a single print device. In this case, printers can be assigned different priorities so that jobs sent to the higher-priority printer are printed first.
- *Print job management*—Administrators can pause, cancel, restart, reorder, and change preferences on print jobs waiting in the print queue.
- *Availability control*—Administrators can configure print servers so that print jobs are accepted only during certain hours of the day.

To configure a print server, you just need to share a printer. After a printer is installed, right-click its icon, click Printer properties, and then click the Sharing tab. The Sharing tab of a print server's Properties dialog box contains the following options:

- *Share this printer*—When this check box is selected, the print server is shared. By default, everyone is assigned print permissions to shared printers.
- *Share name*—By default, it's the name of the print server in the Printers folder. You can enter a shorter share name or one that's easier to remember.
- *Render print jobs on client computers*—When this check box is selected (the default setting), client computers process the print job and send it to the print server in a

format that's ready to go directly to the print device. If this option isn't selected, more processing occurs on the print server.

- *List in the directory*—This option is shown if the computer on which the printer is being shared is a member of a Windows Active Directory domain. When this check box is selected, the print server is displayed in Active Directory and can be found by Active Directory searches. By default, this option isn't selected.
- *Additional drivers*—When a client connects to a shared printer, the printer driver is downloaded to the client from the server automatically when possible. You can click this button to install different printer drivers on the server to support different Windows versions.

Sharing Files and Printers in Linux

Linux supports Windows file sharing by using SMB in a software package called *Samba*. Depending on the Linux distribution, you might have to install this component. On a Linux system with Samba installed, you can share a folder using the Samba Server Configuration GUI tool (see Figure 10-7) or by editing the /etc/samba/smb.conf file. When you use the GUI tool to configure Samba, changes to the smb.conf file are made automatically. Figure 10-8 shows part of the smb.conf file after the folder named Folder1 has been shared using the GUI tool.

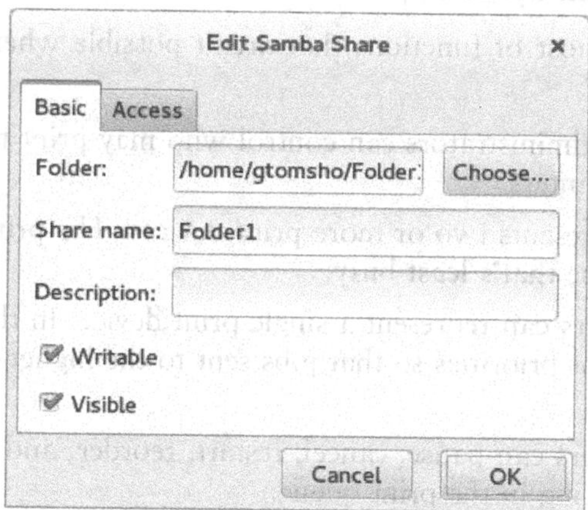

Figure 10-7 Sharing a folder in Linux

Source: Linux

```
[Folder1]
        path = /home/gtomsho/Folder1
        read only = no
;       browseable = yes
        guest ok = yes
```

Figure 10-8 The smb.conf file

Source: Linux

Once a folder is shared in Linux, it can be accessed by another computer using the UNC path; for example, to access the shared folder named Folder1 on a Linux server named LinuxSrv from Windows, you would type the UNC path \\LinuxSrv\Folder1 into a File Explorer or Run box.

Printer sharing in Linux is straightforward after Samba has been installed. When you create a printer in Linux, it's shared automatically. To configure additional printer sharing options, you must edit the /etc/samba/smb.conf file and look for the line that starts with "[printers]."

Accessing Shared Files in Linux To access shared files on another computer from a Linux client, you can use the Files tool and browse the network. If you see the computer that contains the shared files, click the computer's icon and enter your credentials, if necessary. Otherwise, click Connect to Server in the left pane and enter the path to the server. You must preface the path with *smb:* so Linux knows you are trying to connect to an SMB share (see Figure 10-9).

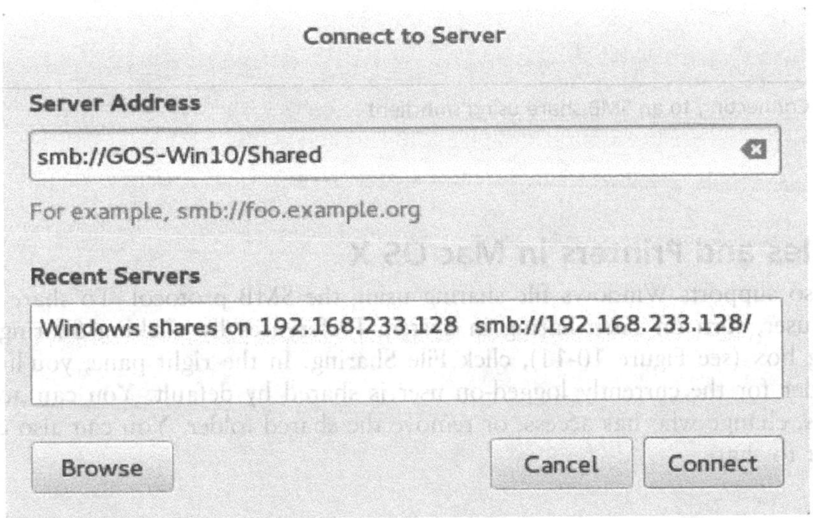

Figure 10-9 Connecting to an SMB share in Linux

Source: Linux

Linux also comes with a command-line program called *smbclient* for accessing SMB shares. To use smbclient, type *smbclient //servername/share* and press Enter. You will see a prompt for *smb*, from which you can enter commands to upload and download files. To see a list of these commands, type *?* and press Enter at the smb: \> prompt (see Figure 10-10).

```
[gtomsho@localhost ~]$ smbclient //gregs-mac.local/folder1
Enter gtomsho's password:
Domain=[GREGS-MAC] OS=[Darwin] Server=[@(#)PROGRAM:smbd PROJECT:smbx-347
smb: \> ?
?              allinfo        altname        archive        backup
blocksize      cancel         case_sensitive cd             chmod
chown          close          del            dir            du
echo           exit           get            getfacl        geteas
hardlink       help           history        iosize         lcd
link           lock           lowercase      ls             l
mask           md             mget           mkdir          more
mput           newer          notify         open           posix
posix_encrypt  posix_open     posix_mkdir    posix_rmdir    posix_unlink
print          prompt         put            pwd            q
queue          quit           readlink       rd             recurse
reget          rename         reput          rm             rmdir
showacls       setea          setmode        stat           symlink
tar            tarmode        timeout        translate      unlock
volume         vuid           wdel           logon          listconnect
showconnect    tcon           tdis           tid            logoff
..             !
smb: \>
```

Figure 10-10 Connecting to an SMB share using smbclient

Source: Linux

Sharing Files and Printers in Mac OS X

Mac OS X also supports Windows file sharing using the SMB protocol. To share a folder with another user, turn on File Sharing in System Preferences by clicking Sharing. In the Sharing dialog box (see Figure 10-11), click File Sharing. In the right pane, you'll see that the Public folder for the currently logged-on user is shared by default. You can accept the default settings, change who has access, or remove the shared folder. You can also choose a different folder to share.

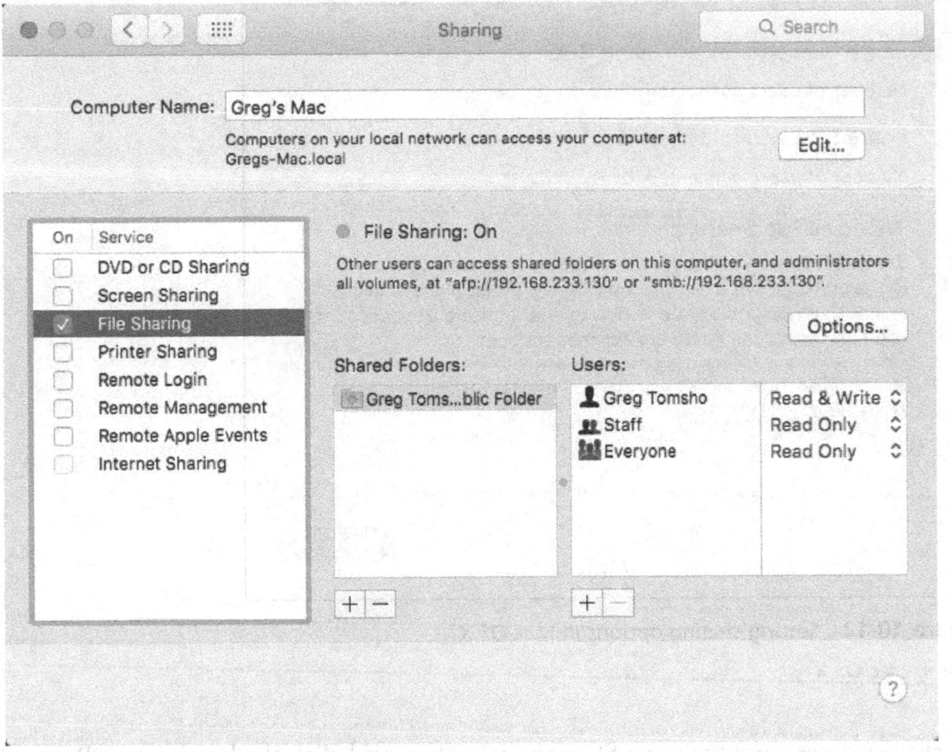

Figure 10-11 Sharing a folder in Mac OS X

Source: Mac OS X

After you have chosen the folder you want to share and set the permissions, click Options to turn on sharing for SMB if you want to share your files with Windows or Linux users. For Windows file sharing, you must enable sharing for each user (see Figure 10-12).

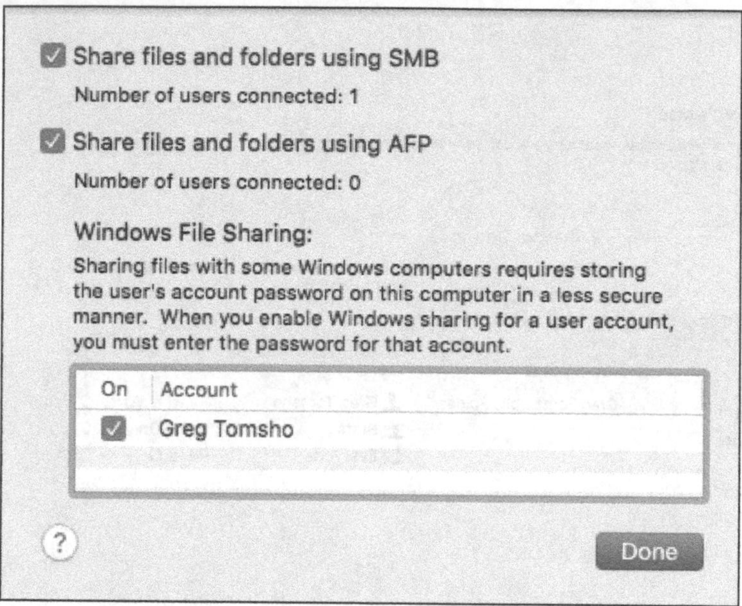

Figure 10-12 Setting sharing options in Mac OS X

Source: Mac OS X

To share printers, use the same Sharing dialog box and click the box next to Printer Sharing. In the right pane, you are presented with a list of printers you can share. Select the printers you want to share and the users with whom you want to share them.

Accessing Shared Files in Mac OS X To access shared files on another computer from a Mac OS X client, click Go and then click Network to browse the network. If you see the computer that contains the shared files, click its icon and enter your credentials, if necessary. Otherwise, click Go, click Connect to Server, and enter the path to the server. You must preface the path with *smb:*, as with Linux. Once connected, you will see the computer in the Network browse window, so you won't need to connect to it each time you want to access shared files on the server.

Managing User and Group Accounts

If you share files and printers, you'll usually want to control access to those shared resources through user accounts, group accounts, and permissions. Working with user accounts is one of an administrator's key tasks. User accounts are the link between people and network resources, so user account management requires both technical expertise and people skills. When users can't log on to the network or access the resources they need, IT staff members get the phone calls. Your understanding of how user accounts work and how to configure them can reduce the frequency of these calls. User accounts have two main functions in a network:

- *Provide a method for users to authenticate themselves to the network*—Using a username and password is the most common way for users to log on to a network and gain access to network resources. This process is called **authentication**. User accounts can also contain restrictions about when and where a user can log on. Administrators use user accounts to assign permissions to network resources and define the types of actions a user can perform on the system, such as installing software, configuring hardware, or accessing files. This process is called **authorization**. Many tasks require elevated access, such as administrator access in Windows or root access in Linux.
- *Provide detailed information about a user*—User accounts can hold information such as a user's phone number, office location, and department. This information can be used in a company directory or by the IT department to identify users for support purposes.

Group accounts are used to organize users so that resource permissions and rights can be managed more easily than working with dozens or hundreds of user accounts. For example, an administrator can make a group account for each department in the company and add the users in each department as members of the corresponding group. Then, when a department creates a shared folder and documents for its users, the administrator just needs to assign permission to the group, which gives all its members the necessary permission. If a user changes departments, the administrator moves the account from one group to another, thereby changing the resources to which the user has permissions.

Account and Password Conventions

In a small network with only a few users and network resources, establishing a naming convention for accounts might be more trouble than it's worth. When you're working with dozens of servers and hundreds or thousands of users, however, a scheme for naming user and group accounts as well as network devices is crucial. For user accounts, considerations for a naming convention include the following:

- Should user account names have a minimum and maximum number of characters?
- Should the username be based on the user's real name? If security is of utmost importance, should usernames be more cryptic and difficult to guess?
- Some OSs distinguish between uppercase and lowercase letters. Should usernames contain both as well as special characters, such as periods and underscores?

There's no right or wrong answer to these questions, but after you devise a policy, you should stick to it so that when it's time to create a new user account, your naming conventions make the process straightforward.

Passwords are also part of creating user accounts. The considerations for password naming conventions include the following:

- *Minimum length*—In environments where a user account is based on a user's real name, all that's needed to access the account is to correctly guess the password. Longer passwords are harder to guess and therefore more secure.

- *Complexity requirements*—Using uppercase and lowercase letters along with numbers and special symbols (such as @, $, and %) makes passwords considerably more difficult to guess, even with password-guessing software.
- *User or administrator created*—In most cases, users create their own passwords after an administrator gives them an initial password. However, to ensure that passwords are complex enough, administrators can use dictionary attacks and other brute-force methods to attempt to crack them.
- *Password change frequency*—Many networks require frequent password changes to enhance security. However, if changes are required too frequently, users are more apt to write down their passwords, which is a major security risk.

There are other considerations for working with passwords, some of which are particular to the OS on which the user account is created. You learn more about password-handling options in the next section.

Group account names also warrant careful planning. The group name should reflect the group membership or the resource to which the group is assigned permissions or rights. For example, the group name might simply be a department name, or it might reflect a resource permission assignment, such as *NAS_4thFloor*, which indicates that group members have access to the NAS server on the 4th floor. In some cases, a group name might reflect the role that group members have in the company, such as supervisors, administrators, or executives. The most important aspect of naming conventions is establishing and sticking to them; only users who are well versed in these conventions should be allowed to create accounts.

Working with Accounts in Windows

This section discusses user and group accounts in Windows Server 2016 with Active Directory; you will also work with accounts in a Windows 10 client OS in the Hands-On Projects at the end of this chapter. A key point to remember when working with accounts in Active Directory is that they're used to log on to the Windows domain and can access resources on all computers that are domain members. By contrast, an account created in a Windows client OS is used only to log on to a particular computer and access resources only on that computer.

When Windows is installed, two users are created: Administrator and Guest. On a Windows Server 2016 domain controller, the Guest account is disabled, and in Windows 10, both Administrator and Guest are disabled. In Windows 10, you create a user with administrator privileges during installation. The Guest account is rarely used and poses a security risk, which is why it's disabled. You can enable the account if you like, but best practices dictate creating new accounts for guest users of your network. The Administrator account has full access to a computer, and in a Windows domain, the domain Administrator account's access is extended to all computers that are domain members. You must carefully consider who can log on as Administrator and who is a member of the Administrators group.

Creating User Accounts in Windows Domains Windows domain users are created in Active Directory Users and Computers (shown in Figure 10-13), in Active Directory Administrative Center (ADAC), or with command-line tools. As you can see, several folders are available for organizing users, groups, and other domain elements. You can also create your own folders, called *organizational units (OUs)*, to match your company's organizational scheme. For example, you can create a folder for each department or create folders that represent office locations. In Figure 10-13, the open folder named Users contains the Administrator and Guest accounts and many of the default groups created when Active Directory is installed. You can create additional users in this folder, but it's better to add OUs and then create users and groups in the OU structure you specify.

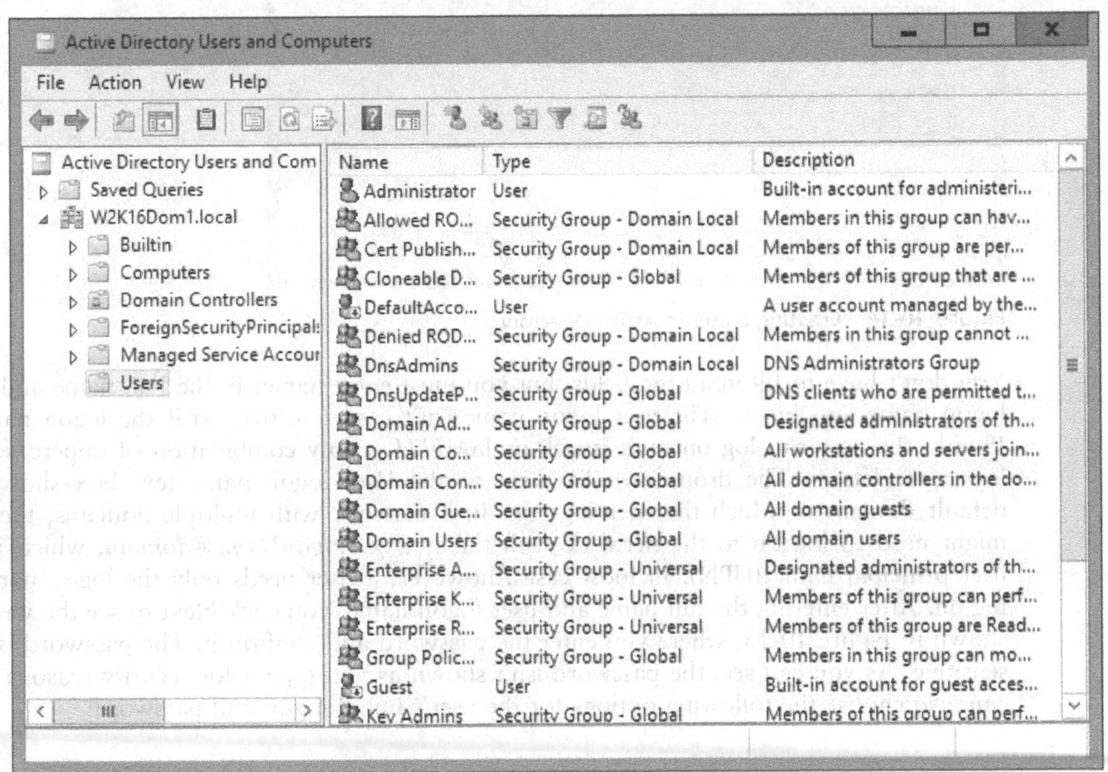

Figure 10-13 The Active Directory Users and Computers management console

To create a user account, select the folder where you want to create it. Right-click the folder, point to New, and then click User, or click the user icon on the Active Directory Users and Computers toolbar. The New Object - User dialog box opens (see Figure 10-14). Everything you create in Active Directory is considered an object.

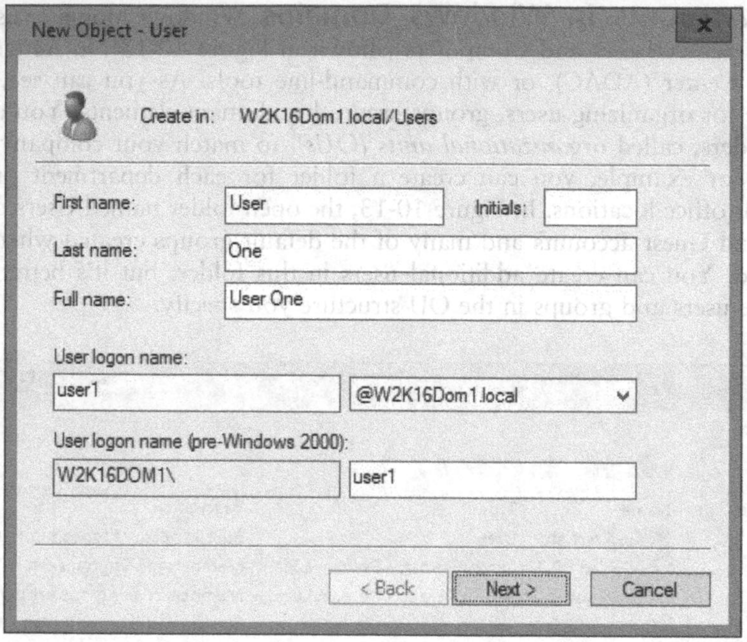

Figure 10-14 Creating a user in Active Directory

You don't have to fill in all the fields, but you must enter names in the Full name and User logon name text boxes. The user logon name isn't case sensitive, so if the logon name is JSmith, the user can log on with *jsmith* or *JSMITH* or any combination of uppercase and lowercase letters. The drop-down list next to the User logon name text box shows the default domain to which the user logs on. In a network with multiple domains, the user might need to log on to the network with the syntax *LogonName@domain*, which is the user principal name (UPN). In most cases, however, a user needs only the logon name to log on. After entering the full name and user logon name, you click Next to see the window shown in Figure 10-15, where you enter the password and confirm it. The password is case sensitive. As you can see, the password isn't shown as you type it for security reasons. You can also choose the following options for the user's initial logon and password:

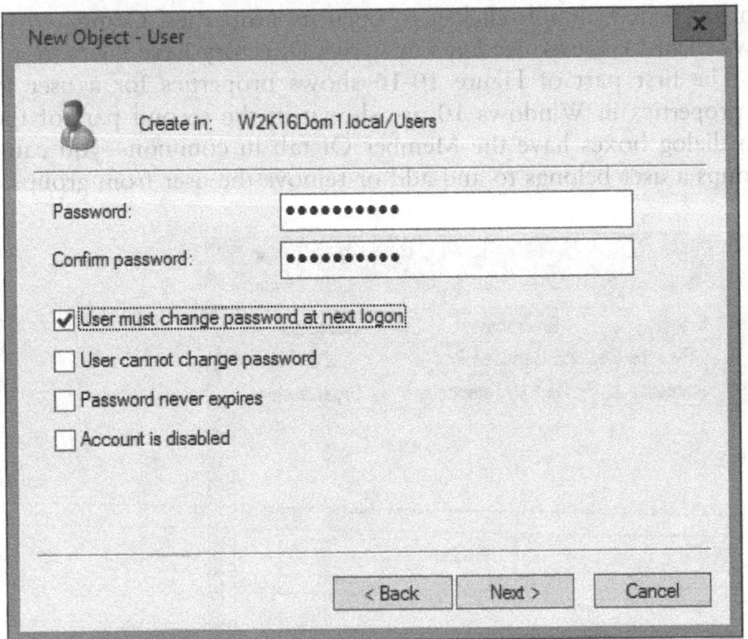

Figure 10-15 Setting the password and additional account options

- *User must change password at next logon*—The user is prompted to change the password at the next logon. Administrators sometimes create accounts with a default password based on the user's name or phone number that must be changed at the next logon. This option can also be set when users forget their passwords and the support staff changes passwords for them.
- *User cannot change password*—When the administrator wants to maintain control of passwords, this option can be set to prevent users from changing their own. It's also used when multiple users have a common generic account for logging on (such as "salesperson").
- *Password never expires*—Users can be required to change their passwords periodically. If this option is set, users aren't subject to the password change requirement.
- *Account is disabled*—If a user account is created several days before it will be used, the account can be disabled at first and then enabled when the user joins the company. In addition, if a user leaves the company or will be gone for an extended period, the account can be disabled. When a user leaves the company, the account is often disabled rather than deleted so that the replacement can use the same account after it is renamed and the password is changed. In this way, the new user has all the same permissions and rights as the previous user.

After a user account is created, double-click it to open its properties. Compared with user accounts in Windows client OSs, user accounts in Active Directory have far more properties you can configure. The first part of Figure 10-16 shows properties for a user in Active Directory; account properties in Windows 10 are shown in the second part of the figure. Notice that the two dialog boxes have the Member Of tab in common—you can use this tab to see which groups a user belongs to and add or remove the user from groups.

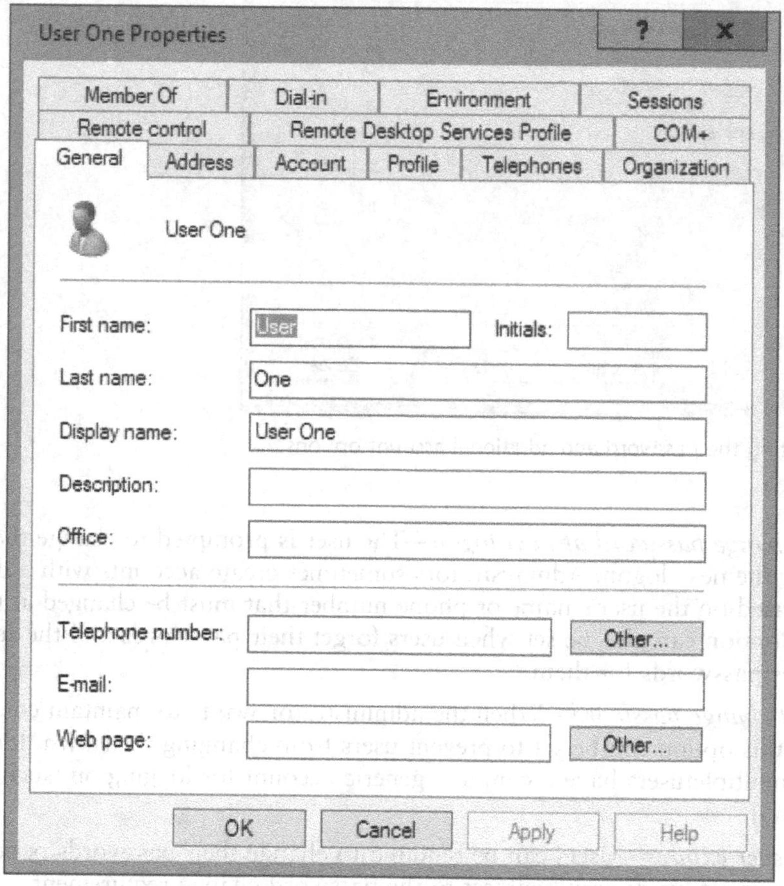

Figure 10-16 User properties in Active Directory and in Windows 10

TestUser Properties

General | Member Of | Profile

TestUser

Full name: TestUser

Description:

User must change password at next logon

User cannot change password

Password never expires

Account is disabled

Account is locked out

OK | Cancel | Apply | Help

Figure 10-16 User properties in Active Directory and in Windows 10 *(continued)*

When a user is added to a group or removed from it, the setting takes effect the next time the user logs on; if a user is already logged on, he or she must log off and log on again.

Creating Group Accounts in Windows Domains Group accounts are easy to create. All they require is a name; after they're created, you can begin adding users as members. The process is similar to creating a user account. In Active Directory, the New Object - Group dialog box looks like Figure 10-17. The "Group name (pre-Windows 2000)" text box is used for backward compatibility with older Windows OSs. The other options, group scope and group type, are used only in Windows domains. The **group scope** lets you create one of three different group types:

- *Domain local group*—This group type can be used to assign permissions to resources only in the domain in which the group is created. Although domain local groups can contain users from any domain, they're used mainly to hold global groups and assign permissions to global group members.

- *Global group*—The default option, global groups contain users from the domain in which they're created, but they can be assigned permissions to resources in other domains in a multidomain network. Their main purpose is to group users who require access to similar resources.
- *Universal group*—This group type is used in multidomain networks; users from any domain can be members and can be assigned permissions to resources in any domain.

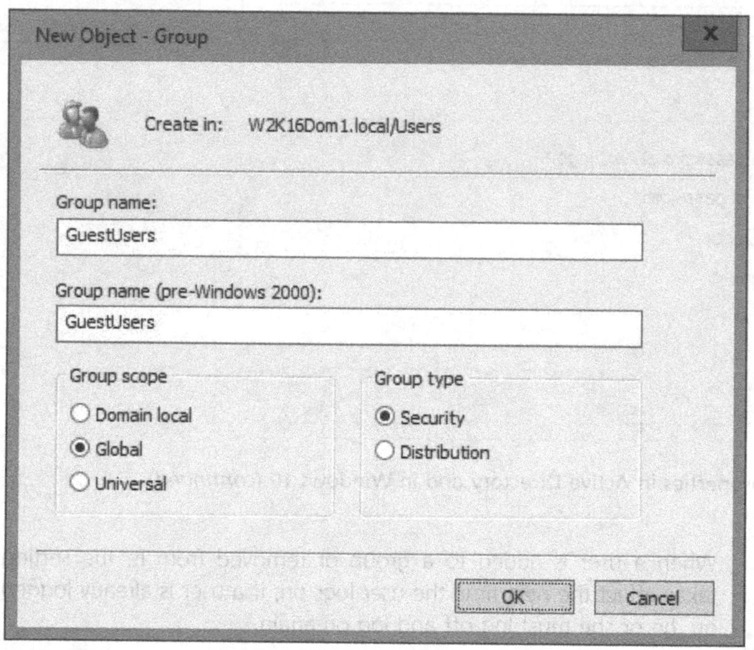

Figure 10-17 Creating a group in Active Directory

A detailed discussion of group scope is beyond the scope of this book. For a complete discussion, see *MCSA Guide to Installing and Configuring Microsoft Windows Server 2012/R2* (Cengage Learning, 2015, ISBN 9781285868653).

The Group type option is set to Security by default. Distribution groups are used only for tasks like sending all group members an e-mail when you run an Active Directory-integrated e-mail program, such as Microsoft Exchange.

Windows Default Groups Aside from groups you create to organize users and assign permissions, Windows defines some **default groups**, which have preassigned rights that apply to all group members. Table 10-1 shows the most important default domain local groups in Windows Server running Active Directory. The table also shows the rights assigned to these groups.

Table 10-1 Some Windows Server default domain local groups

Group	Rights
Administrators	Has complete control over the computer and domain
Account Operators	Can administer user and group accounts for the local domain
Backup Operators	Can back up and restore files that users can't normally access
Guests	Is allowed guest access to domain resources; same access as the Users group
Print Operators	Can add, delete, and manage domain printers
Server Operators	Can administer domain servers
Users	Has the same default access rights that ordinary user accounts have

In addition, Windows Server has numerous default global groups, including Domain Admins, Domain Users, and Domain Guests. These groups apply to entire domains rather than a single machine, and are essentially the same as domain local groups with similar names.

Special Identity Groups Special identity groups, as described in Table 10-2, don't appear as objects in Active Directory Users and Computers or in Local Users and Groups, but they can be assigned permissions and rights. Membership in these groups is controlled dynamically by Windows, can't be viewed or changed manually, and depends on how an account accesses the OS. For example, membership in the Authenticated Users group is assigned to a user account automatically when the user logs on to a computer or domain.

Table 10-2 Some Windows special identity groups

Special identity group	Description
Authenticated Users	Members belong to any user account (except Guest) that can be used to log on to a computer or domain with a valid username and password.
Creator Owner	A user becomes a member automatically for a resource he or she created, such as a folder.
Everyone	Refers to all users who access the system; similar to the Authenticated Users group but includes the Guest user.
Interactive	Members are users who are logged on to a computer locally or through Remote Desktop Services.
Network	Members are users who are logged on to a computer through a network connection.
System	Refers to the Windows OS.
Self	Refers to the object on which permissions are being set.

From the Trenches ...

The author manages a small departmental network and hires students to help with classroom lab maintenance. Sometimes, the tasks performed by students require administrative access to the client workstations. In Windows, a domain administrator has full permissions and rights to all client and server computers in the domain. However, it is not good security practice to give all users domain administrator access. The goal is to give students temporary administrator access to client workstations when they need it but not to provide them with the administrator account username and password. The solution is to use groups wisely. A Global group called clientAdmins is created in the domain; then, using a feature of Group Policy, this group is made a member of the Administrators local group on the client workstations. When students need to perform a task that requires local administrator access, their user accounts are added as members of the clientAdmins Global group. When they log on to client workstations, they have local administrator access. When they finish the task, their accounts are removed from the clientAdmins group and their privileges revert to regular user privileges.

Working with Accounts in Linux

User and group accounts in Linux have the same purposes as in Windows: user authentication and authorization. Linux OSs also have a default user named root who has full control over all aspects of the system. As in Windows, the root user account is used only when you're performing tasks that require root privileges, such as creating additional system users. In fact, some Linux distributions require creating a user during installation because logging on as root isn't allowed; you can access root privileges only by entering a special command.

Most Linux administration takes place at the command line. In its simplest form, user creation is a matter of using the *useradd newuser* command; you replace *newuser* with the logon name for the user account you're creating. Then you create a password for the user with the *passwd newuser* command. Both the logon name and password are case sensitive in Linux.

On most Linux systems, you can't run *useradd* and similar commands unless you're logged on as the root user or you preface the command with *sudo*, as in *sudo useradd newuser*. The *sudo* command, which stands for "superuser do," executes the command with root privileges. If you know you will use many commands that require root privileges, you can change to the root user temporarily with the *su* command (which means "switch user"). This command attempts to switch to the root user when no user is specified, and you must enter the root user's password when prompted.

When some commands are entered with a username, as in *passwd testuser*, the command is executed only for the specified user account. If the commands are entered without a username, they're executed only for the current user. For example, users or administrators can change a user's password with the *passwd* command. You can change user information with the *usermod* command and delete users with the *deluser* command.

The *useradd* command has many options. For example, you can specify a different home directory and assign group memberships. You practice using this command in a Hands-On Project at the end of this chapter.

As with most commands, you can see extensive help for the commands used to create and modify users and groups in Linux by prefacing the command with *man*, as in *man useradd*.

All users must belong to at least one group in Linux. When a user is created, a group with the same name as the user is also created, and the new user is made a member of this group. However, you can create groups and add users to them, just as you can in Windows.

Groups are created with the aptly named *groupadd* command. To add users as members of a group, you can specify this option when you create the user account. You can also use the *useradd username groupname* command or the *usermod* command.

To view the list of users, display the /etc/passwd file's contents with the *cat /etc/passwd* command; to view the list of groups, display the /etc/group file's contents with the *cat /etc/group* command. The *cat* command lists a text file's contents onscreen.

For those who prefer a GUI to manage users and groups, most Linux distributions have convenient graphical interfaces for doing so. In Fedora Linux, the Users tool is available to manage users (see Figure 10-18).

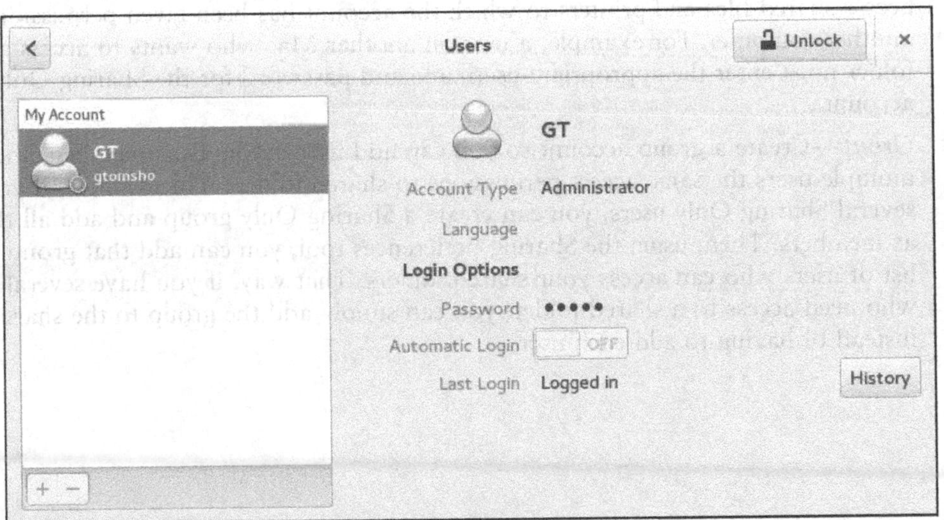

Figure 10-18 The Users control panel in Fedora Linux

Source: Fedora Linux

Many administrators prefer the command-line method for creating users because they can import user information from a text file and add many users at one time by using the *newusers* command.

10

Working with Accounts in Mac OS X

In Mac OS X, you create users and groups using the Users & Groups tool in System Preferences. To create a user, click the plus sign in the left pane of Users & Groups, click the selection arrow next to New Account (see Figure 10-19) to choose the type of account you want to create, and then enter the user's full name, account name, and password. If the user already has an iCloud account, you can use the existing iCloud password or enter a new password. You can also include a password hint.

You can choose one of the following account types:

- *Administrator*—The user has full access to the Mac OS X computer, can create and manage user and group accounts, and can change any of the Mac OS X settings.
- *Standard*—Users can run applications and create files in their home folder but cannot perform administrative actions such as installing devices, formatting drives, and changing network settings. Standard users can install apps and change settings for their own use.
- *Managed with parental controls*—Parental controls can be enforced for users, including which apps they can run, which Web sites they can visit, and how long they can use the computer during a session.
- *Sharing Only*—This type of user cannot log on to the local Mac computer, but can access shared files and printers to which the account has been given permission from another computer. For example, a user on another Mac who wants to access a shared folder must enter the appropriate username and password for the Sharing Only user account.
- *Group*—Create a group account so you can add user accounts as members and assign multiple users the same access permissions to shared folders. For example, if you create several Sharing Only users, you can create a Sharing Only group and add all the users as members. Then, using the Sharing preferences tool, you can add that group to the list of users who can access your shared folders. That way, if you have several users who need access to a shared folder, you can simply add the group to the shared folder instead of having to add each user.

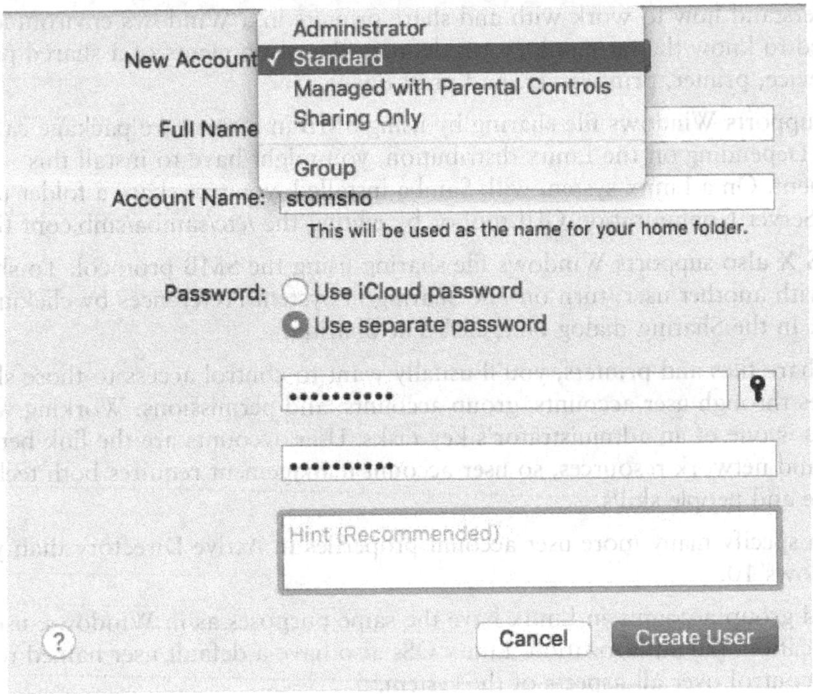

Figure 10-19 Creating a new account in Mac OS X

Source: Mac OS X

This chapter provided basic details for sharing resources in an operating system. A more comprehensive treatment is beyond the scope of this book, but you now have a starting point from which to explore this topic further on the three OS platforms.

Chapter Summary

- File and printer sharing is one reason businesses began to outfit computers with network interfaces and network software. Sharing files and printers with other computers on the network requires a file sharing client and a file sharing protocol The dominant file sharing protocol is Server Message Block (SMB), the native protocol used by Windows; it is also supported by Linux and Mac OS X.
- File sharing in Windows is based on Client for Microsoft Networks on the client side and File and Printer Sharing for Microsoft Networks on the server side. To share files in Windows, you share the folder in which the files are located. Windows assigns default permissions depending on how a folder is shared. Generally, the default share permission is Read for the Everyone group.
- When a user or an application requests a resource—such as a printer or a data file—a redirector intercepts the request and then examines it to determine whether the resource is local (on the computer) or remote (on the network).

- To understand how to work with and share printers in a Windows environment, first you need to know the terminology for defining the components of a shared printer: print device, printer, print server, and print queue.
- Linux supports Windows file sharing by using SMB in a software package called Samba. Depending on the Linux distribution, you might have to install this component. On a Linux system with Samba installed, you can share a folder using the Samba Server Configuration GUI tool or by editing the /etc/samba/smb.conf file.
- Mac OS X also supports Windows file sharing using the SMB protocol. To share a folder with another user, turn on File Sharing in System Preferences by clicking Sharing. In the Sharing dialog box, click File Sharing.
- If you share files and printers, you'll usually want to control access to those shared resources through user accounts, group accounts, and permissions. Working with user accounts is one of an administrator's key tasks. User accounts are the link between people and network resources, so user account management requires both technical expertise and people skills.
- You can specify many more user account properties in Active Directory than you can in Windows 10.
- User and group accounts in Linux have the same purposes as in Windows: user authentication and authorization. Linux OSs also have a default user named root who has full control over all aspects of the system.
- In Mac OS X, you create users and groups using the Users & Groups tool in System Preferences. To create a user, click the plus sign in the left pane of Users & Groups, click the selection arrow next to New Account to choose the type of account you want to create, and then enter the user's full name, account name, and password.

Key Terms

authentication The process of identifying who has access to the network. The most common form of authentication is a logon with a username and password.

authorization The process of granting or denying an authenticated user's access to network resources.

batch file A text file that contains a list of commands you ordinarily type at the command prompt.

default groups Special groups with rights already assigned; these groups are created during installation in a Windows environment.

domain local group A group scope recommended for assigning rights and permissions to domain resources.

global group A group scope used mainly to group users from the same domain who have similar access and rights requirements. A global group's members can be user accounts and other global groups from the same domain. See also *group scope*.

group scope A property of a group that determines the reach of a group's application in a domain—for example, which users can be group members and to which resources a group can be assigned rights or permissions.

Network File System (NFS) The native Linux/UNIX file sharing protocol.

redirector An OS client component that intercepts resource requests and determines whether the resource is local or remote.

Server Message Block (SMB) The Windows file sharing protocol; SMB is also supported by Linux and Mac OS X as Samba.

special identity group A type of group in Windows in which membership is controlled dynamically by Windows, can't be viewed or changed manually, and depends on how an account accesses the OS. For example, membership in the Authenticated Users group is assigned to a user account automatically when the user logs on to a computer or domain.

universal group A group scope that can contain users from any domain and be assigned permissions to resources in any domain. See also *group scope*.

Review Questions

1. Which of the following is the correct syntax for mapping drive letter W to a shared folder named Accounting on the Finance server?
   a. net use W: \\Finance\Accounting
   b. net share W: \\Accounting\Finance
   c. net use W: \\Accounting\Finance
   d. net share W: \\Finance\Accounting
2. A text file that contains a list of commands is called which of the following?
   a. logon process file
   b. service file
   c. task file
   d. batch file
3. Which of the following is the default protocol Windows uses to share folders?
   a. NFS
   b. SMB
   c. WPA
   d. FTP
4. Which of the following is the native Linux/UNIX file sharing protocol?
   a. NFS
   b. SMB
   c. WPA
   d. FTP

5. Which of the following is a native printer sharing protocol used on Linux? (Choose all that apply.)
   a. CUPS
   b. PPP
   c. NFS
   d. LPD
6. Which of the following group scopes can only contain users from the domain in which the group is created?
   a. global
   b. domain local
   c. universal
   d. distribution
7. Which of the following is *not* a Windows share permission?
   a. Read
   b. Write
   c. Change
   d. Full Control
8. Which component of a file sharing client determines whether the resource is local or remote?
   a. redirector
   b. SMB
   c. active directory
   d. UNC path
9. Which of the following correctly specifies a file named salaries.xls in a shared folder named Budget on a server named Accounting when accessing the file remotely from a Windows computer?
   a. \\Accounting.budget.salaries.xls
   b. /Accounting/Budget/salaries.xls
   c. \\Budget.Accounting\salaries.xls
   d. \\Accounting\Budget\salaries.xls
10. What is a storage location for pending print jobs?
   a. print queue
   b. print server
   c. print directory
   d. print path

11. What file can you edit on a Linux system to configure shared folders using Samba?
    a. /samba/smb.cnf
    b. /etc/smb/samba.conf
    c. /etc/samba/smb.conf
    d. /smb/samba.cnf
12. Which of the following is a Linux command to access shared files using Samba?
    a. *netsh*
    b. *samba*
    c. *smbclient*
    d. *nfsclient*
13. Which of the following defines the types of actions a user can perform on a system?
    a. authentication
    b. authorization
    c. logon
    d. permission
14. A user has called you to complain that he does not have access to a file. While on the phone, you add the user to the appropriate group that has permission to access the file. You ask the user to try to access the file again, but he still cannot. What should you do?
    a. Tell the user to log off and log on again.
    b. Delete the user account and re-create it.
    c. Add the user to the permission list for the file.
    d. Shut down the server and restart it.
15. Which group scope can be used to assign permissions to resources only in the domain in which the group is created?
    a. global
    b. universal
    c. domain local
    d. local

Hands-On Projects

Project 10-1: Map a Drive Letter in Windows

In this project, you create a shared folder and then map a drive letter to it. You wouldn't normally map a drive letter to a share on your own computer, but this project shows you how to perform the process without using a second computer.

1. Start your Windows computer and log on.
2. Click **Start**, and then click **File Explorer**. Click **This PC** in the left pane, and then click **Local Disk (C:)**.
3. Create a folder named **MyShare**. Right-click **MyShare**, point to **Share with**, and click **Specific people**. You see that the currently logged-on user has the permission level Owner. You can add users who may access the share in this dialog box, but because only you will access it, click **Share**. You're notified that the folder is now shared, and you see the path listed as *ComputerName*\MyShare, where *ComputerName* is the name of your computer (see Figure 10-20). Click **Done**.

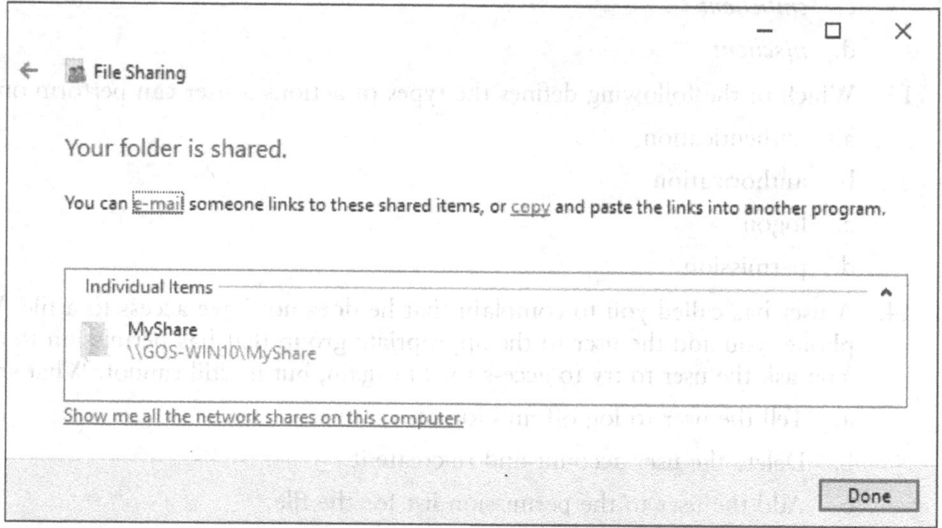

Figure 10-20 Sharing a folder in Windows

4. Click in the Search text box on the taskbar, type **\\localhost**, and press **Enter**. The *localhost* refers to your own computer, so a window opens and displays available shares, including MyShare. Normally, you wouldn't map a drive to a folder on your own computer, and you would replace *localhost* with the name of a server hosting the share. You're using localhost just for practice. Click the search result.
5. In File Explorer, right-click **MyShare** and click **Map network drive**. You can choose a drive letter to map to this share. Click the **Drive** list arrow and click **X:**. Click to clear the **Reconnect at sign-in** check box. If you leave this option selected, the drive is mapped to the share each time you log on. Notice that you can also choose to connect to the share with different credentials (username and password). Click **Finish**.
6. A File Explorer window opens and displays the share's contents (it's currently empty). Close all windows. Click **Start** and then click **File Explorer**. You see the drive letter and share name listed under This PC. Right-click **MyShare (\\localhost) (X:)** and click **Disconnect** to delete the drive mapping. (You might need to press F5 to refresh the File Explorer window and see that the drive mapping has been deleted.)

7. Open a command prompt window. To map a drive letter from the command line, type **net use x: \\localhost\MyShare** and press **Enter**. You should see the message "The command completed successfully." To display current connections to shared resources, type **net use** and press **Enter**.
8. Click in the File Explorer window. The X drive letter is listed under This PC again.
9. At the command prompt, type **net use /?** and press **Enter** to see a list of options for the *net use* command. You can use the */persistent* option to make a drive mapping reconnect each time you log on. You can also connect with a different set of credentials. Type **net use x: /delete** and press **Enter** to delete the drive mapping, and then close the command prompt window. In File Explorer, verify that the drive mapping has been deleted.
10. To create a batch file for mapping a drive, open Notepad and type the following two lines:

```
net use x: /delete
net use x: \\localhost\MyShare
```

11. The first command deletes any existing drive mappings for the X drive. Click **File** and then **Save As** from the menu. In the left pane of the Save As dialog box, click **Desktop**. Click the **Save as type** list arrow, and then click **All Files**. In the File name text box, type **mapX.bat** and click **Save**. Close Notepad. Batch files can come in handy if you need to connect to another computer periodically but don't want a permanent drive mapping. Batch files are especially useful if you need to enter long commands because you don't have to remember and re-enter them each time you need them.
12. On your desktop, double-click **mapX**. In File Explorer, verify that the X drive mapping has been created. Right-click **MyShare (\\localhost) (X:)** and click **Disconnect**.
13. To review what you've learned, write the command to map drive letter G to a share named Accounting on a server named Finance:

____

14. Close all open windows, and leave Windows running for the next project.

10

To learn more about creating and using batch files in Windows, read the TechNet article at *https://technet.microsoft.com/en-us/library/bb490869.aspx*.

Project 10-2: Create and Connect to a Shared Printer in Windows

This project walks you through the process of creating a printer, sharing it, and then connecting to the shared printer. Note that you won't actually connect to a physical printer.

1. If necessary, log on to your Windows computer.
2. Click in the Search text box on the taskbar, type **Devices and Printers**, and press Enter. Click **Add a printer** in the Devices and Printers window. Windows searches for devices. Click **The printer that I want isn't listed.**
3. Click **Add a local printer or network printer with manual settings**, and then click **Next**. In the "Choose a printer port" window, leave the default option **Use an existing port** selected, and then click **Next**. In the "Install the printer driver" window, you would normally select the printer's manufacturer and model, but because there's no physical printer, just accept the default selection and then click **Next**.
4. In the "Type a printer name" window, click **Next**. In the Printer Sharing window, make sure **Share this printer so that others on your network can find and use it** is selected. For the share name, type **MyPrinter**, and then click **Next**. Click to clear the **Set as the default printer** check box (note that you might not see this check box). If you were actually installing a printer, you would click "Print a test page," but for this project, just click **Finish**.
5. To connect to a shared printer, ask your instructor whether a printer share is set up or you can use another student's shared printer. In Windows, you can't connect to your own printer, as you did with the shared folder. Click in the Search text box on the taskbar, type ***computer*, where computer is the name of the computer sharing the printer, and press Enter.**
6. When the window opens, right-click the shared printer and click **Connect**. In the Devices and Printers window, verify that the printer was created. It's listed as "*Printer make and model* on *computer*," where *Printer make and model* is the make and model of the printer and *computer* is the name of the computer on which the printer is shared.
7. Close all open windows but stay logged on if you're continuing to the next project.

Project 10-3: Create Users in a Windows Client OS

In this project, you create a user in the Computer Management console.

1. Log on to your Windows computer, if necessary. There are two tools for creating user accounts in a Windows client OS. One is User Accounts in Control Panel, which is used mostly for home users. The other tool is Local Users and Groups in the Computer Management console. Local Users and Groups gives administrators more control over user properties and has more in common with Active Directory Users and Computers, so it's used in this project.

2. Right-click **Start** and click **Computer Management.** In the left pane, click to expand **Local Users and Groups,** which has two folders under it: Users and Groups. Click **Users** to display a list of users in the right pane (see Figure 10-21). Notice that the Administrator, DefaultAccount, and Guest users in the figure are shown with a black arrow in a white circle to indicate that the accounts are disabled.

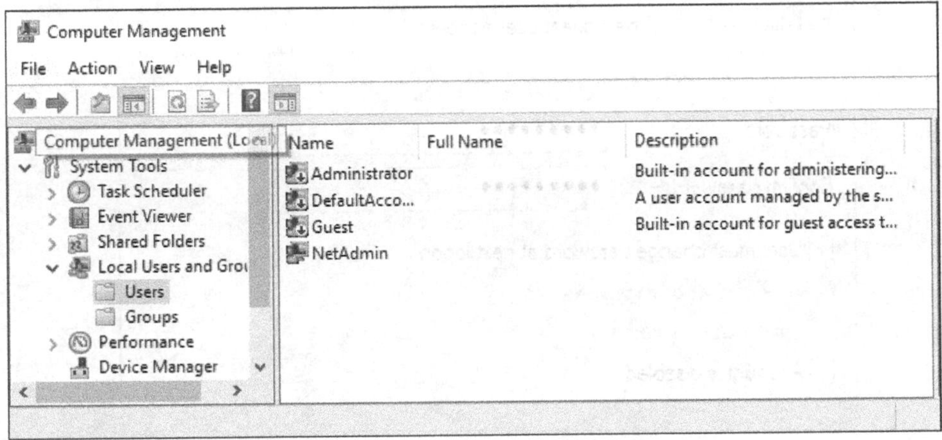

Figure 10-21 Viewing Users in Computer Management

3. Right-click an empty space in the right pane and click **New User.** In the New User dialog box, type **NewGuest1** as the User name. In the Full name text box, type **New Guest User 1,** and in the Description text box, type **A new guest user account.**

4. Type **guestpass** in the Password text box and again in the Confirm password text box.

5. Leave the **User must change password at next logon** check box selected (see Figure 10-22), and click **Create.** The New User dialog box clears so you can create another user. Click **Close.**

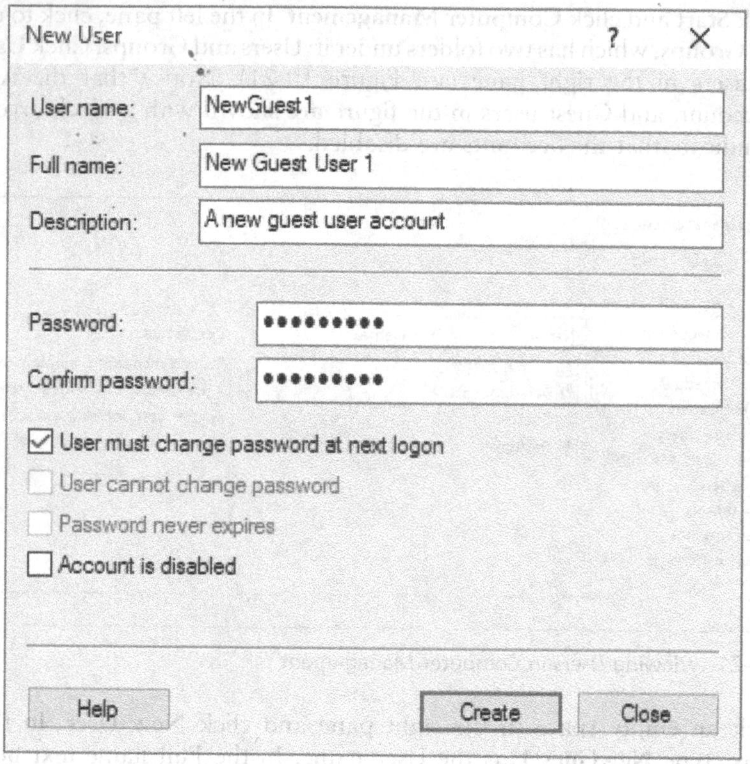

New User

User name: NewGuest1

Full name: New Guest User 1

Description: A new guest user account

Password: ●●●●●●●●●

Confirm password: ●●●●●●●●●

☑ User must change password at next logon

☐ User cannot change password

☐ Password never expires

☐ Account is disabled

Help | Create | Close

Figure 10-22 Creating a user in Windows 10

6. In Local Users and Groups, double-click **NewGuest1** to view its properties. Click the **Member Of** tab. By default, all new users are put in a group called Users; this is also the case when a user is created in Active Directory. Click **Cancel.**
7. Click the **Groups** folder in the left pane to see a list of default groups that Windows creates. Double-click the **Users** group. You'll see a list of users who are members of the Users group, including NewGuest1. You'll probably also see some special groups named Authenticated Users and INTERACTIVE, which are internal groups used by Windows. Click **Cancel.**
8. Log off Windows. When the logon window opens, New Guest User 1 is shown as a user. Click **New Guest User 1.** Type **guestpass** in the Password text box and press **Enter,** or click the arrow to log on. When prompted to change your password, click **OK,** and then type **Password01** in the New password and Confirm password text boxes. Press **Enter** or click the arrow.
9. In the message box stating that the password has been changed, click **OK.** Do not sign in, but leave Windows running for the next project.

Project 10-4: Work with Groups in a Windows Client OS

In this project, you create a group in the Computer Management console and then add a user to the group.

1. Log on to your Windows computer as an administrator.
2. Right-click **Start** and click **Computer Management**. Click to expand **Local Users and Groups**, and then click **Groups**.
3. Right-click an empty space in the right pane, and then click **New Group**. In the New Group dialog box, type **GuestUsers** as the Group name. In the Description text box, type **A group for guest users of this computer.**
4. Click **Add**. Examine the Select Users dialog box shown in Figure 10-23. It's similar to what you see when adding a user to a group in Active Directory.

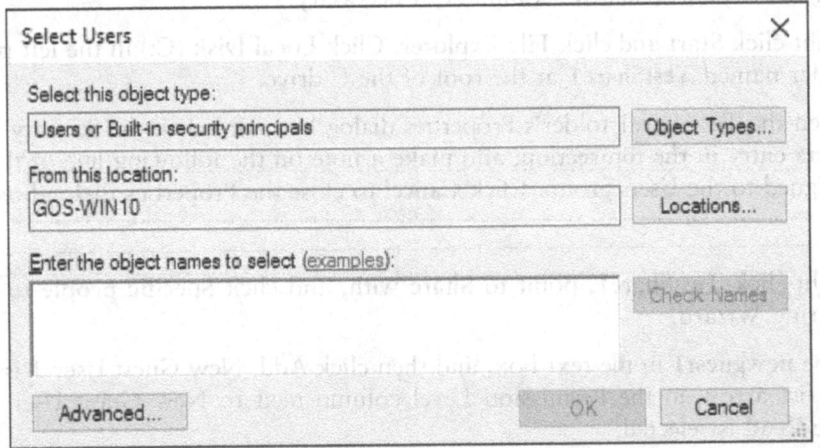

Figure 10-23 Selecting users to add to a group

5. You can use the Object Types button to limit the types of objects Windows displays if you click the Advanced button to search for objects to add to a group. Click **Locations**. You have only one option unless your computer is a member of a domain. If so, you can select objects from the domain; otherwise, you can only choose objects created on your computer. Click **Cancel**.
6. You can type the group members' names in the text box, but to select them from a list, click **Advanced**. Click **Find Now** to list available users and groups you can add as group members. Click **NewGuest1** and then click **OK**. Notice in the Select Users dialog box that the user is specified as *ComputerName\NewGuest1*. *ComputerName* is the name of the computer or domain where the user was created; in this case, it's the computer. Click **OK**.

7. NewGuest1 is listed as a member of the group. Click **Create** to finish creating the group, and then click **Close**.
8. NewGuest1 is now a member of both the GuestUsers and Users groups. Remember that the result of changing group membership takes effect the next time the user logs on. If you wanted to remove NewGuest1 from the default Users group, you would double-click the Users group, right-click NewGuest1, and click Remove. However, doing so removes NewGuest1 from the list of users in the Windows 10 logon window. For now, leave this account as a member of both groups. Log off Windows for the next project.

Project 10-5: Share a Folder and View Permissions

In this project, you use the File Sharing Wizard to see how it sets permissions automatically.

1. Log on to your Windows computer, if necessary.
2. Right-click **Start** and click **File Explorer**. Click **Local Disk** (**C:**) in the left pane. Create a folder named **TestShare1** at the root of the C drive.
3. Open the TestShare1 folder's Properties dialog box, and click the **Security** tab. Click the **Users** entry in the top section, and make a note on the following line of the permissions assigned to the Users group. Click **Cancel** to close the Properties dialog box.

   ____

4. Right-click **TestShare1**, point to **Share with**, and click **Specific people** to start the File Sharing Wizard.
5. Type **newguest1** in the text box, and then click **Add**. New Guest User 1 is added. Click the list arrow in the Permission Level column next to New Guest User 1, and make sure **Read** is selected.
6. Click **Share**. The UNC path for the share is displayed. Click **Done**.
7. Right-click **TestShare1** and click **Properties**. Click the **Sharing** tab, and then click **Advanced Sharing**.
8. Click **Permissions**. The Administrators and Everyone groups have Full Control permission to the share. As you will see in the next step, the NTFS permissions restrict New Guest User 1's permissions to Read & execute, List folder contents, and Read, which effectively allows the user to open and view the file. Click **Cancel** twice.
9. In the TestShare1 folder's Properties dialog box, click the **Security** tab. Click **New Guest User 1**, and notice that the account's NTFS permissions are Read & execute, List folder contents, and Read.
10. Close all open windows and then log off or shut down your Windows computer.

Project 10-6: Work with Users and Groups in Linux

In this project, you create users with the *useradd* command and groups with the *groupadd* command. Next, you add users as members of these groups with the *useradd* and *usermod* commands.

1. Log on to your Linux computer and open a terminal window.
2. At the shell prompt, type **man useradd** and press **Enter** to get an overview of the man pages for the *useradd* command. Press the **Page Up** and **Page Down** keys to scroll through the man pages. Type **q** when you're finished.
3. To view current users on the Linux system, type **cat /etc/passwd** and press **Enter.** Another way to view a text file is with the *less* option. Type **less /etc/passwd** and press **Enter.** Use the arrow keys or Page Up and Page Down keys to scroll through the file. Many of the user accounts you see in this file are system accounts that are not used to log on to the OS. Type **q** to quit.
4. Display the list of groups by typing **less /etc/group** and pressing **Enter.** When you're finished, type **q**.
5. To create a user, type **useradd testuser1** and press **Enter.** If you aren't logged on as root, you see a message stating that permission is denied. Type **su** and press **Enter** to switch to the root user, if necessary; type your password when prompted. The last character in the prompt changes from a $ to a # to indicate that you're now operating as the root user.
6. Type **useradd testuser1** and press **Enter.** To create a password for the user, type **passwd testuser1** and press **Enter.** Type **Password01** and press **Enter.** (Notice that your keystrokes aren't displayed.) You see a message that the password is bad and fails a dictionary check. However, the password is still accepted, and you're prompted to retype it. Type **Password01** and press **Enter** again. You should see a message stating "passwd: all authentication tokens updated successfully."

If you don't enter the same password when asked to retype it, you get a message stating that the passwords don't match, and you're prompted to try again.

7. Create another user with the logon name **testuser2**.
8. Type **less /etc/passwd**, press **Enter**, and page to the bottom of the file, where you see the users you created. Type **q** and then display the group file to see that groups named testuser1 and testuser2 were also created. (*Hint*: Remember that you can use the arrow keys to scroll through recently used commands.)
9. Type **groupadd testgroup1** and press **Enter.** To add **testuser1** to testgroup1, type **usermod -a -G testgroup1 testuser1** and press **Enter.** Repeat the command for **testuser2.** Type **cat /etc/group** and press **Enter** to list all groups. You should see the new group at the end of the file along with a list of its members.

10

10. You can view a user's group memberships with the *groups* command. Type **groups testuser1** and press **Enter**. Testuser1 is listed as a member of the testuser1 and testgroup1 groups.
11. Close the terminal window and shut down the Linux computer.

Project 10-7: Create a User in Mac OS X

In this project, you create users and groups in Mac OS X.

1. Log on to your Mac OS X computer.
2. Click the **Apple** icon and then click **System Preferences**.
3. In System Preferences, click **Users & Groups**. At the bottom of the window, click the lock icon so you can make changes. Type your password when prompted and click **Unlock**.
4. At the bottom of the left pane, click the plus (+) sign, as shown in Figure 10-24.

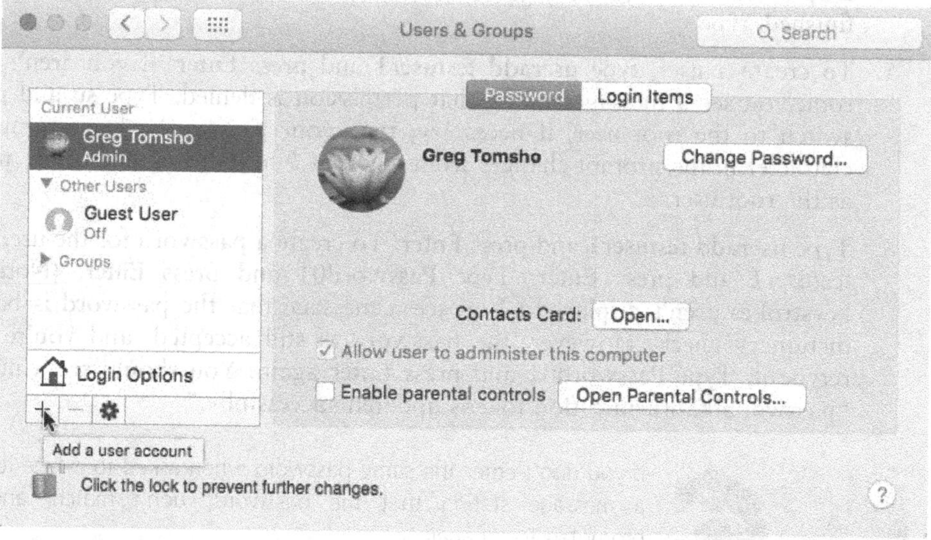

Figure 10-24 Creating a new user in Mac OS X

Source: Mac OS X

5. In the next dialog box, click the list arrow next to New Account to review the account types you can create. In the Full Name text box, type **John Doe**; in the Account Name text box, type **jdoe**. Type **Password01** in the Password and Verify text boxes. Optionally, you can add a password hint.
6. Click **Create User**.
7. Click the plus (+) sign again. In the New Account list box, click **Group**. In the Full Name text box, click **MyGroup** and then click **Create Group**.

8. In the left pane, make sure MyGroup is selected. In the right pane, click the check box next to John Doe to add the account to the group.
9. Close all open windows, but stay logged on if you're continuing to the next project.

Project 10-8: Share a Folder and Assign Permissions in Mac OS X

In this project, you share a folder and assign permissions in Mac OS X.

1. Log on to your Mac OS X computer, if necessary.
2. On the desktop, double-click **Macintosh HD**. Right-click in **Macintosh HD** and click **New Folder**. Type your password if prompted and click **OK**. Click the folder name and rename it **SharedFolder**.
3. Click the **Apple** icon and then click **System Preferences**. In System Preferences, click **Sharing**. In the Sharing dialog box, click the **File Sharing** check box to enable file sharing.
4. Click the plus (+) sign under Shared Folders. Click **Macintosh HD** in the left pane and click **Shared Folder** in the right pane. Click **Add**.
5. In the Sharing dialog box, click the plus (+) sign under **Users**. Click **MyGroup** and then click **Select** (see Figure 10-25).

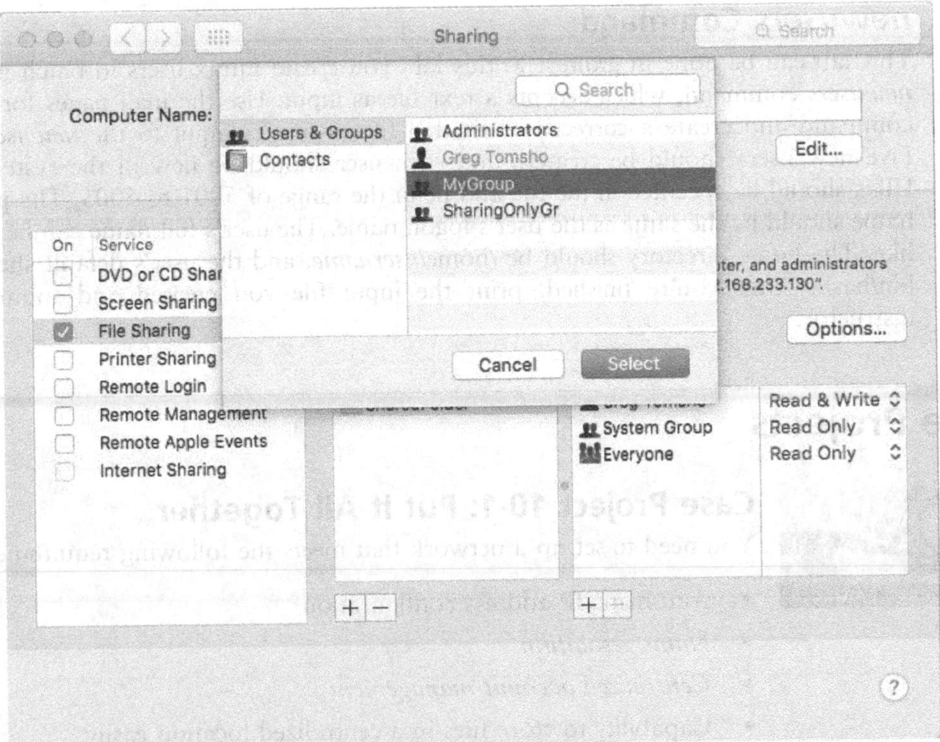

Figure 10-25 Sharing a folder and assigning permissions

Source: Mac OS X

10

6. Notice that the default permission is Read Only for MyGroup. Click the arrow next to **Read Only** in the MyGroup row to see the possible permission settings. Click **Read & Write**. To remove a user or group from the permission list, click the user or group and click the minus (–) sign. Close the Sharing dialog box.
7. Shut down your Mac OS X computer.

Critical Thinking

The following activities give you critical thinking challenges. Challenge Labs give you an opportunity to use the skills you have learned to perform a task without step-by-step instructions. Case projects offer a practical problem for which you supply a written solution. Not all chapters contain Challenge Labs. There is not always a specific right or wrong answer to these critical thinking exercises. They are intended to encourage you to review the chapter material and delve deeper into the topics you have learned.

Challenge Labs

Challenge Lab 10-1: Create Users in Linux with the *newusers* Command

This lab can be done in groups. In this lab, you create Linux users in batch mode with the *newusers* command, which accepts a text file as input. Use the man pages for the *newusers* command and create a correctly formatted file to use as input to the *newusers* command. Five new users should be created, and each user should be new in the system. The users' UIDs should be specified in the file and be in the range of 5001 to 5005. The primary group name should be the same as the user's logon name. The user's full name can be whatever you like. The home directory should be /home/*username*, and the user's default shell should be /bin/bash. After you're finished, print the input file you created and submit it to your instructor.

Case Projects

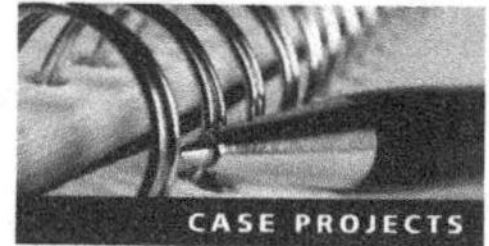

Case Project 10-1: Put It All Together

You need to set up a network that meets the following requirements:

- Automatic IP address configuration
- *Name resolution*
- *Centralized account management*
- Capability to store files in a centralized location easily

Write a memo explaining what services must be installed on the network to satisfy each requirement.

Case Project 10-2: Share Files with Multiple OSs

You have been called in to consult for a company that is running 15 Windows 10 computers, two Linux computers, and three Mac OS X computers. Your boss wants all of these computers to be able to share files. What file sharing protocol do you recommend and why? Should you configure this network as a peer-to-peer network or as a client/server network? Explain your answer.

chapter 11

Operating Systems Management and Maintenance

After reading this chapter and completing the exercises, you will be able to:

- Explain file system maintenance techniques for different operating systems
- Perform regular file system maintenance by finding and deleting unused files and folders
- Perform disk maintenance that includes defragmenting, relocating files and folders, running disk and file repair utilities, and selecting RAID options
- Explain the types of backups and develop a backup plan
- Explain how to install software for best performance
- Tune operating systems for optimal performance

Computer operating systems are similar to cars in that they need regular maintenance to achieve the best performance. A new car, like a new computer, delivers fast response, and every component usually functions perfectly. To keep the car at its best, you must perform regular maintenance, such as changing the oil and performing tune-ups. If you neglect this maintenance, the car's performance suffers and the wear shows quickly. Maintenance is just as important for computers because it does not take long for an operating system, software, and hardware to degrade in performance. Operating system maintenance consists of deleting unnecessary files, tuning memory, regularly backing up files, defragmenting disks, and repairing damaged files. Maintenance is particularly important for networked computer systems because a poorly responding computer has an impact on network operations.

In this chapter, you learn a variety of techniques for maintaining and tuning workstations and servers. One of the most important steps in disk and file maintenance is to start with a well-designed folder structure, which makes finding unused files and folders a straightforward process. Two other important tasks are performing regular backups and running disk maintenance utilities. How and where software is installed is also vital to how a computer performs. Finally, there are tuning options that can immediately enhance performance, such as adjusting virtual memory.

File System Maintenance

Successful file system maintenance is closely linked to a computer's folder structure. On desktop and server operating systems, a well-planned folder structure makes it easy to locate files, update files, share folders and files, back up and archive files, and delete unwanted files. In addition, on server operating systems, well-designed folder structures help network performance and security. The importance of a well-designed folder structure and the default folder structures for Windows, Linux/UNIX, and Mac OS X were described in Chapter 4. As a reminder, here are some basic rules for creating and maintaining a folder structure:

- Keep a manageable number of folders in the root folder.
- Keep operating system files in the default folders recommended by the vendor.
- Keep different versions of software in their own folders.
- Keep data files in folders on the basis of their functions.
- Design home folders to match the functions of users in an organization.
- Group files with similar security needs within the same folders.

Operating system folders are typically placed in the root folder and have appropriate subfolders under a main folder. It's important that you know the locations of system files so you know where to look if you need to troubleshoot a problem with system files. Table 11-1 illustrates typical locations for system files in various operating systems.

Table 11-1 Essential operating system folders

Operating system	Essential system folders at the root level for 32-bit systems	Essential system folders at the root level for 64-bit systems
Mac OS X	bin, dev, etc, Library, Network, sbin, System, var, and Volumes	bin, dev, etc, Library, Network, sbin, System, var, and Volumes
UNIX/Linux	bin, dev, etc, lib, mnt, proc, sbin, and var	bin, dev, etc, lib, mnt, proc, sbin, and var
Modern Windows desktop and server versions	Windows, including the Boot, System, and System32 subfolders	Windows, including the Boot, System, System32, and sysWOW64 subfolders

There are several advantages to leaving operating system files in the folders created by the OS instead of using other folder locations. For example, it is easier for others to help with computer problems as they arise. Also, in organizations that have help desks or support centers, it is easier for support professionals to solve problems with drivers and network access when system files are easy to find. Finally, many software installations expect operating system files to be in their default locations, and these installations work best when it is easy to find specific subfolders and key files related to the operating system.

When you install server operating systems, you may be tempted to hide or rename default system folders as a way to protect them from intruders. However, most intruders will not be deterred by these efforts. A better approach is to understand and implement the security features available in the operating system. One security precaution is to periodically back up OS files in all operating systems, including the system state data in Windows operating systems.

In modern Windows operating systems, such as Windows 10, you can configure system protection to return to a previous system configuration in case one or more system files are deleted or if the installation of a new device causes operating system problems. To configure system protection in Windows 10, right-click Start, click System, and click System protection in the left pane. On the System Protection tab, configure the System Restore settings.

In Windows operating systems, installed software is also tracked in the registry, which contains configuration information as well as information about individual components of a software installation. Thus, it is easier for the operating system to assist when software must be uninstalled or upgraded because the OS can quickly identify and find the relevant components. In Windows desktop and server operating systems, these vital files are kept in the OS's folder and subfolders. For example, these files might be located in the \Windows, \Windows\System, or \Windows\System32 folders. Table 11-2 lists some typical Windows application software components and their associated file extensions. Table 11-3 lists the same types of components for UNIX/Linux and Mac OS X. Application software and operating system enhancements are easier to install when these components are in known locations.

Table 11-2 Examples of Windows-based application software components

File type	File extension	File type	File extension
Application	.exe	Initialization	.ini
ActiveX control	.ocx	Installation	.inf
Backup	.bak	Microsoft Common Console document	.mcs
Bitmap image	.bmp	Microsoft Office settings file	.pip
Compiled HTML help file	.chm	OLE common control (.ocx is now part of the ActiveX control set)	.ocx
Control Panel extension	.cpl	Precompiled setup information	.pnf
Configuration	.cfg	Screen saver	.scr
Data	.dat	Security catalog	.cat
Device driver	.drv	Temporary file	.tmp
Dynamic link library	.dll	Text	.txt
Help	.hlp	TrueType font	.ttf
Help context	.cnt	Virtual device driver	.vxd

Table 11-3 Examples of UNIX/Linux and Mac OS X application software components

File type	File extension	File type	File extension
awk script (for running reports)	.awk	Program header for a C or C++ program	.h
Backup	.bak	Hypertext Markup Language	.html
C program file containing source code	.c	Log file	.log
C++ program file containing source code	.C or .cc	Matlab script	.mat
CGI script for a Web page	.cgi	Object code file	.o
Configuration	.cfg	Perl script/program	.pl
Data	.dat	Python program	.py
Document	.doc	Shell archive	.shar
Emacs Lisp source code file	.el	Scheme source code	.ss
Emacs Lisp compiled file	.elc	Text	.txt
Source code in Fortran	.for or .f	Tape archive (made from the *tar* command)	.tar
Source code in Fortran 77	.f77	Uuencoded	.uue

NOTE

The Windows registry is an extensive database of information about the operating system, including customized settings and software installations. The registry contains data about all hardware components and software. It contains information about Windows services that are started automatically, manually, or are disabled. Desktop configuration data is stored in the registry, as is information about user accounts, group policies, networking, and system boot data. The registry is an essential component of the system state data.

Sometimes, particularly on network servers, several versions of a software application must be available for different uses. For example, an organization may have some users who still use earlier versions of Microsoft Word or even WordPerfect, so these versions must be maintained in case a specific version needs to be reinstalled on a client's computer over the network. In an organization that develops software applications, it may be necessary to keep different versions of compilers or development tools available. Some users may have operating systems that only support 32-bit applications, whereas other users may have operating systems that support 32-bit and 64-bit applications. In these situations, one way to handle having more than one version of the same software is to put different versions in different subfolders under a main applications folder. For example, in Windows Server, you can support different versions of Microsoft Word by having a Program Files folder and subfolders called Word2013 and Word2016. In this case, one version is installed to run locally and the other version is available to clients for network installations. Also, Microsoft 64-bit operating systems offer the Program Files and Program Files (x86) folders to separate 64-bit and 32-bit applications.

Finding and Deleting Files

Having a solid computer file structure makes it easier to find and delete unneeded files on a regular schedule. Files can quickly accumulate and occupy a large amount of disk space—an example is the temporary files created when you install new software and run many types of applications. Most installations create a temporary folder and a set of temporary files that are stored under the root folder or an account's home folder. Some software applications do not completely delete temporary files when the installation is finished. Also, some software applications create temporary files that are not deleted when the application is closed or improperly terminated, either because of a power failure or other malfunction. For example, many word-processing programs create temporary files that are used for backup purposes or to save the most immediate changes.

Web browsers also write an impressive number of temporary Internet files that are not deleted unless you set an expiration date or delete them using an OS utility or browser utility. In most cases, the files can be deleted regularly; however, some **cookies** may be kept because they contain specialized information for accessing particular Web sites. Many cookies are deleted because they only take up space and contain no information the user needs. Some users regularly delete all cookies because new ones are created anyway when users re-access Web sites. Cookies are text files that have the preface *cookie:*—for example, in many Windows operating systems, a cookie created after you access the Microsoft Web site from your account is *cookie:accountname@microsoft.com.* Temporary Internet files often have extensions such as .html, .htm, .jpg, and .gif.

It is a good practice to implement a regular schedule for finding and deleting unneeded files. The following sections explain these methods in different operating systems.

Deleting files is vital for making the best use of disk storage resources, and it can help extend the life of hard disks. One rule of thumb is that hard disk drives should be kept less than 80 percent full. Otherwise, the drive is subject to excessive wear, and is more likely to have problems or fail.

Deleting Temporary Files in Windows

Temporary files accumulate in Windows operating systems and can be deleted using several approaches. In Windows, temporary files are typically located in the \Temp and \Windows \Temp folders, or in users' home folders. Temporary Internet files from Internet Explorer are stored in the Users*accountname*\AppData\Local\Microsoft\Windows\Temporary Internet Files folder.

Temporary Internet files can also be stored in other locations, depending on the operating system, Web browser in use, and individual settings specified by the user.

A convenient way to delete unneeded files in Windows operating systems is to use the Disk Cleanup tool. You can start this tool by typing Disk Cleanup in the search text box on the taskbar and then clicking Disk Cleanup.

When you start Disk Cleanup (see Figure 11-1), it scans your disk to determine the amount of space that can be restored after removing specific types of files. In Windows 8 and later versions, the Disk Cleanup tool is scheduled to automatically run on the system drive where Windows is installed whenever the computer is idle for an extended period.

Figure 11-1 The Disk Cleanup tool in Windows

To quickly delete all temporary files without using Disk Cleanup in Windows operating systems, you can open the Command Prompt window and enter the command *dir *.tmp /s* to list all temporary files that have the .tmp extension. The * works as a wildcard to search for all .tmp files. The */s* switch lists files in subfolders. If you determine that you want to delete all of the listed files, enter the *del *.tmp /s* command. Files that are currently in use will not be deleted.

Windows comes with a Recycle Bin, which contains files that have been deleted. You should regularly open the Recycle Bin and delete its files, which purges them from the system permanently. You can delete files in the Recycle Bin by using the Disk Cleanup tool, but the fastest way to delete these files is to keep the Recycle Bin icon on the desktop, right-click the icon, and then click Empty Recycle Bin on the shortcut menu.

By default, the Recycle Bin can grow to occupy 10 percent of available hard disk storage. Computers that are configured for two or more volumes have a Recycle Bin on each volume. You can resize the maximum allocation for the Recycle Bin by right-clicking its desktop icon, selecting Properties, and configuring the maximum size. When the Recycle Bin is full and you continue to delete files to send to the Recycle Bin, the oldest files in the Recycle Bin are purged first.

Another approach to deleting temporary files in Windows is to use the search function in File Explorer. In File Explorer, go to the root of the drive from which you want to delete temporary files, and then type *.tmp in the search box. When the search is complete, select all the files and press Del on your keyboard.

Deleting Files in UNIX/Linux

You can view UNIX/Linux files by using the *ls* command along with one or more of the following options for listing particular file qualities:

- *-a* lists all files, including hidden files
- -C formats the listing in columns for easier reading
- *-d* lists folders
- *-f* displays files in an unsorted list
- *-F* identifies the list's contents as folders, executable files, and symbolic links
- *-i* displays the inode number for each file (see Chapter 4 for an explanation of inodes)
- *-l* presents a detailed information listing, including permissions and file size
- *-n* displays the user identification numbers (UIDs) and group identification numbers (GIDs) of those who have access to files
- *-r* sorts files in reverse alphabetical order
- *-s* displays the size of files (in blocks)
- *-S* sorts files and folders on the basis of size
- *-t* sorts files and folders based on when they were last modified

For example, to list all files, including hidden files, use the command *ls -a*. If you are only looking for large files, use the command *ls -sa* to show file and folder sizes for all listings, including hidden files. You can use the command *ls -la* to show more detailed information, including file and folder sizes and the permissions associated with each file and folder. Notice that you can combine options, such as using the *-la* option to show detailed information for all files, including hidden files.

Files and folders are deleted in UNIX/Linux using the remove (*rm*) command. Two options commonly added to this command are *-i* and *-r*. The *-i* or interactive option results in a prompt that asks if you really want to delete the file or folder; the *-r* or recursive command is used to delete an entire folder's contents, including all its subfolders and files.

Use the *rm -r* command carefully; it deletes all files and subfolders within a folder. When you delete a folder, you should add the *-i* option, such as in *rm -ir foldername*, so that the operating system asks you to verify the deletion first.

For example, let's say you want to list all files in the /home/mjackson/docs folder that end with .txt so you can determine whether to delete them. You would enter:

ls -a /home/mjackson/docs/.txt*

In the preceding command, the * is a wildcard that lists all files ending in .txt. To delete the files, you would enter:

rm /home/mjackson/docs/.txt*

As another example, assume that you want to delete your /work folder, but first you want to view its contents, including hidden files. As a safety precaution, you also want the command to include a prompt that queries whether you really want to delete the folder and its contents. You would enter the following commands:

ls -a /work

rm -ri /work

TIP

If the /work folder is in your home folder, you can use the ~ symbol to represent your home folder path, no matter what folder you are currently in. In the preceding example, you could enter *ls -a ~/work* and then enter *rm -ri ~/work*.

In the Linux GNOME Files tool, you can delete a file by browsing to the folder that contains it, clicking the appropriate file in the display of the folder's contents, and pressing the Del key on your keyboard.

To find a file, use the *find* command. You can use this command and its various options to find files based on their filenames, file size, and the last time they were accessed or modified. You can also use wildcard characters. For example, to find and print a list of all temporary files modified in the last 30 days, you could enter *find -name temp* -mtime -30 -print*. (Hands-On Project 11-5 shows you how to delete temporary files in UNIX/Linux.)

11

The *find* command has options that let you search for files using several criteria:

- *-atime* for last accessed time
- *-ctime* for last changed time of file attributes
- *-mtime* for last modification time of file data
- *-name* for the filename (wildcards can be used)
- *-print* to print the results of the search
- *-size* for file size (in blocks or bytes; bytes are specified by a *c* after the size value)
- *-user* to find files by ownership

For example, assume that you are looking for a file called *file1* to delete from your home folder. To find the file, you would use the following command:

find ~ -name file1

As another example, consider a server administrator who wants to find all files in the /usr folder that are owned by the user lpadron. To find the files, he would use the following command:

find /usr -user lpadron

To search all folders under the root and find all files owned by user lpadron, enter the following command:

find / -user lpadron

To find all files owned by user lpadron and then delete them, you can use the | symbol with the *rm* command:

find / -user lpadron | rm

Like the Recycle Bin in Windows, the Linux GNOME Files tool offers a trash can for deleting files permanently. The trash can appears in the left pane of the Files tool and is aptly named Trash. Periodically view the contents of Trash and then purge the files by clicking Trash in Files and clicking Empty.

UNIX/Linux provides commands to help you assess the allocation of disk space in a file system. One command is *df*, which provides statistics on the total number of blocks in a file system, the number used, the number available, and the percent of capacity used. While the *df* command provides information for the file system as a whole, the *du* command displays similar statistics for a given folder and its subfolders or for a particular subfolder.

Table 11-4 lists a summary of the UNIX/Linux commands discussed in this section.

Table 11-4 UNIX/Linux commands for finding and removing files

Command	Explanation
df	Reports how disk space is employed, including free and used space on a mounted file system
du	Displays file statistics for a folder and its subfolders
find	Finds specific files and includes these options: • *-atime* for last accessed time • *-ctime* for last changed time • *-mtime* for last modification time • *-name* for the filename (wildcards can be used) • *-print* to print the results of the search • *-size* for file size (in blocks or bytes; bytes are specified by a *c* after the size value) • *-user* to find files by ownership
ls	Lists files and includes these options: • *-a* lists all files, including hidden files • *-C* formats the listing in columns for easier reading • *-d* lists folders • *-f* displays files in an unsorted list • *-F* identifies the list's contents as folders, executable files, and symbolic links • *-i* displays the inode number for each file • *-l* presents a detailed information listing, including permissions and file size • *-n* displays the user identification numbers (UIDs) and group identification numbers (GIDs) of those who have access to files

Table 11-4 UNIX/Linux commands for finding and removing files (*continued*)

Command	Explanation
	• *-r* sorts files in reverse alphabetical order • *-s* displays the size of files (in blocks) • *-S* sorts files and folders by their size • *-t* sorts files and folders based on when they were last modified
rm	Removes files and folders and includes the following options: • *-i* is used to avoid unintentional deletions by prompting the user to verify the deletion • *-r* is used to delete a folder and all of its contents

Deleting Files in Mac OS X

Mac OS X is generally effective in automatically cleaning out many temporary, log, and other files on a regular basis. However, it is still important to find and delete unneeded files periodically to make sure you do not run out of disk space. Mac OS X windows often have a list option that shows files and their sizes. Click the List view button in the window to see file sizes (see Figure 11-2).

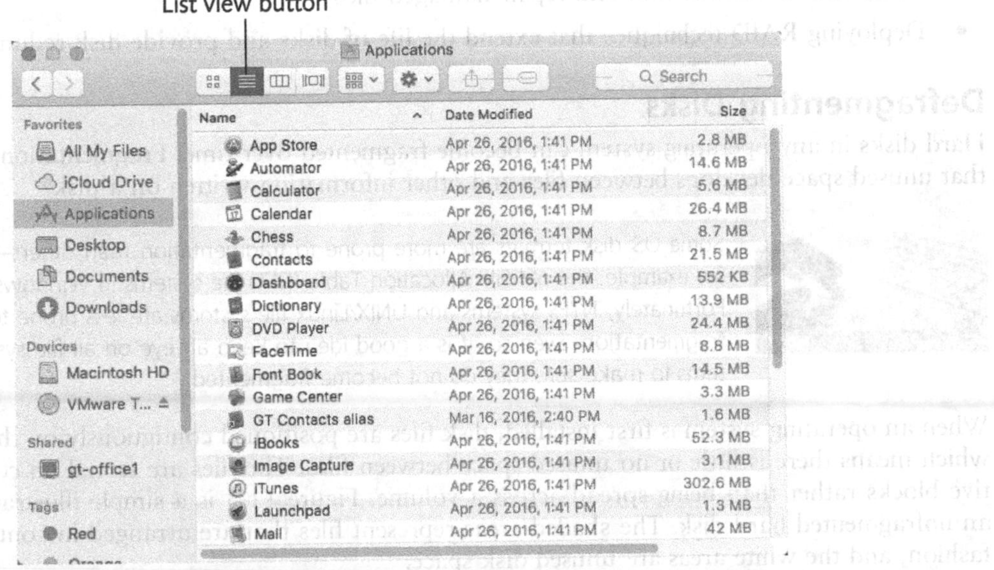

Figure 11-2 Viewing file sizes in Mac OS X

Source: Mac OS X

11

Mac OS X has a Find utility that you can use to find files that are no longer needed. To use the Find utility, click File in the menu bar, click Find, and enter the object of your search in the box with the magnifying glass. Alternatively, you can click the Spotlight icon in the menu bar and enter the search request in Spotlight. When you find an unneeded file, drag it into the Trash. If necessary, you can retrieve the deleted item from the Trash by opening it and moving the item back to a folder or the desktop. Files are not truly deleted until you purge them by emptying the Trash; perform this task on a regular schedule to free up disk space. (You will learn how to empty the trash in Mac OS X in Hands-On Project 11-8.)

Maintaining Disks

In addition to finding and deleting unneeded files, other disk maintenance tasks and techniques are valuable in terms of maintaining the integrity of files and ensuring disk performance:

- Defragmenting disks
- Moving files to spread the load between multiple disks
- Using disk utilities to find and repair damaged files
- Deploying RAID techniques that extend the life of disks and provide disk redundancy

Defragmenting Disks

Hard disks in any operating system can become fragmented over time. **Fragmentation** means that unused space develops between files and other information written on a disk.

Some OS disk formats are more prone to fragmentation than others—for example, the old File Allocation Table (FAT) file systems in Windows. Fortunately, NTFS systems and UNIX/Linux file systems are less prone to fragmentation. Even so, it is a good idea to keep an eye on all file systems to make sure they do not become fragmented.

When an operating system is first installed, disk files are positioned contiguously on the disk, which means there is little or no unused space between files. The files are stored on consecutive blocks rather than being spread across a volume. Figure 11-3 is a simple illustration of an unfragmented hard disk. The shaded areas represent files that are arranged in contiguous fashion, and the white areas are unused disk space.

File 1	File 1	File 2	File 2	File 2	File 2	File 3	File 3	File 3	Free	Free	Free	Free

Figure 11-3 An unfragmented disk

As the operating system deletes, creates, and modifies files, the unused space between them grows and becomes scattered throughout the disk, and the files themselves become scattered throughout the disk (see Figure 11-4). The greater the fragmentation, the more space is wasted. Equally important, the disk read/write head must work harder to find individual files and data in files, which leads to two problems: First, disk performance suffers because it takes the read/write head longer to find information, and it takes longer to find an appropriate unused location on which to write information. The second problem is that the read/write head works harder when there is more disk fragmentation, which increases the chances of hardware failure.

File 1	File 1	File 2	Free	File 2	Free	File 3	Free	File 3	File 2	Free	File 2	File 3

Figure 11-4 A fragmented disk

Defragmentation is the process of removing the empty pockets between files and other information on a hard disk drive. An older defragmentation method is to take a complete backup of a disk's contents and perform a full restore. Some administrators also run a **surface analysis** of a disk before performing the full restore as a means of finding damaged disk sectors and tracks. Some surface analysis tools are destructive to data and attempt to reformat the damaged area to determine if it can be recovered. Other tools are not destructive to data because they relocate information from a damaged disk area to an undamaged location, and then mark the damaged area as off limits so no files can be written there.

As a precaution, back up a hard disk before running a disk surface analysis or defragmenting it. Also, consult the documentation to determine whether a disk analysis tool is destructive to data before you run it. For example, some computer manufacturers provide disk analysis tools on a system troubleshooting disk; these tools perform a format along with the disk surface analysis.

A second option, which is usually easier than backing up and restoring a hard disk, is to run a **disk defragmentation tool**. Some operating systems come with a built-in tool to defragment disks. For example, Windows operating systems come with a disk defragmenter tool called Optimize Drives in Windows 8 and newer versions. Some defragmentation tools can run in the background as you continue to use the operating system. Many also provide a quick analysis of the hard disk and advise whether it is necessary to defragment it. For example, if disk fragmentation is 20 percent or less, the disk does not usually need to be defragmented immediately. Because server operating systems often experience more rapid fragmentation than client operating systems, server administrators should develop a regular schedule to defragment hard disks. Some administrators defragment between once a week and once a month, always during times when no one is on the server other than the administrator. In some situations where a server is under constant and heavy use, such as one used for a client/server or cloud-based application, it can be necessary to defragment disks every few days.

NOTE

In Windows 8, Windows Server 2012, and later versions of both, the disk defragmentation tool defrag.exe is scheduled to run automatically on all volumes when the system is idle, so manual defragmentation is rarely needed.

From the Trenches ...

A new server administrator checked the server at her company and found that the hard drive was severely fragmented. She felt it should be defragmented right away and started the process. To her horror, the defragmentation tool caused the Microsoft Exchange Server process to stop executing on the computer. All e-mail processing was down until the Exchange Server could be rebooted. She quickly learned that defragmentation is safer to run on a server that is taken offline after business hours.

TIP

If a disk contains an error, the Optimize Drives tool in Windows detects the error and requires that it be repaired prior to defragmenting the disk. Errors can be repaired using the *chkdsk* utility, which is discussed later in this chapter.

In UNIX/Linux and Mac OS X, file systems are designed to reduce the need for defragmenting a disk. These file systems first write to a hidden journal, which is loaded into memory; the contents are then written to disk in a linear fashion, not sequentially. Writing in linear fashion means that the data is temporarily stored and written all at one time in contiguous spaces. Writing in sequential fashion means the data is not stored, but is written as soon as it is created to whatever disk areas are immediately open. Using a hidden journal and writing data in linear fashion means that these file systems use methods that minimize fragmentation, which is why defragmentation tools are usually not included with them.

TIP

As with any system, an alternative to defragmenting disks on UNIX/Linux and Mac OS X systems is to perform a full backup and restore.

Moving Disk Files to Spread the Load

Another technique that can help extend the life of disk drives is to spread files evenly across them when there are multiple disks. This technique is used mainly on computers with multiple-user access, such as servers, and on computers with frequent disk activity. Before files are moved, the server administrator examines disk and file activity to determine how to spread files across the disk drives to achieve even loading. Also, files must be moved based on their functions so files that contain related information are on the same drive.

Disk activity is monitored in Windows operating systems using Task Manager, Resource Monitor, and Performance Monitor. Performance Monitor provides the most in-depth information and can be configured to log information to a file so activity can be examined over a longer period of time. For a quick look at current disk utilization, use Resource Monitor (see Figure 11-5).

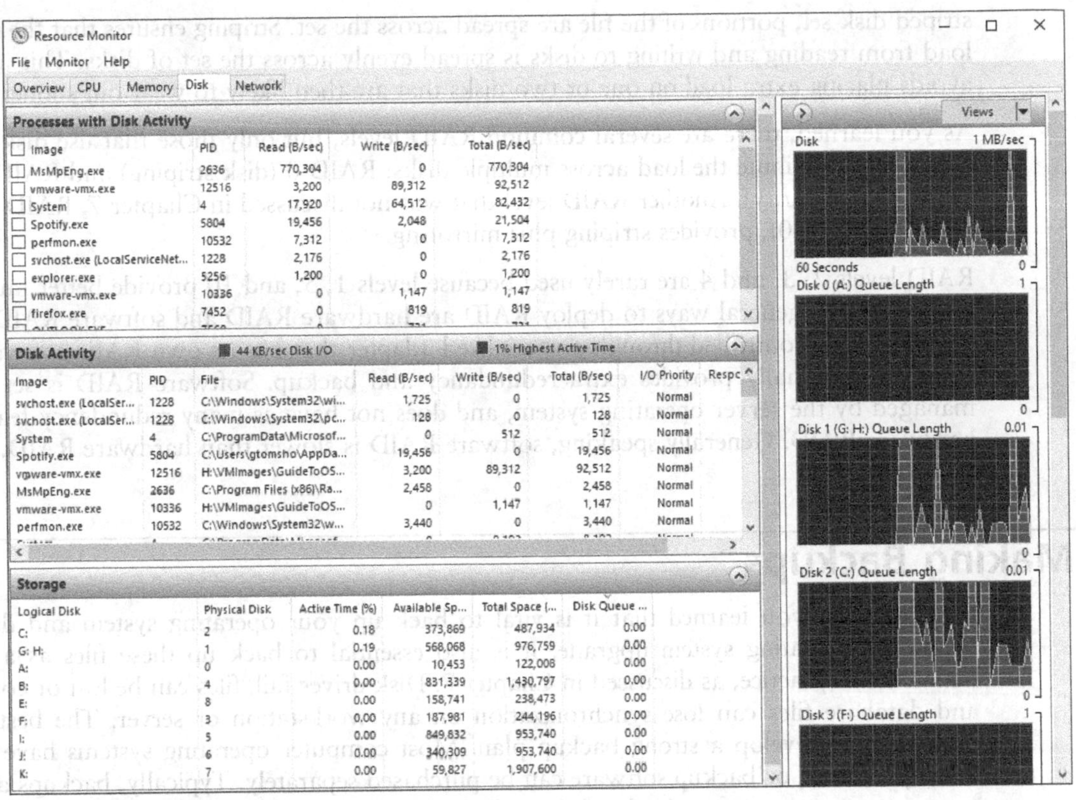

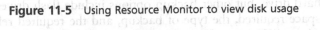

Figure 11-5 Using Resource Monitor to view disk usage

Using Disk Utilities to Repair Damaged Files

Some operating systems have utilities that enable you to repair damaged files and file links. Four examples of these utilities are listed here and were discussed in Chapter 4.

- Disk First Aid in the Mac OS X Disk Utility
- *fsck* and *p_fsck* in UNIX/Linux
- *chkdsk* in Windows

Deploying RAID Techniques

As you learned in Chapter 7, deploying RAID is a technique used by server operating systems and some client OSs for three purposes:

- Increased reliability by providing data recovery when a disk drive fails and extending the useful life of disks
- Increased storage capacity
- Increased speed

This section focuses on how RAID extends the life of a set of disks using **disk striping**, a technique for spreading data over multiple disk volumes. For example, when a file is written to a striped disk set, portions of the file are spread across the set. Striping ensures that the resulting load from reading and writing to disks is spread evenly across the set of disks. This approach avoids placing extra load on one or two disks that are then likely to wear out sooner.

As you learned, there are several common RAID levels, but only those that use disk striping techniques distribute the load across multiple disks: RAID 0 (disk striping) and RAID 5 (disk striping with parity). Another RAID level that was not discussed in Chapter 7, RAID 10 (also called RAID 1+0), provides striping plus mirroring.

RAID levels 2, 3, and 4 are rarely used because levels 1, 5, and 10 provide better fault tolerance. The two general ways to deploy RAID are hardware RAID and software RAID. Hardware RAID is controlled through a specialized adapter that has its own RAID software on a chip, which usually provides extra redundancy and backup. Software RAID is set up and managed by the server operating system, and does not have as many redundancy features as hardware RAID. Generally speaking, software RAID is slower than hardware RAID.

Making Backups

In Chapter 5, you learned that it is vital to back up your operating system and data files before an operating system upgrade. It is also essential to back up these files as a regular maintenance practice, as discussed in Chapter 7. Disk drives fail, files can be lost or corrupted, and database files can lose synchronization on any workstation or server. The best line of defense is to develop a strong backup plan. Most computer operating systems have built-in backup utilities, or backup software can be purchased separately. Typically, backups are written to tape or to a removable hard drive, but other backup options include flash drives, CDs, and DVDs, depending on the space required, the type of backup, and the required reliability of the media. Chapter 7 covers these different media and includes information about their projected life spans.

There are several types of backups. One type is called a **binary backup** because it backs up the disk contents in binary format to create an exact image of the disk contents. The advantages of this type of backup are its simplicity of operation and its inclusion of everything on the disk. The disadvantages are that in many versions, you cannot restore individual files or folders, and that when you perform a restore, the target disk drive must be the same size or larger than the disk drive from which the backup was made.

Another backup type is called a **full file-by-file backup**, in which all of the disk contents are backed up, but as individual folders and files. This type of backup is commonly used on workstations because it enables you to restore a single folder or a set of files without restoring the entire disk's contents. Full file-by-file backups are also performed on servers, depending on the backup scheme that is in place. Some backup schemes call for a full file-by-file backup to be performed at the end of each workday, as long as the total amount of information on the disks is not prohibitive. If the disks hold a great amount of information, it is common to perform a full file-by-file backup once a week and partial backups on the other days of the week.

There are typically two kinds of partial backups—differential and incremental. A **differential backup** only backs up files that have changed since the last full backup. An **incremental backup** backs up any files that have changed since the last full or incremental backup.

The differences between using differential or incremental backups as opposed to full backups depend on the amount of media required for these backups, such as tapes or DVDs, and the number of days of work that must be restored when a complete restore is necessary.

A basic backup scheme for a business might be to perform a full file-by-file backup to tape each Saturday evening and to perform differential backups to tape Monday through Friday. The business might also have four sets of tapes that are rotated each week. The first tape set would be used in week 1, the second tape set in week 2, and so on. In this way, if one tape set goes bad, one of the other tape sets from a previous week can be used to restore a server. In this scenario, if a catastrophic disk failure occurs on Thursday, the business can recover after the disk drive or drives are replaced by restoring the full file-by-file backup from the previous Saturday and then restoring the differential backup from Wednesday night. If the business had been performing incremental backups, it would restore the full file-by-file backup from Saturday and then restore the incremental backups from Monday, Tuesday, and Wednesday.

For small server and individual workstation backups, a simple solution is to use the ability of the native backup software to periodically back up new files and file modifications on the same day they are made. Mac OS X Time Machine, for example, enables you to leave a removable hard drive connected to the computer so it can back up any file changes shortly after they occur. This backup technique can be performed to supplement a full backup. Another option is to always have an internal disk or removable disk connected so that the native backup software automatically performs an image or full file-by-file backup at a scheduled time each day or one day during the week. Windows operating systems enable this type of regular backup.

Some removable disks provide software to perform backups, including software that regularly backs up recent changes to files.

Whether you are a home user, have a client computer in a business, or manage a server, it is important to develop a solid backup strategy. Consider the following elements as you develop your approach:

- *Determine what information needs to be backed up and how often*—Some files, such as the operating system files, need only infrequent backups—for example, after you change the settings on your computer or install new software. More frequent backups are required for other information, such as new word-processing files, spreadsheets, and other documents that you create daily. Develop a plan that enables you to back up the operating system as needed and to back up specific files as often as they are modified or are created.
- *Use scheduling software*—Windows native backup software, Mac OS X Time Machine, open source backup software for UNIX/Linux, and other third-party software can help you schedule backups. Set up the scheduling software to make sure backups are regularly performed so you don't inadvertently miss a backup.
- *Choose the right backup media*—Many kinds of backup media exist, including dedicated internal hard drives for backups, removable hard drives or flash drives, DVDs, and tapes. Choose the media that match your backup needs. For example, if you are a

home user who does not plan to store backups for years and years, a removable hard drive might match your needs. For personal information that needs to be stored for years, such as tax returns and precious family photos, use long-lasting DVDs for backup. If you are a server administrator who needs to back up and store large amounts of data for years or decades, consider using reliable, high-quality tapes and a tape subsystem.

- *Rotate backup media*—Even the longest-lasting backup medium can be damaged or broken accidentally. To protect against failures, rotate the media every week, every two weeks, or once a month, depending on the value of your data. Rotating media means having one or more full sets of media. If you are a home user, you might rotate the media once a month; a server administrator might rotate every week. For example, if it takes four tapes to back up the data files on your server, purchase an extra set of four tapes. Use one set one week and use the other set the second week, and then rotate the two sets every other week. For even better backup assurance, such as for a server in a credit union, purchase three or four sets of tapes so that each set is used only one week per month.
- *Store a set of backups in an off-site location*—Supplement your rotation strategy by storing one full set of backups in an off-site location, such as a bank vault. You might rotate one set to the off-site location once a month. If your home or place of business is damaged by a fire or flood, at least your data will be protected.
- *Regularly use file repair tools and a virus checker*—Regularly run file repair software, such as *chkdsk* or *fsck*, to make sure the data you back up is usable. Also, regularly scan with a virus checker so you do not back up viruses or malware.
- *Investigate third-party backup software*—After you develop your backup plan, you may discover that the backup software that comes with your operating system does not fully match your needs. For example, a server administrator may want to use backup software that helps track all media in a tape rotation or stored off site. In this case, investigate commercial and open source backup software to find a match for your needs.

Optimizing Software Installation

The following list provides some general guidelines for optimizing software installation and uninstallation:

- One aspect of software installation already discussed in this chapter is to plan and set up a well-organized folder structure. The folder structure influences ease of installation, provides the ability to keep different versions in separate places, and enables you to smoothly uninstall software. The following is a checklist of additional guidelines for software installation:
  - Make sure that the software is compatible with your operating system.
  - Check the central processing unit (CPU), RAM, disk storage, audio, video, and other requirements to make sure your computer is a match for the software.

- Find out if there are different installation options, such as one with or without tutoring applications to help you learn the software.
- Use the utilities provided by the operating system for installing or uninstalling applications. In particular, Windows operating systems usually have a Windows-compatible setup program that comes with the software. Also, use the Programs and Features tool in the Windows Control Panel to uninstall applications (see Figure 11-6).

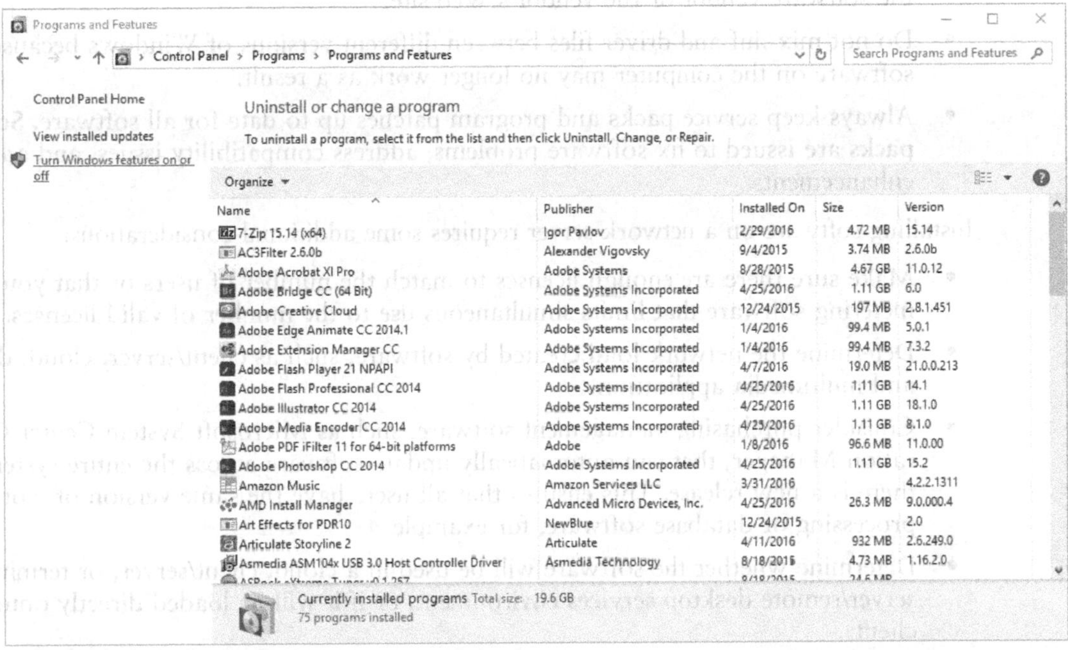

Programs and Features
Control Panel > Programs > Programs and Features
Search Programs and Features
Control Panel Home
View installed updates
Turn Windows features on or off
Uninstall or change a program
To uninstall a program, select it from the list and then click Uninstall, Change, or Repair.
Organize
Name
Publisher
Installed On
Size
Version
7-Zip 15.14 (x64) Igor Pavlov 2/29/2016 4.72 MB 15.14
AC3Filter 2.6.0b Alexander Vigovsky 9/4/2015 3.74 MB 2.6.0b
Adobe Acrobat XI Pro Adobe Systems 8/28/2015 4.67 GB 11.0.12
Adobe Bridge CC (64 Bit) Adobe Systems Incorporated 4/25/2016 1.11 GB 6.0
Adobe Creative Cloud Adobe Systems Incorporated 12/24/2015 197 MB 2.8.1.451
Adobe Edge Animate CC 2014.1 Adobe Systems Incorporated 1/4/2016 99.4 MB 5.0.1
Adobe Extension Manager CC Adobe Systems Incorporated 1/4/2016 99.4 MB 7.3.2
Adobe Flash Player 21 NPAPI Adobe Systems Incorporated 4/7/2016 19.0 MB 21.0.0.213
Adobe Flash Professional CC 2014 Adobe Systems Incorporated 4/25/2016 1.11 GB 14.1
Adobe Illustrator CC 2014 Adobe Systems Incorporated 4/25/2016 1.11 GB 18.1.0
Adobe Media Encoder CC 2014 Adobe Systems Incorporated 4/25/2016 1.11 GB 8.1.0
Adobe PDF iFilter 11 for 64-bit platforms Adobe 1/8/2016 96.6 MB 11.0.00
Adobe Photoshop CC 2014 Adobe Systems Incorporated 4/25/2016 1.11 GB 15.2
Amazon Music Amazon Services LLC 3/31/2016 4.2.2.1311
AMD Install Manager Advanced Micro Devices, Inc. 4/25/2016 26.3 MB 9.0.000.4
Art Effects for PDR10 NewBlue 12/24/2015 2.0
Articulate Storyline 2 Articulate 4/11/2016 932 MB 2.6.249.0
Asmedia ASM104x USB 3.0 Host Controller Driver Asmedia Technology 8/18/2015 4.73 MB 1.16.2.0
Currently installed programs Total size: 19.6 GB
75 programs installed

Figure 11-6 Programs and Features in Control Panel

When you need to remove an application in Windows, always use the uninstall capability in Control Panel. This practice helps to ensure that all components are removed, such as .dll and configuration files, so that the system folders do not become cluttered with files that are no longer needed. If you don't use the uninstall tools and instead simply delete the program's subfolder, such as the one in the Program Files folder, you might see delays in the operating system and other unexpected consequences.

- Check the vendor's "bug" list for the software to make sure the bugs will not affect the way you use it. Bug lists are often posted on the vendor's Web site in the software support area.
- Make sure that the software is well documented and supported by the vendor and that the vendor can provide the required drivers, if applicable.
- Determine in advance how to back up important files associated with the software, and find the locations and purposes of all program and data files, including hidden files.

- Determine whether running the program requires adjustments to page or swap files used by the operating system. (Page files and swap files are discussed in the next section.)
- Find out what temporary files are created by the program and where they are created.
- For Windows-based software, always install the latest versions of components, including .dll, .ocx, .ini, .inf, and .drv files. These files are generally available directly from the software vendor or the vendor's Web site.
- Do not mix .inf and driver files between different versions of Windows because other software on the computer may no longer work as a result.
- Always keep service packs and program patches up to date for all software. **Service packs** are issued to fix software problems, address compatibility issues, and add enhancements.

Installing software on a network server requires some additional considerations:

- Make sure there are enough licenses to match the number of users or that you have metering software that limits simultaneous use to the number of valid licenses.
- Determine the network load created by software, such as client/server, cloud, database, and multimedia applications.
- Consider purchasing management software, such as Microsoft System Center Configuration Manager, that can automatically update software across the entire system when there is a new release. This ensures that all users have the same version of word-processing or database software, for example.
- Determine whether the software will be used in a cloud, client/server, or terminal server/remote desktop services environment, or if it will be loaded directly onto server clients.
- Determine whether the server or client workstations must be tuned for the software in a particular way, such as by modifying page files or registry entries.
- For operating systems that support two or more file systems, make sure the software is compatible with the file system used by the operating system.

Tuning the Operating System

After an operating system is installed, you may notice that it doesn't perform as well as you expected or that performance seems to suffer with time. Just as a car needs periodic tuning, so do desktop and server operating systems. One critical reason for tuning operating systems is that slow workstations and servers have a cumulative impact on a network. Sometimes, poor network performance is not the result of network problems or too little bandwidth; instead, a preponderance of workstations and servers cannot keep up with the network. This is an often overlooked area that can result in significant savings for an organization if addressed. It is much less expensive to tune servers and workstations (often at no cost) than to invest in faster, very expensive network devices such as routers and switches. There are many ways to tune operating systems to achieve better performance, including tuning virtual memory, installing operating system updates and patches, and tuning for optimal network communications.

Tuning Virtual Memory

Most operating systems supplement RAM by employing virtual memory techniques. **Virtual memory** is disk storage used when there is not enough RAM for a particular operation or for all processes currently in use. The operating system can swap to disk (virtual memory) the processes and data in RAM that temporarily have a low priority or are not currently in use. When the operating system needs to access certain information on a disk, it swaps other information to disk and reads the information it needs back into RAM using a process called *paging*. The information that is swapped back and forth from RAM to disk and vice versa is stored in a specially allocated disk area called the **page file,** *paging file*, or **swap file.** (In UNIX/Linux, this area is called the *swap file system.*)

Some operating systems that use virtual memory and paging enable you to tune the page file by adjusting its size. Tuning the page file can result in better operating system performance.

Virtual memory in Windows operating systems is adjusted to set an initial size and a maximum size to which it can grow. Generally, the rule for sizing the page file is to set the initial size to 1.5 times the amount of RAM. The maximum page file size should allow for adequate growth to handle the most active times. In Windows 8, Windows Server 2012, and later versions, the paging file size is configured by default to be automatically managed by Windows (see Figure 11-7). You can change this configuration and specify a size and location for the paging file; however, if you are using a solid state disk (SSD) for the Windows system disk, you should let Windows manage the paging file size. In addition, because the paging file is extensively used, you should locate it on a separate physical disk from the Windows system disk (where the \Windows folder is located). By doing so, you reduce disk contention because the system disk is also heavily used. This advice extends to Linux/UNIX systems—the swap partition should be located on a separate disk from the Linux/UNIX system files. Also, on a Windows system, you can free up considerable space on the system disk by moving the page file to another volume or disk. You learn where to configure the paging file in Hands-On Project 11-3 and in Challenge Lab 11-1.

11

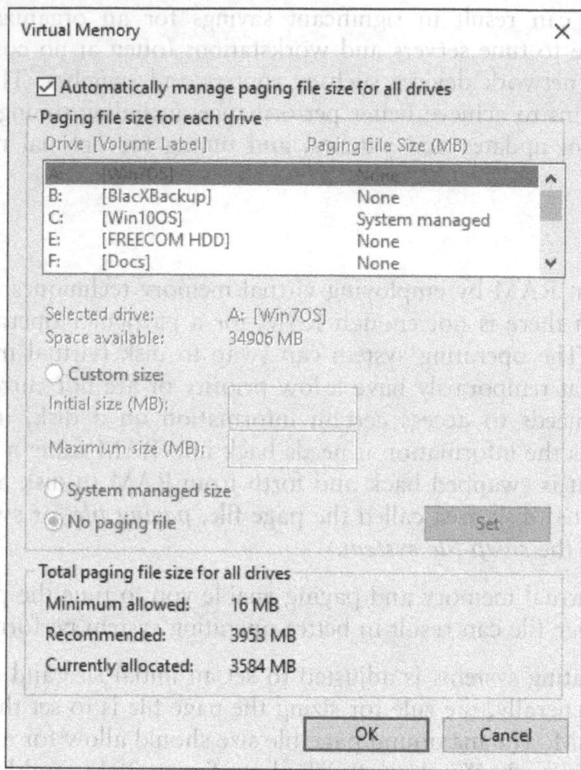

Figure 11-7 Configuring the paging file in Windows

Windows operating systems also offer Performance Monitor for monitoring paging and many other activities, but a discussion of Performance Monitor is beyond the scope of this chapter. To access Performance Monitor, right-click Start, click Computer Management, click to expand Performance in the left pane, and then click Monitoring Tools.

In UNIX/Linux, you can use the *vmstat* command-line utility to monitor paging. Paging in UNIX/Linux is accomplished with a swap file system, which is automatically created when you install most UNIX/Linux distributions. If a swap file system is not already created, you can use the *mkfs* command in Linux to create it. The swap file system is mounted like any other file system. If it is consistently more than 80 percent full, increase its size. Also, if there is a regularly high rate of swapping, consider spreading the swap space over multiple disks on different controllers.

In Mac OS X, there is no option for turning on or configuring virtual memory because it is always enabled. The use of virtual memory is built into the operating system and is not subject to user intervention.

Installing Operating System Updates and Patches

One of the most important ways to keep your operating system tuned is by installing system updates issued by the vendor. Problems with an operating system are often not fully discovered until it has been released and used by thousands, or even millions, of users. Once enough problems are discovered and reported, vendors create updates. For example, you can obtain updates by using the Windows Update utility in all Windows operating systems (see Chapter 5). Windows Update requires an Internet connection and downloads updates from Microsoft's Web site. By default, Windows 10 is configured to automatically download and install updates. Restarts are scheduled during the maintenance window, which is usually around 3 a.m. You can configure Windows Update to notify you when a restart is required rather than restarting automatically (see Figure 11-8). An automatic restart may be okay with a client OS, but you should only restart a server when no client applications are using it.

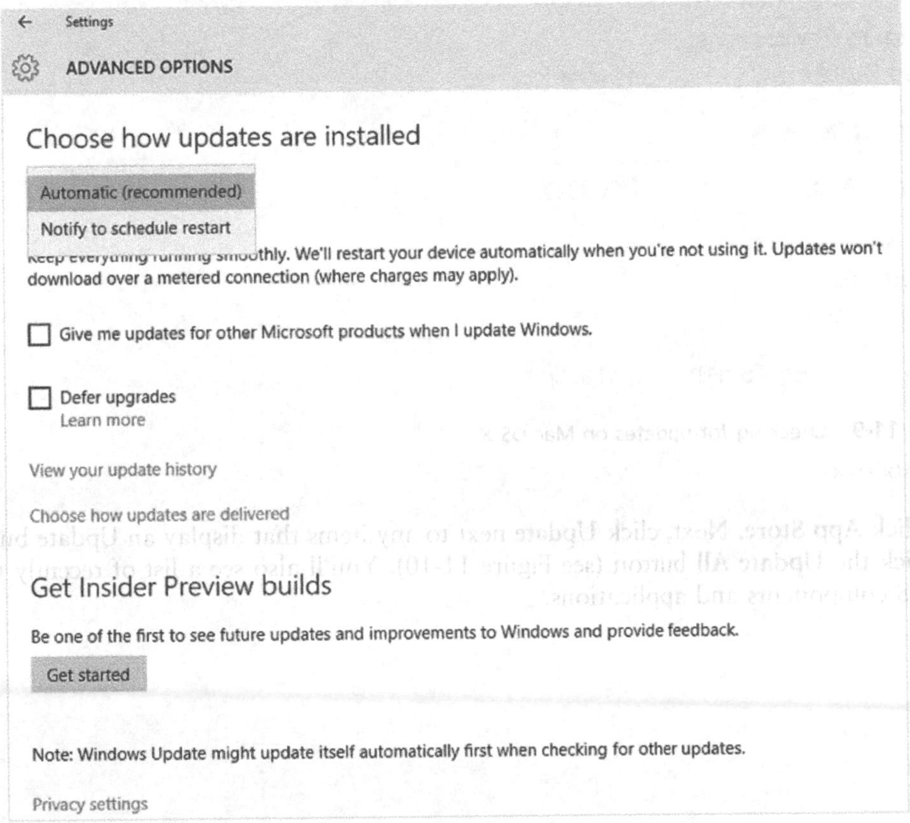

Settings

ADVANCED OPTIONS

Choose how updates are installed

Automatic (recommended)

Notify to schedule restart

Keep everything running smoothly. We'll restart your device automatically when you're not using it. Updates won't download over a metered connection (where charges may apply).

☐ Give me updates for other Microsoft products when I update Windows.

☐ Defer upgrades
Learn more

View your update history

Choose how updates are delivered

Get Insider Preview builds

Be one of the first to see future updates and improvements to Windows and provide feedback.

Get started

Note: Windows Update might update itself automatically first when checking for other updates.

Privacy settings

Figure 11-8 Windows Update

Many Linux distributions with the GNOME desktop have a software update tool that enables you to automatically obtain operating system updates through the Internet. The general steps to start the tool in Fedora Linux with the GNOME desktop are:

1. Click **Activities**.
2. Click **Show Applications**.

3. Click **Software.**
4. Click the **Updates** tab to see if any installed applications or OS files need to be updated.

Mac OS X uses the App Store to deliver updates. As long as the Mac has an Internet connection, the App Store is periodically contacted to look for updates to the OS and installed applications. You can check for updates using the following steps:

1. Click the Apple icon.
2. If any updates are detected, you will see a notification next to App Store (see Figure 11-9).

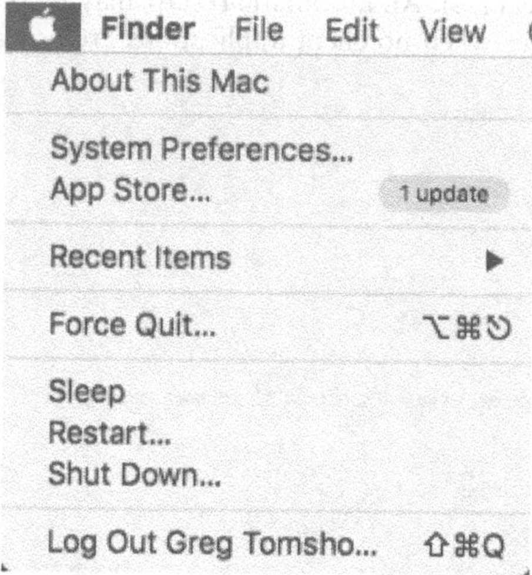

Figure 11-9 Checking for updates on Mac OS X

Source: Mac OS X

3. Click **App Store.** Next, click **Update** next to any items that display an Update button, or click the **Update All** button (see Figure 11-10). You'll also see a list of recently updated OS components and applications.

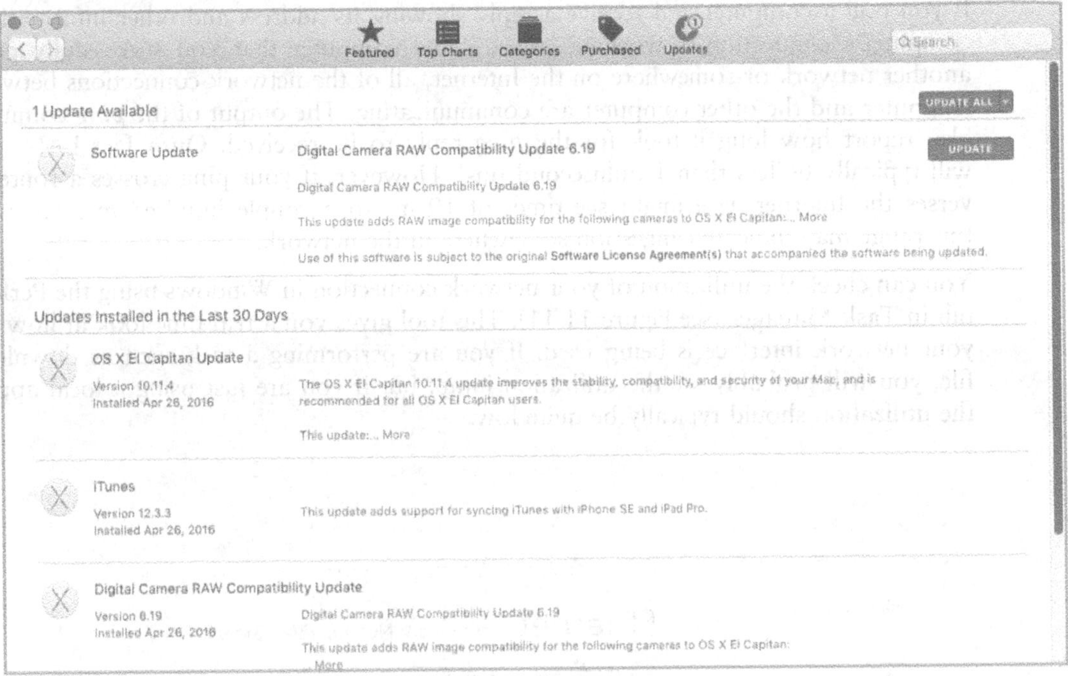

Figure 11-10 Updating Mac OS X

Source: Mac OS X

Sometimes it is helpful to contact the operating system vendor or an independent support organization for help with a system problem. The representative will ask what service releases, upgrades, or patches you have installed, and may request that you install them as the first step in solving the problem.

Tuning for Network Communications

Any computer connected to a network should be checked periodically to make sure that its connectivity is optimized. When a network interface card (NIC) is purchased, it should be of high quality and designed for use in the computer's fastest expansion slot, usually a PCIe slot.

Just as operating systems need periodic patches, so do NIC drivers. Check the NIC vendor's Web site occasionally for updated drivers that you can download and use immediately. Another problem with NICs is that they sometimes have problems that cause them to saturate the network with repeated packet broadcasts, called a *broadcast storm*. Network administrators can regularly monitor the network and individual nodes to make sure they are not creating excessive traffic.

Testing Network Connectivity

Questions often arise about whether the network is working or a particular workstation's network connection is working. Anyone can poll another network device using the *ping* utility, as you learned in Chapter 9. All of the operating systems covered in this book support *ping* as a command-line utility.

If you poll a computer and receive a reply showing its address and other information, your computer's connection is working. Also, if the computer that you successfully poll is on another network or somewhere on the Internet, all of the network connections between your computer and the other computer are communicating. The output of the *ping* command will also report how long it took for the *ping* reply to be received. On a fast LAN, this time will typically be less than 1 millisecond (ms). However, if your ping crosses a router or traverses the Internet, you might see times of 10 ms to a couple hundred ms. Times beyond this range may indicate congestion somewhere in the network.

You can check the utilization of your network connection in Windows using the Performance tab in Task Manager (see Figure 11-11). This tool gives you a real-time look at how much of your network interface is being used. If you are performing a task such as downloading a file, you will probably see the utilization jump, but if you are just using a local application, the utilization should typically be quite low.

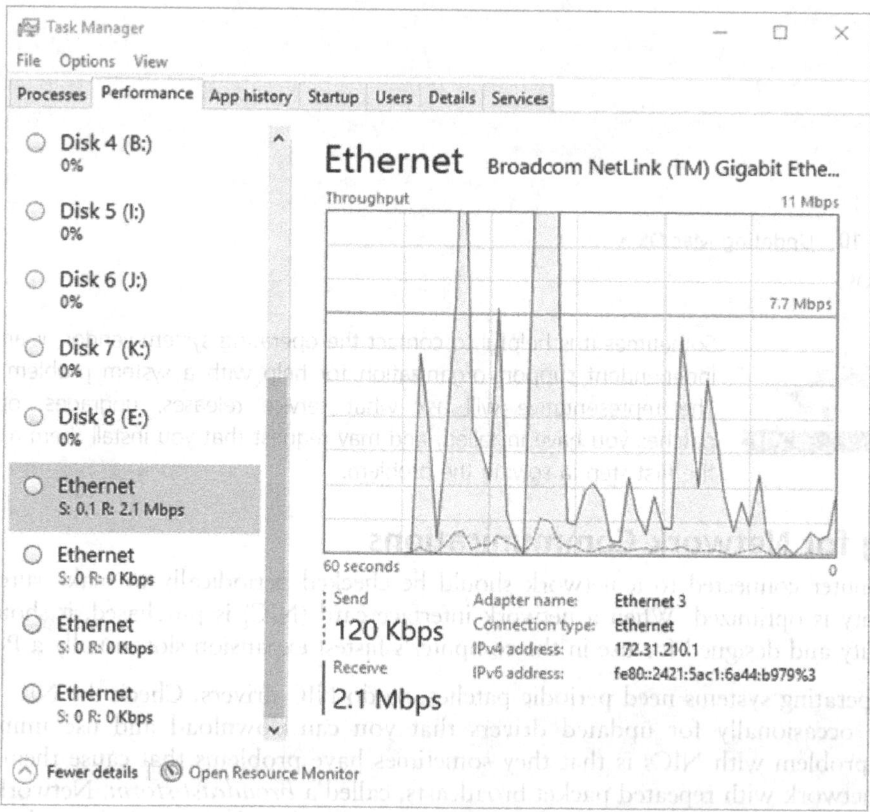

Figure 11-11 Checking network interface utilization in Windows

To check the utilization of your interface in Linux, you may need to download and install a utility such as *netdiag* or *netwatch*, but you can use a simple command-line utility called *ifstat* that is available in most Linux distributions and provides basic statistics for your network interface. On Mac OS X, you can run Activity Monitor and check the Network tab to see which processes are using network bandwidth and to see basic statistics for the number of packets received and sent.

Chapter Summary

- Successful file system maintenance is closely linked to a computer's folder structure. On desktop and server operating systems, a well-planned folder structure makes it easy to locate files, update files, share folders and files, back up and archive files, and delete unwanted files.
- The file structure established on a computer should be easy to maintain over the long term. Keeping files in a logical structure means it is easier to identify files that don't belong, that are out of date, or may be causing problems.
- One important practice for maintaining an operating system is to regularly find and delete unused files. Disk space is often at a premium, and there is no reason to leave unused files on a system because they are easy to delete. To find and delete unused files, use the Disk Cleanup tool in Windows, the *find*, *ls*, and *rm* commands in Linux, and the Find utility in Mac OS X.
- Other ways to maintain disks include defragmenting them, moving files to relatively unused disks, finding and repairing disk problems, and setting up RAID. Some operating systems have built-in utilities that can determine if disks are fragmented and then defragment them. Regularly defragmenting disks is an inexpensive method of extending disk life and improving performance. Disk scan and repair tools are another inexpensive way to address disk problems and prevent them from growing more serious. Equalizing the disk load by periodically moving files is an effective way to extend the life of disks. RAID techniques are also frequently used to extend disk life and to protect data when a disk fails.
- An important part of maintaining a system is to make regular backups. Backups can be vital when a hard disk fails or after you delete files you wish you had retained. Backups can also be used to restore drivers or other operating system files that were damaged or overwritten.
- An important consideration for optimizing software installations is to make sure the software is compatible with the computer hardware and operating system. When uninstalling software, use the uninstall options built into the operating system.
- All operating systems should be tuned periodically. Adjusting paging is one way to tune for better performance. Another way is to keep current with operating system patches and updates. Networked systems should be tuned so that NIC drivers are kept current and checked to ensure that no NIC is causing excessive network traffic. TCP/IP-based network systems include the *ping* utility for testing a network connection.

Key Terms

binary backup A technique that backs up the entire contents of one or more disk drives in a binary or image format.

cookie A text-based file used by Web sites to obtain information about a user, such as the user's name, the user's password to access the site, and information about how to customize the Web page display.

defragmentation The process of removing empty pockets between files and other information on a hard disk drive.

differential backup A method that only backs up files that have changed since the last full backup.

disk striping A disk storage technique that divides portions of each file over all volumes in a set as a way to minimize wear on individual disks.

fragmentation The accumulation of empty pockets of space between files on a disk due to frequent writing, deleting, and modifying of the files and their contents.

full file-by-file backup A technique that backs up the entire contents of one or more disk drives, including all folders, subfolders, and files, so that any of these contents can be restored.

incremental backup A method that only backs up files that have changed since the last full or incremental backup.

page file Also called the *paging file* or *swap file*, an allocated portion of disk storage reserved to supplement RAM when the available RAM is exceeded. See *swap file*.

service packs Software "fixes" issued by a vendor to repair software problems, address compatibility issues, and add enhancements.

surface analysis A disk diagnostic technique that locates and marks damaged disk areas. Some surface analysis tools are destructive to data because they also format the disk. Other tools can run without altering data, except to move it from a damaged location to one that is not.

swap file Also called the *page file*, *paging file*, or *swap file system*, an allocated portion of disk storage reserved to supplement RAM when the available RAM is exceeded. See *page file*.

virtual memory Disk storage used when there is not enough RAM for a particular operation or for all processes currently in use.

Review Questions

1. After you start your Windows 10 computer, you attempt to access your organization's network to open an inventory program, but you can't make a network connection. Which of the following commands tests your computer's ability to connect to the network?
   a. *find net*
   b. *net test*
   c. *ping*
   d. *listen*

2. When examining the contents of the Windows folder in Windows 10, which of the following subfolders would you expect to find? (Choose all that apply.)
   a. sbin
   b. System
   c. etc
   d. System32
3. Your organization's Windows Server 2012 server has 8 GB of RAM but has been running a little slow, so you decide to check the virtual memory configuration. You find that the paging file is located on the C: drive, where Windows is installed. The paging file is about 12 GB. Is there anything you can do to configure the paging file for optimal performance?
   a. Decrease the paging file size to 4 GB.
   b. Move it to another disk.
   c. Increase the paging file size to 24 GB.
   d. No, it is configured optimally.
4. How can you purge a file in Mac OS X?
   a. Send the file to the Trash and then delete it from the Trash.
   b. Right-click the file and click Purge.
   c. Copy the file to another hard drive and then delete it.
   d. Mac OS X files are always purged as soon as they are deleted.
5. You want to check on the size of virtual memory on your Linux computer. Where should you look?
   a. the /vmem folder
   b. the swap file system
   c. the /etc/swapconfig.cnf file
   d. the pagefile.sys file
6. Your Linux workstation runs slowly when you use certain applications. You decide to determine how much virtual memory is used when you run these applications. Which of the following commands enables you to determine virtual memory usage?
   a. *sfiles*
   b. *vmstat*
   c. *netstat*
   d. *vfiles -s*

7. Which of the following utilities in Windows 10 can find and delete temporary files created by programs?
   a. Disk Tracker
   b. Recovery Console
   c. File Manager
   d. Disk Cleanup
8. How do you check for software updates in Mac OS X?
   a. Click the Apple icon and then click App Store.
   b. Click Go and then click System Update.
   c. Click Go, click Utilities, and then click Updates.
   d. Click the Apple icon, click System Preferences, and then click Updates.
9. Which Windows tool lets you monitor paging activity?
   a. Device Manager
   b. Performance Monitor
   c. Disk Management
   d. Storage Spaces
10. In Linux, you are preparing to delete the tprice user account because this user has just left the company. However, before you delete the account, you want to list all files owned by tprice so you can decide which files to keep. What command enables you to view all files owned by the tprice account?
    a. *ls -owner tprice*
    b. *lsuser tprice*
    c. *find / -user tprice*
    d. *scan -owner tprice*
11. Temporary Internet files often have which of the following extensions? (Choose all that apply.)
    a. .html
    b. .cooky
    c. .gif
    d. .htm
12. Which of the following RAID levels involve disk striping? (Choose all that apply.)
    a. level 0
    b. level 1
    c. level 5
    d. level 10

13. How are files stored on the disk when an OS is first installed?
    a. randomly
    b. alphabetically
    c. contiguously
    d. fragmented
14. In Windows operating systems, which of the following methods backs up any files that have changed since the last full or incremental backup?
    a. copy
    b. incremental
    c. daily
    d. differential
15. Which backup scheme requires the fewest tapes to perform a full restore?
    a. full backup plus differential
    b. full backup plus daily
    c. daily backup plus incremental
    d. full backup plus incremental
16. What is the default Windows Update configuration in Windows 10?
    a. manually download, automatic install
    b. automatically download, prompt to install
    c. disabled
    d. automatically download and install
17. When you attempt to access an application in Mac OS X, you see a message that the disk is corrupted. Which of the following tools enables you to examine the disk, find the problem, and attempt to fix it?
    a. Inode Checker
    b. *chkdsk*
    c. Disk First Aid in the Disk Utility
    d. File Checker in the Preferences window
18. Your Windows 10 workstation hard drive seems to be laboring to find files, possibly because you added and deleted hundreds of files without performing any special disk maintenance. What is the most likely problem?
    a. The *defrag* program is not scheduled to run.
    b. The *chkdsk* program is not working properly.
    c. The page file is too small.
    d. Automatic disk cleanup is not working.

19. You use the Internet frequently. What simple step should you perform on a regular basis to maintain your computer?
    a. Tune your Internet browser to automatically shrink all cookies.
    b. Reset the protocol binding order in the Web browser to give priority to HTTP communications because accessing multiple sites can change the binding order.
    c. Check to make sure that your browser's speed is always maintained between 1 Mbps and 20 Mbps.
    d. Use your browser or an operating system utility to regularly delete temporary Internet files.

20. This morning you modified five large data files in your home folder in Linux, and now you want to find and delete the files because you no longer need them. Which of the following commands can you use to list and sort files based on the time they were modified?
    a. *locate -d*
    b. *ls -t*
    c. *rm -m*
    d. *df -d*

Hands-On Projects

Project 11-1: Use Disk Cleanup in Windows

In this project, you use the Disk Cleanup tool in Windows to delete temporary Internet files and temporary files created by applications. You need Administrator privileges for this project.

1. Start and log on to your Windows computer.
2. In the search box on the taskbar, type **Disk Cleanup** and then click **Disk Cleanup** in the search results.
3. In the Disk Cleanup: Drive Selection dialog box, be sure that the drive where Windows is installed is selected, and click **OK**.
4. In the Disk Cleanup for (C:) dialog box (see Figure 11-12), click to select the boxes for **Temporary Internet Files** and **Temporary files**. Remove checks from any other boxes. Click **OK**.

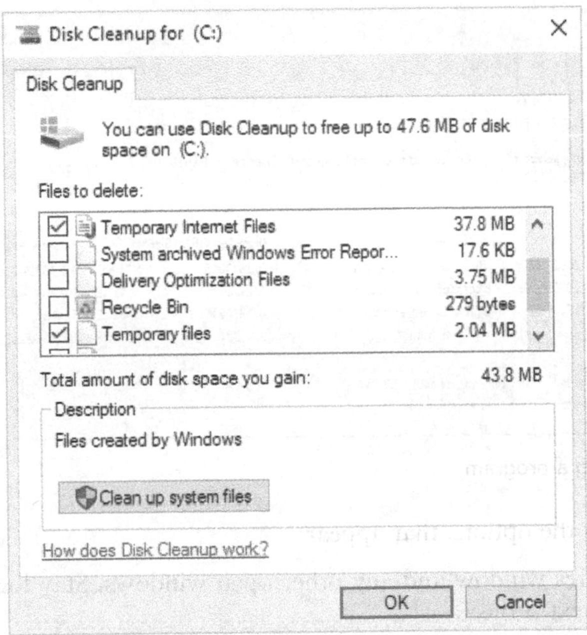

Figure 11-12 Cleaning up files with Disk Cleanup

5. Click **Delete Files** to verify that you want to delete the files. The Disk Cleanup utility begins. Depending on how many files you're deleting, the process could take a few seconds or several minutes.
6. Stay logged on if you are continuing to the next project.

Project 11-2: Use Programs and Features in Windows

In this project, you use the Programs and Features tool in Windows to see options for changing or uninstalling a program.

1. Log on to your Windows computer, if necessary. Right-click **Start** and click **Control Panel.**
2. If Control Panel is in Category view, click the **Uninstall a program** link under Programs. If Control Panel is in icon view, click **Programs and Features.**
3. Click a program in the list (see Figure 11-13). Notice that the option bar just above the list of programs displays the options available for the program. Possible options include Uninstall, Change, and Repair.

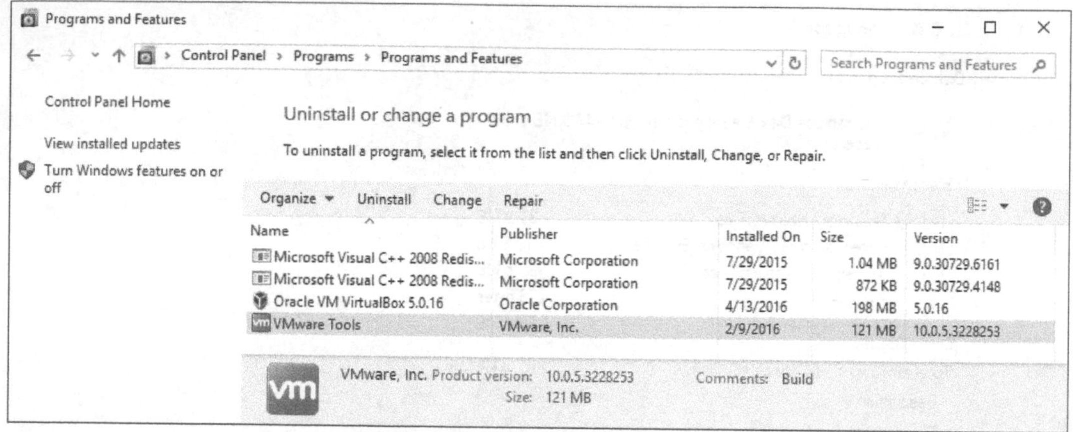

Figure 11-13 Uninstalling or changing a program

4. Click other programs to view the options that appear.
5. Close the Program and Features window and any other open windows. Stay logged on if you are continuing to the next project.

Project 11-3: View Virtual Memory Configuration in Windows

In this project, you view the virtual memory configuration in Windows.

1. Log on to your Windows computer, if necessary. Right-click **Start** and click **System**.
2. Click **Advanced system settings** in the left pane.
3. In the System Properties dialog box, click the **Advanced** tab.
4. On the Advanced tab, click **Settings** under the Performance section.
5. Click the **Advanced** tab in the Performance Options dialog box.
6. Under Virtual memory, you can see the total amount of virtual memory that has been allocated. Click the **Change** button.
7. At the bottom of the Virtual Memory dialog box, notice the minimum, recommended, and currently allocated sizes set for virtual memory.
8. Notice the check box (**Automatically manage paging file size for all drives**) at the top of the dialog box. If you cleared this check box, you could make changes to virtual memory, if needed. For example, you could put the page file on a different physical disk to optimize performance. For now, leave the check box selected. Click **Cancel** to close the Virtual Memory dialog box.
9. Click **Cancel** in the Performance Options dialog box and then click **Cancel** in the System Properties dialog box.
10. Close all open windows but stay logged on if you are continuing to the next activity.

Project 11-4: Check Network Utilization in Windows

In this project, you check network utilization in Windows using Task Manager.

1. Log on to Windows, if necessary. Right-click the taskbar and click **Task Manager**.
2. Click **More details**, if necessary, to see more information in the Performance tab. Click the Performance tab.
3. In the left pane, click **Ethernet**. In the right pane, you see a graph of network utilization on the Ethernet interface. Create some network activity by opening a Web browser and browsing to some Web sites. You should see activity in the graph. Keep the Web browser window open.
4. To see more details of network usage, click **Open Resource Monitor** at the bottom of the Task Manager window. Click the **Network** tab.
5. The top pane displays processes that are using the network. Your browser should be displayed in the list. Browse to some other Web sites, such as Microsoft.com or Espn.com, to create some network traffic. The graphs in the right pane should show plenty of activity (see Figure 11-14).

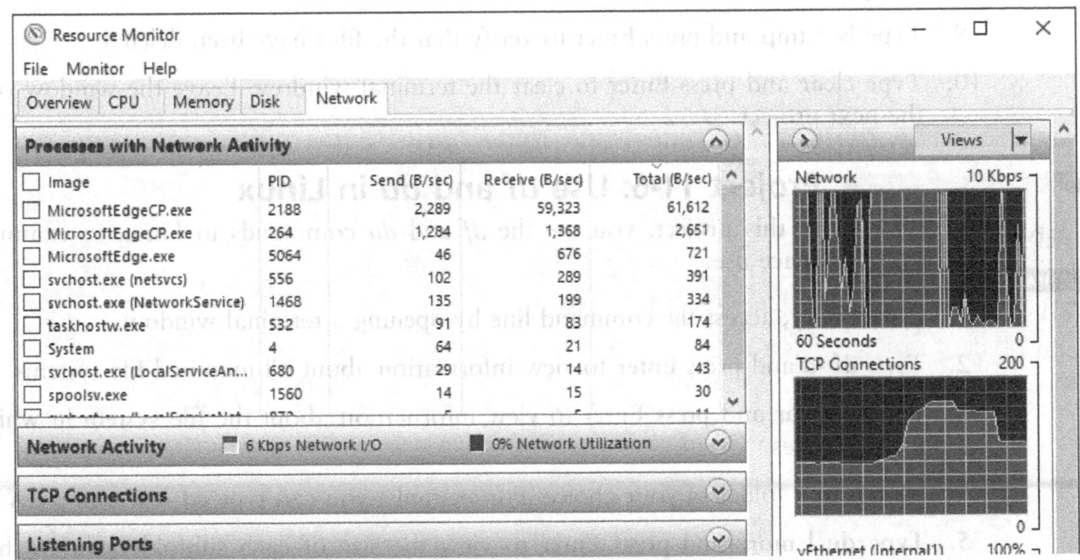

Figure 11-14 Monitoring network activity with Resource Monitor

6. Close Resource Monitor and Task Manager.
7. Close all open windows and shut down Windows.

Project 11-5: Delete Files in Linux

In this project, you create a couple of test files and then practice deleting them in Linux. Log on to your account for this project rather than the root account.

1. Start and log on to your Linux computer. Open a terminal window.
2. Create two files that you can practice deleting. First, type **touch practice1.tmp** and press **Enter**. Next, type **touch practice2.tmp** and press **Enter**.
3. Type **ls *.tmp** and press **Enter**. You can see the files you just created.
4. Type **rm *.tmp** and press **Enter**. If prompted, type **Y** and press **Enter** to confirm the files' removal.
5. Type **ls *.tmp** and press **Enter**. No files are found.
6. Create the two files again by entering the commands from Step 2.
7. Type **find / -type f –name "*.tmp"** and press **Enter**. This command finds all files with the .tmp extension in the entire file system. You may see some "access denied" errors as the *find* command attempts to look in folders for which you don't have permission.
8. To delete all files with the .tmp extension, type **find / -type f –name "*.tmp" -delete** and press **Enter**.
9. Type **ls *.tmp** and press **Enter** to verify that the files have been deleted.
10. Type **clear** and press **Enter** to clear the terminal window. Leave the window open for the next project.

Project 11-6: Use *df* and *du* in Linux

In this project, you use the *df* and *du* commands in Linux to examine disk space use.

1. If necessary, access the command line by opening a terminal window.
2. Type **df -a** and press **Enter** to view information about all mounted file systems.
3. Type **df /var** and press **Enter** to view information about the file system in which that folder resides.
4. Switch to a folder of your choice. For example, you can type **cd /usr** and press **Enter**.
5. Type **du | more** and press **Enter** to view the size of each subfolder within the main folder. Use the Spacebar to advance one screen at a time or type **q** to exit the listing of information.
6. Stay logged on if you are continuing to the next project.

Project 11-7: Use the *fsck* Command in Linux

In this project, you learn more about the *fsck* command in Linux by reviewing its online documentation.

1. Log on to your Linux computer and open a terminal window, if necessary.
2. Type **man fsck** and press **Enter**.
3. Use the **Spacebar** to scroll forward one page at a time or use the **up** and **down** arrows to scroll up or down one line at a time.
4. Unfortunately, you can't run *fsck* while the file system is mounted, but if you use Linux, you should be familiar with this command in case you need to perform file system maintenance. Press **q** to exit the documentation when you are finished.
5. Close the terminal window and shut down Linux.

Project 11-8: Perform Disk Maintenance in Mac OS X

In this project, you empty the trash and use Disk First Aid in Mac OS X.

1. Start and log on to your Mac OS X computer. Click the **Trash** icon on the Dock to view its contents.
2. Make sure there are no files you want to salvage from the trash. If you want to salvage files, drag them out of the trash and into the appropriate folder or folders.
3. Click **Finder** on the menu bar.
4. Click **Empty Trash.**
5. Click **Empty Trash** again to confirm that you want to permanently delete the files.

In Mac OS X, the Trash icon appears either as an empty wire basket on the Dock or as a can with papers inside.

6. Click **Go** in the menu bar, click **Utilities,** and double-click **Disk Utility.**
7. Click **Macintosh HD** in the left pane.
8. Click the **First Aid** button at the top of the Disk Utility window (see Figure 11-15).

11

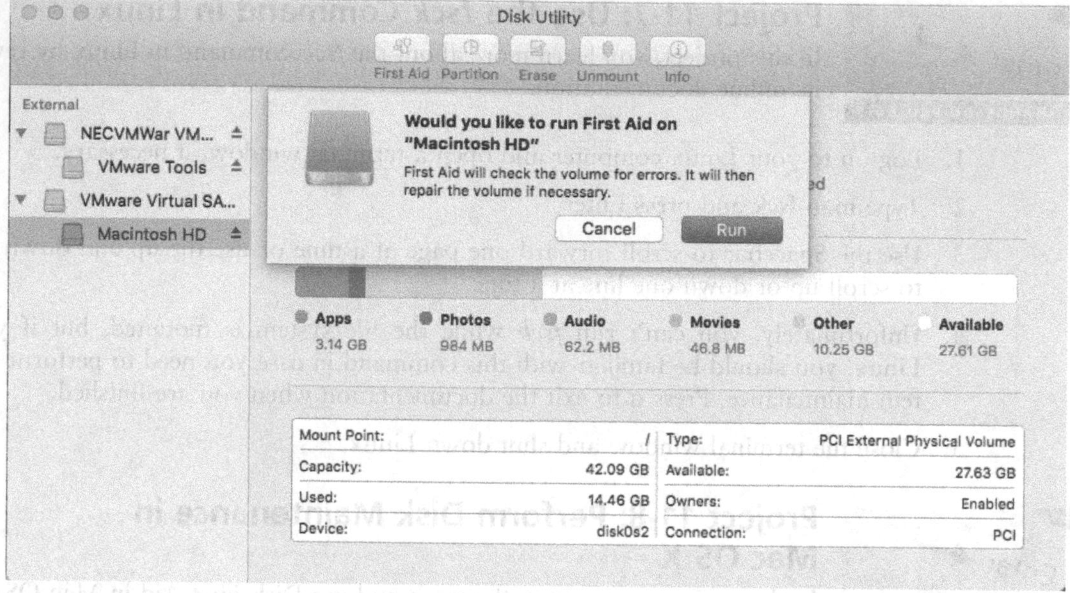

Figure 11-15 The Disk Utility in Mac OS X running First Aid

Source: Mac OS X

9. Click **Run.**
10. Click **Show Details** to see the progress and status.
11. If the disk needs to be repaired, you'll see messages in red and the recommendation to run the Disk Repair utility. If you see this recommendation, click **OK** and then click **Repair Disk.** Otherwise, wait until the verification process is complete and click **Done.**
12. Close all open windows and shut down your computer.

In some cases when disk repair is necessary, the Repair Disk option will not start. In such cases, try starting the disk repair by first booting from the installation DVD and then using Disk Utility from the installation DVD. Another option is to run *fsck* from a terminal window.

Critical Thinking

The following activities give you critical thinking challenges. Challenge Labs give you an opportunity to use the skills you have learned to perform a task without step-by-step instructions. Case projects offer a practical problem for which you supply a written solution. Not all chapters contain Challenge Labs. There is not always a specific right or wrong answer to these critical thinking exercises. They are intended to encourage you to review the chapter material and delve deeper into the topics you have learned.

Challenge Labs

Challenge Lab 11-1: Change Virtual Memory Settings in Windows

In this lab, you will change virtual memory settings on a Windows 10 computer. You want to make your virtual memory a fixed size and, if possible, move it to another physical disk on your computer. Get your instructor's approval if you plan to use classroom computers for this lab. Set the virtual memory to 1.5 times the size of physical RAM and move the page file to a different disk. If you don't have a second disk, move the page file to a different volume. (If you only have one volume, don't move the page file.) Answer the following questions:

- How did you check the amount of RAM installed on your computer?
- What did you have to do before you could change the virtual memory settings?
- What are the advantages of moving the page file to a different disk?

Case Projects

The National Center for Weather Research (NCWR) is funded by 22 state universities and eight foundations to study weather patterns, forecasting, cloud seeding, and other weather phenomena. NCWR's building has a network consisting of 295 workstations, including systems that run Linux, Mac OS X, and Windows 10. There are also Windows Server 2012/R2 servers on the network. All users have access to the Internet.

Case Project 11-1: Discuss Options for Additional Storage

More than 50 users who run Windows 10 are certain they need to purchase additional disks because they are nearly out of space. However, the budget is tight and it is important to eliminate unnecessary purchases. What options can you explain to them before their department heads order new disks?

Case Project 11-2: Repair Disk and File Problems

Your boss hired a new computer professional who formerly worked as a database support specialist in the business office, but who is relatively inexperienced in operating systems. The boss assigned you to train your new colleague. Today you will teach him how to find and repair disk and file problems. Explain the tools available for the following operating systems:

- Linux
- Mac OS X
- Windows 10

11

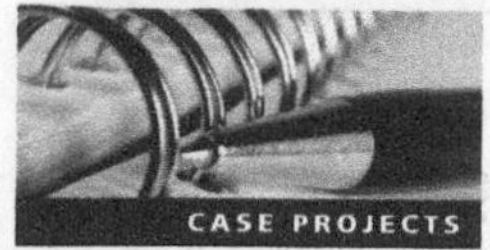

Case Project 11-3: Outline Maintenance Tasks on Mac OS X

The director of publications uses Mac OS X and has been working on so many projects for the past six months that she hasn't had time to perform maintenance tasks. She wants to spend some time tomorrow morning on these tasks. What maintenance tasks do you recommend?

Appendix A

Operating System Command-Line Commands

You can accomplish many tasks by using command-line commands in an operating system, including creating a user account or configuring a network interface card (NIC). Many UNIX/Linux users prefer using commands instead of graphical user interface (GUI) utilities because the commands are so universal and are often quicker to execute. Windows and Mac OS X users often find commands to be powerful, step-saving tools. For example, the Windows *systeminfo* command provides an instant snapshot of the hardware and software used on a computer. The following sections provide tables for quick reference to operating system commands. Two tables are presented for each operating system discussed in this book. For Windows, Fedora/Red Hat Enterprise Linux, and Mac OS X, one table lists general commands and one lists commands that relate to network functions.

Windows Command Prompt Commands

Table A-1 presents general Command Prompt window commands for Windows versions from XP and later, except as noted in the Description column. Table A-2 presents Command Prompt window commands for network functions in Windows. The following steps explain how to open the Command Prompt window in Windows 8.1 and later versions:

1. Right-click **Start**.
2. Click **Command Prompt** or **Command Prompt (Admin)** if the commands require administrator access.

Starting with Windows Vista, Microsoft introduced a powerful new command-line scripting environment called *PowerShell*. PowerShell allows administrators to manage almost every aspect of the OS environment using the command line and PowerShell scripts. PowerShell is a subject for an entire book and is not covered here, but you can learn more about it at *https://msdn.microsoft.com/en-us/library/ms714469%28v=vs.85%29.aspx*.

You can run many commands by typing them in the search box on the taskbar. However, when you use commands in this way, the Command Prompt window often closes before you can view the results of the command. You can also type *cmd* and press Enter in the search box.

To find out more about a general command when you are using the Command Prompt window, type *help* plus the command, such as *help attrib*, and press Enter. To learn more about a network command, such as the *net* command, type *net /?* and press Enter, or type the full command set and */?*, such as *net accounts /?*, and press Enter. To leave the Command Prompt window, type *exit* and press Enter.

The following is only a partial list of commands available in Windows. Many more are available, especially on a Windows Domain Controller. For a full list, see *https://technet.microsoft.com/en-us/library/cc754340%28v=ws.11%29.aspx.*

Table A-1 Windows general commands

Command	Description
assoc	Used to view and change file associations in Windows.
at	Enables you to schedule one or more programs to run at a designated date and time. This command has been replaced by *schtasks* in Windows 8 and later versions.
attrib	Enables you to view the attributes set for a file and to change one or more attributes.
bcdedit	Manages the boot configuration data (BCD) store.
break	Causes the system to check for a break key only during standard operations, such as while making input or output (*break off*) or during all program execution options (*break on*).
cacls	Enables you to view the attributes set for a file and to change one or more attributes.
call	Enables you to call a batch program from another one.
cd or *chdir*	Enables you to change to a different folder or to view the name of the current folder.
chcp	Used to view the currently active code page number or to set a different code page number.
chkdsk	Used to report the disk file system statistics and to correct file system errors such as lost clusters (for FAT and NTFS).
chkntfs	Used to report the disk file system statistics and to correct file system errors such as lost clusters (for NTFS).
cls	Clears the information currently displayed on the screen.
cmd	Used to start a new NT DOS Virtual Machine (NTDVM) session or new command-line session.
color	Sets up the foreground and background screen colors.
comp or *fc*	Enables you to compare the information in two files or in two sets of files to determine the differences in content.
compact	Compresses files and subfolders within a folder or removes the compression attribute.
convert	Converts a FAT-formatted volume to NTFS at the time a server is booted.
copy	Copies files from one disk location to another.
date	Enables you to view the date and to reset it.
del or *erase*	Deletes specified files on a volume.
dir	Lists files and subfolders within a folder.

Table A-1 Windows general commands (*continued*)

Command	Description
diskcomp	Checks the contents of one floppy disk against the contents of another. This command is no longer available starting with Windows 8.
diskcopy	Copies information on a floppy disk to another floppy disk. This command is no longer available starting with Windows 8.
diskperf	Installs, starts, or stops the Performance Monitor/System Monitor disk counters.
doskey	Starts the recall of previously used MS-DOS commands and is used to create command macros.
driverquery	Displays the current device driver status along with the properties.
echo	Shows an associated message or turns screen messages on or off.
exit	Used to close the Command Prompt session.
find	Used to find a designated set of characters contained in one or more files.
findstr	Used to find one or more sets of characters within a set of files.
format	Formats a disk.
fsutil	Configures and displays the file system properties.
ftype	Provides detailed information about file associations and is used to change associations so as to link them with a designated program.
goto	Moves to a labeled line in the batch program.
gpresult	Displays group policy information.
graftabl	Displays characters and code-page switching for a color display monitor. This command is no longer available starting with Windows 8.
help	Provides a list of the Windows command-line commands and is used to display help about a particular command.
icacls	Allows you to display, modify, back up, and restore ACLs (Access Control Lists).
if	Performs conditional processing in a batch routine.
keyb	Enables you to set the keyboard language or layout (only available in Windows XP/Windows Server2003).
label	Modifies the label on a disk volume.
md or *mkdir*	Used to set up a new folder.
mklink	Sets up symbolic and hard links (not available in Windows XP).
mode	Sets up parameters for a device or a communications port.
more	Used to limit the display to one screen at a time so information does not rush by faster than it can be read.
move	Enables you to move files from one disk location to another on the same volume.
openfiles	Displays, queries, and disconnects open files.
path	Used to establish the path or list of folders to search in order to run a program or command.
pause	Suspends processing of a batch file.
popd	Deletes a specified drive letter that was temporarily created by *pushd*.
print	Prints a designated file.
prompt	Modifies the format of the command prompt shown in the Command Prompt window.
pushd	Creates a temporary drive letter to a network resource.
rd or *rmdir*	Deletes a folder or subfolder.
recover	Enables you to try recovering files and data from a damaged or unreadable disk.
reg, regedit, or *regedt32*	Starts the GUI-based Registry editor.

(continues)

Table A-1 Windows general commands (*continued*)

Command	Description
ren or *rename*	Renames a file or a group of files.
replace	Compares files in two disks or folders and synchronizes the files in one to those on another.
robocopy	Utility to copy files and trees (available for Windows XP in the Windows Resource Kit).
sc	Configures and displays services.
schtasks	Schedules commands to run.
set	Shows a list of currently set environment variables and is used to modify those variables.
setlocal	Used to start command process extensions via a batch file, such as for detecting error-level information.
shift	Shifts the position of replaceable parameters in batch files.
shutdown	Allows for shutdown of the computer.
sort	Sorts lines input into a file that is written to the screen or sent to a printer from a file.
start	Starts a new Command Prompt window in which to run a program or a command.
subst	Used to link a path or volume with a designated drive letter.
systeminfo	Provides a wealth of information about hardware and software (not available in Windows 2000).
taskkill	Stops a task from running.
tasklist	Displays all running tasks.
time	Used to view the time of day and to reset it.
title	Modifies the title in the title bar of the Command Prompt window.
tree	Used to show a graphic of the folder and subfolder tree structure.
type	Shows a file's contents on the screen or sends the contents to a file.
ver	Shows the current version of the operating system.
verify	Instructs the operating system to verify that each file is accurately written to disk at the time it is created, copied, moved, or updated.
vol	Used to view the volume label, if there is one, and the volume serial number.
wmic	Displays WMI (Windows Management Instrumentation) information in an interactive command shell.
xcopy	Designed as a fast copy program for files, folders, and subfolders.

A very useful command called *msconfig* starts the graphical System Configuration utility, which enables you to configure files that automatically run when the operating system boots, specify which programs to run at startup, and enable or disable services. You can start *msconfig* from the command line or a Run dialog box.

Table A-2 Windows network commands

Command	Description
ipconfig	Displays information about the TCP/IP setup.
nbtstat	Shows the server and domain names registered to the network (used only on server versions).
net accounts	Used to change account policy settings and to synchronize BDCs (Backup Domain Controllers).
net computer	Adds or removes a computer in a domain.

Table A-2 Windows network commands (*continued*)

Command	Description
net config	Shows the started services that can be configured from this command, such as the Server and Workstation services.
net continue	Resumes a service that has been paused.
net file	Shows the currently open shared files and file locks and is used to close designated files or to remove file locks.
net group	Shows the existing global groups and is used to modify those groups.
net help	Displays help information for the *net* command.
net helpmsg	Used to determine the meaning of a numeric network error message.
net localgroup	Shows the existing local groups and is used to modify those groups.
net name	Used to display, add, or remove computer names that can participate in the Messenger service.
net pause	Pauses a service.
net print	Used to view and manage queued print jobs by computer, share name, and job number.
net send	Sends a message to designated users or to all users currently connected to the server.
net session	Shows the users currently connected to the server and is used to disconnect designated user sessions or all user sessions.
net share	Used to create, delete, or show information about a shared resource.
net start	Shows the started services or is used to start a designated service.
net statistics	Shows the accumulated statistics about the server or workstation service.
net stop	Stops a network service on a server.
net time	Used to synchronize the server's clock with that of another computer in the same domain or in a different domain, or to view the time set on another computer in the same domain or in a different domain.
net use	Shows information about shared resources or is used to configure, connect, and disconnect shared resources.
net user	Used to view, add, or modify a user account set up on the server or in a domain.
net view	Presents a list of domains, the computers and servers in a domain, and all resources shared by a computer in a domain.
netsh	Allows you to display and modify the network configuration.
netstat	Used to display information about the Transmission Control Protocol/Internet Protocol (TCP/IP) session at the server.
nslookup	Queries information on Domain Name System (DNS) servers.
ping	Used to poll another TCP/IP node to verify that you can communicate with it.
tracert	Used to view the number of hops and other routing information on the path to the specified server or host.

Linux Commands

The commands presented in Table A-3 are general Linux commands, and the commands in Table A-4 are network-related commands. If you are using the GNOME interface in Fedora or Red Hat Enterprise Linux, open a terminal window using the following steps:

1. Click **Activities**.
2. Click **Show Applications**.
3. Click **Utilities** and then click **Terminal**.

To close the window, type *exit* and then press Enter. To access documentation for any of these commands, type *man* and the command, such as *man at*, and press Enter. Press Enter to advance through lines in the documentation or press the Spacebar to view pages. Type *q* in the text window to leave it and return to the normal command prompt. Another way to find information about a command is to type *info* plus the command, such as *info at*, and press Enter. Press Enter or the Spacebar to read the information and then press *q* to exit.

Not all commands are available in all installations of Linux. For example, *lpr* and related commands are only available if the *lpr* package is installed. In addition, other commands will be available depending on the packages installed on the system.

Table A-3 Linux commands

Command	Description
at	Runs a command or script at a given time.
atq	Shows the jobs that are scheduled to run.
atrm	Removes a job that is scheduled to run.
awk	Finds and replaces text in a file.
batch	Runs a command or script and is really a subset of the *at* command that takes you to the *at*> prompt if you type only *batch* (in Red Hat Enterprise Linux and Fedora, you should run this command when the system load is at an acceptable level).
cat	Displays the contents of a file to the screen.
cd	Changes to another directory.
cfdisk	Partitions and verifies a hard disk.
chgrp	Changes group ownership of a file.
chmod	Controls file security.
chown	Changes file ownership.
chsh	Sets your login shell.
clear	Clears the screen.
cmp	Used to compare two files.
cp	Copies a file to another directory; you can rename the file at the same time.
cpio	Copies and backs up files to archive them on tape or disk.
crontab	Schedules a command to run at a specific time.
date	Displays the date and time.
df	Shows a report of how the disk space is used.
du	Displays file statistics for a directory and its subdirectories.
dump	Backs up files.
echo	Displays a message on the screen.
fdisk	Formats and partitions a disk.
file	Displays the file type.
find	Finds specific files.
fsck	Performs a verification of the file system.
grep	Searches for a particular string of characters in a file.
groupadd	Creates a new group.
groupdel	Deletes an existing group.

Table A-3 Linux commands (*continued*)

Command	Description
groupmod	Modifies an existing group.
groups	Prints the names of groups for a user.
info	Displays information and documentation about a command or a utility.
kill	Stops a process.
less	Shows the contents of a file, and offers the ability to go back or move ahead in the file.
ln	Creates symbolic file links.
locate	Finds a file.
lpd	Configures a printer.
lpq	Checks a print queue.
lpr	Prints a file.
lprm	Removes print jobs from the queue.
ls	Lists the contents of a directory.
man	Displays documentation in Linux.
mkdir	Creates a directory.
mkfs	Creates a file system (but requires more parameters than *newfs*).
more	Displays text in a file one screen at a time.
mount	Lists the disks currently mounted; also mounts file systems and devices (such as a CD-ROM).
mv	Moves a file to a different directory.
newfs	Creates a new file system.
passwd	Used to change a password.
paste	Merges lines of a file.
pr	Formats a file into pages or columns for printing.
printenv	Prints environment variables that are already set up.
ps	Shows currently running processes.
pwck	Checks the /etc/passwd and /etc/shadow files to make sure password authentication entries are valid.
pwd	Shows the directory you are in.
restore	Restores files (from a dump).
rm	Removes a file or directory.
rmdir	Deletes a directory that is empty.
sfdkisk	Provides information about a partition and can be used to create a partition.
shutdown	Shuts down Linux.
sort	Sorts the contents of a text file.
swapon/swapoff	Turns page file devices on or off.
sync	Forces information in memory to be written to disk.
tar	Archives files.
top	Shows a report of the main, current processes engaging the central processing unit (CPU).
touch	Creates an empty file.
umount	Dismounts a file system.
uname	Shows information about the operating system.
useradd	Configures a new user account.
userdel	Removes an existing user account.

(*continues*)

Table A-3 Linux commands (*continued*)

Command	Description
usermod	Modifies an existing user account.
users	Lists currently logged-in users.
vmstat	Displays a report about virtual memory use.
whereis	Locates information about a specific file, such as a program.
who	Shows who is logged on.

Table A-4 Linux network commands

Command	Description
finger	Provides information about a user.
ftp	Enables file transfers.
ifconfig	Sets up a network interface.
ipchains	Manages a firewall. This command has largely been replaced by *system-config-firewall* on most modern Linux systems.
netstat	Shows network connection information.
nfsstat	Shows statistics for Network File System (NFS) file upload and download activity.
nslookup	Queries information on Domain Name System (DNS) servers.
ping	Polls another TCP/IP node to verify that you can communicate with it.
rcp	Copies files between two computers.
route	Displays routing table information and can be used to configure routing.
showmount	Shows clients that have mounted volumes on an NFS server.
traceroute	Traces the route to the host.
who	Shows who is logged on.
wvdial	Controls a Point-to-Point Protocol (PPP)-based modem dialer.

Mac OS X Commands

The Mac OS X kernel (also called Darwin, the open source core of OS X) is based on Berkeley Software Distribution (BSD) UNIX, which means that you can access a terminal window and execute UNIX commands. To open the Mac OS X terminal window:

1. Make sure Finder is open or click the Finder icon in the Dock.
2. Click **Go** in the menu bar.
3. Click **Utilities**.
4. Double-click **Terminal**.

Tables A-5 and A-6 list commands that you can use in the Mac OS X terminal window. Notice that these commands are nearly identical to those available in Linux, including the use of *man* to read manual pages and *info* to learn more about a command.

Table A-5 Mac OS X commands

Command	Description
awk	Finds and replaces text within a file.
cat	Displays the contents of a file to the screen.
cd	Changes to another directory.
chgrp	Changes group ownership of a file.
chmod	Controls file security.
chown	Changes file ownership.
chsh	Sets your login shell.
clear	Clears the screen.
cmp	Compares two files.
cp	Copies a file to another directory; you can rename the file at the same time.
date	Displays the date and time.
df	Shows a report of how the disk space is used.
dump	Backs up files.
edquota	Edits disk quotas associated with user accounts.
fdisk	Formats and partitions a disk.
file	Displays the file type.
find	Finds specific files.
fsck	Performs a verification of the file system.
grep	Looks for a string of characters in a file.
groups	Displays groups to which a user belongs.
kill	Stops a process.
less	Shows the contents of a file and offers the ability to go back or move ahead in the file.
ln	Creates symbolic file links.
locate	Finds a file.
lpq	Checks a print queue.
lpr	Prints a file.
lprm	Removes print jobs from the queue.
ls	Lists the contents of a directory.
man	Displays documentation.
mkdir	Creates a directory.
more	Displays text in a file one screen at a time.
mount	Lists the disks currently mounted; also mounts file systems and devices (such as a CD-ROM).
mv	Moves a file to a different directory.
newfs	Creates a new file system.
open	Opens a file or folder.
passwd	Changes a password.
pr	Formats a file into pages or columns for printing.
printenv	Prints environment variables that are already set up.
ps	Shows currently running processes.
pwd	Displays the directory you are in.
quota	Displays the disk quota for users.
quotacheck	Verifies the disk quota files, including reporting disk usage.

Table A-5 Mac OS X commands (*continued*)

Command	Description
quotaon/quotaoff	Enables or disables disk quotas.
rcp	Performs a remote copy.
repquota	Makes a report of disk quotas.
restore	Restores files (from a dump).
rm	Removes a file or directory.
rmdir	Deletes a directory that is empty.
scp	Uses a secure version of ftp or rcp (remote copy procedure).
screencapture	Captures the screen image.
sort	Sorts the contents of a text file.
ssh	Uses a secure version of ftp.
sync	Forces information in memory to be written to disk.
tar	Archives files.
telnet	Remotely connects to another computer.
top	Shows a report of the main, current processes engaging the CPU.
touch	Creates an empty file.
umount	Dismounts a file system.
uname	Shows information about the operating system.
uptime	Displays how long the system has been running.
vm_stat	Displays a report about virtual memory use.
whereis	Locates a specific file.
who	Shows who is logged on.

Table A-6 Mac OS X network commands

Command	Description
curl	Transfers data from one server to another.
finger	Provides information about a user.
ftp	Enables file transfers.
ifconfig	Used to set up a network interface.
netstat	Shows network connection information.
networksetup	Sets up and modifies network and system preferences.
nfsstat	Shows statistics for NFS file upload and download activity.
nslookup	Queries information on DNS servers.
ping	Polls another TCP/IP node to verify that you can communicate with it.
route	Displays routing table information and can be used to configure routing.
showmount	Shows clients that have mounted volumes on an NFS server.
traceroute	Traces the route to the host.
who	Shows who is logged on.

Glossary

3D printer A printer that uses an additive process to create one layer at a time of a three-dimensional object.

8.3 filenames An older filename format in which the name of the file can be up to eight characters long, followed by a period and an extension of three characters. See also *extension.*

Accelerated Graphics Port (AGP) A bus standard that has been replaced by the PCI Express or PCIe standard.

access point (AP) A wireless device that serves as the central connection point of a wireless LAN and mediates communication between wireless computers.

activate To register your copy of a Windows operating system, starting with the Windows XP version. Without this activation, you can only run your operating system for a very brief time.

Active Directory The directory service used by Windows servers; a Windows Server installable service that consists of a database of computers, users, shared printers, shared folders, and other network resources and resource groupings used to manage a network and enable users to quickly find a particular resource.

active partition The logical portion of a hard disk drive that is currently being used to store data. In a PC system, the partition that contains the bootable operating system.

ActiveX An internal programming standard that allows various software running under the Windows operating system to communicate with Windows and other programs.

address bus An internal communications pathway inside a computer that specifies the source and target address for memory reads and writes.

address space The number of addresses available in an IP network number that can be assigned to hosts.

advanced intelligent tape (AIT) A tape drive that has an erasable memory chip and a capacity of up to 1.3 TB.

alias In the Macintosh file system, a feature that presents an icon representing an executable file. Equivalent to the UNIX/Linux link and the Windows shortcut.

allocation block In the Macintosh file system, a division of hard disk data, equivalent to the Windows disk cluster. Each Macintosh volume is divided into 2^{16} (65,535) individual units.

alpha software An early development version of software in which there are likely to be bugs, and not all of the anticipated functionality is present. Alpha software is usually tested only by a select few users to identify major problems and the need for new or different features before the software is tested by a broader audience in the beta stage.

Application layer Layer 7 in the OSI model, which provides interfaces that enable applications to request and receive network services. See also *Open Systems Interconnection (OSI) reference model.*

application programming interface (API) Functions or programming features in an operating system that programmers can use for network links, links to messaging services, or interfaces to other systems.

application software A word processor, spreadsheet, database, computer game, or other type of application that a user runs on a computer. Application software consists of computer code that is formatted so the computer or its operating system can translate the code into a specific task, such as writing a document.

arithmetic logic unit (ALU) A component of a CPU that executes instructions.

authentication The process of identifying who has access to the network. The most common form of authentication is a logon with a username and password.

authorization The process of granting or denying an authenticated user's access to network resources.

automatic private IP addressing (APIPA) A private range of IP addresses assigned to an APIPA-enabled computer automatically when an IP address is requested via DHCP but no DHCP server responds to the request. See also *Dynamic Host Configuration Protocol (DHCP).*

backplane A connection system that uses a printed circuit board instead of traditional cables to carry signals.

backup A process of copying files from a computer system to another medium, such as a tape, another hard drive, a removable drive, or a DVD/CD-ROM.

backward compatibility The ability of features from an older chip to function on a newer chip.

bad clusters On a hard disk drive, areas of the surface that cannot be used to safely store data. Bad clusters are usually identified by the *format* command or one of the hard drive utilities, such as *chkdsk* or *fsck.*

bare-metal virtualization A system in which the hypervisor implements OS virtualization by running directly on the host computer's hardware and controls and monitors guest OSs. See also *virtualization.*

basic disk A traditional Windows or DOS disk arrangement in which the disk is partitioned into primary and extended partitions. A basic disk can't hold volumes spanning multiple disks or be part of a RAID.

basic input/output system (BIOS) Low-level program code that conducts basic hardware and software communications inside the computer. A computer's BIOS basically resides between computer hardware and the higher-level operating system, such as UNIX or Windows.

batch file A text file that contains a list of commands you ordinarily type at the command prompt.

batch processing A computing style frequently employed by large systems. A request for a series of processes is submitted to the computer; information is displayed or printed when the batch is complete. Batches might include the processing for all of the checks submitted to a bank for a day, or for all of the purchases in a wholesale inventory system, for example. Compare to *sequential processing*.

Beginner's All-purpose Symbolic Instruction Code (BASIC) An English-like computer programming language originally designed as a teaching tool, but which evolved into a useful and relatively powerful development language.

Berkeley Software Distribution (BSD) A variant of the UNIX operating system upon which a large proportion of today's UNIX software is based.

beta software During software development, software that has successfully passed the alpha test stage. Beta testing may involve dozens, hundreds, or even thousands of people, and may be conducted in multiple stages: beta 1, beta 2, beta 3, and so on.

binary backup A technique that backs up the entire contents of one or more disk drives in a binary or image format.

blade enclosure A large box with slots for blade servers; the box also provides cooling fans, electrical power, connection to a shared monitor and pointing device, and even network connectivity. The actual design depends on the manufacturer.

blade server A server unit that looks like a card that fits into a blade enclosure. Blade servers are intended to save space. See *blade enclosure*.

block allocation A hard disk configuration scheme in which the disk is divided into logical blocks, which in turn are mapped to sectors, heads, and tracks.

block device In the UNIX/Linux file system, a device that is divided or configured into logical blocks. See also *raw device*.

block special file In UNIX/Linux, a file used to manage random access devices that handle blocks of data, including DVD/CD-ROM drives, hard disk drives, tape drives, and other storage devices.

boot block The UNIX/Linux and Mac OS X equivalent of the Windows Master Boot Record (MBR), the area of the hard disk that stores partition information for the disk. For example, on a Mac-formatted disk, the first two sectors are boot blocks that identify the filing system, the names of important system files, and other important information. See also *volume information block*.

boot volume The volume where the \Windows folder is located—usually the C drive, but this location is not mandatory. The boot volume is also referred to as the *boot partition*.

bus A path or channel between a computer's CPU and the devices it manages, such as memory and I/O devices.

cache controller Internal computer hardware that manages the data going into and loaded from the computer's cache memory.

cache memory Special computer memory that temporarily stores data used by the CPU. Cache memory is physically close to the CPU and is faster than standard system memory, enabling faster retrieval and processing time.

catalog b-tree In the Macintosh file system, a list of all files on a given volume. Similar to a folder in the Windows file system.

CD-ROM File System (CDFS) A 32-bit file system used on CD-ROMs and DVDs.

character special file An I/O management file in UNIX/Linux used to handle byte-by-byte streams of data, such as through a USB connection, including printers and network communications.

clean installation An OS installation on a computer that either has no existing OS or an OS that is overwritten by the installation.

client The term used to describe an OS designed mainly to access network resources, a computer's primary role in a network (running user applications and accessing network resources), and software that requests network resources from servers.

client/server systems A computer hardware and software design in which different portions of an application execute on different computers, or on different components of a single computer. Typically, client software supports user I/O and server software conducts database searches, manages printer output, and the like.

cloud computing A networking model in which data, applications, and processing power are managed by servers on the Internet; users of these resources pay for what they use rather than for the equipment and software needed to provide resources.

cloud storage A storage paradigm in which an individual's or company's storage is hosted by a third party and accessed over the Internet.

cluster In Windows-based file systems, a logical block of information on a disk containing one or more sectors. Also called an *allocation unit*.

clustering The ability to share computing load and resources by linking two or more discrete computer systems (servers) to function as though they are one.

command-line interface An interface that enables the user to display a command line from which to enter commands. These interfaces include the Command Prompt window in Windows operating systems and the terminal window in Linux and Mac OS X.

compiler A computer program that takes a high-level language like C# or Java and turns it into assembly code that is executed by the CPU.

complementary metal oxide semiconductor (CMOS) A type of memory that stores a computer's BIOS configuration. A CMOS chip uses a low-power memory technology that is powered by a small battery.

Complex Instruction Set Computing (CISC) A computer CPU architecture in which processor components are reconfigured to conduct different operations as required. Such computer designs require many instructions and more complex instructions than other designs. Compare to *Reduced Instruction Set Computing (RISC)*.

Component Object Model (COM) Standards that enable a software object, such as a graphic, to be linked from one software component to another one.

computer program A series of instructions executed by the computer's CPU.

control bus An internal communications pathway that keeps the CPU informed of the status of particular computer resources and devices, such as memory and disk drives.

control unit (CU) A component of a CPU that provides timing and coordination between the other parts of the CPU, such as the arithmetic logic unit, registers, and system bus.

cookie A text-based file used by Web sites to obtain information about a user, such as the user's name, the user's password to access the site, and information about how to customize the Web page display.

cooperative multitasking A computer hardware and software design in which the operating system temporarily hands off control to an application and waits for the application to return control to the operating system. Compare to *preemptive multitasking*.

core The part of a processor used to read and execute instructions.

creator codes Hidden file characteristics in the Macintosh file system that indicate the program (software application) that created the file. See *type code*.

credentials A username and password or another form of identity used to access a computer.

data bus An internal communications pathway that carries data between the CPU and memory locations.

data fork The portion of a file in the Macintosh file system that stores the variable data associated with the file. Data fork information might include word-processing data, spreadsheet information, and so on.

Data Link layer Layer 2 in the OSI model, which is responsible for managing access to the network medium and delivery of data frames from sender to receiver or from sender to an intermediate device, such as a router. See also *Open Systems Interconnection (OSI) reference model*.

default groups Special groups with rights already assigned; these groups are created during installation in a Windows environment.

defragmentation The process of removing empty pockets between files and other information on a hard disk drive.

defragmenter A tool that rearranges data on a disk in a continuous fashion, ridding the disk of scattered open clusters.

desktop operating system A computer operating system that is typically installed on a PC, usually used by one person at a time, and may or may not be connected to a network. Also called a *client operating system*.

device driver Computer software designed to provide the operating system and application software access to specific computer hardware.

device special file A file used in UNIX and Linux for managing I/O devices. The file can be one of two types: a *block special file* or a *character special file*.

differential backup A method that only backs up files that have changed since the last full backup.

digital audio tape (DAT) A tape system that uses 4-mm tape and has a capacity of up to 72 GB.

digital linear tape (DLT) A tape system that uses half-inch magnetic tapes and has a capacity of up to 1.6 TB.

digital pad An alternative input device frequently used by graphic artists and others who need accurate control over drawing and other data input.

Digital Visual Interface (DVI) A high-quality visual standard for connecting flat-panel LCD displays and digital projectors.

direct-attached storage (DAS) A storage medium directly connected to the server using it. DAS differs from local storage in that it includes externally connected HDDs in an enclosure with a power supply.

directory An organizational structure that contains files and may additionally contain subdirectories under it. A directory contains information about files, such as filenames, file sizes, date of creation, and file type. More commonly referred to as a *folder* in modern OSs.

directory service The software that manages centralized access and security in a server-based network.

disk drive A physical component with a disk interface connector (such as SATA or SCSI) and a power connector.

disk label The UNIX/Linux equivalent of a partition table in MS-DOS or Windows systems. The disk label is a table containing information about each partition on a disk, such as the type of partition, size, and location.

disk quota Allocation of a specific amount of disk space to a user or application with the ability to ensure that the user or application cannot use more disk space than is specified in the allocation.

disk striping A disk storage technique that divides portions of each file over all volumes in a set as a way to minimize wear on individual disks.

DisplayPort A digital interface standard that is projected to replace DVI and HDMI for computers.

Distributed File System (DFS) A set of client and server services to organize distributed shared files into a logical file system.

Distributed Link Tracking A technique introduced in NTFS 5 so that shortcuts, such as those on the desktop, are not lost when files are moved to another volume.

distribution An issuance of UNIX or Linux that is based on a standard kernel, but that also has customizations added by a particular private or commercial development group.

domain A collection of users and computers in a server-based network whose accounts are managed by Windows servers called *domain controllers*. See also *domain controller*.

domain controller A computer running Windows Server with Active Directory installed; it maintains a database of user and computer accounts as well as network access policies in a Windows domain. See also *directory service*.

domain local group A group scope recommended for assigning rights and permissions to domain resources.

Domain Name Service (DNS) An application protocol that resolves domain and computer names to IP addresses, or that resolves IP addresses to domain and computer names.

dot-matrix (impact) printer An impact character printer that produces characters by arranging a matrix of dots.

dots per inch (dpi) Used to measure the resolution of a printer; the number of dots contained in an inch.

driver signing A digital signature that Microsoft incorporates into driver and system files as a way to verify the files and to ensure that they are not inappropriately overwritten.

dye sublimation A printer technology that produces high-quality color output by creating "sublimated" color mists that penetrate paper to form characters or graphic output.

dynamic disk A disk arrangement that can hold up to 128 volumes, including spanned volumes, striped volumes, and RAID volumes.

Dynamic Host Configuration Protocol (DHCP) An Application layer protocol used to configure a host's IP address settings dynamically.

embedded system A computer that has a dedicated function within a larger system, such as a piece of machinery.

encapsulation The process of adding header and trailer information to chunks of data.

Extended (HFS+) A file system released in 1998 with Mac OS 8.1 and the file system used in Mac OS X.

extended file system (ext or ext fs) The file system designed for Linux that is installed by default in Linux operating systems.

extended partition A division of disk space on a basic disk that must be separated into logical drives; it can't be marked active and can't hold the Windows system volume.

extension In MS-DOS and Windows-based systems, the part of a filename that typically identifies the type of file associated with the name. File extensions are typically three characters long and include standard notations such as .sys, .exe, .bat, and so on.

extents b-tree A file system component that keeps track of the location of file fragments, or extents, in the Mac OS HFS file system.

external clock speed The speed at which the processor communicates with the memory and other devices in the computer; usually one-fourth to one-half the internal clock speed.

external commands Operating system commands that are stored in separate program files on disk. When these commands are required, they must be loaded from disk storage into memory before they are executed.

extranet A private network that allows limited and controlled access to internal network resources by outside users, usually in a business-to-business situation.

failover clustering A group of two or more servers configured so that if one server fails, another server can resume the services the first one was providing.

file A set of data that is grouped in some logical manner, assigned a name, and stored on the disk.

file allocation table (FAT) A file management system that defines the way data is stored on a disk drive. The FAT stores information about a file's size and physical location on the disk.

file attributes File characteristics stored with the filename in the disk folder; attributes specify certain storage and operational parameters associated with the file, such as hidden, read-only, archive, and so on.

File Classification Infrastructure (FCI) A system that allows files to be located on servers in an organization based on predetermined naming conventions.

file system A design for storing and managing files on a disk drive; the method by which an OS stores and organizes files and manages access to files on a storage device.

floating point unit (FPU) A component of a CPU that executes floating point mathematical operations.

folder See *directory*.

formatting The process of installing a file system on a disk partition.

fragmentation The accumulation of empty pockets of space between files on a disk due to frequent writing, deleting, and modifying of the files and their contents.

frame A packet with source and destination MAC addresses added and an error-checking code added to the back end. Frames are generated and processed by the network interface. See also *packet*.

full file-by-file backup A technique that backs up the entire contents of one or more disk drives, including all folders, subfolders, and files, so that any of these contents can be restored.

gadgets Small applications for readily accessing information and tools.

gamepad An input device primarily designed for interaction with games. It includes multiple buttons, wheels, or balls to effect movement of a variety of on-screen objects.

global group A group scope used mainly to group users from the same domain who have similar access and rights requirements. A global group's members can be user accounts and other global groups from the same domain. See also *group scope*.

graphical user interface (GUI) An interface between the user and an operating system that presents information in an intuitive graphical format, including multiple colors, figures, icons, windows, toolbars, and other features. A GUI is usually deployed with a pointing device, such as a mouse, to make the user more productive.

group scope A property of a group that determines the reach of a group's application in a domain—for example, which users can be group members and to which resources a group can be assigned rights or permissions.

guest OS The operating system installed on a virtual machine.

GUID Partitioning Table (GPT) A disk-partitioning method that supports volume sizes of up to 18 exabytes.

hard link In Windows versions starting with Windows 2000 and UNIX/Linux, a file management technique that permits multiple folder entries to point to the same file.

hardware The physical devices in a computer, including the CPU, circuit boards (cards), disk drives, monitor, and modem.

header Information added to the front end of a chunk of data so it can be correctly interpreted and processed by network protocols.

Hierarchical Filing System (HFS) An early Apple Macintosh file system storage method that uses a hierarchical folder structure.

High-Definition Multimedia Interface (HDMI) A high-quality visual standard for connecting digital audio and video devices.

high-level formatting A process that prepares a disk partition (or removable media) for a specific file system.

host computer The physical computer on which virtual machine software is installed and virtual machines run.

hosted virtualization A system in which the hypervisor implements OS virtualization by being installed in a general-purpose host OS, such as Windows 10 or Linux, and the host OS accesses host hardware on behalf of the guest OS. See also *virtualization*.

hot fix A procedure used by a file system that can detect a damaged disk area and then automatically copy information from that area to another disk area that is not damaged.

Hyper-Threading (HT) A feature of some Intel CPUs that allows two threads to run on each CPU core simultaneously.

Hyper-V A Windows feature that allows a server to run multiple independent operating systems at the same time and to run multiple virtual servers on one physical server.

hypervisor The component of virtualization software that creates and monitors the virtual hardware environment, which allows multiple VMs to share physical hardware resources.

I/O address range A range of memory addresses used to temporarily store data that is transferred between a computer device or component and the CPU.

in-place upgrade An OS upgrade that overwrites your current OS and maintains your applications, settings, and data.

incremental backup A method that only backs up files that have changed since the last full or incremental backup.

Infrared Data Association (IrDA) A group of peripheral manufacturers that developed a set of standards for transmitting data using infrared light. Printers were some of the first devices to support the IrDA specifications.

infrastructure as a service (IaaS) A category of cloud computing in which a company can use a provider's storage or virtual servers as its needs demand; IaaS is also called *hosted infrastructure*.

inkjet printer A printer that forms characters and images by spraying droplets of ink from a nozzle print head onto the paper.

inode Short for *information node*. In UNIX/Linux, a system for storing key information about files.

input/output (I/O) Input is information taken in by a computer device to handle or process; an example is characters typed at a keyboard. Output is information sent out by a computer device after the information is handled or processed; an example is the display of typed characters on the monitor.

Institute of Electrical and Electronics Engineers (IEEE) An international organization of scientists, engineers, technicians, and educators that plays a leading role in developing standards for computers, network cabling, and data transmissions, and for other electronics areas, such as consumer electronics and electrical power.

instruction set In a computer CPU, the group of commands (instructions) the processor recognizes. These instructions are used to conduct the operations required of the CPU by the operating system and application software.

internal clock speed The speed at which the CPU executes internal commands, measured in megahertz (millions of clock ticks per second) or gigahertz (billions of clock ticks per second). Internal clock speeds can be as low as 1 MHz or more than 4 GHz.

Internet A worldwide public internetwork that uses standard protocols, such as TCP/IP, DNS, and HTTP, to transfer and view information.

Internet Protocol version 4 (IPv4) A connectionless Internetwork layer protocol that provides source and destination addressing and routing for the TCP/IP protocol suite; IPv4 uses 32-bit dotted decimal addresses.

Internet Protocol version 6 (IPv6) A connectionless Internetwork layer protocol that provides source and destination addressing and routing for the TCP/IP protocol suite. IPv6 uses 128-bit hexadecimal addresses and has built-in security and QoS features.

internetwork A networked collection of LANs tied together by devices such as routers. See also *local area network (LAN)*.

interrupt request (IRQ) A request to the processor so that a currently operating process, such as a read from a disk drive, can be interrupted by another process, such as a write into memory.

interrupt request (IRQ) line A channel within the computer that is used for communications with the CPU.

intranet A private network in which devices and servers are available only to users connected to the internal network.

IP address A 32-bit dotted decimal address used by IP to determine the network a host resides on and to identify hosts on the network at the Internetwork layer.

IP Security (IPsec) A way to secure Internet Protocol (IP) traffic by encrypting and authenticating each packet.

journaling The ability of a file system or software (such as database software) to track file changes so that if a system crashes unexpectedly, it is possible to reconstruct files or to roll back changes with minimal or no damage.

joystick An input device shaped like a stick that allows for three-dimensional movement of an on-screen cursor or other object, such as a car, airplane, or cartoon character.

just a bunch of disks (JBOD) A disk arrangement in which two or more disks are abstracted to appear as a single disk to the OS but aren't arranged in a specific RAID configuration.

Kerberos A security system and authentication protocol that authenticates users and grants or denies access to network resources based on a user's log-on name and password. Kerberos creates a unique encryption key for each communication session.

kernel An essential set of programs and computer code built into a computer operating system to control processor, disk, memory, and other functions central to a computer's basic operation. The kernel communicates with the BIOS, device drivers, and the API to perform these functions. It also interfaces with the resource managers.

label printers Special-purpose printers that produce labels only.

laser printer A high-quality page printer design that is popular in office and other professional applications.

level 1 (L1) cache Cache memory that is part of the CPU hardware. See *cache memory*.

level 2 (L2) cache Cache memory that is somewhat slower than L1 cache but is much larger. See *cache memory*.

level 3 (L3) cache Cache memory that is slower than L1 or L2 cache but is much larger. L3 cache is located on the CPU chip on most modern CPUs, and is shared among multiple cores. See *cache memory*.

level 4 (L4) cache Cache memory that is found on some advanced modern CPUs. See *cache memory*.

library A combination of folders that can be in any location on the local computer or the network.

line editor An editor that is used to create text one line at a time.

line printer A printer design that prints a full line of character output at a time; it is used for high-speed output requirements.

linear tape open (LTO) A tape drive used in the high-end server market; it has a storage capacity of up to 1.6 TB.

link-local IPv6 address Similar in function to IPv4 APIPA addresses, link-local IPv6 addresses begin with *fe80*, are self-configuring, and can't be routed. See also *Automatic private IP addressing (APIPA)*.

linked list Used in FAT file systems so that when a file is written to disk, each cluster containing that file's data has a pointer to the location of the next cluster of data.

live migration A feature of virtualization that allows a virtual machine to be moved from one server to another with little or no downtime.

local area network (LAN) A small network limited to a single collection of machines and linked by interconnecting devices in a small geographic area.

local storage Storage media with a direct and exclusive connection to the computer's system board through a disk controller.

localhost A reserved name that corresponds to the loopback address in an IP network. See also *loopback address*.

logical drive A software definition that divides a physical hard drive into multiple drives for file storage.

logical unit number (LUN) A logical reference point to a unit of storage that could refer to an entire array of disks, a single disk, or just part of a disk.

logical volume manager (LVM) A method of creating volumes in Linux that uses physical disk partitions called *volume groups* to create logical volumes.

long filename (LFN) A name for a file, folder, or folder in a file system in which the name can be up to 255 characters in length. Long filenames in Windows, UNIX/Linux, and Mac OS systems are also POSIX compliant in that they honor uppercase and lowercase characters.

loopback address An address that always refers to the local computer; in IPv4, it's 127.0.0.1, and in IPv6, it's ::1. This address is used to test TCP/IP functionality on the local computer.

low-level format A software process that marks tracks and sectors on a disk. A low-level format is necessary before a disk can be partitioned and formatted.

LPT1 The primary printer port designation on many desktop computers; also designated as line print terminal 1.

Macintosh Filing System (MFS) The original Macintosh filing system, introduced in 1984. MFS was limited to keeping track of 128 documents, applications, or folders.

Master Boot Record (MBR) A disk-partitioning method that supports volume sizes of up to 2 TB; an area of a hard disk in MS-DOS and Windows that stores partition information about the disk. MBRs are not found on disks that do not support multiple partitions.

Master File Table (MFT) A storage organization system used with the NTFS file system. The MFT is located at the beginning of the partition.

maximum transmission unit (MTU) The maximum frame size allowed to be transmitted across a network medium.

metadata Information that describes data but is not the actual data.

metropolitan area network (MAN) An internetwork confined to a geographic region, such as a city or county; a MAN uses third-party communication providers to supply connectivity between locations. See also *internetwork*.

microarchitecture The description of the internal circuitry of a CPU that defines characteristics such as the technology used to create the chip, the supported instruction set, and the bit size.

microcode A small program inside a CISC CPU that must interpret and execute each instruction.

Microsoft Disk Operating System (MS-DOS) The first widely distributed operating system for microcomputers, created by Tim Paterson and a team at Microsoft that included Bill Gates. This generic computer code was used to control many basic computer hardware and software functions. MS-DOS is sometimes referred to as DOS.

Microsoft Management Console (MMC) A flexible system that allows server administrators to configure the servers and monitor their function in one place.

migration Moving from one OS to another OS, which may or may not involve implementing a new computer as well.

mount A process that makes a disk partition or volume available for use by the operating system.

multicasting A network communication in which a packet is addressed so that more than one destination can receive it.

multifunction printers Printers that combine printing, scanning, and faxing in one physical device. They can be color inkjet or laser printers.

multiprocessor computer A computer that uses more than one CPU.

multitasking A technique that allows a computer to run two or more programs at the same time.

multithreading Running several program processes or parts (threads) at the same time.

multiuser system A computer hardware and software system designed to service multiple users who access the computer's hardware and software applications simultaneously.

name server A computer that provides the service of name-to-address resolution; for example, it resolves a host and domain name to an IP address.

named pipe In UNIX/Linux, a device special file for handling internal communications, such as redirecting file output to a monitor.

.NET Framework A large library, available to all programming languages supported by .NET, that allows multiple programming languages to use code from other languages.

netbook computers Small portable or laptop computers that have limited computing capabilities and are designed to be lightweight and portable. Netbook computers are generally used for Web access, e-mail, and basic document creation.

network Two or more computers connected by a transmission medium that allows them to communicate.

network client software An application or OS service that can request information stored on another computer.

Network File System (NFS) The native Linux/UNIX file sharing protocol.

network interface card (NIC) A device that creates and mediates the connection between a computer and the network medium.

Network layer Layer 3 of the OSI model, which handles logical addressing and routing of PDUs across internetworks. See also *Open Systems Interconnection (OSI) reference model*.

network protocols The software that defines the rules and formats a computer must use when sending information across the network.

network server software The software that allows a computer to share its resources by fielding requests generated by network clients.

network-attached printer A printer that has a network interface, is connected to the network, and can be accessed by computers on the network via a host name or IP address.

network-attached storage (NAS) A storage device that has an enclosure, a power supply, slots for multiple HDDs, a network interface, and a built-in OS tailored for managing shared files and folders.

New Technology File System (NTFS) The file storage system that is the native system in Windows versions starting with Windows NT.

octet An 8-bit value; a number from 0 to 255 that's one of the four numbers in a dotted decimal IP address.

Open Systems Interconnection (OSI) reference model ISO Standard 7498 defines a frame of reference for understanding networks by dividing the process of network communication into seven layers. Each layer is defined in terms of the services and data it handles on behalf of the layer above it and the services and data it needs from the layer below it.

operating system (OS) A specialized computer program that provides a user interface, file system, services, and a kernel to a computer. An OS runs on computer hardware and facilitates application execution.

optical character recognition (OCR) Imaging software that scans each character on the page as a distinct image and is able to recognize the character.

packet A chunk of data with source and destination IP addresses (as well as other IP information) added to it. Packets are generated and processed by network protocols.

page file Also called the *paging file* or *swap file*, an allocated portion of disk storage reserved to supplement RAM when the available RAM is exceeded. See *swap file*.

pagefile.sys A system file in Windows used as virtual memory; it is also used to store data produced when the system crashes (dump data), which is used for troubleshooting.

partition A logical unit of storage that can be formatted with a file system; it is similar to a volume but used with basic disks.

partition table A table containing information about each partition on a disk, such as the type of partition, size, and location. Also, the partition table provides information to the computer about how to access the disk.

partitioning Blocking a group of tracks and sectors to be used by a particular file system, such as FAT or NTFS. Partitioning is a hard disk management technique that permits the installation of multiple file systems on a single disk or the configuration of multiple logical hard drives that use the same file system on a single physical hard drive.

peer-to-peer network A network model in which all computers can function as clients or servers as needed, and there's no centralized control over network resources.

Peripheral Component Interconnect (PCI) A bus standard that has been replaced by the PCI Express or PCIe standard.

Peripheral Component Interconnect Express (PCIe) A bus standard that has enabled adapter manufacturers to supply one hardware product to a variety of hardware platforms.

physical drive A hard drive in a computer that you can physically touch and that can be divided into one or more logical drives.

Physical layer Layer 1, the bottom layer of the OSI model, transmits and receives signals and specifies the physical details of cables, NICs, connectors, and hardware behavior. See also *Open Systems Interconnection (OSI) reference model*.

pipelining A CPU design that permits the processor to operate on one instruction at the same time it is fetching one or more subsequent instructions from the operating system or application.

pixel Short for *picture element*; the small dots that make up a computer screen display.

pixels per inch (ppi) A unit used to measure the resolution of a display screen; the number of dots (pixels) contained in an inch.

platform as a service (PaaS) A category of cloud computing in which a customer develops applications with the service provider's development tools and infrastructure. After applications are developed, they can be delivered to the customer's users from the provider's servers. PaaS is also called *hosted platform*.

plotter Computer hardware that produces high-quality printed output, often in color, by moving ink pens over the surface of paper. Plotters are often used with computer-aided design (CAD) and other graphics applications.

Plug and Play (PnP) Software utilities that operate with compatible hardware to facilitate automatic hardware configuration. Windows versions starting with 95 recognize PnP hardware when it is installed, and in many cases can configure the hardware and install required software without significant user intervention.

Portable Operating System Interface for UNIX (POSIX) A UNIX standard designed to ensure portability of applications among various versions of UNIX.

power-on self test (POST) Tests, such as memory and hardware component tests, that are run by the BIOS when a computer starts and that must complete before the operating system is loaded. See *basic input/output system (BIOS)*.

preemptive multitasking A computer hardware and software design for multitasking of applications in which the operating system retains control of the computer at all times. See *cooperative multitasking* for comparison.

Presentation layer At Layer 6 of the OSI model, data can be encrypted and/or compressed to facilitate delivery. Platform-specific application formats are translated into generic data formats for transmission or from generic data formats into platform-specific application formats for delivery to the Application layer. See also *Open Systems Interconnection (OSI) reference model*.

primary partition A division of disk space on a basic disk used to create a volume. It can be assigned a drive letter, be marked as active, and contain the Windows system volume.

print job The data or document sent from an application to a printer and accepted by the print spooler.

Print Management Console A console that allows a system administrator to manage printers and printing throughout the network.

print queue A temporary file used to store a print job until it can be sent to the printer.

print spooler A process that accepts print jobs from applications, stores them in the print queue, and then sends them to the printer when the print device is ready.

private cloud Cloud services that a company delivers to its own employees.

privileged mode A feature of the operating system kernel introduced in Windows NT that protected it from problems created by a malfunctioning program or process.

process A program that is loaded into memory and run by the CPU. It can be an application a user interacts with, such as a word-processing program or a Web browser, or a program with no user interface that communicates with other processes and provides services to them.

production computer Any computer used to perform real work; it should be protected from problems that might cause an interruption in workflow or loss of data.

protocol Rules and procedures for communication and behavior. Computers must use a common protocol and agree on the rules of communication.

protocol suite A set of protocols working cooperatively to provide network communication. Protocols are "stacked" in layers, and each layer performs a unique function required for successful communication. Also called a *protocol stack*.

public cloud Cloud services delivered by a third-party provider.

rack-mounted server CPU boxes mounted in racks that can hold multiple servers, each with its own power cord and network connection—and that often share one monitor and pointing device.

RAID 0 volume A volume that extends across two or more dynamic disks, but data is written to all disks in the volume equally; it provides no fault tolerance but does provide a performance advantage over simple or spanned volumes.

RAID 1 volume A volume that uses space from two dynamic disks and provides fault tolerance. Data written to one disk is duplicated, or mirrored, to the second disk. If one disk fails, the other disk has a good copy of the data, and the system can continue to operate until the failed disk is replaced. This volume is also called a *mirrored volume*.

RAID 5 volume A volume that uses space from three or more dynamic disks and uses disk striping with parity to provide fault tolerance. When data is written, it's striped across all but one of the disks in the volume. Parity information derived from the data is written to the remaining disk, which is used to re-create lost data after a disk failure. This volume is also called a *disk stripe with parity*.

raw device In the UNIX/Linux file system, a device that has not been divided into logical blocks. See also *block device*.

read-only memory (ROM) Memory that contains information that is not erased when the power is removed from the memory hardware.

real-time operating system (RTOS) An operating system that receives and processes inputs and produces the required outputs in a specified amount of time.

redirector An OS client component that intercepts resource requests and determines whether the resource is local or remote.

Reduced Instruction Set Computing (RISC) A computer CPU design that dedicates processor hardware components to certain functions. This design reduces the number and complexity of required instructions and often results in faster performance than CISC CPUs. Compare to *Complex Instruction Set Computing (CISC)*.

redundant array of independent disks (RAID) A disk configuration that uses space on multiple disks to form a single logical volume. Most RAID configurations provide fault tolerance, and some enhance performance.

register A temporary holding location in a CPU where data must be placed before the CPU can use it.

registry A Windows database that stores information about a computer's hardware and software configuration.

release candidate (RC) The final stage of software testing by vendors before cutting an official release that is sold commercially. A release candidate is usually tested by a very large audience of customers. Some vendors may issue more than one release candidate if problems are discovered in the first RC.

release to manufacturing (RTM) A version of a Microsoft OS that is officially released to be sold and has gone through the alpha, beta, and release candidate phases prior to official release.

Resilient File System (ReFS) A file system in Windows Server 2012 and later that is used in large file-sharing applications and that can correct some types of data corruption automatically.

resource fork In the Macintosh file system, the portion of a file that contains fixed information, such as a program's icons, menu resources, and splash screens.

resource managers Programs that manage computer memory and CPU use.

root folder The highest-level folder in the structure of files and folders in a file system.

router A device that enables LANs to communicate by forwarding packets from one LAN to another. Routers also forward packets from one router to another when LANs are separated by multiple routers.

scanner A digital image created from a hard copy that is then transmitted to the computer.

sectors Equally sized portions of a disk track. See *tracks*.

sequential processing A computer processing style in which each operation is submitted, acted upon, and the results displayed before the next process is started. Compare to *batch processing*.

Serial ATA (SATA) A common disk interface technology that's inexpensive, fast, and fairly reliable, with transfer speeds up to 6 Gb/s; it is used both in client computers and low-end servers and replaces the older parallel ATA (PATA) technology.

serial attached SCSI (SAS) A newer, serial form of SCSI with transfer rates of up to 6 Gb/s and higher; the disk technology of choice for servers and high-end workstations. See also *small computer system interface (SCSI)*.

server The term used to describe an OS designed mainly to share network resources, a computer with the main role of giving client computers access to network resources, and the software that responds to requests for network resources from client computers.

server-based network A network model in which servers take on specialized roles to provide client computers with network services and to maintain centralized control over network resources.

Server Core A scaled-back version of Windows Server 2008 in which all configurations and maintenance are done via the command-line interface.

Server Message Block (SMB) The Windows file sharing protocol; SMB is also supported by Linux and Mac OS X as Samba.

server operating system A computer operating system usually found on more powerful PC-based computers than those used for desktop operating systems. A server OS is connected to a network and can act in many roles to enable multiple users to access information via e-mail, files, software, and other means.

server role migration An alternative to a Windows server OS upgrade in which you perform a clean installation of Windows Server 2012/R2 and migrate the server roles the old OS version performed.

service A process that runs in the background because there is no user interface. See *process*.

service packs Software "fixes" issued by a vendor to repair software problems, address compatibility issues, and add enhancements.

Session layer Layer 5 of the OSI model, which is responsible for setting up, maintaining, and ending communication sequences (called *sessions*) across a network. See also *Open Systems Interconnection (OSI) reference model.*

shell An interface that enables users to interact with an operating system kernel. The shell enables the user to execute commands. See *kernel.*

simple volume A volume that usually resides on a single basic or dynamic disk.

single-processor computer A computer capable of supporting only a single CPU.

single-tasking A computer hardware and software design that can manage only a single task at a time.

single-user system A computer hardware and software system that enables only one user to access its resources at a particular time.

small computer system interface (SCSI) An older parallel bus disk technology still used on some servers, although it has reached its performance limits at 640 MB/s transfer rates.

snapshot A partial copy of a virtual machine made at a particular moment; it can be used to restore the virtual machine to its state when the snapshot was taken. See also *virtual machine (VM).*

software as a service (SaaS) A category of cloud computing in which a customer pays for the use of applications that run on a service provider's network; SaaS is also called *hosted applications.*

solid-state drive (SSD) A type of storage medium that uses flash memory, has no moving parts, and requires less power than a traditional HDD. It is faster and more shock resistant than a traditional HDD, but it costs more per gigabyte and doesn't have as much capacity as an HDD.

spanned volume A volume that extends across two or more physical disks; for example, a simple volume that has been extended to a second disk is a spanned volume.

special identity group A type of group in Windows in which membership is controlled dynamically by Windows, can't be viewed or changed manually, and depends on how an account accesses the OS. For example, membership in the Authenticated Users group is assigned to a user account automatically when the user logs on to a computer or domain.

Spotlight The new way to search in Mac OS X, starting with version 10.4 Tiger. Spotlight stores a virtual index of everything on the system.

stand-alone computer A computer that doesn't have the necessary hardware or software to communicate on a network.

static IP address A manually configured IP address.

status bits Bits used as part of a folder entry to identify the type of file contained in each entry. The status bits in use are Volume, Folder, System, Hidden, Read-only, and Archive.

storage appliance See *network-attached storage (NAS).*

storage area network (SAN) A storage device that uses high-speed networking technologies to give servers fast access to large amounts of shared disk storage. To the server OS, the storage a SAN manages appears to be physically attached to the server.

storage layout The method used to create a virtual disk with Storage Spaces; the three methods include simple, mirror, and parity. See also *Storage Spaces.*

storage pool A collection of physical disks from which virtual disks and volumes are created and assigned dynamically.

Storage Spaces A new feature in Windows 8/8.1 and Windows Server 2012/R2 and later versions that provides flexible provisioning of virtualized storage.

storage tiering A feature of Storage Spaces that combines the speed of SSDs with the low cost and high capacity of HDDs to create high-performance volumes.

subnet mask A 32-bit dotted decimal number consisting of a contiguous series of binary 1 digits followed by a contiguous series of binary 0 digits. The subnet mask determines which part of an IP address is the network ID and which part is the host ID.

super advanced intelligent tape (S-AIT) A tape system technology that has an erasable memory chip and a capacity of up to 1.3 TB.

super digital linear tape (SDLT) A tape system that uses both magnetic and optical recording and has a tape capacity of up to 2.4 TB.

superblock In the UNIX/Linux file system, a special data block that contains information about the layout of blocks, sectors, and cylinder groups on the file system. This information is the key to finding anything on the file system, and it should never change.

supercomputer A computer that has extreme processing power and speed to handle complex computations that are beyond the reach of other computers.

surface analysis A disk diagnostic technique that locates and marks damaged disk areas. Some surface analysis tools are destructive to data because they also format the disk. Other tools can run without altering data, except to move it from a damaged location to one that is not.

swap file Also called the *page file, paging file,* or *swap file system,* an allocated portion of disk storage reserved to supplement RAM when the available RAM is exceeded. See *page file.*

swap partition In Linux/UNIX OSs, a separate partition on the disk set aside exclusively for virtual memory.

switch A network device that reads the destination MAC addresses of incoming frames to determine which ports should forward the frames. Also, an operating system command option that changes the way certain commands function. Command options, or switches, are usually entered as one or more letters, separated from the main command by a forward slash (/) in Windows and by a dash (-) in UNIX/Linux.

switching table A table of MAC address and port pairs that a switch uses to determine which port to forward frames it receives.

symbolic link A special file in the UNIX/Linux file system that permits a folder link to a file that is on a different partition.

system architecture The computer hardware design that includes the processor (CPU) and communication routes between the CPU and the hardware it manages, such as memory and disk storage.

System V Release 4 (SVR4) A variation of the UNIX operating system. It is very popular today along with the Berkeley Software Distribution (BSD).

system volume A volume that contains the files a computer needs to find and load the Windows OS. See also *volume*.

tar A UNIX file archive utility.

task supervisor A process in the operating system that keeps track of applications running on the computer and the resources they use.

task switching A hybrid between single-tasking and multitasking that permits the user or application software to switch among multiple single-tasking operations.

thermal-wax transfer printer A printer that creates high-quality color printed output by melting colored wax elements and transferring them to the printed page.

thin provisioning A method for creating virtual disks in which the virtual disk expands dynamically and uses space from the storage pool as needed until it reaches the specified maximum size.

thread The smallest piece of computer code that can be independently scheduled for execution.

time-sharing system A central computer system, such as a mainframe, that is used by multiple users and applications simultaneously.

total cost of ownership (TCO) The cost of installing and maintaining computers and equipment on a network. TCO includes hardware, software, maintenance, and support costs.

tracks Concentric rings that cover an entire disk like grooves on a phonograph record. Each ring is divided into sectors in which to store data.

trailer Information added to the back end of a chunk of data so it can be correctly interpreted and processed by network protocols.

Transmission Control Protocol/Internet Protocol (TCP/IP) The most common protocol suite, the default protocol in contemporary OSs, and the protocol of the Internet.

Transport layer Layer 4 of the OSI model, which is responsible for reliable delivery of data streams across a network. Layer 4 protocols break large streams of data into smaller chunks and use sequence numbers and acknowledgements to provide communication and flow control. See also *Open Systems Interconnection (OSI) reference model.*

type code In the Macintosh file system, embedded file information that denotes which applications were used to create the files. Mac OS type codes are used in much the same way as Windows file extensions that identify file types with .txt, .doc, and other extensions. See *creator codes.*

Unicode A 16-bit character code that allows for the definition of up to 65,536 characters.

unique local IPv6 address An address for devices on a private network that can't be routed on the Internet.

Universal Disk Format (UDF) A removable disk formatting standard used for large-capacity CD-ROMs and DVD-ROMs.

universal group A group scope that can contain users from any domain and be assigned permissions to resources in any domain. See also *group scope.*

Universal Plug and Play (UPnP) An initiative of more than 80 companies to develop products that can be quickly added to a computer or network. These products include intelligent appliances for the home. For more information, go to *http://openconnectivity.org/upnp.*

Universal Serial Bus (USB) A serial bus designed to support up to 127 discrete devices with data transfer speeds up to 5 Gbits/s (gigabits per second).

UNIX file system (ufs) A file system supported in most versions of UNIX/Linux; ufs is a hierarchical (tree structure) file system that is expandable, supports large storage, provides excellent security, and is reliable. Ufs employs information nodes (inodes).

upgrade installation An OS installation on a computer that already has an earlier version of the OS; the upgrade replaces the earlier version with a new version, often with the option to retain some or all of the original settings, user accounts, applications, data files, and other existing user files.

User Account Protection (UAP) A feature of some Microsoft operating systems that allows for better protection of user accounts by controlling permissions and limiting the software applications that can be run from an account.

user interface A component of an operating system that provides a method for users to interact with the computer, usually with a keyboard and mouse or touch screen.

VHD file The format that virtual machines running in Hyper-V use for their virtual disks. VHD files can also be created and mounted with Disk Management and used like physical disks.

virtual disk Files stored on the host computer that represent a virtual machine's hard disk.

virtual machine (VM) A software environment that emulates a physical computer's hardware and BIOS.

virtual memory Disk space that stores the least recently used pages of memory when more physical RAM is needed, but not available.

virtual network A network configuration created by virtualization software and used by virtual machines for network communication.

virtual private network (VPN) A private network that is like an encrypted tunnel through a larger network—such as the Internet, an enterprise network, or both—and is restricted to designated member clients.

virtual server A server computer that can be configured to run multiple virtual machines with multiple server or desktop OSs. See *virtual machine*.

virtualization A process that creates a software environment to emulate a computer's hardware and BIOS, allowing multiple OSs to run on the same physical computer at the same time.

volume A logical unit of storage that can be formatted with a file system.

volume information block On a Mac-formatted disk, the sector after the boot blocks. See also *boot block*. The volume information block points to other important areas of information, such as the location of the system files and the catalog and extents trees.

volume label A series of characters, commonly used as a nickname, that identify a volume.

volume mount point An empty folder into which a volume is mounted. See *mount*.

wide area networks (WANs) Internetworks that are geographically dispersed and use third-party communication providers to supply connectivity between locations. See also *internetwork*.

Windows Hardware Error Architecture (WHEA) An architecture that supports memory and cache error recovery without the operating system being aware of the process.

X Window A windowed user interface for UNIX and other operating systems.

Index

J

K

L

M

T